41992

# American Novelists Revisited

A Publication in Women's Studies

Barbara Haber, Series Editor

Edited by
Fritz Fleischmann

# American Novelists Revisited:
Essays in
Feminist Criticism

G.K. Hall & Co.  Boston, Massachusetts

**Library of Congress Cataloging in Publication Data**

Main entry under title:

American novelists revisited.

   1. American fiction—History and criticism—Addresses,
essays, lectures.  2. Women in literature—Addresses,
essays, lectures.  3. Feminism and literature—Addresses,
essays, lectures.  4. Feminism in literature—Addresses,
essays, lectures.  I. Fleischmann, Fritz, 1950–

| PS374.W6A45 | 813'.009 | 82–6097 |
| ISBN 0-8161-9044-5 | | AACR2 |

*This publication is printed on permanent/durable, acid-free paper*

MANUFACTURED IN THE UNITED STATES OF AMERICA

*For Bettie*

# Contents

# Fritz Fleischmann

# Introduction

The original idea for this introduction was to discuss the impact of feminist criticism on the American novel, and to speculate on the open questions and possible future directions in feminist criticism. The idea was abandoned when it became obvious that this was too ambitious an undertaking, considering the fast growth of the field and the variety of new and interesting directions it has taken during the past few years. Instead, this introduction will concern the genesis of this book and its rationale. (The critic's autobiographical voice, after all, is "itself a 'find' of feminist criticism"; Gene Patterson-Black).[1] There are two other reasons for writing a different kind of introduction, one, the collective nature of this effort,[2] and two, the character of the volume itself.

First, I wish to give credit to the people who, through their correspondence and conversations with me, helped to determine the course of the project in its various stages. This book was three years in the making and the research and soliciting of contributors, together with subsequent exchanges, produced a volume of correspondence the size of a small monograph, too precious, I think, to pass over without a word.

Second, the structure of the essays, predictably, pushes the collection rather strongly toward the academic end of "the continuum between the hyper-academic and the totally unbuttoned" (Gene Patterson-Black). A not-so-academic introduction might adjust the balance slightly.

The idea for this book was suggested by Barbara Haber, Editor of G. K. Hall's Women's Studies Program. Concrete plans grew out of conversations we had at the 1978 Berkshire Conference on the History of Women. We discussed the fact that there were still so few synthetic works that dealt with American literary history from a feminist point of view. The most prominent fields of research until then had been critical theory and the rediscovery and evaluation of women's writings. Some reinterpretation had been done in the traditionally accepted canon (predominantly works by male authors), but many major writers had only been touched upon. Much of the 1970s "image of woman" criticism had not sufficiently analyzed the psychological, social, and literary-historical ramifications behind the stereotyped images of women in American literature. Despite some good criticism of individual authors, the existing attempts at critical synthesis seemed to us limited in scope. A coherent rethinking of American literary history, or even of a single genre, was still lacking.

The picture has changed somewhat since 1978, but the raison d'être for an overview (however limited) remains. As Cynthia Secor wrote in 1980, "[revisions] of individual genres are very much what is currently needed." This, then, was to be an attempt at such a revision—a collection of essays on the American novel, treating the works of major authors from a feminist perspective.

Immediately, two problems arose: what is a feminist perspective, and who are the "major authors" of the American novel?

In my letters of solicitation to potential contributors, the following was the core passage: "I see the definition of what is or is not feminist in literary criticism as a major problem (and an exciting and important challenge), not as something that we can now take for granted. That is why, in this collection, I have tried to bring together a variety of interesting critical approaches rather than a homogeneous group, a good mixture of new scholars and more established critics and writers, of both women and men." Variety, eclecticism, not dogmatism, was to be the key. Contributors were encouraged to range afield if they wished; the goal was, in each case, to determine how feminist thinking and expertise had affected a critic's reading of a particular author and, possibly, how the novelist's achievement appeared in the light of feminist criticism. The results of the experiment are reasonably, if not wildly, diverse. No more need be said here, as the essays speak for themselves. With the exception of Nina Auerbach's contribution, reprinted with slight alterations from her *Communities of Women: An Idea in Fiction* (Cambridge, Mass.: Harvard University Press, 1978), all essays are original pieces written for this book.

Discussions with potential and actual contributors elicited a variety of opinions on the nature and viability of feminist criticism, including its terminology. Kay House warned me that she would not use "the current jargon of the feminist criticism . . . in vogue in some quarters." Susan Wolstenholme, who critically examined some of my own assumptions in a long exchange, quoted Marcia Landy who said, "I do not believe that there is a feminist criticism, just as I do not believe there is a black criticism or any criticism of the oppressed which is an umbrella."[3] On the question of whether men can be feminist critics, she wrote, "while a man may believe in feminist ideology and recognize the damage that patriarchy does him as well as women, and while a male critic may take account of feminist ideas, concerns, and questions, still he cannot fully share the same experience of personal exclusion that a woman knows from the inside. To call such a male critic 'feminist,' therefore, is something of a misnomer." Although our discussion started out by exploring the respective positions of female and male readers, it broke off without defining that elusive critter, the feminist critic. I further complicated the issue by asking, "How do we read each other's national literatures?"—a question that I have some reason to think about. The manifest result of our exchange was a new footnote (44) in Susan Wolstenholme's essay on Dreiser, which sums up her position.

The second problem I indicated earlier was the question of the canon, an important feminist concern. Various contributors remarked on how traditional perceptions of the canon as well as individual oeuvres had affected value judgments. John Crowley, writing about William Dean Howells, noted that those portions of Howells's work that have feminist implications are "among the least known and the least discussed of the work. Here as nearly everywhere in American criticism, one detects a sexist bias in what is considered worth discussing." The selection of about fifteen (my original number) novelists for this anthology produced several dilemmas. If one task of feminist scholarship is to re-examine the literary classics, is not this goal of the feminist scholar undermined by taking that very group of works and subjecting it to yet another, albeit feminist, interpretation? Does not the very act of criticizing the canon serve to reinforce it?

When I sent out my first lists of authors for consideration, suggestions were made to add more women writers (Jewett, Freeman, Glasgow, O'Connor, and McCullers were often mentioned), or to drop some (Stowe and Hurston). Rolande Ballorain wondered at a list that included "both male and female writers, already well-known feminists and antifeminists, extremely famous and secondary ones (both in terms of fame and art). Why for instance Hemingway, Fitzgerald, Faulkner and not Welty, O'Connor, McCullers? Why Stowe . . . . not Glasgow, not Nabokov, not Anderson?" Gene Patterson-Black, who contributed the essay on Melville, asked, "Is there enough substance in Melville's work to warrant its position within the canon?" Other critics wanted as "clear" a concept as possible and encouraged me to make a "firm" choice, however defined (*American Literary Scholarship* front runners? the *MLA Bibliography* "top twenty"? college anthology favorites?), for a basis. For a while I challenged colleagues to name the twenty most important American novelists, only to find out that no two could ever agree on more than ten names. It became more complicated as I had to make the choice between present-day writers. Who among the post-World War II generation should be included? This problem was "solved" by the lack of available space; it was finally decided not to include any contemporaries at all. Major figures like Mailer and Bellow had already been discussed by feminist critics, and it was reasonable to assume that younger writers would not be neglected.

The concept of this anthology, then, was to take a new look at novelists from the beginning of the Republic to the middle of the twentieth century.

Authors would have to be identifiable as American,[4] which would exclude someone like Nabokov (but how about Stein?), and as novelists, which would exclude Poe. As for importance, why Brockden Brown and not Dos Passos? Why Crane and not Lewis? Why Stein and not McCullers? Rolande Ballorain, who played our game with the greatest patience, finally came up with thirty-six "greatest artists"—a fine list that did *not* include Brown, Stowe, Howells, Wright, Hurston, and Walker, whom I would have included in my personal list.

Despite the dilemma I have described (re-evaluation versus reaffirmation) and despite the lack of a clear consensus on who should be included, I decided on the novelists who now appear in our table of contents. Besides the obvious choices, it includes some writers who do not now rank as "classics" (Brown, Stowe, Stein, Hurston) but whose critical reputation is on the rise, and others whose very mention, in my experience at least, starts passionate arguments about their merits (Howells, Dreiser, Hemingway). It is, perhaps, easier to say what the table of contents does *not* represent. The rediscovery and re-evaluation of neglected women writers is not a major consideration, nor is a reappraisal of novelists (male or female) with a particular interest in feminism or women. This list is, ultimately, something of a tightrope act between my perception of a critical consensus and my own sense of value; therefore, all responsibility for the final decisions must be mine.

An experiment and not an authoritative collection, this book may be a new planting of possibilities as well as a harvesting of past labors. The process of putting it together has been as interesting as the fact of the book itself, even in the half dozen or so cases where the promise of a beginning did not produce an essay. Two persons, at least, deserve to be mentioned here. Ellen Moers, a pioneer in the field whom I had asked for an essay, answered me two days before her death on 25 August, 1979. I, who did not know her personally, had been unaware that she had been fighting cancer for eleven years, holding her own up to the very end, "maintaining principles," as her husband wrote. Gail Baker, who contributed many ideas to the project in its first stages, was also prevented from contributing an essay by a new appointment in Japan. Her imprint is on the final product nevertheless.

I wish to thank all my contributors for their spirit of cooperation, and my editor at G. K. Hall, Caroline Birdsall, for her patience and productive criticism. My special thanks belong to Elizabeth L. Rose, whose combined skills as a librarian, feminist writer, and critical reader have supported the project from its very beginning. This book is dedicated to her.

F.F.

Boston, Massachusetts
July 1981

## Notes

1. All quotations, unless otherwise indicated, are from letters written to me by contributors to this volume.
2. I wish to thank the following persons for suggesting potential contributors to this project: Daniel Aaron, Elizabeth Ammons, George Arms, Nina Auerbach, Gail Baker, Nina Baym, John Crowley, Laurie Crumpacker, Carol Green, Barbara Haber, Dagmar Loytved, Jane McCabe, Alice Walker, Cheryl Wall, Judith Wittenberg, and Cynthia Griffin Wolff.
3. Marcia Landy, "The Silent Woman: Towards a Feminist Critique," in *The Authority of Experience: Essays in Feminist Criticism*, ed. Arlyn Diamond and Lee R. Edwards (Amherst: University of Massachusetts Press, 1977), p. 16.
4. On this question, as well as the problem of canon in general, see Nina Baym, "Melodramas of Beset Manhood: How Theories of American Fiction Exclude Women Authors," *American Quarterly* 33 (1981): 123–39.

# Fritz Fleischmann

# Charles Brockden Brown: Feminism in Fiction

I

Charles Brockden Brown (1771–1810) is the first novelist to be considered here, because he was the first born. But it would also be appropriate, for other than chronological reasons, to place him at the beginning since he already has a long history of feminist criticism, a history that many would consider disheartening, for it has neither produced a consensus on Brown's feminism nor left much impact on his status in the canon of American writers.

At least three generations of feminist critics have remarked on Brown's women characters; a feminist reading of his novels goes back at least as far as Margaret Fuller's comment that "it increases our own interest in Brown that, a prophet in this respect of a better era, he has usually placed his thinking royal mind in the body of a woman . . . a conclusive proof that the term *feminine* is not a synonym for *weak*."[1] Thomas Wentworth Higginson, a supporter of women's rights and sympathetic biographer of Fuller, noted Brown's "advanced views as to the rights and education of women."[2] The subject, although never ignored by Brown scholars,[3] was picked up again by the generation of feminists who wrote after the passage of the Nineteenth Amendment. In 1925, Augusta Genevieve Violette included Brown in her discussion of "economic feminism," claiming that the radical sentiments in *Alcuin* "express Brown's own feelings on social usages of his time."[4] Mary Sumner Benson, in her pioneering work on women's history published in 1935, wrote of Brown's fictional women that they "could . . . think for themselves" and that "they marked an altered attitude toward women."[5] Dorothy Yost Deegan, in 1951, thought that Clara Wieland and Constantia Dudley "were unusually independent women of their day," and that before Hawthorne, Brown was the only novelist who "dared to present the unmarried woman as somewhat admirable."[6]

If this sounds like a consensus, the impression vanishes with a look at the contemporary critical scene. Brown's place in the American literary canon as "the first writer of prose fiction of which America could boast"[7] appears secure, if the quantity and general quality of recent criticism is any indication.[8] His niche in the American feminist pantheon should also be well established. Not only did he create striking, memorable women characters in his fiction, but he was also the first major writer of the Republic to examine women's rights and roles systematically and sympathetically. On both counts, one would expect far-reaching agreement as to the quality of his achievement as well as to the reasons for his continuing critical appreciation.

But there is no such consensus in Brown scholarship, be it feminist or not. Brown's status as a novelist of rank is still being contested;[9] and although the appreciative majority of his critics agree that his fiction is important because it "examined issues that have remained germane,"[10] there is much disagreement on what those issues are and how they have been presented. Critical opinion on Brown's women is in similar disarray. Its feminist tone re-emerges with the women's movement of the late 1960s and early 1970s and the growth of women's studies as an academic discipline.[11] By the mid-seventies, women as a topic had become academically respectable; the political lines are often no longer clearly discernible.[12] Brown criticism in this period shows how problematic the label "feminist" can be in characterizing critical positions. But the fact remains that an interest or disinterest in the "women's issue" makes a difference in scholarship. Currently, the best arguments for the consistent quality, coherence, and thematic unity of Brown's work come from two critics who pay close and sympathetic attention to Brown's feminist views as well as his women characters, although their tone does not categorize them as political feminists.[13] Brown's own systematic treatment of the issue deserves our attention first.

## II

Anyone who doubts Brown's feminism or his competence as a writer should go back to *Alcuin*. Far from being "an extremely clumsy work"[14] or the product of "an apprentice writer still working out his basic techniques,"[15] it is a small masterpiece, sophisticated and occasionally witty. (Brown had worked on the problem of combining dialogue and narrative as early as 1792, when he wrote the "Henrietta" letters.)[16] Alcuin's preposterous question to Mrs. Carter ("after much deliberation and forethought"!), "Pray, Madam, are you a federalist?" (p. 9)[17] sets the ironic tone that controls the subsequent exchanges.

Alcuin, a city schoolmaster with an active fantasy life, as little money as worldly experience, and but a slender stock of the social graces, descends upon the home of Mrs. Carter, a widow who hosts an intellectual salon for her brother, a physician and "man of letters"; he invites the guests whereas his sister is "always at home" (p. 4). Alcuin's opening gambit is preceded by a careful buildup which establishes the character of the disputants and their social background, creating enough *vraisemblance* to make the discussion realistic. Alcuin is the namesake of Charlemagne's friend and philosopher-teacher, perhaps "to hint that many of [his] opinions . . . should be considered medieval." Mrs. Carter is probably a reference to the famous English bluestocking Elizabeth Carter, "whose views would necessarily be both more modern and more radical."[18]

Mrs. Carter reacts to Alcuin's question about her politics with a smile—and ironic incredulity. Why ask *her*? "We are surrounded by men and politicians. You must observe that they consider themselves in an element congenial to their sex and station" (p. 10). Alcuin jumps to defend the status quo by explaining that, under the existing arrangements, men and women "may all equally be said to stick to their lasts" (p. 10). In so doing, he must also defend women as they now are, ascribing their defects ("perfectly natural and reasonable") to the "limited sphere" in which they properly belong (p. 12). His hostess is far more critical of women and therefore of the circumstances that have made them what they are. This pattern of argument—chivalry/apology versus criticism—follows the distinction Mary Wollstonecraft made in *A Vindication of the Rights of Woman* (1792).[19] As we shall see, such parallels abound. Even the basic analogy is the same: Mrs. Carter derives her demands for women's political rights from the American Revolution and its concomitant documents, just as Wollstonecraft had insisted on equal treatment of women by the French revolutionaries.

Her steadily developing argument is counterpointed by Alcuin's much jumpier tactic of defense and assault that usually gets him to concede a point of principle even while he gains one of circumstance. Alcuin, though mostly the target of irony, is not devoid of wit himself. "You might as well expect a Laplander to write Greek spontaneously, and without instruction," he jokes, as a woman to be learned without an opportunity to learn. But his wit is labored, a warning that he will have to eat his own words.

> I humbly presume one has a better chance of becoming an astronomer by gazing at the stars through a telescope, than in eternally plying the needle, or snapping the scissars [*sic*]. To settle a bill of fare, to lard a pig, to compose a pudding, to carve a goose, are tasks that do not, in any remarkable degrees, tend to instil the love, or facilitate the acquisition of literature and science. Nay, I do not form prodigious expectations even of one who reads a novel or comedy once a month, or chants once a day to her harpsichord the hunter's foolish invocation to Phoebus or Cynthia. Women are generally superficial and ignorant, because they are generally cooks and sempstresses. [Pp. 13-14]

All this he advances to prove that "human beings are moulded by the circumstances in which they are placed. In this they are all alike. The differences that flow from the sexual distinction, are as nothing in the balance" (p. 13). An inch gained, a mile lost; Alcuin's struggle is doomed. He must admit so many single points in order to defend the overall status quo that he becomes hopelessly entangled in his own web. Lee R. Edwards calls Alcuin "the fossil prototype of the much denounced contemporary liberal" (*Alcuin*, p. 98) whose arguments, dismaying to watch, reappear throughout the nineteenth and well into the twentieth century. Some examples:

1. Human nature itself impedes progress. ("It is doubtful whether the career of the species will ever terminate in knowlege" [p. 14].)
2. Unpleasant social tasks are unavoidable. Those who have to carry them out have a right to feel "abundance of injustice," but "it matters not of what sex they may be" (p. 14). "The evil lies in so much human capacity being thus fettered and perverted" (pp. 14-15).
3. Women are excluded from the professions because they don't really care for them. Besides, the professions are in reality demeaning and full of abuse, and hence not terribly desirable in the first place (pp. 16-21). ("It is evident," Mrs. Carter retorts, "that, for some reason or other, the liberal professions . . . are occupied only by men" [p.20]. The assumption that women's lot is more desirable ignores the life of the vast majority.)
4. Should women feel bitter about their exclusion from schools and colleges? Alcuin (a schoolmaster!) wonders "whether a public education be not unfavourable to moral and intellectual improvement" (p. 22).
5. Society and its laws—"which have commonly been male births" (p. 26)—may be defective, but men suffer more than women: "Let us inquire, whether the wives, and daughters, and single women, of each class, be not placed in a more favourable situation than the husbands, sons, and single men, of the same class. Our answer will surely be in the affirmative." The only hope lies in historical progress. "Human beings, it is hoped, are destined to a better condition on this stage, or some other, than is now allotted to them" (p. 28).

With this outlook, Alcuin has the last word of Part I. Like Part II and sections of Part III, it is strongly imbued with Wollstonecraftian rhetoric, even on Alcuin's side, and goes over all the major points from the *Vindication*. The faultiness of women's education, the false delicacy which causes the separation of the sexes in childhood, the socialization of children into sexual roles with different "systems of morality" (p. 24), the inevitable hypocrisy in marriage ("she must hope to prevail by blandishments and tears; not by appeals to justice and addresses to reason" [p.24] –these points are directly, often almost literally, derived from Wollstonecraft, down to Mrs. Carter's caution that she herself is an exception to the picture she has described.

*Alcuin* II moves on to the political and legal rights of women, with Mrs. Carter lecturing more and more, reducing poor Alcuin to inanity. Her cool and systematic destruction of his positions should overcome any remaining suspicions that Brown did not know what he was about. The movement of the text is as follows. Alcuin's repeated question, "Are you a federalist?" is rejected as irrelevant, since the constitution has excluded women from the body politic, together with minors, recent immigrants, paupers, and black people. Here is Mrs. Carter on the poor: they "vary in number, but are sure to increase with the increase of luxury and opulence, and to promote these is well known to be the aim of all wise governors" (p. 33). She gives a spirited defense of democratic government, but Alcuin's attempts to muddle the issue by general reflections are repelled. "I plead only for my own sex"–let other groups fend for themselves; for women "the injury is far greater, since it annihilates the political existence of at least half of the community" (p. 38). Alcuin's faint objection that the marriage laws, by taking away "both the liberty and property of women," deprive them of "independent judgment" in politics, gets Mrs. Carter started on those laws, not without another shot at the "independent judgment" of male officeholders ("Most of them seem not to have attained heights inaccessible to ordinary understandings" [p. 39]). Alcuin sounds a note of humility, admitting his prejudices (men's "teachers have been men"), and proposing women's intellectual equality, even their overall superiority, a kind of higher nature. (His tail is between his legs here, because this is the "specious homage" that Wollstonecraft had criticized.) Nevertheless, he tries hard and ends Part II with the *Vindication*'s analogy between the battle of the sexes and class war. Men's assumption of superiority "is a branch of that prejudice which has so long darkened the world, and taught men that nobles and kings were creatures of an order superior to themselves" (p. 43). At this point, the conversation is interrupted by an intruder "who, after listening to us for some time, thought proper at last to approach, and contribute his mite to our mutal edification" (p. 43).

Parts III and IV, not clearly separated, cover Alcuin's imaginary visit to the "paradise of women," his report of the "voyage" to Mrs. Carter, and a lengthy discussion of marriage. The "paradise of women" is a utopian island of complete gender equality. Alcuin's remarks about sexual distinctions are constantly rebuffed by his guide, who misunderstands them as questions about *anatomical* differences of which Alcuin must be "doubtless apprised"

(p. 50). The views and customs that the visitor reports from his own country are denounced, in good utopian fashion: "Common madness is unequal to so monstrous a doctrine" as gender inequality (p. 62). While the education of children is discussed in Wollstonecraftian terms, Brown prepares the way for Part IV, a Godwinian critique of marriage, by introducing elements from *Political Justice* along the way. "Man" (the term is used generically throughout) "is a progressive being, he is wise in proportion to the number of his ideas" (p. 58), which are products of his environment, creating differences between individuals far greater than those of sex. The utopian island has egalitarian traits ("A certain portion of labor will supply the needs of all. This portion then must be divided among all" [p. 61]). The truth (correct opinions) will automatically change human behavior ("My actions will conform to my opinions" [p. 63]). Alcuin's idea that the oppression of women in his homeland may be a male conspiracy cannot be imagined by the guide, as the introduction of such a system ("by force or persuasion" [p. 64]). is impossible where women are mentally and physically as capable as men.

When Alcuin introduces marriage ("that relation which subsists between human beings in consequence of sex" [p. 64]), he interrupts his narrative for fear of offending Mrs. Carter's sense of propriety. This interruption of almost four pages may seem beside the argument, but it is not. Decorum (what is fit for female eyes or ears) had been recognized by Mary Wollstonecraft as a feminist issue, and it was to remain one throughout the nineteenth century.[20] Here is Brown speaking through Mrs. Carter: "The impropriety methinks must adhere to the sentiments themselves, and not result from the condition of the author or his audience" (p. 65). She insists on her willingness and qualification to discuss marriage, because "the lowest stupidity only can seek its safety in shutting its ears," and "to sophistry . . . the proper antidote is argument" (pp. 67, 68).

Sydney J. Krause has discussed Godwinian attitudes toward marriage extensively in his notes to the KSU *Ormond*.[21] "Fascinatingly," he writes, "whereas in *Ormond* Brown made Godwin a straw man for the criticism of views that disadvantaged women, in *Alcuin* III and IV, he had gone the other way, using Godwinian liberalism *to uphold* women's rights." Mrs. Carter "point by point takes up all of Godwin's revolutionary initiatives, beginning, as Godwin did, with the evils of cohabitation: harmony can be achieved only at the cost of one's individuality; cooperation really means accommodation, which thwarts personal preferences, stultifies reason and inhibits individual judgment; and all of this finally leads to bickering, frustration and unhappiness"; "other objections exactly mirror the Godwinian argument, as with: the inflexible restraints of the contractual relationship, the supreme importance of choice, the need to allow for change and remedy, and, on the positive side, for the supports of free consent, friendship and spontaneity. Seen by themselves, the words might be easily mistaken for Godwin's." Mrs.

Carter defends the idea of marriage as "sacred," but its reality has been made unbearable by unjust laws, which can only be remedied by "unlimited power of divorces" (p. 75). The *Vindication* had suggested that unhappy wives often make good mothers;[22] Mrs. Carter argues that the children suffer more in unhappy marriages than from divorces (p. 85). This goes beyond Wollstonecraft, although it remains true to her method of employing a critique of women's condition and the false ideals of femininity as a critique of society. Where the *Vindication* falls short of supplying a model for a just society, *Alcuin* can draw on the most widely known program for one, Godwin's *Political Justice* (1793; second and third editions in 1796 and 1798). As Professor Krause puts it, "On the requirements of free choice, removal of unnatural constraints and allowance for change," Mrs. Carter's Godwinism "is adamant, and reasserted."

Unfortunately, Mrs. Carter has introduced her whole lecture by warning Alcuin that "[a] class of reasoners has lately arisen, who aim at the deepest foundation of civil society," and that his utopian journey is to be regarded "as an excursion into their visionary world" (p. 68). A little later, she refers to Godwin himself by denouncing "that detestable philosophy which scoffs at the matrimonial institution itself, which denies all its pretensions to sanctity, which consigns us to the guidance of a sensual impulse, and treats as phantastic or chimerical, the sacred charities of husband, son, and brother" (p. 70). In ascribing such views to her, she informs Alcuin, "you would hardly be justified by the most disinterested intentions" (p. 70).

Where does this leave us? How could this be followed by the "boiler plate Godwinism" (S. J. Krause) we have heard? The answer lies, I think, in a game Brown plays with his readers. His frequent disavowals of his radical affiliations have been a persistent problem for scholars. In *Alcuin*, they occur twice, once in the unexpected attack on Godwin and company just mentioned, the other time much earlier, toward the end of Part I. Both times Mrs. Carter has the word, and both times, it appears, she (or Brown) is pulling somebody's leg. *If* Brown is hedging on his radicalism here, as has been alleged, he does so tongue in cheek, relying on his readers' wits and sense of irony. His later works show that he never abandoned his feminism and that he continued to hope for social reform, if not necessarily along Godwinian lines. Why then these disavowals? And why did Brown only publish Parts I and II?

S. J. Krause has followed the writing and publishing history of *Alcuin*,[23] and found that there was much debate on Godwin and the drafts of *Alcuin* among Brown and his closest friends, considerable support at least from Elihu Hubbard Smith (who read Parts III and IV three times in all), and plenty of opportunity for Brown to find publishing space. Yet III and IV did not go into print during Brown's lifetime. We are reminded that "divorce remained so touchy a subject that *Alcuin* III and IV could not even be published posthumously in 1815 without benefit of an extended apology."[24] Brown may have noticed the pattern of critics' reception of Wollstonecraft and Godwin during the 1790s.[25] Those who had read the texts tended to be fairly objective, even in disagreement. The hearsay reaction, on the other hand, which picked up on the vague dangers and alleged moral "looseness" of the "new philosophy," was mostly slanderous and abusive. (The news of Godwin's marriage to Mary Wollstonecraft in 1797 did not help the sincerity of his professed antimatrimonialism; and his publication of the posthumous *Memoirs of the Author of "A Vindication of the Rights of Woman"* the following year, with its exposure of Wollstonecraft's private life, destroyed the moral reputation of both writers.) The obstreperous Mrs. Fielder in *Jane Talbot* is a caricature of such ignorant anti-Godwinism.[26] Brown seems to expect the informed reader to recognize the truth, even as he tweaks the noses of the uninformed by presenting the argument while obscuring its source. That he decided not to publish *Alcuin* III and IV would indicate that he was not entirely sure of his audience, fearing "how grossly his own views might be misunderstood."[27]

To return to *Alcuin* I, and the first instance of this game of hide-and-seek: At the end of a long harangue, Wollstonecraftian in substance as well as imagery (the wife as a fawning dog; Wollstonecraft had specified a spaniel), Alcuin gets suspicious of the picture Mrs. Carter has drawn. "You derive it from some other source than your own experience, or even your own observation." She sweeps the charge aside—"No; I believe the picture to be generally exact"—and embarks on another lecture from the *Vindication*, ending with the purest Wollstonecraft: "Men and women are partakers of the same nature. They are rational beings; and, as such, the same principles of truth and equity must be applicable to both" (pp. 25, 26). Brown gives an ironical turn to the screw each time he puts Wollstonecraft's diction in Alcuin's mouth (as he later makes Mrs. Fielder pick up pseudo-Godwinian vocabulary). This occurs a number of times in *Alcuin*, but nowhere more blatantly than just after Alcuin has smelled the rat. Wollstonecraft had drawn an insistent parallel between the parasitical privileges of aristocrats and women, resulting in warped minds and morals. Alcuin now draws a charming picture of woman's existence ("Yours are the peacefullest recesses of the mansion: your hours glide along in sportive chat, in harmless recreation, or voluptuous indolence. . ." [p. 26], which Mrs. Carter promptly condemns both as unrepresentative of reality and as "a panegyric on indolence and luxury" (p. 27). Alcuin caves in and reverts to Wollstonecraft: "I have only attempted to justify the male sex from the charge of cruelty. Ease and luxury are pernicious. Kings and nobles, the rich and the idle, enjoy no genuine content." In Chapter 9 of the *Vindication*, the most widely quoted section of her book, the author had idolized the middle class. *Vide* Alcuin: "There must be one condition of society that approaches nearer than any other to the standard of rectitude and happiness. For this it is our duty to search; and, having found it, endeavour to reduce any other condition to this desirable mean" (p. 27).

In Part IV, Mrs. Carter adopts Godwin's position on divorce and cohabitation but rejects his outright condemnation of marriage. (This again may be Wollstonecraft turned against Godwin, who himself described his wife as "a worshipper of domestic life.")[28] She ends the discussion with a refusal to discuss what one should do if the commonly accepted form of marriage conflicted with one's "notions of duty" (p. 87): "That indeed, returned she, is going further than I am willing to accompany you." But she reasserts her own, radical redefinition of marriage.

> Marriage is an union founded on free and mutual consent. It cannot
> exist without friendship. It cannot exist without personal fidelity.
> As soon as the union ceases to be spontaneous it ceases to be just. If
> I were to talk for months, I could add nothing to the completeness
> of this definition. [P. 88]

However one looks at Brown's treatment of Godwinism, his own feminist loyalties emerge clearly: "His oscillations themselves become ancillary to this cause. The case for it is that compelling, that simple."[29] The cause Brown makes for women's rights extends to all his novels. It survives even the end of his career as a novelist to turn up again in later writings. Critics have also begun to recognize that "*Alcuin* anticipates Brown's later novels and is consequently at least as noteworthy for its manner as for its matter," thus providing "an early illustration" of, among other techniques, "how Brown could shape his narrative to serve the two separate ends of moral didacticism and psychological realism."[30]

## III

Brown's scattered programmatic statements on writing share a didactic bent. The writer is described as a "moral painter,"[31] a "story-telling moralist,"[32] whose task it is to "exhibit, in an eloquent narration, a model of right conduct."[33] Even if this formula sounds like a recipe for socialist realism, Brown knew how difficult his project was. The depiction of "virtuous activities"[34] could not ignore the limitations imposed upon the actors by their relations with others and by their fragmentary understanding of reality.

Human relations are determined by two main factors, property and sex. "Opinions, relative to property, are the immediate source of nearly all the happiness and misery that exist among mankind." "Next to property, the most extensive source of our relations is sex. On the circumstances which produce, and the principles which regulate the union between the sexes, happiness greatly depends."[35] The social unit that is based on both property and sex is the family. Brown's fictional practice conforms to his theory because the family is a main source of conflict in his novels. Justifying his preoccupation with sexual politics, Brown also establishes his place vis-à-vis the sentimental tradition.

> Fictitious history has, hitherto, chiefly related to the topics of love and marriage. A monotony and sentimental softness have hence arisen that have frequently excited contempt and ridicule. The ridicule, in general, is merited; not because these topics are intrinsically worthless or vulgar, but because the historian was deficient in knowledge and skill.[36]

These are the methods of the "fictitious historian":

> The observer or experimentalist . . . who carefully watches, and faithfully enumerates the *appearances* which occur, may claim the appelation of historian. He who adorns these appearances with cause and effect, and traces resemblances between the past, distant, and future, with the present, performs a different part. He is a dealer, not in *certainties*, but in *probabilities*, and is therefore a romancer. [emphases mine].[37]

The much-discussed question of Brown's "unreliable" narrators is brought into perspective by this stated intention. Whether deceptive or themselves deceived, these narrators hand out probabilities at best; we should never expect certainties from them. (The "narrator"-correspondents of *Clara Howard* and *Jane Talbot* are not excluded since letter writers, by implication, know only part of the truth.) And, of course, this caution automatically qualifies the sentimental formula of virtue in distress, as virtue itself is reduced to a "probability."

"The Man Unknown to Himself" is the subtitle of Brown's first novel, the lost *Sky-Walk*. *Wieland* is subtitled "The Transformation." What is being transformed is human identity, most commonly derived from the family. Wieland is the name of a family.

William J. Scheick has recently commented on "the orphan condition of so many of the characters" in *Ormond*, noting that "the image of the orphan serves as a metaphor for the psychological condition of Americans." Concerned with the origins of knowledge and identity as a theme in *Ormond*, Scheick states that "so long as a person . . . defines himself primarily in relation to the family . . . into which he is born, he can displace questions pertaining to the source of his knowledge and behavior by focusing on the comforting extrinsic biological reference provided by his parents."[38] In *Wieland*, the origination of self in the family is precisely the problem.

Two young orphans, Theodore and Clara Wieland, grow up under the liberal regime of an aunt. Their closest friend is Catharine Pleyel, who later becomes Theodore's wife. Catharine's brother, returned from travel in

Europe, also joins them. After the marriage of Catharine and Theodore, the four live on pastoral estates near Philadelphia in close contact, spending their time in musical activities and enlightened discussion. Mettingen, the Wieland estate, is described as a virtual utopian *locus amoenus*. Clara remembers growing up there with Theodore and Catharine: "The felicity of that period was marred by no gloomy anticipations. The future, like the present, was serene" (p. 21).[39] Not so the past. The happy present is centered on a symbol of the past—the summerhouse on a rock above the river, where the elder Wieland worshipped in somber loneliness and where he found his death, has become a place of joyous community.

In the first three chapters of the novel, Brown constructs a gloomy family history that overshadows the present. Its origins reach far back into the past and the Old World. Clara and Theodore's paternal grandfather was a fallen aristocrat and unsuccessful provider. His son had to be apprenticed to a merchant and engaged in such mind-narrowing labor that "his heart gradually contracted a habit of morose and gloomy reflection" (p. 7). Having accidentally adopted a "bizarre theology,"[40] he spent his life in a "sentiment of fear" and a sense of unfulfilled obligation. After emigrating to America, he married "a woman of a meek and quiet disposition, and of slender acquirements like himself" who could be easily "intimidated into silence" (pp. 9, 10, 15). He died under mysterious and violent circumstances, soon followed by his wife.

This unresolved past, never far from the younger Wielands' consciousness, breaks loose with a vengeance when mysterious voices begin to be heard. We later learn that they are ventriloquist tricks played by Carwin, the serpent in the garden, but their immediate effect is to activate the past. Theodore's extreme identification with his father predisposes him for the madness he develops, during which he believes himself under divine command to kill his family. His madness follows an inherited desire to appease a patriarchal god, transforming the victim from "the glory of his species" (p. 197) into a demented murderer. The transformation is undone by a final flash of recognition followed by suicide, and Theodore dies at his sister's feet.

As critics have noted, this is a flawed transformation, and Theodore is an unsatisfactory hero. He disappears from the narrative for long stretches of time, only to re-emerge as a madman. Far more interesting is the transformation of Clara, the narrator of the story. She, of course, is as little "clear" about the events as Theodore is a "gift of God." But she makes it clear that "*she too* is a Wieland,"[41] and that hers is a family tragedy.

Clara resists the family madness more successfully than her brother, although she is not untouched by it. Portrayed as a woman of extraordinary intellect and firmness of character, she enters the scene as Brown's "new woman." But although she is clearly the strongest of Carwin's victims, the fact of her gender creates specific complications for her. The character also makes sense as the instrument of a larger philosophical design, as a "representative of humanity," as Alexander Cowie has noted, a humanity shown as "cowering in a frightening, lonely, ambiguous universe,"[42] but it is significant that the author of *Alcuin* chose a woman to guide us though this universe. She is an admittedly confused guide. "What but ambiguities, abruptnesses, and dark transitions, can be expected from the historian who is, at the same time, the sufferer of these disasters?" (p. 147). Her confusion arises from a double burden: she is a Wieland and a woman.

Thrown into a universe of male-created madness (the Wieland heritage activated by Carwin's voices), her rational defenses are further weakened by her awakening sexuality. This is a significant aspect for a feminist interpretation, as a closer look at the sexual politics involved will show us. Although Clara herself is an agent in this process, she is primarily an object of manipulation. Her situation is circumscribed, her agency limited by gender. She recognizes the limitations which convention imposes on her and the conflicts which result; her experience and interpretation of her own sexuality are informed by this consciousness.

Clara has relationships with three male protagonists (discounting her uncle, who is not part of her crises): Theodore, Pleyel, and Carwin. Theodore, although a threat, is not involved in the sexual politics; until the final confrontation, he even supports Clara.

She is in love with Pleyel, engaged to another woman who is said to be dead during a crucial stretch of the plot. Clara, like so many of Brown's women, does all the wooing, trying to create situations wherein Pleyel may declare himself. She is restricted by social custom which requires the male to play the active part—a restriction under which Clara chafes but which she finds herself unable to overcome.

> I must not speak. Neither eyes, nor lips, must impart the information. He must not be assured that my heart is his, previous to the tender of his own; but he must be convinced that it has not been given to another; he must be supplied with space whereon to build a doubt as to the true state of my affections; he must be prompted to avow himself. The line of delicate propriety; how hard it is, not to fall short, and not to overleap it! [P. 79]

Later, while writing down the story, she reflects:

> My scruples were preposterous and criminal. They are bred in all hearts, by a perverse and vicious education, and they would still have maintained their place in my heart, had not my portion been set in misery. My errors have taught me thus much wisdom; that those sentiments which we ought not to disclose, it is criminal to harbour. [P. 80]

Right out of Wollstonecraft and *Alcuin*. Clara's problem is that she is dealing with a patriarch of the first order, the cheerful Pleyel. Most critics have treated him as the "nice guy" of the story, the voice of reason and "champion of intellectual liberty" (p. 25) who, alas, becomes another victim of deception. But he is neither nice nor reasonable. His character corresponds to his structural function in the plot, as counterpart to Carwin. They both see women as the Other and indulge in relentless reification of Clara, according to their own needs. (I refer to "the Other" in Simone de Beauvoir's formulation in *The Second Sex* that "humanity is male and man defines woman not in herself but as relative to him; she is not regarded as an autonomous being."[43]) Their needs are diametrically opposite, but their methods are the same. Pleyel, pursued by Clara, puts her on a pedestal as an ideal of womanhood to be admired but not touched (by him *or* anyone else). He prescribes her as a role model to his future wife (p. 123); like Clara, she is to be an exemplum of "that union between intellect and form, which has hitherto existed only in the conceptions of the poet" (p. 121). His own role is that of chivalric adoration. "In the midst of danger and pain, my contemplations have ever been cheered by your image" (p. 123). Carwin's interest, on the other hand, lies in the destruction of Clara's image as this "prodigy" by subjecting her to cruel tests. "I was desirous of ascertaining whether you were such an one" (p. 202). Both commit the "unpardonable sin" of manipulation, doing violence to her personality.

Early in the novel, Clara thinks that "there was nothing to dread from [Pleyel's] malice. I had no fear that my character or dignity would suffer in his hands" (p. 61). But despite his confessed adoration of Clara, Pleyel is quick to jump to horrible conclusions; another twist in his evasion of her pursuit. A "precipitate and inexorable judge" (p. 114), he rejects Clara without a hearing when he thinks she is Carwin's mistress, and he prepares to run away from her, quite literally. Clara is aware of the Kafkaesque "transformation" which women undergo who offend against the moral standard. "The gulf that separates man from insects is not wider than that which severs the polluted from the chaste among women" (p. 113). Now she, despairingly, finds herself subjected to such a transformation by Pleyel; she senses betrayal. "There is a degree of depravity to which it is impossible for me to sink; yet, in the apprehension of another, my ancient and intimate associate, the perpetual witness of my actions, and partaker of my thoughts, I had ceased to be the same" (p. 113).

Pleyel's betrayal, however, is simply the way he treats women. Earlier on, he tries to conspire with Theodore against Clara and Catharine, hoping to persuade him to move his family to Europe. When Clara catches on, Pleyel wants to draw her into the conspiracy in order to keep the secret from Catharine. With arguments almost verbatim from Alcuin's "paradise" guide, Theodore refuses to manipulate the women: they "'are adversaries whom all your force and strength will never subdue.'" Pleyel operates on the assumption "that they would model themselves by [Theodore's] will: that Catharine would think obedience her duty. He answered, with some quickness, 'You mistake. Their concurrence is indispensable. It is not my custom to exact sacrifices of this kind. I live to be their protector and friend, and not their tyrant and foe'" (p. 43). Theodore refuses the patriarchal role which Pleyel wants to exploit. Pleyel's attitudes toward women accord with his monarchist and feudal inclinations (pp. 37-39). Wieland, on the contrary, refuses an inheritance fallen to him by "the law of male-primogeniture" and decides to stay in America, content in "the happiness of mediocrity" (pp. 37, 43).

Like Carwin, Pleyel pries into Clara's papers, using the same excuse that he was "prompted by no mean or selfish views" (p. 128). Like Carwin, he "lie[s] in wait" (p. 133) to satisfy his curiosity. He teases and torments Clara mercilessly about her alleged love for Carwin (pp. 61, 69-70). Although he is engaged to another woman, his jealousy is so strong that Carwin can use it against him: "To deceive him would be the sweetest triumph I had enjoyed" (p. 210). Clara derives "gratification" (p. 235) from her trials, but when she finally gets her Pleyel, all she has to say is that she is "not destitute of happiness" (p. 234). Small wonder.

Carwin is the catalyst for the maddening resurgence of the past and for Clara's sexual awakening. From Clara's perspective, the two go hand in hand, hence her experience of passion is closely allied to madness.[44] Carwin's manipulation of Clara begins with the first mysterious voice heard at Mettingen. Susceptible to supernatural notions as much as her brother, Clara experiences "a thrilling, and not unpleasing solemnity" when she learns about it (p. 35). The second voice, which tells Pleyel that his German fiancée is dead, results in "a sentiment not unallied to pleasure" in Clara, as she increasingly realizes her love for Pleyel: "For though this object of his love be snatched away, is there not another who is able and willing to console him for her loss?" (pp. 48, 46). When Clara finally gets to hear a voice herself, it is Carwin's own natural voice. She is completely overwhelmed by it and loses all self-control: "It seemed as if an heart of stone could not fail of being moved by it. It imparted to me an emotion altogether involuntary and incontroulable . . . I dropped the cloth I held in my hand, my heart overflowed with sympathy, and my eyes with unbidden tears" (p. 52). At first sight, Clara has mistaken Carwin for a "clown," "rustic and aukward" (p. 50). His voice changes her visual perception; now his face has "a radiance inexpressibly serene and potent" (p. 53). Almost paralyzed, she finally rallies to make a sketch of "this memorable visage" (p. 53) and spends half the night staring at it. The next day (which "arose in darkness and storm") is still spent in looking at the sketch. Night brings melancholy premonitions ("Was the tempest that had just past a signal of the ruin which impended over me?")

and anquished thoughts about Theodore's family (p. 54). The sound of her father's clock reminds her of death. Just after midnight, she hears threatening voices in her closet and flees to her brother's house, where she faints, "exhausted by the violence of my emotions, and by my speed" (p. 58).

This sequence shows the skill with which Brown has linked sexuality, madness, and death in Clara's mind. The climax of Clara's first brush with Carwin and her flight to her brother's house is a key scene. Is she succumbing to the family madness? If so, why at this point? It may be that she seeks refuge in the family (her parents'/brother's house), away from her self-sought place in the world (her own house, where she wants to live independently and in control of her own life), since it turns out to be the locus of sexuality and death. But her "ancient security" (p. 60) is gone; there is no way back. This is the meaning of Clara's subsequent dream in which her brother beckons to her across an abyss. Her wish to return to the past is dangerous, for surely she would turn mad.

Clara's dreams and visions show her double fear of sexuality and madness. Even a brief dip into Freudian dream analysis will show the pieces falling into place. (Although Freud has been in bad repute among feminists for confusing culturally conditioned phenomena with anthropological constants, he created important tools for our understanding of human behavior. A feminist analysis must apply the tools properly, not reject them out of hand.) The text itself suggests this approach; an early twentieth-century critic hailed Brown as "the veritable forerunner of the new psychic school of fiction as practiced by the adherents and disciples of the psycho-analytic school."[45] Freud himself defended it: "It sometimes happens that the sharp eye of the creative writer has an analytic realization of the process of transformation of which he is habitually no more than the tool."[46] "Transformation"–indeed! What makes the case so compelling is Clara's own conscious realization of her sexuality as a handicap. She interprets it in Wollstonecraftian fashion; under the existing circumstances, love makes a woman a prisoner, "a passion that will never rank me in the number of its eulogists; it was alone sufficient to the extermination of my peace" (p. 83). (This is only what it does to her psyche; with Mrs. Carter, she might have added that love's consequence, marriage, also makes a woman a physical prisoner.) In a lucid moment, Clara decides to "henceforth intrust my felicity to no one's keeping but my own" (p. 81).

The symbolization process on both levels of creation (Brown's and Clara's) firmly links madness with sexuality. The Wielands' family life centers around a phallic rock overlooking a river (water, a symbol of female sexuality and frequently of birth).[47] Brown places the lovers, Clara and Pleyel, in symbolic landscapes that express their difference. Clara walks in picturesque, garden-like scenes along the Schuylkill; Pleyel, brooding over the alleged death of his fiancée (who has no function in the plot other than to shield him from Clara's desire), seeks out "deformed," "stagnating," "noxious" areas along the Delaware (p. 47). But the symbols that Clara herself creates are more interesting, and central to this discussion.

Whereas Clara's distraction by Carwin's sensual impact comes as an unwelcome and sudden surprise to her, her attraction to Pleyel develops gradually; her awareness of it gains in intensity as she encourages Pleyel to respond to her feelings. After the dramatic sequence ending in her flight from her house, Pleyel moves in with her for protection, "in order to quiet my alarms" (p. 60). Proximity does not create closeness, however, "as it was wholly indifferent to him whether his nights were passed at my house or at my brother's" (p. 60). Clara's famous dream in the summer house by the river takes place some weeks later (p. 61), while Pleyel is still living with her. She falls asleep in an intensely sensual, erotic place characterized by female and male genital symbols; the building is in a "recess" or cave in the riverbank above the river and next to a waterfall. But her dreams are "of no cheerful hue." After a while,

> I . . . imagined myself walking, in the evening twilight, to my brother's habitation. A pit, methought, had been dug in the path I had taken, of which I was not aware. As I carelessly pursued my walk, I thought I saw my brother, standing at some distance before me, beckoning and calling me to make haste. He stood on the opposite edge of the gulph. I mended my pace, and one step more would have plunged me into this abyss, had not some one from behind caught suddenly my arm, and exclaimed, in a voice of eagerness and terror, "Hold! hold!" [P. 62]

It is important to realize that Clara is walking toward her brother in the dream while Pleyel, at this time, is living at her house. She walks away from Pleyel, now one with her house (seat of her sexual longing) but unresponsive to her wooing. Clara repeats in her dream the flight back to her family which she performed in the previous chapter. Her brother is seen as encouraging her, and Clara is ready to fall into the abyss when she is stopped. Although she cannot resist the pull, Clara realizes that Wieland's transformation into a madman has already created a barrier between them. Here is one instance where Theodore's progress toward insanity is noticed, albeit subconsciously, by another protagonist. A dream, says Freud, is always "the hallucinated fulfillment of a wish."[48] Clara wishes to reunite with her brother (her family, her past) in order to regain her "ancient security." In Freudian terms, the gulf represents the censorship that distorts her dream into an anxiety dream. "Anxiety dreams," Freud notes, "are as a rule also arousal dreams; we usually interrupt our sleep before the repressed wish in the dream has put its fulfilment through completely in spite of the censorship."[49]

Even a sexual interpretation of this dream content, which explains the dream as the attempted fulfillment of an incest wish, does not change the fact that Clara sees a danger in her brother. The point is that sexuality (the erotic setting for the dream) triggers the madness latent in the family (the family, to Clara, being identical with Theodore). Clara must resist this double temptation. The "gulf" as Clara's central image is appropriate; to yield is to fall (a falling sensation signifies sexual intercourse), is to succumb to sexuality and madness at the same time. It can only end in death. Clara's *last* use of the image shows its meaning fully developed—the grave. "I will die. The gulph before me is inevitable and near" (p. 228).

After Clara's stunned awakening from the dream, Carwin's threats associate the summer house in the "recess" with the one on the rock, place of her father's mysterious end. The seat of eros becomes the scene of death. Clara is fantasizing her father's death scene while she is being "rescued" by Pleyel (pp. 63-64).

Her increasingly intense association of sexuality with madness and death is shown in her physical surroundings as well as in her fantasies. Her closet, a sexual symbol transformed into the object of her death fantasies, is the place where Carwin hides, where her father's autobiographical manuscript is kept, and where she expects to find her brother. Her fantasies incorporate elements as well as symbolizations of her experience. Her last dream is a mixture of sexual dream symbols: rising and falling, water and fire, mountain and abyss; the only constant is Clara's self-perception as a victim (p. 236).

Once more back to Pleyel and Carwin: both are associated with water, of which Clara has a "hereditary dread" (p. 83). She experiences "floods of passion," her heart "overflowed with sympathy," she is "set afloat upon a stormy sea" or a "sea of troubles" (pp. 50, 52, 151, 68). Carwin is first introduced asking for a drink and receives a cup with which to get water; she sees him from her window standing on a riverbank and, of course, he takes over her summer house by the waterfall. Carwin fits well into this symbolic landscape, but Pleyel is fearful of sexuality. In Clara's fantasy, she sees him in danger of drowning (p. 83), whereas he reacts to her alleged immorality with a "flame of resentment" (p. 134).

Clara has to survive a fire and cross the Atlantic before she can marry Pleyel. After her nervous breakdown, she finds herself the last surviving Wieland. In a similar catharsis, she has to go through a process of complete identification with her brother at his worst moment. "Was I not likewise transformed from rational and human into a creature of nameless and fearful attributes? Was I not transported to the brink of the same abyss?" (pp. 179-80).

In Alcuin's world of male politicians, women has no place; a "paradise" had to be invented for them. The Wieland world is one of male eccentricity where women are both victims and carriers of madness. In *Ormond*, paternal failure starts a young woman's initiation into a world of men where women are objects, where utopian "alternatives" are constructed by misogynists, and where the only happiness comes from the company of other women. Themes from *Wieland* are continued: masculine failure and hubris; a young woman's survival of the "complicated havoc" (*Ormond*, p. 239)[50] created by men; the possibilities of an independent subsistence for women; the support from women's friendships.

Constantia Dudley has had a superior education for a woman; she is intelligent, but not otherwise a "prodigy." Her strength of mind is the result of her unusual upbringing. This proves helpful when her father turns bankrupt, defrauded by a younger man. Constantia's mother (another weak wife) dies of grief; her father moves from drink to blindness and childlike dependence on his daughter, and by the time she meets Ormond, Constantia has reached the bottom of her social decline. She has survived pestilence and poverty, been rescued from a rape attempt, and rejected an offer of marriage which would have ended her economic problems. Since *Ormond* is a novel *about* sexual politics, it is important to consider Constantia's reasons for rejecting her suitor, Balfour.

Her obvious reason is that she has "no sympathy, nor sentiments in common" with Balfour (p. 69); the prospect of economic security is not enough to tip the scales. Constantia's deliberations, according to the narrator, her friend Sophia, are spontaneous and not indebted to any source. "What are the genuine principles of that relation, and what conduct with respect to it is prescribed to rational beings by their duty, she had not hitherto investigated" (p. 68). But her explanations of her decision would be recognized by informed readers as Wollstonecraftian and potentially anti-Godwinian.

> Now she was at least mistress of the product of her own labor. Her tasks were toilsome, but the profits, though slender, were sure, and she administered her little property in what manner she pleased. Marriage would annihilate this power. Henceforth she would be bereft even of personal freedom. So far from possessing property, she herself would become the property of another.

She disdains to manipulate a man by the "soft artillery of blandishments and tears" that Rousseau had recommended and Wollstonecraft criticized. "She would not stoop to gain her end by the hateful arts of the sycophant and"— her potshot at Godwin—"was too wise to place an unbounded reliance on the influence of truth." Her conclusion: "Homely liberty was better than splendid servitude"—another Brownian reminder of the American Revolution (p. 69).

Ormond is introduced as a utopian reformer whose political philosophy is "to be intimately identified with the Godwinian model" (S. J. Krause),[51] nowhere more so than in his views on marriage. A whole chapter is devoted to his political and moral principles, already contrasting "discourse" and "actions" (p. 95), and pinpointing Ormond's "delight" with personal power (p. 96). It concludes with his "belief that the intellectual constitution of females was essentially defective" and that love based on equality does not exist (p. 97). The following chapter proceeds from theory to practice by describing his relationship with the beautiful Helena, who loves him but has to subsist as his kept woman. She is the perfect result of the feminine up-bringing that outraged Wollstonecraft; a textbook case for Drs. Fordyce and Gregory (next to Rousseau, the primary targets of the *Vindication*), she is "calculated to excite emotions more voluptuous than dignified" (p. 98). Yet she is not "silly or ignorant" (p. 98). She has wonderful "accomplish-ments," is a talented, even original, artist, and proves Ormond's equal at chess. But she has not been taught to reason, and Ormond does not encourage it ("he was accustomed to regard her merely as an object charming to the senses"). Her education, likewise, has not prepared her to be self-supporting when her father dies penniless; she must submit to "a life of dependence" (pp. 98–99).

Sophia, always reasonable, does justice to Helena. "Her understanding bore no disadvantageous comparison with that of the majority of her sex, but when placed in competition with that of some eminent females or of Ormond, it was exposed to the risk of contempt" (p. 98). No match for Ormond—yet he expects her to function as an equal in their "voluntary union" and to overcome social "prejudice" by force of reason. To "anni-hilate" those "inconveniences" of social ostracism, "it was only necessary to reason justly" (p. 101). Ormond uses the fiction of equality (basis of every contract) while dictating his own terms—and at the same time insisting that women, by virtue of gender, can never be the equals of men. His whole critique of marriage is based on "the general and incurable imperfection of the female character" (p. 100). To appease Helena's chronic unhappiness, he reasons with her, fully expecting "the influence of truth" to work, with the predictable result that his "maxims were confuted in the present case." In despair, he concludes that "[to] make her wise it would be requisite to change her sex" (pp. 103, 106).

Helena's flaws are those of the society that made her. Only women do her justice; even the critical Constantia grants her "greatness of mind" (p. 139). To Ormond, she is a plaything for his "amusement." "He must occasionally unbend, if he desires that the springs of his mind should retain their due vigor" (p. 108). From the beginning, Ormond is characterized as a pseudo-Godwinian, a coldhearted liar and power-hungry manipulator of men and women. Although his utopian plans remain behind the scenes, it is clear that they follow the same principles and motives as his visible actions. The greatest of Brown's "liberal" scoundrels, he constantly exposes his political designs for what they really are—dishonest power schemes—by his violations of human dignity, particularly that of women.

Enter Constantia, attempting to persuade Ormond that he must marry Helena. She scores in an unexpected quarter. "He was suddenly changed, from being one of the calumniators of the female sex, to one of its warmest eulogists" (p. 131), and he decides to drop Helena for Constantia. After Helena's suicide (her parting letter a model of dignity and logic), Ormond courts (and spies on) Constantia by all the means in his power. It is a *power* struggle. "Ormond aspired to nothing more ardently than to hold the reins of opinion—to exercise absolute power over the conduct of others" (p. 147). His pursuit of Constantia, ending in his rape attempt and death, begins with a recognition of her intellectual equality; but this equality only spurs his need to dominate. It raises the stakes, but does not change his game. His disdain of marriage was based on woman's flawed nature—this basis is gone. Yet, "Constantia was to be obtained by any means" (p. 148), marriage being only a last resort. ("Any means" includes the murder of her father when he appears to be in the way.) Failing to persuade Constantia, he resorts to rape, preceded by ceremonious warnings (pp. 214–15). It is now revealed that Ormond has been a rapist since his youth. Sophia's narration of this background story shows that Brown had an uncanny insight into the mechanics of rape: an act of power, not of sex, woman as pawn in a male struggle for dominance.

> A youth of eighteen, a volunteer in a Russian army encamped in Bessarabia, made prey of a Tartar girl, found in the field of a recent battle. Conducting her to his quarters, he met a friend, who, on some pretence, claimed the victim. From angry words they betook themselves to swords. A combat ensued, in which the first claimant ran his antagonist through the body. He then bore his prize unmolested away, and having exercised brutality of one kind upon the hapless victim, stabbed her to the heart, as an offering to the *manes* of Sarsefield, the friend whom he had slain. Next morning, willing more signally to expiate his guilt, he rushed alone upon a troop of Turkish foragers, and brought away five heads, suspended, by their gory locks, to his horse's mane. These he cast upon the grave of Sarsefield, and conceived himself fully to have expiated yesterday's offence. In reward for his prowess, the general gave him a commission in the Cossack troops. [P. 218]

In his final confrontation with Constantia (following another murder), Ormond sardonically reveals that this logic of power originates in hubris, a form of madness. Ormond, the "secret witness" (the novel's subtitle) of human deeds, assumes the role of God. His motives are impersonal, his actions irresistible. "I am not tired of well-doing," he asserts, despite the ingratitude he has encountered. Being raped, he tells Constantia, will "afford you an illustrious opportunity to signalize your wisdom and your fortitude"

(p. 232). Rejection is something he cannot brook. "What thou refusedst to bestow it is in my power to extort. I came for that end" (p. 233). He is struck by Constantia's penknife and expires at her feet, a fitting climax, as S. J. Krause has observed, "not so much of the traditional battle of the sexes, as a battle over sexism."[52]

The villain slain, Constantia and Sophia sail for Europe. In this novel, as in *Wieland*, "communities of women" (Nina Auerbach) offer the only escape from the mad world of men. Clara Wieland has several women friends: Mrs. Boynton whom she frequently visits; her sister-in-law Catharine, "endowed with an uncommon portion of good sense" (p. 34); and Louisa Conway, murdered by Theodore so cruelly that "*not a lineament remained!*" (p. 157). Clara remembers sadly that Louisa "never met my eye, or occurred to my reflection, without exciting a kind of enthusiasm. Her softness, her intelligence, her equanimity, never shall I see surpassed. I have often shed tears of pleasure at her approach, and pressed her to my bosom in an agony of fondness" (p. 27).

Constantia Dudley develops a great fondness for the aptly named Martinette, growing "daily more enamored of her new acquaintance" (p. 157), although shocked by her friend's sanguinary exploits (as it turns out, she is Ormond's sister) from whose perspective Constantia appears as "a frail mimosa" (p. 160)! But her great love belongs to Sophia. Their reunion throws them into a three-day "state of dizziness and intoxication." Sophia reports, "The ordinary functions of nature were disturbed. The appetite for sleep and for food were [sic] confounded and lost amidst the impetuosities of a master passion. To look and to talk to each other afforded enchanting occupation for every moment. I would not part from her side, but eat [sic] and slept, walked and mused and read, with my arm locked in hers, and with her breath fanning my cheek" (p. 207). Ormond jealously mocks their "romantic passion for each other" (p. 212), but to them, it is a great celebration: "O precious inebriation of the heart! O pre-eminent love! what pleasure of reason or sense can stand in competition with those attendant upon thee? . . . surely thy sanction is divine, thy boon is happiness!" (p. 207).

## IV

Whereas *Wieland* and *Ormond* assume a woman's perspective, *Stephen Calvert*, *Edgar Huntly* and *Arthur Mervyn* have male narrators and deal with problems of young men seeking to establish a place for themselves in the world. This was a theme already developed in the "Carwin" sequel to *Wieland*. The common starting point of these stories is the death or failure of a father (death in *SC* and *EH*, cruelty in "Carwin" and *AM*); in each, the young man's path to success lies through a woman's fortune. The "Carwin" fragment breaks off before the hero's marriage to a rich widow. Stephen Calvert gains a fortune which rightfully belongs to a young woman disinherited by a tyrannical father.[53] Edgar Huntly is willing to marry a young woman when she comes into money; when she loses it, she also loses him. Edgar's sleepwalking *Doppelgänger* Clithero has made a career through a woman's affection—and spoiled it through hubris. Arthur Mervyn even has a choice of two women—and chooses the unattractive, rich widow over the pretty but poor young girl. These plots are complicated, because they also involve issues of cultural and personal identity. Critics of *AM* have tended to see in Arthur's final decision a capitulation, a regression to the security of the womb, a sacrifice of his own potential identity to the maternal embrace, even a "self-abasement."[54] It could be argued in Arthur's defense that his final leap into "matronage" follows the previous failures of "patronage"; as Ludloe in "Carwin," so Welbeck in *AM*, proves treacherous. And yet the matter is more complex than this; for why can't these young men stand on their own feet? A recent critic has recognized the "balance between sex and property" as "basic to *Arthur Mervyn*."[55] Since *AM* is the central and most finished text of this phase, I will use it to demonstrate the problem.[56]

Mervyn is a country boy thrown into the turmoil of the city. He upholds the ideals of country life and experiences the city as a place of fraud, deception, and pestilence. But this simple contrast does not hold. Neither Mervyn's world nor his own character can be drawn in black and white; both are mixtures of good and evil. Arthur's world, like that of Clara and Constantia, "is a world of failed fathers and ruined families,"[57] a world that transcends city and country. Arthur flees from the country where he has become an "alien" (*AM*, p. 21) because of a hostile and jealous father. The elder Mervyn, after the death of his wife, falls for the wiles of a milkmaid (who has also made advances to Arthur) and kicks his son out of the nest. Arthur's fate has a number of parallels in the novel. As Emory Elliott points out, "The fathers of Mervyn, Welbeck, and Achsa desert or abandon their children while those like Mr. Hadwin, Watson, and the elder Lodi die prematurely from disease, crime, and political havoc."[58] The orphaned condition of so many characters is a microcosmic version of the human condition created by the yellow fever, which destroys not only real families but also the human family, the sense of community. Under these conditions, the ethical ideals that Arthur carries so self-consciously on his standard are bound to be subverted by the promptings of self-interest necessary to survival and advancement. Arthur is a mixed character because he must adapt himself to a "culture of contradictions,"[59] like himself the product of the historical moment. "Neither picaresque saint nor complete confidence man, Mervyn, a name suggestive of Everyman, is a symbol of the amoral, unschooled but intelligent individual struggling to survive in the social turmoil of the post-revolutionary age."[60] True, but what about the fact of gender? Is it correct to speak of "Arthur

Mervyn, American"[61] as a representative figure? Women in the early Republic faced special problems not encountered by men, and they face some of them in this novel. We are shown how Arthur slips in and out of the roles of child, lover, and man-of-the-world with little difficulty, whereas a comparably situated young woman, Eliza Hadwin, is confined to the role of dependent. And she is not even much of a victim (despite Arthur's betrayal of her love), if her fate is compared to that of some other young women: Clemenza Lodi, seduced, defrauded, and abandoned in a brothel; Arthur's own sister, seduced, abandoned, and driven to suicide by her father; Eliza's sister Susan, dying from imagined abandonment, and buried by Arthur like a dog.

This hero's interest in women is inevitably property-related, whether his approach to that property follows the route of patronage or matronage. In the patronage model, the property belongs to the real or apparent father (Hadwin/Welbeck), and the young woman represents either access to the property via inheritance (Eliza) or simply an added benefit (Clemenza). In the matronage situation, the woman herself owns the property. These schemes recur with variations in the other major fiction of the same phase. In "Carwin," the adoptive father procures the rich widow for the young man.[62] Edgar's Mary has her own modest fortune (at least for a while); Clithero's adoptive mother prepares a match between her adopted daughter and Clithero. Stephen Calvert's mother has taken up the young woman whose property he inherits from her father; Stephen loses interest in her when he meets a more attractive and wealthy woman. (This woman in turn was adopted by an aunt after escaping from a miserable, arranged marriage.)

In *AM*, the acquisition of property through patronage fails. This does not mean that Arthur does not find a substitute father and mother. But Dr. Stevens (narrator of large portions of the story) and his wife represent an option that Mervyn ultimately rejects—independence and identity through "useful exertion"—and they bear little relation to the property/sex complex. Instead, Arthur's "apprenticeship" takes place under the roof of a man who has a long history of sexually and financially exploiting women. The apprentice, it is true, renounces his master and eventually has a chance to restore some of the damage Welbeck has done. But Welbeck's patronage brings out that aspect of Arthur's character that predisposes him to accept the world's gifts as his due and causes him to spend so much time on his self-stylization as a worthy and "undepraved" recipient. On his first errand for Welbeck, Arthur reflects:

> But what was the fate reserved for me? Perhaps Welbeck would
> adopt me for his own son. Wealth has ever been capriciously dis-
> tributed. The mere physical relation of birth is all that intitles us to
> manors and thrones. Identity itself frequently depends upon a casual
> likeness or an old nurse's imposture. Nations have risen in arms, as

in the case of the Stewarts, in the cause of one, the genuineness of
whose birth has been denied and can never be proved. But if the
cause be trivial and fallacious, the effects are momentous and solid.
It ascertains our portions of felicity and usefulness, and fixes our lot
among peasants or princes. [Pp. 57-58]

This readiness to passively accept a "fate" is in stark contrast to Arthur's
pronounced curiosity and his tendency to play Fate himself by interfering in
the affairs of other people. (A fine testing ground for his chameleon ethics.
"Honest purposes," he reasons, "though they may not bestow happiness
on others, will, at least, secure it to him who fosters them" [p. 270]. Arthur's
quest for a place in the world is marked by this contradiction, which is also
expressed in his changing resolves, his frequent changes of place, his vacilla-
tion between the roles of observer and actor, between naiveté and wisdom.
There are important clues that he even vacillates between gender roles. This
is not your hairy-chested, powerful seducer type. We learn that, back on the
farm, he used to knit stockings and stay away from young men's activities,
reason enough for a neighbor to doubt if all is right with Arthur. He

moped away his time in solitude, never associated with other young
people, never mounted an horse but when he could not help it, and
never fired a gun or angled for a fish in his life. Some people supposed him to be half an idiot, or, at least, not to be in his right
mind; and, indeed, his conduct was so very perverse and singular,
that I do not wonder at those who accounted for it in this way.
[P. 233]

This repudiation of prescribed gender roles is more important than it at first
appears. I have referred to the special problems that women at the end of
the eighteenth century were facing. Not the least of them was an increasing pressure to marry (as women's independent subsistence was more and
more endangered) while, at the same time, their opportunities to marry
dwindled.[63] To advance in the world or simply to obtain a respectable place
in it, women *had* to marry. Whether or not Brown was aware of the historical
trends, whether he picked up the pattern from the sentimental tradition or
any other context, is irrelevant here, because this is so clearly identified as a
feminine pattern of behavior. It is the pattern that Mervyn follows. Amidst
all his waverings, he constantly exhibits androgynous traits (which do not
prevent him from sexist behavior, as we shall see). In the end, he settles for a
typical woman's "career"; he marries a wealthy older person, better educated
and more sophisticated than he. Arthur is "wax in her hand" (p. 428) and
calls her his "mamma," just as a young bride might call an older husband
"daddy." Arthur, it turns out, is Everyman *and* Everywoman, after all; but is
he really the representative American? No, because he is still a man. The

irony of his rise from rags to riches is a double one. He not only chooses a woman's career (the critic's charge of "self-abasement" suddenly gains new dimensions!), but he does so out of a man's arsenal of possible choices. This gives new depth to his much-discussed opportunism—if *he* needs it, how much more a woman? What choices among "honest purposes" does *she* have?

Two more touches from the broad palette of what is perhaps Brown's best novel, one tragic, the other tragicomic. Eliza's rejection by Arthur as a companion and future wife is tragic for her. The decision, typically, is not final until after she has lost her inheritance to a greedy uncle; Arthur's rationalizations of what is to become of her are pitiful (p. 311). But he distances himself from her even earlier, as she appears to be in the way of his plans for a future (p. 293). As Elliott has recognized, "Eliza makes a powerful argument from the position of women's rights for sharing in his years of learning and experience":[64]

> You think me unworthy to partake of your cares and labors; . . . you
> regard my company as an obstacle and incumbrance; . . . assistance
> and counsel must all proceed from you; and . . . no scene is fit for
> me, but what you regard as slothful and inglorious.
>
> Have I not the same claims to be wise, and active, and courageous
> as you? If I am ignorant and weak, do I not owe it to the same cause
> that has made you so; and will not the same means which promote
> your improvement be likewise useful to me? You desire to obtain
> knowledge, by travelling and conversing with many persons, and
> studying many scenes; but you desire it for yourself alone. Me, you
> think poor, weak, and contemptible; fit for nothing but to spin and
> churn. Provided I exist, am screened from the weather, have enough
> to eat and drink, you are satisfied. As to strengthening my mind and
> enlarging my knowledge, these things are valuable to you, but on me
> they are thrown away. I deserve not the gift. [P. 296]

Arthur is "shaken" but not convinced. Eliza ultimately arrives to live as a dependent in Achsa's household, also calling her "mamma," thus becoming a sister/daughter to Arthur. There she appears (small poetic justice) in Arthur's Oedipal dream just before his marriage to Achsa Fielding.

Although tragic to Arthur (and Achsa, who nearly breaks off the engagement), this dream must give a sense of satisfaction, even amusement, to readers who feel qualms about Arthur's success. It hints at the price he may have to pay. The dream is caused by Arthur's sudden panic at the prospect of marriage. Its two parts show the reasons for his panic—fear of sexuality and fear of his "mamma's" past in the shape of her first husband, now to become his "father." (A Freudian interpretation might argue that the dream's "wish" is the appearance of the first husband as an obstacle to the marriage.) Part one, not a proper dream but "a nameless sort of terror," is a replay of

Pleyel's drowning in *Wieland*, this time from the perspective of the victim. "Methinks, that one falling from a tree, overhanging a torrent, plunged into the whirling eddy, and gasping and struggling while he sinks to rise no more, would feel just as I did then" (p. 436). Part two is a visit to Achsa's house, complete with Eliza as parlormaid, only to find Achsa's first husband there.

> What, said he, mildly, is your business with my wife? She cannot see you instantly, and has sent me to receive your commands.
> Your *wife*! I want Mrs. Fielding.
> True; and Mrs. Fielding is my wife. Thank Heaven I have come in time to discover her, and claim her as such.
> I started back. I shuddered. My joints slackened, and I stretched my hand to catch something by which I might be saved from sinking on the floor. Meanwhile, Fielding changed his countenance into rage and fury. He called me villain! bad me avaunt! and drew a shining steel from his bosom, with which he stabbed me to the heart.
> [P. 437]

This classic Oedipal triangle ends a story which had started with one, Mervyn's banishment by his natural father. Ironically, *AM* ends with the young man fantasizing about future fatherhood (p. 446).

## V

In the view of a 1970s feminist critic, "The final resolution of Arthur and Achsa's difficulties offers the maternal role as one possibility in coming to terms with the feminine."[65] This would imply that Brown intended woman as the Other, the nonhuman, the "object" one must come to terms with. It would also mean that the novelist is to be identified with Arthur and the other young men of this phase. That this is patently wrong and that Brown was aware of the punishment such treatment would bring on the heads of the perpetrators is already hinted at in the fate that awaits Arthur in his marriage. Still, Achsa might let him get away with it. The young man in Brown's next novel, *Clara Howard*, is not so lucky.

Brown's last two novels continue to evolve themes that the earlier ones had developed. They represent a high point in awareness, as well as in craftsmanship, technical finesse. They have even been claimed as Brown's "most mature novels."[66] Thematic evolution, as I see it, also accounts for the apparently "regressive" epistolary form that has raised critical eyebrows.[67] Brown's novels began with female narrators (*Wieland/Ormond*), moved on to male narrators ("Carwin"/*SC/EH/AM*), and end now with letters written by both men and women. The form itself is a statement.

The strongest case for *Clara Howard* and *Jane Talbot* as a continuation of earlier efforts was made in a recent essay by S. J. Krause, who finds in them "an extension of the same basic investigation of the 'moral constitution of man' that concerned him" before.[68] His essay places them in the context of Brown's running argument with Godwin and Godwinism. Thus, it finds Clara "a pillar of Godwinian moral theory," "the original Iron Maiden of American literature" who exhibits the absurdities of extreme adherence to "disinterest" (Krause, p. 187). *JT* continues the argument with the result that "Godwin is not just tested, he is corrected; Jane and Colden dispense with theoretical obligations, as it becomes plain that one partner can in no way receive a happiness conferred at the expense of the other's happiness" (Krause, p. 187). To achieve this resolution, Rousseau's radical reliance on feeling is employed as the novelist's "counter-theory" supporting the notion that "acute feelings are heuristic; through the acutest of them we learn virtue" (Krause, p. 191).

This battle of ideas, Godwin versus Rousseau, must be seen in connection with the ongoing battle of the sexes. With respect to both, S. J. Krause's contention can be upheld "that the last two novels are indeed counterparts which have to be read together, in sequence, as they were written, *Jane* in the context of *Clara*. Not only was *Jane* begun almost immediately after *Clara* was finished, but it is its intellectual complement suggesting a progression of where we go from *Clara*, and where we do not. From the negative analysis on which *Clara* ended, we move on to a consideration of alternatives." (p. 202).

In *CH*, the young man continues the game of sex and property, garnished with the usual claims of high-minded disinterest and the most rigorous ethical standards. For the first time, the patronage model seems to work. Edward/Philip, another talented country lad,[69] becomes the protégé of his teacher, Mr. Howard. "He had reason to regard me, indeed, somewhat like his own son. I had no father; I had no property" (XIII, p. 31). Howard leaves the country and returns, years later, with a rich wife and a beautiful, accomplished stepdaughter, Clara, whom he has destined to marry Philip. In the meantime, however, Philip has become engaged to Mary Wilmot, whom he does not love but who loves him and has suddenly come into some money through her brother (this part of the plot is lifted from *EH*). Mary in turn is loved by Mr. Sedley whom she does not love. Almost simultaneously, she finds out that she lost the money (as Mary in *EH*) and that Philip has met Clara, has in fact moved in with the Howards. Mary breaks the engagement to set Philip free for the inevitable and vanishes from the scene. Patronage has superseded matronage; the prize is beautiful, rich, and also in love with Philip. Open season, at last?

Unfortunately, Philip meets what he deserves, a woman who takes him at his word. When he was urging Mary to become his wife, he used the vocabulary of benevolence, as she recalls:

> I was not so base as to accept your hand, without your heart. You
> talked of gratitude, and duty, and perfect esteem. . . . Your reason
> discerned and adored my merits, and the concurrence of the heart
> could not but follow. . . . I doubted not your fidelity, and that the
> consciousness of *conferring happiness* would secure your content-
> ment. [II, pp. 12-13; emphasis mine]

When Clara learns about Mary, she tells Philip that these were, indeed, valid
reasons; that he has to go find Mary and marry her. His earlier claims of
disinterestedness are taken seriously and promptly turn against him. And in
keeping with the "higher nature" that Mervyn and company have routinely
ascribed to the objects of their love, Clara remains adamantly disinterested
herself, yielding no ground to the impulses of self-interest (although she loves
Philip).

Although the basic plot is an elaboration of a catch-22 that Brown had
discussed with his friend William Wood Wilkins around 1792 (boy loves girl
but is loved by another girl),[70] it is significantly transformed by the property
aspect at the time it becomes *CH*. The gentleman doth protest too much—
and has to eat his own words. He tells Clara:

> Your decision has made me unhappy. I believe your decision absurd,
> yet I know your motives are disinterested and heroic. I know the
> misery which adherence to your schemes costs you. It is only less
> than my own. Why then should I aggravate my own? It is the system
> of nature that deserves my hatred and my curses—that system which
> makes our very virtues instrumental to our misery. [III, p. 16]

Whether or not the "system of nature" is Goodwin's moral system or Rousseau's "nature of things" (*Contrat Sociale*), it is reason that Philip is told he
lacks; "Thy spirit is not curbed by reason" (VII, p. 22). Or as the *Vindication*
has it, "to submit to reason is to submit to the nature of things."[71] This does
not mean that Philip is not able or does not try to reason with Clara. "That
conduct which in me is culpable, is no less culpable in others. Am I cruel and
unjust in refusing my love to one that claims it? So are you, whose refusal
is no less obstinate as to me, as mine with respect to another; and who
hearkens not to claims upon your sympathy, as reasonable as those of Mary
on mine" (XXIV, p. 94). But the twisting of words does not help. The moral
tenets that Philip claimed as the basis for his actions are rubbed in his face
until he nearly chokes. Moreover, the re-emerged Mary refuses to take him
back, urging the same reasons. "She was too blind an admirer, and assiduous
a follower of Clara Howard" (XXVI, p. 98). Knight that he is, Philip is sent
on this impossible crusade by his fair lady until he goes insane. She gives in
briefly once, when he nearly dies (from jumping into water!), but she recovers and sends him out again. This time, he goes mad. "Alas, my friend!

you are not in your right mind," Mary informs him. "Disappointment has injured your reason" (XXVIII, p. 112). The dilemma gets resolved only when Mary agrees to marry Sedley. Philip recovers slowly: "In truth, I have been sick;... I have been half crazy, shivering and glowing by turns; bereft of appetite and restless—every object was tinged with melancholy hues" (XXXI, p. 120).

Selfishness masked by high purposes is unmasked by high purposes; by accepting Philip's premises, Clara becomes the Other with a vengeance—she turns nonhuman by living the proposition to its bitter end. Philip feels the nightmare reality of what, normally, would be conventional verbiage; he must "submit to one whom I deem unerring and divine"; "an angel in the heavens like thee, is not a fit companion for a mere earthworm like Philip Stanley" (XVIII, p. 75). Clara, the "heavenly monitor" (XXXI, p. 119), is firmly established as his preceptress who will teach the young man "moral discernment." In her words, "Our modes of judging and our maxims shall be the same; and this resemblance shall be purchased at the cost of all my patience, my skill, and my love" (XXXII, p. 122). A double wedding in sight, Clara writes to Mary, "At present, I must devote myself to console this good lad for his sufferings, incurred, *as he presumes to say*, entirely on my account" (XXXIII, p. 122; emphasis mine).

With respect to our theme, *Jane Talbot* is both summary and resolution of Brown's incredible three-year spell of creativity (1798–1801) that produced all his novels. This comedy has familiar scenes and characters, but the romantic leads have changed. Its greatest innovation is the young man, Colden. He is Brown's epitaph written by himself (with a great deal of wishful thinking), the closest he ever came to a fictional self-portrait. A penniless writer with a suspiciously radical background, he is won to love, marriage, and rational Christianity by Jane who, in turn, changes from a Betsy Thoughtless to a young woman of rational persuasions.

The plot, too, is a synopsis of the familiar. Jane, bereft of her mother as a child, is exposed to masculine failure and tyranny in the persons of her weak father and rakish brother, the latter a cartoon-character misogynist. Jane, an "April girl" who cannot resist an appeal to her emotions, loses half her money to him despite the fact that she knows better—a prefiguration of things to come, for she is a sitting duck for manipulators. Adopted by her aunt, Mrs. Fielder, she follows the advice to marry an older man whom she does not love (Talbot). During his absence, she meets Colden whom she falls to loving and wooing. Although she does not break her marriage vows, a forged letter convinces both her husband and her aunt that she has; Colden is marked as a seducer, and his alleged radicalism is the motive presented by the prosecution. This is the state of affairs when the curtain rises. Talbot is dead, and Jane wishes to marry Colden. Enter the obstacle: Mrs. Fielder, who abhors the young man and his suspected views; she will disinherit Jane if she marries Colden, whereupon the elder Colden (another tyrant) disinherits his son for wanting to marry a poor girl. A conspiracy of the elders, patriarchy and matriarchy coming together in perfect cacophony.

Although Jane's conflict is one between love and duty, the traditional parameters have been discredited. On the one hand, Mrs. Fielder (her "mother") is shown to be as power-hungry and manipulative as she suspects Colden to be; she interprets relationships in terms of power—a form of thinking Jane herself has adopted and must unlearn. Mrs. Fielder raves at Colden that Jane is "an unhappy girl who has put herself into your power" (p. 75);[72] Jane speaks of "my mother's government" (p. 206); at times she promises to "reign" over Colden (p. 93), at other times she slips into a traditional woman's role and craves governance from him. "Let me lose all separate feelings, all separate existence, and let me know no principle of action, but the decision of your judgment; no motive or desire but to please; to gratify you" (p. 91).

On the other hand, Colden is a male feminist who refuses to play any of these games. He wants Jane, not her money. (When interrogated by Jane's brother about "the basis of this engagement," his response is totally deadpan: "Mutual affection, I believe, is the only basis" [p. 123].) He wants Jane to make her own decisions, not follow his; he is firm but unassuming, loving but rational. His lesson is Wollstonecraftian: "It is a farce to call any being virtuous, whose virtues do not result from the exercise of its own reason."[73] Where Jane's worst crimes, in Mrs. Fielder's eyes, are crimes against the family ("the faithless wife and the ungrateful child" [p. 76]), Colden insists that Jane be herself, not a wife or a daughter. In the tug-of-war between Mrs. Fielder and himself, he turns down his final chance to win Jane over to his side; "she has made her election" (p. 212). Jane is a responsible person; this is her choice, which he respects.

Mrs. Fielder's comic ravings about Colden's "radical" views supposedly derived from Godwin are "pure fantasy," as S. J. Krause has shown,[74] and only serve to discredit her, just as her attempts to bribe Colden do. According to her, Colden is

> the advocate of suicide; a scoffer at promises; the despiser of revelation, of providence and a future state; an opponent of marriage, and . . . one who denied (shocking!) that any thing but mere habit and positive law, stood in the way of marriage; nay, of intercourse without marriage, between brother and sister, parent and child!
> [P. 68]

Colden does, in the end, return as a rational Christian to marry Jane, but she has already met him halfway. The "reformation" is mutual, the happy end believable.

Received opinion has it that *Clara* and *Jane* were Brown's last attempts at fiction. Charles E. Bennett has recently pointed out that this is not the case and that Brown developed an interest in historical fiction which lasted well into his last decade.[75] We have already seen that the last two finished novels are no evidence of a "growing conservatism" with respect to Brown's views on women. The surviving fragments of his large-scale project in fictional history show that he placed special emphasis on strong, independent women even then. His magazine articles of the last decade, laboriously nonpartisan as they are, also indicate that he never lost interest in women's issues.

If Brown neither abandoned the pursuit of fiction nor lost his feminist impulse, why did he not finish another novel for the ever-growing audience of women readers in America? The answer must be that he had realized the impossibility of making a living as a writer of fiction—*his* fiction, anyway. *Clara* and *Jane* "were his last-gasp efforts to cultivate a following."[76] In 1801, the year these two appeared, Brown met his future wife whom he married in 1804. Henceforth, unprofitable fiction had to give way to more solid sources of income; an unremunerative career as a novelist was no way to satisfy the demands of a family.

## Notes

1. Margaret Fuller, "Papers on Literature and Art" [1846], in *Critical Essays on Charles Brockden Brown*, ed. Bernard Rosenthal (Boston: G. K. Hall, 1981), p. 63.

2. *Carlyle's Laugh and Other Surprises* (Boston and New York: Houghton Mifflin, 1909), p. 58.

3. See, for instance, Lillie Deming Loshe, *The Early American Novel 1789–1830* (1907; reprint ed., New York: Fredrick Ungar, 1958), Ch. 3; and David Lee Clark, *Brockden Brown and the Rights of Women* (Austin: University of Texas Bulletin No. 2212, 1922).

4. Augusta Genevieve Violette, *Economic Feminism in American Literature Prior to 1848* (Orono: University of Maine Studies, 1925), p. 47.

5. Mary Sumner Benson, *Women in Eighteenth-Century America: A Study of Opinion and Social Usage* (New York: Columbia University Press, 1935), pp. 200–201.

6. Dorothy Yost Deegan, *The Stereotype of the Single Woman in American Novels* (New York: Columbia University Press, 1951), pp. 130–31.

7. *Retrospective Review* 9 (1824), p. 317. Quoted in Rosenthal, Introduction, *Critical Essays*, p. 5.

8. The most useful bibliographies of Brown criticism are Robert E. Hemenway and Dean H. Keller, "Charles Brockden Brown, America's First Important Novelist: A Checklist of Biography and Criticism," *Papers of*

*the Bibliographical Society of America* 60 (1966):349–62; Paul Witherington, "Charles Brockden Brown: A Bibliographical Essay," *Early American Literature* 9 (1974):164–87; Patricia Parker, *Charles Brockden Brown: A Reference Guide* (Boston: G. K. Hall, 1980); Charles A. Carpenter, "Selective Bibliography of Writings about Charles Brockden Brown," in Rosenthal, *Critical Essays*, pp. 224–39.

9. A prominent recent example is Nina Baym, "A Minority Reading of *Wieland*," in Rosenthal, *Critical Essays*, pp. 87–103. In Baym's opinion, "there is no real evidence that [Brown's] novelistic aims were very high" (p. 87); critical emphasis on Brown's ideas ("a list of truisms"), although no valid reason for the high appreciation of his fiction, is caused by "the intense didactic bias" in academic criticism (p. 88).

10. Rosenthal, Introduction, *Critical Essays*, p. 2.

11. See, for instance, Judith Ann Cunningham, "Charles Brockden Brown's Pursuit of a Realistic Feminism: A Study of his Writings as a Contribution to the Growth of Women's Rights in America" (Ph.D. diss., Ball State University, 1971); Mary A. McCay, "Women in the Novels of Charles Brockden Brown: A Study" (Ph.D. diss., Tufts University, 1973); Ann Stanford, "Images of Women in Early American Literature," in *What Manner of Woman: Essays on English and American Life and Literature*, ed. Marlene Springer (New York: New York University Press, 1977), pp. 184–210; Nina Baym, "Portrayal of Women in American Literature, 1790–1870," ibid., pp. 211–34.

12. Examples are Ernest Earnest, *The American Eve in Fact and Fiction, 1775–1914* (Urbana: University of Illinois Press, 1974); Patricia Jewell McAlexander, "The Cultural Dialogue on the Nature and Role of Women in Late Eighteenth-Century America," *Early American Literature* 9 (1975):252–66.

13. Cathy N. Davidson, "The Matter and Manner of Charles Brockden Brown's *Alcuin*," in Rosenthal, *Critical Studies*, pp. 71–86; and Sydney J. Krause, "*Clara Howard* and *Jane Talbot*: Godwin on Trial," ibid., pp. 184–211.

14. William Hedges, "Charles Brockden Brown and the Culture of Contradictions," *Early American Literature* 9 (1974):115.

15. Davidson, "Brown's *Alcuin*," p. 75.

16. This body of work includes the letters between "Henrietta" and "C. B. B." in David Lee Clark, *Charles Brockden Brown: Pioneer Voice of America* (Durham, N.C.: Duke University Press, 1952), pp. 55–107, as well as Brown's correspondence with friends in which "Henrietta" is mentioned. My reference is specifically to Brown's letter "To J. D———n" (MS at the Humanities Research Center, University of Texas at Austin) listed as no. 2 in Charles E. Bennett, "The Letters of Charles Brockden Brown: An Annotated Census," *Resources for American Literary Study* 4, no. 2 (1976):167.

17. All citations in text are from Lee R. Edwards, ed., *Alcuin: A Dialogue* (New York: Grossman, 1971).

18. Edwards, Afterword, *Alcuin*, p. 94.

19. All references are to the second edition of 1792 in the facsimile reproduction of Gregg International Publishers (Farnborough, England, 1970). Its appendix contains Godwin's biography of Wollstonecraft first published in his *Memoirs of the Author of "A Vindication of the Rights of Woman"* (1798), which will be cited hereafter as *Memoirs*.

20. It was also a big headache for a writer addressing a predominantly female audience. Hawthorne's much-maligned diatribe against the "scribbling women" was directed at the sentimental bowdlerization of issues that, in his opinion, called for franker treatment.

21. I wish to thank Professor Sydney J. Krause, general editor of the CEAA/CSE Bicentennial Edition of Brown, for making available to me the resources of the Kent State University Bibliographical and Textual Center and, especially, for permitting me to use his manuscript notes to *Ormond*, which will appear as vol. 2 of the edition. All quotations here are from his lengthy commentary on marriage (passages 140.35–141.2; 141.22–26; 147.24–28 in the KSU *Ormond*), henceforth cited as KSU *Ormond*. I also wish to thank Ms. Bobbie Trowbridge at the center for clerical support during my stay.

22. Wollstonecraft, *Vindication*, p. 59.

23. Krause, KSU *Ormond*.

24. Ibid.

25. See Ralph Wardle, *Mary Wollstonecraft: A Critical Biography* (Lawrence: Kansas University Press, 1951), p. 158 ff.; R. M. Janes, "On the Reception of Mary Wollstonecraft's *A Vindication of the Rights of Woman*," *Journal of the History of Ideas* 39 (1978):293–302; Marcelle Thiébaux, "Mary Wollstonecraft in Federalist America: 1791–1802," in *The Evidence of the Imagination: Studies of Interactions between Life and Art in English Romantic Literature*, ed. Donald H. Reiman et al. (New York: New York University Press, 1978), pp. 195–245. For Philadelphia, see Bertha Monica Stearns, "Early Philadelphia Magazines for Ladies," *Pennsylvania Magazine of History and Biography* 64 (1940): 479–91.

26. Krause, KSU *Ormond*; and Krause, "*Clara Howard* and *Jane Talbot*," pp. 196–97.

27. Krause, KSU *Ormond*.

28. Godwin, *Memoirs*, p. 166.

29. Krause, KSU *Ormond*.

30. Davidson, "Brown's *Alcuin*," p. 75.

31. Most often quoted from Brown's preface to *Edgar Huntly* (1799). See David Lee Clark, ed., *Edgar Huntly, or Memoirs of a Sleep-Walker* (New York: Macmillan, 1928), p. xxiii.

32. Advertisement for *Sky-Walk*, *The Weekly Magazine* (Philadelphia), 17 March 1798, p. 202, reprinted in *The Rhapsodist and Other Uncollected Writings by Charles Brockden Brown*, ed. Harry R. Warfel (New York: Scholars' Facsimiles & Reprints, 1943), pp. 135–36.

33. "Walstein's School of History. From the German of Krants of Gotha," *The Monthly Magazine and American Review* (New York), August–September 1799, p. 408, reprinted in *The Rhapsodist*, p. 151.

34. "Walstein's School," *Rhapsodist*, p. 152.

35. Ibid.

36. Ibid.

37. "The Difference between History and Romance," *Monthly Magazine and American Review*, April 1800, p. 251, reprinted in Alfred Weber, "Essays und Rezensionen von Charles Brockden Brown," *Jahrbuch für Amerikastudien* 6 (1961):185.

38. William J. Scheick, "The Problem of Origination in Brown's *Ormond*," in Rosenthal, *Critical Essays*, pp. 127–28.

39. *Wieland or The Transformation. An American Tale/Memoirs of Carwin the Biloquist (1798)*, Bicentennial Ed. vol. 1, ed. Sydney J. Krause and S.W. Reid (Kent, Ohio. Kent State University Press, 1977). All citations are from this edition.

40. Rosenthal, "The Voices of *Wieland*," in *Critical Essays*, p. 109.

41. Sydney J. Krause, "Romanticism in *Wieland*: Brown and the Reconciliation of Opposites," in *Artful Thunder: Versions of the Romantic Tradition in American Literature* in Honor of Howard P. Vincent, ed. Robert J. DeMott and Sanford E. Marovitz (Kent, Ohio: Kent State University Press, 1975), p. 19.

42. Alexander Cowie, "Historical Essay," KSU *Wieland/Carwin*, p. 348.

43. Repr. in Alice S. Rossi, ed., *The Feminist Papers* (New York: Bantam, 1973), p. 675.

44. James R. Russo has pointed out that Carwin is a notorious seducer in the "Carwin" fragment, where he uses his magnificent vocal gifts to gain control over women ("'The Chimeras of the Brain': Clara's Narrative in *Wieland*," *Early American Literature* 16 (1981):87–88, n. 18). In *Wieland*, the ventriloquist confesses to a "voluptuous temper" (p. 201), but is not physically interested in Clara. He goes to bed with the maid while engaging in a power play with the mistress.

45. Dorothy Scarborough, *The Supernatural in Modern English Fiction* (New York: G. P. Putnam's Sons, 1917), p. 39. Quoted in Cowie, "Historical Essay," p. 347.

46. Sigmund Freud, *The Interpretation of Dreams*, trans. James Strachey (New York: Avon/Discus, 1965), p. 279.

47. Sigmund Freud, *Introductory Lectures on Psychoanalysis*, trans. James Strachey (New York: Norton/Liveright, 1977), p. 153.

48. Freud, *Lectures*, p. 136.

49. Ibid., p. 217.

50. All citations are from Ernest Marchand, ed., *Ormond* (New York and London: Hafner, 1962).

51. Krause, KSU *Ormond*.

52. Ibid.

53. Hans Borchers, ed., *Memoirs of Stephen Calvert* (Frankfurt on the Main: Peter Lang, 1978).

54. Emory Elliott, "Narrative Unity and Moral Resolution in *Arthur Mervyn*," in Rosenthal, *Critical Essays*, p. 159. A good discussion of Arthur's own rationalizations is Warner B. Berthoff, "Adventures of the Young Man: An Approach to Charles Brockden Brown," *American Quarterly* 9 (1957):421–34. On the hero's marriage, Berthoff notes, "there remains something distasteful about his love" (p. 432).

55. Norman S. Grabo, "Historical Essay," in *Arthur Mervyn or Memoirs of the Year 1793*, Bicentennial Ed. vol. 3, ed. Sydney J. Krause and S.W. Reid (Kent, Ohio: Kent State University Press, 1980), p. 474.

56. Subsequent citations are from KSU *Arthur Mervyn*.

57. Elliott, "Narrative Unity," p. 152.

58. Ibid.

59. The term is Richard Chase's in *The American Novel and Its Tradition* (Garden City, N.Y.: Doubleday, 1957); it is discussed in Hedges, "Culture of Contradictions," p. 111 ff. I am indebted to Hedges for the term *matronage* (p. 114).

60. Elliott, "Narrative Unity," p. 143.

61. This is the title of an article by James H. Justus, *American Literature* 42 (1970):304–24.

62. *Adoption*, of course, is not used in any legal sense here.

63. The economic and ideological changes affecting women's lives after the revolution were complex and varied by class and region. Women as independent producers of goods and services lost much of their market, whereas the new manufacturers gave employment to a different group of women. Opportunities for them to marry dwindled as a result of the demographic shifts in this period. There is a massive body of literature on the subject, an impressive proof of the impact of women's history. See, for instance, Mari Jo Buhle, Ann G. Gordon, and Nancy Schrom, "Women in American History: An Historical Contribution," *Radical America* 5, no. 1 (July–August 1971):3–66; Mary P. Ryan, *Womanhood in America: From Colonial Times to the Present* (New York: New Viewpoints, 1975), pp. 85–135; Barbara Mayer Wertheimer, *We Were There: The Story of Working Women in America* (New York: Pantheon, 1977), pp. 50–127; Nancy F. Cott, *The Bonds of Womanhood: "Woman's Sphere" in New England, 1780–1835* (New Haven and London: Yale University Press, 1977):19–62 and passim; Carol Hymowitz and Michaele Weissman, *A History of Women in America* (New York: Bantam, 1978), pp. 64–75, 122–37; Linda K. Kerber, *Women of the Republic: Intellect and Ideology in Revolutionary America* (Chapel Hill: University of North Carolina Press, 1980), Ch. 7 and passim.

64. Elliott, "Narrative Unity," p. 148.

65. Barbara Joan Cicardo, "The Mystery of the American Eve: Alienation of the Feminine as a Tragic Theme in American Letters" (Ph.D. diss., St. Louis University, 1971), p. 45.

66. Paul Witherington, "Brockden Brown's Other Novels: *Clara Howard* and *Jane Talbot*," *Nineteenth Century Fiction* 29 (1974):257.
67. Witherington notes that "Brown came to the epistolary novel when it was being abandoned by other writers" (ibid., p. 267).
68. Krause, "*Clara Howard* and *Jane Talbot*," p. 186.
69. The young man is named Edward Hartley in the first edition, *Clara Howard; in a Series of Letters* (Philadelphia: Asbury Dickins, 1801). He becomes Philip Stanley in the 1807 British edition, and he is Stanley in the edition that was available to me, *Clara Howard; or the Enthusiasm of Love* (Boston: S. G. Goodrich, 1827). The forthcoming KSU *Clara Howard* will use the original name. To facilitate reference, I give letter numbers (in Roman numerals) as well as page numbers.
70. Printed in Paul Allen, *The Life of Charles Brockden Brown*, ed. Charles E. Bennett (Delmar, N.Y.: Scholars' Facsimiles & Reprints, 1975), pp. 44–46.
71. Wollstonecraft, *Vindication*, p. 356.
72. All references are to *Jane Talbot* (Boston: S. G. Goodrich, 1827).
73. Ibid., p. 37.
74. Krause, "*Clara Howard* and *Jane Talbot*," p. 196.
75. Charles E. Bennett, "Charles Brockden Brown: Man of Letters," in Rosenthal, *Critical Essays*, pp. 212–23.
76. Krause, "*Clara Howard* and *Jane Talbot*," p. 185.

# Kay S. House
## with Genevieve Belfiglio

# Fenimore Cooper's Heroines

A feminist reading of Cooper's works, like the twist of a kaleidoscope, not only gives us some new patterns but brings into prominence certain conceptions and intentions that were always there but never appeared so clearly before. With the exception of the Leatherstocking Tales, which have an inner logic and coherence of their own, Cooper's novels reflect his concerns during what a feminist would see as four stages of his career: the early works written or begun before his departure for Europe in 1826, those completed during his European residence, those written after he returned to the United States in 1833, and finally such works as *Jack Tier* (1848) and *The Ways of the Hour* (1850) that seem to have been affected by the women's liberation movement and the Seneca Falls convention of 1848.

Of the three paradigms of feminist thought conveniently identified and illustrated by Gayle Graham Yates,[1] one, the "women's liberationist paradigm" in which "women oppose the masculinist order and sometimes operate as separatists from men," applies, if at all, only to such works as *Jack Tier* and *The Ways of the Hour*. However, Cooper seems to have felt that this particular paradigm was counterproductive and not really in the best interest of women, so the women's liberationist mode is not central to either work and both books have as targets what Cooper felt were greater social evils. The "equalitarian mode" which carries with it an "unspoken acceptance of the masculinist framework" can be found throughout Cooper's career as can, surprisingly enough and perhaps for reasons we have failed to consider, the androgynous paradigm which challenges the conventionally assigned roles of men and women.

To begin with the familiar Leatherstocking Tales, on which Cooper predicted his reputation would ultimately rest, we have to admit that women are peripheral and that Natty Bumppo is not only the central character but the tutelary spirit of the five books. After beginning his existence as an intransigent character in *The Pioneers*, Natty plays a number of roles in the tales, but we can never envision him as a husband. The threat that matrimony poses in *The Pathfinder* is the extinction of Natty's character. Natty's view of Mabel as the "angel in the house," that stereotype being promulgated by both men and women, reveals the danger of such typing to both sexes. To the extent that he considers Mabel superior, all but unattainable, Natty must consider himself a failure. Fortunately for Mabel, Jasper Western has no such delusions, and he can fall in love with the sensible, capable, flesh-and-blood human being she really is.

When not in the grip of culturally sanctioned temporary insanity, Natty is free to interact naturally with women. Like his creator, Natty likes women, which may be a bigger compliment to the sex than loving them would. Rarely does it occur to him that a woman cannot do almost anything that needs to be done, and we should not let his repeated rescues of heroines obscure the fact that their independence, self-reliance, and best energies are often displayed when they aid, or cooperate with, Natty.[2]

Natty is also important as a gauge of the heroine's intelligence. Elizabeth Temple, for instance, enters *The Pioneers* as mistress of the house, a term Cooper uses as the equivalent of master and one that implies, as he makes clear, power.[3] (When the housekeeper viewed Elizabeth's "sweet but commanding features," she "felt that her own power had ended"[4]—as it had.) Elizabeth is the only person in her cultural group capable of reading character and appreciating Natty's true worth, obscured as it is by his manners, low social status, and equivocal actions. By importing a rustic form of chivalry to the frontier, choosing Leatherstocking as her deputy (or knight), and recommending that Richard Jones do the same, Elizabeth proves herself a better judge of character than either Jones or her father. As the one member of the "establishment" with whom Natty can league, furthermore, Elizabeth acts out of principle and disinterestedness even more than he does. That aiding Natty is (after *The Pioneers*) also in their own best interest does not, as I see it, diminish the other heroines' good judgment about his character. It is Cora, in *The Last of the Mohicans*, and not Duncan or David, who remembers Natty's instructions and tries to leave a trail. Judith, in *The Deerslayer*, improves on Natty's hint that the Indians might be impressed by her appearance in the brocade dress and gains some precious time. In short, Natty takes the heroines and their concerns seriously, and they have the wit to respect both his advice and his character.

In addition to their direct relationship with Leatherstocking, the heroines often prove capable of duplicating one of Natty's most essential functions in the tales. Bred by the Moravians, the Indians, and the Effingham family, Natty is able to understand and be of help to all sorts of people who ask his aid. He is the link between redskin and white, between wilderness and settlement, and between past and present. Elizabeth Temple is similarly willing to adventure beyond the conventional limits of her sex and social class, and she is unabashed by the idea that she may be attracted to a man who has some Indian blood. With Cora Munro, the willingness to cross racial boundaries is even more pronounced, and Cora's perception that there are Duncan Heywards who cannot summon such tolerance foretells tragedy.[5] Although Cora's lack of prejudice about Indians is partly based on her knowledge of her own heritage, it is none the less real. With Cora (and Uncas) Cooper exploited an advantage historical romances offer a writer: not only has he hindsight about what was, but he can show as well what might have been. The sheer waste of Cora and Uncas is by no means compensated for by the survival of Alice and Duncan.

The function of the heroine as an effective linking figure is transferred to Mabel in *The Pathfinder*, who joins with Dew-in-June to make an effective military team, and to Hist (aided somewhat by Hettie) in *The Deerslayer*. In *The Prairie*, written before these two books, Cooper expanded the number of competing races, clans, and tribes to the fullest and staged the action with four prominent and representative females: Ellen Wade, Inez Middleton, Esther Bush, and Tachechana, the wife of the Sioux chief. It is here that we get the clearest indication of what Cooper had in mind in making his heroines so flexible and adaptable.

*The Prairie*'s governing concern is with stages of civilization, and its setting is the newly purchased Louisiana Territory. As the opening of the first and fifteenth chapters of the book suggest, this historical event within memory of Cooper's readers offered him an example of incompatible cultures compressed into one space and time more dramatically than colonial or precolonial history had allowed. In the beginning of the fifteenth chapter, Cooper exposed beliefs that seem crucial not only for this book but for a complete understanding of the heroines of all the Leatherstocking Tales.

> The new rulers exercised their functions with discretion, and wielded their delegated authority without offence. In such a novel intermixture, however, of men born and nurtured in freedom, and the compliant minions of absolute power, the Catholic and the Protestant, the active and the indolent, some little time was necessary to blend the discrepant elements of society. In attaining so desirable an end, woman was made to perform her accustomed and grateful office. The barriers of prejudice and religion were broken through by the irresistible power of the master-passion; and family unions, ere long, began to cement the political tie which had made a forced conjunction between people so opposite in their habits, their educations, and their opinions.[6]

We must assume that both Duncan Middleton and Inez share the "irresistible power of the master-passion," but we notice that the responsibility for cultural assimilation falls on the woman; it has been Inez who has taken the biggest step in leaving her cloistered life in Catholic New Orleans to wed an officer of what is in effect an army of occupation. Fragile Inez is a willing intermediary between alien cultures, but she is nemesis for captors (the Bush clan) who take her by force. Genteel, refined almost to the point of disappearance, Inez is, as William Wasserstrom has said, "a woman of peculiar erotic power" who becomes "the center of a plot encircled by crimes of passion."[7]

In dealing with stage theories of civilization,[8] Cooper depicts the position of women in different kinds of societies in a way that matches surprisingly well Henry Adams's study of women's rights a quarter of a century after Cooper's death. Tachechana, living in communal Indian society and lacking protectors strong enough to enforce her claims, has no right either to her child or to her husband. Esther Bush, an Amazon degraded from her former state, asserts her rights as the female head of a clan but gets them only as long as she can find male supporters. Inez, raised to be protected by father, husband, and church, is both provocative and helpless outside of civilization. Ellen Wade seems to be the kind of woman Cooper hoped a republic could produce. She is self-reliant and, like Natty, moves easily from one group to another. Although poverty and the lack of a family of her own have forced her into servitude with the Bush clan, she frees herself (with the aid of allies she has chosen) and marries the man of her choice.[9]

Oddly enough, considering that only communes and clans are intact in *The Prairie*, the social arrangement that emerges as ideal is the family. In concluding, as he thought at the time, the Leatherstocking Tales, Cooper seems to have agreed with Henry Adams's conclusion in the final paragraph of "The Primitive Rights of Women":

> All new discoveries in the record of human development point to the
> familiar facts that the most powerful instincts in man are his affec-
> tions and his love of property; that on these the family is built; that
> no other institution can be raised on the same or on equally strong
> foundations; that for this reason the family is the strongest and
> healthiest of all human fabrics; that it always has and probably
> always will trample every rival system under its feet . . .[10]

In the book, Natty has been a father (not a patriarch) to Paul Hover, Duncan Middleton, Inez, Ellen, and Hard Heart. The latter is actually adopted by Natty and inherits his traps and blessing, while Paul and Ellen offer Natty a home with them as they, like the Middletons, go off to start families of their own. Before his death, Natty reasserts his right to belong to the ex-panded families of the Heyward-Middletons and Effinghams by asking a Christian burial of the former and bequeathing his property to the latter, and a pup descended from his dog, Hector, is the final twist of the family ties. Through affection, tradition, adoption, and the perpetuation of names, the extended family which includes Natty and Uncas endures. While celebrating the family as a unit, Cooper arranges for all the women (with the possible exception of Esther) to be happily married at the end.

Like the heroines of the Leatherstocking Tales, the women characters in other works Cooper wrote before he went to Europe are often inventive, resourceful,[11] alert to natural beauty,[12] energetic (even athletic), and fully aware of who they are and what they want. Occasionally the latter two conflict, as when Kate Plowden, in *The Pilot*, wants Barnstable but explodes when her guardian tells Barnstable he can have her: "'. . . has the daughter of John Plowden no voice in this cool disposal of her person? If her guardian tires of her presence, other habitations may be found,'" she protests, and gains her point.[13] In the same book, Alice Dunscombe, in spite of her love for the Pilot, remains true to herself and loyal to her native land and religion. The third woman in *The Pilot*, however, is one of those "model" heroines that gave Cooper's females a bad reputation. Unlike Alice Munro and Louisa Grant, Cecilia Howard cannot be explained as a function of the plot, and I suspect that she can be attributed only to Cooper's sense of responsibility to his readers. Cooper was very conscious of the extreme mobility of American society, of the number of servants and immigrants aspiring to middle-class status, and of the miseries attendant on wrong choices—particularly matrimonial ones.[14] Cecilia Howard, little as we like her, would have been a safer model than the more attractive Kate, and Cooper repeatedly said that "as a young people, we are essentially imitative."[15]

Cecilia is also housebound during most of the action, and everyone has noticed that the freedom of Cooper's heroines increases as they approach the frontier. Rather than posit some liberating mystique of the wilderness, we might rather conjecture that Cooper's own experience in growing up on the frontier caused him to be, like Natty Bumppo, relatively unconscious of sexually assigned roles. It was to Mrs. Cooper, for instance, and not to his nephew William that he once wrote a letter telling her to break up the household in Florence, ship the baggage by sea, and transport everyone, including what servants she wanted to keep, overland to join him in France. Later in life, he would shop for such domestic needs as kegs of grapes and flattering hats while he was in the city seeing a book through the press; his wife, staying in the country, was responsible for getting crops planted, tenants paid, and hogs butchered. Necessity and common sense, rather than sex, decided who did what just as they had when Cooperstown was still the frontier.[16]

Moving the action of his fiction even farther afield than the wilderness, Cooper invented the sea novel (with *The Pilot*), a genre that should interest feminist critics because of the analogies of women and ships. A perceptive French reviewer of *The Pilot* said that he understood for the first time why ships were referred to as "she" in the English language, and Cooper's sea tales are full of statements like this:

> The two most beautiful things with which we are acquainted are a graceful and high-bred woman entering or quitting a drawing-room, more particularly the last, and a man-of-war leaving her anchorage in a moderate breeze, and when not hurried for time.[17]

A certain ceremonial quality about getting under way gracefully obviously appealed to Cooper, and his smaller ships have even more freedom to maneuver. As Thomas Philbrick has said of one brigantine, "She is resourceful, independent, spirited, daring—everything that orthodox criticism finds wanting in Cooper's female characters."[18] We should also add that this particular brigantine saves the lives of everyone we are interested in. Although the grace, beauty, and sheer witchery of ships are a compliment to women, Cooper's ships also compete with women for the affections of certain seamen. Just as Natty Bumppo found his "sweetheart" in the forest, Tom Tiller had a 'til-death-do-us-part commitment to the *Ariel* in *The Pilot*.

As I indicated at the outset, almost eight years of European residence, during which Cooper became a keen student of comparative cultures, manners, and mores, produced female characters more daring than their predecessors. *The Red Rover*, probably his most popular sea novel, profited from the freedom of the sea to allow the Rover to keep his girlfriend (no "mistress" in Cooper's terms, and certainly not a "lady") on board disguised as a cabin boy. A second book from this period, *The Wept of Wish-ton-Wish*, contains a fine study of an Indian-white marriage and the resulting conflict, largely centered in the person of Ruth Heathcote, of racial prejudice, maternal love, and Puritan belief. Like *The Red Rover*, this book was better received by Old World critics than by Americans, some of whom protested the "revolting mixture" of red and white blood or complained that Cooper did not understand Puritans.

One of my own favorites from the highly experimental batch of books Cooper wrote during this period is *The Water-Witch* (1830). The heroine, Alida de Berbèrie, is attended only by a French valet and occasionally looked after by her corrupt and corrupting uncle, the Alderman van Beverout. Possessed of "a resolute and even a masculine understanding," curiosity, generosity, and disinterestedness, Alida presides unruffled over her own private quarters (*le Cour des Fees*) as they are repeatedly invaded by suitors (like the commander of the British cruiser *Coquette*) or the heavily bearded agent of a smuggler. To the bearded Seadrift (who turns out to be the illegitimate daughter of the Alderman who took advantage of her own mother when *she* was left in his care) Cooper wickedly assigned some standard statements about the inferiority of women.

At one point in the action, Alida disappears (along with "clothes, books, utensils for drawing, and even the lighter instruments of music") from her quarters and spends some time, everyone suspects, aboard the brigantine of the smugglers. Then she just as suddenly reappears, and Captain Ludlow, looking in through the window, sees that

> Alida was seated by a small table of mahogany, deeply absorbed in the contents of a little volume that lay before her. . . . Her dress was a negligée suited to her years; and her whole figure breathed that air of comfort, mingled with grace, which seems to be the proper quality of the sex, and which renders the privacy of an elegant woman so attractive and peculiar. Her mind was intent on the book, and the little silver urn hissed at her elbow, apparently unheeded. [Ch. 23]

As Ludlow and her uncle enter, Alida greets them with composure and the British captain

> scarcely knew which to admire the most, the exceeding loveliness of a woman who was always so beautiful, or her admirable self-possession in a scene that most others would have found sufficiently embarrassing. Alida, herself, appeared to feel no necessity for any explanation.

Alida does not explain her absence, and yet she is no coquette; as the name of the armed cruiser makes clear, coquettes are essentially masculine. Far from enjoying or promoting a rivalry between suitors, Alida tells Ludlow frankly that she will never marry the Patroon of Kinderhook, her merchant uncle's preferred customer. In a book of romance, adventure, and illusion, willful yet admirable Alida emerges as a solid figure. Although her sex is an indispensable part of her character, her character overwhelms her sex. That such a principled being could emerge from the Alderman's milieu Cooper attributes to her French Huguenot ancestry as well as to her own intelligence. (A clue to the Alderman's character—or lack of it—is found in the name he gives his retirement home; he has debased the classical concept of "Otium cum dignitate" to a name more suggestive of hanging up his sexual spurs: "Lust in Rust.")

Cooper blamed the comparative failure of *The Water-Witch* on his attempt to combine too much of the fanciful with the real, but one suspects that Alida's audacity and a heavy sprinkling of foreign languages did not help the book at home. Trying to portray the freedoms and constraints, advantages and dangers he saw in various national cultures during this period, Cooper laid himself open to charges of inauthenticity all around. His characters struck Americans as offensively un-American and yet to English and European critics they seemed to be Americans dressed in Italian, Swiss, and German costumes. Worse yet, for the sake of his subsequent career and a disinterested reading of his later books, a critical review of *The Bravo* (1831) marked the beginning of his long battle with segments of the United States press. At least partly because of his quarrels with various newspaper editors, the tendency to read the books Cooper produced during and immediately after his European residency as political tracts has been dominant.

For example, if read politically with Cooper's role as social critic exclusively in mind, *Homeward Bound* and *Home as Found* (1838) offer us a heroine, Eve Effingham, whose blue-stockinged legs buckle under the load of criticism Cooper gives her to carry. If, however, we can get over our antipathy to models of any sort (an antipathy presumably not shared by women buying etiquette books by the thousands) and read these books from a feminist point of view, they become something different—more interesting and more important.

After seven years of scrutinizing the Old World through anxious American eyes, Cooper had returned to a country that seemed to have changed, in his absence, almost beyond recognition. In styling New York City as "the Emporium" and in describing what passed for culture in the social life there, Cooper detected (half a century before James) a division of duties in American life that assigns to men the job of making money and tending to business while the women are supposed to take care of everything else. If "everything else" seems vague, there is, and was, no remedy and therein lay the problem. The error Americans were tragically making was, to Cooper, not that women were being made responsible for the really important parts of human life but that they were not being equipped to succeed.

Eve Effingham has had a proper education during her years in the Old World, and since she has at the same time been allowed some of the harmless freedoms denied girls in more conventional societies, she emerges as our first "heiress of all the ages," having had the best of both worlds. *Home as Found*, the second volume, was the book Cooper set out to write, but once he got his party on board a packet ship bound for New York from England, "others" to whom the manuscript was being read demanded "'more ship'" until the first volume became, as Cooper said in the preface, "'all ship.'" Actually, Cooper is not entirely right since it is necessary (unfortunately for those readers who care little about shipwrecks and adventures on the western coast of Africa) to read the first volume in order to grasp the character of Eve and her companions. Cooper seems to have divided his own proclivities and ideas between Eve's father and her second cousin, assigning to the father the role of a mild and kindly owner of land in upstate New York and to his cousin, whose past life has been more tempestuous and worldly, a more sophisticated view of life. The house and lands of Edward Effingham are those of *The Pioneers*, so that these books are continuations of that work, and Eve's opportunities are those for which Elizabeth Temple, in her occasional complaints about being cloistered in Templeton, had vaguely yearned without knowing specifically what it was she wanted.

Without being "forward," Eve is far from backward, and one of her first acts is to accost a comparative stranger and ask him to intervene when some shysters from shore (the equivalent of the bounty hunters Huck Finn encounters) attempt to arrest a bridegroom among the steerage passengers. Although she is on guard against "female reasoning," and letting "sympathy . . . get the better of reason," she nevertheless refuses to dehumanize herself and concludes, "'it would require strong proof to persuade me that villainous-looking attorney was engaged in a good cause and that meek and warm-hearted wife in a bad one!'"[19] Eve has a lively sense of the ludicrous, laughs easily, makes puns, and otherwise displays a "self-confidence that did her no injury." Cooper suggests that some of Eve's confidence may come from her association with her French governess, who is "accustomed to depend on herself, coming of a people among whom woman is more energetic and useful, perhaps, than in any other Christian nation. . . ." [HB, Ch. 23] Mademoiselle Viefville and another Frenchwoman aboard help work the capstan bars at one time, and when we look around to see what on earth Eve is doing in this crisis, we find her "folded in" the arms of her old American nurse who forcibly restrains her lest "some accident might occur to injure her" (HB, Ch. 23). The other time that Eve fails the modern reader is when she, like most Cooper females, too quickly (to our minds) consigns her fate to Providence and falls to praying rather than trying to help herself (HB, Ch. 22).

For the most part, however, Eve is a satisfactory character, collaborating (like Emma Woodhouse) with her cousin John and the man she is beginning to love, Paul Powis, in keeping the peace among the ill-assorted passengers and exhibiting neither the "cold sophistication and heartlessness of Europe" nor "the unformed girlishness of America" (HB, Ch. 11). She is flexible, disinterested, and capable of making decisions based on principle, but she is not manipulable. She is, in short, a new kind of woman. Cooper's first paragraph of Homeward Bound gives a clear signal that his interest is in women and their native lands.

> England itself has the fresh beauty of youth, rather than the
> mellowed hues of a more advanced period of life; or it might be
> better to say, it has the young freshness and retiring sweetness that
> distinguish her females, as compared with the warmer tints of Spain
> and Italy, and which, women and landscape alike, need the near
> view to be appreciated.

Two pages later John Effingham focuses the subject more sharply as he replies to Eve's enthusiasm about returning to her native land, "'the land of liberty,'" by retorting, "'After having passed a girlhood of wholesome restraint in the rational society of Europe, you are about to return home to the slavery of American female life, just as you are about to be married!'" Almost five hundred pages later, we get a "near view" of that return.

Once Eve arrives in her homeland, Cooper handles his strategies rather well. He takes upon himself, as one of the money-making sex, the duty of criticizing American males who "consider a wife or a daughter a mere upper servant" and particularly condemns those who spend large sums on lavish entertainments while consequently consigning "their wives and daughters . . . to the drudgery to which the sex seems doomed in this country" (*HAF*, Ch. 1). Although such abuse is most pronounced in the cities, even in the country Eve

> found many of her own sex whom she had left children, grown into
> womanhood, and not a few of them at a period of life when they
> should be cultivating their physical and moral powers, already
> oppressed with the cares and feebleness that weigh so heavily on the
> young American wife. [*HAF*, Ch. 12]

Aware of the old pattern of domestic service combined with education that had given a start to such people as Chaucer and Michelangelo, Cooper believed that service in the family of well-educated people could elevate the servant (as working for the Effinghams had helped Natty Bumppo) while freeing the women of the house. Consequently, Edward Effingham, while in New York,

> made two people comfortable by paying a generous price for a
> housekeeper: his daughter, in the first place, by releasing her from
> cares that necessarily formed no more a part of her duties than it
> would be a part of her duty to sweep the pavement before the
> door; and in the next place a very respectable woman, who was
> glad to obtain so good a home on so easy terms. To this simple
> and just expedient Eve was indebted for being at the head of one
> of the quietest, and most truly elegant, and best ordered establish-
> ments in America, with no other demands on her time than that
> which was necessary to issue a few orders in the morning, and to
> examine a few accounts once a week. [*HAF*, Ch. 1] [20]

Describing Eve as "head" of the establishment was no slip of the pen, for she makes all the important decisions not involving investments. Yet she does not consider herself excluded from the family's finances; learning of a dispute over land to which she has no current legal right, she alerts her father, who does, and "perceiving that things were in the right train, left her father alone. . . ." (*HAF*, Ch. 14). Free to show visiting foreigners around New York, Eve is tolerant of the "'inroad of strangers'" arriving as permanent residents since she assumes that "'many of them . . . ought to be an acquisition to a society that in its nature must be . . . provincial.'" (*HAF*, Ch. 3). She soon wearies, however, of "crowded and noisy balls" and "extravagance" without either "elegance" or "convenience" (for which the modern reader can substitute Las Vegas or Reno), and she and her cousin Grace spend the "remainder of the season quietly cultivating the friendship of such women as Mrs. Hawker and Mrs. Bloomfield, and devoting hours to the improvement of their minds and tastes" (*HAF*, Ch. 8). Mrs. Bloomfield has a first-rate mind and is an excellent conversationalist, and Mrs. Hawker "is a lady in every sense of the word; by position, education, manners, association, mind, fortune, and birth."[21] Because of these women, Eve feels a "glow of triumph" in "letting an intelligent foreigner see that America did contain women worthy to be ranked with the best of other countries" (*HAF*, Ch. 4).

Eve is, during the unfolding story of her love for Paul Powis, frank, even impulsive; she is safe in acting this way since he displays a "profound respect for her character" (*HAF*, Ch. 17) and because

> her attachment to Paul was not the impulse of girlish caprice, but the warm affection of a woman, that had grown with time, was sanctioned by her reason, and which, if it was tinctured with the more glowing imagination and ample faith of youth, was also sustained by her principles and her sense of right. [*HAF*, Ch. 26]

When Paul turns out to be Eve's third cousin (second cousin John's legal heir), Paul gets the Effingham land to hold for their children while Eve receives an equivalent amount in cash and securities. These guarantees of financial independence within marriage, however, are not the important point. For two volumes, Cooper had tried to emphasize his main concern through the other characters who (like the "ado" Henry James was to organize around Isabel Archer) like and admire Eve. On guard against any imputation of inferiority to Eve on any grounds whatsoever, Cooper has tried to show that she fully deserves the respect others feel for her. (Characters who resent her independence and her insistence on keeping her personal affairs to herself, like Steadfast Dodge the newspaperman, condemn themselves.)

Eve's most significant admirer is her cousin Grace, who has grown up in the United States and who comes, in time, to feel her own deficiencies when she compares herself with a woman who has the "'intelligence of a scholar; with all the graces of a woman she has the learning and mind of a man'" (*HAF*, Ch. 20). Grace learns that Eve's "ready and available knowledge" comes not only "almost intuitively, a gift of Heaven" but is also "a just consequence of her long and steady self-denial, application, and a proper appreciation of her duty to herself" (*HAF*, Ch. 20). American women had heard plenty by now about self-denial and duties to others, but the idea of self-denial in the interest of one's duty to one's self seems anachronistic for 1838. By contrast, Grace, "in ill-judged compliance with the customs of a society that has no other apparent aim than the love of display," has "irretrievably wasted" hours and days "in the frivolous levities so common to those of her sex with whom she had been most accustomed to mingle."

In the course of Grace's running comparison, she realizes that Eve, who knows several modern languages, cannot only "'tell you merely what such a phrase or idiom signifies, but what the greatest writers have thought and written.'"

Grace's particularized praise makes clear what Cooper is here attempting. Although *Home as Found* is, as Lewis Leary has said, "America's first extensive novel of manners,"[22] it goes beyond etiquette book notions of manners and moves a long way toward the works of Henry James and Edith Wharton.[23] If one does not wish to leap from Cooper to James and Wharton, Matthew Arnold (who began publishing *Culture and Anarchy* fifteen years after Cooper's death) is the best stepping-stone in between. For Arnold, culture (or civilization) "places human perfection . . . in the growth and predominance of our humanity proper, as distinguished from our animality." Culture is "a study of perfection, and of harmonious perfection, general perfection, and perfection which consists in *becoming* something rather than in *having* something, in an inward condition of the mind and spirit, not in an outward set of circumstances. . . ."[24]

The curiosity for which Arnold was to call, Cooper's heroines had always had; most of them also believed in "making reason and the will of God prevail." They had also had the beauty, sweetness (in Arnold's sense), flexibility, disinterestedness, and generosity that Arnold praised. But the belief in perfection and the "study and pursuit of perfection" through knowing the best that has been written and thought—this education was lacking in Cooper's heroines prior to the arrival of Eve. Culture seeks, said Arnold, "all the voices of human experience . . . of art, science, poetry, philosophy, history, as well as religion." Culture, in Arnold's terms, considers wealth (what the men were devoting their lives to) as "machinery."

> Culture says: "Consider these people, then, their way of life, their
> habits, their manners, the very tones of their voice; look at them
> attentively; observe the literature they read, the things which give
> them pleasure, the words which come forth out of their mouths, the
> thoughts which make the furniture of their minds; would any
> amount of wealth be worth having with the condition that one was
> to become just like these people by having it?"[25]

The dissatisfaction engendered by such a concept of culture, Arnold hoped, might save the future "even if it cannot save the present."

Such passages from Arnold can stand as a gloss of *Home as Found*. The protagonist had to be a woman since women had been given all the responsibility for what I earlier called "everything else," but which we can now see is culture. How much the response of the American press was influenced by Cooper's choice of a woman as protagonist remains a problem open to investigation. What is not in doubt is the fact that the press, ignoring the issues and principles Cooper had raised, launched an ad hominem attack on him.[26] Cooper's attempt to portray a woman—actually, the woman—as the crucial figure in American civilization was hooted down, and by the time Huck Finn lit out for the territory almost half a century later, at the threat of being "sivilized" by Aunt Sally, civilization had come to mean no more than domestication—the housebreaking of boys like puppies.

## Notes

1. *What Women Want* (Cambridge, Mass.: Harvard University Press, 1975), pp. 33–34.
2. Louisa Grant (*The Pioneers*) and Alice Munro (*The Last of the Mohicans*) seem to me largely functions of the plot and aids to the characterization of the heroines. Fully as much a handicap as the weights of a racehorse, they chiefly prove the loyalty and courage of the heroines, Elizabeth Temple and Cora Munro.
3. *Mistress* has become so generally used for a *kept woman* that Cooper's meaning has been lost. In *The Pilot*, for instance, Griffith's question, "'Is it unworthy of a seaman, and a gentleman, to permit the woman he calls his mistress to be so, other than in name?'" makes clear that the power of decision belongs to the woman. In *Home as Found*, Eve Effingham is "mistress" of the family household and her father awaits her signals indicating which persons he, as male head and "master," may invite as guests. When her father's land agent earns her disfavor, she quietly arranges for him to be discharged at the expiration of his contract.
4. *The Pioneers* (Albany: State University of New York Press, 1980), p. 66.
5. Cooper could have had Heyward come from anywhere in the colonies; that he came from the south was Cooper's way of asserting the obdurate reality of prejudices. No such hindrance obviously affected Cora's Scottish father whose prediction, at Cora's funeral, of a future without racial or sexual discrimination is apparently meant to be a recapitulation of his earlier beliefs.
6. Later, the Mexican War brought up the very real possibility that the United States would take over all of Mexico. Writing in *Jack Tier* in the year of that war's conclusion, Cooper warned of the "ages of war" that might be necessary to consolidate such a massive conquest instead of the peaceable amalgamation of cultures he had presumed possible twenty-one years before.
7. "Cooper, Freud and the Origins of Culture," *The American Imago* 17 (Winter 1960), p. 430.
8. For a brief but excellent discussion of stage theory prior to Cooper's own time, see J. A. Leo Lemay's "The Frontiersman from Lout to Hero," *Proceedings of the American Antiquarian Society* 88, part 2

(October 1979), pp. 194–219. Three years before *The Prairie, The Pilot*'s three women were lodged in the former "dormitories of a sisterhood" in St. Ruth's Abbey, and although such a commune proved protective, it allowed no individual, let alone heterosexual, freedoms and was consequently pronounced a "prison" by Kate.

9. Ellen is one of the few female Pygmalions in Cooper's work, and he simply asserts (rather than shows) that she, with the help of Inez and Duncan, later guided her husband to a higher state of civility, education, and public service than he had attained at their marriage. In spite of all the talk about a woman's "influence" at the time, Cooper saw the danger in marrying a man to re-form him, and Mary Wallace (of *Satanstoe*), like the heroine of Catherine Sedgwick's *A New England Tale*, resists such a temptation.

10. *Historical Essays* (New York: Charles Scribner's Sons, 1891), pp. 40–41.

11. In dramatizing a woman's resourcefulness, Cooper gleefully strained the already lax limits of probability the romance allowed. Kate Plowden, for instance, sneaks out of the house to furnish her lover with a set of signal flags and a codebook that turns out to contain some hilariously improbable messages.

12. On board a frigate, Kate Plowden calls the attention of others to "'how beautifully that vapour is wreathing itself in clouds above the smoky line of fog! It stretches already into the very heavens like a lofty pyramid!'" Her aesthetic delight proves a timely warning since what she sees is a tall ship of the enemy. This scene was seized by illustrators, and Kate's speech was often quoted in reviews as proof of Cooper's poetic genius, but no reviewer, to my knowledge, ever noticed that Cooper had assigned the "poetic" response to a woman. (The description occurs in Chapter 33 of a one-volume edition of *The Pilot*.)

13. *The Pilot*, 2 vols. (New York: Charles Wiley, 1824), 2:177 (Chapter 29 of a one-volume edition).

14. James D. Hart's *The Popular Book: A History of America's Literary Taste* (New York: Oxford University Press, 1950) contains fascinating statistics on the rising sales of fiction and etiquette books during the three decades in which Cooper was writing. Cooper's own letters, *The Letters and Journals of James Fenimore Cooper*, ed. James F. Beard (Cambridge, Mass.: Harvard University Press, Belknap Press, 1960–68), contain many references to tragically bad marriages among people he knew, and the miserable life led by the Hutter girls' mother (*The Deerslayer*) speaks for itself.

15. *Recollections of Europe* (Paris: A. & W. Galignani & Co., 1837), p. 22. Although Cooper believed that the "youth" of our country was the reason for imitation, the tendency seems to have continued, as the number of Brett Ashleys now in their eighties suggests.

16. The Italian episode, which would have appalling logistics even today, can be found in *The Letters and Journals of James Fenimore Cooper*, 1:363–64 and the later examples in vol. 6. When it came to writing,

Cooper never indicated that he thought women writers were inferior, as his review of Catherine Sedgwick's *A New England Tale* shows. His promotion of his daughter's writing was constant, and his delight at the success of her *Rural Hours* is recorded in the *Letters and Journals*, 6:195, 237.

17. *Jack Tier*, Pathfinder Edition (New York: G. P. Putnam's Sons, n.d.), p. 405.

18. *James Fenimore Cooper and the Development of American Sea Fiction* (Cambridge, Mass.: Harvard University Press, 1961), pp. 76-77.

19. *Homeward Bound*, Chapter V. Since no text of these books edited to CSE standards is available, I shall henceforth refer to *Homeward Bound* as *HB* and *Home as Found* as *HAF* and cite by chapter only.

20. Domestic chores may be a problem that neither democracy nor socialism can solve. Shen Rong, a prominent woman novelist in China, says that China's "intellectuals are still badly treated despite all the official proclamations about their importance" and adds, "'How can you expect them [female intellectuals] to devote their full energy to the country's modernization when so much effort must go into nothing more productive than standing in line, shopping, housework, minding the children? For example, I need to write, but I must also do housework, and housework really does make a woman stupid. So every day, I have to be clever while being made stupid.'" (Interview with Michael Parks for the Baltimore *Sun*, reprinted in the San Francisco *Examiner*, October 31, 1980.)

21. Cooper's use of the term *female* has been, it seems to me, unjustly derided. *Females* is the only term that covers both girls and women, and Cooper, like James, refused to designate every female a lady. The cook in *Home as Found* is a "lady" according to Aristabulus Bragg (Ch. 9). James was to ask:

> Didn't it appear at moments a theme for endless study, this queer range of the finer irritability in the breasts of those whose fastidiousness was compatible with the violation of almost every grace in life *but* that one? "Are you the woman of the house?" a rustic cynically squalid, and who makes it a condition of *any* intercourse that he be received at the front door of the house, not at the back, asks of a *maîtresse de maison*, a summer person trained to resignation, as a preliminary to a message brought, as he then mentions, from the "washerlady." *The American Scene* (London: Chapman & Hall, 1907), p. 26.

22. *Home as Found* (New York: Capricorn Books, 1961), p. xxv.

23. Anyone not familiar with the views of James and Wharton might start with Blake Nevius, *Edith Wharton* (Berkeley and Los Angeles: University of California Press, 1953), pp. 84-86.

24. "Sweetness and Light," in *Culture and Anarchy*, ed. R. H. Super (Ann Arbor: University of Michigan Press, 1965), pp. 94-95. Italics added.

25. Ibid., pp. 97–98.
26. For example, to quote from a convenient source, one New York paper declared Cooper a "'traitor to national pride and national character'" and hoped that "'the viper so long nourished in our bosoms may shortly leave our shores, never again to disgrace with his presence a land to which he has proved to be an ingrate.'" Warren S. Walker, *James Fenimore Cooper* (New York: Barnes & Noble, 1962), p. 90.

# Nina Baym

# Thwarted Nature:
# Nathaniel Hawthorne as Feminist

I

Although modern feminism has been with us since Mary Wollstonecraft, feminist literary criticism is a product of the resurgent women's movement of the late 1960s. The initial works of feminist criticism analyzed the writings of important male authors and critics in an attempt to uncover the hidden, destructive attitudes toward women that they contained. As one of the few classic authors of the mid-nineteenth century who used women characters extensively in his fiction, Hawthorne—or at least some of his better-known works—figured in their readings. However, his stories presented many problems to the critic who wished to define him as an orthodox espouser of patriarchal attitudes. Consequently, feminists abandoned him for other writers more suited to their aims, and feminist readings of Hawthorne never became more than a minor tributary in the continuous outpouring of Hawthorne studies. More recently, feminist criticism has turned away from male authors entirely, and hence little work on Hawthorne with a feminist stamp has been produced since 1976.

Feminist critics were by no means the first to study Hawthorne's depictions of women. The presence of women characters in his fiction is too pervasive, their role too striking, to be overlooked. But "prefeminist" criticism of Hawthorne that concentrated on his women showed—not surprisingly—little feminist consciousness. Indeed, it often displayed a strong antifeminist bias. Frequently, the prefeminist critics wrote with the intention of uncovering antifeminism in Hawthorne's works, and therefore, curiously, their findings were congruent with those of the feminists. This congruence may be a partial explanation for the relative dearth of feminist work on Hawthorne: in effect, the antifeminists had done the feminists' work for them!

Prefeminist criticism analyzed Hawthorne's women within one of three larger interpretive frameworks. First, the women were discussed as symbols or types of Hawthorne's religious or moral scheme. Second, they were viewed as projections of his sexual psychology. Finally, they were seen to convey an aspect of Hawthorne's social commentary, that concentrating on the role of women in society and contemporary reform movements. None of this analysis saw Hawthorne's intentions with his women characters as mimetic; it treated women as functions controlled by a larger design, whether ideological, psychological, or social. Thus, this criticism coincided with the sense of feminist criticism that "women" in literature were usually not reliable descriptions of women in the real world, but were rather "images" controlled by other concerns.

The prefeminist study of Hawthorne's women found the key to his purpose in particular instances by noting his description of the character's physical appearance. Hawthorne became a prime example of the "dark and fair" polarization of women characters along the axis of guilt and purity, or knowledge and innocence. The dark woman, in discussions of Hawthorne's religious allegory, represented sin and temptation—usually sexual in nature, although pride, secularism, or disobedience were also possible referents. The fair woman represented a contrasting spirituality and grace. In some fictions, the pair were seen to offer the protagonist a choice of damnation or salvation; but in others only one woman appeared, functioning (it was maintained) to imply the entire scheme.

Those critics who saw Hawthorne as a moralist rather than a theologian tended to equate the dark lady with whatever moral qualities they thought Hawthorne disapproved of. Chiefly (since Hawthorne was perceived as a latter-day Puritan) his dark lady was associated with the liberalizing tendencies and the facile optimism that characterized the breakdown of the old New England way. In contrast the fair lady was associated with traditional virtues. Some moralist critics—especially those influenced by New Criticism—looked beyond a simple polarity in Hawthorne's moral ruminations to discern evidence of complexity and ambiguity. They saw how much more attractive and, in some basic sense, "good" the dark ladies tended to be. The fair lady was too often vapid, timorous, prissy, or sanctimonious; such a character seemed unmeet to function as the unequivocal locus of value or virtue in a major author's work. If the spokesmen for ambiguity did not go so far as to challenge the ruling notion of Hawthorne as a moral conservative, they did at least suggest that the polarity of women had some uncertainty built into it.[1]

The psychological approach to Hawthorne grew 'from the perception of ambiguity in his writings; it tended to translate the notion of ambiguity into that of ambivalence and to treat Hawthorne's moralizing as a smokescreen for psychological issues. The psychological approach appropriated the schemes of the moralists for its own uses. Equating the dark lady with sexual experience or sexuality, and the fair with inhibition or repression, psychological critics interpreted Hawthorne as a typical "Puritan" (or more accurately, Victorian) male, afraid of sex and consequently of sexually attractive women, and unable to approach sex without guilt feelings and a certain measure of sadism.[2]

I fault this mode of discourse about Hawthorne's women less for its lack of feminist awareness than for its gross reductiveness, both of the images of women in Hawthorne's work and of the specific texts in which such images appear. Some kind of dark-fair dualism undoubtedly functions in some of Hawthorne's work, but by no means in all or even much of it. Moreover, this polarity has various significances, which are to be derived only from the context and not from a set of prior assumptions about its necessary meaning. In brief, the dark-fair polarity as it has figured in Hawthorne criticism is a critics' creation with relatively little demonstrable utility if insight into Hawthorne's works and mind is the ultimate intention.

The third prefeminist approach to Hawthorne's women has shared with the moralists the conviction that Hawthorne was an author of deeply conservative bent who wrote largely to deplore the liberalizing trends in the thought and society of his time. Hawthorne's depiction of women is seen as motivated by the wish to affirm the traditional views of woman's nature and her place in society, and to criticize contemporary reform movements which were arguing for her equality or emancipation. Hawthorne's alleged objections to feminism and to uppity women were perceived as part of a more general skepticism about social reform, as one article phrased it.[3] Such facts of biography as Hawthorne's intense dislike of Margaret Fuller and his angry epistolary outburst against the "scribbling women" were cited to support this view.[4]

As already suggested, feminist criticism of Hawthorne has been quite comfortable with the treatment of his women developed by prefeminist analysis. The analysis, describing Hawthorne as conservative in his view of women's place, patronizing in his estimate of their capacities, while all the while secretly fearful of their sexual power, identifies precisely the sort of patriarchal mind-set that feminists expect to find in writings by men. And a mode of analysis concentrating on static images of women was common to prefeminist and feminist critics. The chief differences between feminist and prefeminist analysis of Hawthorne have been matters of attitude and evaluation rather than interpretation. Prefeminists praise Hawthorne for qualities to which feminists object.[5] In fact, the suggestion of a minority of critics that Hawthorne's view of women had feminist tendencies has been rejected by both traditionalist and feminist critics of Hawthorne.[6] The chief readings to have taken this unpopular line are by the present writer. As part of the argument in several articles and a book, I have maintained that although women do not always signify the same thing in Hawthorne's many fictions, they usually function in the same way. They represent desirable and valuable qualities lacking in the male protagonist. They offer him the opportunity to attain these qualities through erotic alliance or marriage. The man's invariable failure to take the opportunity is harshly judged by the narrator in fiction after fiction. During the first phase of Hawthorne's career (to 1849), he created male protagonists who suffer from isolation, alienation, and self-absorption;

women offer sociality, self-forgetfulness, connection. A story like "The Bosom Serpent" is typical. Later in his career, Hawthorne created males who were oversocialized and women signifying interior strength, passion, and individuality.[7]

This pattern offers a general guide to Hawthorne's sentiments, especially as they evolved over time, rather than a certain key to all his work. It must be modified where the protagonist of the story is a woman, as in *The Scarlet Letter*. It must also be modified when Hawthorne uses a pair of women, as he does in two long romances, *The Blithedale Romance* and *The Marble Faun*. For if the women form a contrasting pair, then only one of them can offer the corrective; the other must reinforce the weaknesses of the male protagonist. One asks of the pair of women in *The Blithedale Romance* and *The Marble Faun*: which woman plays the corrective role? and for which of her qualities? Since the male's shortcomings in these two late works result from his oversocialization, the woman who is unconventional, defiant of social mores, must represent the ideal. Thus, the woman who has been identified in previous Hawthorne criticism as "bad" (even if ambiguously so) stands in fact for the "good."

In Hawthorne's short fiction, the good women are traditional figures associated with hearth and home, whereas in *The Blithedale Romance* and *The Marble Faun*, they are dramatically less conventional. However in neither the short works or the long romances are these figures mimetic so much as they are signifiers of valuable traits—ideals, to use Hawthorne's language, dressed up in the garments of the real. Therefore, not unless we can link these signifiers which happen to be represented as women to specific women-centered concerns can we validate any kind of feminist approach to Hawthorne's works. As it happens, this link can easily be made, by demonstration that whatever else they may symbolize at different points in Hawthorne's career women always signify their own sex. Therefore, the protagonist who rejects a woman character is rejecting her as a sign of woman as much as he is rejecting her as a sign of various other values.

This linkage, to be sure, means that the psychological critics are right in claiming that the rejection of women is a major, even obsessive, motif in Hawthorne's fiction. What the psychological critics have not grasped is the fullness of Hawthorne's awareness of this obsession, as well as the nature of his represented feelings about it. Unlike machismo authors who join their heroes in boasting about cruelty to women; unlike patriarchal authors who present gestures of contempt or dislike toward women disguised as affection, Hawthorne knows exactly what this sort of behavior means and depicts it as stupid, ugly, and evil. Far from affirming the rightness of traditional patriarchal politics, he sees them as deeply warped.

Ultimately, he holds men and the society that men have created responsible for mistaking neurosis for truth, and elevating error into law, custom, and morality. While condemning these obsessions, however, Hawthorne must represent them, and thus the question of his own motivation as an artist enters his discourse. He must hold himself responsible along with other men for injuries done to women; he inflicts imaginary injuries on imaginary women through the stories he creates, in which women are injured. To some degree, he has a higher degree of responsibility than other men, because he has an awareness that others lack, and because he therefore knows how his moralizing art provides a license to depict what he condemns. His guilt and duplicity as a writer can be richly related to his full apprehension of the suspect ethical status of his achievement as the creator of compelling tales about mistreated women.

It is no wonder that critics have found it well nigh impossible to make the opposing tendencies in his work—the valorization of women, the abuse of women—cohere. The psychological critics have discounted the overwriting of the narrator, as have most feminist critics, including Judith Fetterley in her recent *Resisting Reader* (Bloomington: Indiana University Press, 1978) which characterizes "The Birthmark" as a story about how to murder your wife and get away with it. My own analysis has been too quick to accept the narrator's self-justification at face value. The task of a sophisticated feminist criticism would be to achieve in its discourse the coherence that so improbably exists in Hawthorne's work. Such a criticism would be based on the presumption that the question of women is *the* determining motive in Hawthorne's works, driving them as it drives Hawthorne's male characters. The question of woman is determining because these men are obsessed by their fantasies of women, controlled by them (and, as controllers of women, they engulf women in their fantasies as well).

The idea of a central preoccupation with the controlling power of fantasies of women is interestingly congruent with Hawthorne's preoccupations as critics have traditionally perceived them. It is congruent, for example, with the much discussed question of the conflict/accommodation between the imagined and real, or the real and ideal; with the observed fear that fantasy or obsession will replace reality in the individual's life with eccentricity, alienation, or madness; and with the critics' demonstration of how, in Hawthorne's work, the real is exploited by fantasy with subsequent guilt shared by protagonist and backstage artist. To many critics these recurrent motifs have seemed the central core from which Hawthorne's distressed and distressing fictions have erupted. The feminist reading would simply take such perceptions further, to the discovery of their origin in men's attempts to handle their complex feelings toward women.

The discussion to follow will highlight the connection between the theme of women and other basic Hawthorne concerns, surveying those works in which one woman serves as foil and object for the male protagonist (the short stories and *The House of the Seven Gables*); the two female pairs in *The*

*Blithedale Romance* and *The Marble Faun*; and the triumph of *The Scarlet Letter*, which I attribute directly to the freedom and excitement that Hawthorne experienced through his unique deployment of a woman as his protagonist.

## II

A list of the short stories in which the theme of woman structures the action is, in the main, a list of those short works on which Hawthorne criticism of the last few decades has concentrated. In chronological order these are "Roger Malvin's Burial" (1832), "Wakefield" (1835), "Young Goodman Brown" (1835), "The Minister's Black Veil" (1836), "The Prophetic Pictures" (1837), "The Shaker Bridal" (1838), "Sylph Etherege" (1838), "The Birthmark" (1843), "Egotism, or, the Bosom Serpent" (1843), "Rappaccini's Daughter" (1844), "The Artist of the Beautiful" (1844), "Drowne's Wooden Image" (1844), and "Ethan Brand" (1849). (I omit from this list stories in which women characters have no special gender reference, such as "The Great Carbuncle" or "Dr. Heidegger's Experiment," and stories in which the theme is present but not controlling, as in the minor sexual sadism of "Endicott and the Red Cross," "The Snow Image," and "The Hollow of the Three Hills," or the prurient relation between narrator and female auditors in "Alice Doane's Appeal." Among stories included, only "Sylph Etherege" can be considered minor, and only a few major stories—"My Kinsman, Major Molyneux" (1832), "The May-Pole of Merry Mount" (1836), and "The Legends of the Province-House" (1838 and 1839)—are absent.)

In general terms which, admittedly, require qualification or sophistication in specific instances, these stories narrate the rejection, by a man, of a sexual union with a woman who is either his fiancée or his wife. This rejection affects both man and woman adversely and, in the woman's case, often fatally. Reuben Bourne's slaying of his son may not kill Dorcas, his wife, in "Roger Malvin's Burial" for Hawthorne writes only "She heard him not. With one wild shriek, that seemed to force its way from the sufferer's inmost soul, she sank insensible by the side of her dead boy."[8] But there is no question about the death of Martha in "The Shaker Bridal," or about its cause: "But paler and paler grew Martha by his side, till, like a corpse in its burial clothes, she sank down at the feet of her early lover; for, after many trials firmly borne, her heart could endure the weight of its desolate agony no longer" (9:425); nor about the death of Georgiana in "The Birthmark": "The birthmark—the sole token of human imperfection—faded from her cheek, the parting breath of the now perfect woman passed into the atmosphere, and her soul, lingering a moment near her husband, took its heavenward flight" (10:56); nor about that of Beatrice, killed by two men: "and thus the poor victim of man's ingenuity and of thwarted nature, and of the fatality that attends all such efforts of perverted wisdom, perished there, at the feet of her father and Giovanni" (10:128). The recurrent image of a woman dead at a man's feet and through his efforts cannot be ignored.

What exactly are the efforts that lead to this grim result? In most of the stories written before the Old Manse period, that is, before 1842, the destruction or damaging of the woman seems to result accidentally as a by-product, so to speak, of other intentions. Critics argue endlessly about whether Reuben Bourne meant to kill his son Cyrus, but nobody doubts that the damage to Dorcas was unintentional. As a result of putting on the black veil, either to make a statement to his parishioners or to hide a real secret, Reverend Hooper dooms his fiancée Elizabeth to lifelong spinsterhood; but it does not seem that he devised his plan in order thus to ruin her life. Wakefield, apparently, left home on a whim and not out of malice toward the woman he thereby "widowed"; and he returns after twenty years in the same spirit, not purposefully to bring about, once again, a total disruption of her peaceful life. Young Goodman Brown casts off Faith as a result of his forest experience, but it hardly seems likely that he entered the forest in order to find a pretext for denying her. On the contrary: "Well; she's a blessed angel on earth; and after this one night, I'll cling to her skirts and follow her to Heaven" (10:75).

But does the protagonist not protest too much? The question of a covert intention cannot be entirely absent. If these men did not devise patterns of behavior calculated to destroy the women who love them, they certainly failed signally to think of the possible effect that their plans might have on these women. At the very least—and to this, Hawthorne certainly commits his narrative voice—these are selfish men, basically indifferent to women. That indifference seems to be the source of their killing power so far as women are concerned; its result is the "thwarted nature" described in "Rappaccini's Daughter." Certainly, a supreme selfishness motivates Adam Colburn when he suggests to Martha Pierson, who has waited half a lifetime to marry him, that they join the Shakers. To Adam no sacrifice is involved in sacrificing sexual union; but this is not true for Martha, for whom, with her "woman's heart, and a tender one," there is "something awful and horrible in her situation and destiny" (9:424, 423).

The women in these stories have very slight presences, but these presences are always intensely physical and domestic. In the physical attachment to a man they are fulfilled and offer fulfillment. Thus, Dorcas lives contentedly with her gloomy husband Reuben Bourne and is not sad to leave society with him, "for she felt that it was better to journey in the wilderness, with two whom she loved, than to be a lonely woman in a crowd that cared not for her" (10:357). The physicality of the tie is suggested not only by Martha's agony in a sexless union, but by the "tie" of Faith's pink ribbons and numerous other concrete symbols that link the saving power of the woman with her body and through her body to Nature.

Perhaps the trite critical discussions of head versus heart in Hawthorne's writing will come to mind here—women as heart, men as head. Yet if the "heart" stands for body, and the "head" for rejection of the body, then it seems more accurate to identify the opposition as sexual passion versus the lack of it. The loving heart of woman is closely identified with, even an icono-graphic substitute for, a warm sexuality, whereas the stone man, "The Man of Adamant," the man in whom head predominates, is sexually frozen. The evidence of his coldness, however the evidence is made manifest in action, is what truly kills the woman. To reject her sexually is to reject her fatally. She dies. The man goes on living, but he is merely a shell.

Let us remember here that these stories are making statements not about the real nature of women but about the way in which men imagine them. As is so common in the Judeo-Christian tradition, the woman has become the locus of physicality; what is unusual in these writings is the degree to which the protagonist does not seem to recognize any "temptation" in these women. The body simply does not interest him and the woman who is "in" her body and identified with that body suffers from neglect rather than cruelty. However, the stories associated with the Old Manse era in Haw-thorne's life escalate the man's indifference to an attitude more clearly hostile. And, where women in the earlier group of stories were, apparently, inadvertently caught up and victimized by the man's obsession, woman herself is now the obsession. Retroactively, these two stories force us to inquire if perhaps women were not always, in some disguised sense, the Hawthorne male's obsession.

Specifically, some aspect of the woman is the obsession: some aspect of her body. The hero attempts to purify the woman by separating her in some way from her body. This, as Hawthorne recognizes, is murder: sex-murder. For Aylmer in "The Birthmark," the hand-shaped mark on his wife's cheek becomes the locus of his demonic energies; for Giovanni in "Rappaccini's Daughter," it is the entire physical presence of Beatrice, her very body itself especially as concentrated in her fragrance, her physical perfume, that revolts him. In both these instances, it is impossible to distinguish revulsion from attraction, for exactly to the extent that these men are obsessed, possessed, with the woman's body they are revolted by it. I think we must say that these men actually perceive attraction as what we would think of as its opposite— repulsion. That is to say, they experience a physical sensation which they interpret as repulsion where, to us, it looks exactly like attraction. The intellectual trickery by which one sensation is transformed into or inter-preted as its opposite occurs at a level beneath the awareness of the self-confident protagonist, but not so far beneath awareness as to preclude the faint suggestion that some degree of self-delusion may be involved. And, regardless of the need to speak a guarded language, imposed by the mores of his day and the extreme sensitivity of his subject, the narrator is not deceived.

Hawthorne has engaged here with the moral code that makes sex an unnatural act. Or, more precisely, he is engaged with that part of the psyche— of the male psyche—that perceives sex as an unnatural act and therefore produces such moral codes. But by linking the woman's saving grace and her body inseparably, Hawthorne is indicating that if anything is unnatural, it is the part of the psyche that repudiates human sexuality. He shows us men who, shocked and horrified by the human female body, are driven to dissociate themselves from the entire social fabric as a means of protecting themselves from it. He shows us men for whom evidence of women's sexual responsiveness is sufficient to cause an existential breakdown: "My Faith is gone! . . . There is no good on earth; and sin is but a name. Come, devil! for to thee is this world given" (10:83). But this is not all. He also shows men who, while rejecting real women who unavoidably inhabit physical bodies, substitute fantasies of them that are truly unnatural, fantasies of lust, power, degradation, and control. These fantasies are the outgrowth of the unnatural male psyche.

Certainly we engage here with that familiar modern lament about the growth of mind and self-consciousness in the human being as a result of which he is irrevocably sundered from nature. And in the debate over whether mind is man's glory or his curse, Hawthorne would seem to be taking the "romantic" view that it is his curse. "Woman" would appear to be playing the familiar part of the "Other" in this scheme, and as women suffer in Hawthorne's stories, real women suffer from a peculiar double bind: though made to suffer as bodies, they are denied existence as mind. But Hawthorne is not simply using women to signify nature and the other, and he is not really concerned with abstract romantic self-consciousness. He is suggesting, rather, that the male inability to deal with woman's body is the *source* of all the abstract formulations that function as so many defenses against, and diversions from, the truth. Behind Goodman Brown's religious rhetoric, behind Aylmer's scientific pose, behind Owen Warland's artistic vocation, behind Giovanni's moral crusade, lurk the manifold emotions that prevent men from making connection with women. These emotions, unknowable and unnameable, reach the light of day, as it were, in fantasy. And fantasy is what obsesses Hawthorne as an artist.

This obsession—Hawthorne's obsession—is felt in passage after passage. Consider the initiation scene in "Young Goodman Brown" as an example. In the depths of the forest, the devil delivers his sermon to the novitiates, among whom are Brown and Faith. He catalogs a sequence of "secret deeds" each more awful than the one before. And, "yet, far more than this!" he promises them, "It shall be yours to penetrate, in every bosom, the deep mystery of sin, the fountain of all wicked arts, and which inexhaustibly supplies more evil impulses than human power—than my power, at its utmost!—can make manifest in deed" (10:87). The impulses that produce real crimes originate in fantasy, which is infinitely energetic, infinitely productive. Fantasy becomes as evil as action, perhaps more so.

"The husband cast one look at his pale wife, and Faith at him. What polluted wretches would the next glance shew them to each other, shuddering alike at what they disclosed and what they saw!" (10:88). Although neither Goodman Brown nor Faith has been given a background or a history in any detail, Hawthorne has told us enough about these two so that we can assert with confidence that neither has ever performed any of the evil deeds catalogued by the devil. But they have fantasized—as the devil says, everybody has. The only pollution that the text can imply, at this point in the tale, is the secret pollution of the human bosom, the secret of its fantasies.

Now, if Young Goodman Brown did not "actually" attend a witch's meeting but only dreamed that he did, then that dream—which so prominently features the depiction of his wife as polluted—is itself such an evil fantasy, so the infinite world of fantasy is not escaped by calling Brown's adventure a dream. And so, too, is "Young Goodman Brown" an evil fantasy, featuring so prominently its vision of secret evil and implying so many more awful imaginings than it articulates.

Now Hawthorne did not give all his creative energies in his "early phase"— the years preceding his employment in the Salem customhouse—to the kind of story we have been examining. He alternated between these and light sketches, plotless short pieces which developed a sequence of images and incidents organized sometimes as a procession or a panorama but frequently developed simply as exercises in free association. Modern criticism, however, has characterized most of these sketches as secondary achievements, weak performances, because of their general insubstantiality, triteness, and a prettiness of both matter and rhetoric. Hawthorne's narrator seems to agree, using such images of evanescence for this type of work as snowflakes, dewdrops, or footprints on the sandy shore.

The material that we find at once more powerful and more typical of Hawthorne's imagination consists of the stories of harm. These stories are divorced from the narrator by means of the narrative which he pretends to be purveying rather than creating, and on which he comments, often disapprovingly. Thus, those of Hawthorne's works that we consider to be his best generally include an authorial disclaimer, a suggestion either that Hawthorne was uncomfortable with the material or that he anticipated discomfort or disapproval in his audience. Yet, these "disclaimed" or heavily mediated stories represent, to us, the author's strong achievements! Our own critical judgment appears to support Hawthorne's sense that there is a close but unhealthy relationship between artistic and sexual power. Art is an expression of deformed sexuality, for its obsessive fantasy is that of doing harm to a woman. Sometimes Hawthorne represents this deformity as his own oddity, sometimes as his culture's curse, and sometimes as the nature of men.

A scene in *The House of the Seven Gables* that epitomizes this complex relation of art and sexuality is the one in which Holgrave, the hero, reads a story he has written about his ancestor Maule to the heroine Phoebe. Holgrave's is a particularly nasty example of the typical Hawthorne short story, twice-distanced from its author by an overlay of commentary from the "author" Holgrave and a second layer from the author Hawthorne. The young artisan Maule, summoned to the house of his victorious enemy Pyncheon, takes the opportunity to bring the daughter of the house, Alice, under his control. Though the reader is prepared at first to interpret this behavior as the enactment of Maule's revenge against Pyncheon, with poor Alice an inadvertent victim, the narrative soon makes it clear that the provocation of Alice drives his hatred of Pyncheon clear out of Maule's mind.

And how does Alice provoke Maule? Simply, she looks at him with a glance of undisguised admiration for his physical beauty. But this glance, as the Holgrave narrator quickly comments, is one that "most other men, perhaps, would have cherished as a sweet recollection, all through life" (2:201). But some "diabolic subtlety" leads Maule to interpret this glance of open admiration, which many would take as a tribute, in a different fashion, as a sign of contempt. "Does the girl look at me as though I were a brute beast!" he fumes.

Something in Maule's nature has made him recoil from a simple, natural expression of human sexual attraction; his recoil is rationalized by interpreting Alice's glance as offensive. He links it to pride—and indeed, the narrator Holgrave tells us, Alice was a proud woman, but in no way that was incompatible with womanly integrity. She has, in fact, a womanly tenderness for which "a man of generous nature would have forgiven all her pride, and have been content, almost, to lie down in her path, and let Alice put her slender foot upon his heart" (2:201). Maule's, then, is not a generous nature; unable to respond to Alice's generosity in kind, it brings Alice (through hypnotism) into a lifelong subjugation to Maule's every wish. The possiblity of exchange has been rejected and a relation of dominance and submission substituted. Healthy sex has been transmuted into pornography. Though what Maule actually does to Alice—or what the narrator tells us of it—would not qualify in today's market as pornographic, it is unequivocally cruel. And the spectacle of the proud, virginal young woman forced at any and every moment to do the bidding of a powerful and angry male is, of course, the chief image of Victorian pornography. Yet the worst that Maule does is, apparently, what he does *not* do; having aroused sexual desire and admiration in Alice, he cruelly fails to satisfy her. So, the act that finally kills Alice is his summoning of her to tend his bride on the wedding night, to be a spectator at his sexual union with another woman. Alice has been punished by Maule for being attracted to him, and in *this* respect Hawthorne's story is quite different from normal Victorian pornography, where the subjected woman is one who dislikes her tormenter.

What kind of man is it who would prefer to torture than to please a beautiful young woman who is obviously attracted to him? The Hawthorne narrator suggests—by making Holgrave quite a cheerful and hale young fellow—that it is any young man. And why does he read this strange story to Phoebe? His reading reproduces in Phoebe the kind of submission that Maule's hypnotic powers elicited in Alice; his reading, then, is an exhibition of his power to dominate. Aware of what he is doing, or at least of what is happening, Holgrave is tempted to push his powers further and cement his hold over the young girl, for there is not "any idea more seductive to a young man, than to become the arbiter of a young girl's destiny" (2:212). Maule is thus the dark alter ego of everyman, and Alice is woman as his opportunity. If Holgrave were to act at this crucial moment, he and Phoebe would cease, in a sense, to be themselves and would be transformed into figures in a morbid fantasy. They would become the possessed and driven characters of the story Holgrave has just narrated. In breaking away from the seductive power of his own fantasy, in refusing to appropriate Phoebe to its service, Holgrave saves both of them and earns the Hawthorne narrator's fervent approval.

The motifs of the abuse of women, the power of fantasy, the threat of art, and the guilt of the artist are all entwined in this episode. And the root of it all is, clearly, a man's inability to accept the reality that even the purest and proudest of women have sexual natures.

## III

The appearance of a second woman in Hawthorne's writing corresponds to the introduction of a social dimension to his works. By saying this I do not mean to suggest that Hawthorne had no interest in society in his earlier work. Clearly the separation of the protagonist from society was one measure of his error and tragedy, while the woman was usually identified not only with nature but with traditional social ties. Nor do I mean that later in his career Hawthorne became more of a realist, a mimetic author. I mean rather that society as a concept entered the arena of his fictions as yet another participant in his fantasies. This entrance reflects Hawthorne's later attempts to understand the genesis of his fantasies and particularly to investigate the ways in which they might be accounted for as responses to social pressures or even as social products.

In both *The Blithedale Romance* (1852) and *The Marble Faun* (1859)—
granting that these are very different works of art, separated by significant
years in Hawthorne's life and career—we find a plot that chronicles not
simply the mistreatment and casting off of one woman, but also her supplant-
ing by a second. The second woman is used by the men in the story to
obliterate the first. Essentially, these two correspond to socially acceptable,
and socially disreputable, images of women. The disreputable woman bears
some resemblance to a healthy, natural, vital, fully sexed, radiant goddess,
a figure clearly out of place in a highly structured and inhibited society.
The socially acceptable woman looks something like the stereotypical
Victorian priss. But both the rejected and the acceptable woman are tainted
and polluted by the pornographic imagination. Both are abused, and both are
victimized.

In *The Blithedale Romance*, Zenobia and Priscilla are sisters, contrasted
as presence and absence: Zenobia has everything, Priscilla lacks everything.
Zenobia has personal wealth, womanly beauty, energy, health, intelligence,
success, fame, bearing. Priscilla is poor, plain, weak, malnourished, untalented, simple, obscure. This negation of selfhood is utilized by both
men in the tale, the narrator Coverdale and the antihero (for the novel has
no true protagonist) Hollingsworth, to negate Zenobia. Thus, in the contest
between the two women, Priscilla's negation is seen to be more powerful
than Zenobia's assertion, and this is because true power in the novel resides
in the imaginations of the men. Priscilla is used by the men to obliterate
Zenobia and to protect themselves from their own misogynist rage (when
they become aware of it). "The powerfully built man showed a self-
distrustful weakness, and a childlike, or childish, tendency to press close,
and closer still, to the side of the slender woman whose arm was within his.
In Priscilla's manner, there was a protective and watchful quality. . . . 'Up to
this moment,' I inquired, 'how many criminals have you reformed?' [At an
earlier time Hollingsworth was a reformer of criminals.] 'Not one!' said
Hollingsworth, with his eyes still fixed on the ground. 'Ever since we parted,
I have been busy with a single murderer!'" (3:242-43).

Yet, Priscilla is not a pure woman, for all her resemblance to the dis-
embodied angel of Victorian sensibility. Her two vocations—the deviser of
intricately fashioned purses with hidden openings, much sought after by
fashionable men about town; and the chief performer, as the "Veiled Lady,"
in a mesmeric exhibition under the control of the diabolic Westervelt—are
replete with sexual innuendo.[9] Her veils and concealments are more provocative to the warped male imaginations of Blithedale than Zenobia's
frankly sexual allurements. And one of the ways in which the men punish
Zenobia—the fatally telling way—is to fail to respond to her allurements
and to prefer Priscilla.

And here we see Zenobia's taint, the corruption in this otherwise so strikingly "emancipated" woman. Despite her rhetoric of freedom and her liberal gestures, she lives in and for the admiration of men. Therefore, they retain power over her and she is no less their creature than her sister:

> I looked at Zenobia, however, fully expecting her to resent—as I felt, by the indignant ebullition of my own blood, that she ought—this outrageous affirmation of what struck me as the intensity of masculine egotism. It centred everything in itself, and deprived woman of her very soul, her inexpressible and unfathomable all, to make it a mere incident in the great sum of man. Hollingsworth had boldly uttered what he, and millions of despots like him, really felt. Without intending it, he had disclosed the well-spring of all these troubled waters. Now, if ever, it surely behooved Zenobia to be the champion of her sex.
>
> But, to my surprise, and indignation too, she only looked humbled. [3:123]

Nor does the narrator, however his blood may boil in sympathy for women's wrongs and however he may long for a woman who will really champion her sex, escape the pull of his destructive fantasies: "I—I myself— was in love—with—Priscilla!" (3:247).

Here is a conundrum indeed. Fantasies of women are social products which control the way in which men approach women. Knowing these things, women are still dependent for their sense of reality and value on men and therefore fated to cooperate with, to submit to, these degrading fantasies. Men are helpless to change and yet in control. A woman who could truly be the champion of her sex might make a difference to women and men alike; but how can such a woman be produced in such a society?

In *The Blithedale Romance*, Hawthorne did not engage with the question of the origin of these fantasies, although he clearly was exonerating individual men from blame for them. Witness, for example, the public ritualistic celebrations of the Veiled Lady. However the situation came about, every individual man in contemporary society is born into a world that indoctrinates him—and through his behavior, woman—in its fantasies; each man dreams the dreams of his culture. Thus to some extent the individual artist is also absolved of that burden of lonely guilt which Hawthorne had hitherto imputed to the fantasist. Now, however, he acquires the guilt of his failure to defy the society whose pernicious effects he recognizes. This is certainly the way in which Coverdale fails.

But Hawthorne could not agree that—as the radical transcendentalists among whom he sojourned for a time believed—society was some sort of monstrous accident bearing no relation to the human nature of the human beings who lived within its framework. On the contrary, he was rather in-clined to see society as itself a product of human nature and thus—in a bizarre sense—the most powerful of all fantasies. Seeing both man and society as evil, he was neither romantic nor conservative.

*The Marble Faun* represents his attempt to work back to the cause of society and the human imagination, but his attempt does not succeed. Several myths of origin are offered, one after the other, only to be rejected. Haw-thorne finds it impossible to locate a beginning, a time before the fall, no matter how he tries. He cannot imagine a sexually adult male who is not overshadowed, or to project a future in which the shadows might disappear. Donatello is not a primitive version of man; he is a child. He loves Miriam, adores her, until he possesses her sexually. Then he withdraws from her in revulsion and guilty gloom. Kenyon, after vainly trying to forge some better order out of this misery, turns at last to Hilda, who is Miriam's supplanter in the novel's moral scheme: "Oh, Hilda," he pleads, "guide me home!" (4:461).

Miriam herself, though the most beautiful and appealing woman in the world (and quite probably the best), moves in a fallen universe, and when Donatello unites with her, he makes connection not with the redemptive world of female sexuality but with a patriarchal world of vengeful priests, bleeding corpses, demonic friars—a hideous world of celibate "fathers" based, so it seems, on relentless suppression of the sexual urge in men and women alike. The Roman past is infinitely more corrupt than the present, but the present achieves its "purity" by a ferocious sterilization and sani-tizing of human life. Between these two dreadful alternatives, one catches a glimpse in fantasy of what might have been, of what art might have devoted itself to expressing. But it is glimpsed even as it disappears. "Donatello here extended his hand, (not that which was clasping Miriam's), and she, too, put her free one into the sculptor's left; so that they were a linked circle of three, with many reminiscences and forebodings flashing through their hearts. Kenyon knew intuitively that these once familiar friends were parting with him, now" (4:448). The sculptor (artist) denies his subject, and it deserts him. We assume that once back in America with Hilda he will resume his profession of turning out busts of the popular politicians (the American "fathers") of the day. The vicious circle is unbreakable.

The saddest thing about the sadness of *The Marble Faun*, when the work is put in the context of Hawthorne's own writings, is that the circle had once been broken. Hawthorne had triumphantly transcended the terms of his art in *The Scarlet Letter*. One cannot say that in that story there are no traces of the fantasies that had seemed at once to empower and limit Hawthorne in his other writings. On the contrary, the traces of these fantasies testify all the more to the achievement of the romance in breaking their grip. We can only guess how this achievement might have originated in Hawthorne's life.

We do have Hawthorne's own account of it in "The Custom-House" where, we observe, the Hawthorne narrator accepts the woman's story as his subject and, putting her scarlet letter on his own breast, loses his identity in hers. In return for this giving of himself, "Hester" gave Hawthorne the fullest command of his artistic powers that he had yet known. And, as events proved, the fullest command he was ever to know.

## IV

Although criticism of *The Scarlet Letter* for a long time took Dimmesdale as the central character, it has more recently reacknowledged what was well understood in Hawthorne's own time, that Hester is protagonist and center. The narrator allies himself with her and, despite occasional adverse judgments, devotes himself to her cause. His cause as narrator is to obliterate her obliteration, to force the reader to accept Hester's reading of her letter as a badge of honor instead of a mark of negation. The narrator forces us, just as Hester forces her Puritan townsmates, to see her as a good woman on her own terms. In contrast to the two distorted male personalities who counterpoise her—the one obsessed with revenge, the other with his own purity—Hester appears almost a miracle of wholeness and sanity. While these men struggle with their own egos and fantasies, she has real battles—to maintain her self-respect in a community that scorns her, to stay sane in solitude, to support herself and her child, to raise that child to normal adulthood despite so many obstacles. Curiously, though she has been cast out of society, Hester remains very much in the world, whereas Chillingworth and Dimmesdale at the very center of society are totally immured in their self-absorption. In her inner integrity and her outer responsiveness, Hester is a model and a counterstatement.

Cautiously, Hawthorne advances the notion that if society is to be changed for the better, such change will be initiated by women. But because society has condemned Hester as a sinner, the good that she can do is greatly circumscribed. Her achievements in a social sense come about as by-products of her personal struggle to win a place in the society; and the fact that she wins her place at last indicates that society has been changed by her. Might there be in the future a reforming woman who had not been somehow stigmatized by society? Although in his later works Hawthorne was to answer this question negatively, in *The Scarlet Letter* the possibility, though faint, is there.

There is more to be said about Hester than space allows; let me confine myself to two points: first, the relative insignificance of her relation to Dimmesdale in comparison with her relation to Pearl—the supersession in her portrait of sexual love by maternal love. The downplaying of her passion for Dimmesdale means that—although she continues to love him, and remains in Boston largely on his account—her goodness and her essential nature are not defined by her relation to a man. Hawthorne does not cooperate in the masculine egotism that he excoriates in *The Blithedale Romance* by making Hester a mere event in the great sum of man. Hester is a self in her own right, portrayed primarily in relation to the difficulties in her social situation, in relation to herself, and in relation to Pearl.

Through Pearl, Hester becomes an image of "Divine Maternity" (1:56). But though so signally a mother, she is not a "mother figure." By detaching her from the social milieu that defines and supports the concept of motherhood, Hawthorne is able to concentrate on the relation of Hester to her child without any social implications. In fact, society in this instance wishes to separate the mother and child. By giving her a recalcitrant daughter as child, Hawthorne has even more cleverly set his depiction of motherhood apart from Victorian ideology. What remains is an intense personal relation that expresses Hester's maternal nature in a remarkably role-free way.

But adult love, sexual love, has not been written out of the story by this emphasis, and this is the second point I would stress. At the end of the work Hester expresses the hope "that, at some brighter period, when the world should have grown ripe for it, in Heaven's own time, a new truth would be revealed, in order to establish the whole relation between man and woman on a surer ground of Mutual happiness." The "angel and apostle of the coming revelation must be a woman" who would show "how sacred love should make us happy, by the truest test of a life successful to such an end!" (1:263). These are Hester's ideas rather than the narrator's, but he does not distance himself from her at this point. "Earlier in life, Hester had vainly imagined that she herself might be the destined prophetess." Hester could have had this vain imagining only during the very brief period of her secret affair with Dimmesdale, for once she was stigmatized she could have no further hope of living a life such as she describes. But during their affair, she felt that what they did had a consecration of its own—it was this consecration, then, that she wished to put to the test of a lifetime.

Therefore, what Hester means by "sacred love" is really "sexual love," and she looks forward to the time when sex and love can be united *by men* in one emotion, a time when somehow women can heal the split in the male psyche. As Freud, writing later in the century, was to observe the male inability to feel passion and tenderness toward the same "object," so Hawthorne not many decades earlier found the male's revulsion and fear of sex leading him to separate from women and incapable therefore of love. Hester's letter represents not merely adulterous sex but all sex, and the image of divine maternity becomes even more telling than it seemed at first. Every child testifies to the sexual experience of its mother and is, in a society that finds sex shameful, a shameful object. For Hester to try to return to

Dimmesdale by "undoing" her letter is to return to him incompletely, in a manner that denies sex, denies her child. It is no wonder that Pearl objects.

What one senses here—though how opaquely!—is Hawthorne's tentative engagement with the subject of men and their mothers, his suggestion that the relation between men and their mothers was the deepest and most central core of their lives. The great liberation of *The Scarlet Letter* comes not only from its celebration of a woman, but of a woman who is centrally a mother. I am reminded here of an extraordinary passage from *Our Old Home*, the volume of essays that Hawthorne put together about England in 1863. In a chapter entitled "Outside Glimpses of English Poverty," Hawthorne speaks about the mothers of the Liverpool slums:

> Yet motherhood, in these dark abodes, is strangely identical with
> what we have all known it to be in the happiest homes. Nothing, as
> I remember, smote me with more grief and pity . . . than to hear a
> gaunt and ragged mother priding herself on the pretty ways of her
> ragged and skinny infant, just as a young matron might, when she
> invites her lady-friends to admire her plump, white-robed darling in
> the nursery. Indeed, no womanly characteristic seemed to have
> altogether perished out of these poor souls. It was the very same
> creature whose tender torments make the rapture of our young
> days, whom we love, cherish, and protect, and rely upon in life
> and death, and whom we delight to see beautify her beauty with
> rich robes and set it off with jewels, though now fantastically
> masquerading in a garb of tatters, wholly unfit for her to handle.
> I recognized her, over and over again. [5:283]

This evocation of the mother has almost nothing in common with the normative Victorian image of woman in her place. This mother's place, even in the gutters of Liverpool, is really in the heart, mind, and memory of a man who recognizes his love for her as the most intense feeling he has ever known, a deathless, unquestioning, infinite devotion. An older man looking back on his life, with only a short time left to live, Hawthorne seems to have reached once again beyond the inhibitions of his age and connected with a true and good emotion. If his discovery of the attachment of the child to the mother is like Freud's, the lesson he draws is opposite. No adult life founded on the suppression or perversion of that original love can be happy or healthy; yet society (and Freud in its service) required that men do just that by denying the sexuality of mothers.

Locked into society, the son is powerful in his ability to do harm but helpless to do good. Social betterment must originate with women; but they in turn are made into the creatures of men's power. Those who break out are labeled evil. It will take, indeed, a new revelation to make a change, "at some brighter period, when the world should have grown ripe for it, in Heaven's own time." The time was to be long in coming. The weary writer who put down his pen soon after publishing *Our Old Home* would not be surprised to learn that it has not come yet.

*Notes*

1. The question of Hawthorne's "ambiguity" dominated virtually all the criticism of the 1950s and 1960s, the era of the renaissance of Hawthorne studies. Citations of the pertinent criticism would run to many pages. However, standard readings of Hawthorne as moral conservative can be found in Arlin Turner, *Nathaniel Hawthorne: An Introduction and Interpretation* (New York: Barnes and Noble, 1961); Edward H. Wagenknecht, *Nathaniel Hawthorne, Man and Writer* (New York: Oxford, 1961); Hubert H. Hoeltje, *Inward Sky: The Mind and Heart of Nathaniel Hawthorne* (Durham, N.C.: Duke University Press, 1962); Hyatt H. Waggoner, *Hawthorne, A Critical Study* (Cambridge, Mass.: Harvard University Press, 1955); Roy R. Male, *Hawthorne's Tragic Vision* (Austin: University of Texas Press, 1957); and Richard H. Fogle, *Hawthorne's Fiction: The Light and the Dark* (Norman: University of Oklahoma Press, 1952). These works range from seeing Hawthorne as basically accepting of the conservative vision he saw (Hoeltje) to Hawthorne as despairing (Male).
2. For example, Frederic I. Carpenter, "Puritans Preferred Blondes: The Heroines of Melville and Hawthorne," *New England Quarterly* 9 (1936):253–72; Philip Rahv, "The Dark Lady of Salem," *Partisan Review* 8 (1941):362–81; Rudolph Von Abele, *Nathaniel Hawthorne: The Death of the Artist* (The Hague: Martinus Nijhoff, 1955); Leslie Fiedler, *Love and Death in the American Novel* (New York: Criterion Books, 1960); and Frederic Crews, *The Sins of the Fathers: Hawthorne's Psychological Themes* (New York: Oxford Press, 1966).
3. Darrel Abel, "Hawthorne's Skepticism about Social Reform," *University of Kansas City Review* 19 (1953):181–93.
4. See, for example, Neal F. Doubleday, "Hawthorne's Hester and Feminism," *PMLA* 54 (1939):825–28; Mortin Cronin, "Hawthorne on Romantic Love and the Status of Women," *PMLA* 69 (1954):89–98; Darrell Abel, "Hawthorne and the Strong Division-Lines of Nature," *American Transcendental Quarterly* 14 (1972):23–31; Gustaaf Van Cromphout, "Blithedale and the Androgyne Myth: Another Look at Zenobia," *Emerson Society Quarterly* 18 (1972):141–45; Raymona Hull, "'Scribbling Females' and Serious Males," *Nathaniel Hawthorne Journal* 5 (1975):35–59; and Terence J. Matheson, "Feminism and Femininity in *The Blithedale Romance*," *Nathaniel Hawthorne Journal* 6 (1976):215–26.

5. See, for example, Wendy Martin, "Seduced and Abandoned in the New World," in *Women in Sexist Society*, ed. Vivian Gornick and Barbara K. Moran (New York: Basic Books, 1971), pp. 329–46; Linda Pratt, "The Abuse of Eve by the New World Adam," in *Images of Women in Fiction*, ed. Susan Koppelman Cornillon (Bowling Green, Ohio: Bowling Green University Popular Press, 1972), pp. 155–74; and Judith Fryer, *The Faces of Eve* (New York: Oxford, 1976).
6. See Hyatt H. Waggoner, "Hawthorne Explained," *Sewanee Review* 86 (1978):130–38; and Fryer, *Faces of Eve*, p. 75.
7. See, especially, "Hawthorne's Women: The Tyranny of Social Myths," *Centennial Review* 15 (1971):250–72; and *The Shape of Hawthorne's Career* (Ithaca, N.Y.: Cornell University Press, 1976).
8. *The Centenary Edition of the Works of Nathaniel Hawthorne* (Columbus: Ohio State University Press), 10:360. Subsequent parenthetical citations of volume and page number will refer to this edition.
9. Allan and Barbara Lefcowitz, "Some Rents in the Veil: New Light on Priscilla and Zenobia in *The Blithedale Romance*," *Nineteenth Century Fiction* 21 (1966):263–75.

# Laurie Crumpacker

# Four Novels of Harriet Beecher Stowe: A Study in Nineteenth-Century Androgyny

Feminist critics and historians today identify Harriet Beecher Stowe as a domestic feminist.[1] They suggest that, like her sister, the noted educator Catharine Beecher, Stowe believed in women's stabilizing power within a developing democracy. Certainly, along with Catharine, Harriet saw women offering moral guidance and training a new generation both at the hearth and in the schoolroom. In fact, by the time the sisters published their collaborative work, *The American Woman's Home* (1869), they were proposing school and hearth as the best and only loci for teaching moral values. Like other domestic feminists, they did not believe that women belonged on the podium advocating equal rights with men. Rather, they stated emphatically that women belonged in the home and in the classroom, teaching the ideal of a stable society based on appropriate power for men and women in their separate spheres.

This definition of domestic feminism fits well with the notions of female identity reflected in Stowe's life and work. Still, Stowe would never have identified herself as a feminist, domestic or otherwise. Not only was the term seldom used in the nineteenth century, but Stowe herself did not speak specifically of bettering women's lot. Rather she saw herself as an advocate of evangelical reform throughout society. Thus it is more useful to examine her ideas about women's roles within the context of social transformation, including but not limited to women's rights.

Along with the theoretical problems of designating Stowe a domestic feminist, close examination of her fiction shows this designation to be too static to reflect her changing ideas. Over a ten-year period, the female protagonists in her fiction move from the private, domestic sphere to a larger social context: from private piety to a public ministry, from education at home to public schooling, from the moral education of their family members to social reform movements. Stowe's later synthesis proposes an androgynous individual and a transformed society which provides the male or female individual with both a public and a private role.[2]

Like other nineteenth-century women writers, Stowe saw popular fiction as the most effective way to promulgate her ideology. With major advances in printing technology and in publishing in the early nineteenth century, sentimental fiction could capitalize on a mass market, and domestic novels became early best-sellers. There was thus no more efficient way to disseminate reform, whether abolitionism, temperance, evangelicism, or women's rights, than through the popular fiction of the period. Best-sellers also made money for their authors, and Stowe, Louisa May Alcott, Sarah Josepha Hale, and many other women found this a respectable way to survive. But most important to Harriet Beecher Stowe was the preaching and teaching potential of her books. By virtue of her membership in the Beecher clan, Harriet was a preacher, though denied a pulpit because of her sex. By interest and talent she was also a historian, though denied a university appointment again because of her sex. Her novels allowed Stowe to realize her ambitions at the same time that she augmented her family's income. It was through her writings that she preached the reforms to which she was committed.

In this essay, I will examine the evolution of Harriet Stowe's thinking in her four major novels: *Uncle Tom's Cabin* (1852), *The Minister's Wooing* (1859), *The Pearl of Orr's Island* (1862), and *Oldtown Folks* (1869). In *Uncle Tom's Cabin*, she delineates her philosophy of domestic feminism; in *The Minister's Wooing*, she proposes and describes a female ministry. In *Pearl*, Stowe examines the role of education in creating the ideal woman and man. Finally, in *Oldtown Folks*, she describes the ideal community, truly nurturant of androgynous individuals.

In *Uncle Tom's Cabin* (1852), both black and white women are ideally domestic queens, moral and pious mothers—epitomizing the nineteenth century's "cult of true womanhood," with one significant difference. The strong and effective women of *Uncle Tom's Cabin* reject one of the cult's cardinal virtues; they are neither passive nor submissive. Rather, it is through their activity that their power emerges—most impressively in the brilliant and successful escapes of slave women like Eliza Harris, Cassy, and Emmeline.[3]

Other women in this novel display their female power less dramatically, but more in keeping with their domestic roles, through domestic "faculty," that ability to run a home smoothly and raise children effectively that Stowe eulogizes here and elsewhere in her writings. In this novel, Stowe introduces three women of domestic faculty, two white and the other black: Ophelia Sinclair, Rachel Halliday, and Chloe. Chloe, who is Tom's wife, demonstrates Angela Davis's contention that in the slave community, black women often performed the only unalienated labor because they provided for the survival of their own families.[4] Chloe is a superwoman in this respect. She labors all day in the Shelby kitchen as chef and manager, keeps a clean and pleasant house herself, feeds, tends, and nurtures her own children and does all with that efficiency and skill that Stowe labels faculty. Later in the novel, after

Tom is sold, Chloe goes out to work as a pastry chef and earns the money to buy back her husband. Chloe is strong and she is a resister, counseling Tom not to accept being sold. In domestic faculty, strength, and dignity, Chloe is like two other strong and wise black women in Stowe's novels: Dinah in the St. Clares' kitchen in this novel and Candace, the Marvyns' talented house-keeper in *The Minister's Wooing*.

Chloe is also to be compared with the most outstanding white woman of faculty in this novel, the Quaker matron, Rachel Halliday. Here is Stowe's description of the veritable "paradise" of the Quaker home over which Rachel presides:

> The next morning was a cheerful one at the Quaker house. "Mother" was up betimes, and surrounded by busy girls and boys . . . who all moved obediently to Rachel's gentle "thee had better," or more gentle "Hadn't thee better?" in the work of getting breakfast . . . John ran to the spring for fresh water, Simeon the second sifted meal, and Mary ground coffee . . . Rachel moved gently and quietly about, making biscuits, cutting up chicken, and diffusing a sort of sunny radiance over the whole proceeding generally. . . . This indeed was a home,–home,–a word that George Harris had never yet known a meaning for; and a belief in God . . . began to encircle his heart . . . and fierce despair melted away before the light of the living Gospel.[5]

Stowe is suggesting here not only that the home has the power to convert the unbeliever, but also that certain conditions are optimal for the flowering of the Christian home and for the kind of domestic creativity and female power of women like Rachel and Chloe. Chloe's position arises from the relative gender equality of the slave community where male and female slaves were both oppressed. Gender equality of a different kind characterized nineteenth-century Quaker society where women had throughout the history of the sect been encouraged to testify publicly about their beliefs and might also serve as ministers alongside men.

Unlike the women of faculty in *Uncle Tom's Cabin*, it is the wives of wealthy slave owners who are most passive; and Stowe suggests that their passivity is both a product and a cause of the perpetuation of the corrupt and powerful slave system. Their passivity is the product of the system, because in Stowe's view, it was the feudal, corrupt, class-ridden, slave-owning South that robbed white women of their legitimate power within the family. But women's passivity also contributes to the continuation of slavery as Stowe demonstrates through the character of Mrs. Shelby, the wife of Tom's debt-ridden owner, George Shelby. She discovers that her moral and spiritual superiority cannot stand up against the economic necessity of selling Uncle Tom and little Harry. She tries to dissuade her husband, but it is too late for moral arguments. Only if she had kept informed of family finances, could she have stepped in earlier to prevent her husband's increasing debts. Passivity and ignorance of family economy brought Emily Shelby finally to her helpless position.

Passivity could also be aggressively dangerous for slaves when a white mistress vented her hostility on them. Marie St. Clare, the wife of New Orleans slave owner Augustine St. Clare, is bored, sick, and angry. She becomes one of the worst exploiters of her slaves, causing a young slave mother to neglect her own children to minister to her mistress's constant complaints. But according to Stowe, it is the system that is to blame, a system that dictated for Marie St. Clare a "life of constant inaction, bodily and mental," and left her a "yellow, faded sickly woman . . . who considered herself . . . the most ill-used and suffering person in existence" (p. 159).

In contrast to Marie St. Clare, the active women of this novel have another important and powerful function. They have the ability to render Christianity meaningful in its relation to antislavery doctrine. The influence of Christian women occurs in two ways, both of which Stowe explores in more detail in *The Minister's Wooing* and in *The Pearl of Orr's Island*. Stowe's first example is the dying female child/angel whose life, dying, and death often convert the most recalcitrant sinners. Men are particularly susceptible to this influence, at least in the case of Augustine St. Clare, who is returned to religion and agrees to free his slaves in response to his daughter Eva's death. In contrast, his wife Marie seems oblivious to the message of her daughter's death and in fact becomes a worse oppressor of her slaves after the restraining influence of Eva and then Augustine is removed. But other conversions are precipitated by Eva's death. Topsy, the "morally undeveloped" black child, is converted to "goodness" by Eva's dying message that "Christ loves you"; and it is at her niece's death bed that Miss Ophelia finally understands the message of a Christian love transcending race and class.

In this novel, traditional Calvinism is both softened and "feminized," a common enough trend among the sentimental novelists of the early nineteenth century. Uncle Tom is male, but he is also the prototype of a feminized Jesus. He is endowed with the typical female characteristics of moral superiority, unquestioning piety, loyalty, and worst of all, submission, not to any earthly owner, of course, but to a heavenly master. Finally, like Eva, he is a martyr, dying for the sins of slaveholders. His death accomplishes an even more efficacious conversion than Eva's many triumphs: he affects young George Shelby so dramatically that we are sure that young Shelby, a representative of the new generation of enlightened southerners, will now go forth an antislavery convert. In this novel, Stowe asserts, as she will again and again in her writings, that it is within women's power to define a merciful, approachable God and Son; and Uncle Tom himself is only one very early example of the androgynous Christians she hopes to see dominate ninteenth-century religion.[6]

In *Uncle Tom's Cabin*, women's power extends beyond their capacity to redefine Calvinism; because they are mothers, they are also able to conquer racism. It is important to recognize that although this is an antislavery novel that raises the issues of racism, Stowe could still be considered racist by today's standards.[7] Her black characters embody virtually every racial stereotype from the constant burlesque humor of Sam and Andy, to Tom's "childlike simplicity" and his Christian passivity and acceptance of suffering. Some of her limitations are understandable because Stowe's views on slavery and the characteristics of black people developed within the context of the Beecher family who, though strongly against slavery, were not immediate abolitionists of the Garrisonian persuasion. They were, in the early years, colonizationists, believers in a Liberian home for gradually freed and educated ex-slaves. In fact, Lyman Beecher's antipathy to radical abolitionism precipitated the dissolution of Lane Seminary in 1835, when Theodore Weld attempted to turn it into a radical abolitionist center. Only after the Fugitive Slave Law (1850) and "Bloody Kansas" did Stowe and many of her family begin to support more rapid abolition of slavery.[8]

As a writer, Harriet Stowe's views about slavery were strongly influenced by her reading of slave narratives, particularly the memoirs (1849) of an escaped slave and minister, Reverend Josiah Henson, whom Stowe met in Boston in the late 1840s and whose story provided a model for Uncle Tom. In *Uncle Tom's Cabin*, George Harris is a somewhat closer copy of the great abolitionist, Frederick Douglass, whose memoirs were published in 1845. Conversations with the religious feminist and abolitionist, Sojourner Truth, in Amherst in 1845 obviously influenced Stowe's portrayal of strong black women like Chloe in *Uncle Tom's Cabin*, Milly in *Dred*, and Candace in *The Minister's Wooing*. And most impressive for a northern white woman of Stowe's era was her recognition of a large part of her own racism and her attempt to modify it in the character of Ophelia Sinclair in *Uncle Tom's Cabin*.

Miss Ophelia, the Vermont-born cousin of Louisiana-bred Augustine St. Clare, is a flawed woman in two related respects: she had never learned to be warm and nurturant, and she cannot bear to be physically close to black people. When young Eva St. Clare ran from one to another of the slaves on her father's New Orleans plantation, embracing and kissing them, Ophelia "afterwards declared [it] fairly turned her stomach" (p. 168). Like Stowe and many other northern antislavery advocates, Miss Ophelia is only completely comfortable with antislavery doctrine in theory; in practice, she knows she has considerable prejudice to overcome.

In this novel, Stowe has her own spokesman, Augustine St. Clare, discuss northern prejudice:

I know the feeling among some of you northerners well enough . . .
but custom with us does what Christianity ought to do,—obliterates

the feeling of personal prejudice . . . you loath them as you would a
snake or a toad, yet you are indignant at their wrongs. You would not
have them abused; but you don't want anything to do with them
yourselves. [P. 182]

Thus Stowe attributes Ophelia's discomfort to her New England upbringing.
In contrast, her cousin Augustine, raised by a black woman in the South, has
absolutely no aversion to physical proximity with his slaves. Although Stowe
identifies completely with Augustine's antislavery principles, it is to her credit
that she creates Miss Ophelia to represent her own limitations as a New
Englander. Stowe insists at the same time that change is always possible but
only through religious conversion. To prove this theory, Stowe has Ophelia
undergo a conversion experience under the guidance of saintly Eva and in
response to the massive nurturing needs of the black child, Topsy. Her conversion is so effective that she adopts Topsy and takes her home to grow up
in Vermont.

Topsy, you poor child . . . don't give up! I can love you, though I am
not like that dear little child. I hope I've learnt something of the love
of Christ from her. I can love you; I do. [P. 305]

Stowe has thus solved both of Ophelia's major problems—having conquered
her physical aversion to black people and made her a mother at the same
time. Stowe's further implication is that white people, especially northerners,
have a real problem with racism, but they must and can change. The route to
change is through active exposure to black people and through the new
convert's recognition of the true meaning of Christian love in action.

It is this capacity to change that Ophelia's New England upbringing has provided. Village democracy has taught her that all classes have rights and that
the most fundamental right is liberty. In addition, Miss Ophelia believes in
getting things done—she has the faculty of running the most efficient household, and her practicality convinces one that she will raise Topsy successfully
(by her lights), and that she will also take every opportunity to spread the
antislavery word.

Other women of strength in this novel are those who have suffered most
as women and as mothers. The maternal sufferers feel driven to protect their
children from the evils of the system. Eliza Harris and Cassy are the clearest
examples of this kind of strength. Eliza needed only the certain knowledge
that her little Harry was to be sold to pay Mr. Shelby's debts, and although
certain that she had little chance of success, she was ready to run away. As
a younger woman, Cassy had been driven to madness by the sale of two of
her children and had administered a lethal dose of laudanum to her third
child to prevent another separation. It is largely the reawakening of her
maternal feelings, her desire to protect the younger woman Emmeline from

Simon Legree's lustful advances, that causes Cassy to devise a brilliant and dangerous escape plan at the end of the novel.

Separation of mother and child could have an equally powerful effect on the male child. Augustine St. Clare tells his cousin that his "mother had been all that stood between me and utter unbelief for years" (pp. 143-44). Since her death, Augustine has lost his religious faith but has the opportunity to regain it with Tom and Eva's help. Simon Legree is not so fortunate. His mother died while he was at sea, and after her death he lost all impulse to goodness. Without a mother, he is powerless to control evil impulses and his lust for women. In *The Rungless Ladder*, Charles Foster suggests that it is this leitmotif of mother-child separation that makes the tragedy of slavery a personal one, both for the author (who had recently lost one son) and for her largely female American reading public.[9]

It was also her belief in the *power* of mothers that gave Stowe license, and in fact obliged her, to write this novel—to speak out on the moral wrongs of slavery. In her introduction to the 1878 edition of *Uncle Tom*, Stowe quoted a letter from Swedish author Frederika Bremer: "It was the work I had long wished for . . . that I thought must come in America, as the uprising of the woman's and mother's heart on the question of slavery."[10] Like Angelina and Sarah Grimké, Stowe thought women to be in a unique position to reach other women and mothers; and it was important to reach them because they were charged with the moral guidance of the nation. One of her novel's greatest achievements was its statement to women that they had the power to convert others to antislavery and also a major responsibility to fight both slavery and other injustices. They were to follow the lead of the author, herself a wife and mother, in taking action against slavery. As it turned out, it was only a matter of time before other obvious injustices, especially to women, would engage those female reformers and demand their organized action.

The publication of *The Minister's Wooing* in 1859 marked a further step in the evolution of Stowe's thinking about new roles for women. In this novel, Stowe suggests that once women make an active commitment to reform, they face certain obstacles. One of the worst of them is the relative insignificance of good works or benevolent actions in the Calvinist scheme of salvation. Thus, in *The Minister's Wooing*, Stowe devotes herself to redefining Calvinism as a necessary first step before proposing her own solution: a female ministry which would change Calvinism at the same time that it allowed women a public role as active reformers and as mystics and preachers.[11]

The plot of this novel is thin and secondary to the exploration of these theoretical theological issues. What happens in the novel is that we meet the widow Katy Scudder who provides room and board for the minister Samuel Hopkins, an early protégé of Jonathan Edwards. The Widow Scudder's

Newport cottage is a domestic shrine graced by the presence of her only daughter, a saintly young woman named Mary. Mary is smitten with the unregenerate sailor James Marvyn, whose apparent loss at sea throws her into deep mourning, largely because she fears that he died unconverted. Reeling from this blow and bound by a strong sense of filial and religious duty, she acquiesces in her mother's wish that she marry Hopkins. Of course, James returns; the village gossip reveals Mary's true love; Hopkins releases her; and she marries James Marvyn. We leave Mary setting up housekeeping and raising a son of the new dispensation. A subplot involves Mary's French-Catholic friend, Virginie, who only narrowly and with Mary's help, escapes seduction by Jonathan Edwards's grandson, Aaron Burr.

Mary is clearly the central actor in the novel even though it purports to be about ministers and the religion of men. But before she can fully develop Mary's religious potential, Stowe must present a convincing critique of the Calvinist legacy she inherits. In one of her most famous passages, Stowe describes her sense of the problems with Edwardsian Calvinism:

> There is a ladder to heaven, whose base God has placed in human affections . . . through which the soul rises higher and higher . . . till she outgrows the human, and changes as she rises into the image of the divine . . . At the very top . . . blazes dazzling and crystalline that celestial grade where the soul knows self no more . . . this Ultima Thule of virtue has been seized upon by our sage [Hopkins] as the *all* of religion. He had knocked out every round of the ladder but the highest, and then pointing to its hopeless splendor, said to the world, "Go up thither and be saved."[12]

The goal is clear and so is the problem—how to ascend the slippery "rungless ladder." These are the problems that plague the unregenerate characters in this book: Aaron Burr, Ellen Marvyn, and James Marvyn. Dr. Hopkins's preaching is sterile, empty, and useless in confronting their massive doubts.

Hopkins has failed to help James Marvyn find religion, and when Mary suggests that he talk further with the minister, James tells her why he won't:

> "Hang, Dr. Hopkins! . . . Now, Mary I beg your pardon, but I can't make head or tail of a word Dr. Hopkins says. I don't get hold of it, or know what he would be at." [P. 22]

Later Hopkins is sure that he has a chance to convince the grandson of his mentor Jonathan Edwards. But he fails again with Aaron Burr, though here Stowe does not blame him any more than she blames the circumstances of Burr's life, the series of deaths in his family, which robbed him of fatherly and grandfatherly ministry and, even more importantly, of the pious example of his mother.[13] We have to wait until Burr reappears as Ellery Davenport in *Oldtown Folks* before Stowe explains that only a loving mother's teaching could have interpreted Jonathan Edwards's abstractions for Burr. Unloved and untaught, Burr was left susceptible to rationalism which robbed him of both religious piety and moral scruples.

For Stowe personally, the most significant failure of the old Calvinism appears in Hopkins's total inability to comfort the grief-stricken mother of James Marvyn after she learns of his death. In this instance, Stowe is describing her own grief at the hands of Calvinism when she faced her two sons' deaths. Charley Stowe was too small a child to have been converted, and Henry had not yet experienced conversion when he drowned in 1857. Because Hopkins can make no compromise with the harsh doctrines denying salvation to the unconverted, he has nothing to offer Ellen Marvyn, who is a sad, frustrated intellectual, already sliding away from religion. Stowe had seen her own father's failure to comfort her older sister Catharine (also a frustrated intellectual) after her fiancé's death in 1822. But Ellen Marvyn is more like Stowe herself than like her sister who totally rejected Calvinism after this early crisis. Stowe and Ellen Marvyn find comfort, not from Calvinism and its ministers, but through the ministry of other women.[14] Only Candace and Mary Scudder can comfort Ellen Marvyn and save her from madness.

> "Mary," she said "I cannot, will not be resigned! Dr. Hopkins says
> that this is all best . . . for a greater and final good . . . It is not
> right!" At this moment Candace . . . suddenly burst into the
> room . . . "Come ye poor little lamb," she said, "come to old
> Candace! . . . I knows our Doctor's a mighty good man, an' larned—
> But, honey, that won't do for you now . . . dar just a'n't but one
> t'ing to come to an' dat ar's Jesus. Jes' come right down to whar
> poor ole black Candace has to stay allers—it's a good place, darlin'!
> Look right at Jesus." [P. 195]

Mary and Candace could save Ellen when Hopkins could not partly because they share her grief—Mary as James's lover, and Candace as the woman who raised him; but they also bring to their task new and significant additions to the current theology. Candace is especially effective because she combines a supposedly black mysticism with her intellectually incomplete grasp of Hopkins's theology. Most importantly, she infuses every aspect of religion with her compassion, her sense of humor, and her ability to render revealed religion concrete.

Having criticized the fathers' Puritanism and outlined a feminized alternative, Stowe examines women's personalities for those characteristics that render them the best exponents of the new theology. Women's characteristics are divided between the domestic strengths which we saw in the characters of Rachel Halliday and Chloe of *Uncle Tom's Cabin*, and the mystical spirituality which Little Eva merely foreshadowed in the earlier novel. In this novel, women continue to play two of their traditional Biblical roles—the roles of Lazarus's sisters, Martha and Mary. Martha prepared the food for Jesus and washed the dishes while Mary sat and listened to him speak; Jesus informed Mary that she had "chosen the good part." Stowe is considerably more sympathetic than Luke to the struggling Marthas among women, eulogizing three of them in this novel.

Katy Scudder is the best example. She embodies so much of the domestic faculty that she is a near-perfect housekeeper.

> The Widow Scudder was one of the sort of women who reigned queens in whatever society they move; nobody was more quoted, more deferred to, enjoyed more unquestioned position than she . . . she was one of that much-admired class who in the speech of New England, are said to have "faculty,"—Faculty is Yankee for savoir faire, and the opposite virtue to shiftlessness . . . To he who has faculty [sic], nothing is impossible. [P. 1]

True faculty is also accompanied by a proper élan, the ability to *appear* unharried and unhurried. And faculty also allows one to provide for others, to practice unselfish Christian benevolence.

> She who hath faculty is never in a hurry, never behindhand. She can always step over to distressed Mrs. Smith, whose jelly won't come,—and stop to show Mrs. Jones how to make her pickles so green,—and be ready to watch with poor old Mrs. Simkins, who is down with the rheumatism. [P. 2]

Another woman of faculty is Miss Prissy, the village seamstress. She is the *unmarried* working woman who is both skilled in her work and proud of all aspects of her essential role in the community.

> You may have heard of dignitaries . . . but I assure you, you know very little of a situation of trust or importance compared to that of the dressmaker in a small New England town . . . Among the most influential and happy of her class was Miss Prissy Diamond . . . she laughingly boasted of being past forty and her merry flow of spirits and ready abundance of gayety, song and story apart from her professional accomplishments made her a welcome guest in every family in the neighborhood. [Pp. 107-8]

Each of these Marthas seem to function best without a man. Of course, both devote themselves to the care of the minister, but they are unencumbered by a male *head* of the household and, of course, by a man's sexual demands.

Candace, the freed slave in the Marvyn family, is the third woman of faculty in this novel. She takes care of everyone, including her nearly helpless husband, Cato. "She was a powerfully built, majestic black woman, corpulent, heavy with the swinging majesty of motion like that of a ship in a ground swell" (p. 63). Candace introduces one of Stowe's main points about women because she is not only an efficient housewife but also a natural mystic, a good Christian, and a superb preacher and counselor. Like Milly in *Dred*, her character probably owes a great deal to Stowe's knowledge of Sojourner Truth, who spent most of her life as an itinerant preacher.

It is only after her minute description of the domestic queens in this novel that Stowe offers a new synthesis. Mary Scudder is the character who embodies *both* domestic faculty and mystical spirituality. Early in the book her room is described as symbolizing the combination: neat and tidy, filled with products of her own handiwork yet also containing a small altar, the location for her prayers and meditations. In this novel, Mary is the primary example of female ministry, and she has a matrilineal heritage. Mary's father had died early, and her only memories are of her mother's teaching. Her inheritance is really not from Johathan Edwards but from Sarah Edwards, whose piety caused Jonathan to seek her hand in marriage and later to choose his wife's conversion experience as an example of a near-perfect conversion.[15]

Pious and mystical in character and by spiritual lineage, Mary is still able to render the minister's abstractions concrete and convert James Marvyn where Hopkins failed. Her success is hardly surprising in Stowe's view, for she tells us that "where theorists and philosophers tread with sublime assurance, woman often follows with bleeding footsteps; (but) women are always turning from the abstract to the individual, and feeling where the philosopher only thinks." (p. 15). It is not that Mary lacks an intellectual understanding of Calvinism; though not his equal in understanding theoretical religion, she can hold her own in a conversation with Hopkins. Stowe is suggesting instead that though Hopkins may be a superior theoretician, Mary is the superior minister because she has the ability to render the truths of religion real and powerful to each individual.

Mary is the near-perfect female minister because she can understand theology and experience the transports of piety, and she is able to translate her piety into action. She saves others from immorality and teaches by her own self-sacrifice the true nature of Christian benevolence. Finally, as priestess, she converts those whom ministers fail to reach. Once Mary marries James—now a pious man—and establishes her own home, she has gained *all* the accouterments of a true saint. She combines domestic faculty with piety—Martha's qualities with Mary's—in the woman's shrine, her home. She is now ready to continue with her ministry within her own family as teacher to her children and a "mother in Israel" to the community. Stowe describes this bliss in her closing chapters:

> The fair poetic maiden, the seeress, the saint, has passed into that appointed shrine for woman, more holy than cloister, more saintly

and pure than church or altar—a Christian home. Priestess, wife and mother, there she ministers daily in holy works of household peace, and by faith and prayer and love redeems from grossness and earthliness the common toils and wants of life. [P. 321]

In Mary, Stowe has not only found a place for women within the new Protestantism, she has given them the central role as evangelists and ministers.

In subject matter and style, *The Pearl of Orr's Island* belongs both before and after *The Minister's Wooing*, and in fact, Stowe began this "Maine story"[16] before and finished it after *The Minister's Wooing* was published. She divided the work accordingly, devoting the first seventeen chapters to an examination of childhood and the second half to a sentimental account of the heroine's death. The discussion that follows concentrates on the earlier child-rearing section of the novel because it is here that many of the author's concerns about women's private and public lives coalesce. In *Pearl*, Stowe seeks to answer two important questions: Are male and female traits inherited or acquired? If they are acquired, as she hints early is her belief, what kinds of child-rearing practices are best calculated to develop a child's individual talents? How does a mother raise a potential female minister, or even more difficult, the husband for a female minister?

As Stowe asks theoretical questions about child-rearing, she obviously sympathizes with hard-working mothers, and at the same time, she seeks to make these mothers aware of the importance of their role. She knows the "secret agonies . . . [of those] who receive the infant into their bosom out of the void unknown . . . what perplexities,—what confusion! . . . and frail, trembling, self-distrustful mothers are told that the shaping and ordering not only of this present life, but of an immortal destiny is in their hands" (p. 188). This work is an essential part of the quartet I have chosen to discuss. After describing the domestic queens and reformers of *Uncle Tom's Cabin* and the female minister of *The Minister's Wooing*, Stowe needed to focus on early childhood education to investigate and instruct in proper methods of raising a good Christian man or woman.

Stowe chose Orr's Island carefully as the setting for this novel about child-rearing. She knew the island well from her tenure in Brunswick, Maine; and it represented all of the best elements of rugged, isolated seacoast communities—as yet untouched by industry or urbanization. Perhaps best of all, men were less important in these communities (though not so totally lacking as in Sarah Orne Jewett's later Maine novels) because of their frequent absences.

The young men have all left: for the sea, the northern lumber country, the city, the West. The men at home are either too old (Zephanniah Pennel), too unassertive (Captain Kittridge) or too much "sicklied o're with the pale cast of thought" (the minister) to wield much power. Thus, Orr's Island is a matrifocal community where widows and spinsters, lonely wives and sweethearts can play leadership roles without significant male interference, and Stowe has free rein to experiment with a near gynocracy—at least in domestic, religious, and community affairs. Only politics and commerce remain, and these are as distant as the men whose callings they are.

In this novel, Stowe's discussion of innate and acquired gender differences moves far beyond the ideas then current in either the popular literature, ladies' books like *Godey's*, or the "Christian nurture" teachings of minister Horace Bushnell. Sarah Hale, editor of *Godey's*, and Horace Bushnell taught that women belonged in a totally separate sphere from men and that there is "a basic and enduring opposition between the values of domesticity and much of society."[17] Harriet's sister, Catharine, differed fundamentally from Hale and Bushnell because, rather than isolating women in a totally separate sphere at home, Beecher "saw the home as an integral part of a national system, reflecting and promoting mainstream American values."[18] Stowe agreed with her sister that women belonged at home but that the home should be absolutely central to the community. What intrigues Stowe in this novel is whether women and men are born destined for separate spheres or whether, as she suspects, they are conditioned to fill certain gender roles.

From the beginning it is clear that to Stowe superior intellect is not an innate masculine characteristic. Mara is soon discovered to be smarter than Moses. Because she has "finer senses, a finer mind" she is allowed to learn Latin and Greek with Moses instead of embroidery and fine needlework. At age seven, "whatever book Moses reads, forthwith she aspires to read too, and though three years younger, reads with a far more precocious insight" (p. 122). Is Mara's intelligence compatible with womanliness? Stowe says yes. "Those who contend against giving woman the same education as man do it on the ground that it would make the woman unfeminine, as if Nature has done her work so slightly that it could be so easily raveled and knit over" (p. 122). Stowe then explains that, because "there is a masculine and feminine element in all knowledge," women should study what men study and will "extract only what their nature fits them to see" (p. 123). The argument then is that women deserve the same educational opportunities as men; only then will it become clear exactly what each sex is capable of.

In spite of Mara's interest and intelligence, however, she receives only a short seminary education, whereas Moses, without aptitude or interest, may go to college and beyond if he wishes. The minister questions this injustice when he asks Zephanniah Pennel if he will give Moses a "liberal education." Pennel answers, "'Let 'em feel their own way, and then if nothin' will do but a fellow must go to college, give in to him—.'" But, adds the Captain, "'Now, there's Mara! . . . she's real sharp set after books . . . That child thinks too much and feels too much and knows too much for her years . . . But she's a woman . . . and they're all alike. We can't do much for

them, but let them come up as they will and make the best of it'" (p. 153).
And there ends any hope Mara might have for a higher education.

Other disappointments are in store for Mara because of her sex. She is
not allowed to think of seagoing adventures. When Moses goes on his first
voyage, Mara laments, "'How I wish I were going with you! . . . I could do
something, couldn't I—take care of your hooks or something?'" Moses
answers with typical male nonchalance, "'Pooh! . . . you're a girl; and what
can girls do at sea? You never like to catch fish—it always makes you cry
to see 'em flop.'" Not only must Mara stay at home when Moses goes adven-
turing, but she must also endure his constant disparagement of her sex. When
Moses seeks to settle another dispute by saying "'Well, well you are young
yet . . . and only a girl besides,'" Mara protests, "'I'm sure he oughten't to
feel so about girls and women. There was Deborah as a prophetess and
judged Israel . . .'" (p. 147). But Stowe hastens to inform us that this is
only a thought, not a spoken dissent.

Like Mara, Stowe is chagrined about women's options. She has Mara
ponder the situation: "He was handsomer, cleverer and had a thousand
other things to do and think of—he was a boy, in short, and going to be a
glorious man and sail all over the world, while she could only hem handkerchiefs . . . and sit at home and wait for him to come back" (p. 149). Stowe
also sees the lack of female models for a young girl to emulate. In the novel,
the children's reading list includes Plutarch's *Lives*, and Mara asks the seemingly inevitable question, "'Are there any lives of women?'" The minister
answers "'No, my dear, in the old times, women did not get their lives
written'" (p. 152). Stowe's biography of Mara is of course her attempt to
begin to even the score and to suggest that the definition of greatness for
women might differ from the classical definitions of the heroic for men.

Although, like Mara, Stowe is irate at male disparagement of women's
talents, she is not ready to suggest public action. Mara achieves power and
ultimately her revenge through traditional women's means. Mara's triumph
is her moral and spiritual superiority which she proves through the ultimate
moral victory of renunciation, of complete self-sacrifice for another—in this
case, the selfish Moses. Throughout the book, she takes care of his every
need and, by her anonymous intervention, even saves him from turning an
adolescent prank into a crime. Her ultimate sacrifice is to die for him; to
see him reborn a Christian at her deathbed is her final reward. Her revenge
is to die before they have even exchanged a kiss!

Once Stowe has made it clear that she believes that education and not
birth is responsible for most of the positive and negative characteristics
usually linked to gender, she turns to a discussion of the importance of good
mothering. She approaches the subject with some urgency, realizing that
nineteenth-century mothers face challenges different from those of their
grandmothers, and that child-rearing guidelines are needed. Because by the

early nineteenth century, industrialization had moved much of women's productive labor from home to factory, for middle-class women especially, work at home was more supervisory than productive. Nineteenth-century wives and mothers were also more likely than their grandmothers to be living in a nuclear family without other women to provide aid and without the presence of their husbands who were now more often working outside their homes. Child-rearing manuals took cognizance of those changes as the century progressed. The 1830's manuals by William Alcott, Lydia Maria Child, and others emphasized the authority of the father in the home.[19] The popular teachings in the 1840s of minister Horace Bushnell and *Godey's Lady's Book* editor Sarah Josepha Hale were a considerable improvement for women, because they concentrated on the centrality of the mother in all domestic matters.[20] But Bushnell and Hale also suggested that women had an "organic" (innate) instinct for motherhood. This instinctive understanding of how to proceed was supposed to lessen the difficulties of child raising for all "normal" women. On this point, Harriet Beecher Stowe agreed with her sister, Catharine Beecher; they both rejected the notion of organic motherhood. Beecher maintained that one needed training and common sense to be a good mother; reliance on intuition was simply unrealistic and too risky for such an important task as raising responsible citizens. Stowe agreed and was also well aware of the conflict for women in too strictly adhering to Bushnell's tenets of Christian nurture. What if one simply were not gifted with child-rearing skills although a mother? Stowe's answer was a practical guide in *Pearl* with three test cases for mothering and three quite different children on whom to experiment.

The three "mothers" are Mary Pennel (actually the heroine's grandmother), Mrs. Kittridge, Sally's mother, and Roxy Toothacre (no one's biological mother but everyone's aunt). Neither Mrs. Kittridge nor Grandma Pennel is a "natural-born" mother. Mrs. Kittridge is too harsh and Mrs. Pennel is too soft. Mrs. Kittridge believes in the old Calvinist doctrine that children are born willful and disobedient, needing to have their wills broken early. She feels that "'nothin' straightens out children like work'" (p. 35). Mrs. Kittridge's regimen has exactly the opposite effect from that intended. The lively energetic Sally sits at her tasks with "her large well-marked eyebrows . . . bent in a frown, and her large black eyes . . . surly and wrathful" (p. 31). Sally learns only to be deceitful and exceedingly clever in avoiding those jobs that she hates.

On the other hand, Mrs. Pennel is too permissive; a gentle woman herself, she is unable to deny her children anything. Her granddaughter, Mara, is unharmed by her permissiveness as she too is delicate, sensitive, and acquiescent. It is with the willful, adopted orphan, Moses, that Mrs. Pennel's gentle tactics fail. Moses is the true test case, an unknown quantity of mysterious Latin origin. In addition, he is a boy with all the puzzling and difficult attributes that maleness posed for the nineteenth-century mother. Mrs. Pennel's conflicts about Moses were common ones for gentle mothers who had been taught that they were naturally gifted with nurturing talents. "Was it not her duty, as everybody told her, to break his will while he was young? — a duty which hung like a millstone round the peaceable creature's neck, and weighed her down with a distressing sense of responsibility" (p. 100). The questions emerge: Can sweet-tempered Grandma Pennel raise this willful, disobedient male child? Can Harriet Beecher Stowe deal with these characteristics when they arise among her own sons? These are the soap-opera themes that caused every mother to turn eagerly to the next chapter for another answer to these daily domestic dilemmas.

Stowe's answer to Mrs. Pennel and to Mrs. Kittridge is that good mothers, like good Christians, are made, not born. The best mother in this novel is the spinster, Aunt Roxy Toothacre, who had developed her skills through years of practice with other people's children. Aunt Roxy and her sister Aunt Ruey are the women in this community who are most gifted with every kind of domestic faculty. "It was impossible to say what they could not do," from dressmaking to laundry, upholstering, quilting, and nursing "all kinds of sickness . . .":

> Many a human being had been ushered into life under their auspices, trotted and chirruped in babyhood . . . clothed by their handiwork in garments gradually enlarging from year to year, watched by them in the last sickness, and finally arrayed for the long repose by their hands. [P. 18]

These women are the "cunning women" of the community, "given the title of 'aunt' . . . showing the strong ties of relationship which bind them to the whole human family. They are aunts to human nature generally. The idea of restricting their usefulness to any one family would strike dismay through a whole community" (p. 18). They are the foremothers of the later Down-East priestesses, Mrs. Goodsoe and Almira Todd, in Sarah Jewett's fiction.[21]

Miss Roxy is particularly skilled as a counselor and as a child-care expert. To Mrs. Kittridge, she suggests allowing Sally a bit more fun. She advises Mrs. Pennel to tighten up her discipline and to leave Moses to Mr. Pennel whenever he becomes unruly. Her guiding principle (and also Harriet Beecher Stowe's) is that children are not all the same; thus, no one system of discipline can work for every child. She puts her philosophy concisely to Mrs. Kittridge. "'All children . . . ain't alike . . . This 'un [Mara] ain't like your Sally. A hen and a bumble-bee can't be fetched up alike, fix it how you will'" (p. 35). How comforting to beleaguered mothers these words could be. And how helpful for unmarried women who, Stowe suggests, have an important function in society and a right to involvement with the children of the community. Like her own sister Catharine, who was a mother to Harriet, single women could have value far surpassing the usual connotations of "old maids."

The female ministry is another topic of concern in *Pearl*, though to a lesser extent than in *The Minister's Wooing*. Mara Pennel's power to convert both Moses and Sally extends beyond her death because she leaves the legacy of her pious example and the memory of her saintly deeds. She has succeeded, as did Mary Scudder, where the minister failed—in teaching Moses to feel his religion, and she has reaffirmed women's central role in religious ministry. In doing so, she also reflects changes in Stowe's religious thinking during this period.

During the 1860s, Stowe converted to Anglicanism, a return to the church of her mother Roxanna Foote. Stowe's move to the Anglican church was accompanied by an intensification of her belief in the importance of a female ministry and by her need for a more feminized divinity. Thus, Mara probably speaks for her creator when she explains near the end of the novel that "God has always been to me not so much like a father as like a dear and tender mother." She goes on to catalog the motherly attributes of her God who "has always been loving" to her, who has been a confidante to whom she could tell all her "joys and sorrows," a divinity who watched over her while she slept, and one to whom she could confide her secrets about her lover (p. 322). This was the Mother God to whom Harriet Beecher Stowe turned more often as she endured yet another tragedy—the death by drowning of her son Henry.

Finally, the death of Mara Pennel in *Pearl* has an even greater significance than simply to convert Moses and Sally and to bless their future together. Mara dies of consumption; she has, in Susan Sontag's metaphor,[22] been consumed by the demands on women in her society, demands that have had nothing to do with her potential as an intellectual, an artist, a naturalist, and a minister. She has died of lack of options, consumed by social expectations for women. Stowe is saying that nineteenth-century society is not yet ready for the Mara Pennels and Mary Scudders, the new women of the post-Revolutionary War era. Not only must the individual change through proper child-rearing, so also must the society in which the new individual will make her home. To this theme—redefining the community as well as the individual— Stowe devotes the last novel of this quartet, *Oldtown Folks.*

*Oldtown Folks* has been characterized variously as a community study, as a history of New England, and as a comparative study in religions.[23] Although Stowe describes particular communities in detail; models major characters on eighteenth-century Massachusetts ministers, educators, and even on Vice-President Aaron Burr; and argues theology long and well, this novel is actually an attempt to describe an ideal community which nurtures the new nineteenth-century individual she has been at pains to describe in the preceding three books. In the earlier books, female ministers and their male counterparts found it difficult if not impossible to live in a male-dominated society. Where then might Stowe find an alternative, a community in which nonstereotyped males and females might grow and flourish? Her answer is to turn first to the past. *Oldtown Folks* is set in 1780s Natick and Needham, Massachusetts, and in Litchfield, Connecticut. In these communities, Edwardsian Calvinists like Grandmother Badger and Dr. Moses Stern coexist with liberal Arminians like Parson Lothrop, with Anglicans like Dorothy Lothrop and Harry and Tina Percival, with New Divinity preachers like the Reverend Avery, and even with doubters and skeptics like Mehitable and Jonathan Rossiter and the worst doubter of them all, Ellery Davenport. (It has been assumed that these characters are loosely modeled on the following real-life individuals: Stern on Nathanael Emmons, minister in Franklin, Mass., 1773–1827; Jonathan Rossiter on Litchfield Academy educator John Pierce Brace; Davenport on Aaron Burr; and Avery on Lyman Beecher.)

All of the religious themes and historical characters serve in *Oldtown Folks* to illuminate Stowe's central concern, the examination of a community as a nurturant place for androgynous individuals. In her insistence on a community's vitality in this respect, Stowe is uniquely female and most universal. She tells us of her concern with nurturing and fertility when she states that her "object in this book is to show . . . New England in its *seed-bed*, before the hot suns of modern progress had developed its sprouting germs into the great trees of today." It is "that particular time of its [New England's] history which may be called the Seminal Period [1780 to 1800]."[24] Even more importantly, it is a place—the New England village community exemplified in this novel by Natick (Oldtown), Needham (Needmore), and Litchfield (Cloudland). What these communities have in common is that all have a central female leadership, usually the grandmothers and "old maids" of the town. Each village is also for Stowe a religious community, where she can examine the transition from eighteenth-century New England Calvinism to the feminized Christianity which Stowe sees as the new wave of her century.

In Oldtown, only Grandmother Badger practices and preaches Edwardsian Calvinism, and she does so in a manner that Edwards would have admired—with heartfelt conviction and benevolent actions, the warm emotional variety of Calvinism that Mary Scudder and Mara Pennel exemplified in earlier novels. Based on Joseph Bellamy's interpretations of Edwards, which are set forth in "Grandmother's Blue Book,"[25] Grandmother's religion is held in stark contrast to that of minister Moses Stern. Stern's ministry is modeled on the destructive preaching of Nathanael Emmons which had driven Catharine Beecher irretrievably away from Calvinism. Emmons had preached the funeral sermon for Catharine's fiancé, Stephen Fisher, and had offered no hope that Fisher had received mercy at the last. Emmons's fictional counterpart, Moses Stern, drives Emily Rossiter away from the church into skepticism and then to the life of a fallen woman, after his funeral sermon has denied hope for Emily's favorite brother.

Very different are Grandmother's more tolerant sermons and her benevolent actions. As in *Pearl*, the contrast is most pronounced with issues of child raising. A disciple of Moses Stern, Miss Asphyxia Smith, has taken in the orphaned Tina Percival and attempted to raise her according to the strict Calvinist belief that children are born sinful, needing harsh discipline and hard work to break their wills and make them "God-fearing" adults. She defends her methods to Grandmother Badger:

> "Yes Mis' Badger, I defy her to say I han't done well by her, if she says her truth; for I say it now, this blessed minute . . . [that] that 'ere child . . . had everything pervided for her that a child could want—a good clean bed and plenty o' bedclothes and a good whole clothes to wear, and her belly full o' good victuals every day; an' me a teachin' and a trainin' on her, enough to wear the very life out o'me,—for I always hated young uns . . ." [P. 268]

In fact, she is only raising Tina as she was raised. "'I was a fetchin' on her up to work for her livin' as I was fetched up. I hadn't nothing more'n she an' just look at me now; . . . I've got as pretty a piece of property . . . as most any round; and all I've got . . . is my own arnin's, honest, so there'" (p. 268). Miss Asphyxia has not done badly for herself; after all, in her day, an unmarried woman rarely owned land and managed her own farm. She is actually trying to teach the orphan girl to survive as she has. But Grandmother Badger makes it clear that something crucial is missing:

> "Why, you've done what you'd no business to . . . you'd no business to take a child at all; you haven't a grain of motherliness in you. Why, look at natur', that might teach you that more than meat and drink and clothes is wanted for a child. Hens brood their chickens . . . cows lick their calves . . . it's *broodin'* that young creature wants; you hain't a bit of broodin' in you; your heart's as hard as the nether millstone. Sovereign grace may soften it someday, but nothin' else can . . ." [P. 269]

Stowe is reinforcing the point she made in *Pearl*, that motherhood is hardly an innate womanly instinct. Rather it is a vitally important and difficult job for which a woman is truly "elected"—granted the divine grace to make a success of the task.

As for the Emmons variety of Calvinism, Miss Asphyxia has the final word. She blames her personal harshness on the religion that denied her election: "'Mis' Badger does think I've got a heart of stone. I should like to know how

I'm to have any other when I ain't elected, and I don't see as I am, or likely to be'" (p. 27). Grandmother Badger's Calvinism provides a kind of transition to the future with its insistence on demonstrating piety through acts of benevolence. But it is an option only for those strong enough to feel fairly certain of their election. New directions must be found.

The ultra-Arminianism of Parson Lothrop is worse yet. Diluting and liberalizing Calvinism to the point where anyone can be saved, Arminianism leaves one without an analysis of evil in the world. In this book, Stowe proposes two future alternatives. The first is the old Calvinism reinterpreted through the softer, more feminized "New Divinity" of Mr. Avery who could be Lyman Beecher or Harriet's brother, Henry Ward Beecher. The second is the Anglican Church which in this novel, as in the author's life, becomes a comfortable new home for many disenchanted children and grandchildren of the eighteenth-century Calvinists. In *Poganuc People* (1878), Stowe explains further:

> The nucleus of the Episcopal Church in any place . . . gladly
> welcomed to their fold any who, for various causes, were discon-
> tented with the standing order of things. Then, too, there came to
> them gentle spirits, cut and bleeding by the sharp crystals of
> doctrinal statement, and courting the balm of devotional liturgy
> and the cool shadowy indefiniteness of more aesthetic forms of
> worship.[26]

Quibbling over doctrinal points is less important to Stowe in this novel than maintaining the importance of religious tolerance and a feminized and more nurturant form of Christianity demonstrated through charitable acts. In *Oldtown Folks*, the female religious leaders are also community leaders. The center of Oldtown is Grandmother Badger's kitchen, "a great wide roomy apartment, whose white sanded floor was always as clean as hands could make it" (p. 104). In the home of an eighteenth-century farmer, the kitchen was still the main family room, not yet relegated to a back location or staffed by servants as many nineteenth-century kitchens were to become. "By the side of the ample blaze we sat down to our family meals, and after-wards, while grandmother and Aunt Lois washed up the tea things, we all sat and chatted by the firelight." On a typical Sunday night, neighbors drop by, and the talk ranges from religious issues to politics to ghost stories. In Grandmother Badger's kitchen, black servants and Indian neighbors also share the meals and the talk. When bedtime approaches, the author con-cludes, "So passed an evening in my grandmother's kitchen,—where religion, theology, politics, the gossip of the day and the legends of the supernatural all conspired to weave a fabric of thought" (p. 125).

Grandmothers have the experience of life and mothering without the burden of yearly childbearing and daily child care. They have both the knowledge and the time to exercise power wisely. Thus it is not surprising that they are the center from which radiate the spokes of the community wheel. Horace says of Grandmother Badger, "My grandmother was in my view a tower of strength and deliverance . . . one of those wide awake, earnest active natures whose days were hardly ever long enough for all that she felt needed to be done . . . She had very positive opinions on every subject and was not at all backward in the forcible and vigorous expression of them" (pp. 64–65). Grandmother Kittery also dominates her Boston household with her quiet dignity and near saintliness. She is the example of Stowe's contention that grandmothers are often "the connecting link between heaven and earth" (p. 347).

In stark contrast to Grandmother Badger is her daughter, Horace's mother, Suzy Holyoke. She *had* been "one of those bright, fair, delicate New England girls," Horace recalls. But "how quickly they become withered and bedraggled. My mother's gayety of animal spirits, her sparkle and vivacity all went with the first year of marriage. The cares of housekeeping, the sickness of maternity and nursing, drained her dry of all that was bright and attractive." Horace further describes her as "a little, quiet, faded, mournful woman, who looked on my birth and that of my brother Bill as the greatest of possible misfortunes" (p. 59). Marriage and childbearing have totally depleted her strength, ruined her health and beauty, and blotted out her vivacity. We never hear from her again in the novel! For Harry's mother, the daughter of a poor country curate, marriage to a wealthy Englishman must have seemed a welcome escape from impoverished spinsterhood. It had proved far different, however, after her husband had left her in failing health with two small children to provide for. Hepsy Lawson has changed from an energetic young woman into a terrible scold after marrying ne'er-do-well Sam Lawson and raising six children by herself. Crab Smith's wife is both verbally and physically abused by her husband; she is an eighteenth-century battered woman. Stowe's sympathy clearly goes out to these overworked, undervalued wives and mothers. By marrying, they have lost their autonomy and gained a wretched existence.

These married women have personal significance for the author, because they mirror one of her own conflicts. How many children should a woman have, in order to mother them well, support them, and still keep her health and sanity? New research on the letters between Harriet and Calvin Stowe suggests that Harriet's frequent long absences may have been part of her attempt to limit her family's size.[27] Certainly, Calvin Stowe's laments about Harriet's absence from their bed support the conclusion that Harriet was concerned about the need for abstinence as a form of birth control. Without family limitation, as Stowe suggests in her letters and novels, a woman's health and spirits were sure to be broken. In *Oldtown Folks*, rearing and raising two boys are enough to break Suzy Holyoke's spirit; and there is little doubt that Hepsy Lawson's scolding results as much from the size of her family as from her husband's inability to hold down a job. No wonder grandmothers, who are beyond the dangers of pregnancy, and spinsters have a happier lot and a more powerful social role than wives and young mothers.

Like the grandmothers, the "old maids" are a cheery, assertive, and indipendent group. After adopting Tina, Miss Mehitable Rossiter enjoys motherhood without its pains. Horace's spinster aunt Lois occupies an important position in the Badger family—second in command to Grandmother with ample opportunity to mother the three boys in the household. Miss Deborah Kittery also enjoys a management position in her Boston household. She suggests that independence is the best part of spinsterhood. Commenting that her sister, Dorothy Lothrop, is obliged to parrot her husband's political views, she asserts, "'But I, Deborah Kittery, who was never yet in bondage to any man, shall be free to have my say to the end of my days'" (p. 323).

In this novel, Stowe adds a special tribute to her own spinster sister, Catharine Beecher, in the character of Minerva Randall, perhaps the most glowing old maid in New England literature before Mary Wilkins Freeman's "New England Nun." Miss Nervy is Mr. Rossiter's housekeeper and the Latin teacher at Cloudland Academy (modeled on Miss Pierce's Academy in Litchfield, Connecticut). Raised on the Down East coast, this "Maine Mermaid" is already learned in the ways of survival. In addition, she combines domestic faculty with a very good mind and, unencumbered with a husband and offspring, she is free to teach and mother all of the academy students.

> Miss Nervy was about the happiest female person whose acquaintance it has ever been my fortune to make. She had just as much as she wanted of exactly the two things she liked best in the world,— books and work, and when her work was done, there were the books and life could give no more. [P. 445]

The happy spinsters in this novel, like Miss Ophelia in *Uncle Tom's Cabin*, Miss Prissy in *The Minister's Wooing*, and the Toothacre sisters in *Pearl*, provide a critique of what Stowe saw as the wrongs of Victorian marriage: loss of independence for women and excessive childbearing. These women may also reflect the author's own longings for a life freed from family demands.

The spinster aunts and the grandmothers are models for and nurturers of the next generation, and it is the young people in *Oldtown Folks* who demonstrate what the new generation of men and women might be. Stowe suggests that they can be different, that they may include men and women who are better able to fulfill their potential as talented people, regardless of their sex, and that they will also be able to marry and raise children without being destroyed in the process. Feminized religion and more equal education will effect necessary changes in their lives. Because they have experienced egalitarian education and friendships with male schoolfellows, Stowe believes that women of the new generation will make better marriage choices, will live in more democratic families and will choose men whose sexual control will enable them to practice family limitation.

Stowe suggests that Tina's first disastrous marriage to Ellery Davenport might never have taken place had she received an education commensurate with her talents. Like Mara Pennel, Tina Percival and Esther Avery are intellectually equal if not superior to their male companions. Horace admits that Tina "'had ... quite as good a mind and was fully capable of going through our college course with us having walked thus far.'" Harry reminds Horace that Esther is "'ahead of us both in Greek and Mathematics.'" But instead of going on to college, Tina and Esther must do nothing, as Harry puts it, but "wait the coming man." Horace agrees that it makes no sense that Tina has nothing to do with her fine mind but "to make a frolic of life." He goes on: "'Why couldn't she as well find the coming man while she is doing something? ... Esther and you found each other while you were working side by side, your minds lively and braced, toiling at the same great ideas, knowing each other in the very noblest part of your natures ...'" (p. 521). The worst of it, suggests Stowe, is that an unoccupied mind may fall prey to danger. "When such a gay creature of the elements as Tina has nothing earthly to do to steady her mind ... it throws her open to all sorts of temptations from that coming man." (p. 523). Stowe is making her strongest statement yet for women's education. If Tina had continued in school instead of entering society, she might not have fallen victim to Ellery Davenport's charms; instead she might have waited patiently for the right man, whom Horace believes to be himself, to finish school and marry her.

Finally, Stowe answers the ultimate nineteenth-century objection to coeducation. Would not learning beside each other subject the morally weak of both sexes to irresistible temptation? "Even so, my friends," answers Stowe, "but flirtations and love affairs among a nice set of girls and boys ... where love is never thought of, except as leading to lawful marriage, are certainly not the worst things that can be thought of." She concludes, "On the whole, I cannot think of a better way to bring the two sexes together, without the false glamour which obscures their knowledge of each other, than to put them side by side in the daily drill of a good literary institution" (pp. 488–89).

Education for women, their religious ministry, their roles in the family and in maintaining the community—these are the critical concerns for Stowe in *Oldtown Folks*. Her analysis is careful and thorough; her conclusions are inescapable. She believes that networks of women are the infrastructure essential to community survival and change. The community, in turn, owes women the education and political rights they both deserve and need in order to continue their service. The closer and more intricate her analysis of community structure becomes, the more Stowe drops the sentimental trappings of many other Victorian novelists. In *The Rungless Ladder*, Charles Foster suggests that her style becomes "masculine." After praising *Oldtown Folks* as "large, comprehensive, and various," Foster adds, her "vision was primarily shrewd, witty, and—there would seem to be no other word—masculine."[28] Although I will leave it to Mr. Foster to explain why wit and shrewdness are masculine attributes, I should like to follow up his additional suggestion that some of Oldtown's characters are, like its creator, neither clearly male nor female, but often a combination of the two.

Stowe's use of a male narrator is the first inkling that the author's perspective is not limited to traditional female expression. In this novel, Horace Holyoke fills important needs for Stowe as a writer. Like Augustine St. Clare in *Uncle Tom's Cabin*, he is her spokesman, acting as the scientific observer she wished to be. In both novels Stowe is asking a mass audience not only to listen to but also to believe her as she discusses subjects like the slave trade and theology, subjects usually assumed to be outside a woman's knowledge and intellectual comprehension. She reasoned that a male spokesman might provide the necessary authority to convince a skeptical audience.

Horace Holyoke and Augustine St. Clare are also "feminized" men. Augustine's poetic soul and naturally decent inclinations have been fostered by a saintly mother's care and an angelic daughter's death. But Augustine cannot act, and his brand of manhood cannot even survive in the corrupt soil of the male-dominated, slave-owning South. In contrast, Horace, the child of intellectual, unworldly parents, thrives in the woman-dominated community of *his* childhood. Horace describes himself as a "spiritual type of man," a friend and counselor to his women friends. "Some men," he says, "have a faculty of making themselves the confidants of women. Perhaps they have a certain amount of the feminine element in their own composition . . . I think I had this power" (p. 487). Stowe is demonstrating for her female readers the kind of androgynous menfolk they too may raise if they take seriously their work as educators and moral arbiters. She also suggests that such a son may turn out to be a great comfort to the women who raised him in this manner.

Tina Percival also has her androgynous moments, and like Mara Pennel's, they involve her dissatisfaction with limits on female opportunities and options. Horace reports, "I think the girl was sincere in the wish she often uttered, that she could be a boy, and be loved as a comrade and a friend only . . . 'O, Horace!' she would say . . . 'if I were only Tom Percival, I should be perfectly happy! but it is so stupid to be a girl'" (p. 487). Her attempts to be friends with boys or even to study with male teachers always result in declarations of romantic love from these males. Were she not female, she believes, her nature might be perceived as more rational, less necessarily romantic. The exciting world of male companionship and work might then be opened to her.

Of all the young people in Oldtown, Harry Percival is the most spiritual and emotional. Stowe tells us that "his conclusions were all intuitions. His religion was an emanation of the heart . . . and not a formula of the head" (p. 483). These characteristics, inherited from his Episcopal mother, enable him to convert Esther Avery where her minister father has failed. Harry begins, as Mary Scudder and Mara Pennel had, by loving the potential convert.

> In such an hour Esther saw that she was beloved!—beloved by a
> poet soul . . . his simple faith in God's love was an antidote for her
> despondent fears . . . She was a transfigured being. [Pp. 482–83]

His talent is one hitherto perceived by Stowe as female—that of injecting feeling into religion and thereby reaching hearts otherwise unmoved by more traditional methods of ministry.

The development in Stowe's novels from the female ministry of Mary Scudder and Mara Pennel to the feminized male ministry of Harry Percival raises questions about Stowe's vision of transformed Christianity. She saw that Christianity had been dominated for centuries by male priests and their theology. In her view, female influence was urgently needed:

> Woman's nature has never been consulted in theology. Theological
> systems, as to the expression of their great body of ideas, have, as
> yet, been the work of man alone. They have had their origin, as in
> St. Augustine, with men who were utterly ignorant of moral and
> intellectual companionship of women, looking on her only in her
> animal nature as a temptation and a snare. [P. 446]

But Stowe's ultimate goal was neither a feminine nor a masculine religion but an androgynous theology, combining her father's Calvinism with her mother's Anglicanism, and encompassing the best of both modes. In the hands of female preachers and feminized men, an androgynous theology seemed best suited to meet nineteenth-century needs.

In this novel, the most interesting and complex androgynous character is Esther Avery, who, as the daughter of Lyman Beecher's stand-in, Mr. Avery, could be either Catharine (Esther) Beecher or the author herself. From the beginning, she is never described in traditional female terms. Rather, Stowe tells us,

> Esther was one of those intense, silent repressed women, less like a
> warm, breathing, impulsive woman . . . than some half-spiritual

organization, every part of which was a thought . . . She had inherited all the strong logical faculties . . . which are supposed to
be more particularly the characteristics of man. [Pp. 455-56]

As Esther had also inherited "exquisite moral perceptions" from her female ancestors, she was a victim of the "internal strife of a divided nature. Her heart was always rebelling against the conclusions of her head" (p. 456). Stowe maintains that Esther's conflict can only be resolved by reuniting her divided selves. This resolution is accomplished on a spiritual level through her own personal conversion experience and her acceptance of Anglicanism as a religion of love. Thus, like her creator, Esther returns to the religion of the mothers, the Anglicanism of Harry's and Harriet's mothers. She has rejected the Calvinism of her own and the author's father.

Esther's schizophrenia also needs a personal and emotional cure, which occurs when she marries Harry. Their marriage unites his emotional, spiritual nature with her more rational being, bringing head and heart together in a reversal of the eighteenth-century equation of female-heart and male-head. Their union creates a model Christian family at the same time that it com-pletes an androgynous Christian personality. Stowe describes her vision of the perfected human personality in terms of the Platonic ideal: "The only perfect human thinker and philosopher who will ever arise will be the MAN-WOMAN, or a human being who unites perfectly the nature of the two sexes"[29] (p. 456). Esther and Harry's marriage presents another intriguing possibility in the family tangles which Stowe is investigating. Harry may well stand also for Harriet, in which case his union with Esther has the added dimensions of reuniting the sisters Catharine and Harriet Beecher and their particular characteristics.

There was a vision of personal fulfillment for Harriet Beecher Stowe in the conclusion of her last major novel. Esther and Harry's marriage cured the divided self, reunited the sisters Harriet and Catharine, and created a model Christian family. As if this were not enough, their marriage also repre-sented a reunion between the evangelical Calvinism of Stowe's father, Lyman Beecher, and the Episcopal heritage of her mother, Roxanna Foote. Thus Stowe's vision of a new androgynous Christianity for the nineteenth century is a triumphant resolution of a long-standing personal conflict. She has effected a reconciliation between her parents and an affirmation of their offspring as heirs to the best of two religious traditions and as creators of a third.

In the four novels I have considered and in the years they span (1852-69), Harriet Beecher Stowe's concepts of women's sphere and influence in Ameri-can life grew and broadened. For her the home remained the center from which a woman gained and exercised her power. Stowe's orientation was still domestic. But through her writings and over the years, she had continued to assert woman's claim to greater access to the community's educational resources and to the moral and political authority which was her right. Considered in this light, she was always a feminist. The real change in the author's domestic feminism is the movement from the feminization theme of the earlier novels to an androgynous ideal for men and women in the later works. In communities led by women and female-trained men, she believed, education and religion could both create and maintain this androgynous ideal in American society.

## Notes

1. For recent examinations of Stowe's feminism, see Ann Douglas's chapter on Stowe in *The Feminization of American Culture* (New York: Alfred A. Knopf, 1977). Douglas contends that Stowe was a feminizing and sentimentalizing influence on American culture. See also Ellen Moers, *Literary Women* (New York: Doubleday & Co., 1976) where Stowe is designated an "epic" writer. Elizabeth Ammons sees Stowe as both feminist and revolutionary in her essay, "Heroines in *Uncle Tom's Cabin*," in *Critical Essays on Harriet Beecher Stowe*, ed. Elizabeth Ammons (Boston: G. K. Hall, 1980). Kathryn Kish Sklar first discussed domestic feminism in print when she applied the term to Harriet's sister, Catharine, in *Catharine Beecher: A Study in American Domesticity* (New York: W. W. Norton & Co., 1973 and 1977). Dorothy Berkson sees Stowe as committed to "humanizing society" through "feminine values" in her essay, "Millennial Politics and the Feminine Fiction of Harriet Beecher Stowe," in *Critical Essays*, ed. Ammons (pp. 248–53).

2. Dorothy Berkson has pointed out that after the completion of the four novels considered here, Stowe produced three distinctly nonfeminist works: *My Wife and I* (1871), *We and Our Neighbors* (1873), and *Pink and White Tyranny* (1871). Berkson suggests that because these novels followed the Beecher-Tilton scandal (1872), they may have reflected Stowe's reaction to the radical feminism of Victoria Woodhull, Elizabeth Cady Stanton, and her half-sister Isabella Beecher Hooker, all of whom were involved in accusing Henry Ward Beecher of adultery. This hardly explains the appearance in 1878 of *Poganuc People* (a novel that continued to support the matriarchal values of the earlier novels), but may offer further evidence of the conflicts between family loyalty and feminist and revolutionary ideology that informed Stowe's entire life. Berkson, "Millennial Politics," passim.

3. Elizabeth Ammons analyzes the revolutionary potential of these active black and white women and concludes that Stowe looks to "feminine values as the foundation for ethical revolution in America." Ammons, *Critical Essays*, n. 1, p. 163.

4. Angela Davis, "Reflections on the Black Woman's Role in the Community of Slaves," *The Black Scholar* 3 (December 1971):2-15.

5.  Harriet Beecher Stowe, *Uncle Tom's Cabin* (New York: Washington Square Press, 1964), p. 143–44. All subsequent page references to this novel will appear in the text and will refer to this edition.

6.  Ammons discusses the significance of Uncle Tom as a feminized Jesus and calls him a powerful "heroine" of *Uncle Tom's Cabin*. I agree that he is a prototype of Stowe's androgynous Christian who later appears more fully developed in the character of Harry Percival in *Oldtown Folks*. Ammons, *Critical Essays*, p. 158.

7.  The accusation of racism was first developed in James Baldwin's essay, "Everybody's Protest Novel," *Partisan Review* 16 (June 1949):578–85.

8.  The Lyman Beecher/Theodore Weld controversy of 1835 is described in detail in Gerda Lerner, *The Grimké Sisters from South Carolina* (New York: Schocken Books, 1977), pp. 117–25. Lerner explores further distinctions between Beecher antislavery doctrine and radical abolitionism in her discussion of the letters between Sarah Grimké and Catharine Beecher, wherein Beecher objects to a *public* role for antislavery women.

9.  Charles H. Foster, *The Rungless Ladder: Harriet Beecher Stowe and New England Puritanism* (New York: Cooper Square Publishers, 1970), p. 39.

10. Quoted in Foster, *The Rungless Ladder*, p. 58.

11. For an excellent discussion of Stowe's critique of Calvinism in this novel, see "The Bruised Flax Flower" in Foster, *The Rungless Ladder*, pp. 86–128. See also Lawrence Buell, "Calvinism Romanticized: Harriet Beecher Stowe, Samuel Hopkins, and *The Minister's Wooing*," in *Critical Essays*, ed. Ammons, pp. 244–59. Buell discusses the emergence of a female minister in the person of Mary Scudder.

12. Harriet Beecher Stowe, *The Minister's Wooing* (Ridgewood, N.J.: Gregg Press, 1968), pp. 49–50. Subsequent references to this book will appear in the text and will refer to this edition.

13. The historical Aaron Burr was the son of Esther Edwards and Aaron Burr. His father was an evangelical Presbyterian minister and the second president of Princeton. When Aaron was two, his father died and six months later his grandfather, Jonathan Edwards, and his mother also died; in another six months, his grandmother, Sarah Edwards, was dead. For further discussion of the Burr family, see Carol Karlsen and Laurie Crumpacker, eds., *The Journal of Esther Burr* (forthcoming from Yale University Press).

14. Later in the nineteenth century, the New England writer, Sarah Orne Jewett, developed further the notion of a female ministry. See especially the character of Almira Todd in her 1896 book, *The Country of the Pointed Firs* (Garden City, N.Y.: Doubleday & Co. 1956). Jewett always credited Stowe with inspiration in writing her own fiction.

15. Stowe makes this heritage clear when she compares Mary to Sarah Edwards in this novel. See Stowe, *The Minister's Wooing*, pp. 150-51.

16. *Maine story* is Stowe's term for this novel. Quoted from a letter by the author dated 29 July 1852 in Introductory Note to Harriet Beecher

Stowe, *The Pearl of Orr's Island* (Ridgewood, N.J.: Gregg Press, 1967), p. vii. Subsequent references to this novel are given in the text and refer to this edition.

17. This is Kathryn Sklar's view which she develops in Sklar, *Catharine Beecher*, p. 162.

18. Ibid., p. 163.

19. William Alcott, *The Young Housekeeper* (1838), and Lydia Maria Child, *The American Frugal Housewife* (1832).

20. Horace Bushnell, *Christian Nurture* (1847), and Sarah Josepha Hale, editor, *Godey's Lady's Book* (1837–77).

21. Sarah Orne Jewett, "The Courting of Sister Wisby," in *The Oven Birds*, ed. Gail Parker (Garden City, N.Y.: Doubleday & Co., 1972), pp. 217–34, and *The Country of the Pointed Firs*, passim.

22. Susan Sontag, *Illness as Metaphor* (New York: Farrar & Straus, 1978).

23. Two particularly helpful essays on *Oldtown Folks* are Charles H. Foster, "New England Looking Glass," in Foster, *The Rungless Ladder* and Introduction to Harriet Beecher Stowe, *Oldtown Folks*, ed. Henry F. May (Cambridge, Mass.: Harvard University Press, Belknap Press, 1966), pp. 3–43.

24. Harriet Beecher Stowe, Preface, in *Oldtown Folks*, p. 47. Subsequent page references will appear in the text and refer to the same edition.

25. The reference is to Joseph Bellamy, *True Religion Delineated* (1750).

26. Harriet Beecher Stowe, *Poganuc People: Their Loves and Lives* (New York: Fords, Howard, Hulbert, 1878), p. 27.

27. See Mary Kelley, "At War with Herself: Harriet Beecher Stowe as Woman in Conflict within the Home," in *Woman's Being, Woman's Place: Female Identity and Vocation in American History*, ed. Mary Kelley (Boston: G. K. Hall, 1979), pp. 201–19.

28. Foster, *The Rungless Ladder*, p. 202.

29. This quotation is used by David S. Reynolds to establish Stowe's concern with androgyny rather than feminization. See his essay, "The Feminization Controversy: Sexual Stereotypes and the Paradoxes of Piety in Nineteenth-Century America," *New England Quarterly* 53, no. 1 (March 1980):96–106.

# Gene Patterson-Black

# On Herman Melville

Until his 1856–57 visit to Europe and the Middle East, Herman Melville appears to have suffered from a self-hatred which he simultaneously acknowledged, in the form of a Byronesque Ishmaelism that makes his literary narrators invariably outcasts, and denied, projecting the repressed self-hatred as misanthropy and misogyny, whose mirrored reflections appear in his work as androphobia and gynophobia.

Melville's increasingly profound involvement with a psychological atmosphere so permeated with self-hatred led him to the verge of a nervous collapse. The nature of this collapse is recorded in "Shelley's Vision," "Venice," and "In a Bye-Canal," as well as in a journal entry on Titian's women.

The bulk of Melville's work was written during the period in which his self-hatred and its projections and reflections clouded his perspective of the world around him, as he came increasingly to recognize. *Mardi* (1849) and *Pierre* (1852) show the dual projections of the ego, the Taji or Pierre who whispers "I love you" to Yillah or Lucy, and of the self-hater reflected both in its androphobic (male-identified) forms as the avenging sons of the patriarchal high priest or the male-cousin Glendinning, and in its gynophobic (female-identified) forms as Hautia and Isabel.

*Clarel* (1876) shows a distinct break in this psychological pattern and reflects what Melville had made of the nervous collapse undergone twenty years previously. Fraternity and toleration are the keynotes of male relationships in this book. Misanthropes exist in its pages only, so to speak, in retrospect, and Melville's understanding of the self-hater mechanism is objectified in his portrait of Mortmain. More significantly, *Clarel* does not exhibit the mirrored self-hatred that underlies the gynophobia of Melville's earlier work: Yillah has her Hautia, Lucy her Isabel, but Ruth has no shadow counterpart.

In *Mardi, Pierre,* and *Clarel,* his three romantic novels—which form a separate genre apart from his adventure novels—Melville spends more time on the psychological state of the hero, couched in terms of the dialectic of rational philosophy and concerned primarily with the state of his soul, than on the hero's pursuit of the heroine which, although providing a spring for the plot, is merely tangential in each case. This reveals what is essentially

Melville's own lack of interest in women—a disinterest I have found women to reciprocate—and points up the fact that although men often think they are being attentive to women, their major concern is, in fact, themselves.

But, as was often the case with Melville, Melville was the first to point this out. The seriocomedy of "I and My Chimney" and "Jimmy Rose" arises from conflicts in which the wife tries to budge her husband out of his set, self-centered ways—efforts that the husband, with self-conscious condescending irony, perceives as the set, self-willed ways of the wife. But it is the very give-and-take of these stories that indicate that, in his own life, Melville's ego had been preparing itself for the confrontation with the self-hater that, we may surmise from "Shelley's Vision," occurred in Rome in February, 1857.

The foregoing are some of the considerations that form the framework for the discussion of Melville that follows. Another is that the Melville canon as it is taught—focusing on *Moby-Dick, Billy Budd*, "Bartleby," and "Benito Cereno"—has crystallized around works in which women do not figure, thereby producing a distorted concept of Melville's work as a whole and producing a general reading public that assumes that Melville did not write about women. The major critical stance—that it is male and academic hardly needs mention—that forms this curriculum and this common assumption is that Melville's chief interest was in melodramatizing philosophical questions into a tediously studied "quarrel with God."

But to limit our understanding of Melville to this single facet is to do him a disservice. Many of Melville's superior pieces are simply overlooked because they do not fit our preconceived notions of him, and an acknowledgement that many of his works involve a domestic or would-be domestic setting will, one hopes, help balance both the critical emphasis and the curricular focus. But we must hasten to add that Melville's interest is directed primarily toward women as wives rather than women as autonomous and equal persons. (In fact, even in his examination of women as persons in "Tartarus of Maids"—where, despite the fact that it presents the situation of the mill "girls" as an emblem, not only of the demeaning industrial usages of women, but of their demeaning usage as quasi-industrial baby-factories—the narrator's obvious sympathy does not lead him beyond objectification.[1] His relationship remains an I/it rather than an I/Thou one, which keeps Melville from ever moving from an examination of women's condition to an examination of women's rights as a shared human issue. In fact, this objectification of women leads Melville easily into condescending sentimentalities, as is shown with especial truth in his examinations of women's poverty, which is invariably linked with certain elements of the picturesque. "The Piazza" is especially blatant in this regard.)

But neither should this objection blind us to Melville's achievement in his tales of "domestic adventurers."[2] The husband and wife in "The Apple-

Tree Table" have a relationship as subtle, one feels, as that between Mr. and Mrs. Bennet in Jane Austen's *Pride and Prejudice.*

However, while arguing that Melville's canon is more varied than is generally appreciated, we must not shirk reassessment of the peculiar lacks it does have. For instance, although an extended family was important in maintaining Melville during his own life, such a group does not appear in his work. Of Melville's heroes, only Pierre and Timoleon have mothers whose existence is of any moment to the plot. Melville had two sons, but none of his male characters does, although several of his domestic adventurers have daughters, as Melville did himself. Melville's unwillingness to probe the father/son relationship from the father's perspective arises not only from his reluctance, post-*Redburn*, to place himself imaginatively in his father Allan's position but from his own experience: Malcolm, his firstborn, died at the age of eighteen; a coroner's jury ruled that his death from a bullet wound in the temple was accidental rather than self-inflicted. Stanwix, his secondborn, ran away to Central America where he lived as a beachcomber, much as Herman had done in Tahiti, later taking up dentistry in San Francisco; he too predeceased his father, dying at the age of thirty-five. Perhaps Billy Budd's benediction "God bless Captain Vere" is Melville's own forgiveness of both Allan and himself as fathers.

The importance of the father/son relationship to Melville at every stage of his career as a writer should not blind us, however, to the fact that the husband/wife relationship figures as large in his writings. His own forty-four-year marriage to Elizabeth Shaw, whom he wed when he was twenty-eight, seems to have been a genuinely sustaining one,[3] and in forming any critical estimate of Melville's "development" as a writer, we should perhaps pay thoughtful attention to W.H. Auden's conclusion that he sailed at last into the haven of his wife's arms.

# I

*And slowly I began to understand that father-wounded sons never recover, never confess, never remember; slowly, I began to understand why women can never satisfy the longings of boys who are starved for their fathers; why women can never exorcise the grief of men, lured by their fathers into wanting the impossible: revenge, reunion, redemption.*

Phyllis Chesler, *About Men*

If there is a master key to understanding Herman Melville, I believe Chesler's statement presents it. Taken in aggregate, Melville's work mingles objective and intuitive probings of the wound and gains its cumulative power from the drama of the healing that takes place over the nearly fifty-year span of Melville's life as a writer.

Herman Melville spent the first ten years of his life in comfortable surroundings. Born in New York City, 1 August 1819, the third of eight children and the second son, his boyhood was passed in the ever more fashionable homes into which his father, prospering as an importer of French dry goods, successively moved his family. Although Allan Melville once characterized his son in a family letter as "backward in speech and somewhat slow of comprehension," their relationship appears, by all accounts, to have been an affectionate one. The preference for the older son, however, that Melville attributes to the mother in his poem "Timoleon," printed in 1891, seems to have been shared by the father in regard to Herman's gifted elder brother Gansevoort.

In 1830, as the result of poor investments, Allan Melville was wiped out. After a false start at re-establishing himself in Albany, the home of his wife's family, but inextricably "burdened with debts and hopeless responsibilities,"[4] Allan Melville suffered a physical and nervous breakdown in mid-January, 1832. After two weeks of a derangement his brother Thomas described to their father as "maniacal," Allan died. Herman was twelve years old at the time.

> His death was the direst and most decisive event emotionally of
> Herman Melville's early life. Deprived of an idolized father on the
> very verge of adolescence, the boy Melville underwent—can there
> be any doubt?—an emotional crisis from whose effects he was never
> to be wholly free. . . . He was to spend much of his life divided
> between the attempt to retaliate upon his father for this abandon-
> ment and the attempt, a still more passionate one, to recover the
> closeness and the confidence of happy sonhood.[5]

Hired out to surrogate fathers, Herman spent the next year working with his maternal uncle as a bank clerk and the year after as a clerk in his brother Gansevoort's fur retailing shop; much of the year he was fifteen was spent working for his paternal uncle Thomas on his farm at Pittsfield, Massachusetts. After a stint of schoolmastering, which did little to improve his circumstances or alleviate his sense of loss, Melville went to sea—Ishmaelism becoming for him a means whereby he could simultaneously acknowledge, romantically, and distance, ironically, the pain of his bereavement.

The clearest picture of this bereavement comes in *Pierre*, published in 1852, twenty years after Allan Melville's death:

> His father had died of a fever; and, as is not uncommon in such
> maladies, toward his end, he at intervals lowly wandered in his mind.

At such times, by unobserved, but subtle arts, the devoted family
attendants had restrained his wife from being present at his side. But
little Pierre, whose fond, filial love drew him ever to that bed; they
heeded not innocent little Pierre, when his father was delirious; and
so, one evening, when the shadows intermingled with the curtains;
and all the chamber was hushed; and Pierre saw but dimly his
father's face; and the fire on the hearth lay in a broken temple of
wonderful coals; then a strange, plaintive, infinitely pitiable, low
voice, stole forth from the testered bed . . . The child snatched the
dying man's hand; it faintly grew to his grasp; but on the other side
of the bed, the other hand now also emptily lifted itself, and emptily
caught, as if at some other childish fingers. Then both hands
dropped on the sheet.

Melville had published his first picture of the aftermath of his father's
death in *Redburn, His First Voyage*, three years earlier in 1849. Written
as a potboiler after the failure of *Mardi*, which had been published at the
beginning of that same year, this "little nursery tale," as Melville described
*Redburn* in a letter to Richard Henry Dana, Jr., is a bewildering patchwork
of seemingly straightforward autobiographical statement and adroit obfusca-
tion about Melville's own New York-to-Liverpool voyage and return undertaken ten years previously in 1839. In the chapter entitled "He Contemplates
Making a Social Call on the Captain in His Cabin," Melville parodies the
emotional anxieties into which his Ishmaelism, his conscious sense of his
unfatheredness, led him.

I had heard that some sea-captains are fathers to their crew; and so
they are; but such fathers as Solomon's precepts tend to make—severe
and chastising fathers, fathers whose sense of duty overcomes the
sense of love,[6] and who every day, in some sort, play the part of
Brutus, who ordered his son away to execution, as I have read in our
old family Plutarch.

Redburn's greatest disappointment, however, arises not from the futility
of his attempt to find another father but from his betrayal by his father
himself, or rather, his betrayal by his father's green morocco guidebook
to Liverpool.

My intention was in the first place, to visit Riddough's Hotel, where
my father had stopped, more than thirty years before; and then,
with the map in my hand, follow him through all the town, according to the dotted lines in the diagram. For thus I would be performing a filial pilgrimage to spots which would be hallowed in my eyes.

This pilgrimage, which Melville himself actually undertook, is to be a species of initiation into mysteries Redburn felt himself equipped to understand: "Great was my boyish delight at the prospect of visiting a place, the infallible clew to all whose intricacies I held in my hand." Redburn's faith in the power of this sacred talisman to transmit to him the wisdom and charisma his father had won through a rite of passage Redburn hopes to replicate reflects that species of magic that father-deprived sons expect will someday miraculously operate to redress their deprivation. It quickly becomes obvious that the guidebook that had served Allan usefully is useless to his son. It is not the change in the cityscape itself that most depresses Redburn, but Herman's realization of his own inability to measure up to and to spiritually reconnect himself with his father, which in turn breeds a case of the hypos in which Redburn unbreeds himself with a nihilism not entirely comic.

> Yes, in this very street, thought I, nay, on this very flagging my
> father walked. Then I almost wept, when I looked down on my
> sorry apparel, and marked how the people regarded me; the men
> staring at so grotesque a young stranger, and the old ladies, in beaver
> hats and ruffles, crossing the walk a little to shun me. How differ-
> ently my father must have appeared; perhaps in a blue coat, buff
> vest, and Hessian boots.[7] And little did he think, that a son of his
> would ever visit Liverpool as a poor friendless sailor-boy. . . . My
> own father did not know me then; and had never seen, or heard, or
> so much as dreamed of me. And that thought had a touch of sadness
> to me . . . you are indeed friendless and forlorn. Here you wander a
> stranger in a strange town, and the very thought of your father's
> having been here before you, but carries with it the reflection that,
> he then knew you not, nor cared for you one whit.

The failure of his father's guidebook—and, as a subtheme, since Melville's hero-worship of the father amalgamated itself to his Dutch Reform worship of God-the-Father, of the "one Holy Guide-Book" which Redburn's father had recommended to him as one that "will never lead you astray, if you but follow it aright"—did not keep Herman from dedicating this record of his maiden voyage to another maiden voyager: "To My Younger Brother, Thomas Melville, Now a Sailor on a Voyage to China." Melville is ironic about his elder brother Gansevoort's attempts to function *in loco parentis*: "He accompanied me part of the way to the place, where the steamboat was to leave for New York; instilling into me much sage advice above his age, for he was but eight years my senior." In fact, Gansevoort was but four years Herman's senior and had died at thirty in 1846, three years before *Redburn* appeared. Herman, eleven years Thomas's senior, was perhaps being sardonic in the dedication, though he was probably in deadly earnest about warning his younger brother of the danger of too-trustingly overestimating the legacy of which father-deprived sons may have been deprived.

The following passage from *Pierre*, which prefaces the deathbed scene quoted earlier, shows a later understanding of how a son's maturity may alter his perspective on a father.

> Blessed and glorified in his tomb beyond Prince Mausolus is that mortal sire, who, after an honorable, pure course of life, dies, and is buried, as in a choice fountain, in the filial breast of a tender-hearted and intellectually appreciative child. For at that period, the Solomonic insights have not poured their turbid tributaries into the pure-flowing well of the childish life. . . . But if fate preserves the father to a later time, too often the filial obsequies are less profound; the canonization less ethereal. The eye-expanded boy perceives, or vaguely thinks he perceives, slight specks and flaws in the character he once so wholly reverenced.

## II

Although, as Chesler states, the longings of boys starved for their fathers may be impossible to satisfy, Melville, throughout his work, shows us a man seeking his satisfaction through other men.

It is perhaps one of the fundamental differences between Melville and Hawthorne and, at root, the most crucial aspect of their essential incompatibility that whereas Melville's psychological makeup lends support to Chesler's contention, Hawthorne's was aligned with the opposite view. In a footnote to his essay "Hawthorne and Melville: An Inquiry into Their Art and the Mystery of Their Friendship," Sidney Moss suggests that

> While Hawthorne often used his fiction to repair his moral failure, he is more confessional than penitential in *The Marble Faun*, if we take Kenyon's view toward Donatello to have any connection with Hawthorne's view toward Melville. "I do not pretend to be the guide and counsellor whom Donatello needs," Kenyon says to Miriam, though he recognizes Donatello's "bitter agony": "for, *to mention no other obstacle*, I am a man, and between man and man there is always an insuperable gulf. They can never quite grasp each other's hands; and therefore man never derives any intimate help, any heart sustenance, from his brother man, but from woman—his mother, his sister, or his wife."[8] [Emphasis mine]

Melville too alludes to this debate on whether it is woman or man who can provide the needed psychological solace. That, in fact, this drama may have had at some point in their relationship a real-life enactment seems probable from Melville's portrait of Hawthorne in *Clarel*, where this scene plays itself out between Clarel and Vine, the latter engaged in one of Melville's own favorite ploys, conversation-as-avoidance:

> Prior advances unreturned
> Not here [Clarel] recked of, while he yearned—
> O, now but for communion true
> And close; let go each alien theme;
> Give me thyself!
>                     But Vine, at will
> Dwelling upon his wayward dream,
> Nor as suspecting Clarel's thrill
> Of personal longing, rambled still. . . .
> Thought [Clarel], How pleasant in another
> Such sallies, or in thee, if said
> After confidings that should wed
> Our souls in one:—Ah, call me *brother*!—
> So feminine his passionate mood
> Which, long as hungering unfed,
> All else rejected or withstood.

All else. As if only Hawthorne, fifteen years his senior, could fill the void left by Allan's death. But, aware that Hawthorne was too reticent for the robust frankness his own nature required, Melville attributes to Vine the rebuke, "None lives can help ye . . . Go, live it out"—perhaps the very advice Hawthorne had given him in the dunes at Liverpool, the reticent Hawthorne masking in his own journal whatever desperation may have led Melville to his declaration that he had "pretty much made up his mind to be annihilated."

Vine's unspoken rebuke continues:

> But for thy fonder dream of love
> In man towards man—the soul's caress—
> The negatives of flesh should prove
> Analogies of non-cordialness
> In spirit.

But, with an ambiguity which may mask what was once a hopefulness, the scene proceeds:

> But, glancing up, unwarned [Clarel] saw
> What serious softness in [Vine's] eyes
> Bent on him. Shyly they withdrew.
> Enslaver, wouldst thou but fool me
> With bitter-sweet, sly sorcery,

> Pride's pastime? or wouldst thou indeed,
> Since things unspoken may impede,
> Let flow thy nature but for bar?

And as if recoiling from attributing to Vine a latency and its bar which he himself may have felt, Clarel's self-hater turns on him:

> Nay, dizzard, sick these feelings are;
> How findest place within thy heart
> For such solicitudes apart
> From Ruth?

Thus the psychological reality of Melville's need for comfort from another man, incompatible with Hawthorne's insistence that such comfort come from a woman, plays itself out into self-directed homophobia. (Thus, when Rolfe, speaking later to Clarel of Derwent, says "Things all diverse he would unite: / His idol's an hermaphrodite," "the student shrank." The interview does not end, however, with a rebuke, but with the advice of the wise old man which Melville had become by looking back at the experience of his youth: "Indulgence should with frankness mate:/Fraternal be: Ah, tolerate!"

This scene between Clarel and Vine may help us understand a later one in which Clarel comes upon Vine suddenly and unobserved.

> Could it be Vine, and quivering so?
> 'Twas Vine. He wore that nameless look
> About the mouth—so hard to brook—
> Which in the Cenci portrait shows. . .
> A trembling over of small throes
> In weak swoll'n lips, which to restrain
> Desire is none, nor any rein.

Whatever is causing these small throes, it is enough to convince Clarel "no more need dream of winning Vine / Or coming at his mystery."

The context of this passage leads one to suspect that Melville has detected in Hawthorne a self-hater whose projections he wished to be no target for. In the canto "The High Desert," only two hundred lines earlier, Vine, bored and restless, picked up bits of

>                       porous stone,
> And crushed in fist: or one by one,
> Through the dull void of desert air,
> He tossed them into valley down;
> *Or pelted his own shadow there.* [Emphasis mine]

And as the cavalcade resumes its march forty lines—lines in which Clarel has heard "the blast of Roncesvalles" tolling for his ideals of the heroic and Rolfe has identified the carillon of the monastery at Mar Saba[9]—after Clarel's detection of Vine,

> They saw, in turn abrupt revealed,
> An object reared aloof by Vine
> In whim of silence, when debate
> Was held upon the cliff but late
> And ended where all words decline:
> A heap of stones in arid state.

The heap is "a cairn" in the eyes of the Roland-mourning Clarel, which he interprets as "a monument to bitterness."

If, on a philosophical level, *Clarel* is a narrative ringing the changes on the relationship between the faith of the logical mind and the immediate experience of the heart, on a psychological level, it is an exploration of the "longing for solacement of mate" which cankers the happiness of the male characters of this epic. In the Epilogue to *Clarel*, the philosophical debate between faith and reason is resolved within a greater perspective which subsumes the two:

> But through such strange illusions have they passed
> Who in life's pilgrimage have baffled striven—
> Even death may prove unreal at last,
> And stoics be astounded into heaven.

But in the immediate psychological world of the end of the poem, Clarel, unable to be fraternal and thus deprived of the solace of "the soul's caress" from a man, widowed before his marriage by Ruth's death, leaving behind "Dusked Olivet," is last seen fading into the chiaroscuro. "And, taking now a slender wynd," the atmosphere growing archaic, he "vanishes in the obscurer town."

The Sire de Nesle thus departs upon his journey.

Set in all-male environments, frequently but not invariably nautical, the bulk of Melville's fictional world is an intensely masculine one wherein various paradises of bachelors in which these exorcisms and satisfactions can uninhibitedly occur border misanthropic infernos in which damnation replaces exorcism and frustration becomes the universal absolute of all relationships.[10]

As Melville observed in *Redburn*, "there is no misanthrope like a boy disappointed," and we may read his work up through *The Confidence Man* (1857) as an elaboration of this statement. Herman's closeness to his father is that Edenic state toward which he is ever drawn to return, a reunion achieved, if only covertly, in the closeted interview between Vere and Billy.[11]

This desired closeness has, throughout Melville's work, physical overtones which have led to a number of homosexual interpretations. Besides the "comic predicament" of Queequeg's "bridegroom clasp" from which Ishmael extricates himself "by dint of much wriggling, and loud and incessant expostulations upon the unbecomingness of his hugging a fellow male in that matrimonial sort of style," there are such ambiguous passages as this one from *White-Jacket*: "We main-top men were brothers, one and all; and we loaned ourselves to each other with all the freedom in the world." Or this, from the chapter "A Squeeze of the Hand" in *Moby-Dick*, which has been cited as some sort of group masturbation:

> Squeeze! squeeze! squeeze! all morning long; I squeezed that sperm till I myself almost melted into it; I squeezed that sperm till a strange sort of insanity came over me; and I found myself unwittingly squeezing my co-laborers' hands in it, mistaking their hands for the gentle globules. Such an abounding, affectionate, friendly, loving feeling did this avocation beget; that at last I was continually squeezing their hands, and looking up into their eyes sentimentally; as much as to say,—Oh! my dear fellow beings, why should we cherish any social acerbities, or know the slightest ill-humor or envy! Come, let us squeeze hands all round; nay, let us all squeeze ourselves into each other; let us squeeze ourselves universally into the very milk and sperm of kindness.
>
> Would that I could keep squeezing that sperm for ever! For now, since by many prolonged, repeated experiences, I have perceived that in all cases man must eventually lower, or at any rate shift, his conceit of attainable felicity; not placing it anywhere in the intellect or fancy; but in the wife, the heart, the bed, the table, the saddle, the fire-side, the country; now that I have perceived all this, I am ready to squeeze case eternally. In thoughts of the visions of the night, I saw long rows of angels in paradise, each with his hands in a jar of spermaceti.

Yet surely the passage is one in which the emphasis is on felicity rather than promiscuity and which carries the tone of Melville's spiritual utopianism at its most playful.

The same may be said of Melville's archetype of the Handsome Sailor. Billy Budd has been viewed as the major icon in the American literary homosexual pantheon,[12] but a closer analysis shows that the primary emphasis is, again, emotional and social:

> In the time before steamships, or then more frequently than now, a stroller along the docks of any considerable seaport would occasionally have his attention arrested by a group of bronzed mariners, man-of-war's men or merchant sailors in holiday attire, ashore on liberty. In certain instances they would flank, or like a bodyguard

quite surround, some superior figure of their own class, moving among them like Aldebaran among the lesser lights of his constellation. That signal object was the "Handsome Sailor" of the less prosaic time alike of the military and merchant navies. With no perceptible trace of the vainglorious about him, rather with the offhand unaffectedness of natural regality, he seemed to accept the spontaneous homage of his shipmates.

It may be closest to the mark to say that in Billy Budd, Melville has projected an image of his ideal physical self, just as in Jack Chase, he has projected an image of his ideal social self—for why should we not identify ourselves with our own best archetypes? Both Jack and Billy show the harmonious balance between physical beauty and social frankness and likability. Both Jack and Billy are the object of an uncoerced, spontaneous homage, despite the fact that the maintop democracy of Jack Chase exists amid a world of floggings under a military hierarchy and the Handsome Sailor lives under the eye of the ship's chief of police. Melville was intrigued by this concept of a man, king by nature rather than by government, the ideal government being the democracy of friends, the brotherhood of mystics keeping metempsychotic watch in the maintops or masquing at Mar Saba. Always the mystery of brotherhood and kingship.

And always the neglect to include women in this circle.

This ideal of relations with equals remained unrealizable so long as Melville remained in the grasp of father-longing, for there is a basic inequality between father/son, donor/recipient, dominant/subordinate. Yet Herman had seen Allan at ease among equals and kept this too as a model for male friendships—as well as their shunning of him after his bankruptcy, as Jimmy Rose's former friends shun him or as Timon's do him. And although Melville too sought the equality of peers, his Ishmaelian narrators always have to remind themselves that they are "one of that crew," for their tendency is to view themselves as outcast gentlemen forced into slumming and always on the lookout for a father's spontaneous approval, an approval that raises them to equality. Only when they find fellow gentlemen, such as Redburn mistook Captain Riga to be, as "Paul" took Doctor Long Ghost to be, or as Jack Chase proved to be, do they show themselves at ease—an ease that has something about it of that snug life prior to Allan's bankruptcy and death. It is no accident that Long Ghost and Chase assimilate to themselves the well-read conversation and well-traveled perspective of Melville's father.

Yet such idealized expectations sooner or later become frustrated, and with frustration comes anger; and with anger, hatred; and with hatred directed against a reverenced and hence taboo object, guilt; and with guilt, self-hatred. And the displacement of this self-hatred makes it impossible to maintain peer relations since one cannot love one's neighbor as oneself if one does not love oneself.

In a story such as "The Fiddler," we see Melville's acute awareness that Hautboy, a frank, cordial man, is also a man who has made peace with the self-hatred which could have overwhelmed him following the prodigy stage of his youth—as Melville may have felt he had outgrown the applauded-prodigy stage of his literary career which the successes of *Typee* and *Omoo* epitomized.

It is between projected self-hatred and the frank self-acceptance which is the basis for true social equality that Melville hovered in the early years of the 1850s.

By the time he had concluded work on *The Confidence Man*, Melville's misanthropy so pervaded his personality that his family feared it would lead him to complete destruction. "In 13 years," as his wife noted in her bio-graphical memorandum about him, "he had written 10 books besides much miscellaneous writing." His family arranged for him to take a vacation in Europe and the Holy Land, and in October, 1856, with funds supplied by his father-in-law, Melville accordingly set sail.

In November, he visited Hawthorne in Liverpool, where he was American consul, and, as Hawthorne recorded, "told me he had 'pretty much made up his mind to be annihilated.'" If such a frame of mind is suicidal, it is also a frame of mind in which former obsessions too may lose their will to live.

In February, 1857, Melville visited Shelley's tomb in Rome. "Went from Caracalla to Shelley's grave by natural process," he noted in his journal. "Shelley's Vision," the poem this visit initiated, did not appear until 1891, the year of Melville's death, in *Timoleon*, a volume privately printed in an edition of twenty-five copies. It is unclear at what point between 1857 and 1891 this poem was given its final form; but during these years, Melville finally was able to exorcise the self-hatred which had been his virtually lifelong companion.


Shelley's Vision

Wandering late by morning seas
When my heart with pain was low—
Hate the censor pelted me—
Deject I saw my shadow go.

In elf-caprice of bitter tone
I too would pelt the pelted one:
At my shadow I cast a stone.

When lo, upon that sun-lit ground
I saw the quivering phantom take
The likeness of St. Stephen crowned:
Then did self-reverence awake.

## III

In surveying Melville's work chronologically, one senses a distinct break in tone following his journey to Europe and the Middle East in 1856-57. There is a tolerance of humanity, his own and that of others, which is, for all his angered, anguished quarreling with God about the human condition, lacking prior to this time. "Shelley's Vision," remarkable as it is as a record of self-forgiveness, of the truth that hatred of the self can be forgiven only by the self, is merely the first in a series of reconciliations which occurred within the span of Melville's journey.

On April Fool's Day, 1857, Melville arrived in Venice, where he remained for six days. Venice, like Lima with its women mysteriously cloaked in their saya-y-mantas, had always been emblematic for Melville of sexual intrigue. The rather prudish Ishmaelians of Melville's earlier work have a curiously repressed quality about them, and even though Taji will commit symbolic parricide to attain Yillah, Melville's heroes are more apt to be impressed by ladies' men than to be ladies' men. In fact, one of the reasons Jack Chase cuts such a dashing figure is that although he abandoned ship at Lima "to draw a partisan blade in the civil commotions of Peru, and befriend, heart and soul, what he deemed the cause of the Right," some attribute his behavior to "love of some *worthless* signorita" (italics added).

However the two poems that seem to have resulted directly from Melville's 1857 visit to Venice, "Venice" and "In a Bye-Canal" which head the section of *Timoleon* entitled "Fruit of Travel Long Ago," reveal how the repression of his earlier years is beginning to lift under the influence of his self-forgiveness.

Here, for instance, is his impression of Venice itself:

### Venice

With Pantheist energy of will
The little craftsman of the Coral Sea
Strenuous in the blue abyss
Up-builds his marvellous gallery
    And long arcade,
Erections freaked with many a fringe
    Of marble garlandry,
Evincing what a worm can do.

Laborious in a shallower wave,
  Advanced in kindred art,
A prouder agent proved Pan's might
When Venice rose in reefs of palaces.

The operative image in this poem, it seems to me, is the contrast between Pantheist energy which has fueled the abstract philosophical arguments at which Melville's aloof and isolated heroes have been both speculator and spectator, and Pan's might. This poem in some ways commemorates Melville's acceptance of his Pan-self, not the great god whose death has been rumored, but the fructifying masculine deity who is the antithesis of the damning self-hater. After years of denial, Melville finally acknowledges to himself that he is also Pan.

The acknowledgement of Pan leads Melville to use this image in other poems in *Timoleon*. "The Archipelago," which takes as its subject the isles of Greece, shows not only Pan but also the South Seas, as "Venice" had in its use of this pair of images.

But perhaps the most complex use of Pan as an emblem of sexual energy occurs in Urania's lament in "After the Pleasure-Party":

Could I remake me! or set free
This sexless bound in sex, then plunge
Deeper than Sappho, in a lunge
Piercing Pan's paramount mystery!

The dynamic sense is reminiscent of Ahab who, longing to reach the philosophical absolute, lunges to break through the wall of Moby-Dick's forehead, but with its *plunge, lunge,* and *piercing,* the vocabulary is that of male sexual activity and rather surprising to find in a woman's monologue. The remaking of which Urania speaks has its physical impulse in her envious desire to be as attractive as the young peasant woman who had attracted the attentions of the man Urania craves. But its psychological impulse is toward union and intimacy beyond sex, such as Clarel felt toward Vine, and for such fulfillment, physical gender, which Melville himself viewed as a barrier, is circumvented by a dual voicing of simultaneously active and passive sexual roles, a dual voicing that dismisses all physically grounded logical distinction. Such dual voicing had also occurred in Melville's rapturous "Hawthorne and His Mosses" (1850):

I feel that this Hawthorne has dropped germinous seeds into my
soul. He expands and deepens down, the more I contemplate him;
and further and further, shoots his strong New England roots into
the hot soil of my Southern soul.

This androgynous-like dual voicing in "After the Pleasure-Party" is the only clear place in Melville's work where he acknowledges that women too have sexual imperatives; his sympathetic portrayal of Urania's imperatives is a far cry from his gynophobic depictions of women's imperatives in Hautia, who is the distinct embodiment of Yillah's sexual imperatives, just as Isabel is the embodiment not only of Lucy's but of Pierre's father's sexuality.

If we would speak of Melville's "testament of acceptance," we need to expand it to include his acceptance of women's sexuality. And if "After the Pleasure-Party" is the "final" statement of this theme, "In a Bye-Canal" is the first.

### In a Bye-Canal

A swoon of noon, a trance of tide,
The hushed siesta brooding wide
    Like calms far off Peru;
No floating wayfarer in sight,
Dumb noon, and haunted like the night
    When Jael the wiled one slew.

(This image of Jael, who drove a nail through Sisera's forehead, is the image of the demonic sexuality of women which is abandoned by the end of the poem. It is interesting, in terms of the poem's allusions, that the movement from demonic to human in Melville's perception of female sexuality is carried by a movement from Biblical to pagan images of women.)

A languid impulse from the oar
Plied by my indolent gondolier
Tinkles against a palace hoar,
    And, hark, response I hear!
A lattice clicks; and lo, I see
Between the slats, mute summoning me,
What loveliest eyes of scintillation,
What basilisk glance of conjuration!
    Fronted I have, part taken the span
Of portents in nature and peril in man.
I have swum—I have been
Twixt the whale's black flukes
    and the white shark's fin;
The enemy's desert I have wandered in,
And there have turned, have turned and scanned,
Following me how noiselessly,
Envy and Slander, lepers hand in hand.
All this. But at the latticed eye—
"Hey! Gondolier, you sleep, my man;

Wake up!" And, shooting by, we ran;
The while I mused, This, surely now,
Confutes the Naturalists, allow!
Sirens, true sirens verily be,
Sirens, waylayers in the sea.

In his study, *The Poetry of Melville's Later Years*, William Bysshe Stein, after drawing attention to the pun "palace hoar," continues his analysis of this poem by saying:

> The quick reaction of the pander-gondolier, of course, betrays the pretense of his sleeping. Now having caricatured a romantic episode in Venice, Melville turns around and addresses all those frustrated Don Juans disillusioned with the timidity of the adventurer. For the knowledgeable reader, he reserves a friendly wink, a zesty double-entendre—"waylayers." Added to the pun secreted in the title, it plainly demonstrates that the poet is not to be confused with the persons in the poem. He knows how to joke—with combined seriousness and levity.[13]

We need not attribute to the narrator of the poem the intention of finding a prostitute which Stein assumes as the premise of his reading. The crucial point seems to be that suddenly confronted with female sexuality, the narrator is thrown into panic. This panic, however, is not a sustained one, for there is a certain ambiguity in the source of this panic. The woman's sexuality provokes not only the gynophobic response that Melville's projected self-hatred had hitherto induced, the response that conjures a "basilisk glance," but also a response to her "loveliest eyes of conjuration." And as a footnote, we may here quote another of the poems from the *Timoleon* volume, "The Marchioness of Brinvilliers":

He toned the sprightly beam of morning
  With twilight meek of tender eve,
Brightness interfused with softness,
  Light and shade did weave:
And gave to candor equal place
With mystery starred in open skies;
And, floating all in sweetness, made
  Her fathomless mild eyes.

What seems at first a conventional poetic exercise describing a woman's eyes takes on dimension when placed next to "In a Bye-Canal." The poem on the Marchioness has a male authority throughout. The "He" which opens the poem is, presumably, God-the-Father as Creator. It also reminds us how men objectify and thus control women, hedging women's movements and meanings within male stereotypes. The Marchioness's eyes do not threaten as the Venetian eyes do. Yet in the concluding quatrain of "In a Bye-Canal," which Stein fails to quote or to comment upon, the narrator, released from his panic, dismisses along with it the sense that the demonic is the predominant aspect of female sexuality:

> Well, wooed by these same deadly misses,
> Is it shame to run?
> No! flee them did divine Ulysses,
>     Brave, wise, and Venus' son.

Thus Melville simultaneously acknowledges woman's fructifying Venus energy, but displaces it into a sexually nondemanding relationship between mother and son.[14] But that Melville responded to the Venus energy he acknowledged other than as a son is clear from his journal entry for 5 April, the day before his departure from Venice:

> Walked to Rialto. Look up & down G. Canal. Wandered further on.
> Numbers of beautiful women. The rich brown complexions of
> Titians women drawn from Nature, after all. (Titian was a Venetian)
> The clear rich golden brown. The clear cut features, like cameo.–
> The vision from the window at end of long narrow passage.

The drama is clear. Without the aid of Stein's "pander-gondolier," Melville has gone out and "looked" in the main public areas of the Rialto and the Grand Canal and then wandered farther on. And having found a woman, choosing from "numbers," he is fascinated with her skin, commenting knowingly that Titian—whose most famous work is perhaps "Venus and the Lute-Player"—has drawn his women from life after all. The final sentence is clearly meant as a private talismanic statement to remind Melville of some particularly epiphanic "vision."

## IV

Although the reader familiar only with the Melville of *Moby-Dick*, "Bartleby," and *Billy Budd*, may assume that women play only a negligible role in Melville's work, in fact, they comprise a rather extensive, though depressing, catalog. In the notes that follow, the reader should bear in mind that although women have a presence in Melville's work, they have no voice. Only with Urania and with Mary Glendinning do we overhear a woman's thoughts. In all other cases, we know the women only through the perspective of male commentators within the novels and stories. Although Melville shows, more clearly, perhaps, than he intended, the sorts of expectations that women endured in nineteenth-century America, he shows no women of achievement.

And when a woman, such as Urania, does achieve success, it is belittled, Melville attributing to Urania a self-hatred based on her dissatisfaction that her accomplishment is in the "male," intellectual realm of astronomy, rather than in the "womanly" realm of catching a man's eye.[15]

Yillah, in *Mardi*, represents an extreme case of woman as victim of male expectation. The old priest who has held her captive ever since she can remember (the matriarchy in bondage to the patriarchy, just as Israel had been in bondage in Egypt—these "imaginal" linked analogies reveal a personality obsessed with correspondences, the correspondences presenting the ambiguities which Melville, not always consciously, one feels, wove into his work)[16] had, in fact, already charted through this chartless voyage of a book a path for her from her birth as the distillation of the dew from a flower to her death in the cavernous vortex. With the barbaric Samoa, Yillah is portrayed as a gentle tamer: "Now, as everywhere women are the tamers of the menageries of men [Yillah as latent Circe], so Yillah in good time tamed down Samoa to the relinquishment of that horrible thing in this ear and persuaded him to substitute a vacancy for the bauble in his nose." Jarl, who sees her as "a sort of intruder" between himself and Taji, vents his jealousy through a self-righteous misogyny which views Yillah, stereotypically, as "an Ammonite siren." Taji perceives her as neither Circe nor siren, projecting his glimpses of these disturbing undercurrents onto the character of Hautia, but rather as a damsel in distress; and his first action is to rescue her—though not with the intention of setting her free, but rather of changing her warder. In the chapter innocuously entitled "A Fray," which is a euphemism for parricide, Taji kills the patriach, "old Aaron," her warden, whom he has met in the preceding chapter, "Sire and Sons."

> Remorse smote me hard; and like lightning I asked myself whether
> the death-deed I had done was sprung from a virtuous motive, the
> rescuing of a captive from thrall, or whether beneath that pretense
> I had engaged in this fatal affray for some other and selfish purpose,
> the companionship of a beautiful maid. But throttling the thought,
> I swore to be gay.

These are exactly the same sorts of guilty accusations Pierre levels at himself regarding his "rescue" of Isabel. But in *Pierre* the murdered parent is the mother, for Pierre is already living in the paradisical patrimony of Saddle Meadows, living, moreover, with his mother in his father's place, but disguising the incestuous undercurrents by a camp humor in which he and his mother address each other as brother and sister.

In *Mardi*, Taji spends the remainder of the tediously overlong novel alternately, while ostensibly seeking Yillah, seeking his own safety amid an all-male entourage and fleeing the male fury of the avenging brothers—just as Babbalanja (Melville's elder persona, as Rolfe is Melville's elder persona to his younger persona Clarel who is still, like Taji, seeking his Yillah, Ruth, after the author has disposed of her father) alternately seeks solace in Bardiana and endures his unrepressible demon Azzageddi. In *Mardi* the question of whether the hero will be punished by the avenging brothers is left ambiguous: "Churned in foam, that outer ocean lashed the clouds; and straight in my white wake headlong dashed a shallop, three fixed specters leaning o'er its prow, three arrows poising. And thus pursuers and pursued fled on over an endless sea." In *Pierre* there is no doubt that the avenging guilt has caught up with Melville. In the novels of 1849 and 1852 and the poem-narrative of 1876, Melville punishes parricide, thus absolving himself of ever plotting it, even fictitiously, by denying the young men their maidens. In almost hysterical guilt, Melville discovers Yillah in a whirlpool similar to the one into which the old Aaron would have thrown her. Pierre, Isabel, and Lucy are discovered wound around each other in death in a final tableau which owes its power to the Laocoon. And Ruth is reclaimed by "the bier Armenian" of patriarchal funeral custom. Clarel, like Taji, has spent his time of separation from his Beloved traveling and chatting and smoking and drinking with his buddies. Confronted by the attractiveness of both bachelor congeniality and domestic conjugality, the newly married author of *Mardi* was indecisive, nor had the older author of *Clarel* settled the matter absolutely in his mind. (We may see in Annatoo, Samoa's stereotypical termagant wife, Melville's displacement of some of his own confused hostility toward the wife and family he felt were tying him down, making it necessary, as he wrote his father-in-law, for him to write books "as jobs, being forced to it, as other men are to sawing wood"—referring to the writing of *Redburn* and *White-Jacket* in a single summer following the commercial disaster of *Mardi* that spring. "And while," he adds in a petulant? stoic? resigned? relieved? voice, "I have felt obliged to refrain from writing the kind of book I would wish to.")

But he could not refrain from dwelling on what most concerned him, nor from transplanting sequences of interior argument into the framework his stories set up for the linked analogies of the repressed.

Consider the diptych "The Paradise of Bachelors and the Tartarus of Maids." The paradise is a comfortable club, redolent in good cigars, fine wine, congenial conversation—all the appurtenances designed to mellow men into transcendent chumminess. The tartarus is a paper mill, a whitewashed factory building "like some great white sepulchre" which stands "not far from the bottom" of Devil's Dungeon, a high mountain hollow through which Blood River flows, a hollow approached up a canyon called the Mad Maid's Bellowspipe and through "a Dantean gateway" called Black Notch. The narrator, who has also narrated "The Paradise of Bachelors," is a seedsman brought to the factory to buy envelopes in which to mail his seed. (Melville's comparison of spired Temple Church in London and the factory "with a rude tower—for hoisting heavy boxes—at one end" anticipates the church/factory, spiritual/commercial antithesis which Henry Adams developed in the image of the Virgin and the dynamo, though in Melville's formulation, the woman is the victim of factories rather than the font of grace.)

The first panel of Melville's diptych is an ecstatic apostrophe to bachelor congeniality, the second is premised first on the image of woman as prisoner subservient to the biological imperative of motherhood, and second on the question of career and family which harried Melville at the time. It being apparent that he could not afford to be a writer and maintain his family, he was constantly on the verge of giving it up and petitioning the government for a sinecure. Which, he asked himself, is the greater progeny, books or children?

As a writer whose work had not been selling well lately, Melville could not enthusiastically endorse books. In *Pierre* he punishes himself for being a writer. Both Bartleby and the seedsman see the futility of written communication, see the delusion of it ever amounting to much.

> Dead letters! does it not sound like dead men? Conceive a man by nature and *misfortune* [emphasis mine] prone to a pallid hopelessness, can any business seem more fitted to heighten it than that of continually handling these dead letters, and assorting them for the flames? For by the cart-load they are annually burned. Sometimes from out the folded paper the pale clerk takes a ring—the finger it was meant for, perhaps, moulders in the grave; a bank-note sent in swiftest charity—he whom it would relieve, nor eats nor hungers any more; pardon for those who died despairing; hope for those who died unhoping; good tidings for those who died stifled by unrelieved calamities. On errands of life, these letters speed to death.
>
> Looking at that blank paper continually dropping, dropping, dropping, my mind ran on in wonderings of those strange uses to which those thousand sheets eventually would be put. All sorts of writings would be writ on those now vacant things—sermons, lawyers' briefs, physicians' prescriptions, love-letters, marriage certificates, bills of divorce, registers of births, death-warrants, and so on, without end. Then, recurring back to them as they here lay all blank, I could not but bethink me of that celebrated comparison of John Locke, who, in demonstration of his theory that man had no innate ideas, compared the human mind at birth to a sheet of blank paper, something destined to be scribbled on, but what sorts of characters no soul might tell.

And children? Cupid, "a dimpled, red-cheeked, spirited-looking, forward little fellow, who was rather impudently, I thought, gliding about among the passive-looking girls—like a gold fish through hueless waves—yet doing nothing in particular that I could see," despite vague imputations of sexual harassment of the female workers, leads the seedsman on a tour of the factory, cheerfully pointing out the analogies between making paper and making babies. It begins, to male observation, in the testes, "two great round vats . . . full of a white, wet, woolly-looking stuff, not unlike the albuminous part of an egg, soft-boiled." "'Look,'" says Cupid, "'how it swims bubbling round and round, moved by the paddle here. From hence it pours from both vats into the one common channel yonder,'" and thus into "a room, stifling with a strange, blood-like, abdominal heat, as if here, true enough, were being finally developed the germinous particles lately seen." This womblike room contains the machinery to process the sperm/pulp into paper. The machine's nine-minute cycle from pulp to paper duplicates the nine-month cycle from impregnation to birth.

To verify the time of the process, Cupid has the seedsman mark the material as it enters the machine, which the seedsman does by writing Cupid's name on the embryonic paper. And Melville further points up the gestation analogy by providing the machine/womb with an attendant midwife, an elderly, sad-looking person formerly a nurse.

> I saw a sort of paper-fall, not wholly unlike a water-fall; a scissory
> sound smote my ear, as if of some cord being snapped; and down
> dropped an unfolded sheet of perfect foolscap, with my "Cupid"
> half faded out of it, and still moist and warm.

Even the mark man makes genetically on his children is half-faded at their birth and becomes fainter and fainter as the blank sheet is scribbled over by the child's experience.

This sense of futility as writer and parent leads Melville to identify with the futility of woman's position, both in the factory and in the biological scheme.

The seedsman systematically surveys the faces of the mill girls on his arrival: "A face pale with work, and blue with cold." "At rows of blank-looking counters sat rows of blank-looking girls, white folders in their blank hands, all blankly folding blank paper." At the embossing machine he glances "from the rosy paper to the pallid cheek." At the machine that rules the lines onto blank foolscap, "I looked at the first girl's brow," who fed the blank paper into the machine, "and saw it was young and fair." "I looked at the second girl's brow," tending the ruled paper as it comes from the machine, "and saw it was ruled and wrinkled."

"All this scene around me," the narrator explains, "was instantaneously taken in at one sweeping glance." As the narrator proceeds "to unwind the heavy fur tippet from around [his] neck . . . the dark-complexioned man, standing close by, raised a sudden cry." The narrator's cheeks are frost-bitten from his January drive to the factory. "'Two white spots,'" the man tells him, "'like the whites of your eyes'"—by which he has taken in the scene, the narrator, unlike the other men in the story who have highly colored complexions, assuming the characteristic pallor of the mill girls. The man rubs snow on the narrator's cheeks, and "soon a horrible, tearing pain caught at my reviving cheeks. Two great blood-hounds, one on either side, seemed mumbling them. I seemed Actaeon."

Although the narrator may feel sympathy for these women, subservient not so much to their own biological imperatives as to men's (phallic) engines and men's demands for their products—the seedsman's demand for envelopes, the father's demand for progeny, either books or children, by which he can imprint his name and ideas upon the world—the narrator can never assume their burdens, he can only profane their mysteries, and for this he is subjected to Actaeon's punishment.

Although Melville's own male guilt may have developed as a result of his observation of women's place, his sense of that place was perhaps generated by comparison of their impoverishment with his own—for like Ishmael, Melville was not cast out alone, but with his mother; in order to keep themselves from becoming shabby genteel, those who suffer a reverse of fortunes become quite expert on distinguishing minute instances in which that border might have been crossed, even though one still pretends to a good exterior.

We may gain a sense of the humiliation which the reduced circumstances in which his family lived after Allan's bankruptcy and death caused Melville by his account of Redburn's voyage down Hudson to New York. The scene is, significantly, couched in terms of exclusion from the paradise of bachelors which Melville had first glimpsed in his father's heyday.

> As years passed on, this continual dwelling upon foreign associations, bred in me a vague prophetic thought, that I was fated, one day or other, to be a great voyager; and that just as my father used to entertain strange gentlemen over their wine after dinner, I would hereafter be telling my own adventures to an eager auditory.

The scene upon the Hudson River steamer is reminiscent to Redburn only of the unlikelihood that he shall ever play a role such as his father in such a gathering.

> For several hours, I sat gazing at a jovial party seated round a mahogany table, with some crackers and cheese, and wine and cigars. Their faces were flushed with the good dinner they had eaten; and mine felt pale and wan with a long fast. If I had presumed to offer to make one of their party; if I had told them of my circumstances, and solicited something to refresh me, I very well knew from the peculiar hollow ring of their laughter, they would have had the waiters put me out of the cabin, for a beggar, who had no business to be warming himself at their stove.

The humiliation of reduced circumstances is again depicted when, in order to buy a seaworthy wardrobe, Redburn is forced to sell his brother's fowling-piece at a pawnbroker's. It is this experience which seemingly opens his eyes, and sympathies, to the poverty of others.

> At one of the little holes, earnestly talking with one of the hook-nosed men, was a thin woman in a faded silk gown and shawl, holding a pale little girl by the hand. As I drew near, she spoke lower in a whisper; and the man shook his head, and looked cross and rude; and then some more words were exchanged over a minia-ture, and some money was passed through the hole, and the woman and child shrank out of the door.

In another incident in the shop, when one of the pawnbrokers accuses a young man of attempting to sell stolen goods, another "poor woman in a nightcap, with some baby-clothes in her hand, looked fearfully at the pawn-broker, as if dreading to encounter such a terrible pattern of integrity."

But Melville's most vivid descriptions of poverty are reserved for the poverty of Liverpool, descriptions which, incidentally, follow Redburn's discovery of the treachery of his father's guidebook, as if to underscore the point that each new realization of his unfatheredness sensitizes Redburn to further suffering.

Hearing what seems "the low, hopeless, endless wail of some one forever lost" while walking through Launcelott's-Hey, Redburn

> advanced to an opening which communicated downward with deep tiers of cellars beneath a crumbling old warehouse; and there, some fifteen feet below the walk, crouching in nameless squalor, with her head bowed over, was the figure of what had been a woman. Her blue arms folded to her livid bosom two shrunken things like children, that leaned toward her, one on each side.

Despite his efforts, Redburn is unable to procure help for them and, returning after several days had passed since first observing them, "found that the vault was empty. In place of the woman and children, a heap of quick-lime was glistening."

Melville's observation of women's poverty extended to the poverty that exists in the country. Isabel, like Delly Ulver, is its victim until Pierre rescues her; however, in keeping with the romanticism of the novel, that poverty is merely picturesque, its melodrama heightened by the tale of Delly's illegiti-mate child, its death, and her pathetic devastation. The same sentimentalizing is true as regards Marianna in "The Piazza." She, an orphan, has recently lost her brother and is living alone in a house to which the story's narrator is drawn by his desire to see "that far cot [cottage] in fairy-land" whose window he sees glinting in the sunlight.

Suddenly looking off, I saw the golden mountain-window, dazzling like a deep-sea dolphin. Fairies there, thought I, once more; the queen of fairies at her fairy-window; at any rate, some glad mountain-girl; it will do me good, it will cure this weariness, to look on her.

The reality is somewhat other than the narrator has anticipated:

Pausing at the threshold, or rather where threshold once had been, I saw, through the open door-way, a lonely girl, sewing at a lonely window. A pale-cheeked girl, and fly-specked window, with wasps around the mended upper panes.

But this does not deter the narrator's romanticism.

I spoke. She shyly started, like some Tahiti girl, secreted for a sacrifice, first catching sight, through palms, of Captain Cook. Recovering, she bade me enter; with her apron brushed off a stool; then silently resumed her own. With thanks I took the stool; but now, for a space, I, too, was mute. This, then, is the fairy-mountain house, and here, the fairy queen sitting at her fairy window.

For her acute depression, the narrator can offer no remedy but "prayer and pillow," not even when Marianna tells him that her weariness might leave her "if I could but once get to yonder house"—the narrator's own, which she sees through a haze of distance which "made it appear less a farm-house than King Charming's palace."

Although the narrator offers Marianna no practical help of any sort,[17] he is content to let her serve as an emotional stimulus for his writing. The writer sticks to his piazza.

It is my box-royal; and this amphitheatre, my theatre of San Carlo. Yes, the scenery is magical—the illusion so complete. . . . But, every night, when the curtain falls, truth comes in with darkness. No light shows from the mountain. To and fro I walk the piazza deck, haunted by Marianna's face, and many as real a story.

This same sort of passivity is exhibited by Hunilla, the Chola widow of "The Encantadas" (collected as one of *The Piazza Tales*), whose husband and brother are shipwrecked before her very eyes:

The real woe of this event passed before her sight as some sham tragedy on the stage. . . . So instant was the scene, so trance-like its mild pictorial effect, so distant from her blasted bower and her common sense of things, that Hunilla gazed and gazed, nor raised a finger or a wail. But as good to sit this dumb, in stupor staring on that dumb show, for all that otherwise might be done.

Here again we see Melville's own Bartleby-ism, the melancholy of a student of Burton's *Anatomy*, "a man by nature and misfortune prone to a pallid hopelessness," extended to define the human condition for both sexes.

In Melville's second diptych, "Poor Man's Pudding and Rich Man's Crumbs," like the first, "The Paradise of Bachelors and the Tartarus of Maids," one panel depicts London and the other the impoverished Northeast which Melville would have seen firsthand around Arrowhead. The London panel of this diptych, however, shows not the conviviality of the feasting bachelors, but the sordid dispensation of the crumbs of their feast. The men in "Rich Man's Crumbs" no longer have the immunity to poverty that the bachelors of the Temple seem to enjoy, for they too queue up for the remains of the Lord Mayor's dinner; nor are women excluded from the feast any more than the beggar women with their hint of Redburn's Liverpool are excluded from the queue.

And William and Martha Coulter, the Squire's tenants in "Poor Man's Pudding," share a poverty which only women had endured in the American panel "Tartarus of Maids." But Melville goes further, advancing his Bartleby-ism against the Young America mentality he had butted heads with in *Pierre*:

> The native American poor never lose their delicacy or pride; hence, though unreduced to the physical degradation of the European pauper, they yet suffer more in mind than the poor of any other people in the world. Those peculiar social sensibilities nourished by our peculiar political principles, while they enhance the true dignity of a prosperous American, do but minister to the added wretchedness of the unfortunate; first by prohibiting their acceptance of what little random relief charity may offer; and, second, by furnishing them with the keenest appreciation of the smarting distinction between their ideal of universal equality and their grindstone experience of the practical misery and infamy of poverty—a misery and infamy which is, ever has been, and ever will be, precisely the same in India, England, and America.

However, like Marianna and Hunilla, Martha is most depressed not by physical poverty but by bereavement:

> "William loves me this day as on the wedding-day, sir. Some hasty words, but never a harsh one. I wish I were better and stronger for his sake. And, oh! sir, both for his sake and mine" (and the soft, blue, beautiful eyes turned into two well-springs), "how I wish little William and Martha lived—it is so lonely-like now. William named after him, and Martha for me."

And it is perhaps their bereavement rather than their poverty that makes Melville, the bereaved and impoverished orphan, most sympathetic to women

of this sort: it is an outlet of self-pity disguised behind the genteel sentimentalities of his day. Not all of Melville's portraits of marriage, however,
have the ashen hue of "Poor Man's Pudding."

But the road to husbandhood runs from adolescent awakening through
suitorhood, and the instances of adolescent discovery are, as one would
expect, for the most part in Melville's juvenile work, *Typee* and *Omoo*. In
these stories, the behavior of the suitor is mimicked; the immediate object,
however, is not matrimony but rather the eternal adolescent work of developing familiarity with the dynamics of male-female relationships.

In *Typee* and *Omoo*, Melville feels obliged to excuse his lack of intentions
by references to the transient nature of his sojourn and to defend his attachment to Fayaway by Europeanizing her. She is blue-eyed, as Yillah will be
(and Melville is preparing himself for the role of Taji, remarking "the natives
multiplied their acts of kindness and attention towards myself, treating me
with a degree of deference which could hardly have been surpassed had I
been some celestial visitant"). Fayaway's tattooing is not as extensive as is
usual; the shoulder bands "always reminded me of those stripes of gold lace
worn by officers in undress,and which were in lieu of epaulets to denote their
rank" (note the masculinization of the female).

"Fayaway—I must avow the fact—for the most part clung to the primitive
and summer garb of Eden"; her main attraction, however, is not physical but
emotional: Melville felt her to be supportive of him. "Of all the natives she
alone seemed to appreciate the effect which the peculiarity of the circumstances in which we were placed had produced upon the minds of my companion and myself." The last we see of Fayaway, she is "violently weeping"
at Melville's departure, but her companionship has been supplanted: Melville's
native friend Marheyo "placed his arm upon my shoulder, and empathically
pronounced the only two English words I had taught him—'home' and
'mother.'" Thus Melville flees what some commentators persist in calling his
dream of Eden, drawn by the power of western sentimentalities already
assimilated.

The conflict Melville felt between the natural and the sentimental appears,
for instance, when he goes to bathe:

> Somewhat embarrassed by the female portion of the company, and
> feeling my cheeks burning with bashful timidity, I formed a primi-
> tive basin by joining my hands together, and cooled my blushes
> in the water it contained; then, removing my frock, bent over and
> washed myself down to the waist in the stream.

Yet his own sentimental modesty does not prevent a sidelong glance toward
"the young girls springing buoyantly [another masculinization of the female]
into the air, and revealing their naked forms to the waist."

Melville's relation with Fayaway is, imaginatively, at least as evidenced by his text, comfortable enough that they can go boating and smoking together—smoking being elsewhere the most sacred totem of male bonding in Melville's iconography.

> Fayaway and I reclined in the stern of the canoe, on the very best terms possible with each other; the gentle nymph occasionally placing her pipe in her lip, and exhaling the mild fumes of the tobacco, to which her rosy breath added a fresh perfume. Strange as it may seem [*sic!*], there is nothing in which a young and beautiful female appears to more advantage than in the act of smoking. How captivating is a Peruvian lady swinging in her gaily woven hammock of grass, extended between two orange trees, and inhaling the fragrance of a choice cigarro!

(Melville has already hinted at Peruvian intrigue in this conjunction of atmospheres: "Her feet, though wholly exposed, were as diminutive and fairly shaped as those which peep from beneath the skirts of a Lima lady's dress"—this in the catalog of Fayaway's parts which includes her Yillah-blue eyes.)

In their own way, *Typee* and *Omoo* are a diptych depicting Melville's sexual adolescence in the South Seas. Although uneasiness gives way to spontaneous discovery in *Typee*, in *Omoo* we see all efforts to establish presexual contact thwarted. And although the narrator of *Typee* has had his male ego bolstered by Fayaway's attentiveness, this is not to be the case with the narrator of *Omoo*:

> I think it was the second day of our confinement, that a wild, beautiful girl burst into the Calabooza, and, throwing herself into an arch attitude, stood afar off, and gazed at us. . . . Whenever anything struck her comically, you saw it like a flash—her finger leveled instantaneously, and, flinging herself back, she gave loose to strange, hollow little notes of laughter, that sounded like the bass of a music-box, playing a lively air with the lid down.
>
> Now I know not, that there was any thing in my own appearance calculated to disarm ridicule; and, indeed, to have looked at all heroic, under the circumstances, would have been rather difficult. Still, I could not but feel exceedingly annoyed at the prospect of being screamed at in turn, by this mischievous young witch, even though she were but an islander [*sic*]. And, to tell a secret, her beauty had something to do with this sort of feeling. . . .
>
> Ere her glance fell upon me, I had, unconsciously, thrown myself into the most graceful attitude I could assume, leaned my head upon my hand, and summoned up as abstracted an expression as possible.

Though my face was averted, I soon felt it flush, and knew that the
glance was upon me: deeper and deeper grew the flush, and not a
sound of laughter.

Delicious thought! she was moved at the sight of me. I could
stand it no longer, but started up. Lo! there she was; her great hazel
eyes rounding and rounding in her head, like two stars, her whole
frame in a merry quiver, and an expression about the mouth that
was sudden and violent death to any thing like sentiment.

The next moment she spun round, and, bursting from peal to peal
of laughter, went racing out of the Calabooza; and, in mercy to me,
never returned.[18]

This sort of maliciousness is directed not only toward *Omoo's* adolescent
narrator, but to the adult Doctor Long Ghost who attempts to engage Loo,
the daughter of their host, while she is reading her Bible. She ignores him,

but it would never do to give up; so he threw himself at length
beside her, and audaciously commenced turning over the leaves. . . .
the doctor rather frightened at his own temerity, and knowing not
what to do next. At last, he placed one arm cautiously about her
waist; almost in the same instant he bounded to his feet, with a cry;
the little witch had pierced him with a thorn.

Or again: The narrator, spying a missionary's wife and daughter, "a pretty,
blond young girl," taking the evening breeze, resolves on

a courteous salute, to show my good breeding if nothing more. . . .
"Good evening, ladies," exclaimed I, at last, advancing winningly; "a
delightful air from the sea, ladies." Hysterics and hartshorn! who
would have thought it? The young lady screamed, and the old one
came near fainting.

But this apparition is nothing compared to what the narrator sees only
two paragraphs after Loo repulses Long Ghost.

One day, taking a pensive afternoon stroll along one of the many
bridle-paths. . . I was startled by a sunny apparition. It was that of a
beautiful young Englishwoman, charmingly dressed, and mounted
upon a spirited little white pony. . . . Stepping to one side, as the
apparition drew near, I made a polite obeisance. It gave me a bold,
rosy one; and then, with a gay air, patted its palfrey, crying out,
"Fly away, Willy!" and galloped among the trees.

The narrator's and eventually Long Ghost's pursuit leads them several days
later to Mr. Bell's sugar plantation where the episode evaporates, its incipient
adultery powerless before the circumstances of Mrs. Bell's married life.

> A stranger approached. He was a sun-burnt, romantic-looking European. . . . This was Mr. Bell. He was very civil; showed us the grounds, and, taking us into a sort of arbor, to our surprise, offered to treat us to some wine. . . . Now all this was extremely polite in Mr. Bell; still, we came to see *Mrs.* Bell. But she proved to be a phantom, indeed; having left the same morning for Papeetee, on a visit to one of the missionaries' wives there. I went home much chagrined. To be frank, my curiosity had been wonderfully piqued concerning the lady. In the first place, she was the most beautiful white woman I ever saw in Polynesia. But this is saying nothing. She had such eyes, such moss-roses in her cheeks, such a divine air in the saddle, that, to my dying day, I shall never forget Mrs. Bell. The sugar-planter himself was young, robust, and handsome. So, merrily may the little Bells increase, and multiply, and make music in the Land of Imeeo.

Thus do interlopers excuse themselves with prayers for the increase of the husband. But thus excluded, how do young men win their wives? We have already seen of what Taji's courtship of Yillah consisted. Pierre's engagement to Lucy seems less the result of his own entreaties than of entrapment by his prospective mother-in-law.

> The first cup of coffee had been poured out by Mrs. Tartan, when she declared she smelt matches burning somewhere in the house, and she must see them extinguished. So, banning all pursuit, she rose . . . leaving the pair alone to interchange the civilities of the coffee. . . . Pierre looked from Lucy to his boots, and as he lifted his eyes again, saw Anacreon on the sofa on one side of him, and Moore's melody on the other, and some honey on the table, and a bit of white satin on the floor, and a sort of bride's veil on the chandelier. Never mind though—thought Pierre, fixing his gaze on Lucy—I'm entirely willing to be caught, when the bait is set in Paradise, and the bait is such an angel.

And their betrothal is marked by such cutesinesses as Pierre shaking down a flower that had reposed itself on Lucy's pillow and "conspicuously" fastening it "in his bosom," exclaiming "I must away now, Lucy; see! under these colors I march," while she thrills "Bravissimo! oh, my only recruit," and Pierre entering a "formal declaration and protest" that "when we are married, I am not to carry any bundles, unless in cases of real need; and what is more, when there are any of your young lady acquaintances in sight, I am not to be unnecessarily called upon to back up and load for their particular edification."

Melville's collusion with such sentimental clichés is seen in his revision of Israel Potter's autobiography. Potter simply states, "Despairing of meeting with a favourable opportunity to return to America ... I became more reconciled to my situation, and contracted an intimacy with a young woman whose parents were poor but respectable, and who I soon after married."

Melville's version depicts a narrator injured, as *Typee*'s narrator had been, and marrying his solacing Fayaway, but with consequences that only emphasize the bondage of additional financial responsibilities attendant on marriage, which led Melville to his famous outburst, "Dollars damn me."

> As stubborn fate would have it, being run over one day at Holborn Bars, and taken into a neighboring bakery, [Israel] was there treated with such kindness by a Kentish lass, the shop-girl, that in the end he thought his debt of gratitutde could only be repaid by love. In a word, the money saved up for his ocean voyage [to return to his native America] was lavished upon a rash embarkation in wedlock.

And how is marriage itself depicted? In "I and My Chimney" it is depicted as a contest of stubborn wills—the wife wishing to remodel the house by removing its central chimney, the husband defending it as a companionable fellow smoker. In fact, the male camaraderie is so emphatic that the chimney becomes a phallic extension of the narrator, and the story is often read as a sly attack on castrating women.

The contest of wills in "Jimmy Rose" between husband and wife is over the choice of wallpaper in the largest parlor. Whereas the wife in "I and My Chimney" sought to enlist male help against her husband, primarily in the person of an architectural engineer, the wife in "Jimmy Rose" can claim as re-enforcements two daughters and the family maid. And although the husband-narrator prevails in each of these tales, one does not sense that his victory is either complete or permanent.

"The Apple-Tree Table, or Original Spiritual Manifestations" is the only domestic piece in Melville's fiction that reaches a mutually satisfying conclusion, and this through the instrumentality of the wife. Although the narrator would like to think himself rational and objective, he is still frightened by the bogeyman projected from his reading of Cotton Mather. His wife, whom he dubs "Mrs. Democritus," is the paragon of pragmatic common sense. When, after the "seraphical bug" has rapped its way out of the table, the husband announces, "Well, then, wife and daughters, now that it is all over, this very morning I will go and make inquiries about it," his daughter Julia cries, "Oh, do, papa, do go and consult Madame Pazzi, the conjuress." "Better go and consult Professor Johnson, the naturalist," says his wife. Although Melville personifies the spiritual realm by a female figure and the scientific by a male, the fact remains that it is through the efforts of both husband and wife, and primarily the wife, that the education of their daughters, and the family maid, is accomplished.

This working relationship between husband and wife is rare, however, in Melville's work. Ruth's parents in *Clarel*, Nathan and Agar, have come to the Holy Land together, impelled by Nathan's Zionism, Agar, Melville's representative of the stereotype of the reluctant pioneer, following him from duty rather than from her own conviction or enthusiasm and, like Ruth, dying of grief following Nathan's murder by Arab terrorists.

Yet late in his life, Melville seems to have started voicing his own "testament of acceptance" of himself as husband. The antagonism of married couples depicted with such immediacy prior to 1856 had, by the publication of *Clarel* in 1876, been distanced into the objective account of Nathan and Agar. And the movement from the emotional and psychological uncertainties of newlyweds to the familiarity of long-married couples appeared in his late poems.

"The Figure-Head," published in the section entitled "Minor Sea Pieces" in *John Marr and Other Sailors*, privately printed in 1888, is retrospective and elegiac, following a couple from marriage to death:

> The *Charles-and-Emma* seaward sped,
> (Named from the carven pair at prow,)
> He so smart, and a curly head,
> She tricked forth as a bride knows how:
>     Pretty stem for the port, I trow!
>
> But iron-rust and alum-spray
> And chafing gear, and sun and dew
> Vexed this lad and lassie gay,
> Tears in their eyes, salt tears nor few;
>     And the hug relaxed with the failing glue.
>
> But came in end a dismal night,
> With creaking beams and ribs that groan,
> A black lee-shore and waters white:
> Dropped on the reef, the pair lie prone:
>     O, the breakers dance, but the winds they moan!

*John Marr* also includes the rambling "Bridegroom Dick," which appears to be a conversation between a retired sailor and his wife, but on closer examination proves essentially a monologue—garrulous, almost senile, reminiscences about other men, ending with this stanza:

My pipe is smoked out, and the grog runs slack;
But bowse away, wife, at your blessed Bohea;
This empty can here must solace me—
Nay, sweetheart, nay; I take that back;
Dick drinks from your eyes and he finds no lack!

Recalled to an awareness of his wife's presence, the bridegroom seeks to soothe his bride with the gallantry typical of the inattentive husband.

## V

Auden may be right that Melville sailed at last into the haven of his wife's arms. There is, after all, something romantic about Melville's courtship of Elizabeth Shaw—he, tanned and handsome, recalling his South Sea adventures to his sisters and their friend—she listening and, perhaps, recalling for Melville Shakespeare's line "She loved me for the dangers I had passed . . ."

And of their settled domesticity, we have this sketch by Arthur Stedman which appeared in the New York *World* the week following Melville's death:

> His favorite companions were his grandchildren, with whom he delighted to pass his time, and his devoted wife, who was a constant assistant and advisor in his work, chiefly done of late for his own amusement. To her he addressed his last little poem, the touching "Return of the Sire de Nesle."

Whether this "L'Envoi" is actually Melville's last poem is a moot question. It does serve as a concluding poem in the *Timoleon* volume, which, as we have seen, included "Shelley's Vision," "In a Bye-Canal," and "After the Pleasure Party."

The Sire de Nesle would have been a near-contemporary of his fellow countryman Montaigne, an author to whom Melville turned late in his life, characterizing him in *Billy Budd* as a writer who, "free from cant and convention, honestly and in the spirit of common sense philosophizes upon realities." The references to Kaf, in Oriental legend the range of mountains encircling the world which serves as the chief abode of the jinns, and to Araxes, the Oxus River forded by Alexander the Great, point up not only the journeys of the Sire but something of Melville's own estimation of the nature of his own wanderings. And of what he has come to value most in his life.

L'Envoi

The Return of the Sire de Nesle
A.D. 16—

My towers at last! These rovings end,
Their thirst is slaked in larger dearth:
The yearning infinite recoils,
  For terrible is earth!

Kaf thrusts his snouted crags through fog:
Araxes swells beyond his span,
And knowledge poured by pilgrimage
  Overflows the banks of man.

But thou, my stay, thy lasting love,
One lonely good, let this but be!
Weary to view the wide world's swarm,
  But blest to fold but thee.[19]

## *Notes*

1. For a concise discussion of this problem, see John Stoltenberg, "Sexual Objectification and Male Supremacy," *M: Gentle Men for Gender Justice,* no. 5 (Spring 1981):5, 30–31.
2. See Judith Slater, "The Domestic Adventurer in Melville's Tales," *American Literature* 37 (1965):267–79.
3. This view is not universally held. Writing of Mrs. Melville's biographical memorandum of her husband, Raymond M. Weaver states in *Herman Melville: Mariner and Mystic* (New York: George H. Doran Co., 1921) that it "reveals more about Mrs. Melville than of the subject it purports to treat. . . . He had been a busy man, and he came to be a sick one. Such is Mrs. Melville's *apologia* for her husband. And the limitations of her piety and imagination that narrowed her vision to this were, I believe, among the prime instigating causes to provoke in Melville the emotional crisis which she was pitiably unable to understand." See also Amy Elizabeth Pruett, "Melville's Wife: A Study of Elizabeth Shaw Melville" (Ph.D. diss., Northwestern University, 1969).
4. Newton Arvin, *Herman Melville* (New York: William Sloane Associates, 1950), p. 22.
5. Ibid., p. 23.
6. A major theme of Byron's *The Two Foscari*.
7. This concern with boots has appeared earlier, when Redburn, wondering what life would be like for boys in foreign lands, contemplates

"whether their papas allowed them to wear boots, instead of shoes, which I so much disliked, for boots looked so manly."

8. Sidney Moss, *Hawthorne and Melville: An Inquiry into Their Art and the Mystery of Their Friendship*, Literary Monographs, no. 7, ed. Eric Rothstein and Joseph Anthony Wittereich, Jr. (Madison: University of Wisconsin Press, 1975) pp. 45-84.

9. *Saba* is Hebrew for "father" and Melville, capable of punning on Margrave in a poem on Christmas, must have meant this to signal a marring of the father as well as the passing of the heroic.

10. Sidney Moss's quotation of John Ciardi's gloss on *The Inferno* seems equally applicable here: "The souls of the damned are locked so blindly into their own guilt that none can feel sympathy for another, or find any pleasure in the presence of another." Moss, "Hawthorne and Melville," p. 49.

11. The most immediate statement of the nature of this interview is to be found in the chord sequence by which Benjamin Britten depicts it in his opera *Billy Budd*.

12. See, for instance, Dennis Kelly, "Melville as Size Queen," in *Chicken* (San Francisco: Gay Sunshine Press, 1979), pp. 44-45.

13. William Bysshe Stein, *The Poetry of Melville's Later Years: Time, History, Myth, and Religion* (Albany: State University of New York Press, 1970), pp. 115-16.

14. Melville must have been aware that Ulysses was not only the son of Venus but the father of Telemachus, the father-neglected son par excellence of classical mythology. Chesler again: "Consider: If it were natural for fathers to care for their sons, they would not need so many laws commanding them to do so. Fathers would not have to be tempted into it by offers of immortality, empire, or God's love."

15. Mary Glendinning's self-sufficiency is punished even more grotesquely: "Presently, as she paced the room in deep, rapid thought, she became conscious of something strange in her grasp, and without looking at it, to mark what it was, impulsively flung it from her. A dashing noise was heard, and then a quivering. She turned; and hanging by the side of Pierre's portrait, she saw her own smiling picture pierced through, and the fork, whose silver tines had caught in the painted bosom, vibratingly rankled in the wound."

16. "Imaginal" psychology, with its emphasis on Jungian archetypal method, has proved a fruitful approach to interpreting Melville's work. See, for instance, James Baird, "Puer Aeternus: The Figure of Innocence in Melville," in Cynthia Giles, ed., *Puer Papers* (Irving, Texas: Spring Publications, 1979), pp. 205-23.

17. The "picturesqueness" of poverty is another means of disempowering the women caught in it.

18. Nor was this sort of thing unknown in the pre-Fayaway days on *Typee*, but without the malice implicit in *Omoo*: "The house was nearly filled with young females, fancifully decorated with flowers, who gazed upon me as I rose with faces in which childish delight and curiosity were

vividly portrayed. After waking Toby, they seated themselves round us on mats, and gave full play to that prying inquisitiveness which time out of mind has been attributed to the adorable sex. . . . Long and minute was the investigation with which they honored us, and so uproarious their mirth, that I felt infinitely sheepish; and Toby was immeasurably outraged at their familiarity."

19. It may have been the sentiment of this concluding stanza that inspired W. H. Auden's "Herman Melville," whose 41 lines may be the most concisely insightful criticism of Melville's mind and work ever published. The poem begins:

Towards the end he sailed into an extraordinary mildness,
And anchored in his home and reached his wife
And rode within the harbour of her hand.

# Rolande Ballorain

## Mark Twain's Capers: A Chameleon in King Carnival's Court

*"He is a chameleon; by the law of his nature, he takes the color of his place of resort."*

"What Is Man?"

*"The last quarter of a century of my life has been pretty constantly and faithfully devoted to the study of the human race—that is to say to the study of myself, for in my individual person, I am the entire human race compacted together."*

*Autobiography*

Speaking of the rows of books of Mr. Galsworthy and Mr. Kipling, V. Woolf remarks in a famous passage of *A Room of One's Own*: "Do what she will, a woman cannot find in them that fountain of perpetual life which the critics assure her is there. It is not only that they celebrate male virtues, enforce male values and describe the world of men; it is that the emotion with which these books are permeated is to a woman incomprehensible" (Ch.6). Had she been concerned with American writers, she could have added Mark Twain, who read *Kim* every year, to her list. For this is exactly what a woman feels when reading Twain, the Mark Twain celebrated and perpetuated by his male readers and critics; the Twain of the first period, before, according to them, he produced second-rate works; the Twain of the frontier, of the yarns and tall tales, of the West, of Hannibal; the humorist, the story-teller, the great man who introduced the Western vernacular to world literature; one of the great American writers, who wrote one of the two or three great masterpieces of American literature. ("What else do we have," they say, "*Moby Dick*?" And then?) I must confess something: I have never shared that extraordinary admiration. Is it because I am a woman and have no sense of humor? Is it because I am French? ("You French people cannot feel all the subtleties, all the allusions, Twain is so deeply American." Well, then, he cannot be universal.) But I happen to think that *The Scarlet Letter, The Red Badge of Courage*, James's novels, *Lolita*, to mention only a few among dozens of books written by other men, are more deserving of the name of masterpieces. After feeling a guilty conscience and pangs of remorse about my reactions to Twain, I decided it might be worthwhile to probe into all his works and his cult and see what I could discover. So one of the purposes of this essay is to try to consider the whole bulk of the works of Twain, not only *Huckleberry Finn,* and particularly the second period; and to confront Twain and his male critics. They share some characteristics. They all put Huck on a pedestal. They, each in turn, offer a unique and global interpretation of their idol. Twain is the writer of the West, of the frontier; he is a humorist; he was cramped by wife and life; he is an artist, a master of language. They all neglect what he wrote after 1885 and particularly the two works that he considered his best and most important. "He thought the mawkish *Joan of Arc* and the second-rate *The Prince and the Pauper* his best work," contemptuously states Bernard DeVoto in his introduction to *The Portable Mark Twain.* They also all enjoy enumerating his many defects: his bad taste, his structural weaknesses, his inconsistencies and contradictions, his sexual squeamishness, his philosophical pretension, his meanness.[1] Is it that all his shortcomings have to be forgiven because he originated a fundamental American pattern? But they never dare say clearly that that pattern is precisely the creation of a woman-excluding world, of an all-boys world, englobing writer, characters, and male readers in pure masculine complicity. That is an obsessive line of American fiction; and it was perceived by Leslie Fiedler even before the contemporary wave of feminist criticism underlined it. And that pattern makes Twain universal for obvious reasons. But that is only a level-one reading of Twain, that only considers "manners," and not literary "mystery." Twain cannot be limited to that. No writer, unless he is truly minor, can. Twain (two) just cannot be interpreted in one way. He loved too much to change roles. The study of the main structures and patterns of his whole opus, especially of the neglected second period, brings to light the capital role of *Joan of Arc* in his work, as well as the necessity of avoiding a unique global interpretation of that work. It shows that Twain was only American in part, but essentially the last American writer to write according to the oldest European tradition, the carnivalesque vision of the world and of art.

*Level One Reading:*
*American "Manners," or Twain's Reader Abroad*

Twain's misogyny is so blatant that one can wonder whether he was joking when he wrote in his Preface to *Tom Sawyer* that he hoped "men and *women*"[2] would not shun the book, since his plan was to "pleasantly remind adults of what they once were themselves"; though, of course, immediately after, in the first chapter, addressing the reader, he refers him to the time "he was a boy." What woman could think she was once Becky Thatcher, a mere onlooker, when Tom is the center of the stage all the time? She passively follows him, fears, cries, applauds: he is the leader. Pretending he was showing "real" children and not simply stereotyped models of goodness, Twain demonstrated what male and female roles must be. Tom is the prototype of the "boy"; Twain's world is an all-boys' world. That is a first unifying pattern of his work at a level-one reading. A boys' world is not a man's world. A boy is opposed to a girl. A man includes the human being in him. A boy is a type; a child is an individual. A boy is already made into the masculine role. A child is pre/a/sexual; a boy is sexualized. The boys appear in many shapes in Twain. On board "The Quaker City," "the innocents" include sixteen or eighteen ladies counted at the beginning, but rarely mentioned afterwards, while the other excursionists, "three ministers of the gospel, eight doctors, several military and naval chieftains with sounding titles, an ample crop of 'Professors' of various kinds," etc. . . . very soon become "all the other boys" laughing at "Mr. Mark Twain" in the kid-glove episode, confronting American values and the Old World, some of them achieving "the glory of lighting their cigars by the flames of Vesuvius."[3] The miners of Nevada in *Roughing It*, the Marion Rangers of "The Private History of a Campaign That Failed," the experienced steamboatmen on the Mississippi, even the knights of King Arthur's court and the soldiers of Joan are all boys. An interesting dialogue takes place in *A Connecticut Yankee*: "Don't forget the cowboys, Sandy." "Cowboys?" "The knights, you know, you were going to tell me about them."[4] In *Personal Recollections of Joan of Arc*, the boys are first the faithful who follow Joan from the beginning: the Scholar, Sieur Louis de Conte, her biographer, the supposed writer, the Paladin, Noël Rainguesson, and the d'Arcs; but also "the gang of soldiers" that was her army. A boy is indeed forever. He can be a child like Tom Canty and the friends of the young Prince; in his teens, like Tom and Huck and the children dreaming of being pilots on the Mississippi; a young man: "I was eighteen and the other youths were from one to four years older—young men in fact," says Louis de Conte,[5] or a fully grown man like the travelers or the miners. For it is not age, but the adoption of a set of values that came to make up the typical American male, Westerner or Yankee, even Southerner, which defines the boy. Certainly, writing about them, Twain only used Woolf's "male side of the brain." The boys' world is made of males in groups[6] united by bonds that have nothing to do with latent or overt homosexuality, as Fiedler said, but rather with the refusal of the sexualized state and a strong wish to perpetuate the presexual state of the androgynous child, a wish that we also find in many writings by women. Indeed the pleasures of such life are innocent in all meanings: they exclude sexuality associated with woman, sin, and dirtiness; they wish to perpetuate the paradise of a precivilized golden age, the condition Adam knew before Eve intruded into Eden. They are clearly defined several times: in "A Campaign That Failed"; in *Roughing It*: "And it was comfort in those succeeding days to sit up and contemplate the majestic panorama of mountains and valleys spread out below us and eat ham and hard-boiled eggs while our spiritual natures reveled alternately in rainbows, thunderstorms, and peerless sunsets. Nothing helps scenery like ham and eggs. Ham and eggs, and after these a pipe—an old, rank, delicious pipe—ham and eggs and scenery, a 'downgrade', a flying coach, a fragrant pipe and contented heart—these make happiness. It is what all the ages have struggled for."[7] Cardiff Hill where the Douglas Mansion stands, Jackson Island, and the raft are areas diminishing as time goes by, where the boy is "free and comfortable," "kind of lazy and jolly laying off comfortably all day, smoking and fishing and no books to study"; but it always gets "lonesome" there, and the company not of Eve, but of other men, to do something, to start acting on the world, to play, mostly to show off to, is first required. For the boys have Twain's temperament; he did believe in the importance of temperament, and his was the "sanguine temperament":[8] all fire and flames, doing, active, noisy, enterprising, thinking afterwards, creating, playing, stirring things. He was, they are extroverted: the dominant American male type. If they can't act on the world, they dream of doing it, talk and brag. Twain was himself in turn a boy, a printer, a prospector, a miner, a reporter, a pilot, a lecturer, a businessman, a publisher, "an author for 20 years and an ass for 55":[9] a full *actor* in all meanings, and loving to be applauded and celebrated at that. That lively actor, physical fighter, successful winner is the image of man that was imposed on American men by people like Twain. That conception of "virility" ignores weakness, softness, gentleness, sentiment.

It is in *Roughing It*, the most spontaneous of his works, that Twain spelled out his conceptions most clearly in a passage often referred to as expressing nostalgia for the past.[10] He exalts the gone population of the bygone days with a lyricism not to be found again before *Joan*. In fact it is an enthusiastic exaltation of the males verging on the ridiculous: he speaks of "a peerless and magnificent manhood," of "an assemblage of two hundred thousand young men," "the very pick and choice of the world's glorious ones," "the most gallant host that ever trooped down in the startled solitudes of an unpeopled land." It is easy to oppose the terms referring to "beautiful manhood" and to the rest of humanity on that page:

| BEAUTIFUL MANHOOD | THE OTHERS |
|---|---|
| • driving, vigorous, restless | • simpering, dainty, kid-gloved weaklings |
| • stalwart, muscular, dauntless: young braves, brimful of push and energy | • women, children, gray stooping veterans |
| • royally endowed with all attributes | |
| • erect, bright-eyed, quick-moving, strong-handed young giants | • slow, sleepy, sluggish-brained sloths |

- the finest population
- a splendid population
- pioneers
- getting up astounding enterprises
- magnificent dash and daring
- recklessness of cost or consequences
- rough, happy
- a wild, free, disorderly, *grotesque* society
- Men

- aristocrats
- "biled shirts"
- juvenile, feminine

The superabundance of words to praise "men" contrasts with the few vague opposite characteristics, evidently summed up by the word "feminine." But even the roles traditionally associated with women are refused to them in a world that excludes them, for Twain insists, "men cooked and washed and sewed their own buttons"! This page expresses a deep nostalgia for the past and for an Eve-excluding paradise lost.

For this praise of manhood and of boys' companionship goes along in Twain with an absence of substantial feminine portraits and a scattering of misogynist comments of the rudest sort. In his *Autobiography* and *Notebooks*, his remarks on the women he happened to meet are often not only unfair but gross lies. Mrs. Aldrich was a favorite target; he himself recognizes at one point that he might have been biased against her.[11] Contemporary readers would get a wrong idea of Harriet Beecher Stowe or Isabella Hooker if they confined themselves to reading Twain.[12] Olive Logan and Kate Field should have been "house-emptiers," he says, reproaching them mostly with not being celebrated; he does not care about their messages as lecturers: they were active in reform movements and the women's cause and were also an actress and a novelist. Put together, his remarks form a catalogue of clichés in which narrow nationalism, racism, and sexism combine at their worst. All foreign women are dirty or ugly, the grisettes are "homely" and eat "garlic and onion"; the Nazarenes are "homely," too, the Moroccan women are ugly, the Milan women are "unwashed peasant girls," the Palestine women are not "fastidious enough" for him; as to the French women, of course, they "suffocate with nastiness" and are all harlots.[12] The American woman alone, and occasionally the Englishwoman too, are in all places, in all circumstances, beautiful—and pure. But all women, even the Americans, suffer from the unpardonable sin: while supposed to be BeckyThatcherlike passive spectators of men's heroism or talk, they have the audacity to talk, necessarily, too much. In *A Connecticut Yankee*, Sandy is "a flow of talk." "Her clack was going all day." "She could grind and pump, and churn and buzz by the week, and never stop to oil up or blow out. And yet the result was just nothing but wind. She never had any ideas, any more than a fog has. She was a perfect blatherskite; I mean for jaw, jaw, jaw, talk, talk, talk, jabber, jabber, jabber."[13] In the *Notebooks*, one finds this entry: "Two men talking. It is the nature of women to ask trivial, irrelevant and pursuing questions. Yes, and to think they have logical, analytical minds and argumentative ability."[14] In *Adam's Diary*, the first entry reads: "This new creature with the long hair is a good deal in the way. It is always hanging around and following me about. I don't like this; I am not used to company. I wished it could stay with the other animals." Two days after: "I wish it would not talk; it is always talking"; and more significantly: "Built me a shelter against the rain, but could not have it to myself in peace. The new creature *intruded*." In man's world, woman is barely tolerated; she belongs with the other animals; she is no equal partner; she can't join the club.

Another traditional form of misogyny in Twain is the product of the paternalism of Victorian times, roughly dividing women into two categories: the pure/the impure; the married and mothers/the unmarried and lovers or "concubines"; the Virgin and Saint (Joan)/the harlot (all other French women: Joan will chase the "bad women" from her camp); the civilizing, clean, beautiful American women/the dirty, ugly other women, the corrupting French; his wife and daughters/the others. The first are extolled by their men who put them on pedestals since they are their properties. Twain could not tolerate any gross conduct (Bret Harte's, for instance) to Mrs. Samuel Clemens. He settled her in a house with children, made her a housekeeper, his secretary, while the household was centered on him and his needs. Neither Susy nor Jean could become independent adults: they died still connected with the house; when Jean died, his greatest regret was that he was going to be left alone again, and that his last dream of settling down in a cozy family life with her had disappeared. Like the Brontës' father, he survived most of his family. Though his wife was to him "the most honest, the most beautiful, the most perfect creature," allowed to criticize his manuscripts, apparently she had no brains and was unable to judge of moral matters and art, since he felt he had to expurgate her readings: *Gil Blas* and *Gulliver's Travels* would offend her, and even *Don Quixote* had to be "prepared for her as usual."[15] This pattern is so common that it is unnecessary to insist on it. That simplism led him, however, to commit at least two remarkably ridiculous productions: a revised version of the story of Heloise and Abelard in which Heloise becomes a poor victim raped by the man who has stepped out of his role of protector of pure womanhood; and "In Defense of Harriet Shelley," probably inspired by Harriet Beecher Stowe's *Lady Byron Vindicated*, which could almost make Twain appear as a feminist in his gallant support of the betrayed wife if one did not soon discover that what ails him most—totally ignoring Shelley's views on marriage—is that some men and women could, by their very lives and theories, attack the fundamental pillar of society and of his own little world: the institution of marriage. His nasty remarks about

Godwin, Mary Godwin, and all free and bold thinkers can seem surprising to those who see him as a challenger of racism against blacks and Jews, an iconoclast who attacked the Established Church, the monarchies of Europe, and the corruption of Washington, but who ignore his admiration for the Emperor of Russia and Napoleon III, and his hatred of the "Injuns," and of communism and socialism. About the women's movement of the time he says very little; the women he knew who were involved, he disparaged. When he finally concedes women ought to get the vote, it is with the most conservative arguments typical of many Americans at the time. White American women must get the vote to counterbalance the colored people and the ignorant immigrants.[16]

Those views interfered with his treatment of Laura Hawkins, the most elaborate of his portraits of white American women. The other woman in *The Gilded Age*, Ruth Bolton, is a feminist, but she was entirely conceived by Charles Dudley Warner.[17] She wishes to study medicine, asserts she wants to be something, to have a profession, "to be independent"; then her "love would be a free act and not in any way a necessity"; "women are put in a box," she says. Ultimately, Ruth will convince Philip, the man she loves; at no moment is the character made to be ridiculous: Twain does not meddle with her. On the contrary, Laura was his creation; but Chapter 18 dealing with her fake marriage, her betrayal by Selby, and the ensuing transformation that was to make her a criminal, had to be handled by Warner. From that chapter on, Twain's views are mixed with Warner's and produce a strange compendium. At no moment in the book does either Twain, or Warner, when he takes charge, clearly accuse society, or more directly, Selby of having victimized Laura. Even Dickens, in the case of Little Emily, manages to persuade the reader that he keeps some distance from the mores of a society that entirely condemns the woman who is first an "angel" and then is made to "fall," and he clearly names the responsible man. But once she learns of Selby's deceit, Laura, almost magically, turns into an entirely dark contriver to end up a murderess, transforming parts of the novel into melodrama. In Chapter 18, we find the following passage: "Nature must needs be lavish with the mother and creator of men, and center in her all the possibilities of life. And a few critical years can decide whether her life is to be full of sweetness and delight, whether she is to be the vestal of a holy temple, or whether she will be the fallen priestess of a desecrated shrine. There are women, it is true, who seem to be capable neither of rising much, nor of falling much, and whom a conventional life saves from any special development of character." That vision of woman as either "a vestal" or "a fallen priestess" defines her only in relation to her sexuality, channeled into the holy function of marriage and motherhood or perverted by passion and sex. That passage also reveals a possible reason for the absence of women from Twain's novels: if only those who rise much (the saints?) and those who fall much (he would not speak of them) did not have a conventional life saving them from "special development of character," then he felt there was nothing to say of the mass of ordinary women, impossible literary subjects—a position which, we shall see, goes beyond the matter of Twain's misogyny and involves a conception of fiction different from the novelistic level of manners. So, even for Warner who could create Ruth, Laura is a contaminated person. In other words, Ruth, who will marry and so keep in line, can be accepted as a feminist, but Laura, who won't, must be depraved, and her attempts at independence must be of the "wrong" sort. In Chapter 18, it is said that not only had she read many books with false ideas of romance and heroism, "but along with these ideas she imbibed other very crude ones in regard to the emancipation of women." In chapters 39, 41, and 46, written by Warner, women's rights are condemned in relation to Laura: "She may have heard, doubtless she had, similar theories of the tyranny of marriage and of the freedom of marriage." When the murder is committed, the newspaper of the day prints the following news: "This morning occurred another of those shocking murders which have become the almost daily food of the newspapers, the direct result of the socialistic doctrines and woman's rights agitations, which have made every woman the avenger of her own wrongs, and all society the hunting ground for her victims," a comment apparently approved by the novelists. In Chapter 58, written by Warner, Laura, acquitted, is at a loss to find a living and is offered a frequent occupation of the time, a lecture tour. "What should I lecture about?" she asks. "Oh, why, woman—something about woman, I should say; the marriage relation, woman's fate, anything of that sort. Call it The Revelations of a Woman's Life; now, there's a good title." There is irony there, but Warner still considers lecturing a possible way out for Laura. Not so with Twain who finishes her off quickly, eliminating her in the cruellest way, first by killing her character, then her personality, by making her recant, then fail, then die. In Chapter 60, she is made to long for a more womanly attitude: "a strong yearning came upon her to lay her head upon a loyal breast and find rest from the conflict of life, solace for her griefs, the healing of love for her bruised heart"; and then, "Love," she said, "was a woman's first necessity." Twain adds: "Love being forfeited, one solution was left to her, fame, applause, the applause of the multitude." "She would turn to that final resort of the disappointed of her sex, the lecture platform." To him, lecturing, no doubt, was reserved for his sex to thrive on, as he himself did. Stepping into public and political life for a woman could only mean being frustrated in her love life. But that is not all. Twain stages an exit for his character that is a real revenge for the murder of the male. Stepping on the platform on her first night, she finds "a vast, brilliant emptiness," "coarse men and coarser women" who only hiss her. After that humiliation, of course, she can only die: her heart, "stubborn" but "repenting," just stops.

That end reveals Twain's meanness about certain subjects, woman's emancipation in particular.

No other complete female portrait emerges from his work. Only some passing figures here and there, such as the sixteen traveling ladies of *The Innocents Abroad*. In *Roughing It*, history helps the novelist: "Woman" was a "rare spectacle" in those days (Ch. 57). Mary, Tom Sawyer's cousin, a child too, seems rather on the adult side since her only brief function is to make him recite and to go to church with him. Amy Lawrence and Becky Thatcher are dull little girls seen from the point of view of the boy. In *Huckleberry Finn*, Mary Jane is barely sketched; she only plays the role Huck assigns to her. Among grown women, Aunt Polly, the widow Douglas, Miss Watson (too cumbersome, she is made to die), Aunt Sally, Mrs. Loftus are all reasonable asexual entities seen only through the eyes of the lads, centering their lives on them, busy with feeding, cleaning, scolding, educating them, and crying for and over them. Obviously they could not live without the lads, so important their "civilizing" function seemed to be. But after all, that is all their society left them with. And the point of view chosen by the novelist, the boy's, justifies the absence of reference to the total person. So, we know nothing about their clothes, their bodies, their feelings, tastes, friends; when they meet other adults, it is to speak of the boys. Thinking of Peggotty and Miss Trotwood, one then admires Dickens's art. In *A Connecticut Yankee*, we can find two women; but Morgan is the Fay, and we saw Hank Morgan's comment on his companion Sandy. We are left with two cases that we shall dismiss for the moment: Roxana, majestic, "full of character," "shapely, intelligent, comely, even beautiful," full of drive, enterprise, the masterworker of the situation, challenging all conventions. But black—all male critics insist on this (yet they never add about Jim, "but" he is black). Joan, that case of "gyneolatry,"[18] perfectly beautiful, intelligent, pure, noble, the constant presence, the prime mover of the action, is no creation, she is historical. *Joan of Arc* is not a novel, but a biography. She is no woman; Twain insists, she is a virgin, another "vestal" of some "holy temple," the purest of the pure, the martyr already, the saint almost. She is also in part the portrait of the beloved Livy, and the same terms are used in the biography and in the *Love Letters*. So she is in many ways on the side of venerable women. Finally, neither man nor woman, rather both (as we shall see), Joan is above all "the most extraordinary person the human race has ever produced" ("Saint Joan of Arc"), "the most noble life that was ever born into this world save only One" (Preface). A female Christ figure then, opposed to the satanic mysterious stranger. Unique. She is no woman then; the woman is Eve.

All this being said, well known, and admitted, reflections come to mind that temper this image of Twain as a misogynist.

First, he was a product of his time. Cooper, Melville, Dickens, Galsworthy, Conrad, Kipling were mostly interested in men. Hawthorne, James, Thackeray, Hardy had more "of the woman" in them and so are more complete writers. In the 1870s and 1880s, no male novelist frankly took sides with the women's movement.[19] As to the pattern set in the boys' stories, it was very common at the time and had been initiated before him; he only imitated in fact. Aldrich's *The Story of a Bad Boy* had appeared in 1869; Eggleston, in *The Hoosier Schoolmaster* (1871), used the Indiana vernacular before Twain ever thought of using seven types of dialects. Warner published *Being a Boy* in 1878. Twain knew those works. *Peck's Bad Boy and His Pa* appeared in 1883, and Howells's *A Boy's Town* in 1890. In all those stories, parents are nonexistent, boys live to parade in front of girls or to eliminate them. Hannibal, like Flat Creek, Rivermouth, Boy's Town, Boyville, later Whilomville and Lawrenceville, is a masculine world, where challenge, action, pranks, fights, lickings dominate. The "real" boy is in fact the bad boy—indeed the future delinquent. More reflective than the others, Howells in *A Boy's Town*, underlines the opposition betwen "outward boy" and "inner boy," and complains: "The boy *has* to be a boy," he must conform to an image imposed from the outside; the child lives a more secret life, "the cloud-dweller's life," and is made to feel ashamed of it and keep it a secret (Ch. 16). Howells was very conscious of the fact that the various episodes described in his novel—"the river," "schools and teachers," "circuses and shows," "guns and gunning," the pleasures of hunting, the Indian myth—were all contributing to forming a generation of extroverted boys needed at the time, and to creating the fundamental myths of American literature and culture.

Another set of reflections leads us to consider Twain's evolution and his intellectual inconsistencies. He should have engendered inconsistent critics like himself. I myself accept the charge of inconsistency; it is fitting in this case. So after having called Twain a misogynist, I immediately add he was also just the opposite of one. My evidence is not Joan, that admirable girl—and French at that!—but less obvious examples, for the moment. If Hank, the Yankee, says of Sandy: "She was a perfect blatherskite," he immediately adds: "but just as good as she could be." And at the end of the book, the astounded reader discovers that through some magic trick, they are married and have a child, and that Hank says: "Ah, Sandy, what a right heart she had, how simple and genuine and good she was! She was a flawless wife and mother . . . People talk about beautiful friendship between two persons of the same sex. What is the best of that sort as compared with the friendship of man and wife where the best impulses and the highest ideals of both are the same? There is no place for comparison between the two friendships; the one is earthly, the other divine."[20] This was written at least nineteen years after the author's marriage to Olivia Langdon. In *Adam's Diary*, in the same way, ten years later, Adam concludes in his last entry: "After all these years,

I see that I was mistaken about Eve in the beginning; it is better to live out-side the Garden with her than inside without her. At first I thought she talked too much; but now I should be sorry to have that voice fall silent and pass out of my life. Blessed be the chestnut that brought us together and taught me to know the goodness of her heart and the sweetness of her spirit." Those qualities are still of the heart, not of the mind; but that confession of the need for a company more essential than man's is far from the rejection of *Roughing It*. Clemens has become mature. Certainly. But that comment shows that Twain's criticism of women is essentially based on traditional jokes; women can be more roughly handled by worse misogynists; in the twentieth century, when sexuality invades fiction, they will even become mere sex objects. I am not bothered by Twain's "sexual squeamishness" (or James's refusal to dwell on sexuality); for him, as for many other people, sex must have been a private matter; he was perfectly happy with his wife; that was his life, not literature. And I happen to think, as a twentieth century person, that it is almost a relief, now, to be able to read writers who avoided seeing only sex in women and had other things to say. In brief, Twain's attitude toward women seems to be the familiar: "difficult with, impossible without." All in all, there is worse criticism of men in his works, and even of boys, than of women and girls. And that from the very beginning.

Indeed, he has no fully convincing portraits of men either. Huck and Tom are kids. Jim is as black as Roxy—even more; and he is just as disguised as she is. Pap Finn, so darkly horrible, belongs to melodrama. The Yankee is a type, no more an individual, Hank Morgan, than Gulliver or Samuel Butler's Higgs. Tom Canty and Edward are children. Pudd'nhead plays a minor role in spite of his philosophy. No. 44 is omnipresent but has too much of Satan in him—or of the magician. Judge Driscoll, Senator Dilworthy, Colonel Sellers, Colonel Selby, Colonel Shelburn, the Grangerford men? The King? (which?) The Duke? We don't know their lives; they are sketches, attitudes, moments, roles. There are no real women; there are no real men in his work. Because he was not interested in psychology; he was after something else. Not so much humor or not only humor, but making people act, showing them as a magi-cian might, in certain situations, confronting certain possibilities. In the same way, there are as many biting remarks on male individuals, and on men gen-erally, as on women. Cooper, Paul Bourget, Bret Harte to mention a few, were scathingly and unsparingly scorched alive in essays that were almost libels. If to him Frenchwomen are all harlots, Frenchmen are "savages," "gorillas," "hybrids," the last link between "man and the monkey."[21] The male "Injuns," the senators, the men in power through the centuries, the soldiers-murderers, the men of the clergy who could burn Joan alive, are all *men*, not women. What is man? Nothing much ultimately, almost a "rat"; "dirt," Satan says; and Satan, fittingly, looks like a "boy" for "that is what he is."[22] Clearly for Twain, Man is man; with woman alone lies the hope of some regeneration. This civilizing process has always been derided by Twain's critics, who have harped on the image of his "taming" wife taking profanity out of his manuscripts and probably all the pep too, while all his autobiographical writings suggest that Twain appealed for that sort of influence and that anyway, he was the greater influence of the two. It is, in fact, Twain himself who, clearly, from the beginning, rejects the image of the "rough" boy. Even in 1872, in *Roughing It*, he deplores that "the rough element predominates and that a person is not respected unless he has killed his man."[23] At the same time, that type of man is a coward. The boys playing at being soldiers in "A Campaign That Failed" cannot bear to see their first dead man, and one of them, the narrator, confesses: "My campaign was spoiled. It seemed to me that I was not rightly equipped for this awful business, that war was intended for men and I for a child's nurse." In the same vein, in a letter to J.H. Burroughs written November 1, 1876, Twain writes about himself: "Ignorance, intolerance, egotism, self-assertion, opaque perception, dense and pitiful chuckle-headedness, and an almost pathetic unconsciousness of it all. That is what I was at 19–20, and that is what the average Southerner is at 60 today. Northerners too of a certain grade." Himself too? The boys, anyway. But it is in *Joan of Arc* that the debunking of the myth of the boys is accomplished.

At the beginning of the biography, in Book I, Chapter 4, an episode taking place during Joan's childhood reveals a new essential quality of her character, bravery, as well as the first signs of the fundamental things Twain will accomplish in the disguise of Louis de Conte. In the village of Domrémy, the boys and the girls talk about the King and the Queen and about how France could be dragged so low. Noël, Pierre, and the Paladin start *talking*, wishing they were able to go and fight: "Oh, are we never going to be men!" "If I could only be a soldier now!" "There are some who, in storming a castle, prefer to be in the rear; but as for me, give me the front row or none; I will have none in front of me but the officers." The girls in turn wish they were men too, to save their country: "Pooh!" said the Paladin "girls can brag, but that's all they are good for." Little Joan arrives, and they all laugh at the idea that she, too, might wish to go to the battlefield. The Paladin keeps imagining her as an officer, or a captain: "Certainly it was a funny idea—at that time—I mean the idea of that gentle creature, that wouldn't hurt a fly, and couldn't bear the sight of blood, and was so girlish and shrinking in all ways, rushing to the battle with a gang of soldiers at her back." Twain has evidently inserted this episode intentionally, as well as the next one. Behind the Fairy Tree appears the head of Crazy Benoist, "ragged, hairy, and horrible," raising an ax as he comes. All flee except Joan who stops and begins to talk with him. When they all come back, Joan stands with the ax in her hand. Everybody hugs her, but she goes and hides "to get relief from the embarrassment of *glory*." The boys begin to *talk* again to give account of their cowardice, "telling the brave things they would say and the wonders they would do" if it happened again. That reveals Joan's self-forgetfulness; it is also a reversal of traditional roles and a bitter satire of the "boy." No wonder then that Joan, who was afraid about how to obey the Shadow's command, about how she could "talk with men, be comrade with men-soldiers,"[24] finally became their general and transformed them from braggarts to heroes accomplishing great feats. When she is a prisoner and thus absent, they lose and are nothing. Woman is not only to be followed because she is selfless and animated by the best and the highest, but without her, man is nothing. This is one of the clear messages of the book for those who perceive it is not only a historical biography, but Twain's invention too. In Book II, Chapter 3, after a five nights' walk, the men are surprised to see she is the only one alert: "There, it shows you how men can have eyes and yet not see. All their lives those men had seen their women folks hitched up with a cow and dragging the plow in the fields while the men did the driving. They had also seen other evidences that women have far more endurance and patience and fortitude than men—but what good had their seeing these things been to them? None . . . a great soul with a great purpose can make a weak body strong and keep it so." So Joan is not really unique; her qualities are also those of women. Joan turns the Paladin into a courageous soldier, and La Hire, the "tough old lion," "a cyclopedia of sin," riding by her side, becomes "tame and civilized." All men "wondered at her," and then they "worshipped," as Twain did with his wife; all men with women; Adam with Eve.

Which throws a new light on *Huckleberry Finn*. If "the nomadic instinct," the free life on the raft and in the woods, "lighting out into the territory" is not to be "cramped up and civilized" by women, it also, always, gets "lonely," and expeditions to the woods or on the Mississippi always alternate with visits to the shore—which is also civilization, but the boys' civilization this time. For there are no women on shore, there is no place for them in a world of murders, fraud, profit, lynching, cowardice, egoism; all the people they meet are men. Aunt Sally appears only at the end of the trip after that initiation into male violence. All the others play at being men; they are all the more bragging and violent as they are no real braves. As Shelburn says, "The average man's a coward." Clearly, if the raft is a momentary solution, it is more a help to get away from man's world, Pap's gun and snakes, than from woman's world, the widow's regular meals; women have power only over the household and the school; all the rest depends on men and is irrevocably rejected.

Mark Twain's world is an all-American male world, but it could not be otherwise in his time. That is a first unifying pattern of his whole opus. It is not because of a strong conscious antifeminism on his part: he hated men as much as he hated women; he loved women more. A "sanguine temperament" can only love or hate. In fact he rather oscillates between the masculine and the feminine worlds, two poles that alternately attract, confront, and reject each other. The passing from one to the other, the constant *intrusion* from the feminine into the masculine, or the masculine into the feminine reveals more of Twain than the study of these worlds. And so, one must show two other fundamental structures in his whole corpus. They lead to a level-two reading of his works. The first structure appears in the confrontation of the dates of publication, times of composition, and periods covered by his most important works. It brings to light a constant movement away from the present toward the past, from America to Europe. The second structure consists of the multiplication and metamorphosis of opposed poles, the masculine and the feminine worlds, man and woman, being, with past and present, only two of many pairs included in that structure. Brought together, these two structures point to a third pattern in which Twain's specificity must be found: confrontation and intrusion, transgression and disguise. Twain was a chameleon. He took the colors and the forms of the world he moved in, a King's Court, nothing less, King Carnival's Court. He cavorted along, changing patterns, wearing all the masks of His Majesty's Pranksters, chameleonlike. And that was much more the realization of the wildest dreams of young Sam Clemens than being "only" a humorist, cramped up by America's so-called civilization.

*Level Two Reading:*
*Literary "Mystery," or Twain, the Mysterious Stranger*

Let us begin by examining the following list of Twain's long works, classified according to their dates of publication.[25]

| TITLE | PUBLICATION | COMPOSITION | PLACE AND PERIOD | |
|---|---|---|---|---|
| The Innocents Abroad | 1869 | Mar.–Apr. 1868 | Europe | June–Nov. 1867 |
| Roughing It | 1872 | 1872 | U.S. | 1861–1867 |
| The Gilded Age | 1873 | Winter 72–May 73 | U.S. | 1840s–1870s |
| Tom Sawyer | 1876 | 1870–July 1875 | U.S. | 1830s or 1840s |
| A Tramp Abroad | 1880 | 1878–1880 | Europe | 1878–79 |
| The Prince and the Pauper | 1881 | 1877–1881 | England | 1547 |
| Life on the Mississippi | 1883 | 1875–1882 | U.S. | 1) 1857–1861 |
| | | | | 2) 1882: M.T. |
| | | | | 3) 1542 on: |
| | | | | Mississippi |
| Huckleberry Finn | 1885 | July 76–Sept .83 | U.S. | 1830s–1840s |

| | | | | |
|---|---|---|---|---|
| *A Connecticut Yankee* | 1889 | 1886–1889 | England | 1) 1470: Th. Malory<br>2) 6th Century |
| *Pudd'nhead Wilson* | 1894 | 1890s | U.S. | 1) 1830–<br>1853–55 |
| *Joan of Arc* | 1896 | 1893–1895 and ten years research | France | 1412–1431 |
| *The Mysterious Stranger* | 1916–1969 | | | |
| Version A:<br>St. Petersburg Fragment | | 1897 | U.S. | 1840s |
| Version B:<br>The Chronicle of<br>Young Satan | | Nov. 1897–<br>Sept. 1900 | Austria | 1702 |
| Version C:<br>Schoolhouse Hill | | Nov.–Dec. 1898 | U.S. | 1840s |
| Version D:<br>No. 44 The<br>Mysterious Stranger | | 1902–1908 | Austria | 1490 |

One notices several things studying this table. First, the oscillations in space and time from America to Europe and from present to past. The settings and the periods first alternate, but the ascension toward the past is almost systematic. If Twain's favorite periods were 1840-1880 and the fifteenth and sixteenth centuries (he ignored the seventeenth after 1601 and disliked the eighteenth), the movement backward is steady and irreversible. In *The Innocents*, he speaks of the year 1867, and in *Roughing It*, of the time between 1861 and 1867; with *The Gilded Age, Tom Sawyer, A Tramp Abroad, Life on the Mississippi, Huckleberry Finn*, and *Pudd'nhead Wilson*, we move further back between the 1830s and the 1870s. In the remote past, the action of *The Prince and the Pauper* takes place in 1547; then the history of the Mississippi River is told from its discovery by de Soto in 1542, since de Soto was "the first white man who ever saw the Mississippi River"; the Connecticut Yankee is moved back to the sixth century, but in fact to Thomas Malory's 1470 vision of it; then Joan of Arc's life takes us to between 1412 and 1431; *The Chronicle of Young Satan* version taking place in 1702 is abandoned for a further move back to 1490. Critics generally say that Twain was unable to carry on in his best vein, the rendering of Western America, since "the tank ran dry." It is not only that; he was also deeply fascinated and attracted by the past from the very beginning; he had in fact two and even several "tanks." Indeed, in July 1870, an article of his was published in *The Galaxy*, "The tournament in A.D. 1870,"[26] about a medieval tournament organized in Brooklyn, a confrontation that will be reversed in *A Connecticut Yankee*. *The Innocents Abroad* is as much about the past of the various countries visited as about the reactions of contemporary American tourists to them. The crucial period for the development of this pattern is between the years 1875 and 1883. Of those eight years, seven years were needed to compose *Life on the Mississippi* and *Huckleberry Finn*. *The Prince and the Pauper* took only four years and was ultimately published before the other two. Clearly enough, he felt more at ease in 1547 than in the nineteenth century. *Life on the Mississippi* is a turning point, for it is as much about Clemens's past (recent, in 1882, more distant in 1857-61) on the Mississippi, as about the river's past. A study of the composition of the four versions of *The Mysterious Stranger*, as revealed to us by William Gibson,[27] also shows that twice the Hannibal environment was proving a sterile hunt and was discarded in favor of a past European setting. Version A was revised and worked into Version B, and references to the 1840s disappeared; then Version C, also written relatively quickly, is left aside together with its allusions to Clemens's Hannibal boyhood; and No. 44 is made to play his magic and satanic tricks in the Austria of 1490.

Notice too that with the years, Twain spent more and more time writing his works. That is a well-known fact. It is generally supposed to mean that he had problems with the structures of his works, problems of inspiration, as he himself often states, or personal problems in his life. He probably did. But why not consider too, in a more positive way, that the writer aimed at a greater artistic effort to elaborate something more important to him than the mere reproduction of reality and of his own experience? That was too easy game for him. His first three works were written extremely quickly; practically no time separates the lived experience and its reproduction in written words; they all come from notes, and the process involved is journalistic and documentary; Twain was merely telling about himself, what he knew. With *Tom Sawyer* and *Huckleberry Finn*, literary personae appear; invention, combination is more important. He insisted on it in his Preface: "Huck Finn is drawn from life; Tom Sawyer also, but not from an individual—he is a *combination* of the characteristics of three boys whom I knew, and therefore belongs to the *composite order of architecture*." The latter expression is worth pondering, not to search for the real names of those three boys and so maintain Twain at the duplicating level, but because it reveals his mind was then mostly interested in the "composite" level of true invention, and in manipulating reality. This relatively easy transition is followed by greater and greater imaginative effort, more sophisticated "combinations" and confrontations, characters more and more distant from the ordinary and the conventional: a pair of twins, a black woman, a martyr dressed as a man, Satan in gracious guise.

Then if, as he said in "What Is Man?" and "Pudd'nhead Wilson's Calendar," "Training is everything," man's training is "toward higher and higher, and even higher ideals," and that is worth "any man's thought and labor and diligence." With such views, no doubt Twain considered that he had to elevate himself from himself, his youth, his past, or the time of his past, toward the past of the United States and of Europe, then the past of humanity, its very origin which led him, of course, to the philosophical vein of the end of his life, to considerations about Satan, Adam and Eve, lost paradises, in a backward quest from manners to mystery, from the anecdotal to the essential.

Finally, it appears that in several works, Twain was more interested in putting present and past side by side, in confronting them, than in dwelling upon one particular period. In his introduction to his *Autobiography* (which is, as all his readers know, *not* chronological), he insists on what he considers the originality of his method: "I intend that this autobiography shall become a model for all future autobiographies when it is published, after my death, and I also intend that it shall be read and admired a good many centuries because of its form and method—a form and method whereby the past and the present are constantly brought face to face resulting in contrasts which newly fire up the interest all along like contact of flint with steel." The point is in the contrasts. The innocents must go abroad; the 1840s must be compared with the 1870s; medieval times must clash with the modern period; even 1490 has to face the endless procession of the past back to Arthur, and even Noah and Eve, conjured up by 44, the magician who moves the clock backward (oh! Carroll, oh! Wells) at the end of *The Mysterious Stranger*.

Confrontation between America and Europe, Present and Past if a unifying structure of Twain's works, is only one of many other confrontations between extremes or opposites. Many are the opposed poles in his work. The young man and the old man (dialogue of "What Is Man?"); the Yankee/King Arthur; the nineteenth/the sixth centuries; the Pauper/the Prince; more generally, the powerful and corrupted/the people, the crowd; the peasants of Hannibal and Domrémy/the courts of kings; Huck and Jim, the natural men/Tom, the dreamer and the knight; naive Huck and Jim/the frauds, the Duke and the Dauphin; reality/dream; the white man/the black man; Joan's saintly actions/the mysterious stranger's satanic ones; the humorous and the vernacular/the romantic, the rhetorical, and the sentimental; the anecdote/the essay; the burlesques, the satires/autobiography, biographies. One can go on endlessly. In short, the grotesque and the sublime. The oldest literary tradition. Twain plays endlessly with those poles: he juxtaposes them, hesitates, mixes, mars one with the other, consciously confronts them to fire up a new interest. He launches a man in Hadleyburg and revels in describing the ensuing disorder and corruption; a Satan or a Saint, both magicians, appear in the middle of a town or a country and food, cats, and men are metamorphosed. This is what has been taken for disorder, incoherence, inability to keep in a fixed track; whereas it is exactly what Twain is up to: transgression, disguise, intrusion. There is no Mark Twain; there is a Sam Clemens that invented a mask, Mark Twain, and spent his time playing at being Sam Twain or Mark Clemens and intruding into the bodies and clothes of the people he created. That structure explains many aspects of his work usually considered as shortcomings. Take the famous end of *Huckleberry Finn*, for instance. It is fitting that Tom Sawyer's wild schemes and "style" should so complicate a simple escape, as it is fitting that the raft drifting toward free territory is made in fact to head South; as it is fitting that the little nest of the raft should be interfered with by the violence of the shore and of the river, themselves intruded upon and violated by the elaborations of the two frauds from the river. In that light, Roxy's interference, from the outside, substituting one boy for the other and putting each in the other's environment, symbolically represents the plottings of the dark magician, the writer, who interferes with his characters, transfers them into new, invented, combined settings to see what might happen. All the more since black Roxy, in fact, looks white. Joan of Arc, entering upon the scene of the Hundred Years War, a girl, intruding into a man's world, alters it completely with her very personal set of values. In the same way, the boys Tom and Huck intrude upon the world of adults when spying in the churchyard and testifying in court; just as Huck is intruded upon when seized by the benevolent widow or captured by awful Finn. There is no end to those infinitely combined games. Joan herself and her world of goodness has to be meddled with by the Satanic world—if one may say so!—of the Established Church that will take her to the stake. Intrusion from one world into another necessitates the mixture of tones, the marring of the serious by the comic, of the heroic by the burlesque, of the sublime by the parodic. It carries with it the need for alteration of identity and for disguise. In such a perspective, reality is never stable; and being a fraud, wearing a mask, lying, is the only possible way of expressing the real. So the fraud is the emblem of such a representation of the world. Huck's several identities are well known ("Sarah Mary Williams George Elexander Peters"), he is even Tom Sawyer while the latter is Sid. Joan of Arc is Joan the Bashful, the Beautiful, and the Brave at Domrémy. She then becomes Joan the Maid, the Maid of Orléans, is made Lady du Lys by the King (a title quickly rejected), and we all know she shall be Joan the Saint, metamorphosed by the flames of the stake. Jim is disguised by the Duke (himself a humbug about to pass off as Uncle William Wilks, after having been the actor Garrick the Younger playing Romeo) dressed up in "King Lear's outfit," of course a fake one, only "a long curtain-calico gown, and a white horsehair wig and whiskers," with his face painted all blue, like a drowned man, supposed to be a "Sick Arab—but harmless when not out of his head" (Ch. 24).

Till 1885, Twain mostly plays with transferring his males from one male world to another male world and so with disguising them as other males. The innocent American becomes a brutal uncivilized chauvinist abroad; the pioneers of *Roughing It*, according to circumstances, turn into silver-miners, journalists, secretaries like their creator, or into desperadoes, bullies, outlaws, Mormons, Chinese, nabobs. Tom becomes a knight, a pirate, the real witness of a real murder. The prince and the pauper, the Yankee and Arthur merely confront two male civilizations. But with *Huckleberry Finn, Pudd'nhead* and *Joan of Arc*, a new pattern emerges, corresponding to the greater sophistication of Twain and to the assertion of the first pattern I spoke of. He multiplies the intrusion of the male element into the female world, or of the female element into the male world, with slightly different purposes and effects. In *Huckleberry Finn*, Twain is more interested in acting, which explains the intrusion of the Duke and the Dauphin onto the raft. It is immediately transformed into a stage with its wooden boards, its main actors (the two intruders) substituted for the first owners now playing subsidiary roles, and the wigwam serving as curtains and backstage. In Elizabethan times, perpetuated on the raft, actors were all men, and so it is appropriate that the supposed Duke of Bilgewater, in turn, printer, doctor, theater actor, phrenologist, lecturer, and the exiled rightful King of France, also doctor "for cancer and paralysis," fortune teller, preacher "missionaryin' around," should first think of disguising themselves into actors; the duke turning the king into "Edmund Kean" playing Juliet, finds the right argument to convince him: "Besides, you know, you'll be in costume, and that makes all the difference in the world." It does indeed. Costume makes the man . . . and the woman. Huck cannot fool Mrs. Loftus: a girl "throws her knees apart" trying to catch something in her dress; her dress has *trained* her to behave like a girl, to be a girl. In the same way, Joan's "male attire" will make a man of her. Which can only mean that being male or female is as much the result of conditioning as of nature. In *Pudd'nhead*, disguise is again used to show that training is everything, that men are only playing a part decided for them from the outside. The exchange brought about by Roxy substituting for her son, Valet de Chambre (henceforward called Tom Driscoll), Tommy Driscoll or Thomas à Becket, her master's son (henceforward called Chambers), involves exchange of identities, environment, social class, race, complicated by the fact that Roxy's real son looks white, though he has black blood. In Chapter 4, that first switch of identities brings forth a metamorphosis in Roxana herself. So far a slave of the whites, but as a mother, a queen, she becomes a slave to her son turned into her new master; even if she is made a free woman in Percy Driscoll's will: "All that was left was master, master pure and simple, and it was not a gentle mastership. She saw herself sink from the sublime height of motherhood to the somber depths of unmodified slavery." A situation which reminds us of *Une Vie* by Maupassant, a writer with whom Twain has much in common. From Chapter 10 to Chapter 16, Tom Driscoll uses disguise as a way to hide his crimes; in his "suit of girl's clothes," he raids Patsy Cooper's and escapes wearing his mother's clothes, looking like a "stoop-shouldered woman." In Chapter 19, when he kills Judge Driscoll, he blackens his face with burnt cork, thus disguising himself into "the nigger in him," and escapes in his suit of girl's clothes. In that novel, Count Luigi, a good man, passes for an assassin; Tom, a murderer, for an honest man; Roxy when honest, for a thief. Only our fingerprints can stand proof for our real identities; the games of life, circumstances, training can falsely transform all the rest: race, sex, relationships, "gait, attitudes, gestures, bearing, laugh, manners"; the real heir of the Driscolls, his estate restored to him, can only feel at home and at peace "in the kitchen."

In *Joan of Arc*, Twain brought his ideas, and his disguise pattern, to their highest achievement. Joan is first a "flawless, ideal, perfect," "entirely unselfish" person confronted with a world of curs (the King), rascals, low and debased ingrates (the English and the French), traitors (the Church). She is a peasant from a village brought to Court, like the pauper. But she is mostly a girl in a man's world; and a much better man than any man. In Twain's "Saint Joan of Arc," she is shown as having "military genius, leonine courage, incomparable fortitude, a prodigy of a mind," and also an orator's gift, an advocate's gift, a judge's gift, a statesman's gift. She was ignorant and became a commander-in-chief; she was "a cattle-pasturing peasant," and she crowned a king. Her father is the first to accuse her of "unsexing" herself. History has shown how wearing "male attire" was also held against Joan by her judges. But Twain repeats that famous accusation again and again and obviously defends her on that point in the most modern way. He even becomes her champion for that. For one obvious reason: he cannot but defend disguise. In the long tradition of misogynist literature, woman's make-up, her artifice, her love for dressing, acting, lying is constantly reviled. Not so with Twain. He emphasizes the fact that the court touched upon "the matter of her apparel," asked her to wear a woman's dress; she is ultimately reproached for "doing man's work in the wars and thus deserting the industries proper to her sex"; she is made to promise to resume "the male habit," then is reproached for not doing it. Finally when she is brought to the stake, it seems that her fundamental heresy is not her refusal to accept the law of the Established Church (and her substituting for it her own personal intuitive contact with the Deity, a belief of American Transcendentalists, by the way), but her refusal to keep to the role assigned to her by her society, by men and religion. She is burnt because she is a woman. If one sees that in Joan, her male attire is central. She is a peasant girl who dresses as a soldier in armor, and then even in prison she dresses like a man. This is the other reason for which Twain champions her. He and she think that among men, it is not only more becoming to dress like a man (in Part I, Chapter 9, a court allows her "to wear men's clothes, since she must do the work of a man and soldier"), but (since "costume makes all the difference in the world") that dressing like a man, she will become one. And an even better one than they are, for she is a better person; so she is more entitled than men to wear men's clothes. At the end of Chapter 21, she says that the Bastard and La Hire are real men, but the Council, who wish to stop her in her progress are only "disguised ladies' maids." Moreover, after all her achievements, Joan wishes to go back to her village if she could get out of prison (Part II, Chapter 7). Then, she says, she would wear her woman's clothes again; in the prison, it is impossible. They knew, Louis de Conte insists (Chapter 12), that one of the reasons was that "soldiers of the guard were always present in her room whether she was asleep or awake and that the male dress was a better protection for her modesty than the other." A very modern way of seeing the advantages of a very convenient garb. One can understand why Twain called that work "the apple of my eye."

There are other reasons. It is a pity that book has been so neglected by American readers and critics. One may guess why. It is about History; about French and English History; about a woman, and a Frenchwoman; matters of no immediate concern to Americans. They refused to follow Twain and to rehabilitate Joan as Quicherat had done, then Michelet. They decided those matters had to be irrelevant to the "best Twain" as they had decided to define him. I maintain that it is only by considering that work seriously (and *The Prince and the Pauper* as well), and not separately, but along with the other works of Twain, that one can begin, if one is interested in that writer, just begin to understand what he was really up to. Moreover one is surprised to see how well written the biography is, how elegant it is, how easily it reads from beginning to end, how even humor is smoothly mixed into it and never jars with lyrical passages, how tenderness pervades it. Clearly Twain felt very much at ease with it. Because he could harmoniously reconcile here the opposite poles of his work and find in history a confirmation of ideas important to him. History gave him the narrative line, so that the "tank" could not "run dry." History was bringing proof that the wildest dreams can come true. Already Tom Canty, who dreamed of seeing the real Prince or of becoming one himself, had started imagining in his dreams he was one, then acted being one, "organizing a royal court" in which, daily, "the mock prince was received with elaborate ceremonials borrowed by Tom from his romantic readings," an acting that worked such an effect on him that he began "to *act* the prince, unconsciously." The double meaning of "to act" shows the elaborate process of disguise and reality in Twain. To the point that Tom's personality has changed: "His speech and manners became curiously ceremonious and courtly, to the vast admiration and amusement of his intimates." When he meets the Prince for good, and in spite of himself is made to be the Prince, his dream has come true. He is metamorphosed into one. And the real Prince on English roads with Hendon—suggesting Don

Quixote and Sancho, and announcing Joan and La Hire—discovers his country and tries to save his nation. All those elements are found in *Joan of Arc* too, but carried further. For Twain is aware that Tom Canty's adventure was only fabricated by him and so remained a dream for the two of them, creator and persona. But Joan, the peasant, dreamed of saving her land, of getting to the King's Court and even of crowning him; and she did it for real, in history, not in a romance! She, a girl, accomplished in reality the wildest of all the dreams of the Toms and Edwards and Sams, and she became celebrated! Tom Canty and Edward VI of England are ten; Tom Sawyer is twelve; Huck is thirteen, fourteen; Joan is sixteen to nineteen when she acts. They all are presexual. Huck, a boy, disguises himself as a girl; Joan, a girl, disguises herself as a man. All are children trespassing into the world of adults, judging it, wishing to bring order to it. In fact, only a child can be a real civilizing force, neither man nor woman; and only a villager issued from the golden age. Last, *Joan of Arc* helped Twain to put all his great ideas into action. All his prejudices against the French, against even the English, against the Church against monarchy reappear, but organized into constructive criticism. Joan's life is a demonstration of the validity of his conception of "training." Before Joan, the French had lost all courage; when she told them the necessity of urgent action, they changed; once she was gone, they became low and vile again. Joan herself, an ignorant girl, is given an army which believes in her, and thus makes her the Maid of Orléans; believing in herself (through the sponsorship of the Voices), she does accomplish wonders. Put in a man's world, she does better than any man. But once put into prison, treated as a heretic, isolated from her friends, she becomes a lonely person, "an apostate," "an idolater," a "friendless poor girl" who could only die even if in martyrdom. Those two contrasting images of the Maid correspond to the two volumes of Sieur de Conte. The last idea that Twain illustrates here is what he asserts in "What Is Man?" also. Man is nothing, all his ideas come from the outside. What could come from the outside more than the Voices? For neither in the biography nor in the essay does Twain justify Joan's extraordinary actions by the miracle of God's intervention. On the contrary, he keeps saying that there is no possible explanation for "the Wonder of all Ages," "the Riddle of the Ages": "All rules fail in that girl's case." The young man asks the old man: "Consider the man who stands by his duty and goes to the *stake* rather than be recreant to it." The old man answers: "It is his make and his training. He has to content the spirit that is in him, though it cost him his life."[28] Ultimately then, Joan only satisfied the spirit that was in her, whether originated by the Voices of St. Catherine and St. Marguerite or by that most commendable feeling (to Twain), his last compliment, at the end of the book: "the genius of patriotism." "She was patriotism embodied, concreted, made flesh and palpable to the touch and visible to the eye."

The importance of disguise; the confrontation of two worlds, the serious and the comic, the sublime and the grotesque; his popular laughter; his profanities place Mark Twain into the tradition of writers whose vision of the world is "carnivalesque." I am using that word in Mikhaïl Bakhtin's sense. Much of what Bakhtin says and shows for Dostoyevsky and Rabelais applies to Twain as well.[29] The serious comic genre, he says, has deep affinities with the folklore of Carnival; it does not belong to a set traditional form, but is defined by its own inventing and deliberate experimenting; it is characterized by the multiplicity of tones, the refusal of stylistic unity, the use of all literary genres—letters, manuscripts found and translated, dialogues, parodies, caricatures, satires—the use of living dialects and jargons. Bakhtin insists on one particular genre of the "carnivalesque": the Menippean Satire, born in Antiquity, transformed, Proteanlike, in Medieval times. Its most important characteristics are the following: the taking over of the comic element; an extreme freedom of invention even when dealing with historical or legendary characters; the symbolic and idealistic combined with the grossest naturalism; a new type of experimental fantastic; the observation from an unusual point of view (and here Bakhtin mentions Rabelais, Swift, and Voltaire); madness, split personalities, doubles, dialogues between two men (the young man and the old man) or a man and his conscience (it is appropriate that it is in the story, "Facts Concerning the Recent Carnival of Crime in Connecticut," that Twain conceives this dialogue). All these are forms of it. The Menippean Satire loves scandal, eccentrics, outrage, profanity ("*1601*"); it is made of violent contrasts: an emperor becomes a slave, rise and fall, wealth and poverty. It includes elements of social utopia (*A Connecticut Yankee*). Bakhtin concludes by speaking of the deep organic unity of all those aspects. Reading this, Mark Twain's readers have recognized how perfectly it applies to him and how there lies the deep unity of his work. The Menippean Satire is associated with "literary carnivalization." Carnival is of and for the people; Twain repeated he wrote for the masses. It is the time of reversal of usual hierarchy and power, the time of free relationships, eccentricity, misalliance, profanation. It is situated in a Court (the ideal little world of a novelist): King Arthur's Court, Offal Court, Charles VII's Court; it celebrates a King who has to be enthroned and dethroned. Need I recall the abundance of kings in Twain's work? Living or dead, true and frauds, literary kings, disguised kings. Then, Joan's crowning of her King appears in a new light: "To Joan of Arc, the peasant girl, Charles VII was no King until he was crowned; to her, he was only the Dauphin; that is to say the heir. If I have ever made her call him King, it was a mistake; she called him the Dauphin, and nothing else until after the Coronation. It shows you as in a mirror—for Joan was a mirror in which the lowly hosts of France were clearly reflected—that to all that vast underlying force called the "people" he was no King but only

Dauphin before his crowning, and was indisputably and irrevocably King after it" (Book II, Chapter 33). So, before the Coronation, he was as much a fraud as the Dauphin, supposed son of Louis XVI in *Huckleberry Finn*. The ceremonial of "dethroning" is also symbolically described in the first chapters of *The Prince and the Pauper*, particularly in Chapter 3, when the children changed clothes, "the little Prince of Wales was garlanded with Tom's fluttering odds and ends, and the little Prince of Pauperdom was tricked out in the gaudy plumage of royalty." Carnival implies travesty, masks, a general desacralizing tone, a negative denunciation with a sociopolitical meaning. Parody is its tone, laughter its aim, deflating, debunking are its own creations, its game. Laughter stops at nothing: men and women are no longer sexualized and individualized, but masks and puppets. Heaven and Hell, the earth are jokes. In the Middle Ages, the exceptional vitality of the genre gave birth to new forms; lives of Saints (Joan), dialogues, philosophical tales, regional expressions appeared. All those can be found in Twain who, in turn experimented with a few more things of his own. All must be seen together as an organic whole.

So Mark Twain laughed at men and women, used the vernacular, and spoke of American regions. But that was only one form of his genius which must be integrated into the whole. His critics have been wrong in extolling that aspect to the point of separating it from the rest of his work. For he was not only an American writer, but one of the last truly European writers in America. He dared not recognize it; perhaps he was totally ignorant of what he was doing; he was so celebrated as an American. But he repeated he admired Rabelais and Cervantes more than any other writers and must have dreamed of belonging with them and their tradition. As an American writer, more than the ancestor of Hemingway or of Salinger, he prefigures the Southerners, the circuses and the freaks, the grotesques of Capote, McCullers, Goyen. Tom Driscoll, disguised as a girl, seen through the windows by Pudd'nhead, or Jim as King Lear, with his white wig, look more like Capote's Randolph disguised as a marquess seen by Joel Knox through a window, than anything else. And 44 the magician has much in common with Goyen's Redeemer, Mr. de Persia, and with Addis Adair.[30] In the world of Carnival, there are indeed no women; there are no men either; only masks and freaks, players wearing masks, actors capering about. In such a Court, the creator always takes all shapes, assumes all roles, chameleonlike, "the entire human race compacted together," playing with the world, confronting its opposites, doing, inventing, destroying, and burning kings and himself on the stake, to be born forever again in a new garb, playing new pranks.

January 1981

## Notes

1. Examples of that sort of criticism can be found in H. Nash Smith, ed., *Mark Twain. A Collection of Critical Essays*, (Englewood Cliffs, N.J.: Prentice Hall, 1963). In his introduction, Smith speaks of the "structural defects in both *A Connecticut Yankee* and *The Mysterious Stranger*" (p. 9). Leo Marx, in his essay "The Pilot and the Passenger" says the following "There is no way, within the convention, to treat the beautiful and the murderous rivers as one. The style imposes a hopeless bifurcation of experience. In the second half of *Life on the Mississippi*, consequently, the past and the present, the beautiful and the actual, the benign and the tragic are discrete compartments of life. *The result is not literature but a disorderly patchwork*" (p. 55). As the reader will discover reading my essay, it is precisely because the work is "a disorderly patchwork" that it is literature. Other examples can be found in practically all forewords or afterwords to editions of Twain's works. In his afterword to *A Connecticut Yankee* (New York: New American Library, 1963), Edmund Reiss says the book is "confused and ill-organized, attempting to do too many things at the same time" (p. 321); "Twain never solves or decides anything" (p. 326); "Throughout, the humor so confuses the book that it is hardly possible to find a consistent tone or attitude" (p. 327); "Twain bathes everything in a grotesque low humor that may seem out of place, a weakness in the book" (p. 329). Leslie Fiedler in his afterword to *The Innocents Abroad* (New York: New American Library, 1966) says that the author "continually risks disaster because of his uncomfortable closeness to the persona he has assumed" (p. 489); "He shares especially the bad taste of his generation" (p. 482). Leonard Kriegel, in his afterword to *Life on the Mississippi* (New York: New American Library, 1961) begins by saying that Twain's readers consider that book "as one of the indisputably great works in the Twain canon," adding that most of Twain's critics "have also directed attention to its numerous artistic defects." In his foreword to *Roughing It* (New York: New American Library, 1962), he insists on Twain's "sexual squeamishness," "sexual prudishness," "sexual inhibitions" (pp. 22, 25).
2. All italics in this essay and in the notes are mine.
3. *Innocents Abroad*, p. 234.
4. *A Connecticut Yankee*, p. 91.
5. *Personal Recollections of Joan of Arc* (New York: Harper & Row, 1896, 1899, 1924), p. 54.
6. The expression "males in groups" refers to the characteristics described by Lionel Tiger in his book *Men in Groups*, (New York: Random House, 1969).
7. *Roughing It*, p. 114.
8. For Twain's ideas about temperament and the "sanguine temperament" in particular, see F. Anderson, M.B. Frnak, and K. M. Sanderson, eds., *Notebooks, Vol. 1, 1855–1873* (Berkeley, Los Angeles, and London:

University of California Press, 1975), p. 21–23, Twain's entry on "The Sanguine Temperament," June–July 1855; Charles Neider, ed. *The Complete Essays of M. Twain* (New York: Doubleday, 1963), essay entitled "The Turning Point of My Life," pp. 477–85; and Charles Neider, ed., *The Autobiography of M. Twain*, (New York: Harper & Row, 1975), pp. 334–37.

 9. See "Letter to an Unidentified Person," 1890, in *The Portable Mark Twain*, ed. Bernard DeVoto, (New York: Viking Press, 1968), p. 775.

10. See, in particular, Van Wyck Brooks's essay, "M. Twain's Humor" in Smith, *A Collection of Essays*, p. 15.

11. For Twain's comments on Mrs. Aldrich, see *Autobiography*, (pp. 388–97). Justin Kaplan, in *Mr. Clemens and M. Twain* (New York: Pocket Books, 1968), p. 366, tells how Twain referred to Harriet Beecher Stowe as the "maniac," as well as paying her other compliments. The reader will find allusions to Isabella Beecher Hooker in Mark Twain's *Love Letters to His Wife*, ed. Dixon Wecter (New York: Harper and Row, 1949). See, for instance, this comment when she retires from the feminist movement: "She has been blandly pulling down the temple of Woman's Emancipation and shying the bricks at the builders," (Oct. 3, 1872) p. 180. See, also, allusions to Olive Logan and Kate Field in *Autobiography*, pp. 177–79. The reader will find it interesting to compare Twain's judgments with the biographies of the three women in *Notable American Women 1607-1950: A Biographical Dictionary*, 3 vols., ed. Edward T. James, Janet Wilson James, and Paul S. Boyer (Cambridge, Mass.: Harvard University Press, Belknap Press, 1971).

12. References to women in Twain are numerous. The allusions I make come from *The Innocents Abroad* and *A Tramp Abroad*, passim. The allusions to French women (and to French men) come more particularly from "The French and the Comanches" from the manuscript of *A Tramp Abroad* in *Letters from the Earth*, ed. Bernard DeVoto (New York: Harper & Row, 1974), pp. 146–51; and from F. Anderson, L. Salamo, and B. L. Stein, eds., *Notebooks, Vol. II, 1877-1883* (Berkeley, Los Angeles, and London: University of California Press, 1975), pp. 316–27. In those pages can be found the following comments: "France has usually been governed by prostitutes"; "French are the connecting link between man and the monkey"; "The nation of the filthy-minded"; "Scratch an F & you find a gorilla. Take America by & large & it is the most civilized of all nations. Pure-minded women are the rule"; "Scratch a F & you find a savage . . . a Fw & you find a harlot"; etc.

13. *Connecticut Yankee*, p. 78.

14. *Notebooks* Vol. II, May–July 1877 p. 17.

15. Cf. *Love Letters*, 27 December 1869, to Livy: *Gil Blas* "would sadly offend your delicacy." On *Don Quixote*, 1 March, 1869, "I am sorry enough that I did not ask you to let me prepare D.Q. for your perusal . . . D.Q. is one of the most exquisite books that was ever written . . . but neither it nor Shakespeare are proper books for virgins"

(p. 76). And in the same letter, on *Gulliver's Travels*: "If you would like to read it, though, I will mark it and tear it until it is fit for your eyes."

16. On Godwin and Mary Godwin, see "In Defense of Harriet Shelley," in *The Complete Essays*. For Twain's comments on the Emperor of Russia, Napoleon III, and Napoleon Bonaparte, see *The Innocents Abroad, Notebooks, Essays,* passim; on the Jews, see more particularly "Concerning the Jews," in *Complete Essays*, pp. 235-50. On the women's movement, see *A Connecticut Yankee*, Ch. 40, or "The Temperance Crusade and Woman's Rights" in *Complete Essays*, p. 664-68.

17. All my references concerning Twain's and Warner's contributions to *The Gilded Age* come from Bernard Poli, *Mark Twain Ecrivain de l'Ouest, Régionalisme et Humour* (Paris: Presses Universitaires de France, 1965), Part II, Chapter 5.

18. An expression of DeVoto: "a debauch of gyneolatry," in his introduction to *The Portable M. Twain*, p. 16.

19. My impressions on this point are based on Teresa Kieniewicz's paper "Novelists' Views on Women's Rights and Careers in the 1870s and 1880s" read at the Workshop on American Women's Search for Identity, 15 April 1980, at the E.A.A.S. Biennial Conference in Amsterdam. Kieniewicz teaches at the University of Warsaw.

20. *A Connecticut Yankee*, p. 290. *Adam's Diary* was written in 1893.

21. On Frenchmen, see note 12.

22. Cf. *The Mysterious Stranger* (New York: New American Library, 1962) p. 170: "Why actually I look like a boy for that is what I am."

23. *Roughing It*, p. 255.

24. *Joan of Arc*, Book I, Ch. 46, p. 69.

25. I must thank the editors of the *Notebooks* for their commentaries, as well as B. Poli and W. Gibson for his introduction to *The Mysterious Stranger* (Berkeley and Los Angeles: University of California Press, 1970,) pp. 1-35, in particular, pp. 4-11; it is from their works as well as from the information provided by Twain in his own *Notebooks* and *Autobiography* that I draw all information concerning dates in this table, except for the periods covered by *Pudd'nhead Wilson, The Gilded Age,* and *Life on the Mississippi*. If there are errors, they must be mine.

26. Cf. Poli, *Mark Twain*, p. 348, n. 8.

27. See note 25.

28. "What Is Man?" in *The Complete Essays*, p. 359.

29. I refer the reader to M. Bakhtin's works in French, for this is the language in which I have read him: *La Poétique de Dostoievski* (Paris: Editions du Seuil, 1970) [First published in Russia in 1929, then a second time in Moscow in 1963]; *L'Oeuvre de François Rabelais* (Paris: Gallimard, 1970) [First published in 1965] *Esthétique et théorie du roman* (Moscow: 1975, Paris: Gallimard, 1978). The brief and incomplete summary I make for the readers who might not be acquainted with his works comes mostly from Chapter 4 of *La Poétique de Dostoievski*.

30. Mr. de Persia and Addis Adair are characters in William Goyen's *Come the Restorer* (New York: Doubleday, 1974). On Goyen's vision of the writer as a magician, see my "Interview with W. Goyen," *Delta*, no. 9 (November 1979):3–45, in particular, pp. 27–28, in which Goyen alludes to King Arthur. Capote's characters appear in *Other Voices, Other Rooms* (1948).

# John W. Crowley

# W. D. Howells: The Ever-Womanly

*The fact is* I *was the serpent who tempted Eve. In that way I learnt
so much about women—started early.*
Howells to Charles Dudley Warner, 23 August 1876

W. D. Howells would never forget two bits of advice he received in his youth.
The first came from Henry D. Cooke, owner of the *Ohio State Journal*, who
admonished reporter Howells in 1859 for having written a "too graphic paragraph" about a murderously jealous husband. "Never *never* write anything
you would be ashamed to read to a woman," Cooke exhorted; and Howells
felt "lastingly ashamed of what I had done, and fearful of ever doing the like
again, even in writing fiction."[1] Two years later, en route to Venice to
assume his consulship (the opportunity that launched his literary career),
Howells stopped in Cambridge to consult his Brahmin mentor James Russell
Lowell. As a parting thought, Lowell averred that there were unworthy
women but that "a good woman was the best thing in the world, and a man
was always the better for honoring women."[2]

Howells never did write a novel he was ashamed to have read by a woman,
and since the American audience for fiction was predominantly female, most
of his readers *were* women.[3] And although he was criticized for his unvar-
nished portraits of female characters, he always did honor women in his
fashion. Aside from Henry James, no male American writer of the late
nineteenth century wrote more often or more perceptively than Howells
about what he liked to call (after Goethe) the "Ever-Womanly." What one
reviewer observed in 1882 could stand for Howells's entire career. "It is a
trite remark, or at least so evident a statement of fact that it should by this
time be trite, that every new story which Mr. Howells writes is a new study
of women".[4] Quite deliberately. Howells cast his literary fate with women,
declaring in *Heroines of Fiction* (1901) that "novelists are great in proportion to the accuracy and fulness with which they portray women"[5] By this
standard, Howells himself knew that he fell short of his idols: Austen, George
Eliot, Tolstoy.

Since his death in 1920, Howells has seldom been judged to measure up by any standards. Even the Howells revival of the 1950s made few converts. Now, when only true believers would claim greatness for Howells as a novelist, his reputation may still depend—in a way he could not have foreseen—on women. Howells has been barred from the canon of "major American authors" for many of the same reasons and by many of the same tactics that have been used by male critics to exclude nineteenth-century women writers; and as feminist critics reconstruct that canon, there may be a place in it for W. D. Howells.

## I

Howells's attitudes toward women were rooted in his childhood neuroticism. "If heaven lies about us in our infancy," he wrote in a passage canceled in the typescript of *A Boy's Town* (1890), "hell borders hard upon boyhood, and the air of its long summer days which men look back to so fondly is sometimes foul as if with exhalations from the Pit."[6] Howells's Swedenborgian parents believed, and taught their children to believe, in a "hell, which each cast himself into if he loved the evil rather than the good, and that no mercy could keep him out of without destroying him, for a man's love was his very self."[7] Young Will Howells resolved to escape the Pit by always loving the good, and he set himself on strict watch against the slightest of childish transgressions. The boy believed that teasing was fiendish, that angry and vengeful feelings summoned evil spirits to his side, that "wicked words were of the quality of wicked deeds, and that when they came out of our mouths they depraved us, unless we took them back" (*YMY*, p. 21). During his early years, Howells lived in nearly constant fear. When he was not stabbing himself with guilt for real or imagined sins, he was peopling the nooks and corners of his home with "shapes of doom and horror" (*ABT*, p. 18). Superstitions, nightmares (some recurrent), death fantasies, sexual dreads, phobias, insomnia, headaches, vertigo, bouts of homesickness—these were the torments of Howells's "very morbid boyhood," as he would call it himself (*YMY*, p. 79).

In 1854, at the age of seventeen, he succumbed to "nervous prostration" in the form of an hysterical, but nonetheless harrowing, attack of hydrophobia. This climactic adolescent breakdown was followed by several milder relapses, and in his adult life Howells guarded himself from threatening emotions. Just the same, he collapsed psychologically more than once, and so did his wife and their elder daughter Winifred—and, years later, their younger daughter Mildred. The 1880s, the years of Howells's highest achievement in fiction, were punctuated by crisis: Howells broke down while writing *A Modern Instance* (1882) and later while writing *The Rise of Silas Lapham*

(1885); Winifred developed apparently hysterical symptoms in 1881, went up and down throughout the decade, and finally died of organic and psychic causes in 1889; Elinor, who was always high-strung, never recovered from this blow and became a lifelong invalid.

Howells's neuroticism lends itself to a psychoanalytic investigation, but this is not the place to go into details. I shall merely sketch the outlines of Howells's case and then state some bald conclusions that must be substantiated elsewhere.[8] Evidently, Howells's emotional upheavals had their origins in unresolved Oedipal conflicts and in earlier, oral-stage abandonment fears. A representative childhood memory epitomizes his underlying psychodynamics. In *Years of My Youth* (1916), Howells recalled an instance of the "tragical effect" of his father's "playfulness." As a very small boy, he had been incited by William Cooper Howells to play a practical joke on his mother. "My father held out to me behind his back a rose which I understood I was to throw at my mother and startle her." Unfortunately, when the rose struck her head, Mary Dean Howells, who had little sense of humor anyhow, mistook it for a bat. She whirled about, spied her son "offering to run away," and made him "suffer for her fright," while her husband tried to calm her, gravely entreating, "'Mary, Mary!'" She could not forgive her son at once; and the boy, whose love for her was "as passionate as the temper I had from her," ached with remorse. Later, after he had gone to bed, she stole upstairs to console him, telling him "how scared she had been, and hardly knew what she was doing; and all was well again between us" (*YMY*, p. 20).

In offering this example of his father's "humor"—which "made life easy for him" but which "could not always have been a comfort to her" (*YMY*, p. 19)—Howells implies that he resented his father's treatment of his mother. He also resented his father's having put him up to a prank that was no comfort either to the son or his mother—a prank, on the contrary, that temporarily severed the bond between them. The Oedipal theme is plainly figured here, both in its aspect of rivalry between father and son for the mother's love and in its aspect of mutual aggression. The father's incitement of his son's aggression (throwing the rose) is an oblique retaliation against the son and his mother. The threat of further retaliation keeps the son's Oedipal rage in check. In effect, it is displaced in the son's narrative as it was in his child's mind; it appears three paragraphs later, in Howells's remembering that he once "came out with the shocking wish that he [his father] was dead" (*YMY*, p. 21).

More important for my present purposes is the bearing of the rose-throwing incident on Howells's relationship with his mother. Obviously, he craved the love that had put a happy ending to this "tragical" event. The sweet intimacy of that reconciliation was equaled on those occasions when the boy's physical ailments and his homesickness earned him favored treatment. With her evenhanded policy of child rearing, Mary Dean Howells "would have felt such a preference wicked" under any other circumstances (*YMY*, p. 25). But there was "rich compensation" for any suffering boy in the "affectionate petting" his mother gave him when sickness removed him from the "rough little world" of boys and restored him to her care again. "Then she makes everything in the house yield to him ... She is so good and kind and loving that he cannot help having some sense of it all, and feeling how much better she is than anything on earth ... [In] his weakness, his helplessness, he becomes a gentle and innocent child again; and heaven descends to him out of his mother's heart" (*ABT*, p. 236).

Such regressive fantasies of fusion with the mother coexisted, on one hand, with fear of engulfment and annihilation by her—as in Howells's recurrent childhood vision of the "inevitable oncoming of a vast, impalpable something that seemed to be rolling toward me to surround and swallow me up in enormous airy billows"[9]—and, on the other hand, with fear of separation from her. The same mother who petted him might, with her passionate temper, reject him violently, as in the rose-throwing incident. Both fears (of annihilation and separation) gave rise to repressed rage toward the mother. As Howells's oral-stage ambivalence accrued Oedipal significance, his dread of being surrounded and swallowed up came to symbolize fear of castration as well as of engulfment. In adolescence, as he struggled to free himself from the bonds of family life and from his increasingly possessive mother, Howells expressed his ambivalence toward her more overtly; and he began to displace it upon other women, first his favorite sister Victoria and ultimately upon his wife and daughters.

In Howells's anthology chestnut, "Editha" (1905), George Gearson is depicted as the prey of two women (his mother and his fiancée), vying for hegemony over his mind and spirit.[10] Despite their polarly opposite views of warfare, Mrs. Gearson and Editha are shown to be sisters under the skin; they represent two faces of a single imago, the castrating mother. Gearson escapes their clutches only by dying in a war he does not believe in, by committing what seems like unconscious suicide. Howells's imaginative act of killing off Gearson in "Editha" reflects a triad of unconscious impulses that drove him throughout his life: of escape from women's power, of revenge on women for having that power, of self-punishment for wanting such revenge. But, like Gearson, Howells masochistically courted women's domination. He sought emotional support from the women he feared, and this need prevailed over his concealed misogyny by means of a compensatory reaction-formation. That is, Howells defended against his repressed rage toward threatening women by consciously stressing their benevolence, by proclaiming "the fact of woman's moral and spiritual superiority" over man.[11] Such a psychic reversal, of course, was practiced on a mass scale in Victorian America (and since); it is one of the sources of the cultural myths of exalted womanhood—whether in the avatar of the angel in the house, the pedestaled virgin, or, more prosaically, the Gibson Girl—which informed the fiction of his male contemporaries.

## II

Like any introspective person, Howells was not merely a slave to his repression. Our recognizing his unconscious misogyny should not blind us to his conscious identification with women, his compassion for women's suffering, and his sensitivity to their needs. Howells told an interviewer in 1895 that he had lately come "to think that the differences we see between men and women are due very largely to their bringing up—to their education." Boys and girls begin to be differentiated when they are very young, he added. "The girl is not allowed the freedom a boy has. Many of the things he does she is warned against . . . it's our version of the Chinese foot-binding."[12]

In his own youth, Howells had witnessed the binding effects of sexual differentiation on his sisters, particularly Victoria, with whom he shared a discontent with the village limits of Jefferson, Ohio, as well as a dream of escape into a world of "wealth, of fashion, of haughtily and dazzlingly, blindingly brilliant society, which we did not unconveniently consider we were altogether unfit for" (*YMY*, p. 107). Yet, when their father took them to Columbus in 1857, only Will remained there. Columbus could not match their fantasy of cosmopolitan splendor, but it did afford Will Howells a foothold in "the great world" beyond Jefferson. For Victoria, who had gone along not to begin a career but to keep house for the men, there would be no fit place outside the village home. After a few weeks, she "went back to those bounds where her duty lay"—to the lifelong care of her brain-damaged brother Henry (*YMY*, p. 108).

During his Columbus years, Will kept a journal just for Vic, so that she might taste his freedom vicariously. With unwitting cruelty, he reminded her in 1859 of the days when they had "comforted each other in our hard task of making bricks without straw for those Jefferson Egyptians," and he resolved some day "to rescue my kindred out of the bondage."[13] Vic must have taken this figure of speech more literally than Will had ever intended; for he was compelled a month later to dampen the hopes he had raised, giving Vic elaborate reasons—of the same sort he had rejected himself—why she should see the "silver lining" in her Jefferson cloud (*SL*, 1:24-25). Painfully conscious of the depth of Vic's misery in Jefferson and yet helpless (and, finally, unwilling) to rescue her, Howells guiltily counseled her to resignation.

Howells might have had Vic in mind as he wrote to Oliver Wendell Holmes, Jr., in 1861, of a young woman who had come to learn the printing business in his father's shop. She had been beautiful, witty, intelligent, refined, well read, "a woman who could have shone most brilliantly in any society." But she was also poor. The only alternative to a life of labor beneath her talent and dignity seemed to be marriage; and after three years in the print shop, lacking a better match, she became engaged to a man who was her inferior in everything but age. Then she fell ill and died—a fate that Howells regarded as cruelly merciful. "But for her, what else remained?" he asked Holmes, rhetorically. "Either a monotonous drudgery through life at the trade she detested, or a domestic round of tasks and stupid little duties. She could not have been religious. She did not believe enough.—She could not write well enough, or would not write ill enough to achieve that doubtful splendor and distinction of female authorship. From her nature, I think, motherhood would not have made her happy, for though passionate, I do not think she had much affection—though here I may wrong her. What then? Only death—" (SL, I:73-74).

Howells's slur on female authors, reminiscent of Hawthorne's notorious complaint about the damned mob of scribbling women, betrays a widely felt male resentment of women's competition in the literary profession, a resentment for which Howells later compensated in his sponsorship of women writers. Early and late, however, he was aware of the possibly tragic consequences of any woman's aspiring, without independent means, to other than a domestic life. A woman was not brought up to support herself, Howells believed, but to be supported in marriage.[14] Should she contract a marriage of unequals, there would be little to relieve her from the drudgery of the domestic round in even the best of situations. If she were neither religious enough to accept her misery as a means to grace, nor maternal enough to find fulfillment in children, nor talented enough to bear literary offspring, she might as well be dead. Reform, then, lay in the direction of improving woman's lot within marriage. As Sidney H. Bremer observes, Howells "feared that the American home was being threatened," but he located the threat "not in female emancipation, but in the enslavement of American women to an isolated, trivialized domesticity."[15] But Howells's commitment to women's emancipation was informed by his unwavering allegiance to the cult of female superiority.

When asked by an interviewer in 1894 why his women characters were "always so much more admirable" than his men, Howells promptly replied: "Because women are better than men. A good woman is beyond the imagination of even a good man, and a bad woman is as good as the average of the other sex." Then he added, "It's because women are mostly outside of our infernal economic system."[16] As he explained ten years later in another interview, "our women are superior to our men" because of the sexual differentiation in their upbringings. Women are given "better opportunities for self-cultivation"; their education is "prolonged far beyond the years of their brothers in the formative period; and later in life they have leisure to develop, shielded by their husbands, their mankind, who wage the battle with the world that absorbs all their energies." Echoing Veblen's *Theory of the Leisure Class*, which he had favorably reviewed in 1899, Howells described how woman's isolation in the domestic sphere both nurtured her finer nature and bred her discontent:

> Honestly speaking, the average American—the rushing, money-making, preoccupied man of business—is a stick. He is chivalric, devoted, true as steel, he means generously well, but the graces of the higher intellectual and emotional life are strange to him. Now, Mrs. A., discovering in Mrs. B.'s home the same lack she vaguely feels in her own, concludes that it is the inferiority of the sex: their very isolation forces our women to flock together. The semi-consciousness of a void is transmuted into activity, the boundless energy of the American woman, perhaps not always wisely expended, but beneficial as the safety-valve none the less. This dim realization of something lacking is, perhaps, responsible in part for our women's adoration of foreign nobilities: here is an ideal made tangible, real—maybe the very thing that is wanting to make whole their own mankind.[17]

The sexual division of labor, Howells realized, was creating a gap between men's and women's lives that was potentially destructive to American society. Ideally, men should "have more time for the social graces, for education, for closer companionship with their wives." Women should have outlets for their "boundless energy" more culturally productive than consuming conspicuously or reading pernicious romantic novels, and they should have objects more worthy of their adoration than foreign nobilities. Within the void of domesticity, women's higher instincts were given either to atrophy or, worse, to hyperdevelopment. Like some of Howells's women characters, as Bremer says, they tended "to become dependent, closeted idealists who judge the public activities of their spouses according to an abstract morality that they themselves have no opportunity to test."[18]

Howells hoped that ways could be found to transfuse the moral vitality of American women into the body of American life. Women must be motivated, as Edwin H. Cady puts it, "to give the best of their gifts to a sorrowfully needy world."[19] Indeed, they must be encouraged to achieve their evolutionary destiny. Howells wrote in 1905, "It is to no purpose that the modern girl is so tall, unless she stoops to raise mankind into a finer ether than it now breathes even when standing tiptoe on its own feet." Is it "wholly unimaginable," he asked, that in the "farthest future, when the suffrage and coeducation shall have become almost prehistoric events of her development, there shall be a type of womanhood, to which the ultimate type of manhood shall be as the drone is to the queen bee?"[20]

In sum, the goal of Howells's political and literary activities in support of women was to bring them more fully into the nondomestic world, but not so far that they would abandon domesticity. Since Howells could not imagine a world without traditional domestic structures, and since he feared woman's losing her "moral superiority" outside the home, Howells wished to revitalize the family. Some career women might uplift the male world with their presence in it, but most women would continue to exert a crucial but indirect influence by civilizing their husbands and sons at home. Thus, Howells opposed those reformers, such as G. Stanley Hall, who urged the transformation of female education into professional training. Howells acknowledged the logic and even the justice of such ideas, but he thought that they would subvert the family. To him, the fault lay with the American system of domesticity, not with domesticity itself:

> It is because women have, in the hideously egoistic and erroneous
> development of our commercial civilization, been obliged so often
> to *make* the homes they were bidden keep to, that we now find
> them the rivals (alas! sometimes the victorious rivals) of men, not
> only in the graces, but the industries, the arts, the sciences. The part
> they play (it is very like working) has been less chosen than forced
> upon them by the brutal and entirely man-made conditions of the
> life which prevails throughout the world ironically calling itself
> Christendom; and their schools cannot do better than continue to
> fit them for it, until their brothers shall imagine some gentler and
> juster economy, in which they shall be each chosen a wife by a
> husband worthy of her, and dwell with him in a home of their com-
> mon creation, safe from want and the fear of want.[21]

As Gail Thain Parker suggests, Howells's entrusting women's future to "their brothers" was "certainly not a feminist scenario."[22] He did not envision a room of one's own within the home of their common creation. In this, Howells was very much a man of his time, and not surprisingly, we may glimpse questionable motives behind his public pronouncements on behalf of women.

## III

Howells's conservatism about domesticity and female education colored his attitudes toward women's suffrage and the women's movement in general. He had been far from sympathetic at first. In 1871, for instance, after his father had published an essay critical of "Mrs. Woodhull and Her Set," Howells was quick to congratulate him: "I think your article on the Women's

Rights trollops is very good. What an abomination they are!–" (*SL*, I:386).[23] And he recalled in 1909 that in the "fashionable" society of twenty years before, George William Curtis had been the only man and Julia Ward Howe the only woman who believed in women's suffrage. "Of course there were many other gifted and excellent people in the 'best,' or cultivated, society who believed in it, and one may typify these by the names of Frances Willard and Elizabeth Cady Stanton without dread of the ridicule which such a little while ago would have attached to the mere mention of their names."[24] Whatever he had thought twenty years earlier, Howells had seen the justice of the cause himself by 1909. Three years later, at the age of seventy-five, he went so far as to march up Fifth Avenue in a suffrage parade.

More important than this symbolic gesture was Howells's advocacy of suffrage in the columns of his influential "Editor's Easy Chair." As Robert L. Hough observes, many of Howells's comments "came at a period of low fortunes for the suffragettes, that is between 1896 and 1910," during which years "not a single state granted full political rights to women."[25] Thus, Howells's support, as temperate and occasionally temporizing as it was, meant a great deal; and he possessed the courage to defend even the confrontational tactics of the English suffragettes.

Howells was at least as sympathetic toward men's anxieties as toward women's rights, however. To him, granting woman the vote symbolized man's humiliating admission of his defeat at ruling the world humanely. Furthermore, enfranchising women was a calculated risk. Ideally, it would fulfill the best hopes of mankind through the moral intervention of womankind. But it might, without bearing fruit of its own, blight "the exquisite flower of chivalry which has been nurtured by the countless acts of self-devotion, and is our one truly precious heritage from the feudal ages."[26]

In Howells's column after the suffrage victory in England in 1918, it is clear that if he was allied with women in principle, he was allied with men at heart.[27] His emphasis fell upon the emotional consequences for men, especially the opponents of woman's suffrage: "The men who most warmly contested it will not be the first to deny that their reasons against suffrage remain as valid as ever. It is still true, or as true as ever, that woman's sphere is the home; that when she steps outside of this realm of her proper sovereignty men cannot render her the chivalrous homage that they have always shown her when she is nicely dressed . . . It can even continue true that she did not really want the vote, and that she has not only won it in spite of herself, but that men have given it her in an illusion of her fitness which it will remain forever too late to dispel." Woman must remember the anguish her new status has inflicted upon some men, so far as it has removed her from the pedestal to be man's equal even in menial tasks. "He may well warn her that . . . if she permits herself to shine his shoes she degrades him below the dignity of manhood. At every step of her advance beyond her natural sphere she will still more embarrass him, and he can only entreat her not to humiliate herself as well as him."

The cost to men, however, will be a good investment so long as women hold up their part of the bargain. "In return for the right they have yielded men claim the right to what is best in the minds and hearts of women. They claim their motherly self-sacrifice, their wifely devotion, their sisterly truth, and the best they can offer in the equality of service and sufferance." Howells admitted that men have "no claim to this return from the *gratitude* of women," since women "owe them nothing for the payment of a just due." But he felt that men might rest assured that women would repay them simply out of the goodness of their hearts, "because it is women's nature to give wherever it is man's need to receive, and nobly to forget that his need is not his desert."

Two years later, in nearly the last column he would write, Howells confessed that his faith had been shaken by a reading of Judge Robert Grant's recent book on the rise of divorce.[28] Grant, who had given fictional shape in *Unleavened Bread* (1900) to the male fantasy of the New Woman as predatory bitch, had noticed in his courtroom that woman seemed to be intent upon enlarging the sphere of her independence by "'experimenting with herself and with man—experimenting with a vengeance.'" Grant had detected "'a lurking growth in the feminine mind that the sexual relations may be casual without detriment to the eternal scheme of things.'" Some women, it seemed, were even capable of giving birth out of wedlock without feeling a twinge of shame. Howells worried that this "rather revolting instance" might not be "the most revolting instance" of the "renewed matriarchy" toward which American culture might be headed. Woman's desire to "'live her own life,'" Howells rued, "has its effect in raising her to a selfish supremacy as yet unequalified by those endeavors for moral reform which the friends of her political equality had promised themselves from her. These had hoped that woman's suffrage would, for instance, immediately involve the endeavor to rid civilization of the social evil which neither science nor religion had hitherto availed against. But apparently there has been no generally concerted movement against this horror; women's rule has left this where it found it, or where men's rule had kept it from the beginning of time." Instead, Howells saw "a constant extension of divorce," which he interpreted as an ominous proof of "woman's enjoyment of her greater freedom through its extension as a gift from men or a spoil of her increasing power."

These views of an octogenarian near death reflect Howells's lifelong ambivalence toward women, the same ambivalence that I have linked to his unconscious fears. Gail Thain Parker, in a most trenchant essay on Howells and feminism, arrives by a different psychoanalytic route at conclusions similar to mine, asking whether Howells's sexual egalitarianism was not "in fact tainted by a desire to get even with the opposite sex" (p. 144).[29]

Although Howells's "realistic canons were never consciously aimed at sabotaging the woman's movement in America," Parker concludes, such feminist leaders as Elizabeth Cady Stanton, Frances Willard, and Gertrude Atherton were "not far wrong when they sensed that Howells was an enemy" (p. 161). Yet even Parker concedes that "there is a strong element of truth" in Edwin H. Cady's more sanguine view of Howells: "A feminist in the best of all senses, he wished to help women become freer psychologically and intellectually, more honest, more mature, more realistic, healthier" (p. 233). Certainly, as Parker allows, this is "a description of intention that Howells himself would have recognized" (p. 144)—one that he carried out most fully in his literary career.


## IV


In a review of Howells's early novel, *A Foregone Conclusion* (1875), Henry James praised Howells for creating women who are "always most sensibly women; their motions, their accents, their ideas, savor essentially of the sex; he is one of the few writers who hold a key to feminine logic and detect a method in feminine madness."[30] Yet, as the *Literary Digest* reported thirty-seven years later, "One sometimes hears that women are not always satisfied with the women of his books. They think there are depths or remote recesses of womanly psychology that are beyond him."[31] The truth about Howells's achievement, like his career itself, lies between these statements. In fact, Howells provided a fair and accurate description of his own work in his judgment of Anthony Trollope's. "He has not shown the subtlest sense of womanhood; his portraits do not impart the last, the most exquisite joy; it is not the very soul of the sex that shows itself in them; but it is the mind, the heart, the conscience, the manner . . . Trollope has shown them as we mostly see them when we meet them in society and as we know them at home."[32]

To reveal the "very soul of the sex," as James tried to do, was somewhat contrary to Howells's realistic principles. Always wary of subliminal consciousness, including his own, Howells consistently relied on the dramatic method to reveal his characters' minds, hearts, and consciences by means of depicting their manners; and he eschewed the probing of interior states that gives the American romance its psychological depth. That is not to say that Howells's fiction lacks psychological penetration, only that it reaches the depths indirectly, sometimes almost inadvertently, by focusing (to turn Freud's phrase) on the psychopathology of the commonplace. As a result, we most often see Howells's women as he met them in society and as he knew them at home; and in the process we may discover a great deal about the underlying structures of American society and the American home.

Howells's fictional treatment of women has large cultural implications, for he was a representative man of his age (perhaps *the* representative male writer) and an extraordinarily faithful reflector of America's sexual arrangements. For example, as Gary A. Hunt has shown, *Their Wedding Journey* (1872), Howells's first long fiction, expresses "a reality that can't be quite definitely spoken"—namely, the sexual repression and the conflicts of sexual identity that inhabited "the suppressed underside of the Victorian mind."[33]

The same underside is visible in any number of later Howells novels, especially the dozen or more centrally concerned with courtship and marriage. There is no space here to expand on any of these novels, but I should point at least to four of the lesser-known ones that would repay deeper attention than they have customarily received: *Dr. Breen's Practice* (1881), *A Woman's Reason* (1883), *The Coast of Bohemia* (1893), and *Miss Bellard's Inspiration* (1905). All of these fictions concern women who are torn between the attractions of marriage and their desire (or need) to work, whether as a physician, a journalist, a milliner, a painter, or a teacher.

All of the women finally subordinate themselves to men and abandon their careers; and, if read superficially, these novels present themselves as easy targets for a demystifying feminist attack. Judith Fryer, for instance, asserts that "Dr. Breen is a sympathetic figure, but as a lady doctor, she is first of all a lady, for Howells could not conceive of a woman . . . being seriously dedicated to her work."[34] Elizabeth Stuart Phelps, about to publish her own novel about a woman physician (*Dr. Zay*), complained to Howells in 1881, "I don't feel that Dr. Breen is a fair example of professional women; indeed, I know she is not for I know the class thoroughly from long personal observation under unusual opportunities." But Phelps recognized, as Fryer does not, that Howells has made it "clear to any fine eye" that Grace Breen's failure is "the failure of an individual, not of a cause."[35] In other words, if Howells did not conceive of *this* woman's being seriously dedicated to her work, it was because he understood how cultural conditioning had rendered her, and any woman like her, incapable of such dedication. The neurotically crippled daughter of a degenerate New England tradition, Grace Breen has been raised not to heal others but to rive herself with a scalpel-keen Puritan conscience. Like Helen Harness, in *A Woman's Reason*, Dr. Breen cuts a pathetic figure as a career woman because she has been bred to be a lady, a wife, and a moral conservator.

In Howells's novels, only extraordinarily independent and talented women, such as Alma Leighton in *A Hazard of New Fortunes* (1890), manage to have careers, and then only at the cost of isolation and misunderstanding. Even Alma Leighton, at one point in her life, would willingly sacrifice herself to the egoist Angus Beaton. Another artist, Cornelia Saunders in *The Coast of Bohemia*, finds after marriage that she is destined to be the material of her husband's art rather than the creator of her own. "'Oh, you'll be in all his imaginative pictures, now, Mrs. Ludlow,'" she is told by Wetmore, Alma Leighton's former art instructor. "'That's the fate of the wife of an imaginative painter. But you really must get him to keep you out of his portraits.'"[36] Otherwise, an older Cornelia might share the fate of Marion Alderling in "Though One Rose from the Dead" (1903). Having abandoned her own painting to become the model for her husband's Madonna portraits, she gradually dissolves herself into his work. "'You know how some women, when they are married, absolutely give themselves up, try to lose themselves in the behoof of their husbands?'" her husband reflects after her death. "'I don't say it rightly; there are no words that well express the utterness of their abdication.'"[37]

As a novelist, Howells recognized, as profoundly as Phelps herself in her brilliant *Story of Avis* (1877), the risk of such self-abnegation for the artist-woman. As an editor, Howells did everything he could to prevent it by fostering the careers of promising women writers. When he was planning to inaugurate the "Contributors' Club" in the *Atlantic* in 1876, he wrote to E. C. Stedman, "If you know any bright women who are disposed to write in the Club, invite them for me."[38] He kept his own eyes open for new talent. In 1869, for example, while he was temporarily in charge of the *Atlantic*, Howells accepted a story entitled "Mr. Bruce," by one "A. C. Eliot": this was to be Sarah Orne Jewett's first appearance in the magazine (*SL*, I:337n.). Other beneficiaries of Howells's encouragement included Alice Brown, Rose Terry Cooke, Mary Wilkins Freeman, Mary Noailles Murfree, Harriet Prescott Spofford, and Charlotte Perkins Gilman.

Howells's dealings with Gilman were typical. In 1890, out of the blue, he sent her a letter of praise for her feminist poem, "Similar Cases," comparing it favorably to *The Biglow Papers*. Her joyful reaction is a measure of Howells's literary authority. "There was no man in the country whose good opinion I would rather have had. I felt like a real 'author' at last."[39] Then, after Gilman's "Yellow Wall Paper" had been rejected by Horace Scudder at the *Atlantic* (as "so terribly good that it ought never to be printed"!), Howells pulled some strings: "I could not rest until I had corrupted the editor of *The New England Magazine* into publishing it."[40] Thirty years later, he saved the story from the oblivion of the back issue by reprinting it in his anthology, *The Great American Short Stories* (1920). All the while, he had been following Gilman's career. As he told Joyce Kilmer in an interview in 1914, he did not believe that the women's movement had yet found "adequate literary expression," but that "the best things that have been said about woman suffrage in our time" had been said by Charlotte Perkins Gilman. He recalled having admired her handling an audience of heckling Single Taxers: "She had a retort ready for every interruption. She stood there with her brave smile and talked them all down."[41]

Howells had no patience with the idea that women writers were "limited." When he was asked once, "What place are women to take in the literary field?" he looked "as nearly disgusted as his unfailing good nature would allow" and retorted crisply, "Why, the place they can get." Woman may not look at life from a man's point of view, he explained, "but that's no reason she doesn't see it as clearly. One hears platitudes about woman's lack of breadth and power of generalization. They say she is intense but within narrow bounds, that her genius is better suited to the short story than to the novel. I call that nonsense."[42]

V

Over the years, as Howells took women writers and readers as seriously as men, as he championed women in his criticism and portrayed them in his fiction, he became closely identified with women in the eyes of his contemporaries. To the debunking generation that followed him—to those men who impugned the worth of his fiction and embalmed him in the image of the snuff-colored Dean of American Letters—Howells seemed to be genteelly "womanish" himself. Frank Norris caricatured Howellsian realism as "the drama of a broken teacup, the tragedy of a walk down the block, the excitement of an afternoon call, the adventure of an invitation to dinner."[43] H. L. Mencken sneered that Howells was "an Agnes Repplier in pantaloons" and that his novels had been "fawned over" by "lady critics" who would no more question them than they would "Lincoln's Gettysburg speech, or Paul Elmer More, or their own virginity"—perhaps because Howells's "uninspired and hollow books" contained no more ideas "than so many volumes of the *Ladies' Home Journal*."[44] To Sinclair Lewis, in his Nobel Prize address, Howells was "one of the gentlest, sweetest, and most honest of men, but he had the code of a pious old maid whose greatest delight was to have tea at the vicarage."[45] According to his detractors, Howells had a fetish for tea. John A. Macy, one of the revisionist literary historians, asked, "Is he not, after all, a feminine, delicate, slightly romantic genius . . .?" If life is a tempest in a teapot, Macy continued, then Howells is "one of its finest and most faithful recorders. But he puts the emphasis on the teapot and not on the tempest . . ."[46] Such reactions to Howells have damaged his reputation for years; he has suffered at the hands of sexist critics for his "guilt" by association with women.

This association makes positive sense, however, if we accept the idea that realism of the Howellsian sort has remained an indispensible mode of expression for women. Ann Douglas, in her recent attack on Harlequin Romances, acknowledges that in the current age of deconstruction, realism as a form for fiction has been deemed to be as bankrupt as the psychological and philosophical assumptions that underpin it: "Recently, male scholars and observers have commented profusely on modern man's post-Freudian destabilized 'narcissistic' ego, what could be called the transfusion self."[47] But

Douglas wonders, as "the male observers and scholars usually do not," whether their observations apply equally to the female psyche: "Might it not be closer than the male's to the older Freudian ego model with its implications of a coherent narrative of the self and a predictable dynamic of conflict?" Douglas notes that women have been able "to regenerate, free from any effective charges of anachronism, the more traditional forms, like the novel, the memoir, and the narrative, whether in film or fiction, treated as passé by their male contemporaries." Such totalizing narratives have value, Douglas argues, because "biography is the base fantasy life of 'healthy' people, the product of the profound hope that our lives be complete and entire and, most of all, shaped . . ."

Douglas's defense of contemporary feminist realism argues implicitly for the continuing value of nineteenth-century realism and for the construction of a canon that reclaims American women realists as well as those male realists, such as Howells, who have shared their denigration and neglect. The literary sons and daughters of Jewett, Phelps, Freeman, and Gilman, of Brown, Cooke, Murfree, and Spofford have an opportunity to reciprocate Howells's generosity and justice to the women writers of his time. We need not blink at Howells's limitations as a Victorian man in order to see his strengths as a writer. For all his ambivalence toward women, for all his talk about the "Ever-Womanly," Howells still managed to see through some of the sexual stereotypes and to work through some of the emotional barriers that bound his fellows.

## Notes

1. David J. Nordloh, ed., *Years of My Youth and Three Essays* (Bloomington: Indiana University Press, 1975), p. 126. Other quotations are documented in the text by use of the abbreviation, *YMY*.
2. David F. Hiatt and Edwin H. Cady, eds., *Literary Friends and Acquaintance* (Bloomington: Indiana University Press, 1968), p. 79.
3. "The man of letters must make up his mind that in the United States the fate of a book is in the hands of the women. It is the women with us who have the most leisure, and they read the most books. They are far better educated, for the most part, than our men, and their tastes, if not their minds, are more cultivated . . . If they do not always know what is good, they do know what pleases them, and it is useless to quarrel with their decisions, for there is no appeal from them. To go from them to the men would be going from a higher to a lower court, which would be honestly surprised and bewildered, if the thing were possible." "The Man of Letters as a Man of Business" (1893) in *Literature and Life*, Library Edition (New York: Harper, 1911), p. 21.

4. Clarence L. Dean, "Mr. Howells's Female Characters," *Dial* 3 (October 1882):107.

5. *Heroines of Fiction*, 2 vols. (New York: Harper, 1901), 1:190.

6. The typescript is in the Houghton Library; it is quoted by permission of the Harvard College Library and of William White Howells for the heirs of the Howells Estate. No republication is authorized without these same permissions.

7. *A Boy's Town* (New York: Harper, 1890), p. 12. Other quotations are documented in the text by use of the abbreviation, *ABT*.

8. In my book in progress, to be titled, *W. D. Howells: The Psychological Juggle*.

9. "Contributors' Club," *Atlantic Monthly* 45 (June 1880):860.

10. "Editha" was collected in *Between the Dark and the Daylight* (New York: Harper, 1907).

11. "Editor's Easy Chair," *Harper's Monthly* 111 (October 1905):794.

12. Ulrich Halfmann, ed., *Interviews with William Dean Howells* (Arlington, Texas: American Literary Realism, 1973), pp. 46–47.

13. George Arms et al., eds., *W. D. Howells, Selected Letters, Vol. 1, 1852–1872* (Boston: Twayne, 1979), p. 21. Other quotations are documented in the text by use of the abbreviation, *SL* 1.

14. Howells believed, however, that the single life should not stigmatize a woman. He told an interviewer in 1895: "Why should the fact that a woman doesn't marry be a criterion of her worth any more than it is of a man's? I know people joke about old maids, but it's just tradition. It comes out of the emptiness of people's minds. By far the greater number of old maids are sensible, full of thought, and most estimable. They have more time than married women, and on an average have done more studying and reading, and are mentally more controlled and intelligent." Halfmann, *Interviews*, p. 49.

15. "Invalids and Actresses: Howells's Duplex Imagery for American Women," *American Literature* 47 (January 1976):599. This article is an excellent treatment of the types of women in Howells's fiction; see also Bremer's "William Dean Howells' Ingenues and the Road to Marriage," *American Literary Realism* 12 (Spring 1979):143–50. For a fuller account of recent studies on Howells and women, see my essay, "Howells in the Seventies: A Review of Criticism, Part II," *ESQ: A Journal of the American Renaissance* 25 (Fourth quarter 1979): 235–39.

16. Halfmann, *Interviews*, p. 42. In 1892, in answer to the charge that he had created no noble women, Howells replied: "This criticism always seems to be extremely comical. I once said to a lady who asked me, 'Why don't you give us a grand, noble, *perfect* woman?' that I was waiting for the Almighty to begin. I think that women, as a rule, are better and nobler than men, but they are not perfect." Halfmann, *Interviews*, p. 17.

17. Halfmann, *Interviews*, p. 74.

18. Bremer, "Invalids and Actresses," p. 600.

19. *The Road to Realism: The Early Years, 1837-1885, of William Dean Howells* (Syracuse, N.Y.: Syracuse University Press, 1956), p. 233. Other quotations are documented in the text.
20. "Editor's Easy Chair," *Harper's Monthly* 111 (October 1905):797, 794.
21. "Editor's Easy Chair," *Harper's Monthly* 103 (November 1901):1006-7.
22. "William Dean Howells: Realism and Feminism," in *Uses of Literature*, ed. Monroe Engel (Cambridge, Mass.: Harvard University Press, 1973), p. 161. Other quotations are documented in the text.
23. Although Howells was indignant about the sexual freedom advocated by such radicals as Victoria Woodhull, he was consistent enough to be repelled by the sexual double standard. He fulminated to S. L. Clemens during the presidential campaign of 1884, in which a burning issue was Grover Cleveland's liaison with a widow and his bastard by her: "As for Cleveland, his private life may be no worse than that of most men, but as an enemy of that contemptible, hypocritical, lopsided morality which says 'a woman shall suffer all the shame of unchastity and a man none,['] I want to see him destroyed politically by his past. The men who defend him would take their wives to the White House if he were President, but if he married his concubine—'made her an honest woman'—they would not go near him!" Henry Nash Smith and William M. Gibson, eds., *Mark Twain—Howells Letters* (Cambridge, Mass.: Harvard University Press, 1960), p. 503.
24. "Editor's Easy Chair," *Harper's Monthly* 118 (May 1909):967.
25. *The Quiet Rebel: William Dean Howells as Social Commentator* (Lincoln: University of Nebraska Press, 1959), p. 100.
26. "Editor's Easy Chair," *Harper's Monthly* 111 (October 1905):796.
27. "Editor's Easy Chair," *Harper's Monthly* 136 (February 1918):450-53.
28. "Editor's Easy Chair," *Harper's Monthly* 140 (March 1920):566-68.
29. Howells's suppressed resentment of women is detectable in such "Easy Chair" remarks as: "A main difficulty with the Eternal Womanly has always been that she has to be temporarily provided for. The care falls not only upon her, but upon her brother, the Secular Manly, who has a good deal to do in looking after himself in a sphere where he finds her intruded while awaiting her apotheosis. He does not complain of it; she is an agreeable guest, and he has a fine faith in the poet's notion that she will draw him beyond, draw him onward and perhaps upward, when she goes. But it is natural that he should be somewhat excited in looking out for her wants and tastes, and imagining occupations and amusements for her; and not unnatural that in certain circumstances he should be willing to let her do something to pay for her board." *Harper's Monthly* 103 (November 1901):1004.
30. *North American Review* 120 (January 1875):212.
31. "A Woman's Tribute to Mr. Howells," *Literary Digest* 44 (9 March 1912):485.
32. *Heroines of Fiction*, 2:137.

33. "'A Reality That Can't Be Quite Definitely Spoken': Sexuality in *Their Wedding Journey*," *Studies in the Novel* 9 (Spring 1977):31.

34. *The Faces of Eve: Women in the Nineteenth-Century American Novel* (New York: Oxford University Press, 1976), p. 207. Of course, Howells's choice of a heroine like Grace Breen *is* symptomatic of his ambivalence toward women. Fryer is half right in perceiving the negative side of this ambivalence, but she reduces a complex novel to a simple, antifeminist tract. For richer readings of *Dr. Breen's Practice*, see Gail Thain Parker, "William Dean Howells: Realism and Feminism" in *Harvard English Studies 4: The Uses of Literature* (Cambridge, Mass.: Harvard University Press, 1973), pp. 133–61; Alfred Habegger, "W. D. Howells and the 'American Girl,'" *Texas Quarterly* 19 (Winter 1976): 149–56; Paul John Eakin, *The New England Girl* (Athens: University of Georgia Press, 1976), pp. 97–104.

35. Manuscript letter of 2 November 1881 in the Houghton Library; quoted by permission (see note 6).

36. *The Coast of Bohemia* (New York: Harper, 1893), p. 338.

37. *Questionable Shapes* (New York: Harper, 1903), p. 209.

38. George Arms and Christoph K. Lohmann, eds., *W. D. Howells, Selected Letters*, Vol. 2, *1873–1881*, (Boston: Twayne, 1979), p. 141n.

39. *The Living of Charlotte Perkins Gilman* (1935; reprint ed., New York: Harper, 1975), p. 113.

40. "A Reminiscent Introduction," in *The Great American Short Stories* (New York: Boni & Liveright, 1920), p. vii. No doubt, Howells was so receptive to "The Yellow Wall Paper" because the experiences of its nameless central character so painfully recalled to him the psychological terrors of his own daughter. Winifred Howells had died just the year before while taking a "rest cure" with Dr. S. Weir Mitchell, the same physician who had treated Gilman. Indeed, as she later told Howells, Gilman intended "The Yellow Wall Paper" as a protest against Mitchell's methods.

41. Halfmann, *Interviews*, p. 115. According to Gilman's autobiography (p. 220), the speech that Howells heard was given in Chicago on 14 February 1896.

42. Halfmann, *Interviews*, p. 56.

43. "A Plea for Romantic Fiction," *The Responsibilities of the Novelist* (1903; reprint ed., New York: Hill & Wang, 1967), p. 280.

44. "The Dean," *Prejudices, First Series* (1919); reprinted in *Howells: A Century of Criticism*, ed. Kenneth Eble (Dallas: Southern Methodist University Press, 1962), pp. 95, 97.

45. "The American Fear of Literature," in *The Man from Main Street*, ed. Harry E. Maule and Melville H. Cane (New York: Random House, 1953), p. 15.

46. *The Spirit of American Literature* (1911; reprint ed., New York: Boni & Liveright, n.d.), pp. 288–89.

47. "Soft-Porn Culture," *New Republic* 183 (30 August 1980):25–29.

# Nina Auerbach

## *The Bostonians:* Feminists and the New World

> *It isn't Boston—it's humanity!*
> Henry James, *The Bostonians*

Women today want to be the first and only generation to seize the time. Our contemporary Elizabeth Janeway exults: "Suddenly, and really for the first time, it is women who are in the forefront of change . . . For reality is on our side. We are working with history and not against it."[1] But ominously for us, this triumphant alliance has been forged and broken before. At the end of the nineteenth century, history's majesty seemed to many men a waning thing, reduced to the "babble, babble" Tennyson's aged patriarch curses in "Locksley Hall Sixty Years After" (1886).

> Poor old Heraldry, poor old History, poor
>   old Poetry, passing hence,
> In the common deluge drowning old political ,
>   common sense! [ll. 249-50]

In the face of this pervasive exhaustion, institutionalized feminism held the promise of historical youth; fighting disenchantment, male authors as well as female crusaders turned for the first time to the vision of the female community as a new, if equivocal, source of power.

Thus, Henry James's *The Bostonians* anticipates Elizabeth Janeway's excitement at this new possession of reality by women.[2] As our own century came into view, James allowed his feminists to converge with history by invoking a reality that seemed as irrevocably present then as it does today, though we who were supposed to solidify it have only recently managed to rediscover it. At the same time, James's feminist vision was his compromise with historical change.

For he recoiled from the mass commercial ugliness of a democratic revolution. As he saw the lower classes, "their yearning toward the superior world makes up their very substance. Unlike the Flaubert of *Un Coeur Simple* . . . he could see nothing but pathos and unreality in states of penury and servitude . . . The appurtenances of poverty were 'the merciless signs of mere mean stale feelings.' Poverty was the total failure of the human."[3] In the struggling proletariat, James sensed a coming "common deluge" that threatened to drown the private and fastidious perceptions of art; thus, the woman's revolution may have brought about an uneasy marriage between his social guilt and his aesthetic instincts. Shrill-voiced or hardhearted as the new woman may have been, her ascension seemed preferable to the garbage of mass lower-class culture that surged below her. Unnatural as her coming reign might be, it would at least maintain good taste.

To many, *The Bostonians* seems a stillborn anomaly in the Jamesian canon. James regretfully found no place for it in the definitive New York edition of his work, which was his own gesture toward public definition; and his later critics have floundered in finding a language in which to discuss it or even a tone on which they can agree. To one it is "a long, cold, and distinctly unpopular novel"; to another it is "admirably open, wonderfully funny, and humanly attractive."[4] No doubt one's critical perspective depends on one's human judgment of the central passion of the novel: Olive Chancellor, an inhibited Boston Brahmin who seeks sisterhood and salvation in the woman's movement, is stricken with an obsession to possess beautiful, pliant Verena Tarrant. Daughter and subject of a sleazy mesmerist with whom she is performing when we first meet her, Verena is endowed with the gift of compelling talk. Gripped with excitement, Olive buys the girl from her parents, thus initiating a bond which through Verena's mellifluous, magnetic speeches promises to make the fortunes of the feminist movement and to purchase Olive's happiness forever. The women's only antagonist is Olive's cousin Basil Ransom, a displaced Southerner adrift with medieval ideas in progressive New England, who falls in love with Verena and vows to restore her to her "normal" sphere of ornamental privacy.

Whether the emotion between Olive and Verena is human or inhuman, it is not as solitary a thing as it seems. In making the novel's psychic pivot "one of those friendships between women which are so common in New England," James captured a moment in which New England women were not only yearning to find Platonic elevation in each other, but were exhorted by men to do so. In 1885, the year in which *The Bostonians* was completed, a book appeared in Boston which held such friendships up to women as the crown of life: "If one-tenth of the efforts which women now make to fill their time with amusements, or to gratify outward ambition, were devoted to personal improvement, and to the cultivation of high-toned friendships with each other, it would do more than anything to enrich and embellish their lives, and to crown them with contentment."[5]

In its crowning claims for sisterhood *The Bostonians* could be an alternative sequel to the rich all-sufficing New England matriarchy of Louisa May Alcott's *Little Women*. Alcott and James knew each other. Their philosophic fathers both orbited dreamily around the beaming Emerson, and in 1865, when he was twenty-two, James wrote a respectful, if qualified, review of Alcott's *Moods* for *The North American* and lectured her sententiously in private, "as if he had been eighty and I a girl."[6] Jo March's plaintive allegorizing of her noble sister—"Beth is my conscience, and I *can't* give her up. I can't! I can't!"[7]—is echoed in Verena's drier tribute to Olive: "You do keep me up . . . You are my conscience" (p. 159). The "marriage" Olive envisions between them has the same corporate self-completeness as the mutually balancing circle of the March sisters:

> To Olive it appeared that just this partnership of their two minds—
> each of them, by itself, lacking an important group of facets—made
> an organic whole which, for the work in hand, could not fail to be
> brilliantly effective . . . Olive perceived how fatally, without
> Verena's tender notes, her crusade would lack sweetness, what the
> Catholics call unction; and, on the other hand, how weak Verena
> would be on the statistical and logical side if she herself should not
> bring up the rear. Together, in short, they would be complete, they
> would have everything, and together they would triumph. [P. 160]

Olive is echoing Alcott's faith that a solitary woman is a fragment of a greater female whole, an irresistible mystical body with the power to cleanse history.

There is a more distinct echo of Alcott in *The Tragic Muse* (1889-90), in the humiliating fiasco of aspiring tragedienne Miriam Rooth's first audition before the great Madame Carré, which she later recoups through indefatigable work and overweening confidence. In *Jo's Boys* (1886), Meg's hoydenish daughter Josie gives an equally embarrassing performance before the great actress Miss Cameron, whose beloved protégée she later becomes. For Alcott and James, histrionic ability takes almost interchangeable theatrical and political forms; these young women auditioning before the queens of their sex represent the grooming of political as well as artistic power.

If James adopted Alcott's voice and vision in his "very *American* tale," he was intimately aware of another female community in his adopted England: Elizabeth Gaskell's Cranford, with its self-depreciating power. *Cranford* was a beloved artifact in Cambridge, Massachusetts, where James lived as a young man. Writing to Gaskell in 1855, Charles Eliot Norton, James's mentor and first editor, endows it with the status of holy writ as it prepares his sacred father for a better world:

During the summer of 1853 as my Father's life was gradually drawing to its peaceful close, there was little left for those who loved him
to do but endeavour to amuse the listless and languid hours of
decline. It was then that your Cranford, which had been read aloud
(and much of it more than once) in our family circle when it first
appeared in "Household Words," was again read to him and gave him
more entertainment and pleasure than any other book. It was
indeed, I think, the last book that he cared to hear. You may
imagine what sacred associations it now possesses for us,—and how
glad I am, and I speak for my Mother & sisters as well as for myself,
to have the opportunity to express our gratitude to you for it.[8]

Reviewing Gaskell's career for *The Nation* in 1866, James placed *Cranford* as
a work "manifestly destined in its modest way to become a classic."[9] This
witty phrase captures precisely the book's blend of the overweening and the
shrinking, the imperial and the demure, and casts it in the America idiom that
was James's. *The Bostonians*, one strange fruit of this idiom, is part of a distinct tradition and carries its antecedents, both from England and New
England, before it. Moreover, in James's total vision of his country, the world
of women that is his Boston spreads out over the land he sees as his personal
past and the historic future.[10] The focus of the novel sharpens in the context
of James's total geography, where the might of collective American womanhood steps forth as history's irony and its promise.

If The American Girl did not exist, James would have had to invent her as
a personification of the United States more appealing and appalling than
Uncle Sam. While New England women tended to see themselves as a glorious
America within America—Julia Ward Howe's *Reminiscences* equates the discovery of her own sex with "the addition of a new continent to the map of
the world"[11]—to James, women were simply, and ambiguously, America
itself, a land whose men had disappeared either into soldiers' graves or into
something mysterious and inconsequential called "business." His writings
abound in obsessive references to the domination of America by women,
references of an oddly insistent but uncertain tone, as if this female world is
too important and unprecedented to be captured by familiar definitions.

James's personal and national ambivalence crystallizes around the death
of his mother and his simultaneous (to him) abandonment by his mother
country, out of which *The Bostonians* was born: "The disappearance of the
home in Quincy Street, the now permanent absence of a Cambridge hearth, is
probably the single deepest emotion out of which *The Bostonians* sprang . . .
*The Bostonians* was the novel in which James wrote out the hidden emotional
anguish of the collapse of his old American ties, and he coupled this with a
kind of vibrating anger that Boston should be so unfriendly as to let him
go."[12] His capacity for dependence and disgust seemed rooted in his mother,

and he reacts to her death in visions where mother and country seem perceived interchangeably, as centers of transcendent comfort or cosmic vertigo.
He greets her loss first with an Emersonian eulogy: "Her death has given me
a passionate belief in certain transcendent things—the immanence of being
as nobly created as hers—the immortality of such a virtue as that—the reunion
of spirits in better conditions than these. She is no more of an angel today
than she had always been; but I can't believe that by the accident of her
death all her unspeakable tenderness is lost to the beings she so dearly loved.
She is with us, she is of us—the eternal stillness is but a form of her love."
Twenty years later, he confronts the family graves in Mount Auburn Ceme-
tery on a bleak Cambridge evening in which "the highest deepest note of the
whole thing" is a note of loss and numbness: "But why do I write of the all
unutterable and the all abysmal? Why does my pen not drop from my hand
on approaching the infinite pity and tragedy of all the past? It does, poor
helpless pen, with what it meets of the ineffable, what it meets of the cold
Medusa-face of life, of all the life *lived*, on every side. *Basta, basta!*"[13] The
land of swaddling angels is now haunted by Gorgons, women who are equally
transcendent, but devouring.

But angel and Gorgon cannot be reduced to Mrs. James alone. This vacilla-
tion between renewal and decay, birth and blight, beginnings and endings,
reflects the historical tone of feminized, turn-of-the-century New England as
well as the psychic idiosyncrasies of James's reaction to it. In "The Relation
of College Women to Social Need," Vida Scudder writes of educated women
as a new, saving race, their unprecedented numbers revealing "the harmony
of dramatic purpose that runs through the evolution of history . . . The time
passionately demands new life-force, new mind-force, consecrated to the
study of social evil and the lessening of social distress. The college woman,
prepared by combination of nature and training to react on life from a new
point of view, appears for the first time."[14] But for Van Wyck Brooks, looking backward, this New England that seemed to Scudder restored and renewed was a valley of the dry bones, its possession by women a sign of the
death rather than the evolution of history: "The bony fingers of ageing spinsters dominated the village scene, where one might have supposed the end
of the world was at hand."[15]

With the ascendancy of woman to apocalyptic force, the anchor of home
is supplanted by the pervasive communality of the hotel. In *The American
Scene* (1904-5), James stands before the "gorgeous golden blur" of the
Waldorf-Astoria, contemplating the sumptuous fruit of the death of home:
"The moral in question, the high interest of the tale, is that you are in presence of a revelation of the possibilities of the hotel—for which the American
spirit has found so unprecedented a use and a value; leading it on to express so a
social, indeed positively an aesthetic ideal, and making it so, at this supreme
pitch, a synonym for civilization, for the capture of conceived manners

themselves, that one is verily tempted to ask if the hotel-spirit may not just be the American spirit most seeking and most finding itself." "Here was a social order in positively stable equilibrium. Here was a world whose relation to its form and medium was practically imperturbable; here was a conception of publicity *as* the vital medium organized with the authority with which the American genius for organization, put on its mettle, alone could organize it."[16] This replacement of home by hotel as a point of "positively stable equilibrium" in a society made up of dizzying changes is at one with the spread of women over the social life of the land. The hotel nationalizes Louisa May Alcott's dream of perpetual sisterhood, with the result that no homely little cottage remains to lure the lone male from dreams of glory. The community of women has gorgeously communized American life.

Ironically, this appropriation of social life by women, which James regards with such fascinated horror, was originally (and perhaps disingenuously) intended as a holding action against the public push of feminism. In 1850 a pious woman exhorted her gentle readers to leave the inexorable power of government to men and to be content with the nobler sphere of society: "May not we, the women of America, mould our social life by our intelligent convictions into a form which shall make it the fit handmaid of our political life in its grand simplicity and lofty aims?"[17] This decorous resignation will become for James an overwhelming national monument:

> The phenomenon may easily become, for a spectator, the sentence written largest in the American sky: when he is in search of the characteristic, what else so plays the part? The woman is two-thirds of the apparent life—which means that she is absolutely all of the social. . . . The woman produced by a woman-made society alone has obviously quite a new story—to which it is not for a moment to be gainsaid that the world at large has, for the last thirty years in particular, found itself lending an attentive, at times even a charmed ear. The extent and variety of this attention have been the specious measure of the personal success of the type in question, and are always referred to when its value happens to be challenged. "The American woman?—why, she has beguiled, she has conquered the globe: look at her fortune everywhere and fail to accept her if you can." [Pp. 346-47]

The imperial conquest by the American female, product of a kind of social parthenogenesis whereby the male is bred out of the race, is the United States—and thus the future—itself. Though *The American Scene* finds with relief that Washington is still a male bastion in a female nation, James is uneasy with such reassuring divisions as Maria McIntosh's between lofty little social life and its ruthless political counterpart. In "Pandora" (1884), a story written the year *The Bostonians* was begun, social and political life converge disturbingly in the person of Pandora Day, "the latest, freshest fruit of our great American evolution. She is the self-made girl!"[18] In the course of her story, Pandora effortlessly conquers Washington society until she bullies America's affable, silly president into appointing her fiancé minister of Holland. There are some nervous jokes along the way about Pandora herself being made a foreign minister, and when we observe her fiancé's obliging facelessness at the end, we realize she has effectively become one. As a "woman produced by a woman-made society," this "self-made girl" could never have been made by a man, though by the end she is able to make one. Containing in her name both a threat and a promise, the mythic Pandora Day is an amalgam of "certain transcendent things" James associated with his mother country. *The American Scene* describes women "in peerless possession" of his powerful homeland. *The Bostonians* lives through such a spreading possession, with its capacity for transcendence and the "cold Medusa-face" of its power.

With the partial exception of the hypnotically intense relation between Olive and Verena, the larger community of women in *The Bostonians* has none of the lovingly personal solicitude of its antecedents in *Little Women* and *Cranford*: with the exception of the first scene in the dim parlor of Miss Birdseye, the fuzzily selfless abolitionist, figurehead of the movement, whose guests straggle suspiciously around while their benevolent hostess wonders who these people are she has invited, we are scarcely permitted to see the collective entity of womanhood we are told will sweep over the world. The female community is an abstraction. For its guiding spirit, Olive Chancellor, feminism's main drawback is the intrusion of other women: "Miss Chancellor would have been much happier if the movements she was interested in could have been carried on only by the people she liked, and if revolutions, somehow, didn't always have to begin with one's self—with internal convulsions, sacrifices, executions. A common end, unfortunately, however fine as regards a special result, does not make community impersonal" (pp. 113-14). On the face of it a contradiction in terms, this goal of impersonal community is the heart of Olive's mission. She dreams not of sisterhood, but "that a woman *could* live on persistently, clinging to a great, vivifying, redemptory idea, without the help of a man" (p. 393)—and ideally, one presumes, without the intercession of another woman. The impersonality of her private Utopia carries Olive beyond womanhood as her century defined it, endowing her with the monumental constriction of an institutional body: "A smile of exceeding faintness played about her lips—it was just perceptible enough to light up the native gravity of her face. It might have been likened to a thin ray of moonlight resting upon the wall of a prison" (p. 8).

It is easy enough to give this image a Freudian tinge and to visualize poor crazy Olive as the prisoner of her own unnatural desires and twisted aspirations; but if Olive is inmate, she is given the status of prison as well. The image that introduces her reminds us that in the last third of the nineteenth century, a fervent New England cause was separate "matriarchal" prisons, such as the one at Sherburne which Louisa May Alcott described with excitement in 1879: "Went with Dr. W. to the Woman's Prison, at Sherburne. A lovely drive, and very remarkable day and night. Read a story to the four hundred women, and heard many interesting tales. A much better place than Concord Prison, with its armed wardens, and 'knock down and drag out' methods. Only women here, and they work wonders by patience, love, common-sense, and the belief in salvation for all." The bleak smile with which Olive greets her antagonist is an emblem of this corporate female self-sustainment which will preside over the world of the future and uplift it.[19]

The institutional weight with which Olive is endowed on her first entrance is reinforced by the book's title, which suggests that with all their qualifications and conflicts, Olive and the rest are at one with their time and place. This union of Olive with her age defines the accuracy of her catty sister's first characterization: "She is very honest, is Olive Chancellor; she is full of rectitude. Nobody tells fibs in Boston; I don't know what to make of them all" (p. 3).

Olive's relentless honesty is a part of her undivided fusion with her life: "There are women who are unmarried by accident, and others who are unmarried by option; but Olive Chancellor was unmarried by every implication of her being. She was a spinster as Shelley was a lyric poet, or as the month of August is sultry" (p. 18). Like her dream of an impersonal community, Olive's asexuality is an allegiance that moves beyond humanity: "I have said that it was Miss Chancellor's plan of life not to lie, but such a plan was compatible with a kind of consideration for the truth which led her to shrink from producing it on poor occasions" (p. 288). Her "consideration for the truth" as a thing beyond the contingencies of the moment removes her from the secretly subversive enclaves of earlier Victorian women. Divorced from herself like the vaporously impersonal Miss Birdseye, Olive acts as a yardstick of honesty in all its grotesqueness, bestowing for a time the apparently omniscient perspective of which Miss Birdseye's name is a witty emblem: "Olive had taken [Verena] up, in the literal sense of the phrase, like a bird of the air, had spread an extraordinary pair of wings, and carried her through the dizzying void of space. Verena liked it, for the most part; liked to shoot upward without an effort of her own and look down upon all creation, upon all history, from such a height" (p. 79). The very ludicrousness of this image of Olive as American eagle carries a certain authenticity. "A woman without laughter," Olive may be funny as she takes to herself a God's-eye view, but nothing in the book says she is false.

From his opening drawl, "I pretend not to prevaricate" (p. 4), Basil Ransom "as a representative of his sex" (p. 5) is associated with a dissimulation that is traditionally feminine.[20] Far from expressing his gallant love of "the sex," the florid chivalry with which he smothers every woman he meets (and, in the case of Mrs. Luna, becomes smothered himself) is the honey of a universal rage: "Chivalry had to do with one's relations with people one hated, not with those one loved" (p. 403). This belated admission corroborates Olive's most paranoid and seemingly unbalanced observations: "Olive disliked [men] most when they were least unpleasant" (p. 294). "He didn't love [Verena], he hated her, he only wanted to smother her, to crush her, to kill her—as she would infallibly see that he would if she listened to him. It was because he knew that her voice had magic in it, and from the moment he caught its first note he had determined to destroy it" (p. 390). Without doubt Olive's speech is hysterical, but it is nevertheless an honest echo of Basil's involuntary response to Verena's voice in the night: "Murder, what a lovely voice!" (p. 366). What seems deranged in Olive is her explicit formulation of the duplicitous Basil's buried life.

Basil is not only a liar, but a carrier of lies. Like the relic-obsessed narrator of *The Aspern Papers* (1888), he contaminates the shabby but genuine integrity of a community of women with the seductive lie of love. At a key moment in the novel, he confronts the incorruptibly honest Miss Birdseye with the advantages of deceit: "'Do you wish me to conceal—?' murmured Miss Birdseye, panting a little . . . 'Well, I never did anything of that kind'" (pp. 225-26). Backed to the wall, she submits only in the name of that "truth" of which she is a disheveled exemplar: "Well, I believe in the victory of the truth. I won't say anything" (p. 226). Though the truth seems sadly unvictorious in this novel, at least as it is usually read, Olive's dismissal of men as "poor creatures" is quietly sanctioned by the reality James creates, since Basil is the most attractive man we see, while his ornate fantasy about women as decorative objects for private consumption is given the lie by every woman in the novel, of whom none but Verena is decorative and none but Olive's carnivorous sister, Mrs. Luna, lives a private life.

Serpentine landscapes seem to follow Basil. When he takes Verena for an idyllic walk in Central Park in order to initiate her into the "contempt and brutality" that make up his conservative doctrine, the two "[thread] the devious ways of the Ramble, [and lose] themselves in the Maze" (p. 335). Her conversion to his alternate truth is introduced by another image of random, floundering falsity. As she sees him "waiting for her at a bend of the road which lost itself, after a winding, straggling mile or two, in the indented, insulated 'point,' *where the wandering bee droned through the hot hours with a vague, misguided flight*, she felt that his tall, watching figure, with the low horizon behind, represented well the importance, the towering eminence he had in her mind" (p. 397; emphasis mine). The droning directionless bee Verena is becoming takes poignancy from the certainty with which Olive scans history from Miss Birdseye's perspective in her plan to appropriate it "like a bird of the air." The bare view of the Charles River with which Olive is associated carries by contrast with Basil's lost and devious associations the authority of its honest ugliness.

Basil's role as the source of lies is associated with his isolation in time and place. No South is left to validate his identity; his plantation and his homeland have been destroyed in a war he thinks was incited by female abolitionists from New England.[21] And he is locked into an ideology that is "about three hundred years behind the age." His lie is less personal than historical, for in this novel, truth is the partner not of morality, nature, and sanity, but of history as James perceives it. Too many critics have dismissed Olive's perceptions because they see her as neurotic:[22] in the face of this pervasive historicity, her "new truths" are vindicated by the bushels of letters she receives on Cape Cod, while Basil sits alone in his law office in New York, waiting for someone to need him.

The truth upheld by the female community in the person of its representative Olive is the truth of an age whose religion is publicity and its concurrent theatricality. The age is defined by Olive's uncharacteristically witty response to Boston theatergoing: "It was not so religious as going to evening-service at King's Chapel; but it was the next thing to it" (p. 119). The spiritualistic miasma that clings to Boston's feminist communities aligns them with a "truth" that is public and transcendent.[23] As it is defined in the novel, truth is one's theatrical debut on the stage of history.

This inseparability of history and the theater is not unique to James's America: in the England of *The Princess Casamassima* (1886) and *The Tragic Muse* (1889-90), the entanglement between politics and the stage simply is more glamorously dazzling than that of London's earnest and shabby American cousin. The three major novels of the 1880s grow out of a single vision and set of concerns, in which the Old World and the New illuminate each other in the suspicious similarity of their national and histrionic performances. Donald David Stone's otherwise exhaustive account of James in the 1880s oversimplifies in its contentions that "history is a mirage, for James's main characters, which they escape by disavowing" and "art is an illusion which lasts, while history is a reality which passes."[24] Neither James nor his protagonists can escape a narrowly defined "history" for a private Skinner box of "art." The overarching irony of all these novels is the extent to which the confinements of history and the freedom of art pervade and create each other, and the characters who try to separate them can only be damned by losing both.

In *The Princess Casamassima* the initiation of the artist is at one with that of the incendiary. "Mr. Vetch had on a great occasion, within the year, obtained for the pair an order for two seats at a pantomime, and to Hyacinth the impression of that ecstatic evening had consecrated him, placed him for ever in the golden glow of the footlights."[25] Young Hyacinth Robinson's vision of his destiny is as prescient as the young Wordsworth's in Book IV of

*The Prelude*. His shift to the golden glow of political footlights does not even require a shift of vocabulary: "Hyacinth waited for the voice that should allot him the particular part he was to play. His ambition was to play it with brilliancy, to offer an example—an example that might survive him—of pure youthful, almost juvenile, consecration" (p. 233).

Hyacinth's formal consecration to the cause of revolution is the result of a flamboyantly theatrical speech, and his final suicide is an equally stagy/ political gesture which deftly makes him a martyr to both parties. We learn of it in a wonderfully grandiose curtain line: "Mr. Robinson has shot himself through the heart. He must have done it while you were fetching the milk" (p. 511). In a novel soaked in the aura of footlights, the Princess herself is of course the primary diva, embodying the worlds of politics and the stage from the moment we first see her at the theater, a covert revolutionary outshining the actors. But though the Princess incarnates the complex performances of public life, her companion Madame Grandoni speaks with the same intimate authority as Olive's sister did: "Christina has many faults, but she hasn't that one [of lying]; that's why I can live with her. She'll speak the truth always" (p. 210). Immersing her private needs in "the golden glow of the footlights" of a political mission, she generates, grotesquely, honesty and truth. She is an illuminatingly inverted descendant of Tennyson's Princess Ida, who, in her equally gorgeous confluence of feminism, education, and art, was simply, compellingly false. By the time we reach James's Olive Chancellor and Princess Casamassima, a woman's entrance in the historical theater introduces an undeniable new truth which no dashing intrusion of a prince can gainsay.[26]

The budding actress Miriam Rooth in *The Tragic Muse* is James's final confrontation of the public woman in this group of novels. Though Miriam is not a secret political organizer, she is subtly balanced against her analogue, the thoroughly political Julia Dallow, whose irritated fiancé asks wearily of her pageant of house parties: "Must you *always* live in public, Julia?"[27] Similarly, Peter Sherringham, whose role is that of a more civilized Basil demanding that the public woman subside "naturally" into being private and possessed, defines the monstrosity of the perpetually performing Miriam: "It struck him abruptly that a woman whose only being was to 'make believe,' to make believe that she had any and every being that you liked, that would serve a purpose, produce a certain effect, and whose identity resided in the continuity of her personations, so that she had no moral privacy, as he phrased it to himself, but lived in a high wind of exhibition, of figuration— such a woman was a kind of monster, in whom of necessity there would be nothing to like, because there would be nothing to take hold of" (p. 150).

But when Peter confronts Miriam with his discovery that she is a monster, her answer is the calm: "'Yes, perhaps,' the girl replied, with her head on one side, as if she were looking at the pattern. 'But I'm very honest'" (p. 167). As with Olive and the Princess, honesty is born, not submerged, in the public woman, an assertion made with greater assurance in each of the three novels. The most assured, ebullient, and untragic of the trilogy of the 1880s, *The Tragic Muse* rewrites and exposes the controversial ending of *The Bostonians*, in which Basil invades the New York theater where Verena is about to give a crucial speech, breaks her frail will, and steers her into marriage, leaving Olive to mollify the enraged audience as Verena secretly weeps under her hood.

In *The Tragic Muse*, Miriam and Peter replay in a comic key the backstage confrontation between Verena and Basil. Here, however, the performing woman can assert the integrity of her existence: Miriam/Verena not only refuses to marry Peter/Basil, but meets his soothing platitudes with a series of elegantly stinging retorts that are unfortunately beyond the perpetually mesmerized Verena. Her final turn of the screw is her selection of the unsavory Basil Dashwood as her husband-manager. Like Matthias Pardon in *The Bostonians*, Dashwood embodies the shrewd professional acumen of the untalented; it may be James's final comment on the romance of the old South and the public supremacy of the male sex to bestow Basil's name on a petty operator who gets the girl and gives up his career to manage hers. The lucidity and grace of the later novel lend shape to some of the convolutions of the earlier one.

*The Tragic Muse* opens with the portentous announcement that "all art is one" (p. 16), and the art of politics is included in this statement of theme. As one essay puts it: "Actor and politician have this in common, that they can only function in relation to an audience; that to catch this audience both speak and feign 'parts' that have been written and devised for them by others—they must be what they are not." In its sense of this alliance between two public arts that tell a perverse but immutable "truth," *The Bostonians* is indeed "a backstage drama—will the show go on?"[28]

Seen in this context of performance and triumphant theatricality, the relation between Olive and Verena is less purely a matter of submerged eroticism than it may seem. Its "unnatural" intensity is a consequence not simply of its implicit alliance with "the love that dare not speak its name," but of the magically unnatural generation of creativity and art, the love between impresario and star. The eighties and nineties abounded in impassioned, unnatural unions such as those between Henry Irving and Ellen Terry, Henry Higgins and Eliza Doolittle, Svengali and Trilby, whose agents literally invade each others' personalities to produce the "new truth" that is not a child. In depicting such a relation between two women, James made the process of mutual identification more subtle and complex, for when Olive flings herself onstage after Verena's defection, her desperate appearance suggests that of the archetypal mousy understudy who becomes a star.

James has carefully prepared us for a surprising triumph on Olive's part. Shortly after the widely quoted passage on her masochistic hunger for martyrdom, he adds quietly: "Olive had a fear of everything, but her greatest fear was of being afraid. She wished immensely to be generous, and how could one be generous unless one ran a risk? She had erected it into a sort of rule of conduct that whenever she saw a risk she was to take it; and she had frequent humiliations at finding herself safe after all" (p. 14). In a sense, Olive's greatest martyrdom would be personal acclaim by the audience she despises; but her fastidiousness hides the yearning of the secret ham. At the gathering at Miss Birdseye's, she gibbers nervously to Mrs. Farrinder: "I want to enter the lives of women who are lonely, who are piteous. I want to be near to them—to help them. I want to do something—oh, I should like so to speak" (p. 36). And later on, the thorough trooper Verena evaluates one of Olive's self-forgetting harangues: "Why, Olive, you are quite a speaker yourself! ... You would far surpass me if you would let yourself go" (pp. 139-40). For Olive, letting herself go and letting Verena go may be equally therapeutic means of realizing her vision of woman standing alone and "clinging to a great, vivifying, redemptory idea"—which she spreads over her age.

If the impresario Olive is a secret star, pliant Verena is closer to Trilby than to Victoria Woodhull. She enters the novel performing under her father's mesmeric influence, and in her subsequent conversions to Olive's new truth and Basil's old one, she vacantly replaces the compulsion of Selah Tarrant's initial Svengali. When she falls under Basil's counterspell at the end of the novel, she explains her abdication in the Trilby-like phrase, "I was paralyzed" (p. 460). Basil sees her not as the medium of an ideology, but as a complete performer; he drinks her voice in with no sense of the words it utters. In their futile debate toward the end of the novel, both dismiss the mighty "cause" as if it were mere program music: "'I confess I should like to know what is to become of all that [talented] part of me, if I retire into private life, and live, as you say, simply to be charming for you. I shall be like a singer with a beautiful voice (you have told me yourself my voice is beautiful), who has accepted some decree of never raising a note. Isn't that a great waste, a great violation of nature?' ... 'Believe me, Miss Tarrant, these things will take care of themselves. You won't sing in the Music Hall, but you will sing to me; you will sing to every one who knows you and approaches you'" (pp. 401-2).

This recurrent impression of Verena as a singer in her passive, compulsive response to the influence of others may not be purely coincidental. James became friendly with George du Maurier in 1884, the year *The Bostonians* was begun; ten years later the stunning success of *Trilby* as novel and play was a bitter pill: "'See what it is to take the measure of the foot—as we say— of the gross Anglo-Saxon public,' he remarked to Daudet. 'The rare Meredith is not that kind of shoemaker—nor,' added Henry, 'the poor James.'"[29]

James's rare ungraciousness presumably stems from the fact that years before, he himself had been offered the idea for *Trilby*—and rejected it. In 1889 he wrote in his notebook: "Last evening before dinner I took a walk with G. du Maurier, in the mild March twilight (there was a blessed sense of spring in the air), through the empty streets near Porchester Terrace, and he told me over an idea of his which he thought very good—and I do too—for a short story—he had already mentioned [it] to me—a year or two ago, in a walk at Hampstead, but it had passed from my mind. Last night it struck me as curious picturesque, and distinctly usable: though the want of musical knowledge would hinder *me* somewhat in handling it."[30] But it is just possible that the success of *Trilby* stung him so much not because he had refused the idea of a beautiful mesmerized girl who is a mere "subject" for the "sacred fire" of others, but because he had already taken and transplanted it from music to politics in a novel of his country that no one had liked.

Verena's kinship to Trilby further undermines the authenticity of Basil's chivalry and his love: conventional marriage offers only escape from the truth of the performing self. Moreover, males lack the power to endow a woman with fulfillment, for in a world where the public faces of art and politics are so nearly interchangeable, the men must struggle for billing in an increasingly feminized history, as we see the journalist Matthias Pardon doing throughout: "Besides, it was a woman's question; what they wanted was for women, and it should be by women. It had happened to the young Matthias more than once to be shown the way to the door, but it had not hitherto befallen him to be made to feel that he was not—and could not be—a factor in contemporary history; here was a rapacious woman who proposed to keep that favorable setting for herself" (p. 147). Olive's banishment of Pardon has the historical audacity of Elizabeth Cady Stanton's "woman herself must do this work," and under this stern injunction the men equate surviving at all with getting one's name in the paper. If the struggle for existence is the struggle to break into print, "it is to the world of Matthias Pardon, and Selah Tarrant, we have to look for the most consistent portrait of the age."[31] Tarrant's hope of heaven embodies the pathos of these peripheral men: "The wish of his soul was that he might be interviewed; that made him hover at the editorial elbow" (p. 106).

In his awareness that a self-promoting society requires him to publish or perish, Basil Ransom is no different from the grubbier Tarrant and Pardon. If his obsessive dogmatizing links him to Olive, his feeling that the acceptance of a single essay by an obscure periodical makes "an era in my life" sufficient to justify his existence forges a stronger link with the other men in the novel, who in their pathetic print-bound obscurity anticipate the tenants on Gissing's New Grub Street. Indeed, Verena's first involuntary tenderness for Basil comes when he exposes to her his humiliatingly unpublished state: he reminds her of her unpublished father, whom she is accustomed to pity and obey. It is no wonder that in the final abdication of her flight with him, her mother springs out of her habitual torpor and hurls herself upon Verena in a "furious onset" of rage, prayers, and tears: she knows better than Olive the hopelessness of such a marriage. Rather than marrying the "normal" antago- nist and double of twisted unnatural Olive, Verena retreats to the home cycle by eloping with a more romantically colored version of her shady father.

It is as debatable as the nature of history itself whether "the age" in *The Bostonians* belongs to its scrambling men, who maintain a tenuous identity as long as they have the hope of seeing their names on a page, or to the visionary gleam of its women. For Basil, "it's a feminine, a nervous, hysteri- cal, chattering, canting age . . . which, if we don't soon look out, will usher in the reign of mediocrity, of the feeblest and flattest and the most preten- tious that has ever been" (p. 343). Allowing Basil his own hysterical and cant- ing tone, "the age" we see does seem implacably possessed by its variegated women.[32] But insofar as Olive embodies it, its "chattering, canting" rhetoric disappears into the silence that is associated with her throughout. The mutuality of her "dumb embrace" with Verena (p. 310) is held against Basil's surely more "hysterical" concept of marriage: "if he should become her husband he should know a way to strike her dumb" (p. 329). At Marmion, Dr. Prance describes the women's nervousness as stillness: "you can hear the silence vibrate" (p. 416). Shortly thereafter, we do: "Verena leaned her head back and closed her eyes, and for an hour, as nightfall settled in the room, neither of the young women spoke. Distinctly, it was a kind of shame" (p. 425). The silence defines the shame, of their intensity and of Verena's betrayal. But most portentous is the "quick, complete, tremendous silence" which greets Olive's appearance onstage at the end, where the book leaves her.

This silence in which the private and the public meet is a majestic question mark. It is so common to assume that Olive's first performance is her lifelong humiliation[33] that critics of James seem infected by the intensity of her own self-hate: "I am going to be hissed and hooted and insulted!" (p. 463). But perhaps, after all, the waves part for Olive. The dramatic hush she creates looks forward to that moment in *The Turn of the Screw* (1898) when the governess first sees an apparition: "It was as if, while I took in, what I did take in, all the rest of the scene had been stricken with death. I can hear again, as I write, the intense hush in which the sounds of evening dropped. The rooks stopped cawing in the golden sky and the friendly hour lost for the unspeakable minute all its voice."[34] Such a silence marks an unnatural change in the universe. The ghost in the garden, Olive on the stage, reveal an invasion of commonality by an equivocal power that must change the present and the future and throw the past in new perspective. Whatever the value of such an invasion, it is an irrevocable emergence.

The very end of the novel juxtaposes Olive's "rush to the front" with Verena's hidden tears. This important moment seems to repeat itself in a majestic passage written in 1905 for the New York edition of *The Princess Casamassima*, in which the Princess repudiates Hyacinth's adoration: "And she turned from him as with a beat of great white wings that raised her straight out of the bad air of the personal. It took her up too high, it put an end to their talk; expressing an indifference to what it might interest him to think of her to-day, and even a contempt for it, which brought tears to his eyes" (p. 495). This quasi-mystical ascent away from nature and regret crystallizes the expectant, theatrical silence of Olive's debut. "Like the heroine that she was" (p. 462), she seems to balloon into the purity of history, while "the bad air of the personal," with concurrent lies and tears, mourns its loss.

James's historical prophecy about women sweeping over and embodying his virgin land has been muddled by the subsequent diminution of feminism after the vote was finally gained. It was easy for later writers to assume that feminism was as morbid an eruption to James as it seemed to them, but a remark he made about the British suffrage movement in 1908 might stand as as his own diagnosis of his Bostonians: "All the signs of the beginning of a great movement, in spite of the ease of ridiculing them for desiring martyrdom on such cheap terms, 'for the terms *are* cheap.'"[35] The martyrdom, not the movement, is legitimately ridiculous; this female thirst for self-destruction has recently been given the soberer, more secular label, "fear of success." James's freedom from defensive derision is underlined by the fact that, in 1908, passionate support began in Boston for the militant suffragists in England; a torpid New England party was revivified by its adoption of British tactics and its adulatory response to the Pankhursts.[36] Though by that time the novel was a far-off failure to him, James may have remained a Bostonian despite himself. His respect for the new militancy of the crusade exposes the sadly anachronistic and ahistorical nature of some later assumptions about his attitudes: "[T]he doctrinaire demand for the equality of the sexes may well seem to promise but a wry and constricted story, a tale of mere eccentricity . . . It would seem to be susceptible only of comic treatment, and the comedy it seems to propose is not of an attractive kind[.]"[37] Lionel Trilling's unattractive laughter is a measure of what our century has lost. For James, women's demands were less funny than inexorable. The bitter comedy lay in the movement's self-subversion of its own strength.

When Olive furiously mounts the stage, readers may assume, consciously or unconsciously, that James wrote out a terrible prevision of his own devastating debut ten years later, when, as the author of *Guy Domville*, he was so "hissed and hooted and insulted" that he never recovered from the exposure. In Leon Edel's magnificent description of James's entrance, the theater and politics converge irrevocably in the crisis of the author's adult life:

> He brought James on, leading him by the hand. The novelist, having
> heard applause, came forward shyly, hesitantly; and at that moment

the gallery exploded. Jeers, hisses, catcalls were followed by great waves of applause from that part of the audience which esteemed James and had recognized the better qualities of the play. *The two audiences had declared war.* The intellectual and artistic elite answered the howls of derision; the howls grew strong in defiance. This was an unusual kind of passion in an English theatre, where feelings were so seldom expressed. "All the forces of civilization in the house," Henry later wrote to his brother, "waged a battle of the most gallant, prolonged and sustained applause with the hoots and jeers and catcalls of the roughs, whose roars (like those of a cage of beasts at some infernal zoo) were only exacerbated by the conflict."[38]

For Edel, the trauma of James's life was an incident in the British class struggle, as the "two audiences," the elite and the roughs, battled for possession of the innocent artist. His excruciating debut was a symptom of the class war in his adopted country; but Olive's equally vulnerable entrance in the city she personifies is a touchstone of American feminism, particularly in its Bostonian incarnation. For Boston feminism, American womanhood was the transcendent triumphant fact that swept over differences of class, age, and race: "True empathy based on experiences common to sex rather than on those particular to class, ethnic origin or religion was the ultimate goal."[39] The one far-off divine event in Olive's life seems less a private sexual captivation of Verena than a breaking out of Brahminism into this mystical solvent of "true womanhood." Its consummation is left poised at the end of the novel, but this "great, vivifying, redemptory idea" of womanhood as a common purging wave over the social war differentiates James's "very *American* tale" from its poignant British echo in his life.

## Notes

1. Elizabeth Janeway, *Between Myth and Morning: Women Awakening* (New York: William Morrow & Co., 1975), pp. 138–39, 144.
2. Henry James, *The Bostonians* (1884; reprint ed., New York: Modern Library, 1956). Future references to this edition will appear in the text.
3. F. W. Dupee, *Henry James* (1951 ; reprint ed., New York: William Morrow & Co., 1974), p. 122.
4. Leon Edel, *Henry James, The Untried Years: 1843–1870* (Philadelphia and New York: J. B. Lippincott Co., 1953), p. 202; and Charles Thomas Samuels, *The Ambiguity of Henry James* (Urbana: University of Illinois Press, 1971), p. 106.
5. William Rounseville Alger, *The Friendships of Women* (Boston: Roberts Brothers, 1885), p. 364.

6.  Ednah D. Cheyney, ed., *Louisa May Alcott: Her Life, Letters, and Journals* (Boston: Roberts Brothers, 1890), p. 165. For more on Alcott as an exemplar of New England feminism, see my discussion in *Communities of Women: An Idea in Fiction* (Cambridge, Mass.: Harvard University Press, 1978), pp. 55–73.

7.  Louisa May Alcott, *Little Women* (1868–69; reprint ed., New York: Grosset & Dunlap, 1947), p. 204.

8.  5 June 1855; quoted in A. B. Hopkins, *Elizabeth Gaskell: Her Life and Work* (London: John Lehmann, 1952), pp. 225–26.

9.  *The Nation* 2 (22 October 1866):246.

10.  See John Henry Raleigh, *Matthew Arnold and American Culture* (Berkeley and Los Angeles: University of California Press, 1961), p. 42: "Both [Arnold and James] were convinced that the future lay in the hands of America."

11.  Quoted in Judith Becker Ranlett, "Sorority and Community: Women's Answer to a Changing Massachusetts, 1865–1895," (Ph.D. diss., Brandeis University, 1974), p. 72.

12.  Leon Edel, *Henry James, The Middle Years: 1882–1895* (Philadelphia and New York: J. B. Lippincott Co., 1962), p. 144.

13.  9 February 1882 and 19 March 1905; F. O. Matthiessen and Kenneth B. Murdock, eds., *The Notebooks of Henry James* (New York: Oxford University Press, 1947), pp. 41, 320–21.

14.  Quoted in Ranlett, "Sorority and Community," p. 160.

15.  Van Wyck Brooks, *New England: Indian Summer, 1865–1915* (New York: E. P. Dutton & Co., 1940), p. 469.

16.  Henry James, *The American Scene* (Bloomington and London: Indiana University Press, 1968), pp. 102, 105. Future references to this edition will appear in the text.

17.  Maria J. McIntosh, *Woman in America: Her Work and Her Reward* (New York: D. Appleton & Co., 1850), p. 57.

18.  Leon Edel, ed., *The Complete Tales of Henry James*, 6 vols. (London: Rupert Hart-Davis, 1963), 5:396.

19.  8 October 1879; Cheyney, *Louisa May Alcott*, p. 322. See also Ranlett, "Sorority and Community," Ch. 3; and Estelle B. Freedman, "Their Sisters' Keepers: An Historical Perspective on Female Correctional Institutions in the United States: 1870–1900," *Feminist Studies* 2 (1974):77–95. A depressing reminder of how far we have or have not come from Alcott's exuberant "salvation for all" is Rose Giallombardo's *Society of Women: A Study of a Women's Prison* (New York and London: John Wiley & Sons, 1966). According to Giallombardo, the total desolation of these women without men is less sexual than social; deprived of their sole means of attaining status, the women have evolved an elaborate masquerade in which some of them strut about in elaborate drag, even at times assuming the role of a strict, respectable paterfamilias, and order the others about. Life is thus tolerable and familiar once more because it holds at least the charade of salvation through a man. "The hardest part of living in a prison is to live with

other women," says one; all seem to agree that a world without men is an anticommunal jungle (pp. 99–100).

20. See Irving Howe's introduction to the Modern Library College Edition of the novel, p. xvi: "while Basil Ransom is ready to talk about the proper place of women, who are for him the solacing and decorative sex, James is far too much of a realist to suggest that they can or ever will again assume this place: even Ransom's lady relatives in Mississippi, deprived of their darkies, have been reduced to hard work." Howe's exposure of Basil's inadequacies is a good antidote to Lionel Trilling's erection of his sadism into a cultural norm, though Howe and Basil are oddly at one in their detestation of Boston's feminists.

21. In *The American Scene*, pp. 414–17, James ironically corroborates Basil's sexual vision of history in his portrait of the South as an analogue of Boston, "a sick lioness," overrun by women.

22. See, among many, Howe, p. xxiii; Samuels, pp. 97–99; Theodore C. Miller, "The Muddled Politics of Henry James's *The Bostonians*," *Georgia Review* 26 (Fall 1972):336–46; and Robert C. McLean, *"The Bostonians*: New England Pastoral," *Papers on Language and Literature* 7 (Fall 1971):374–81.

23. See R. Laurence Moore, "The Spiritualist Medium: A Study of Female Professionalism in Victorian America," *American Quarterly* 27 (May 1975):200–221, for the historical links between spiritualism, feminism, and the theater. For Moore, spiritualism was one of the few avenues by which women could take center stage, while being able to deny responsibility for their entranced assumption of public power.

24. David Donald Stone, *Novelists in a Changing World: Meredith, James, and the Transformation of English Fiction in the 1880s* (Cambridge, Mass.: Harvard University Press, 1972), pp. 84, 306.

25. Henry James, *The Princess Casamassima* (1886; reprint ed., New York: Harper & Row, 1968), p. 35. Future references to this edition will appear in the text.

26. Stone, *Novelists in a Changing World*, pp. 302–3, discusses some similarities between Olive and Christina, and innumerable critics have linked the forbidding spinster to such lovable Jamesian creations as Isabel Archer, Julia Dallow, and Milly Theale, as well as to her more seemingly wholesome antagonist, Basil Ransom.

27. Henry James, *The Tragic Muse* (1889–90; reprint ed., New York: Harper & Brothers, 1960), p. 212. Future references to this edition will appear in the text.

28. D. J. Gordon and John Stokes, "The Reference of *The Tragic Muse*," in *The Air of Reality: New Essays on Henry James*, ed. John Goode (London: Methuen & Co., 1972), p. 92; and David Howard, *"The Bostonians*," ibid., p. 71.

29. See Edel, *Middle Years*, p. 81; and Leon Edel, *Henry James, The Treacherous Years: 1895–1901* (Philadelphia and New York: J. B. Lippincott Co., 1969), p. 153.

30. 25 March 1889; *Notebooks*, p. 97. On p. 98, the editors quote some remarks by du Maurier corroborating James's account, with du Maurier's significant addition: "'Well,' I said, 'you may have the idea and work it out to your own satisfaction.'"

31. Howard, "Bostonians," p. 67.

32. Compare Florimond's similar extended soliloquy in "A New England Winter" (1884), which begins: "He felt at moments that he was in a city of women, in a country of women" (*Tales*, VI, 142). Florimond's diagnosis is correct, but his dismay is called into question by the flimsy and pretentious nature of his career as "an impressionist." In the final analysis, the women who pass him back and forth among them represent less a sinister sexual conspiracy than the force of greatest integrity.

33. See, for instance, Elizabeth Schultz, "*The Bostonians*: The Contagion of Romantic Illusion," *Genre* 4 (March 1971):45–59; and Graham Burns, "*The Bostonians*," *The Critical Review* 12 (1969):45–60.

34. Henry James, *The Turn of the Screw* (New York: W. W. Norton & Co., 1966), p. 16.

35. Quoted in Leon Edel, *Henry James, The Master: 1901–1916* (Philadelphia and New York: J. B. Lippincott Co., 1972), p. 383.

36. See Sharon Hartman Strom, "Leadership and Tactics in the American Woman Suffrage Movement: A New Perspective from Massachusetts," *The Journal of American History* 62 (September 1975):296–315.

37. Lionel Trilling, "The Bostonians," in *The Opposing Self* (New York: Viking Press, 1955), pp. 109–19.

38. Edel, *Treacherous Years*, p. 79; my italics.

39. Ranlett, "Sorority and Community," p. 120.

# Elizabeth Ammons

# Cool Diana and the Blood-Red Muse: Edith Wharton on Innocence and Art

For a number of reasons, Edith Wharton is unusually important to any feminist revision of American literary history. She is an author of the first rank and a woman. She spent her life writing about women and issues affecting women. Her career, because she did not publish in the mid-nineteenth century or begin her work in the 1920s, is underestimated in the current, rather skewed literary demography. Her fiction took a conservative turn after 1920, which, like similar shifts in the careers of Sinclair Lewis and Willa Cather, raises basic questions about war and misogyny in twentieth-century literature.

Wharton's career also is fascinating biographically. Her work, like that of many women artists, flowered when she was in the middle of life (around forty) rather than in her twenties or thirties. Also suggesting patterns that may be peculiar to female experience, gender and class clash at some important points in her life; and certainly her expatriation is connected both to being a woman and to the profession of writing. Not least important is untangling her complicated feelings (as opposed to her thoughts) about being female—how she felt about her mother, about being childless, about friendships with other women, about relationships with men.[1]

Indeed, there are so many issues that any short essay has to be selective. What I would like to do here, therefore, is talk in detail about one book, *The Age of Innocence*, a best-seller in 1920 and recipient of the Pulitzer Prize. I have chosen it because it is a pivotal book in Wharton's career and one in which several of the issues I have mentioned collect.[2]

After *The Age of Innocence*, critics agree, the quality of Wharton's long fiction changes. The line of exceptional work beginning with *The House of Mirth* in 1905 and running through *The Fruit of the Tree* (1907), *Ethan Frome* (1911), *The Reef* (1912), *The Custom of the Country* (1913), and *Summer* (1917) ends in 1920. After that there is an occasional book of extraordinary accomplishment (some argue that *The Mother's Recompense*, for instance, is one), but by and large the early books greatly overshadow the novels Wharton wrote in the twenties and thirties: *The Glimpses of the Moon* (1922), *The Mother's Recompense* (1925), *Twilight Sleep* (1927), *The*

*Children* (1928), *Hudson River Bracketed* (1929), and *The Gods Arrive* (1932). *The Age of Innocence* marks the end of Edith Wharton's major period. It also marks the end of her Progressive Era fictions; and, as I hope to explain here in my discussion of the polarized portraits of the American girl and the woman artist in *The Age of Innocence*, the novel comments significantly on its author's personal situation. *The Age of Innocence* is one of the clearest expressions we have of Edith Wharton's frustration as an American woman writer.

Because *The Age of Innocence* culminates years of criticism on Wharton's part of America's treatment of women, it may be useful to summarize the concerns that preceded it. In *The House of Mirth*, the best-selling novel that secured her reputation as a popular yet serious writer in 1905, Edith Wharton had attacked—to use language current at the time—the "parasitism" of marriage for women. The novel is set in fashionable, wealthy New York at the turn of the century, and it studies the predicament of beautiful Lily Bart, who does not want to be anyone's wife but knows that she must nevertheless marry in order to remain financially and socially secure. Because she resists marriage, she ends up ostracized, destitute, and finally, dead.

Wharton's next three books, *The Fruit of the Tree, Ethan Frome*, and *The Reef*, are equally cheerless. *The Fruit of the Tree* (1907) is about a New Woman of exceptional intelligence and integrity, Justine Brent, who marries the liberated young man of her dreams only to have him eventually subordinate her to the memory of his dead first wife Bessy, a childish and utterly self-centered person. In *Ethan Frome* (1911), a grim modern fairy tale for adults, Wharton's two female figures finally merge into one awful image of woman as cripple; isolated from the world at large, Zeena Frome and Mattie Silver, like Ethan's mother before them, turn into invalids and madwomen— physical and mental ruins. Wharton's heroines in *The Reef* (1912), Anna Leath and Sophy Viner, attempt to change their lives: Sophy wants to find economic independence; Anna seeks erotic liberation. Each fails and not because her goal is unworthy; they fail because, as Wharton sees it, economic independence and sexual liberation are forbidden to women. Anna and Sophy end as they began: limited, unrealized people.

As if determined to write about a woman succeeding, indeed triumphing, rather than being crushed, Wharton in *The Custom of the Country* (1913) created Undine Spragg: smart, brash, ruthless. Required to marry, she plays the marriage market as skillfully as her male counterparts play the Wall Street market. Wharton loads the book with mercantile rhetoric to emphasize the crass, profit-seeking character of marriage, an institution in which women are property. Instead of resisting as Lily Bart does, Undine—aptly named for a money-making hair-curler (but also, of course, for the ancient temptress and nemesis of men, the siren)—goes through husbands like ambitious men go through jobs: with an eye on profit and advancement. She thus turns the system to her own advantage and, alone among Wharton's heroines, manages to shape her own fate. She does so, however, because she is unscrupulous; and though Wharton in many ways seems to have enjoyed charting Undine's devastating sweep through the upper reaches of old New York and sedate French society, Undine was clearly no solution to the problems Wharton had been exploring. She might be relief, vicious relief; but she was certainly no role model.

*Summer*, published in 1917, returns to the more usual, if depressing, Wharton vein. The novel, set in rural, impoverished New England, is about a very young woman's desire to escape the restrictions of village life, epitomized for her by her guardian, a man old enough to be her father. For one summer, her seventeenth, she does escape both emotionally and sexually. But the price she pays is marriage to the very person she most wanted to escape, her paternal guardian. Pregnant by another man, penniless, and without any skills to market, Charity Royall can see no alternative but to marry protective Mr. Royall. Thus, in this last book before *The Age of Innocence*, the father literally becomes the husband; there is not even the pretense of marriage as a union of equals at this primitive, and therefore unusually bold-faced, level of society.

*The Age of Innocence* brings to a close, brilliantly, this early line of fiction on what had been known in the United States for more than seventy years as "the woman question." Themes and issues that Wharton had begun exploring even before *The House of Mirth* echo and twine until *The Age of Innocence*, rich by any standard, has the unmistakable texture and depth of a masterwork. Wharton was looking backward both in historical time and in personal time when she wrote the book; she revisited in the wake of World War I the old New York of her girlhood and of America's adolescence, and, as in the world of *Summer*, the moral locale of *The Age of Innocence* has a sharp edge to it. The war had shaken Wharton. She lived in France throughout the fighting, working tirelessly on behalf of the French war effort, and she was constantly and personally aware of the devastation: the dying, the agony of widows and orphans, the razing of homes and monuments and, it seemed, culture itself. When the fighting was over, she turned, for relief no doubt, to her past and recreated in *The Age of Innocence* the New York of her youth. This is not to say that the book is nostalgic or escapist. It is, rather, an autopsy.

Wharton's plot is simple enough. About to announce his engagement to May Welland, who is one of old New York's loveliest virgins, Newland Archer—who is also a product of convention in the age Wharton dubs Innocent: the American 1870s—meets the Countess Olenska. She is not innocent. Originally an old New Yorker herself (though never a particularly conforming one), she has endured ten years of a miserable foreign marriage, and she has now returned to get a divorce and build a new life, one independent and wholesome, in the United States. Inevitably Archer falls in love with her. He then marries May out of duty, is unhappy, hopes to make Ellen his mistress, is disappointed. Although she loves him, the countess knows what it means to be a "kept" woman: lying, hiding, constantly hating oneself—and she would rather leave America than lead such a life. Her family, which has been trying to get rid of her, is relieved to see her go. Her desire to get a divorce; her living in a Bohemian quarter of the city; her open friendships with men who are married or engaged to other women—each is an unpardonable transgression. Old New York ceremoniously sends the Countess Olenska back to Europe, and Newland Archer is left to live out his conventional life with his conventional wife, May. The book ends twenty-five years later with Newland, now a widower, gazing up at the Countess Olenska's window in Paris but deciding not to go up. He is afraid to upset his memories, afraid to see Ellen in the flesh.

As soon as Wharton named her hero Archer, she insisted upon comparison with her good friend Henry James's *The Portrait of a Lady* (1881). Both novels are set in the American 1870s, both contrast American and European values, both have as a central figure an American named Archer who is highly susceptible to Continental charm and mystery. Yet the comparison of most interest to me here is not between the two Archers, Isabel and Newland, but between the two American girls, Isabel and May, each of whom is, in a sense, the author's title character. Just as the "portrait" James paints applies most directly to Isabel Archer, so Wharton's title *The Age of Innocence*, which she took from a Reynolds portrait of a child, applies most directly to May, a character as frozen in endless childhood as the painter's little girl. As Cynthia Griffin Wolff notes, Wharton's painterly title strengthens this novel's connection to James.[3] But in its substitution of a little girl for a lady, it also, as I will go on to explain, emphasizes the great distance between them.

Henry James's American girl—adventurous, ignorant, virtuous, self-assured—was the pride of America by the time Wharton began publishing novels at the turn of the century. If the image had shocked the nation in *Daisy Miller* in the 1870s, by the late nineties the type was such a commonplace, imaginatively, that it was a staple of popular culture. The ingenuous American girl was the heroine of best-selling novels—Gertrude Atherton's *Patience Sparhawk and Her Times* (1894) is an excellent example—and she was so frequently the centerpiece of cultural analyses that in *Land of Contrasts: A Briton's View of His American Kin* (1898), James Fullarton Muirhead (author of Baedeker guides to Great Britain and the United States) could routinely remark on the type in his chapter, "An Appreciation of the American Woman":

> Put roughly, what chiefly strikes the stranger in the American
> woman is her candour, her frankness, her hail-fellow-well-met-edness,

her apparent absence of consciousness of self or of sex, her spontaneity, her vivacity, her fearlessness. If the observer himself is not
of specially refined or delicate type, he is apt at first to misunder-
stand the camaraderie of an American girl, to see in it suggestions of
a possible coarseness of fibre. . . . But even to the obtuse stranger of
this character it will become obvious—as to the more refined observer
*ab initio*—that he can no more (if as much) dare to take a liberty
with the American girl than with his own countrywoman. The plum
may appear to be more easily handled, but its bloom will be found
to be as intact and as ethereal as in the jealously guarded hothouse
fruit of Europe. He will find that her frank and charming com-
panionability is as far removed from masculinity as from coarseness;
that the points in which she differs from the European lady do not
bring her nearer either to a man on the one hand, or to a common
woman on the other. He will find that he has to readjust his standards, to see that divergence from the best type of woman hitherto
known to him does not necessarily mean deterioration; if he is of an
open and susceptible mind, he may even come to the conclusion
that he prefers the transatlantic type![4]

Edith Wharton did not share Muirhead's enthusiasm. In *The Fruit of the
Tree*, published thirteen years before *The Age of Innocence*, she first offered
extended comment on the American girl in the character Bessy Westmore,
who is vivacious, ignorant, brave, and, Wharton emphasizes, pathetically
shallow. Bessy has energy but no knowledge, imagination but no depth. For
all her robust self-confidence, she is an extremely limited creature. As Wharton has an attractive older woman ruefully observe, Bessy is "one of the most
harrowing victims of the plan of bringing up our girls in the double bondage
of expediency and unreality . . . and leaving them to reconcile the two as
best they can, or lose their souls in the attempt."[5] This description could as
easily apply to Isabel Archer as to Bessy Westmore, with the major difference that, where James is fascinated to see how the reconciliation will be
attempted, Wharton is disgusted by the problem's even existing. She does not
see the American girl as America's noblest creation, the nation's most interesting contribution to modern civilization. She sees her as the nation's failure,
the human victim of a deluded obsession with innocence.

May Welland is Wharton's rarefied version of the stereotype. Unsoiled by
life, May is always connected with white: her virginity, mentally and emotionally, cannot be touched. She is permanently pure. Likewise, Wharton
implies, she is permanently juvenile. She has a fresh "boyish" quality that
brings to mind the "invincible innocence" of her middle-aged mother, and
suggests that May too will go through life sexually unaware and armed in
innocence (pp. 142, 190, 146).[6] To be sure, she is vigorous physically—she

rides, rows, plays lawn tennis, wins archery competitions—but even this healthiness is deceptive, for the allusions Wharton surrounds May with are lifeless. She walks beside Archer and "her face wore the vacant serenity of a young marble athlete" (p. 142); at another point her smile, we are told, is "Spartan" (p. 293). Elsewhere and most pointedly, Wharton says, the "faculty of unawareness was what gave her eyes their transparency, and her face the look of representing a type rather than a person; as if she might have been chosen to pose for a Civic Virtue or a Greek goddess" (p. 188).

The goddess Wharton associates with May is Diana, virgin deity of the hunt. Wearing a "white dress, with a pale green ribbon about the waist and a wreath of ivy on her hat," May wins her archery match with "Diana-like aloofness" (p. 210). Later she enters a ballroom "tall and silver-shining as a young Diana" (p. 306). Similarly, at the van der Luydens' reception for Ellen Olenska,"in her dress of white and silver, with a wreath of silver blossoms in her hair, the tall girl looked like a Diana just alight from the chase" (pp. 65–66). In May, Wharton takes selected virtues of the American girl: her innocence, her physical vigor, her cheerfulness and vivacity, her wholesomeness and self-confidence, and links them to a forever virginal goddess of death. Newland, with a shiver, wonders of May: "What if 'niceness' carried to that supreme degree were only a negation, the curtain dropped before an emptiness?" (p. 211). May Welland *is* empty. She is, in addition, living at the pinnacle of American society, America's Dream Girl.

Wharton insists that innocent May is both ancient and artificial. In spite of her athletic freedom and bright modern cheeriness, she is as old as patriarchy itself. Newland is depressed as he tries to imagine a comradely marriage with the Wellands' daughter: "he perceived that such a picture presupposed, on her part, the experience, the versatility, the freedom of judgment, which she had been carefully trained not to possess" (p. 44). He realizes further that, because "of this elaborate system of mystification" to which girls are subjected (which might well come from one of "the books on Primitive Man that people of advanced culture were beginning to read"), May has no depth: "she was frank, poor darling, because she had nothing to conceal, assured because she knew nothing to be on her guard against" (pp. 45–46). Yet Newland knows that "untrained human nature was not frank and innocent; it was full of the twists and defenses of an instinctive guile. And he felt himself oppressed by this creation of factitious purity," which, ironically, has been manufactured solely for his pleasure (p. 46).

In Wharton's version, the American girl is not spontaneous. She has been taught to be frank and self-assured as proof of her innocence (which is simply the ancient patriarchal value of virginity served up, of course, in nineteenth-century language). She is as manufactured an image of femininity as any other. She may look, in the guise of Isabel Archer or Daisy Miller, like a brand new independent creature; but take away James's infatuation with the American girl's illusion of freedom (and that is all Isabel or Daisy has, of course: the illusion of independence), and we have May Welland. The innocent American girl was a pernicious ideal, Wharton, looking back on the nineteenth century, felt compelled to say.

The issue here is larger, of course, than simply a difference of opinion between Edith Wharton and Henry James. Wharton was attacking an entire tradition when she entered May Welland in the lists of nineteenth-century American girls. Indeed, by the turn of the century, William Dean Howells, the most respected man of letters in America, was so convinced of the moral centrality of feminine virtue in fiction and life that he devoted two volumes to the study of women in nineteenth-century novels. His *Heroines of Fiction* (1901) argues, in his own words, "my prime position that the highest type of novelist is he who can most winningly impart the sense of womanhood."[7] That "sense of womanhood" most consistently admired by Howells in this book—as in his own fiction—always has the essential ingredients of the American girl. The preferred Howells heroine, who captures what *Heroines of Fiction* repeatedly calls the "Ever-Womanly," is fresh, intelligent, self-confident, and morally irradiating.

Subsequent criticism has followed Howells's lead. Paul John Eakin's *The New England Girl: Cultural Ideals in Hawthorne, Stowe, Howells, and James* (1976) maintains that in the nineteenth century, "woman functioned as an all-purpose symbol of the ideals of the culture: the official repository of its acknowledged moral code, and she appears accordingly as a redemptive figure in the era."[8] Eakin is building here, by his own admission, on William Wasserstrom's earlier study, *Heiress of All the Ages: Sex and Sentiment in the Genteel Tradition* (1959), which traces images of women in American novels from James through the twenties, looking in particular at the way the American girl is used symbolically, in fact messianically, to embody American idealism. As Eakin explains the premise he shares with Wasserstrom: "As the country moved toward more secular ways, a fiction arose which explicitly proposed its heroines as cult objects. . . . The value of these young women was measured by their power to redeem the individual, to regenerate society, through love."[9] Thus Wasserstrom, for example, concludes that Maggie Verver, the American girl of James's *The Golden Bowl* (1904), is the quintessential American heroine because she miraculously "combined the qualities of a nymph and a nun [and thus] finally reconciled all antitheses; she fulfilled the American dream of love, the dream of all the ages."[10]

It should not be surprising that Edith Wharton disliked *The Golden Bowl*.[11] In *The Age of Innocence*, she argues against the sentimentality of idealizing an "innocent" American woman; she argues against the masculine tradition celebrated by James and Howells and Wasserstrom and Eakin. In the first place, she knows that the price of innocence is diminished humanity for women. In the second place, she argues that the "natural" American girl

May Welland (like Bessy Westmore before her) is in fact not natural at all; she is an artificial product, a manufactured symbol of patriarchal authority. Yet in their surveys of the subject, neither Eakin nor Wasserstrom takes Wharton's criticism into account. Eakin stops with James and does not discuss Edith Wharton. Wasserstrom cites Wharton's dislike for May[12] but fails to see that May is Maggie shown from a different angle than James's. The result, as has often occurred because of superficial (or non-) treatment of women writers, is perpetuation of a distorting thesis about American literature, in this case the idea that major nineteenth and early twentieth-century American novelists, except for Hawthorne, idealized a virginal American girl. In fact, Edith Wharton did not.

Ironically, it may be that the tradition Edith Wharton was more in sympathy with, whether she realized it or not, is the popular one described by Nina Baym in *Woman's Fiction: A Guide to Novels by and about Women in America, 1820-1870*. The novels Baym analyzes do not celebrate innocence or idealize ignorance. Nor do they abstract women into a cultural "value." Their objective is realism and the story they tell is pragmatic: how to create for oneself a healthy adult female identity. Typically these novels "chronicle the 'trials and triumph' (as the subtitle of one example reads) of a heroine who, beset with hardships, finds within herself the abilities of intelligence, will, resourcefulness, and courage sufficient to overcome them."[13] The goal of these women's novels, like Wharton's decades later, is to examine female experience in fact and in its full social context. The difference is that where earlier women customarily offered a happy resolution to the heroine's struggle to construct an identity that mediated between the extremes of perpetual passive dependence and total (and hence antisocial) independence, Wharton, writing from the vantage point of a world no longer nineteenth-century in its basic assumptions about the primacy of family and the home, repeatedly found no happy resolution to offer. Her heroines—Ellen Olenska is a good example—seek informed active adulthoods only to find that America insists on perpetual daughterhood, eternal innocence.

Wharton's disdain for innocence as a female ideal is passionately expressed in the characterization of Ellen Olenska. She is everything May is not. She is complicated, flawed, sensual, curious, and creative. In important ways, she reflects the artist Edith Wharton trying to make a place for herself in America and failing.

Only once did Wharton make a woman writer a major character in one of her long fictions. At the beginning of her novel-writing career in *The Touchstone* (1900), she shows Margaret Aubyn, a brilliant and well-known author, being thrown over by Stephen Glennard in favor of an unthreatening, conventional young woman when it comes to marriage. Rejected, Margaret leaves America for England, where she dies. The rest of the book traces Glennard's inexcusable exploitation of Margaret after her death: in order to make money to marry, he sells the dead novelist's letters to him, which were personal. The novel condemns Glennard's dastardly behavior and ends with his remorseful confession of guilt to his wife.

As even a sketch suggests, *The Touchstone* is a melodramatic book and for that reason not very successful. Still, it is important autobiographically. Wharton had been publishing for eight years when the novel appeared, and she was not yet widely known; nevertheless, the fear of success that she invests in Margaret Aubyn's predicament is obvious. At the beginning of what would be a long and enormously successful career as a novelist, Wharton had chiefly fear and resentment to express about the woman writer's situation. There is nothing but discord between Margaret Aubyn's two lives. Publicly, she is brilliant, successful, and acclaimed. Personally, and in payment for that public success, she is lonely, humiliated, and punished, indeed—killed. She dies because Glennard rejects her; Glennard rejects her because she is such a brilliant and successful artist. Turn that around, and the message is clear: what a woman risks in daring to live as an artist is life itself.

As a rule, Edith Wharton avoided the subject of the woman writer. She was a proud and private person—she did not talk about her disastrous marriage to Edward Wharton; she kept her affair with Morton Fullerton so secret that not until her papers at Yale were opened in the late 1960s did biographers even know about it. She was similarly guarded about her feelings as an author. She did the ordinary things: sat for publicity photos, clipped reviews, fought with editors to get more money, wrote a memoir, *A Backward Glance* (1934), that is polite and uninformative. How she really *felt* about being a writer she expressed only very indirectly. If her first novel is remarkably direct—anger and anxiety are on the surface—it is the exception. After it, Wharton abandoned the woman writer as a character for long fiction. Perhaps she was afraid of revealing too many of her innermost feelings, perhaps she realized that writers writing about writers usually produce boring books. In any case, after *The Touchstone*, Edith Wharton continued to think about the woman artist in a few of her novels but the figure would not appear again as a writer. Sophy Viner in *The Reef* is an aspiring actress. Anne Clephane in *The Mother's Recompense* is a painter. And neither is an artist in the deepest sense. They are young, gifted women whom Wharton wishes well but in whom she does not, as she had with Margaret Aubyn, invest herself. The only artist with whom she does that again, twenty years after she started writing novels, is Ellen Olenska.

Ellen is not an artist in any narrow, sheerly production-oriented sense of the word. She does not paint, sing, write, dance, or act—although as a child she did most of those things. Indeed, old New York vividly remembers her "gaudy clothes" and

high color and high spirits. She was a fearless and familiar little
thing, who asked disconcerting questions, made precocious comments, and possessed outlandish arts, such as dancing a Spanish
shawl dance and singing Neapolitan love-songs to a guitar. Under the
direction of her aunt [Medora] ... the little girl received an expensive but incoherent education, which included "drawing from the
model," a thing never dreamed of before, and playing the piano in
quintets with professional musicians. Of course no good could come
of this. [P. 60]

Small wonder that Ellen, who was as wild and gorgeous a child as Hawthorne's Pearl in *The Scarlet Letter*, shows up at the opera at the beginning of
*The Age of Innocence* in, as Newland's grown sister describes it, a strange
dress of "'dark blue velvet, perfectly plain and flat—like a nightgown.'"
Newland's mother feigns shock at her daughter's reference to a bedroom and
remarks, "'What can you expect of a girl who was allowed to wear black satin
at her coming-out ball?'" (p. 40). Ellen's opera costume offends because it is
dramatic and sexy (one suspects the same was true of the earlier black satin).
She sits engrossed in *Faust*, "revealing, as she leaned forward, a little more
shoulder and bosom than New York was accustomed to seeing" (p. 15).

As an artist Ellen's medium is life itself. She moves into her aunt's dilapi-
dated house on unfashionable West Twenty-third Street and, without commo-
tion or a lot of money, changes it into something original. Newland looks
around him and

what struck him was the way in which Medora Manson's shabby
hired house, with its blighted background of pampas grass and
Rogers statuettes, had, by a turn of the hand, and the skillful use of
a few properties, been transformed into something intimate,
"foreign," subtly suggestive of old romantic scenes and sentiments.
He tried to analyze the trick, to find a clue to it in the way the chairs
and tables were grouped, in the fact that only two Jacqueminot
roses (of which nobody ever bought less than a dozen) had been
placed in the slender vase at his elbow, and in the vague pervading
perfume that was not what one put on handkerchiefs, but rather
like the scent of some far-off bazaar, a smell made up of Turkish
coffee and ambergris and dried roses. [Pp. 71–72]

Ellen Olenska, receiving Newland here in an erotic red-velvet gown (trimmed
with black fur [p. 105]), is exotic and passionate. Although she is not beautiful—she is thin and pale, on occasion haggard—she creates beauty around
herself, automatically. She has the visual artist's instinct for interesting
statement.

Ellen's life is also fertile intellectually. She prizes good conversation even more than the heirloom jewels and priceless antiques that she married into. Stimulating talk is for her (as it was for Wharton) a necessity of life, and she settles on West Twenty-third Street because she chooses to live among writers and actors. The odd move horrifies her relatives. They "had simply, as Mrs. Welland [May's mother] said, 'let poor Ellen find her own level'—and that, mortifyingly and incomprehensibly, was in the dim depths where . . . 'people who wrote' celebrated their untidy rites. It was incredible, but it was a fact, that Ellen, in spite of all her opportunities and her privileges, had become simply 'Bohemian'" (p. 260). Unreclaimable in the opinion of conservative upper-class New York, the Countess Olenska is given a dinner—"the tribal rally around a kinswoman about to be eliminated from the tribe" (p. 334)— and banished.

Her banishment, in keeping with old New York's impeccable good manners, is smooth and subtle. It even looks as if Ellen could stay in America and be happy if she wished. The family has tried to force her exit by forbidding divorce and then cutting her allowance severely—giving her no alternative but to return to her husband. Then at the last moment her grandmother, ignoring family pressure, offers Ellen a home with her. This may look appealing, but in fact, it is a sorry substitute for the freedom Ellen craved. She came to America to get a divorce, to live as an independent woman. The best she can achieve, however, is life as her grandmother's companion/dependent (with Newland propositioning her on the side). The only choice she has, in other words, is such a compromise that Wharton's point seems clear: there is no independent life available to this woman in America. The best she can do is grown-up little girlhood. Not surprisingly, Ellen turns down her grandmother's offer, and the original plan succeeds (with the help of a well-placed lie by May: she claims to be pregnant before she is positive in order to thoroughly close Ellen out of Newland's life). Forbidden a divorce and cut off from financial independence as long as she stays in the United States, Ellen is put in the position of having no good alternative but to leave. She is effectively—though politely, of course—gotten rid of.

With Ellen's exit Edith Wharton, living in France, repudiated the America of her youth and said important things about herself as an artist. Most obviously, Ellen's elimination exposes old New York as a barbaric and paranoid culture. Far from the model of genteel security that Wharton and others must have considered it during the nineteenth century, the New York of her girlhood is a frightened, primitive place in *The Age of Innocence*. And what is feared is Ellen Olenska. The woman of intellect and artistic disposition is such a threat that she must be expelled. Equally significant is the fact that Ellen is not alone. Behind her stands eccentric Aunt Medora, who raised her; behind Medora is her formidable grandmother, old Catherine Mingott. Medora is tolerated only because she lives on the fringe of society and is not as smart or creative as Ellen—also, she is no longer a sexual threat; Catherine is accepted because she has been assimilated through marriage (she has literally been incapacitated, being so fat that she can barely move without assistance). What is crucial is that these women—Catherine, Medora, Ellen (later Fanny Beaufort is added)—suggest a line of female unconventionality and vitality which has not been totally eradicated by the cultural preference for May Wellands, and one so powerful that, when irrepressible by co-option or ridicule (the methods used to keep Catherine and Medora within bounds), it requires the extreme remedy of exile. In this respect, the "matriarchal" line that Catherine Mingott heads is no sham (p. 13). There is an implication of awesome female energy and creativity that, given a chance, could explode old New York. Wharton agrees with the established order on this: Ellen Olenska, and by association Wharton herself, *is* a threat.

Biographically, the identification between Wharton and Ellen Olenska is unmistakable. Both are women and passionate. Both are alienated from their old New York roots. Both value original, inquisitive conversation above all other sorts of social intercourse and need to create around themselves physical environments that are beautiful and interesting. Both are sexually experienced women who have had love affairs in Europe with slightly younger men while still married to men totally unsuited to them (this we know of Wharton and suspect of Ellen). Both seek divorces. Both—unlike their relatives—prize the life of artistic and intellectual achievement above all other lives. Both end up leaving America (in each case for Paris). The parallels are so strong that one must believe that Wharton spoke to one degree or another of her own situation, emotionally, when she wrote of Ellen's exile. At the very least, *The Age of Innocence*, published in 1920, says that in Wharton's opinion upper-class America had long ago made it impossible for the woman of sexual, intellectual, and artistic energy—that is, the woman such as Wharton herself—to live at home.

On this subject of Ellen's expatriation, it is particularly interesting to look at certain changes Wharton made in the novel. She left three outlines for *The Age of Innocence*.[14] In the earliest, marked "1st Plan" by Wharton, Archer breaks his engagement to May and marries Ellen, who quickly finds life with him deadly. Wharton's plan says:

> When they come back from their honeymoon, & she realizes that for the next 30 or 40 years they are going to live in Madison Ave in winter & on the Hudson in the Spring & autumn, with a few weeks in Europe or Newport every summer, her whole soul recoils, & she knows at once that she has eaten of the Pomegranate Seed & can never never live without it.
>
> She flies to Europe, & Archer consents to a separation. He realizes dimly that there is no use struggling with her. He arranges

his own life as best he can, & occasionally goes to Europe, & usually calls on his wife, & is asked to dine with her. She is very poor, & very lonely, but she has a real life.[15]

In this first plan, Ellen leaves Archer and America of her own free will. Likewise, in the next prospectuses, she leaves instead of being expelled. In each, Archer marries May out of duty, as in the published book, but then has an affair with Ellen, who eventually leaves because she is bored. In the second plan, "both get tired—she of the idea of living in America, he of the idea of a scandal & a dislocation of his life."[16] In the third plan, "Mme. Olenska, on her side, is weary of their sentimental tête à tête & his scruples, & they finally go back [from Florida, where they have their affair], & the story ends by Mme. Olenska's returning to Europe."[17] In all three prospectuses, Ellen decides she is tired both of Archer and of living in America. She rejects the United States, not the other way around.

In the published novel, Wharton discarded all three plans by having America reject Ellen more than vice versa; and I want to suggest that both the plans and the finished version, although they conflict, reflect the author's own estrangement from the land of her birth. Wharton left America early in the twentieth century of her own free will, much like the Ellen Olenska of the prospectuses, presumably because she found her native land dull and confining personally and artistically—not unlike James before her and Hemingway after her. In this respect Hawthorne's famous complaint that the United States was too young, too traditionless to foster great art was Wharton's as well; so she left. She did not hate her country or feel aggrieved; she simply needed an older, richer environment in which to live and work. Having spent large portions of her youth in Europe, she settled abroad. This, I think, is the Wharton who planned *The Age of Innocence*, who in three different prospectuses had Ellen leaving America because it was too shallow for her.

Added to this idea of mere discontent in the finished book, however, is the idea that Ellen leaves because she is forced to leave: the idea that the new world, at least in its upper reaches, actively conspires against the woman of intellect and artistic talent. Between the prospectus and the published novel, Wharton changed the fable at the center of *The Age of Innocence*. The plan was to say that the woman artist finds America narrow, confining. But the book goes further and offers another and more profound criticism, namely that America finds the creative woman dangerous *because* she is female and therefore ostracizes her. In the finished novel, Wharton does not make Ellen simply bored—simply a victim of stultifying upper-class American culture; rather, in Ellen's tragedy, she specifically links American contempt for art and the life of the mind to the national fear of female independence. In the remembered America of *The Age of Innocence*—the America of Wharton's "formative" years—May Welland's forays into the world of athletic achievement are applauded while Ellen Olenska's desire to live among artists and writers is met with horror. This is a fundamental split. The realm of Diana, chaste and rule-bound, is open to women. The world of art, dangerously sexual and full of mystery and adult knowledge, is denied. Wharton's America is not the land of liberty when it comes to the woman of artistic and intellectual disposition. Ironically, Europe, the "old world," though hardly perfect, offers more freedom.

How accurate this criticism is objectively is debatable. One could point out that Willa Cather and Ellen Glasgow developed and prospered as writers at the same time as Wharton and neither expatriated (Glasgow even came from much the same social class as Wharton). One could also point out, though, that Cather's *A Lost Lady*, published just three years after *The Age of Innocence*, wages much the same criticism as Wharton's novel, and Kate Chopin, another contemporary, clearly did feel censured—indeed exiled—for her art twenty years earlier. But whatever the large historical truth for women,[18] the subjective truth for Edith Wharton in 1920 seems to have been that the woman artist was exiled, banished, from her homeland.

Edith Wharton had no story to rival Ellen's in the remaining decade of her career. The idea that America had rejected the woman artist—expressed in *The Touchstone* but then buried for twenty years—surfaced in her work at the same time that she began to deteriorate as an artist. True, the deterioration is partially explained by the fact that Edith Wharton, born in 1862, was getting old by 1920; also, as I explain at length elsewhere, she was permanently changed by the war, as was America.[19] But added to those facts and raising questions for American women writers in general is the fable of ceremonial death at the heart of *The Age of Innocence*. Ellen's banishment means that the woman artist is despised by ruling-class America. It means that the woman of unusual intellect and talent is rejected, symbolically killed.

It should be added that in writing this particular fable at the beginning of the Roaring Twenties, Edith Wharton, writing out of her own feelings of alienation, was acutely prophetic. The twenties, as even the most cursory literary survey will show, did not generate women writers in the United States. New talent was not nurtured. Indeed, the American twenties were to be another and, if possible, even more blind Age of Innocence for all women not inclined to model themselves on the newest version of the American girl, the flapper. Ellen Olenska, figuratively speaking, *was* about to be exiled once again.

The image that opens *The Age of Innocence* perfectly anticipates Wharton's theme. The novel begins with a performance of *Faust*, and it is the soprano Christine Nilsson, not any of the male artists, that Wharton asks us to imagine on stage. We are required to enter the novel with a real woman artist in mind. To reinforce the point, we later watch Wharton's fictional characters attend a production of Boucicault's *The Shaughraun* with Ada

Dyas in the female lead. Still later, it is *Romeo and Juliet* with Adelaide Neilson as Juliet. These references to opera and theater serve the obvious purpose of strengthening realism in the novel. Christine Nilsson, Ada Dyas, and Adelaide Neilson did play New York in the 1870s. At the same time, the inclusion of real women who made their living as artists is, in this particular book, revealing. These women are independent. They are not American. Finally (and most complicated), they are actresses—not writers or painters or sculptors. They are women who make their living playing roles. Wharton emphasizes in each case that there is a real woman on stage pretending to be a woman she is not, pretending to be a *naif*. The only women artists valued in *The Age of Innocence* are those who act out—literally—the culture's insistence on feminine innocence. The irony, of course, is that while old New York plots the punishment of Ellen Olenska, it pays to see these other unconventional women masquerade as ingenues. Clearly, magnificent Christine Nilsson playing Marguerite parallels Ellen Olenska trying to "play" May Welland—with the difference that Nilsson, by all accounts, was brilliant at the task. Dressed all in white,[20] she was able to make audiences believe that she was innocent, artless. Ellen Olenska could not. Seen in this light, she is exiled for choosing to identify herself with the artist rather than the role—for making the same inevitably alienating choice that Edith Wharton made. On stage, in the world of make-believe, female passion and feminine innocence might be one. In real life, the two, like Ellen and May in *The Age of Innocence*, were enemies.

## Notes

1. The most recent biographies are R. W. B. Lewis's *Edith Wharton: A Biography* (New York: Harper & Row, 1975) and Cynthia Griffin Wolff's psychoanalytic and critical study, *A Feast of Words: The Triumph of Edith Wharton* (New York: Oxford University Press, 1977). For earlier biographies and criticism, see Marlene Springer's annotated bibliography, *Edith Wharton and Kate Chopin: A Reference Guide* (Boston: G. K. Hall, 1976).
2. For full-length discussion of Wharton's work from a feminist perspective see my book, *Edith Wharton's Argument with America* (Athens: University of Georgia Press, 1980). My discussions of *The Age of Innocence* in the book and in this essay complement but do not duplicate each other.
3. Wolff, *Feast of Words*, p. 312.
4. James Fullarton Muirhead, *Land of Contrasts* (Boston: Lanson, Wolffe & Co., 1898), pp. 50–51. James was so well known on the subject that Muirhead can casually refer to him: "The American girl, as Mr. Henry James says, is rarely negative; she is either (and usually) a most charming success or (and exceptionally) a most disastrous failure" (p. 48).

5.  Edith Wharton, *The Fruit of the Tree* (New York: Charles Scribner's Sons, 1907), p. 281.

6.  All quotations are from Scribner's paperback edition of the novel: Edith Wharton, *The Age of Innocence* (New York: Charles Scribner's Sons, 1968).

7.  William Dean Howells, *Heroines of Fiction*, 2 vols. (New York: Harper & Brothers, 1901), II:43.

8.  Paul John Eakin, *The New England Girl: Cultural Ideals in Hawthorne, Stowe, Howells and James* (Athens: University of Georgia Press, 1976), p. 5. Although Eakin's announced focus is New England's version of the American girl, his inclusion of James's girls from New York State (Daisy, Isabel) indicates that the focus is not rigid.

9.  Ibid., p. 6.

10. William Wasserstrom, *Heiress of All the Ages: Sex and Sentiment in the Genteel Tradition* (Minneapolis: University of Minnesota Press, 1959), p. 98.

11. See Lewis, *Edith Wharton*, p. 144.

12. Wasserstrom, *Heiress of All the Ages*, p. 64.

13. Nina Baym, *Woman's Fiction: A Guide to Novels by and about Women in America, 1820–1870* (Ithaca, N.Y.: Cornell University Press, 1978), p. 22.

14. This manuscript material, available in the Edith Wharton Collection at the Beinecke Library, Yale University, is conveniently summarized and quoted by Alan Price in "The Composition of Edith Wharton's *The Age of Innocence*," *Yale University Library Gazette* 55 (July 1980):22–30.

15. Ibid., p. 24.

16. Ibid., p. 26.

17. Ibid., p. 27.

18. American women writers as a group at the turn of the century are the subject of my next book, on which I am currently working with the aid of a grant from the National Endowment for the Humanities.

19. See Ammons, *Edith Wharton's Argument*, Chs. 6 and 7.

20. Helen Headland, *Christina Nilsson: The Songbird of the North* (Rock Island, Ill.: Augustana Book Concern, 1943), p. 140.

# Carol Hurd Green

# Stephen Crane and the Fallen Women

Stephen Crane, who died at twenty-nine, was always a young writer. Nowhere is his youth more apparent than in his attitude toward women. In a letter to an early love, Nellie Crouse, he wrote of himself:

> So you think I am successful? Well I don't know. Most people con-
> sider me successful. At least, they seem to so think. But upon my
> soul I have lost all appetite for victory, as victory is defined by the
> mob. I will be glad if I can feel on my death-bed that my life has
> been just and kind according to my ability and that every particle
> of my little ridiculous stock of eloquence and wisdom has been
> applied for the benefit of my kind. From this moment to that death-
> bed may be a short time or a long one but at any rate it means a
> life of labor and sorrow. I do not confront it blithely. I confront it
> with desperate resolution. . . . I do not expect to do good. But I
> expect to make a sincere, desperate, lonely battle to remain true to
> my conception of my life. . . . It is not a fine prospect. I only speak
> of it to people in whose opinions I have faith. No woman has heard
> it until now.[1]

The tone is stylishly world-weary, the voice that of an eager, appealing, and literary self-absorbed youth whose infatuation with himself is clear. He professes himself infatuated as well with Nellie, but the measure of his regard is in the assurance that she is worthy of his confidence.

In Crane's poetry and fiction, such self-absorption and high intentions leave women out of serious consideration; they are never more than images. And the images are those seen from a perspective of adolescence: women are mothers or crabby-teacher figures or gossips, sexless and shapeless, manu-facturing and exerting authority, or—if they are young and shapely—seduc-tresses, or (like Grace Fanhall in *The Third Violet*) the stuff of which roman-tic dreams are made. In the presence of women, men are driven to nonsense, silence, impotence, or guilt. Women, too, fall prey to members of their own sex; there is not among them the loyalty of brotherhood that Crane, the "preacher's kid," created as a faith. It was that capacity for loyalty that redeemed men; without it, all women—not just the prostitutes who fascinated Crane—were fallen women.

Some could be rescued, if the man was sufficiently intrepid and the woman suitable for rescuing. It is not new to point to the recurrence in Crane of the rescue motif. In 1950, John Berryman set out to explain the pattern of Crane's relationships with women.[2] He noted the writer's attraction to older, often unattainable, and sometimes morally dubious women and his continuous fascination with prostitutes, culminating in his common-law marriage to Cora Stewart, proprietor of the Hotel de Dream, a brothel in Jacksonville, Florida. Berryman offered a Freudian explanation, seeing Crane as an example of the man described in Freud's "A Special Type of Choice of Objects Made by Men" (1910). Such a person seeks a woman in whom another man has some "right of possession," and/or one who is to some extent "sexually discredited" and whose "fidelity and loyalty" are open to doubt. The lover, intense and sincere, will manifest, in his compulsion to repeat such relationships, a desire to rescue the woman.[3]

Daniel Hoffman, in his book on Crane's poetry, agreed. He saw Crane's attachment for his early loves—Helen Trent, Nellie Crouse, Lily Brandon Munroe—as well as for a number of demimonde figures as confirmation of Berryman's analysis, and also emphasized Crane's wish to rescue them from "plights sometimes imaginary."[4] For Hoffman, however, the explanation of Crane's behavior was not to be found solely in psychology, but also in religion. Crane's "mode of interpreting experience" can be seen as deeply influenced by his Methodist heritage. In Hoffman's view, this heritage created in the young author a profound moral anxiety about sexual love, leading him to believe that "to love is to be damned."[5] Further, Hoffman points out, in Crane's poetry the blame for this damnation is consistently placed on the woman; she is the aggressor and seductress, he is the victim.

Like the fiction, Crane's poetry pays relatively little attention to women; Crane's imagination functions best in the world of men. When the poetry does concentrate on women, it reveals a simultaneous fascination with and revulsion from female sexuality, and a mingling of images of nineties' decadence with the petulance of a failed lover. Three poems are especially relevant here: the series of verses titled "Intrigue" from the *War Is Kind* volume,[6] the poem from the same collection that begins "On the desert,"[7] and the undated brief verse, "A naked woman and a dead dwarf."[8] "Intrigue" provides the most direct illustration of Hoffman's point about the transference of blame: the hand-wringing anguish and the accusations of infidelity swirl and spit out among verses of sentimental exaggeration.

> Thou art my love
> And thou art a weary violet
> Drooping from sun-caresses.

Answering mine carelessly
Woe is me.

. . .

Thou art my love
And thou art the ashes of other men's love
And I bury my face in these ashes
And I love them
Woe is me.

. . .

Thou art my love
And thou art a priestess
And in thy hand is a bloody dagger
And my doom comes to me surely
Woe is me.

The images are self-absorbed and angry. They sink to bathos—"I weep and I gnash/And I love the little shoe/The little, little shoe"—and seldom rise beyond self-pity. The theme is struck here, as it will be frequently throughout Crane's work: women, being incapable of fidelity, make men into fools. Being without honesty, they make mockery of men's attempts to transcend human limits. Like the "little man" who inhabits so much of Crane's fiction, the lover is reduced to posturing and pomposity:

God give me loud honors
That I may strut before you, sweetheart
And be worthy of—
—The love I bear you

to fantasies of brutality:

And I wish to be an ogre
And hale and haul my beloved to a castle
And there use the happy cruel one cruelly
And make her mourn with my mourning

and of chivalry:

I have heard your quick breaths
And seen your arms writhe toward me;
At those times
—God help us—
I was impelled to be a grand knight.

But that, too, leads to self-mockery: the knight would "Swagger and snap my fingers,/And explain my mind finely."[9]

The woman here, as in "On the desert," is like a snake: her arms "writhe" toward her lover. The echo of the Garden of Eden, the tempting snake, is combined with the popular nineties image of the sinuous Salomé in the shorter poem. "On the desert" is a silent movie of the seductress and her victims, the "squat and dumb" men who are hypnotized into powerlessness by her. Sinister and deadly, she and the snakes work their will: "[S]low things, sinuous, dull with terrible color/Sleepily fondle her body/Or move at her will, . . .

> And over the sand serpents move warily
> Slow, menacing and submissive,
> . . .
> But always whispering, softly whispering.
> The dignity of the accurséd;
> The glory of slavery, despair, death
> Is in the dance of the whispering snakes.

Caught in her trap, the men have left only paradox—the glory of the fall, of slavery, despair, and death, a romantic, self-destructive bondage to sex, to woman.

The risk of being made a fool of, of being false to oneself, dominates Crane's view of men's fate in the presence of women. In "A naked woman and a dead dwarf " he strips both parties to the essentials. The man is the fool in cap and bells, truly the little man, the dwarf—and perhaps a more exact figure of impotence—and the woman is naked.

> A naked woman and a dead dwarf;
> Wealth and indifference.
> Poor dwarf!
> Reigning with foolish kings
> And dying mid bells and wine
> Ending with a desperate and comic palaver
> While before thee and after thee
> Endures the eternal clown—
> —The eternal clown—
> A naked woman.

Here the little man is clearly identified with the artist. "Ending with a desperate comic palaver," he endures the final humiliation. The woman survives.

The temptation to autobiographical readings of Crane's portraits of women is strong. But it is less fruitful to see this poem as simply Crane being angry in advance at his wife for outliving him than to see it within the context of the destructive tension between honesty and dishonesty, morality and immorality, the making of art and its destruction, that Crane sees as the relation between man and woman. In that relation, man and especially man as artist (there are no creative women in Crane) is driven into posturing and fantasy or forced into silence and self-betrayal.

The experiment in form that his poems represented apparently freed Crane to express the deeper associations of ideas and emotions that governed his imagination—bitterness, irony, and anger as well as a high romantic self-image are all more openly expressed. The fiction was a different matter: the stories were written to attract a large reading public and to earn him a living. There were forms ready to hand—the tract, the adventure story, the small-town tale—and he turned to them, while transforming each to suit his purposes. In so doing, Crane modified his portrayal of women but did not turn away from his conviction that they were the troublemakers, noisy, disloyal, and destructive.

Only passive women, those who could be rescued by men and be properly grateful for it, like Marjory Wainwright in *Active Service* (1899) or the bride who came to Yellow Sky, were exceptions. They allowed men to find and express their better selves: the married Jack Potter, Sheriff of Yellow Sky, defeats Scratchy Wilson once and for all, and without violence. His bride, "not pretty, nor . . . very young," the bearer of a "plain, under-class counte-nance," and rescued by Potter from the drudgery of being someone's cook, looks on. Rufus Coleman, the sophisticated, hard-drinking editor of the Sunday edition of the yellow *New York Eclipse*, rushes off to save Marjory and her parents from a terrible fate in the midst of the Greco-Turkish war. She, well trained in the modesty becoming a lady, maintains her dignity and transforms him into a figure of innocent happiness; *Active Service* ends in a romantic fade-out clearly designed to please the serial-reading audience for whom, in the rush of trying to finish the novel and pay his bills, Crane in the end designed the book.[10]

*Active Service* was originally to be a "big book" about the Greco-Turkish war, benefiting from Crane's experience as a war correspondent. But between 1897, when he began the book, and 1899, when, in failing health, he hurried to complete it, the focus changed. The war becomes a faint backdrop to a tale of chivalry and of the war between the sexes. Coleman is in love with Marjory, whose professor father takes her to Greece to get her away from her unsuitable suitor, only to plunge her, his wife, and the students he brought along into danger. Coleman, dashing off to the rescue, encounters on ship-board Nora Black, the "queen of comic opera," who then throws up her London theatrical engagement to pursue Coleman and add his scalp to her belt. Nora is the only seductress in Crane's fiction, indeed the only openly sexual woman, and she is put properly in her place. She tries everything, even open seduction, plying Coleman with strong drink as she entertains him, dressed in a "puzzling gown of . . . Grecian silk," in her subtly lighted room. On the verge of succumbing—"to go to the devil with this girl was not a bad fate"—he is saved by the thought of Marjory, whose name Nora had had the effrontery to mention: his face "instantly stiffened and he looked like a man suddenly recalled to the ways of light."

The book's main interest is in the glimpses it gives of Crane's conception of the journalist's role. Many, however, have found extra interest in comparing Nora Black to Cora Stewart Crane, Crane's common-law wife. He had first met her in 1896 in Jacksonville, Florida, where he had gone preparatory to covering the insurrection in Cuba. Twice married and once divorced, Cora Stewart was the owner of the Hotel de Dream, a successful brothel. "The lady was handsome, of some real refinement, aloof to most,"[11] until she met Stephen Crane, with whom she fell deeply in love. He reciprocated. Older than he by some five or six years, eager—as her letters suggest—to care for him and yet tantalizingly unconventional, Cora Stewart had obvious attractions for the young writer who had put such energies into rebellion.

As her biographer suggests, Cora Stewart shared Crane's delight in defying the rules. "One of the greatest pleasures of having been what is called bad is that one has so much to say to the good. Good people love hearing about sin," she wrote.[12] She had flaunted convention by walking out on her well-to-do English husband, Donald Stewart, when he refused her a divorce, and even more by making her way to Jacksonville and establishing her business there. She also shared Crane's romanticism, both its decadent side:

> Sometimes I like to sit at home and read good books, at others I must drink absinthe and hang the night hours with scarlet embroideries. I must have music and the sins that march to music[13]

and its idealism:

> Love illumined by truth, truth warmed through and through by love—these perform for us the most blessed thing that one human being can do for another.[14]

Cora Stewart also wryly recognized certain "limits of decorum," both in romantic relationships and in business. "Zeus has unquestioned right to Io," she noted, "but woe betide Io when she suns her heart in the smiles that belong to Hera." She married her lovers, she was always seen in public with a woman companion, Mrs. Ruedy, and she promoted the Hotel de Dream as a place primarily for good food and good conversation. No hard liquor was served, and Cora Stewart maintained her dignity and her privacy, while charming men with her wit and conversation.

In Stephen Crane she believed she had found the love she had sought. He would be her "guiding star. . . . I never realized true happiness or joy until I met you."[15] Acting on this belief, she gave up what was an established social position of sorts in Jacksonville, followed Crane to the Greco-Turkish war (from which she also sent dispatches to the New York *Journal*, writing as Imogene Carter), and then went to live with him in England as his wife. The courtship and the marriage were marked by separations and struggles and, ironically, by a persistent anxiety about the face of propriety to be shown to the outside world. Pretenses of legal marriage were retailed to friends and relatives; the bohemians, and apparently Stephen Crane in particular, could not confront Victorian society head on. Life in England was often difficult. Both were extravagant, and both loved to entertain. But the guests came in increasingly unmanageable numbers, and while Stephen Crane played host and, later, "Baron Brede" (they lived from February 1899 in Brede Place in Sussex), Cora worried about the bills, about his health, and about ways to insulate him from his friends so he could work. She also carried on their social and his business correspondence, and helped the orphaned children of the improvident Harold Frederic.

Hardest for Cora Crane must have been the realization that Stephen Crane was not content with their life. Early on, he had described to her his belief in the evanescence of love:

> Love comes like the tall swift shadow of a ship at night. There is for
> a moment, the music of the water's turmoil, a bell, perhaps, a man's
> shout, a row of gleaming yellow lights. Then the slow sinking of this
> mystic shape. Then silence and a bitter silence—the silence of the
> sea at night.[16]

When war broke out in Cuba, Crane left England as fast as he could; he did not return for nine months, and his silence was indeed bitter to Cora. She had to abandon the dignity she so prized to write frantic letters to the United States seeking his whereabouts and to publishers seeking money to pay their bills. He returned to England and to her very slowly. Eighteen months later he was dead. Cora Crane returned to Jacksonville but her moment was past; she was never able to re-establish herself successfully in business, made a disastrous marriage, and died in her mid-forties in 1910.

The "Intrigue" verses, with their apparent allusions to Cora Crane and her past, were written in Cuba during Crane's long silence. He may also have returned to the writing of *Active Service* there, completing it when he came back to England. In its new conception as a romantic story, it too takes swipes at Cora. Nora Black is not simply a portrait of Cora; the character probably owes something to the actress Amy Leslie whom Crane had befriended and who had turned against him, as J. C. Levenson has pointed out.[17] But there is the echo of the name, the presence of the aged companion, like Cora's Mrs. Ruedy who had moved to England with her, and the biographical parallel of Nora Black's work as a "correspondent" during the Greco-Turkish war. The mixture of styles, sophisticated and crudely vulgar, was also characteristic of Cora Crane, as Levenson notes.

Nora is by far the liveliest woman in the novel and one of the liveliest women in any of Crane's fiction. But she is also soundly defeated for her sins. She arrives on the scene in Greece on her "fat and glossy horse," echoing the black riders, the "ride of sin," of Crane's early poem.[18] Twice within minutes of her appearance, Coleman tells her pointedly that she is playing the devil. Like the woman addressed in "Intrigue," she comes trailing a string of past conquests. The poet's antagonist/lover is, in one of the worst metaphors in American poetry, "the beard on another man's face." Nora fares better, but her aggressive behavior and her fickleness put her beyond the pale. Crane may not have been able to rescue his past loves from the lives they had chosen instead of him, but Rufus Coleman will rescue and marry Marjory, and Nora Black will have to go off in search of her little Greek prince. Art is better than life.

Nora and the faithless lover of "Intrigue" share with the other women in Crane's poetry and fiction an inability to be honest—with themselves or, most important, with others. For Crane, honesty and its attendant virtue loyalty were the only means to redemption. In a much-quoted letter to John Hilliard, probably written in 1896, Crane spelled out his creed:

> I understand that a man is born into the world with his own pair of
> eyes, and he is not at all responsible for his vision—he is merely
> responsible for his quality of personal honesty. To keep close to this
> personal honesty is my supreme ambition. . . . This aim in life
> struck me as being the only thing worth while. A man is sure to fail
> at it, but there is something in the failure.[19]

Crane's formulation here parallels a distinction made earlier by his father, the Reverend Jonathan Townley Crane, regarding the relation between the neutral passions of human beings and their responsibility for self-control. In *Holiness the Birthright of All God's Children* (1874), the elder Crane noted that "to be human is to be endowed with appetites and passions, innocent in themselves but unreasoning, required to be guided by the intellect and the conscience and controlled by the will." His example was Eve, who was to be condemned, not for her desire for the forbidden tree, but for her decision to yield.[20] The premium put by both father and son on the exercise of choice and strength of will is reflected in Crane's assessment of his characters. Circumstances are no excuse, Crane often reiterated—the poor and the dependent have just as much chance to be virtuous. The daughters of Eve clearly have a harder time of it. Self-control, fidelity to a vision of personal honesty and responsibility are not among their gifts.

Contrast, for example, groups of women and men. When men gather in Crane, they are seen to understand each other and to possess a comprehension of the large issues that precludes any unnecessary conversation. When women gather, it is to cackle and rant, to exult in disaster. When Maggie has been found drowned in the East River for her sins, her mother and her acquaintances convene:

> "Yer poor misguided chil' is gone now, Mary, an' let us hope it's fer deh bes'. Yeh'll fergive her now, Mary, won't yehs, dear, all her disobed'ence? All her tankless behavior to her mudder an' all her badness? She's gone where her ter'ble sins will be judged." . . . Two or three of the spectators were sniffling, and one was loudly weeping. . . . "She's gone where her sins will be judged," cried the other women, like a choir at a funeral.
> "Deh Lord gives and deh Lord takes away," responded the others.
> "Yeh'll fergive her, Mary!" pleaded the woman in black. The mourner . . . shook her great shoulders frantically, in an agony of grief. . . . Finally her voice came and arose like a scream of pain.
> "Oh, yes, I'll fergive her! I'll fergive her!"[21]

When Dr. Trescott, the hero of "The Monster," determines on the path of righteousness toward the faceless Henry Johnson, he provides the women of Whilomville with a chance to make noise:

> "Have you heard the news?" cried Carrie Dungen, . . . Her eyes were shining with delight.
> "No," answered Martha's sister Kate, . . . "What was it? What was it?"
> Carrie appeared triumphantly in the open door. "Oh, there's been an awful scene between Doctor Trescott and Jake Winter. I never thought Jake Winter had any pluck at all but this morning he told the doctor just what he thought of him." . . . "Oh, he called him everything. Mrs. Howarth heard it through her front blinds. It was terrible, she says. It's all over town now. Everybody knows it."
> "Didn't the doctor answer back?"
> "No! Mrs. Howarth—she says he never said a word . . . But Jake gave him jinks, by all accounts."
> "But what did he say?" cried Kate, shrill and excited. She was evidently at some kind of feast.[22]

Compare the sound of these scenes among women with Crane's account of men facing situations of moral and physical danger. Loyalty and brotherhood characterize the quiet communion of the men in "The Open Boat":

> The hurt captain, lying against the water-jar in the bow, spoke always in a low voice and calmly; but he could never command a more ready and swiftly obedient crew than the motley three of the dinghy. It was more than a mere recognition of what was best for

the common safety. There was surely in it a quality that was
personal and heartfelt. And after this devotion to the commander of
the boat, there was this comradeship, that the correspondent, for
instance, who had been taught to be cynical of men, knew even at
the time was the best experience of his life. But no one said that it
was so. No one mentioned it.[23]

The silence there is profound, even sacred; the men understand without
speaking, as they do in the stress of battle in *The Red Badge of Courage* and
others of the war stories. There are shrieks and cries there, but they are
mechanical—the sounds of war machines—or the cry of pain and the shout
of victory. While Maggie's death is celebrated by cannibalistic din, the death
of Jim Conklin, through which Henry Fleming learns both the enormity of
his sin and his path to redemption, is framed in silence:

His spare figure was erect; his bloody hands were quietly at his side.
He was waiting with patience for something that he had come to
meet. He was at the rendezvous. They paused and stood, expectant.
There was silence.[24]

Crane's two early fictions about women, *Maggie* and "George's Mother,"
are loud with the sound of women, betraying their children and bemoaning
their betrayal by them. *Maggie* was written when Crane was twenty-one; he
published it himself a year later in 1893. He sent copies off to Hamlin Garland and to William Dean Howells, conscious that his small book was in the
vein of realism that the older writers prized and hoping that his gesture of
literary rebellion—as he saw it—would win him approval. The dedicatory note
to Garland was repeated in other copies with only slight modification. Anticipating the reader's shock, he insisted that the book set out to show

that environment is a tremendous thing . . . and frequently shapes
lives regardless. If one proves that theory, one makes room in
Heaven for all sorts of souls (notably an occasional street girl) who
are not confidently expected to be there by many excellent
people.[25]

This attempt to "épater les bourgeois," it scarcely needs saying, is a very
limited one. *Maggie* is essentially a tract, written by the son of a gentle
Methodist. Crane's father had left the Presbyterian church because he could
not accept the doctrine of infant damnation, but he was nonetheless a strin-
gent moralist. Writing in the wake of John Brown's raid on Harper's Ferry,
Jonathan Crane had reminded slaves that, whatever their condition, they
could feel wronged but must not do wrong, that is, they must not engage in
violent revolt.[26]

His son condemned Maggie to death with the same regretful stringency. As Leslie Fiedler pointed out many years ago,[27] Crane took few chances with respectability in his book. By making Maggie so clearly working class, he ensured that her fall into prostitution and her suicide would not unduly disturb the reader. Indeed, the pattern of Maggie's fall might have come directly from the pages of the genteel reformers of the purity crusade. They saw that low wages and the resulting poor living conditions tempted young women to seek for something more. They warned, too, as had Crane's father,[28] against the dangers of alcohol and of popular entertainment, especially the melodramas of the kind to which Pete took Maggie. The first National Purity Congress, held in Baltimore in October 1895, heard many addresses on the relation between alcohol and prostitution and was warned by Josiah Leeds that "impure stage spectacles" bore a direct relation to the spread of the Social Evil.[29] B. O. Flower, editor of the *Arena*, reminded the gathering that the extremes of wealth and poverty to be found in cities could lead only to evil:

> Extreme wealth produces too frequently indolence, high living, the indulgence in wines and liquors, all of which tend to deaden the conscience and stimulate the sensual in man's nature, while the poor, huddled together in overcrowded tenements, lose to a great extent that refinement and modesty so necessary to the development of virtue, and the multitudes of poor girls who are forced to make a living and who are underpaid, too frequently find themselves at the mercy of their employers or are driven through insufficient wages to add to their earnings by yielding to the demands of the men who possess means or influence.[30]

Although Crane expressed only fierce contempt for the do-gooders and reformers, especially against Frances Willard and her temperance crusade,[31] his understanding of what led a girl into the life was exactly what one might expect from a well-brought-up young man. His behavior was rebellious: he associated with prostitutes and women of the demimonde as a way of proving his bohemianism, even though it brought personal risk. But when challenged, he responded out of his background. He defended the honor of Dora Clark, accused of soliciting, and appeared in police court on her behalf. The result was fierce attacks on him by the New York press and personal ostracism. He explained his claim to be married to a woman charged with soliciting: "If it were necessary to avow a marriage to save a girl who is not a prostitute from being arrested as a prostitute, it must be done though the man suffer eternal ruin."[32]

Crane understood the language and the rules in a way that slum inhabitants could not; his rescue attempts could be successful, but Jimmie, Maggie's brother, could not perform the same service for her. He had "an idea that it wasn't common courtesy for a friend to come to one's house and ruin one's sister. But he was not sure how much Pete knew about the rules of politeness." Jimmie's sense of right and wrong is more than his mother or her friends possess, but the comment is nonetheless an easy joke at Jimmie's, and ultimately at Maggie's, expense.

In ascribing Maggie's downfall to what were a conventional set of causes— poverty, the harsh life of the shopgirl, the search for some excitement in a tedious and difficult life—Crane followed a pattern. He breaks it, however, by placing much of the blame for Maggie's fate on the women of the slums. Maggie herself becomes quickly and improbably accomplished in the ways of the streets, knowing to which men to appeal and which to avoid:

> A girl of the painted cohorts of the city went along the street. She threw changing glances at men who passed her, giving smiling invitations to men of rural or untaught pattern and usually seeming sedately unconscious of the men with a metropolitan seal upon their faces.[33]

But Crane makes clear that she is neither successful nor willing at the game; her life as a prostitute is chiefly an occasion for hypocritical self-righteousness on the part of the other female inhabitants of the slums.

As an assault on Christian hypocrisy, Crane liked to recall the attacks on his mother by others when she took in a mother and her child born out of wedlock.[34] Women are incapable, Crane clearly believed, of true charity ("Charity is a toy of women," one poem begins) and even of the kindness and loyalty that should go without saying for an innocent child, and particularly of a mother for her child.[35] Mary Johnson, Maggie's mother, is a drunk, a grotesque, a figure of the angry and malevolent goddess of evil. Her tangled hair calls up the image of the snake, but her threat is not sexual. Her sexuality is only material for a police station joke: "'Mary, the records of this and other courts show that you are the mother of forty-two daughters who have been ruined. The case is unparalleled in the annals of this court.'" Mary Johnson devours her daughter in her dogged pursuit of her own survival, gorging on self-righteousness and feasting on the clichés of bourgeois morality to justify herself. Her neighbors eagerly join her ravening outbursts, outdoing one another in imaginary tales of Maggie's promiscuity and keening complacently over her death (see above, p. 233).

George's mother, in the story of that name, would seem to be the opposite of Mary Johnson in every way. Neat, clean, and sanctified, a fierce temperance advocate, she works to retain respectability in the face of the looming threats of the slums. Also unlike Mary Johnson, she rejects the other women who come rapaciously ready to join in denunciation of her "wild son. They came to condole her. They sat in the kitchen for hours. She told them of his wit, his cleverness, his kind heart."

But her sanctity and her conception of motherhood are almost as noisy and destructive as Mary Johnson's. She swings from grotesque flirtatiousness to hellfire threats toward George. Obsessed with her own need for him and for his conformity to her idea of what a son should be, she forces him to a prayer meeting and, when that fails, resorts to the final weapon—she dies. Guilty George suffers the drunk's punishment: staring at the wallpaper above his mother's death bed, he sees the brown roses "like hideous crabs crawling upon his brain." His mother has succeeded, not in reforming him, but in giving him a permanent case of guilt.[36]

As has often been noted, one source of this story is an incident between Crane and his mother, Helen Peck Crane.[37] A more fierce Methodist than her husband, she once inveigled her son into attending a prayer meeting; he agreed because he was drunk. The mingled message that the figure of George's mother offers—she invites all the clichés about being brave and pathetic and full of faith, while also uncomprehending of her son—comes perhaps from the story's source. It is not just that Crane uses his mother as a source, but that his perspective here and in *Maggie* remains that of youth, of the son. These women demand to be paid attention to, and their children must heed or suffer.

The sexless, noisy, gossiping women return in "The Monster." Written in 1897 but not published until 1899, this story is a powerful blending of the sun-dappled fiction of the small town with an exploration of its potential for evil. Whilomville—a permutation of Port Jervis, New York, where Crane spent some happy years—was the setting for many of his most whimsical stories: "The Angel Child," "The New Mittens," and others appearing later under the title of *Whilomville Stories* (1900). Most have an edge to them, an awareness of the social hypocrisy in the town, but only in "The Monster" did he use the town as a setting for a morality play. The story turns on a complex moral problem, the question of Dr. Trescott's responsibility to his black serving man, Henry Johnson, who had saved the life of Trescott's son, Jimmie, in a fire. Henry became not only mad but a faceless monster. The question, as Trescott sees it, is one not of charity but of justice.

Henry Johnson is a grotesque of an archetypal kind, a figure at once human and nonhuman. Before the fire, the town could classify Henry with the other blacks in the town and thus dismiss him. Now, faceless, he is suddenly the unknowable in their midst, and they react with anger and resentment. Henry cannot respond, so they direct their fury at Trescott, who refuses to allow Henry to disappear from their lives.

The social life of Whilomville is run by strict if unspoken rules, with clear divisions between the men and the women. The men meet in Reifsnyder's barbershop where they discuss the issues involved in Trescott's determination to help Henry Johnson at whatever risk to himself. Although frightened, the men are at least aware of the importance and value of Trescott's decision;

they can understand the abstract considerations that motivate him, although incapable of such courage themselves. The women, however, cannot even begin to understand. They gather in the backyards and kitchens only to gossip, telling tales of those frightened by Henry and whipping themselves into a frenzy of excitement over the affair.

> The overplus of information was choking Carrie. . . . "And, oh, little Sadie Winter is awful sick, . . . And poor old Mrs. Farragut sprained her ankle in trying to climb a fence. And there's a crowd around the jail all the time . . ."
> Kate heard the excited newcomer, and drifted down from the novel in her room. . . . "Serves him right if he was to lose all his patients," she said suddenly, in blood-thirsty tones. She snipped her words out as if her lips were scissors.[38]

The men of Whilomville are doubly impotent, before their own inarticulateness and moral inadequacy in the face of Trescott's virtue, and before the simplistic fury of the women. Like the squat and dumb men on the desert, they are made fools of by the women. They take refuge in blaming them. Asking Trescott to send Henry away, the men chorus to each point in their argument, "It's the women."

Like Mary Johnson and the raucous women of the slums, if less coarse, the women of Whilomville are morally and socially deformed. Cannibalistic in their devouring of reputations, they are capable of common action only to destroy. As in *Maggie*, their chief victim is another woman, Grace Trescott, the doctor's wife, who sits alone, bereft and foolish amid her unused teacups as the story ends.

Chief among the women is the "old maid" figure of Martha Goodwin. In several ways, Martha Goodwin resembles the "feminine mule" of Port Jervis whom Crane described in an 1894 letter. That woman had "no more brains than a pig," but whenever "she grunts something dies howling. It may be a girl's reputation or a political party or the Baptist Church but it stops in its tracks and dies." Crane's longtime animus against this woman seems, both in his letter and in his later fictional reincarnations of her, in excess of the cause. He had taken a fifteen-year-old girl out for a buggy ride on Sunday: "Monday the mule addresses me in front of the barber's and says 'You was drivin' Frances out y'day' and grunted. At once all present knew that Frances and I should be hanged on twin gallows for red sins." The "big joke" in all this, Crane gleefully goes on, is that

> this lady in her righteousness is just the grave of a stale lust and every boy in town knows it. She occurred ruin at the hands of a farmer when we were all 10 or 11. But she is a nice woman and all her views of all things belong on the table of Moses.[39]

Crane's own self-righteousness, and his pleasure in rehearsing the adolescent snicker over the woman's fate, suggest this attack as a mirror image of the attitude toward women's sexuality seen in the poems. He used this episode with little modification in his early romantic novel, *The Third Violet*, and his obsession with women's past loves has been noted in "Intrigue" and *Active Service*. In "The Monster," he draws again on the episode and the image to create the contradictory figure of Martha Goodwin. Like the feminine mule, Martha has opinions on every large issue and "argued constantly for a creed of illimitable ferocity." She emphasized her opinions with a sniff, which her antagonists received "like a bang over the head, and none was known to recover." She is also and "simply the mausoleum of a dead passion." Her fiancé had died young of smallpox, "which he had not caught from her," and she lives on in the house of her sister and brother-in-law. She is their victim: while her sister Kate is upstairs with her novel, Martha does nearly all the housework "in return for the privilege of existence." Desexed, she can stir up the ashes of passion only in the denunciation of others. But while the women tremble before her savage attacks, they are in "secret revolt" against her. Vulnerable in her dependency, sexless, and without a male defender, "she remained a weak, innocent, and pig-headed creature, who alone would defy the universe if she thought the universe merited the proceeding."[40]

The anger the other women do not dare express openly to Martha, fearful of her sniff, they vent on the unfortunate Grace Trescott, who has developed no sharp tongue to defend herself. Instead she attempts to continue the calls and the teas, the genteel rituals of the town, hoping to retain some of the order that has been broken by her husband's determination. Grace Trescott bears the burden of Dr. Trescott's commitment to justice, his recognition, incomprehensible to the women, that loyalty demands sacrifice. It is her lot to join in that sacrifice without understanding it.

*Maggie* and "The Monster" are the most vivid illustrations of Crane's conviction of women's incapacity for loyalty, indeed, for moral abstractions of any kind. It is in their disloyalty to each other that women are inferior to men and unredeemable. Not for them the "subtle brotherhood" that allows men to save themselves through mutual self-sacrifice, nor the moment of self-discovery that enables them to transcend past mistakes, as Henry Fleming does, and go on toward redemption. When Maggie reaches the point of self-discovery, it is too late to do anything but, conventionally, to throw herself in the East River. The other women do not reach such a moment.

Crane's happiest letters are to his old schoolmates at Claverack. That boarding school experience seems to have established for him an ideal of companionship and loyalty, a team spirit, that no relationship with a woman or among women could ever match. And, it seems, his view of women never matured far beyond that level of experience. For most of his brief career, the solution was to remove himself, as artist and as man, to the battlefield and the decks of ships, to places where women could not follow.

## Notes

1. Stephen Crane to Nellie Crouse, 26 January 1896, in R. W. Stallman and Lillian Gilkes, eds., *Stephen Crane: Letters* (New York: New York University Press, 1960), p. 103.
2. John Berryman, *Stephen Crane* (New York: William Sloane Associates, 1950), pp. 298–304.
3. Ibid., pp. 299–300.
4. Daniel Hoffman, *The Poetry of Stephen Crane* (New York: Columbia University Press, 1957), pp. 106–7.
5. Ibid., p. 126.
6. Fredson Bowers, ed., *The Works of Stephen Crane* (Charlottesville: University Press of Virginia 1969–), vol. 10, *Poems and Literary Remains* (1975), poems 96–105, pp. 64–69.
7. Ibid., poem 79, p. 51.
8. Ibid., poem 132, p. 87. The figure of the dwarf in the poem and his identification with the artist seem to show the influence of Poe's "Hopfrog."
9. Writing to women, Crane was always eager to explain his mind finely. His letters to Nellie Crouse (see above) are full of pronouncements on life and literature. See also Stephen Crane to Lily Brandon Munroe, March 1894[?], in Stallman and Gilkes, *Letters*, pp. 31–33.
10. On 25 March 1899, Crane sent a note to his agent, Paul Revere Reynolds, urging him to pursue the sale of serial rights and telling him: "For your own edification and also for business reasons I think it should be announced that Coleman simply drowns all opposition and marries Marjory." Quoted by J. C. Levenson in Introduction to Bowers, *Works*, vol. 3, *The Third Violet and Active Service* (1976), p. liv.
11. E. W. McCready to B. J. R. Stolper, 22 January 1934, in Stallman and Gilkes, *Letters*, p. 340. McCready was a correspondent for the New York *Herald*; he was in Jacksonville with Crane, and they were ship-mates during the Spanish-American War.
12. Quoted in Lillian Gilkes, *Cora Crane: A Biography of Mrs. Stephen Crane* (Bloomington: Indiana University Press, 1960), pp. 50–51.
13. Ibid., p. 55.
14. Ibid., p. 57.
15. Ibid. Lillian Gilkes sees Cora Stewart as ready to be rescued by Crane.
16. Stephen Crane to C. E. S., January 1897, in Stallman and Gilkes, *Letters*, p. 138. The letter was written shortly after Crane was rescued from the shipwreck described in "The Open Boat." The image reflects that

experience but also, as Hoffman points out, Crane's reading of Longfellow.

17. J. C. Levenson, Introduction to *Active Service* in Bowers, *Works* 3:liv–lv.

18. "Black riders come from the sea," in Bowers, *Works* 10:poem 1, p. 3.

19. Stephen Crane to John Northern Hilliard, January 1896[?], in Stallman and Gilkes, *Letters*, p. 110.

20. Rev. J. T. Crane, *Holiness: The Birthright of All God's Children* (New York: Nelson & Phillips, 1874), pp. 92–95.

21. "Maggie," in Bowers, *Works*, vol. 1, *Bowery Tales* (1969), pp. 76–77.

22. "*The Monster*," in Bowers, *Works*, vol. 7, *Tales of Whilomville* (1969), p. 59.

23. "The Open Boat," in Bowers, *Works*, vol. 5, *Tales of Adventure* (1970), p. 73.

24. Bowers, *Works*, vol. 2, *The Red Badge of Courage* (1975), p. 57.

25. *Letters*, p. 14.

26. Rev. J. T. Crane, *Christian Duty in Regard to American Slavery* (Jersey City, N.J.: R. B. Kashow, 1860).

27. Leslie Fiedler, *Love and Death in the American Novel*, rev. ed. (New York: Dell, 1966), p. 247.

28. Among Reverend Crane's published writings are *An Essay on Dancing, Arts of Intoxication*, and *Popular Amusements*.

29. Josiah Leeds, "The Relation of the Press and the Stage to Purity," in *The National Purity Congress: Its Papers, Addresses, Portraits*, ed. Aaron M. Powell (1896; reprint ed., New York: Arno Press, 1976), pp. 320–27. See also Edwin R. A. Seligman, ed., "The Social Evil with Special Reference to Conditions Existing in the City of New York: A Report Prepared (in 1902)," in *Prostitution in America: Three Investigations, 1902–1914* (New York: Arno Press, 1976); Jane Addams, *A New Conscience and an Ancient Evil* (New York: Macmillan, 1914); David Pivar, *Purity Crusade: Sexual Morality and Social Control, 1868–1900* (Westport, Conn.: Greenwood Press, 1973).

30. B. O. Flower, "Some Causes of Present Day Immorality and Suggestions as to Practical Remedies," in Powell, *National Purity Congress*, p. 314.

31. Crane told Catherine Harris that "Frances Willard is one of those wonderful people who can tell right from wrong for everybody from the polar cap to the equator. . . . I have loved myself passionately now and then but Miss Willard's affair with Miss Willard should be stopped by the police." Quoted in Stallman and Gilkes, *Letters*, p. 133n. In her address to the National Purity Congress, Willard singled out the bicycle for praise as it would bring men to drink milk and would also keep them "away from the theatre or the saloon." *National Purity Congress*, p. 127.

32. Quoted in Hoffman, *Poetry of Stephen Crane*, p. 101.

33. *Maggie*, p. 68.

34. See the account of Willis B. Clarke's visit with Crane in Stallman and Gilkes, *Letters*, p. 242.

35. In a letter to Nellie Crouse, 12 January 1896, Crane explained: "The final wall of the wise man's thought is Human Kindness of course. If

the road of disappointment, grief, pessimism, is followed far enough, it will arrive there." It was also in this letter that he said he was "minded to die in [his] thirty-fifth year." Stallman and Gilkes, *Letters*, p. 99.

36. On this point, see also Brenda Murphy, "Women with Weapons: The Victor in Stephen Crane's *George's Mother*," *Modern Language Studies* 11 (Spring 1981):88–93.

37. See the Willis B. Clarke notes in Stallman and Gilkes, *Letters*, pp. 242–43.

38. "The Monster," p. 52.

39. Letter to an unknown recipient, December 1894, Stallman and Gilkes, *Letters*, p. 42.

40. The echo here is of Crane's poem in *War Is Kind*: "A man said to the universe:/'Sir, I exist!'/'However,' replied the universe,/ The fact has not created in me/'A sense of obligation.'" Bowers, *Works* 1:poem 89, p. 57.

# Susan Wolstenholme

# Brother Theodore, Hell on Women

> *Sometimes he wept for the general human condition*
> *But he was hell on women.*
>
> *He had never loved any women, he confessed,*
> *Except his mother whose broken shoes, he*
> *In childhood, had once caressed,*
> *In the discovery of pity.*
>
> Robert Penn Warren, *Homage to Theodore Dreiser*

In his acceptance speech for the Nobel Prize that Dreiser thought *he* deserved, Sinclair Lewis paid homage to *Sister Carrie* as having descended upon "housebound and airless America" to give fresh air to "our stuffy domesticity."[1] Lewis's use of domestic imagery to describe the world that received Theodore Dreiser's work both recalled the publishing problems that beset the young Dreiser and anticipated the critical battle that would follow for over half a century.

It has become a popular cultural myth to perceive Dreiser as Lewis portrayed him, as a great energetic, virile force that descended upon a female-dominated, enervated literary world. But this myth is as dubious as it is demeaning to women. Recent critics have suggested that the old story of Mrs. Doubleday's acting as guardian of America's literary morals is apocryphal;[2] and seven years after Dreiser's quarrels with the original publisher of *Sister Carrie*, Dreiser himself became director of the Butterick "Trio" of women's magazines, the *Designer, New Idea Woman's Magazine*, and the *Delineator*, and editor of the last, which a recent Dreiser critic has called "one of the silliest and most syrupy publications in the history of women's magazines."[3] He himself may well have been responsible for rejecting manuscripts on the same prudish grounds as those attributed to Mrs. Doubleday, for, as he wrote to a correspondent, he was "personally opposed in this magazine [*Delineator*] to stories which have an element of horror in them, or which are disgusting in their realism and fidelity to life," and he urged that material have "a truly uplifting character."[4] If one can speak of confrontations between male and female literary values and manners at the time, these confrontations were surely not external to the psyches of the men who dominated the literary world.

Repercussions of the myth that Dreiser came as a great phallic force to liberate male literary strength have shaken not only critical evaluations of Dreiser but the entire literary canon. In an essay originally written after the publications of *The Bulwark* and later reprinted in *The Liberal Imagination*, Lionel Trilling deals with these implications. Because of Dreiser's "force," says Trilling, and because he knows "low life," critics have mistakenly given him license to generalize without earning his conclusions and therefore he is used to valorize an anti-intellectual current in American literature. One can see why, then, in comparison with Dreiser, such a writer as Edith Wharton is dismissed by Alfred Kazin, for example,[5] not simply because she is a woman but because her careful artistry is alien to this aesthetic.[6]

Feminist readers of Dreiser must revise traditional notions of Dreiser's place in the canon, but they also have a new vantage point for seeing his work. As a "resisting reader," to use Judith Fetterley's term, a contemporary reader can perceive the profound implications for feminism in Dreiser's fiction. This fiction at its best arises not from hostility toward women or from great phallic strength but from a powerful struggle between male and female psychical values, a struggle perceptible within the fiction rather than in the outside literary world, a struggle that Dreiser at his best confronted honestly and humanely.

In *The Mermaid and the Minotaur*, Dorothy Dinnerstein argues that our prevailing sexual arrangements, rooted in mother-dominated infancy, are destructive to both men and women because, for both male and female children, these arrangements give rise to deep-seated passionate ambivalences toward sexuality. From these arrangements originates, for both male and female children, deep-seated antipathy toward women, along with passionate attachment, arising from one's primary relationship with one's mother. Consequently, adult women in our society are the targets of great primary rage from both men and women; and both men and women, for slightly different reasons, experience a rather precarious sense of identity.

Both Dreiser's life and his work exemplify these deep-seated, passionate ambivalences and this precarious sense of identity.[7] Dinnerstein's analysis begins to explain some of the paradoxes in both Dreiser's life and his work: that he was a notorious womanizer while intensely devoted to his mother and sisters; that he could devote his first two novels to sympathetic portraits of women and in his acknowledged masterpiece sympathize with the murderer of a pregnant woman; that he could fill two volumes with stories of women breaking free of societal bonds but still write the three-volume saga of a hero who treats women as objects.

Robert Forrey has explained the biographical roots of the Oedipal structuring principle in Dreiser's work: "His rejection of his father—whom he held responsible for the suffering and humiliation of his impoverished childhood—and his identification with his mother and women were probably the crucial psychological events of his life, for they affected not only his personality and sexuality in a decisive way but his political and religious belief and his art as well."[8] Forrey's "French Freudian" analysis, though it takes account of the entire Oedipal drama, gives the psychic weight of the role of the father. But although, as Forrey reminds us, the French unconscious may be Oedipal "through and through," the American unconscious is at least equally dominated by a "mother complex" that Freud's terms explain only partially.[9]

Dinnerstein's analysis reinterprets the Oedipal triangle to offer a fuller explanation of the "mother complex." During early childhood, both girls and boys develop a strong attachment to their primary caretaker, generally the mother, an attachment with a strong erotic component for both sexes. Later, for the boy, "resentment of the father's claims upon the mother threatens to interfere with . . . attachment to his newly interesting and powerful male parent."[10] Consequently, he directs new rage not only against this powerful male parent but also against his mother, who in the child's eyes is at least equally powerful; and this new difficulty "is likely to coalesce with certain longer-standing grievances, rooted in the inevitable frustrations of infancy, that had been part of his feeling for her from the beginning."[11]

Robert Penn Warren has remarked that *Sister Carrie, Jennie Gerhardt*, and *An American Tragedy* were written "under the aegis of the mother," whereas *The Financier, The Titan,* and *The Stoic* were written "under the aegis of the father."[12] The imagery Warren invokes enlightens the psychological dynamic worked out in these novels. The *aegis* was Zeus's shield, borne by Athene, and later given by her to Perseus to be used in defeating the Gorgons. When Athene later reclaimed the shield as her breastplate, she continued to wear on it the head of Medusa.

In Dreiser's Cowperwood novels, the father's "aegis" protects the protagonist from that same threatening, primitively awesome female power suggested in the myth. For a man, the trilogy fulfills the infantile wish of escape from mother-domination; Frank Cowperwood is the modern equivalent of the successful conquering hero-son. The narrative voice in this novel is very close to the protagonist. The real-life Cowperwood, Charles Tyson Yerkes, was a hero to Dreiser, for such a businessman, as Dreiser saw it, could "do as he pleased"—that is, he might successfully circumvent maternal restriction. Cowperwood's motto is "I satisfy myself."

The famous early scene of the squid and the lobster portends Cowperwood's later dealings in the financial world, as critics have suggested. But its place as a pivotal incident in Frank's childhood suggests that in Frank's psychic development it might also have more primal significance. As the lobster lives on the squid, Cowperwood concludes that men live on men—but Frank isn't really sure. He hesitates before reaching the conclusion. What lived on men?

> Was it other men? Wild animals lived on men. And there were
> Indians and cannibals. And some men were killed by storms and
> accidents. He wasn't so sure about men living on men; but men did
> kill each other.[13]

Finally, when he lights on the idea of slavery as explaining how men live on other men, it is with an air of relieved triumph—and he runs home to tell his mother. Children, locked into symbiotic relationships with their mothers, perceive their mothers as devouring them at the same time that they themselves are torn between the wish to devour their mothers and the wish to preserve them as a source of nourishment. Thus, little Frank Cowperwood's relieved discovery that men live on men serves as a defense against his infantile fear that women might. No wonder Frank is so excited by his discovery!

"The squid couldn't kill the lobster—he had no weapon." What this "weapon" might signify is abundantly clear to any reader of Freud. Whereas the hard, armored lobster and its claws suggest the phallus as "signifier of desire," the squid resembles Dinnerstein's "mermaid" in its symbolic overtones—as representative of "the dark and magic underwater world from which our life comes."[14] But the squid Dreiser describes is not a terrifying creature at all; it is rather "pale and waxy in texture, looking very much like pork fat or jade" (*The Financier*, p. 4). In the presence of the lobster's "weapon," the squid is perceived as powerless and as solely a source of nourishment. For the only way to detoxify the infantile fear that women will live on men is to turn the image around.

As Perseus used the reflecting surface of the original "aegis" literally to turn around the Medusa's image, so that what was threatening to him instead destroys her, in the trilogy the infantile threat of female domination is turned around to assure Cowperwood's victory. Perseus then used his phallus-like sword to behead the Medusa; Cowperwood uses the business world.

Appropriately, at the end of the chapter where this incident appears, Frank Cowperwood ponders how he should get along in this world. He has reached the age when he seeks to turn the "shield" of his father's world against his mother-dominated young life. At the end of the chapter, he concludes that "he was sure he would like banking; and Third Street, where his father's office was, seemed to him the cleanest, most fascinating street in the world" (*The Financier*, p. 6). The adjective *cleanest* makes sense if the reader acknowledges the psychic significance of the chapter's events. His father's world is "clean" because it enables him to escape from the "dirty" world of the flesh represented to him by home and mother, dirty because, as

Dinnerstein suggests, this world reminds one of the constraints of mortality and also because it represents the part of his own nature that a man must suppress if he is to be as successful as Cowperwood will be.[15]

But Clyde Griffiths in *An American Tragedy* also seeks an "escape" from what he perceives as female-imposed demands. His escape, without the assurance of the father's "aegis," suggests more fully and clearly the dark implications of both the male adolescent's problem and its threat to women under prevailing sexual arrangements. The psychological significance of the murder of Roberta Alden is made explicit when he first contemplates that means of "escape," in a dream where Dreiser uses a set of images similar in their implications to those of the incident of the lobster and the squid.

Clyde dreams first that he is beset by "a savage black dog that was trying to bite him."[16] Escaping that menace by waking up, he then sleeps again to find himself in "some very strange and gloomy place, a wood or a cave or narrow canyon between deep hills." He leaves the cave by a "promising" path, but that path disappears; and his way back is blocked by "an entangled mass of snakes that at first looked more like a pile of brush." Finally, he turns around again to be confronted by a huge "horned and savage animal . . . its heavy tread crushing the brush." Crying out, Clyde awakens.

This dream seems at first to suggest only that dangers beset Clyde wherever he turns. But the elements of the dream suggest why Clyde sees his situation as so horrible. The lobster and the squid are safely enclosed in a tank, but Clyde's dream does not provide him with a safe vantage point. The black biting dog suggests castration anxiety. In the second dream, the three terms used to describe the place where Clyde finds himself, "a wood or a cave or narrow canyon between deep hills," are apparently not alike except that all suggest female genitalia. Escaping from the frightening but nonetheless fairly safe womblike enclosure, Clyde encounters the Medusa-like cluster of snakes.

Freud tells us that "the terror of Medusa is . . . a terror of castration that is linked to the sight of something."[17] Freud explains that the Medusa's snakes "replace the penis, the absence of which is the cause of the horror. This is a confirmation of the technical rule according to which a multiplication of penis symbols signifies castration."

Freud explains the magical effect of the Medusa's head, its turning the spectator to stone, as a "transformation of affect" that offers consolation to the spectator: "He is still in possession of a penis, and the stiffening reassures him of the fact." In the appearance of the "horned and savage animal," the same transformation of affect is evident. Another parallel: though both the appearance of the horned animal and the petrification of the spectator counteract the threat of the Medusa (Dreiser even tells us that the heavy tread of the animal crushes the same "brush" that the snakes at first resemble), both also threaten the spectator-victim. Clyde's dream, then, suggests both that his own penis, as a defense against the Medusa-snakes, has betrayed him; and at the same time, that the father as alternative to the mother, represented by the Medusa according to Freud, is equally terrifying.

For Dreiser's men, the presence and strength of the father's "aegis" marks the difference between success and the most horrifying defeat. Whereas Frank Cowperwood's father provides him with a "clean" alternative to mother-domination, Clyde Griffiths's father is a failure in Clyde's eyes because he provides no safe clean world as a refuge for Clyde. The character of Lester Kane in *Jennie Gerhardt* foreshadows Frank Cowperwood in many ways: like him, Lester Kane is a businessman; and like him, his "perversion" regarding women is that he is attracted to their resistance and to difficulty in working out relationships with them. But he is unlike Cowperwood in that he is more completely mother-dominated. He never escapes from the murky world of the lobster and the squid to the "clean" world of his father's business. One result is that in business he cannot become as successful as Cowperwood or even as his brother Robert; he is not, as Robert notes, "snaky" enough.[18] The other result is that he adopts Jennie as mother to him: "These years of living with Jennie had made him curiously dependent upon her. Who had ever been so close to him before? His mother loved him. . . . His father—well, his father was a man, like himself" (*JG*, p. 216).

Though Dreiser has been labeled a "naturalist" and his strength has been perceived in his presenting a mechanistic, amoral system, some critics[19] have perceived that his view is sentimental, humanistic, and moralistic. All of his novels written under "the aegis of the mother" suggest a war between these two systems of perceiving reality. In *Jennie Gerhardt*, the gap between these two systems must have become clear to Dreiser as resolving this confrontation eluded him. Originally *Jennie Gerhardt* had a happy ending; but, according to Robert Elias, "Lester's not marrying Jennie and the death of Jennie's child were incidents Dreiser had to contrive in revising his novel, to give the story a 'poignancy' which the original tone demanded but which he had not been able to maintain."[20] The original ending of the novel, though it may have been more sentimental, would have been appropriate to one of the competing sets of values implicit in it. For two-thirds of its length, the novel is a rewriting of the Patient Griselda tale. Dreiser's problem in writing the novel was closely related to his perception of society's ambivalence toward women's role in our own culture.

As Frank Cowperwood is one kind of ideal man to Dreiser, Jennie Gerhardt is his ideal woman, but it is instructive to note the difference between the male and female ideals. Whereas Cowperwood represents complete escape from the dark mermaid world of the mother and the ability to subjugate feminine energy to male will, Jennie represents that mermaid world itself; and that world is both comforting and terrifying.

Early in the novel, Dreiser notes the inconsistency of society's glorification of the mother role under certain conditions and its detestation of this same role if these conditions are not met: "Certain processes of the all-mother, the great artificing wisdom of the power that works and weaves in silence and in darkness, when viewed in the light of the established opinion of some of the little individuals created by it, are considered very vile. We turn our faces away from the creation of life as if that were the last thing that man should dare to interest himself in, openly" (*JG*, p. 98).

Nonetheless, Dreiser himself seems to bear this same ambivalence toward maternity. Jennie's mother in the novel's opening chapter performs two roles: to work to provide food for her family, and to admonish: "'Don't forget to rub into these little corners,'" she tells Jennie. "'Look here what you've left'"; "'You mustn't stare at people when they pass'" (*JG*, p. 6-7). Jennie inherits the same mother role, both beneficent and admonishing.[21] She plays a maternal role to her siblings; and both seductions, the first by Senator Brander and the second by Kane, are motivated not by sexual attraction or even, as in Carrie Meeber's case, by the desire to advance herself, but by the need to provide for her family. When she bears her own child early in the novel, her only role becomes to be mother to her, for she has no other job; she never becomes a wife; and although she is mistress to Brander and to Kane, there is no emotional force of engagement with either man. She resists both until the need to provide for the family overwhelms her. She seems curiously detached from Brander throughout their relationship; and his death signifies to her not so much the loss of a vital relationship in her life as the loss of the person who would continue to provide for her family, including now her biological child. She does grow fond of Lester Kane, but even here her feeling is motivated to a great extent by the good he has done her family. Finally, as she provides for her parents as they have never been able to provide for her, she becomes "mother" even to them.

By the terms of the novel, Jennie becomes for Lester the embodiment of the "all-mother"; and it is her role as mother that makes her, as critics have perceived, the ideal woman Dreiser never found.[22] But the dream that she fulfills for a man has nightmare implications for him: he cannot operate in the socially accepted "male" mode if for him a woman occupies the center of his life. Lester lives with Jennie in a womblike, timeless world, which, nonetheless, is affected by the events of the external time-bound world. In Lester's infantile fixation, he denies that time will ultimately deny him his inheritance; so Jennie must become the admonishing mother to remind him. His marriage allows him to manage a woman as Jennie could not be managed; it puts his relationship with a woman in socially accepted terms partly because it allows him to subordinate a woman to his "clean" business activities, and so it represents his escape from the dark but emotionally satisfying mother-dominated world to the business world of his father and brothers.

Therefore, he suddenly gathers great energy in the business world and quickly rises.

For all her self-abnegation, Jennie becomes an Angel of Death, presiding over the deaths of her mother, her father, her daughter, and finally Lester— appropriately, because she embodies life-and-death forces with which Lester's wife has lost connection. But Dreiser establishes in this novel the merits of these forces; he maintains something positive even in Jennie's role as Death Angel. Further, he makes clear why society is unfair to force a woman to assume such a burden, for Jennie herself suffers not as a superpowerful but as a human being. In the original ending of the novel, Jennie and Lester live out a fantasy, the inverse of the Cowperwood fantasy. In that fantasy the threat of maternity is apparently neutralized; consequently, the ending is both "happy" and sentimental. But in the published ending of the novel, one sees the human, female consequences of a status quo where women are made to bear such an "ideal." After all, the "little individuals" created and limited by "certain processes of the all-mother" who consider this force "very vile" are in power.

In the Cowperwood trilogy, the actual terms of such power are explicitly laid out. As Lester Kane lives the fantasy of a nearly perfect symbiotic relationship with mother, Frank Cowperwood lives the fantasy of complete escape both from maternal domination, threatening because the mother is perceived as a devouring creature, and from paternal authority, threatening because the father is perceived as castrator. Forrey suggests that Cowper- wood's defiance of the father is only posturing because the son cannot escape castration as long as he sees the father as "the other"; Forrey notes, more- over, that Cowperwood's virility is asserted but never authenticated.[23]

Dreiser "authenticates" his hero's virility only in a series of shadow pictures, in Cowperwood's relationships with women. For such a man as Cowperwood, as Dinnerstein suggests, "what makes life under the dominion of other males livable, is in part his ownership of [women]."[24] Cowperwood is successful because, unlike Clyde Griffiths and even unlike Lester Kane, he can so completely separate his needy, childish self from the self that goes forth each day to an exclusively male world. "Even in the efforts man makes to *overthrow* male tyranny [over males] . . . he rests on the vassalage of women," Dinnerstein tells us.[25] Consequently, Cowperwood is never without a woman. Dreiser tells us that Cowperwood becomes interested in girls the year of his first business transaction or a little earlier (*The Financier*, p. 19). Later his sexual liaisons are overlapping rather than serial because he cannot risk being without the security of such an arrangement.

Cowperwood's relationships with women, so necessary to his business success, are clearly modeled on his relationship with his mother, as Dreiser implies early in *The Financier* (see p. 30). His three most important relation- ships, with Lillian, Aileen, and Berenice, suggest in turn the psychological dimensions of the stages of Cowperwood's career. Lillian, older than Frank, is a mother figure; Aileen, though younger than he, is the most nearly his contemporary; Berenice is a daughter figure. But Dreiser also plays the inversions implicit in each of these roles:[26] the mother-figure is, as Dinnerstein suggests she must be, childish. During his courtship of Lillian, Cowperwood picks her up like a child; this action symbolically neutralizes the primitively awesome power she embodies and with which she cannot be comfortable, and also portends the dependent childish role a woman must assume in marriage.

Aileen is the most conflicted of the three because of her anomalous position—the only woman to be both mistress and wife to Cowperwood, she is also mother to the child imprisoned within him and child to his fatherlike mastery of the world—and therefore the most completely robbed and destroyed. In her the need to be both child and mother clash, and she can be nothing but victim. Berenice is safer in her daughter role, though she must still emulate maternal authority. Significantly, only Lillian, the maternal figure, bears children to Cowperwood; Aileen's parents appear in *The Financier*, but they disappear in the later books; and Berenice is represented as having a mother—but no father, for Cowperwood assumes that role.[27]

Cowperwood's art collection in the trilogy reflects his relationship with women. During the early days of his affair with Aileen, Cowperwood arranges a little votive shrine to beauty in the house on North Street for her, where he gathers rare art objects (*The Financier*, p. 161); and when they are married, she perceives that her position must be that of a "radiant, vibrating *objet d'art*."[28] Later Cowperwood hangs her trophylike portrait in his Chicago art gallery, where she presides over the riches that conceal the ruin of her life. But Cowperwood has no affectionate loyalty to the items in his collection, including the women; he replaces them as he can afford finer and finer pieces. Finally, in the scene where Cowperwood declares to Aileen his lack of love for her, Aileen pauses before one acquisition—appropriately, a Raphael Holy Family, in which she takes note of the Madonna (*The Titan*, p. 456) and notes the Virgin's vapid insufficiency for a contemporary woman like herself. Cowperwood's sense of art moves him continually toward more artistic women—Rita Sohlberg, Stephanie Platow, and finally Berenice Fleming, successively finer examples of the Madonna.

Love and art are so closely associated in the trilogy because both, in addition to being social and financial assets, become means for Cowperwood to deny the fundamental fact of mortality. As Dinnerstein suggests, maternal power is particularly threatening because it forces confrontation with this fact. Cowperwood's freedom to replace any woman who cannot give him what he requires fulfills the infantile fantasy of having the power to demand perfect satisfaction from the mother; he believes that he really can satisfy himself. Like his drive for financial power, his control of women and ownership of art confer on him the omnipotence that children imagine themselves to have. Significantly, in the trilogy only the women characters grow old.[29] Love and art are bound to be illusory for Cowperwood so long as he refuses to acknowledge the suggestion of mortality implicit in both.

The movement of plot in the three novels invites the reader to disregard time. The trilogy moves not diachronically but dialectically, as Warren suggests[30] This same dialectical movement occurs also in *An American Tragedy*; but there the dialectic is biologically prescribed, tied to time and bound with it. In the trilogy, the dialectical method allows Dreiser to create in Cowperwood a fantasy character who can operate heedless of the restrictions embodied in the mother. His career—his financial dealings, relationships with women, successive houses, art galleries, and acquisitions—become ways of living what the terrifying and exciting incident of the lobster and the squid suggests.

In *A Gallery of Women*, the form of the work itself, a collection of portraits, acts like the fictional "gallery" that Dreiser has Cowperwood create within the fictional world of the trilogy. In effect, Dreiser as author builds for himself the same sort of gallery he attributes to the fictional businessman with whom he so closely identified himself. Though some critics have noted that the *Gallery* suggests Dreiser's devotion to "the study of female psychology,"[31] it would be more accurate to describe the *Gallery* as a study of a man's relationship to women, with the emphasis on the male observer. Warren is much closer to the mark when he describes the *Gallery* as "a sort of trophy room in print." His metaphor is again brilliantly suggestive. The "Gallery" is at least as much like a shooting gallery as a picture gallery; and what is striking about the work is not so much the psychology of the women as the psychology of the curious narrator who points to the many portraits to tell their stories, as the Duke of Ferrara in Browning's poem pointed to the portrait of his last Duchess.

In some of the sketches—for example, "Reina"—this narrator seems merely priggish. In others, like "Olive Brand," the narrative voice suggests fear of the protagonist's sexuality, fear that appears not to be under the author's control. The narrator seems unaccountably unaware of some of the most evident suggestions of the stories he tells. For example, the narrator appears not to recognize that Lucia, in volume I, has unresolved Oedipal problems. "Emmanuela," in volume II, presents the classic male fantasy of a frigid woman's suppressing a rape fantasy. But below the smugness, one senses that the narrator's impetus to tell about this life springs not from a desire to justify himself but from a troubled need to make sense of a mutual failure: "I had really wanted," he tells us sadly at the end, "to share her life."[32] Even if the reader perceives that the responsibility for his failure to have done so rests as much with him as with her, the sincerity of the wish is evident.

None of the portraits in the *Gallery* is entirely successful; all read more like the sketch of a novel that was never written than a finished work. Some of the least successful are the most essayistic, where Dreiser indulges, as he is wont to do, in pseudophilosophy and rhapsodizes on the vicissitudes of life and its meaninglessness. Nonetheless, these less successful sketches do suggest the force behind the work as a whole.

"Ida Hauchawout" is one such unsuccessful sketch. Ida is first dominated and exploited by her father, then by a husband. She dies giving birth to a (sex undisclosed) child, who dies with her. In the funeral scene, she almost disappears in a description of a gaudy, overdecorated room. She herself becomes, finally, one more tasteless ornament in a tasteless coffin. Her life only puzzles the narrator. He does not deal with the clichés well, but he knows enough to ask how one can deal with such clichés at all: "The crude and defeated Ida. And this fumbling, seeking, and rather to be pitied dub with his rhymes. Myself, writing and wondering about it all" (p. 658).

"Ernestine" is likewise essayistic; likewise, the narrator is troubled and torn. The central conflict, between Ernestine and the narrator, is really a shadow image of a conflict apparently within the narrator himself. Ernestine, like Carrie Meeber and like Stephanie Platow in the trilogy, is an actress. She is presented with the choice of continuing her stage career, a choice that will entail a loveless, ruthless, promiscuous life, or remaining mistress to the man she loves—and little else. The narrator appears sympathetic to her dilemma, but he is also afraid of her potential power. After wavering between the two for some time, she finally opts for her career; she is aware in so choosing that she will have to use sex to advance her career.

Dreiser seems unaware of his own ambivalence toward the dilemma that confronts Ernestine. At one point he agrees with "a famous critic of international repute—a student of types and personalities," who says that the American girl "seems to realize more than do her sisters of almost any other country to-day, that her business is to captivate and later dominate the male. . . . Now I do not count that as being inferior or stupid. To me it is being effective" (*Gallery*, p. 532). Indeed it is, given Dreiser's code whereby one does what will accomplish one's goals, and given that in the society he depicts, women are prevented from gaining goals except through men. But that this idea troubles Dreiser is clear. He can't even state it in his authorial voice but instead introduces a character, of whose credentials he must make a point, expressly for the purpose of making the statement.

Later there is an unmistakable note of condemnation when he expresses a similar sentiment. He speaks of actresses—"female adventurers" he calls them—who must "sell themselves to the highest bidders or fall, and quite uniformly they sold themselves. They had no essential refinement." He perceives that they chase men who are "bounders and dubs and wasters like themselves" (*Gallery*, p. 555). But he fails to acknowledge that the difference between the male and female "adventurers" is that the males are in power.

Yet this very issue is what troubles the narrator throughout this story. The preoccupations in *A Gallery of Women*—the limits of responsibility, the definition of power relationships—are the same themes used, with greater artistic control, in Dreiser's better work. Despite its artistic limitations, the much-neglected *Gallery* is a rich source for critical inquiry, a work that may shed some light on the author's better-known work. Dreiser suggests, apparently unaware of the implication, why Hollywood must create a "little girl" type for the films such women as Ernestine make. When Ernestine begins to age, the film world, which cannot recognize mortality, discards her. She returns to the scene of her earlier life with her lover and, having failed to gain power over her life, exercises it over her death by committing suicide. "I thought I understood," says the narrator in the concluding paragraph. "Or did I?" (*Gallery*, p. 564). Her former lover is "very sad," and the suggestion is that so is the narrator.

That problematic narrative distance in *A Gallery of Women* was prefigured in Dreiser's first novel; for in many ways *Sister Carrie* is a portrait that has escaped the confines of a "gallery." Here, the narrative voice assumes an identity and becomes a character in the novel as the narrator attempts to arbitrate between his mechanistic, amoral philosophy and that sentimental, humanistic one to which he is also drawn. Like the portraits in *A Gallery of Women*, Carrie's story has feminist implications: Carrie does better for herself than if she had followed a more conventional path; and the novel suggests that the single life can be worth living whereas the married life often is not.[33] But Dreiser undercuts these implications. Earlier critics perceived Carrie to be unsympathetic and Hurstwood to be the source of the novel's power.[34] Critics accorded tragic stature to Hurstwood, but they perceived Carrie herself to be lacking the human possibilities that make such stature possible.[35] She becomes a comic character, just as within the novel she becomes a comic actress. The narrative voice of Dreiser, counterposing the "tragedy" of Hurstwood as a reproach to Carrie, seems to indicate that Carrie's success suggests her own emptiness.

The character Ames seems to speak for the narrator and to suggest the same thing to Carrie directly. But Ames—like the narrator of the *Gallery* portraits, who always takes seriously the women he encounters—does not trivialize Carrie herself but only her role as comedienne. He advises her to take her own power seriously and to use it as a real artist might, to represent "the world's longing."[36] He proposes to Carrie that she employ her talent neither in tragedy nor in comedy, but in "comedy drama."

Likewise, neither is this novel tragic, as it might be if Hurstwood were really at its center (and if it acknowledged a greater degree of personal responsibility), nor is it comic, as it might be perceived if Carrie were at its center. It is, as Leslie Fiedler has called it, "sentimental"; and its center is the authorial presence that, inspired by sentimental, lower-middle-class values, becomes an "avenging brother" to Carrie.[37] The fraternal authorial voice at the center of the novel can make of Carrie what the fraternal character Ames, who is confined within the limits of the novel's fictional world, can only suggest to her. That voice, as it "explains, justifies, persuades, and interprets for the reader,"[38] acts as intermediary between the reader and Carrie.

What the reader learns about Carrie herself is different in kind from what she or he learns about Hurstwood. Though the dynamics of Hurstwood's troubled marriage are laid out in some detail in several scenes, we meet Carrie only after she has left her family at home. Though she is "sister" to Minnie, the relationship—except in the scene recounting Minnie's dream— seems to have little intensity; the relationship does not account for her later career, though Hurstwood's marriage, divorce, and theft have a great deal to do with his. Indeed, Carrie hardly appears at all to be "sister" in any significant sense to any character in the novel. She sheds her family easily. Though she has a few pangs of conscience when she takes up residence with Drouet, their values do not seem to affect her, and they do not exert any claims on her, either to censure her conduct or to share in her later success.

Carrie does not really exert control over Hurstwood; rather, he relinquishes power over himself to her. The relationship between them reverses the lobster-squid relationship; the squid, consumed by the lobster, then controls the lobster. Hurstwood becomes a failure because he cannot control this lobster-squid relationship like Frank Cowperwood and because Carrie Meeber refuses to submit to the squidlike role that Jennie Gerhardt submits to.[39] Hurstwood allows his prey literally to starve him.

If the narrator evokes our sympathy for Hurstwood's position, he does not tell us that Carrie is responsible for it, merely that Hurstwood *perceives* that she is somehow responsible. Though Carrie tries to help Hurstwood when she learns of his condition, he resents her help. But this narrative voice is a problem because at times it seems to function from within Hurstwood, though it does not function within Carrie.

In the final chapter, the weather functions much as it does in James Joyce's short story "The Dead" to suggest a unity in diverseness of which only the narrator is aware. This voice begins superior to the action of the story and then moves, in turn, into Hurstwood's consciousness and then Carrie's. But it enters Carrie's consciousness only in a far less specific way.[40] The narrator maintains a certain distance when he turns to her in her Waldorf suite with her roommate. He is aware of implications in their words and actions that they are not always aware of. As Forrey remarks, the unknown man they observe falling in the snow suggests a parallel with Hurstwood. But though Carrie intuitively sympathizes with suffering, and though the book she is reading gives her some understanding of it, she lacks the perspective to understand what is going on under her window.

Dreiser goes on to assemble all the principals on stage: Drouet appears, and then the Hurstwood family. The very artificiality of his technique calls further attention to the narrator's unseen presence. With each scene the narrative voice changes, approaching parody: Drouet is merely foolish; the Hurstwood women are dangerous and hateful. He moves back to Hurstwood, again moving in from a wide-angle perspective, and shows his suicide. When he moves to Carrie, though he begins in her mind, he moves quickly into his own perspective. Finally he closes in his own voice, in a final tearful apostrophe, both admonishing and sympathetic.

The narrative voice that emerges in *Sister Carrie* is an attempt to mediate between dual systems of perceiving reality that Dreiser never fully integrated. Such a voice is not as directly present in *An American Tragedy*, but the same war between opposing systems is, if anything, more evident in Dreiser's greatest work. Attempting to arbitrate among the views of Alfred Kazin, F. O. Matthiessen, Lionel Trilling, and Robert Penn Warren, Charles Thomas Samuels defines the problem for *An American Tragedy*. "Dreiser is caught," says Samuels, "between a mechanism that denies responsibility and thereby a fully human response and a humanistic ethic which can only convince us of Clyde's profound guilt."[41] Samuels maintains that the novel is a failure, not, as Trilling says, because of a failure of style, but because of a failure of ethics at its very center.

In *An American Tragedy*, as in the Cowperwood trilogy, Dreiser identifies himself with his protagonist as he does not in *Sister Carrie* or *Jennie Gerhardt*. Scholarship has suggested[42] that the early life of Clyde Griffiths resembles that of the young Theodore Dreiser more than that of Chester Gillette, the real-life protagonist of the story on which the novel is based; and this identification is the source both of power in the novel and also of the problems many critics have dealt with. Here, narrative voice is more completely subordinated to the demands of characterization. Clyde Griffiths as character becomes arbiter of systems of values, like the narrator of *A Gallery of Women* and *Sister Carrie*. He himself first voices the question that many critics after him have tried to resolve: is he a guilty murderer or an innocent victim?

Because Clyde is at the center of this novel, the reader is drawn in to identify with him—unless the reader becomes Fetterley's "resisting reader." For the issue of the murder of a pregnant woman has feminist implications. Irving Howe reads the novel: "As we are touched by Clyde's early affection for Roberta, so later we participate vicariously in his desperation to be rid of her. We share his desire with some shame, but unless we count ourselves among the hopelessly pure, we share it."[43] Or, Fetterley's resisting reader might respond, unless we are women. And Howe's argument suggests why one must resist: the implications of the novel are not restricted to the extreme case in which one might be murdered: "In the particular case upon which he drew for *An American Tragedy*, the young man did kill his pregnant girl; but Dreiser must nevertheless have realized that in the vast majority of such crises the young man dreams of killing and ends by marrying."[44]

This statement, horrifying as it is, is nonetheless validated in Dreiser's autobiographical novel *The "Genius"* where the idea of killing Angela Blue is displaced onto her and made into a suicide wish. Eugene Witla, unable himself to contemplate actual murder, nonetheless fantasizes: "To think of her under the water of little Okoonee, with its green banks, and yellow sandy shores. . . . How would it be with her if she were really below those still waters? How would it be with him? It would be too desperate, too regretful. No, he must marry her."[45] In *The "Genius"* the young man does precisely what Howe suggests, though he refuses to acknowledge the murder as his own idea. (It is certainly not a coincidence that the imagined manner of death in *The "Genius"*—drowning—is the same as the actual manner of death in *An American Tragedy*, for reasons I will suggest below.) Angela Blue considerately takes from Witla's shoulders the guilt for imagining murder by framing the death wish herself; finally, she even more considerately takes from him the need to murder her by dying in childbirth. In *The "Genius"* Witla is relieved of such responsibility. But in *An American Tragedy* the issue of responsibility serves to focus the sexual questions at the core of the novel, questions that begin to be suggested long before Roberta Alden is murdered but which become sharpest with the murder.

Under the legend "God is Love," on the window of the Griffiths's combination home-mission, is the line "How Long Since You Wrote to Mother?" (*AAT*, 1:9). The sign is appropriate, for the novel works out the rather startling implications of this clichéd sentiment. Like Mrs. Gerhardt, and in spite of her mission work by the side of her husband, Mrs. Griffiths is inspired with an order of spirituality different from the conventionally religious order; Dreiser's women have not established that nineteenth-century link with religion that puts them on a pedestal in charge of the civilizing values of society. In the opening scene, as the Griffiths family gather on the street to proselytize, Mrs. Griffiths "more than any of the others stood up with an ignorant, yet somehow respectable air of conviction. If you had watched her . . . you would have said: 'Well, here is one who, whatever her defects, probably does what she believes as nearly as possible'" (*AAT*, pp. 4-5). And Mrs. Griffiths, like Jennie and Mrs. Gerhardt, believes in her family and her children above all else.

Dreiser's fictional fathers, both Griffiths and old Mr. Gerhardt, are consumed, on the other hand, with religious fervor, a burning vision of heaven and hell. But their passion is nonetheless cold at heart, for it makes them inhuman. It causes them to reject simple acts of love and mercy that bind families together. Clyde rejects his father's "vision"; at the same time, he perceives women to be dangerous.

From the outset of his life in Kansas City, women act as restricting forces to call Clyde to account—literally to financial account as they deal quite frankly in sex and money. His first sweetheart Hortense wants money in exchange for her favors; his mother wants the same money for the family, specifically for his pregnant sister Esta. Later in Lycurgus, his reflections suggest that he holds Hortense responsible for his disaster in Kansas City— even though the entire episode that resulted in the death of a little girl had been managed by boys.

Though Clyde is trapped by the consequences of his own filial and sexual impulses, he continually tries to evade these consequences, as Witla does more successfully. Dreiser's primary concern of course is with Clyde; as Ellen Moers suggests, "if he had conceived the 'Tragedy' as the destruction of a pregnant girl by a man who finds her claim upon him an inconvenience; and if he had seen the Americanness of the Tragedy as consisting of the emotional casualties, inevitably female, of a mobile society, then *An American Tragedy* would have been a very different, far more conventional novel (perhaps another *Jennie Gerhardt*)."[46] Nonetheless, Dreiser makes clear that for women there can be no such evasion as Clyde contemplates for himself. Though the issue of "responsibility" in the novel is a problematic one, the novel does suggest one clear set of responsibilities: that of mothers for their children. Clyde's mother naturally seeks support for Esta, just as Esta must provide for her child, and finally as Roberta, who cannot escape the "claims" of her pregnancy as Clyde contemplates escaping, must be responsible for her child and Clyde's. Given the social conditions, the "Americanness" of the Tragedy, women's biological circumstances are made into a trap to ensnare both women and men like Clyde.

Dreiser's concern is Clyde's response to this trap: rage that the women equally caught dare not or cannot express. This rage is directed against the women that Clyde perceives, mistakenly, to be responsible for the trap. Clyde comes to perceive Roberta's passion for him, her pregnancy, and finally her very existence solely in terms of a violent threat to himself, a threat that can be met only by an act of equal violence. Clyde's fears are the same fears of engulfment by women that Dinnerstein describes. Dreiser describes these fears in similar terms: unless Clyde can escape Roberta's demands, "this other world from which he sprang might extend its gloomy, poverty-stricken arms to him and *envelop* him once more, just as the poverty of his family had enveloped and almost *strangled* him from the first" (*ATT*, II:12-13; emphasis mine). This "other world" is ostensibly the world of poverty and insecurity; but the terms in which it is described imply that it also suggests the dark fearful mermaid world from which life springs. By displacing his fear fantasy onto Roberta and drowning her, he destroys that part of himself that is drowning in a sea of "female" problems.

Clyde's claim to innocence rests on the fact that he does not *deliberately* strike Roberta or push her. What he does is strike out blindly, for he is overcome by "a tide of submerged hate, not only for himself but Roberta—her power—or that of life to restrain him in this way" (*AAT*, 2:77). His blow externalizes the hatred he has for "his own failure," Dreiser tells us—that part of him sufficiently dominated by maternal influence to make him incapable of freeing himself. Roberta is not, to Clyde, at the moment of this blow, Roberta at all, but the embodiment of what he perceives as female forces that entrap him.

More clearly than Clyde's original cold-blooded plan could possibly suggest, Clyde's blind thrust suggests that he is striking out at the great pregnant mother-force. One might suggest that those critics who exonerate Clyde do so on the grounds that Clyde only expresses the culturally normal hatred for women and what they represent. To suggest that Clyde is guilty of murder is to hold men responsible for their expressed hatred for women.

Dreiser does not suggest that the solution to the problem is simple. Clyde's action is both horrifying and futile because Roberta herself, like Jennie Gerhardt, is not really a terrible powerful force but only a mortal woman. Ironically, the location of the murder is within a great primeval forest, a vaginal symbol like the forest in Clyde's dream; and having killed Roberta, Clyde still finds himself in the middle of that forest. Clyde therefore becomes a victim himself because, like Roberta, he too is made to bear an onus that is not his. Drowning Roberta kills her vulnerable mortal self; it does not destroy the force that is drowning Clyde, and that force reappears as The Law, ostensibly the chivalric champion of women but in fact part of the same system of oppression that made the murder possible in the first place.

Roberta and Clyde are both scapegoats: Roberta, of society's hatred for women; and Clyde, of men's shame at having such hatred. Clyde's tragedy is that he is made into the unwilling champion of men's hatred for women. And just as Clyde does not kill Roberta *as Roberta*, Clyde is not condemned as the Clyde whose character we have come to know. The prosecution invents a *persona*, the seducer-murderer, to be killed. To counter their charge, Clyde's lawyers invent an alternate fictional version of Clyde, equally false. Appropriately, to counter the opposing woman-murderer *persona*, they stress Clyde's attachment to his mother.

In prison Clyde cannot determine whether he is guilty or innocent because guilt and innocence have become meaningless terms in the fictional world he lives in at the same time that that world lives by these terms. He himself is torn; for to a certain extent, he still subscribes to the philosophy represented by his mother and the Reverend McMillan. At the same time, he continues to hold women responsible for his destruction.[47] He feels he is a help-less victim because he had been "tortured . . . by Roberta with her determina-tion that he marry her and thus ruin his whole life . . . burned with that unquenchable passion for the Sondra of his beautiful dreams . . . harassed, tortured, mocked by the ill fate of his early life and training. . . . How could they judge him, these people, all or any one of them, even his own mother . . . ?" (*AAT*, 1:392).

Clyde's disclaimer of responsibility rests on the assumption that he cannot define himself except in relation to a woman. Under a parent's "aegis," one must, as Warren remarks of Clyde, "have things done for him,"[48] like a baby. Dreiser sets critics' teeth on edge because his lovers address one another in baby talk; but such a mode of conversation is appropriate for them, for they are permanently infantilized. Clyde perceives Sondra Finchley, who returns his baby talk, as totally nondemanding, whereas Roberta is all-demanding (*AAT*, 2:57); the two women share the role that one's mother, paradoxically, always plays. But in spite of the apparent inevitability of the trap Clyde finds himself in, Dreiser makes clear that to disclaim responsibility as Clyde does is merely to echo the same societal disclaimers that make a system of male-female mutual victimization possible. And though the novel's final scene sug-gests that such a tragedy may be repeated, for nothing essential has changed from the opening scene, a muted hope is suggested by Clyde's final ability to perceive his separation from his mother and to accept his death.

Part of Clyde's tragedy thus stems from his position, as Ellen Moers ex-pressed it, "not only as a solitary young American on the make but also as someone's brother and someone's son."[49] In contrast, Caroline Meeber, sister though she is called, is just exactly a "solitary young American on the make." What seems to be necessary but is impossible in Dreiser's fictional world is to define oneself autonomously but to retain the capacity and the insight for human compassion.

What one early reviewer wrote of the second edition of *Sister Carrie* might have been said by earlier critics of *An American Tragedy* or any of Dreiser's novels: "Amid the thousands of anaemic novels that come out like a flood, written by ladies, for ladies of both sexes, here is a book written by a man, obviously intended for men."[50] Whatever Dreiser's intended audience, his actual audience has been reconstituted. One feminist critic, Marcia Landy, suggests:

> A further look at literature, a look which goes beyond the uncover-ing and acceptance of the basic mythology of female subordination to the male and which questions its existence, should provide more information about the social reasons for the myth, how it functions, and about the kind of world it portrays, a world which may have seemed inevitable or necessary to the writer and his society but

certainly not to the contemporary reader, not to women and perhaps not even to men.[51]

Dreiser merits this further look.

What is remarkable for the feminist reader of Dreiser is that he so honestly dealt with his own primal rage and rarely reduced either men or women to the simple level of "victim" or "villain." In all his fiction, Dreiser deals with an issue of vital concern to women, the issue of power. He acknowledges and accepts the idea that women can have power; women like Jennie Gerhardt and Carrie Meeber and Mrs. Griffiths endure, like Dilsey. Although men perceive women's power as threatening, the problem lies not in some inherent female destructiveness, for both men and women share a death-wish, but rather in structures that force sexual power to be used destructively. Dreiser himself speaks from the position of being "someone's brother and someone's son"; but for him as an artist such a position becomes liberating even if problematic. He points to the problems inherent in our social sexual arrangements; and although speaking from a male perspective, he is clearly aware that both men and women are victims. If, as Forrey remarks, Dreiser stood at one time for "brotherhood, allied with motherhood, against fatherhood," he is, if not a feminist, at least a fellow traveler, allied with feminists in a struggle against patriarchy. For his initial impulse in writing a novel was to tell the story of a sister.

## Notes

1. *The Man from Main Street*, ed. Harry E. Maule and Melville H. Cane (New York: Random House, 1953), p. 8.
2. See Jack Salzman, *Theodore Dreiser: The Critical Reception* (New York: David Lewis, 1972), pp. xv–xviii.
3. James Lundquist, *Theodore Dreiser* (New York: Frederick Ungar, 1974), p. 25.
4. Cited by Robert H. Elias, *Theodore Dreiser: Apostle of Nature*, emended ed. (Ithaca: Cornell University Press, 1970), p. 140.
5. *On Native Grounds*, abridged ed. (New York: Anchor, 1956), pp. 53–68.
6. In fact, Wharton and Dreiser have much in common: both are centrally concerned with the problem of quickly changing economic patterns and the lack of manners and morals in the culture. Robert Lehan suggests only some of the bases for comparison between *Sister Carrie* and *The Custom of the Country* in *Theodore Dreiser: His World and His Novels* (Carbondale: Southern Illinois University Press, 1969), pp. 252–53. The comparison need not be, as it is in Kazin's essay, at Wharton's expense.
7. The woman reader must resist, partly because although she may share a precarious sense of identity, this particular identity is male. But as

Dinnerstein suggests, male and female precarious identities are mirror images of one another and equally hazardous.

8. Robert Forrey, "Theodore Dreiser: Oedipus Redivivus," *Modern Fiction Studies* 23 (Autumn 1977):343.

9. One Frenchman, Régis Michaud, has remarked that the "mother complex" is "the American complex par excellence" and suggests that this American "mother complex" is difficult for Europeans to understand. See *The American Novel Today: A Social and Psychological Study* (Boston: Little Brown, 1928), p. 20.

10. Dorothy Dinnerstein, *The Mermaid and the Minotaur* (New York: Harper & Row, 1976), p. 48.

11. Ibid., p. 49.

12. Robert Penn Warren, *Homage to Theodore Dreiser* (New York: Random House, 1971), p. 131.

13. Theodore Dreiser, *The Financier* (1912; reprint ed., Cleveland: World Publishing Co., 1940), p. 5. Subsequent citations from *The Financier* refer to this edition and are cited in the text.

14. Dinnerstein, *Mermaid*, p. 5.

15. See Dinnerstein, *Mermaid*, Ch. 7, "The Dirty Goddess," especially pp. 147–49.

16. Theodore Dreiser, *An American Tragedy*, 2 vols. (New York: Boni & Liveright, 1925), 2:27. Subsequent citations from *An American Tragedy* refer to this edition and are cited in the text.

17. Sigmund Freud, "Medusa's Head," in *Sexuality and the Psychology of Love*, ed. Philip Rieff (New York: Collier Books, 1978), p. 212. The manuscript of this essay is dated 14 May 1922; coincidentally, Freud wrote this sketch during the time Dreiser must have been working on *An American Tragedy*. Though he could not have known this essay, Dreiser had read *The Interpretation of Dreams* and other works by Freud—see Ellen Moers, *Two Dreisers* (New York: Viking, 1969), pp. 260–70—and may well have been aware of the symbolic implications of the dream. But conscious or not of the particular symbolic significance of what he was doing, Dreiser used dream material suggestive of the universal symbol systems Freud describes.

18. Theodore Dreiser, *Jennie Gerhardt* (New York: Harper & Brothers, 1911), p. 300; repeated p. 412. Subsequent citations from *JG* refer to this edition and are cited in the text.

19. For example, Leslie Fiedler in *Love and Death in the American Novel*, rev. ed. (New York: Dell, 1967).

20. Elias, *Apostle of Nature*, p. 154.

21. Fiedler calls Jennie the "eternally offended" mother (p. 253).

22. I am suggesting not that Jennie Gerhardt's origin as a character was in Dreiser's own mother (as well as his sister), as Warren and others have suggested, though that may well be, but that Jennie's character is perceived as universally maternal. What is interesting is that any specific characteristics of an individual who is a mother, especially one's own

mother, become for Dreiser subsumed under the more general traits attributed to "Mother."

23. Forrey, *Theodore Dreiser*, pp. 350–52.

24. Dinnerstein, *Mermaid*, p. 191.

25. Ibid., pp. 196–97.

26. Dreiser made an interesting slip when he was finishing *The Stoic* in his last days that suggests the extent to which he unconsciously conflated women's roles. He calls Cowperwood's daughter at his funeral Anna (p. 271); whereas in fact in *The Financier*, her name is Lillian, after her mother. In *The Financier*, Cowperwood's *sister* is named Anna.

27. Cowperwood's relationship with Lillian parallels Eugene Witla's relationship with Angela Blue in *The "Genius"* which Forrey terms "an act of regression" (p. 352). Likewise, Cowperwood's relationship with Berenice parallels Witla's relationship with young Suzanne Dale.

28. Theodore Dreiser, *The Titan* (1914; reprint ed., New York: New American Library, 1965), p. 40. Subsequent citations from *The Titan* refer to this edition and are cited in the text.

29. Warren, *Homage*, p. 152, remarks that only Aileen does; but in fact, though Aileen ages the most because we see her over the longest period of time, Lillian changes from an attractive young wife to a bovine matron, and Berenice grows from a silly schoolgirl to a sophisticated *femme fatale*.

30. Warren, *Homage*, p. 78

31. See, for example, Lundquist, *Dreiser*, p. 49.

32. Theodore Dreiser, *A Gallery of Women*, 2 vols. (New York: Liveright, 1929), 2:720. Subsequent citations refer to this edition and are cited in the text.

33. See Cathy N. and A. Davidson, "Carrie's Sisters: The Popular Prototypes for Dreiser's Heroines," *Modern Fiction Studies* 23 (Autumn 1977): 395–407.

34. See, for example, James T. Farrell, "Dreiser's *Sister Carrie*," in *The Stature of Theodore Dreiser*, ed. Alfred Kazin and Charles Shapiro (Bloomington: Indiana University Press, 1955), pp. 182–87; see also Michaud, *American Novel*, p. 103.

35. Lundquist says Carrie is no more capable of tragedy than a chipmunk (*Dreiser*, p. 32).

36. Theodore Dreiser, *Sister Carrie*, Norton Critical Ed. (New York: Norton, 1970), p. 356.

37. Fiedler, *Love and Death*, p. 249.

38. William J. Handy, "A Reexamination of Dreiser's *Sister Carrie*," in the Norton Critical Ed. of *Sister Carrie*.

39. Though *Sister Carrie* is not immoral or even amoral—Fiedler points out that Dreiser condemns both Carrie and Hurstwood (pp. 251–52)—it is threatening, because it makes a spectacle of the failure of the traditional dominating men's role and the abdication of the traditional maternal women's role. Dreiser's claims to the contrary, however, the

book was not really "suppressed"; and, as Salzman points out, it did not receive a bad press so much as an inadequate one.

40. The statement that Carrie's reading makes her understand the worthlessness of her former life is tied to the narrator's remarks in the novel's final paragraph rather than to anything we know about Carrie's mental processes. Earlier in the novel, Dreiser similarly uses Carrie's mind to express the narrator's ideas. Handy notes (p. 525) that when Carrie observes to Mrs. Hale that "no one is ever happy," her statement is "an expression of the unseen presence of the author," rather than a convincing observation from Carrie's character.

41. Charles Thomas Samuels, "Mr. Trilling, Mr. Warren, and *An American Tragedy*," in *Dreiser: A Collection of Critical Essays*, ed. John Lydenburg (Englewood Cliffs, N.J.: Prentice-Hall, 1971), p. 169.

42. See Lehan, *Dreiser: His World*, pp. 142–69.

43. Irving Howe, "Dreiser and Tragedy," in Lydenburg, *Collection*, p. 151.

44. Ibid., p. 148. Though Fetterley, *The Resisting Reader: A Feminist Approach to American Fiction* (Bloomington: Indiana University Press, 1978), implies that the "resisting reader" is a female reader, the question of whether a reader's gender affects his or her reading of a particular work (and if it does, how) poses a problem that reader-response criticism might explore further. Possibly a male reader with raised awareness could likewise resist this novel's premises, without that reader's counting himself among the "hopelessly pure." Such investigation might consider the relationship between the conscious resistance to a novel's premises that Fetterley considers, and the unconscious "resistance" that Norman Holland and others have suggested helps to determine every reader's reading style.

45. Theodore Dreiser, *The "Genius"* (New York: New American Library, 1967), pp. 176–77.

46. Moers, *Two Dreisers*, p. 213. Moers's statement suggests interesting questions: why would a "female" emphasis make such a novel "conventional"? What "conventions" of fiction or of culture are linked to such a story? And what are the implications of such "conventions"?

47. Dreiser apparently held women responsible for Clyde's destruction. Moers cites a letter (p. 199), written in the summer of 1924, in which Dreiser writes, "I'm to where the factory girl and the rich girl in Clyde's life are enlarging and by degrees destroying him."

48. Warren, *Homage*, p. 135.

49. Moers, *Two Dreisers*, pp. 213–14.

50. In Salzman, *Critical Reception*, p. 31.

51. Marcia Landy, "The Silent Woman: Toward a Feminist Critique," in *The Authority of Experience: Essays in Feminist Criticism*, ed. Arlyn Diamond and Lee R. Edwards (Amherst: University of Massachusetts Press, 1977), p. 17.

# Sharon O'Brien

# Mothers, Daughters, and the "Art Necessity": Willa Cather and the Creative Process

Since its inception, as Judith Fetterley observes, feminist literary criticism has been a "growing, changing, constantly self-transforming phenomenon characterized by a resistance to codification and a refusal to be rigidly defined or to have its parameters prematurely set."[1] But despite its eclectic, rapidly shifting nature, certain trends in feminist criticism can be discerned. In its early stages, most critics, trained in the techniques of formalist literary analysis, naturally focused on the texts themselves despite their awareness that literature could not be separated from culture or biography. Much early work was thus of the "images of women in fiction" variety. Such analyses provided scholars with a useful taxonomy of recurrent female stereotypes, most often those employed by male writers who consciously or unconsciously revealed the male vision of woman as Other; whether a female character was Goddess, Mother, or Temptress, she reflected male desires or fears rather than autonomous selfhood.[2] Since this beginning, feminist critics have deepened and varied their approaches to literature as more acquire the interdisciplinary skills that work in women's studies requires, going beyond issues of imagery and characterization to explore the complex links among writer, culture, and text. Two of the most promising and potentially fruitful approaches are summarized in Cheri Register's recent review essay on feminist criticism in *Signs*.[3] Since I employ both methods in my work on Cather, I will briefly detail them here.

The first approach, centering on the question, Is there a female aesthetic? combines formalist analysis with cultural contexting to determine whether the woman writer and her work reflect distinctly female experience or perceptions. In *The Madwoman in the Attic*, Sandra Gilbert and Susan Gubar argue persuasively that the woman writer in patriarchal culture experiences self, authorship, and creativity differently. Facing a male literary tradition that excludes her, unlike her male counterpart she suffers a feminine "anxiety of authorship" rather than Harold Bloom's Oedipal "anxiety of influence."[4] Gilbert and Gubar find a "distinctively female literary tradition" connecting Austen, the Brontës, Eliot, Rossetti, and Dickinson. Forced to invert or subvert the images of women inherited from a patriarchal tradition as well as forge a new definition of the artist, these authors create fiction embodying the "woman writer's own discomfort, her sense of powerlessness, her fear that she inhabits alien and incomprehensible places."[5]

Growing up in Victorian America when the dominant culture assigned women to the home and men to the world and social conventions and literary traditions conspired to relegate women writers to subordinate status, Willa Cather suffered the same anxiety of authorship Gilbert and Gubar see afflicting her British predecessors. How could one be a woman and a great writer at the same time? This dilemma plagued Cather during her twenties and thirties; until she resolved it she could not commit herself fully to her craft. Her first solution was to repudiate her gender and identify with men, which she did flamboyantly and overtly during her adolescent masquerade as "William Cather, jr.," later more discreetly and covertly. Obviously male identification was not a satisfactory answer to her search for identity and vocation. Despite her yearnings she was not male, and as long as she devalued her gender she devalued herself; as long as she devalued herself she did not have the self-confidence to embark seriously on the writing of fiction. Reconciliation of the conflict between feminine identity and artistic vocation was an arduous process. Although she wrote her first short stories in her early twenties, Cather did not complete her first major novel until she was forty. To understand her long apprenticeship and to evaluate patterns in the major fiction concerning woman's search for autonomy and creativity, it is necessary to consider the forces that caused and prolonged Willa Cather's anxiety of authorship—as well as those that allowed her to overcome it.

Patriarchal culture and male literary tradition are not the only forces affecting the woman writer. The other important recent development in feminist literary criticism is psychoanalytic rather than cultural in orientation, concerned with the woman writer's sources of support and strength as well as oppression. Inspired by recent studies combining feminist with psychoanalytic perspectives such as Dorothy Dinnerstein's *The Mermaid and the Minotaur* and Nancy Chodorow's *The Reproduction of Mothering*, feminist critics are displaying new interest in the mother/daughter relationship and in the impact of mothering—and being mothered—on women's lives, identities, and creative expression. As Register points out, viewing "the mother-daughter relationship as a creative source for women can enhance our work in a number of ways."[6]

Such an approach is central to understanding the connection between Willa Cather's life and work. Just as her mother dominated her early years, so themes deriving from the mother/child configuration dominate her fiction. As one of her recent critics astutely noted, Cather's bond with her mother provided her with a "source of conflict" central to her creativity.[7] Her mother provided Cather with a source of support as well as conflict, for this mother/daughter bond—like most—was marked by intense ambivalences and contradictions.[8] The daughter's wish to separate was countered by the desire to remain fused; the drive for an autonomous self was countered by the fear of abandonment and loss. Unlike most women, Cather did not escape the psychodynamics of the mother/daughter bond in her intimate relationships. As a woman whose primary intimacies were with other women, Cather never relinquished the support and nurturance the daughter gains from the mother which, as Chodorow argues, many heterosexual women must forgo since men are culturally and psychologically induced to seek rather than offer nurturance. She also never escaped the accompanying fear that in same-sex intimacies she was losing adult separateness, since she did not have the barrier of gender to differentiate herself from the women she loved. Although the extent to which Cather's bonds with women were overtly sexual is not clear given the scant evidence available, her fiction reveals that she found sexuality and passion troublesome forces. Cather's heroic, creative characters channel their passions into transcendent objects—land, the family, religion, art— whereas her doomed or limited characters indulge in sexual or romantic passion. This essay will explore some of the critical problems that Cather's emotional orientation toward women presents to the feminist critic. Simultaneously identifying with women as subjects and viewing them as objects, Cather created both complex, autonomous heroines struggling toward self-definition and creative expression like Alexandra Bergson and Thea Kronborg, and archetypal female figures that reflect the (usually male) viewer's needs and preoccupations, like the maternal Ántonia Shimerda or the seductive Lena Lingard. Hence any feminist reading of Cather's fiction confronts a paradox: a novel like *The Song of the Lark* (1915) with its triumphant, independent artist-heroine seems feminist before its time, whereas *My Ántonia* (1918)—appearing only three years later—may at first seem as sexist as *Light in August*, with Antonia the idealized Earth Mother the precursor of Faulkner's bovine Lena Grove. Understanding Cather's psychological and emotional conflicts can help us resolve such paradoxes without having to view her as the unwitting captive of male views of women.

In the first half of this essay, I will be intertwining these two approaches in examining Cather's struggle to combine the seemingly contradictory identities of "woman" and "artist," uniting cultural and psychological analysis in assessing her response to a patriarchal culture and literary tradition as well as analyzing her relationship with her mother and the other women whom she loved. In the second half of the essay, I will consider the major fiction in the light of the issues I have raised, concentrating on those major texts that are most pertinent to the questions I am asking. Of course in this brief space I can only suggest approaches to Willa Cather's life and work, not offer a comprehensive overview. I hope to demonstrate one way for a feminist critic to assess the complex interplay among culture, life, and text.

I

As a young woman, Willa Cather associated creative achievement with maleness because she looked for it in culturally sanctioned and prestigious forms: the novel, the poem, the concerto. In later years, however, she recognized the underground stream of female creative expression. Long before the current feminist movement helped us discover the artistry concealed in the sampler or the quilt, Willa Cather understood that female creativity had been forced to flow in acceptable and unobtrusive domestic channels. "The German housewife who sits before her family on Thanksgiving Day a perfectly roasted goose, is an artist," she declared in 1927.[9] Although Cather realized it only in retrospect, during her rural childhood in the Shenandoah Valley farming village of Back Creek, Virginia, where she was born in 1873, she had been surrounded by such un-self-conscious women artists. The old women who helped out at the Cather farmhouse during busy seasons—sewing, quilting, preserving—were not only accomplished craftswomen, they were the first storytellers the child encountered. Indigenous artists, in their conversation they were the preservers and transmitters of culture, myth, and folklore. Entranced by their vivid talk, Willa Cather would creep under their quilting frames and listen for hours. Her maternal grandmother Rachel Boak taught her to read and write, thereby providing another unconscious resource for Cather's eventual reconciliation of feminine identity and artistic vocation, since the child's mastery of language and expression was connected with a female presence. When the Cathers moved to the Nebraska Divide in 1884, the nine-year-old Willa encountered more women she would later recognize as artists—the immigrant farm wives who combined storytelling craft with creative skill at women's life-sustaining tasks of cooking, gardening, preserving. Although this exposure to strong, creative women could not counter the culture's association of professional artistry with maleness, it was a resource on which Willa Cather could draw, a tradition of female creativity to which she could look with pride—when she knew how to look.

Willa Cather's own mother, Virginia Boak Cather, was more the spoiled southern lady than the hard-working, self-denying rural farm wife. Beautiful, charming, and imperious, she was the dominant presence in the family, overshadowing her milder husband Charles Cather. A paradoxical woman, she whipped her children to maintain household order while allowing them great freedom in their personal lives.[10] Although she must have found Willa's fondness for male dress trying, she nevertheless saw to it that her eldest daughter had a room of her own, an attic bedroom which reappears in Cather's fiction as the space for autonomy, creativity, and nurturance. She also supported her daughter's wish to attend the University of Nebraska. Evidently Virginia Cather inspired the same devotion in her children the southern belle traditionally evoked in her doting admirers. According to

Edith Lewis, the woman who shared Cather's life for forty years, all the children worshipped their mother and dreaded her displeasure.[11] Like the others, Willa bought her gifts to win her favor—delicate clothing, perfume, flowers, all tributes to her mother's beauty.

Willa Cather's relationship with her mother was intense and conflicted. For her as for all children, growing up required a process of separation and individuation, defining the self against the mother with whom the infant was once merged. The process was fraught with ambivalence. Increasing autonomy meant increasing loss, independence was accompanied by fears of abandonment and yearnings to return. Throughout childhood as well as the rest of her life, Cather sought to reconcile the competing needs that separation from the mother brought, trying to balance autonomy—her need for a separate, creative self—with nurturance—her need for close, sustaining human bonds. As Nancy Chodorow and Jane Flax have pointed out, the process of separation and identity formation and the balancing of needs for autonomy and nurturance are far more complex for girls than for boys.[12] Unlike her brother, the girl does not have the barrier of gender to sever identification with the mother; hence forming her own identity is more difficult, there being less clearly demarcated ego boundaries between daughter and mother than between son and mother. And whereas men can combine the joys of autonomy and nurturance by having both a professional career and a domestic life where they are nurtured, most women must sacrifice autonomy for nurturing relationships—or sacrifice nurturance for independence. Willa Cather's early memories and her crude, heavily psychological first short stories reflect these conflicts, centering on the mother/daughter bond and the accompanying issues of separation and individuation, independence and loss, autonomy and nurturance. But before turning to the fiction, we must consider a dramatic episode in Willa Cather's life which will illuminate these conflicts: her adolescent male impersonation period. Her four-year masquerade as William Cather reveals how cultural and psychological pressures conspired to delay her attainment of identity and vocation, preventing her temporarily from realizing the alliance between femininity and creativity the Back Creek storytellers embodied.[13]

One of Cather's earliest childhood memories concerned her adopting an identity that "horrified" her genteel southern mother. The five-year-old Willa, expected to please a visiting judge who was paying her chivalrous compliments, announced defiantly that she was not a little girl but a "dang'ous nigger," simultaneously rejecting her mother's standards of ladylike behavior and declaring her separate identity.[14] When Cather was fourteen, newly arrived in the small prairie town of Red Cloud, Nebraska, she adopted another persona that must also have horrified Virginia Cather. Announcing her disdain for the female sex and her membership in the male, Willa cropped her hair to crew-cut length, donned shirts and trousers, and

baptized herself anew as "William Cather, jr." or, reflecting her career interests, "William Cather, M.D."[15] She continued this male role playing for the
next four years. Her sustained performance had multiple sources, cultural as
well as psychological. The cultural ones are most evident. In Red Cloud, she
encountered expectations for female behavior she found confining and
unacceptable. As a gifted, independent, spirited girl who intended to be a
doctor, Cather rejected a female identity requiring passivity, deference, and
submissiveness as well as a role requiring domesticity. Possessing personal
traits such as ambition and assertiveness which her society deemed male
and desiring a role in the male territory outside woman's domestic sphere,
she chose to repudiate her gender rather than her personality or aspirations.
Her male masquerade reflected identity conflict, not confusion. Cather
pretended to be male because she knew she was female—and in Victorian
America, being female meant being confined and regulated.

An angry rejection of a confining sex role was only one source for Cather's
rebellion. She was also acting in a psychological drama, propelled by the inner
needs for self-definition all girls face in adolescence—some contradictory,
most doubtless unconscious. The masquerade, connected with the adolescent's need to define identity, reflects her complex and ambivalent relationship with her mother. As Nancy Chodorow points out, during adolescence
the girl engages in a psychological "replay" of the issues that characterize
the Oedipal phase—merging, separation, sameness, identity.[16] The girl wants
to separate from mother and form her own identity, yet she dreads the loss
of the mother's love; moreover, the mutual identifications characterizing the
mother/daughter bond complicate the process. In addition, the daughter must
confront her emerging sexuality, continue to identify with her mother's sex
role while transferring her erotic interest to men. Willa's metamorphosis into
William was a creative, daring way of mastering the psychological and emotional difficulties adolescence posed. As William Cather she could reject the
mother she perceived as indifferent (the phase began when Virginia Cather,
ill after the birth of a male child, could not care for her daughter's hair and
Willa had it chopped off). She could also flout her mother's standards of
ladylike dress and appearance while at the same time separating from her by
adopting an opposed identity; clearly as William Cather she was not the same
as her mother. Of course, the extremity of her action suggests the underlying
fear that she *was* the same. Her transformation satisfied other conflicting
needs. She wanted to strike out at her mother, just as she had "horrified"
her by declaring herself a "dang'ous nigger," but she also wanted to continue
to seek her love. As William Cather she could do this, competing with the
men her mother preferred—her father, her brothers, perhaps the newborn
male sibling. Her male identification thus reflects her failure to transfer her
emotional/erotic needs from women to men, the process that in heterosexual
women occurs during the Oedipal stage and is "replayed" during adolescence.

Her William Cather solution to identity problems was obviously temporary, and Willa Cather abandoned male dress and coiffure after two years at the University of Nebraska. But a more feminine external appearance did not signify the end of identity conflict. She was still not happy about being a woman; during her college years, she abandoned thoughts of medicine and began to aspire to the artist's lofty role—which was, she realized, a male preserve. America's "scribbling women" who invaded the literary marketplace during the nineteenth century did not offer her an acceptable tradition. Their fiction she considered trashy, commercial, and woefully limited to women's subjects like romance and domesticity. Such writers could not be literary forebears for a young woman now entranced by the Emersonian notion of the artist as godlike Creator.[17] The artists she worshipped in this category—Carlyle, Shakespeare, James—were male. "Artist" and "woman" seemed contradictory identities also because Cather doubted that women could subordinate their need for human affection to the austere demands of art. "Art of every kind is an exacting master," she wrote, accepting only "human sacrifices"; if an artist were to do anything worthwhile, he must make human relationships a "secondary consideration."[18] Male artists could make this sacrifice, but had any woman "ever really had the art instinct, the art necessity?" she wondered. Liberty and solitude were the two "wings of art," but what woman could deny her need for human bonds, even if they kept her earthbound?[19]

Cather did meet several actresses and opera singers during her years in Lincoln and Pittsburgh who had committed themselves to artistic careers, but they could not compensate for an insufficient female literary tradition. Operas needed sopranos, plays demanded actresses, but American letters did not require participation by female writers. Moreover, the actresses and opera singers she knew were performers, not original creators of texts; her situation was different. There were a few literary women she admired, although none were American: Austen, the Brontës, in particular the "great Georges"—Eliot and Sand. But these last, whom she respected the most, she considered "anything but women"—anomalies, deviants, perhaps male impersonators like William Cather. Given the choices, being "anything but" a woman was preferable to being female. Willa Cather's youthful advice to women writers who wished to escape the limitations of their traditional sentimental and domestic subject matter reveals how strongly she had internalized the male aesthetic. When a woman writer leaves behind romantic subject matter and attempts a "stout sea tale" or a "manly battle yarn"—then, the young woman concluded, she might expect "something great" from a female author.[20] Abandoning her male persona had solved nothing, since in aspiring to the writer's role she once again encountered forbidden territory and sexual polarization. Women writers were limited, male writers were universal; to escape female limitations, a woman had to write like a man. But advocating men's subjects for women writers—or attempting them herself—was in effect resuming her William Cather disguise. Manly battle yarns were not the answer.

Cather's view that human relationships were draining forces threatening to autonomy and creativity was not merely a theoretical argument. Although Cather's Nebraska classmates later described her as a loner who had no friends and wanted none, in fact she had several close friends in college as well as an intense and sometimes turbulent intimacy with Louise Pound, a classmate who later became a well-known philologist and folklorist as well as the first woman president of the Modern Language Association.[21] The few existent letters reveal the formerly rebellious William Cather in the role of the moody, beseeching lover—at times jealous, insecure, passionate, depressed, self-pitying.[22] Eventually Louise Pound terminated the relationship, and Cather was devastated for a while. As Carroll Smith-Rosenberg has shown, such intense and romantic friendships between women were common in Victorian America.[23] Close, caring, and compassionate, these intimacies were often the primary emotional bonds in women's lives. In most cases not genitally sexual, these relationships were socially acceptable and considered compatible with woman's role as wife and mother.

But Cather's attachment to Pound had a different quality from the close, secure intimacies Smith-Rosenberg found prevalent in the 1840s and 1850s. Her letters, which were written in the early 1890s, bear out Lillian Faderman's contention that by the late nineteenth century, as women increasingly left the home for college and the professions and Havelock Ellis's and Krafft-Ebbing's work on human sexuality appeared, women's romantic friendships seemed increasingly suspect, ultimately deviant: Americans had discovered lesbianism.[24] Although Cather's letters reveal emotional rather than physical passion, they do reflect an uneasiness that a woman would not have felt in the 1840s. It was unjust, she wrote Pound, that feminine friendships should be unnatural.[25] Her protest suggests an underlying anxiety. Forty years earlier, it would not have occurred to a woman that her intense feelings for a female friend might be "unnatural."

It is possible to debate whether Cather's attachment to Louise Pound and later her primary relationships with Isabelle McClung and Edith Lewis were lesbian if we insist that the term imply genital sexuality. There is no evidence in the remaining letters or in Edith Lewis's discreet memoir, *Willa Cather Living*, that these bonds were sexual as well as emotional, although the fiction reveals Cather's familiarity with the allure and the danger of sexual passion. But such a distinction does not concern me here. Two points are central: Willa Cather invested herself emotionally in other women, and in keeping with the comment to Pound that such intimacies were unnatural, she did not portray them in her fiction. Hence we find her disguising and camouflaging her deepest attractions, which are always translated into heterosexual attachments. Such fictional disguise, which as we will see raises complex interpretive problems, reveals her awareness that female intimacies are not appropriate subject matter for fiction. (By contrast, her mentor Sarah Orne Jewett who had a "Boston marriage" or stable ménage with Annie Fields during a more innocent era made women's friendships the primary subject of her fiction; she could not understand why Cather chose male personas to express romantic yearning for female characters.)

Willa Cather's first short stories, written between 1892 and 1902, embody both the cultural and the psychological stresses we have been discussing. Aesthetically crude but psychologically revealing, they are worth considering both for the insights they provide into the young writer's inner life and for their anticipation of the major fiction, where she would explore similar themes with far greater control, detachment, and artistry. Cather chose Nebraska settings and immigrant protagonists in several of these stories which expose the harshness of prairie life as well as the social and economic injustices crushing the immigrant farmers. But despite her subject matter she was no Hamlin Garland. Like many young writers, her deepest concern is herself rather than her characters or the social issues she attempts to raise. The prominent motifs in this fiction—the child searching for a maternal figure, the association of erotic and maternal love, the dangers of passion—are her own enduring preoccupations, although here as in her novels she portrays all intense erotic or emotional bonds as heterosexual.

Cather's choice of male protagonists in several of these early stories—among them "Peter," "Lou the Prophet," "The Clemency of the Court," "The Elopement of Alan Poole," "The Burglar's Christmas"—suggests that she was still captive of a culture relegating women to subordinate status. If she could not be a male writer, she could at least create male characters whose universal dilemmas would lift her fiction above that of the scribbling women. The one story featuring a strong, admirable heroine—"Tommy, the Unsentimental"—reveals Cather's continued association of positive human qualities with the male sex. The boyish heroine receives Cather's approval; blunt, intelligent, resourceful, Tommy is, Cather assures us, "unfeminine."[26] Her foil, the shrinking, delicate, childlike Miss Jessica who "wore violet perfume and carried a sunshade," is useless and ridiculous, Cather's caricature of Victorian America's ideal woman. The author had not progressed too far beyond her William Cather phase. The human qualities she admired she still considered male.

While "Tommy" reveals the cultural pressures contributing to Cather's identity conflict, paradoxically the stories featuring male protagonists reflect the psychological and emotional dynamics of the mother/daughter bond. In drawing on intensely personal and unconscious material, Cather opted for disguise, projecting herself into male characters—another reason for their prevalence in this fiction. What was she concealing? Let us briefly consider one early story that reveals her inner conflicts with almost embarrassing

directness: "The Burglar's Christmas." The surface plot is appallingly sentimental. A starving, destitute young man named William (Cather's adolescent pseudonym) is driven by hunger and desperation to rob a fashionable
Chicago mansion on Christmas Eve. Obsessed with obtaining food, he slips
upstairs and surreptitiously enters a richly furnished bedroom, opens a
dressing-case and begins pocketing the rings, watches, and bracelets he finds.
Suddenly the thief discovers a disturbingly familiar object: the silver drinking
mug he used as a little child! Before he or the reader has time to puzzle this
out, his mother enters the room. It is her bedroom, this is his parents' house.
(The reason for the unlikely coincidence and the son's ignorance of his
parents' whereabouts is later awkwardly and unconvincingly explained.)
An angelic presence, his mother embraces her prodigal son, forgives all and
assures him of her undying, unconditional love while she gets him dinner.

Despite its glaring aesthetic deficiencies, "The Burglar's Christmas" is a
crucial story in the Cather canon because its psychological themes connect
both to her life and to her later fiction. They center on issues of nurturance,
separation, and identity. Having failed at an autonomous adult existence,
William returns home to possess and be possessed by his mother who offers
endless nurturance. But he must pay the price of regression for regaining this
bliss; the twenty-four-year-old man becomes a small child finding "refuge
and protection" in his mother's arms. At the story's end, he seems to have
traveled even farther back into the past, for the "rich content" he experiences
sitting by a warm fire with hunger satisfied and sleep descending suggests the
infant's satiated pleasure more than the little boy's happiness. He has returned to the oral stage, the period in human development symbolized by the
baby's silver drinking mug.

The story's imagery of the theft suggests that this is an Oedipal as well as a
pre-Oedipal fantasy, for the mother is an erotic as well as a nurturing figure:
the son guiltily steals along passageways and corridors, finds his way to the
"darkened chamber" where the "jewels and trinkets were kept," forces open
his mother's dressing case, and begins stealing her jewels. Such imagery hardly
needs commentary. But one does not need the resources of Freudian theory
to see the eroticism in this mother/child reunion. Not only does the mother
seem beautiful and seductive to the son, with her "superb white throat and
shoulders" and her "impetuous and wayward mouth," but their embraces
are also marked by intense sensuality (his mother's kiss "burnt him like
fire"). Cather seems to be describing the reunion of long-separated lovers, not
mother and son.

In following her protagonist back to childhood and infancy, Cather reveals
both the identity problems Chodorow finds in the mother/daughter relationship and the conflict between autonomy and nurturance that Jane Flax
analyzes. In regaining his mother, William loses a separate identity. "'We are
of one blood,'" his mother tells him. "'Even as a child, I felt your likeness

to me . . . I have lived all your life before you. You have never had an impulse that I have not known, you have never touched a brink that my feet have not trod.'" The mother's terrifying declaration of their sameness becomes psychologically more understandable when we take William as a mask for Willa; the fusion then suggests the mutual identifications existing between mother and daughter. The protagonist's inability to balance autonomy and nurturance also suggests the mother/daughter configuration. On his own, he is starving and destitute; independence means emotional abandonment. But in returning to his mother's love, he must abandon adult separateness and independence. This seemingly clichéd piece of magazine fiction, a senti-mental reworking of the prodigal son motif, thus in fact reflects the author's unconscious desires and fears. The text's artlessness is connected with her lack of control of her material as well as her technical inexperience. There is no controlling authorial presence in the story, no separation between the author's and the character's viewpoint, no criticism of his urge to regress—in fact the rapturous ending implies that we are to read William's sinking into passive gratification as positive. Of course, the biographical parallels are suggestive but not complete, for in writing the story and expressing the fantasy, Cather resisted the regressive impulses to which her protagonist succumbed. But the fact that the fantasy is presented uncritically with the young author unaware of what she is concealing and revealing demonstrates that Cather did not yet have mastery over her material, either psychologically or technically.

Other early stories reveal similar psychological themes. In "The Clemency of the Court," the orphaned Russian immigrant Serge finds that he can return to his idealized mother only in death and dies assuming the fetal posi-tion; in "The Elopement of Alan Poole," the hero unites with his sweetheart only as he is dying and she, a "little Madonna of the Hills," assumes the mother's role ("'Oh my boy! my boy!' Nell cried as she rocked herself over him as a mother does over a little baby.")[27] Regaining the mother/lover is thus literally equated with death in these stories, in contrast to the meta-phoric death William achieved as he slid into passive nonbeing. The mother figure in all the stories is alluring because she offers love and nurturance, but terrifying because she threatens loss of self; to regain the infant's precon-scious oneness with the mother is to be obliterated, to die. Since Cather connects maternal and erotic love, the sexual drive has a threatening regres-sive component, similarly leading to self-annihilation and ultimately the obliteration of death. Although drawing on childhood drives and conflicts, doubtless these early stories owed something to Cather's contemporary relationship with Louise Pound.

This immature early work raises critical problems that will persist in the major fiction. In "Elopement," for example, is Cather revealing her hostility to adult heterosexual passion and to her male rivals by killing off the male lover? Or, if Alan is a mask for herself, is she revealing her own discomfort with the erotic/emotional drives? Or both? (The same questions can later be asked of the lovers' murder in *O Pioneers!*) Clearly the interpretation shifts if we consider the male protagonist a mask for a female author who must disguise homosexual themes to her audience and perhaps to herself. Another problematic pattern that will persist is Cather's occasional portrayal of women characters in traditional stereotypic guises, women as Other. For example, Nell, the "Madonna of the Hills," is the idealized virgin/mother one might expect to find in fiction by a male writer. Like other aspects of her early work, this figure will reappear in novels like *My Ántonia* and *A Lost Lady* where Cather consciously explores the ways in which men (or women?) invest women with meaning.

The fear expressed in Cather's early journalism and fiction that human relationships must be sacrificed for art must have lessened in 1899. In that year she met Isabelle McClung, the beautiful daughter of a Pittsburgh judge who was to be her great love. With Isabelle Cather found a sustaining affection that promoted rather than impeded creativity, since Isabelle was devoted to nurturing her friend's talent; she also discovered a loving maternal presence whom she did not have to share with father or siblings. Isabelle continued to support Cather's creative life until her marriage to violinist Jan Hambourg in 1916. Even after Cather moved to New York and was sharing an apartment with Edith Lewis, she would return to Pittsburgh and Isabelle to write. Shortly after their meeting, Isabelle invited Cather to move into the McClung household; the two women shared a bedroom but Isabelle provided her friend with an attic study where she could be alone to write, so Cather had spaces for both intimacy and solitary work. Achieving the delicate balance between nurturance and autonomy with a motherly friend who wanted her to write, Cather experienced a creative explosion. She published six stories the year after meeting Isabelle and two books shortly after—*April Twilights* (1903), a pallid collection of poems, and *The Troll Garden* (1905), a collection of short stories containing her first work of real literary merit.

Whereas the early stories were either stilted imitations of other writers or barely disguised personal fantasies, in *The Troll Garden* stories, Cather created fully realized characters who are not merely projections of the author's inner conflicts. Unlike the regressive William, for example, the rebellious Paul in her well-known short story "Paul's Case" who greedily seeks beauty amid Pittsburgh's grimy commercialism exists in a thickly textured, realistic world. Cather was drawing on her own rebellious adolescence in creating this character, but she was not limited by her own experience; hence Paul exists outside of herself and thus can exist for the reader. This successful, well-crafted story reveals the connection between her technical and personal advances. Paul is driven by the same regressive urges that sent William home to mother; his lust for music, fine wine, and delicate clothes masks an urge for passive gratification, not active creation, in a world of "basking ease." But in this story, Cather manages point of view beautifully, maintaining a consistent ironic detachment from her character, a critique of his capitulation to the regressive pull that seemed so enticing in "The Burglar's Christmas." The story reveals her in control of her material, both psychic and literary.

Most of the stories in the collection concern art and artists, exploring in particular the external and internal forces that cause artists to succeed or fail. As in her college journalism, the great artists are men—Harvey Merrick in "The Sculptor's Funeral," Hugh Treffinger in "The Marriage of Phaedra," Raymond d'Esquerré in "A Garden Lodge," Adriance Hilgarde in "'A Death in the Desert.'" But the stories also demonstrate progress in Cather's resolution of feminine identity with artistic vocation. Revealingly, the male artists are all absent or dead, and the author is more interested in the failed artists who are her protagonists—all female. Katherine Gaylord, Aunt Georgianna, and Caroline Noble are her first significant female protagonists who are neither mannish Tommys nor silly Miss Jessicas; nor are they stereotyped figures seen only through men's eyes. Although they do not equal the men's artistic achievements, it is important that Cather is now writing about women who possess creativity—albeit creativity that is denied, distorted, or repressed by cultural pressures and psychological necessities. The female characters' defeat reflects Cather's understanding of the difficulties facing the woman artist, including that of confronting a patriarchal artistic tradition (suggested by the absent or dead male artists in the stories), but the fact that they possess creative gifts at all reveals her new awareness that women are not innately limited as artists, an insight that can be connected with her development of her own creative powers and growing artistic self-confidence. Moreover, Cather's choice of female protagonists in four of the seven stories shows a new interest in exploring female identity and experience. The decision reflects her increasing identification with her own sex.

A crucial turning point in Cather's resolution of feminine identity and art came a few years after *The Troll Garden* was published when she met Sarah Orne Jewett, then celebrated for *The Country of the Pointed Firs* as well as her other stories of Maine life. Their brief friendship was central in Cather's decision to commit herself to the artist's vocation. On assignment in Boston for *McClure's* magazine (she had moved to New York to work for S. S. McClure in 1905), Cather met Jewett at the gracious Charles Street home of Annie Fields in 1909. As a gifted American woman writer whom Cather revered, Jewett embodied the female literary tradition the younger woman had been seeking. She was, to use Gilbert and Gubar's term, the literary "foremother" who provides the daughter/artist with a tradition and a lineage. In addition, as a well-bred New England lady, Jewett was not "anything but" a woman; she was, Cather later commented approvingly, "a lady, in the old high sense," perhaps a northern version of Virginia Cather's southern lady.[28] In any case, for a brief time Jewett was model, mentor, and mother for her young protégée, offering support and encouragement for her work, proffering literary advice, and delicately suggesting that Cather leave her draining magazine job to devote herself solely to her writing. Jewett also predicted Cather's ultimate literary direction. One day, she thought, Cather would write about her "own country" and embody Nebraska's land and people in fiction just as Jewett had honored her beloved Maine.[29] Jewett's influence continued after her death a year later. Her memory inspired Cather finally to embark on her first novel in 1912. After paying a pilgrimage to Jewett's house in South Berwick, she "felt goaded," she told a friend. "It was as if Miss Jewett's spirit, which filled the place, had warned her that time was flying."[30]

Cather knew she had to take the final step, quit her job and commit herself to writing, and yet she was understandably fearful. Even if it now seemed possible that a woman could be a great writer, as a single woman who had to make her own living she was reluctant to give up a secure income. In 1912 she managed a compromise and took a leave from *McClure's* to write *Alexander's Bridge*. She was not yet ready to trust herself and turn to her "own country," though, for the novel with its international settings and drawing room conversations shows her still in the grip of Henry James. Cather later disparaged the novel, viewing it as the apprentice writer's awkward, imitative venture and comparing it unfavorably to *O Pioneers!*[31] It seemed a bastard child to the mature writer, and in the Library Edition of her fiction, she denied *Alexander's Bridge* its rightful place, offering *O Pioneers!* as her "First" novel. The plot was largely conventional, a mid-life crisis superimposed on a romantic triangle. Bartley Alexander, a successful middle-aged bridge builder, is torn between his American wife and everything she stands for (self-discipline, professional success, adult responsibility) and his English mistress and everything she stands for (self-gratification, romance, youth). His yearning to recapture his own youth through Hilda proves Bartley's moral/psychological flaw. In the novel's melodramatic and symbolically inevitable conclusion, the similarly flawed bridge he has been building collapses, and he is drowned in the St. Lawrence River.

Although the novel's settings are artificial and the dialogue stilted, its themes connect with some of Cather's enduring preoccupations; it is not as atypical as she would have us think. Alexander is the heroic, creative individual of pioneer force and energy, anticipating Alexandra Bergson, Thea Kronborg, and Godfrey St. Peter, but unlike them, he is driven by the urge for romantic love that Cather finds so disastrous. Bartley displays the urge to recapture his lost youth that links him with other Cather protagonists like Jim Burden and Godfrey St. Peter as well as the regressive William. But although the author sympathizes with Bartley's wish to retrace time, she surrounds him with imagery of flux and change—oceans, rivers, clocks—that remind the reader that time and adulthood cannot be denied. As in "Paul's Case," the distance between author's and character's point of view reveals Cather's technical and psychological growth; she projects some of her deepest desires into Bartley, but is detached from them at the same time.

Like much of Cather's fiction, the novel poses some perplexing interpretive problems when regarded from a feminist perspective. Cather again chooses a male protagonist to explore erotic and regressive drives, and the women in his life are flat, stereotypic figures: the patient wife, the enticing mistress. Does this mean that Cather was still captive of a patriarchal culture and literary tradition and thus was choosing a male protagonist and women characters as conceived by men in order to seem "universal" rather than limited and feminine? Or was Bartley another mask for the female writer who had to camouflage her own "unnatural" intimacies in fiction? Do the female stereotypes reveal the author's psychological and emotional realities rather than her slavish adherence to patriarchal images of women, since for her women did embody her desires and fears and were thus objects as well as subjects? Perhaps all these possibilities are true, with cultural and psychological forces intersecting to produce a novel that seems to have sexist patterns linking it with works by male writers for whom woman is Other. In her later novels like *My Ántonia* and *A Lost Lady*, Cather is more aware of the way men project meaning onto women and interpret them in terms of their own needs and fears. That process in fact becomes the subject of both novels.

## II

In 1913 Cather took Jewett's advice and decided to write about her "own country," the Nebraska farmland and its immigrant settlers. In combining memory with imagination, she created the first novel she later felt was her own. *O Pioneers!* celebrates the pioneer-immigrants who tamed the stubborn land and founded a civilization; it is Willa Cather's epic. The heroic protagonist is a woman who makes the land flourish when the men around her have failed, broken in spirit by the soil's resistance to cultivation. Alexandra Bergson is a new heroine both in American literature and in Cather's fiction: strong, autonomous, creative, she is neither the female figure of male fantasy nor a doomed heroine like Chopin's Edna Pontellier or Wharton's Lily Bart who cannot achieve self-definition in an oppressive society. Alexandra's triumph reflects the author's. Although the novel is not directly autobiographical, since Alexandra is artist as well as pioneer, her achievement reflects Cather's now successful welding of the formerly mutually exclusive identities, artist and woman. Accepting her gender, newly confident of her creative powers, freed from subservience to the male literary tradition (there is no trace of James's influence in the novel, which fittingly is dedicated to Sarah

Orne Jewett), Cather could at last create a heroine who redeems the failed female artists in *The Troll Garden*.

Alexandra is the novel's supreme artist. Her selfless passion for the land, which she regards with "love and yearning," rather than the men's antagonism, parallels the unselfish love Cather thought the artist must have for subject matter.[32] As a farmer/artist, Alexandra creates order and beauty in the natural world, shaping and forming what was chaotic and barren: "it is in the soil that she expresses herself best" (p. 84). Later her childhood friend and suitor Carl Linstrum makes the artist/pioneer equation explicit. "'I've been away engraving other men's pictures,'" he tells her, "'while you've stayed here and made your own'" (p. 116). Cather reverses the pattern of *The Troll Garden*: the woman is now the authentic creator, the man the mere copyist. In her bond with the fertile soil—the dominant maternal presence in the novel—Alexandra the artist/daughter combines autonomy and merging with something beyond the self. With the soil she can both assert the self and give it up, imposing order in cultivation and fusing physically and spiritually with the soil, feeling its "joyous germination" in her own body (p. 204). Alexandra both nurtures the land and receives sustenance from it, playing the roles of both mother and daughter. But in losing the self in joyous identification with the land, she does not suffer William's regressiveness or Alan Poole's obliteration; this merging with a maternal force, which allows her to be separate and connected at the same time, leads to flourishing life rather than self-annihilation—just as giving up the self in the act of writing did for Willa Cather. (The artist should be "so in love with his subject matter," she commented, that "he forgets 'self' in his passion."[33]) In creating a female hero who is artist as well as pioneer, Cather reveals a new awareness that her creative "foremothers" extended back beyond Sarah Orne Jewett to the strong rural women she had known in childhood and youth, the immigrant farm wives who introduced her to narrative. A lineage of creativity links mother and daughter in the novel as well. Mrs. Bergson, the immigrant farm wife, makes a garden in the desert as soon as she arrives, just as her daughter Alexandra would do on an epic scale.

Alexandra ultimately discovers a nurturing relationship in addition to her tie with the land. At the novel's end, depressed by the murder of her brother Emil and Marie Shabata, she acknowledges her need for human companionship and turns to her ever-faithful friend and suitor Carl for support and affection. But their union will not contain the destructive force of sexual passion. "'When friends marry, they are safe,'" Alexandra reassures herself, envisioning a future protected from the dangerous forces that destroyed Marie and Emil (p. 309).

Cather wrote *O Pioneers!* when she realized that two previously written short stories should be combined: "Alexandra," a 1911 version of the heroine's taming of the soil, and "The White Mulberry Tree," a tragic tale written a year later in which a crazed Bohemian farmer kills his wife, Marie, and her young Swedish lover—the source for the lovers' subplot. She felt a "sudden inner explosion and enlightenment" when she realized the two stories belonged together; obeying a command that seemed to issue from the tales themselves, she combined them to create her "two-part pastoral."[34] Many critics feel that the fusion of the two fictional elements is imperfect, with the lovers' subplot an unnecessary diversion. But as I have argued elsewhere, the stories are linked thematically.[35] Both are parables about passion. Alexandra Bergson's taming of the soil chronicles the heroic results of passion regulated and channeled into the land rather than into human relationships, while the lovers' doom records the destructive outcome of sexual passion indulged and unleashed. Like "The Elopement of Alan Poole," the subplot reflects Cather's uneasiness with romantic/erotic love, which she portrays here as narcissistic, solipsistic, and regressive. Marie and Emil fall in love with the images they create of each other and are most intense when they are separated. Thus they do not really connect with anything or anyone beyond their own egos, in contrast to the self-transcendent Alexandra.

Alexandra should please any feminist critic or reader looking for full-bodied, complex, autonomous female characters who transcend stereotypes traditionally defining and limiting women. Her portrayal suggests that Willa Cather, although politically never aligned with feminist causes, imaginatively had broken the cultural molds circumscribing female identity. But a perplexing inconsistency emerges for the feminist critic in considering Marie Shabata, the impetuous heroine whose self-indulgent romanticism leads to destruction. At first she seems to be more complex than the stereotypic temptress; warm, generous, and vibrant, she was, as Carl tells Alexandra, "'the best you had here'" (p. 305), and throughout the novel Cather portrays her sympathetically. And yet at the novel's end, we learn that the tragedy was caused by Marie; Carl, who is the voice of reason and psychological insight in the novel, tells Alexandra that "'There are women who spread ruin around them through no fault of theirs, just by being too beautiful, too full of life and love. They can't help it'" (p. 304). The generalizing rhetoric ("There are women who . . .") reveals that Marie is being categorized as the seductive Eve who spreads ruin among men. Evidently Emil and Frank do not share moral responsibility for the tragedy. Why does a woman writer both challenge the traditional stereotypes confining women and reinforce them in the same novel? It is possible that at the time Cather was only partially free of cultural views of women, and her inconsistency determined the characterization of the contrasted women. On the other hand, it is likely that her portrayal of Marie reveals her own unacknowledged conflicts, since here as elsewhere in her fiction she portrays all attraction as heterosexual. Since in life she both identified with women and viewed them as objects of desire, in fiction she could portray women both as autonomous, three-dimensional female subjects and as stereotyped or idealized objects of fear or longing.

In writing *O Pioneers!* Cather experienced the creative process in a new way. Instead of consciously controlling and shaping her material, she felt that the book wrote itself. Powerful forces seemed to be using her as their agent, and she yielded to a nonrational force she called the "wisdom of intuition."[36] This self-abandonment to a powerful force and joyous loss of self in the creative process Cather connected with the novel's composition suggests that she was letting down psychic barriers. With her internal conflicts surrounding identity and vocation resolved, the writing of fiction could be an expansive process of "letting go with the heart."[37] From now on she found writing blissful. The joy Cather experienced in the creative process is connected with her achievement of harmony between conflicting psychic opposites. In writing she could be both connected to a larger force and separate, balancing needs for nurturance and autonomy. In *My Ántonia* she defined happiness as being "dissolved into something complete and great" (p. 18), and all her comments on the creative process suggest that she found such self-annihilation in merging with loved subject matter or characters, just as Alexandra thrilled in fusing with the land. But like Alexandra, Cather could also maintain separateness; such loss of self was neither regressive nor final. Hence in writing, Cather resolved the conflict we have seen as particularly intense in mother/daughter relationships.

The creative process provided nurturance as well as self-dissolution; like Edith Wharton, Cather characteristically used the language of starving and feeding to describe the act of writing. The writer without a subject is starving or half-nourished, the writer who finds her material is nourished and sustained.[38] But if the writer is the nourished child (the relationship of writer to subject matter is like that of baby to the "mother's breast," Cather once commented), she is also the mother, creating the book as child and nourishing its characters.[39] Cather thus also used metaphors of gestation, birth, and separation to describe her relationship to her novels, referring to the way she "fed" characters in creating them.[40] Once Cather could give herself up to the creative process in this way, having resolved the conflicts that had kept "woman" and "artist" apart, her novels followed in a steady stream. After the long apprenticeship period ended with *O Pioneers!* there would be no creative dry spells. Her next novel, *The Song of the Lark* (1915), appeared two years later. In it Cather introduced another strong, creative heroine to American literature; Thea Kronborg might have been Alexandra Bergson's sister.

At last sure of her creative powers after discovering both her "own country" and the creative process in *O Pioneers!* Cather wrote her most autobiographical novel in celebrating the woman as artist. Although ostensibly based on the career of opera singer Olive Fremstad, *The Song of the Lark* owes more to Cather's discovery of the "art necessity" within herself. Thea's slow, stumbling growth as an artist parallels Cather's own laborious discovery of identity and vocation; in addition, Thea's mystic turning point—her sojourn at Panther Canyon where she undergoes a conversion experience to art—directly reflects Cather's trip to the Southwest where she saw the ruins of the Cliff-Dwellers in Walnut Canyon, an experience that deeply stirred her and later "took root and grew and flowered in her mind into artistic creation" when she returned to the East and wrote *O Pioneers!*[41] In choosing to make her alter ego Thea a singer, Cather revealed her now firm wedding of femininity and creativity. As a gifted soprano, Thea can not separate her art from her body. Anatomy does not relegate woman to a restricted destiny; gender is the basis of artistic expression. The pattern of Cather's journalism and early fiction is reversed here: the novel's male characters are worshippers at Thea's shrine.

Thea's artistic triumph involves personal costs, for her personal life wanes as her artistic life flourishes. Art is not incompatible with feminine identity here but it is with the feminine role as culturally defined, for the artist cannot be answerable to the demands of human relationships requiring female self-abnegation. But the options Cather gives her heroine—the artist's solitary devotion to her craft and a possibly confining marriage—were not the only ones available to the author. Cather was constrained from giving Thea the possibility she had chosen for herself, an intimate relationship with a nurturing woman friend. Whereas Thea triumphs alone, Cather wrote *The Song of the Lark* while tended by Isabelle McClung and Edith Lewis, who filled Isabelle's role in New York.

But Cather does grant Thea her mother and the land. Bearing some resemblance to Virginia Cather, Mrs. Kronborg recognizes Thea's specialness and promotes her talent, providing her a private space for creativity within the house—Thea's beloved attic room, a duplicate of Willa Cather's. Thea also has the land to which she escapes for freedom and self-expression. The sand hills that she loves anticipate the topography of Panther Canyon, as Thea seeks out a feminine landscape with a "great amphitheater" called "Pedro's Cup," "cut out in the hills" along with "winding ravines . . . full of soft sand."[42] Like Alexandra she draws physical and spiritual strength from this affinity.

Nowhere is Thea's life-sustaining union with the land's maternal power more dramatic than in her journey to the Southwest, where she spends days in Panther Canyon, home of the ancient Cliff-Dwellers; it is, as Ellen Moers observes, "the most thoroughly elaborated female landscape in literature."[43]

> The canyon walls, for the first two hundred feet below the surface, were perpendicular cliffs, striped with even-running strata of rocks.

> From there on to the bottom the sides were less abrupt, were
> shelving, and lightly fringed with *piñons* and dwarf cedars. The
> effect was that of a gentler canyon within a wilder one. The dead
> city lay at the point where the perpendicular outer wall ceased and
> the V-shaped inner gorge began. There a stratum of rock, softer than
> those above, had been hollowed out by the action of time until it
> was like a deep groove running along the sides of the canyon. In
> this hollow (like a great fold in the rock) the Ancient People had
> built their houses of yellowish stone and mortar. [P. 297]

Thea explores the "long horizontal grove" and finds among the ruins of the
Cliff-Dwellers' houses a safe, protected retreat where she lingers for days:
a "cave," a "rock-room" where she can touch the stone roof with her finger
tips (p. 298). The feminine imagery surrounding this "nest in the high cliff"
suggests both Thea's attic room and her "Cup" in the sand hills. Cather does
not associate Thea's withdrawal into her womb/cave with regressiveness; she
is not William who seeks only passive, infantile merging with the mother. Her
journey is a mythic return to the primitive, maternal sources of life and
energy to gain strength for her return to the world, the cave a place for
rebirth rather than death. Her retreat into the rock-room is the heroine's
equivalent of the epic hero's journey to the underworld, and Thea emerges
from her interlude with maternal powers whole, integrated, and ready to
commit herself to art.[44]

Willa Cather makes the linkage between this landscape and feminine
creative power even more explicit when Thea discovers shards of pottery
crafted by the Indian women. She uncovers a connection between herself
and her long-dead artistic foremothers, for in crafting pots to hold the
precious water, the Indian women were both sustaining life and expressing
artistry; their vessels were beautiful as well as functional. Bathing in a nearby
stream, Thea feels "a continuity of life that reached back into the old time,"
back to the Indian women who held life in their jars just as they created it in
their bodies (p. 304). This continuity provides her with a connection to
feminine creativity outside the patriarchal artistic tradition.[45] Thea recognizes her resemblance to her foremothers: "In singing one made a vessel of
one's throat and nostrils and held it on one's breath, caught the stream in a
scale of natural intervals" just as the Indian women caught the stream of
water and life in their jars (p. 304).

In writing *My Ántonia* (1918), considered by many critics her finest
novel, Cather drew once more on the past for inspiration, this time transforming her childhood memories of the Bohemian farm girl Annie Sadilek
into artistic expression. In Ántonia Shimerda, Cather offers a different
version of the creative woman. Like Alexandra and Thea, she is linked with
the land and its generative power, but Ántonia does not self-consciously

shape or transform its energies into art. Like Cather's farm wife whose Thanksgiving meals rivaled novels and operas, Ántonia is linked with the un-self-conscious, ongoing creative processes of life. Connected with fertility and nurturance, she tends her children and her garden with equal care. When Jim Burden returns to her farmhouse after a twenty-year absence, he sees the miracle of birth she suggests re-enacted before his eyes. After leaving the fruit cave with Ántonia, he looks back to see her children "running up the steps together, big and little, tow heads and gold heads and brown, and flashing little naked legs; a veritable explosion of life out of the dark cave into the sunlight."[46] The use of the womb/cave image implies her difference from Thea. In *The Song of the Lark*, the cave was the retreat from which the daughter was reborn as autonomous artist; here it reflects the mother's powerful fertility. Jim's meditation on Ántonia's transcendent meaning further suggests her alliance with the life force: "she had only to stand in the orchard, to put her hand on a little crab tree and look up at the apples, to make you feel the goodness of planting and tending and harvesting at last" (p. 353). By the end of the novel, Ántonia is an archetypal figure, the Earth Mother who nourishes all life. "She was a rich mine of life," Jim reflects, "like the founders of early races" (p. 353).

Jim's romantic vision of Ántonia as the mother of sons who stood "tall and straight" makes any simplistic feminist reading of the novel suspect. Ántonia is strong and admirable and she endures (despite missing teeth and weathered skin), but like Faulkner's Dilsey or Lena Grove, she is not a complex human being but a mythic figure viewed through male eyes. Jim's construct (the book is *My Ántonia*), she is not an autonomous subject but another version of woman as Other. But Cather, unlike Faulkner, is not promoting a romanticized male myth about women; whereas Faulkner creates Lena, Jim creates the mythic Ántonia. The reader has seen her realistically described in the early chapters and so is aware of how Jim transforms her in the final pages of the novel. In the unusual Introduction where Cather introduces Jim Burden to the reader as the actual author of the novel, she stresses that *My Ántonia* is *his* version of Ántonia when she has him change the title from *Ántonia* to *My Ántonia*, the addition suggesting both possession and subjectivity.

Critical debate has centered on whether Jim's deification of Ántonia is positive or not, and hence on whether he is a reliable narrator. Although most critics trust Jim's perceptions and see the novel as a celebration of Ántonia and the American frontier, in a provocative, ground-breaking article Blanche Gelfant argued that Jim's perceptions are untrustworthy. Beset by sexual fears, she contends, he eulogizes the asexual mother Ántonia and shuns the sensual Lena, celebrating childhood and the past because he is afraid to grow up. Thus his romanticizing of Ántonia stems from his own inadequacies. "He can love only that which time had made safe and irrefragable—his memories," and thus Jim "succumbs to immobilizing regressive needs."[47] Gelfant's article illuminates patterns in the novel unnoticed by other critics that reveal the fear of sex and passion we have seen in "The Elopement of Alan Poole" and *O Pioneers!*: Pavel and Peter's terrible story of the bride fed to the wolves; Jim's fight with the phallic snake whose "loathsome, fluid motion" makes him sick (p. 45); Jim's disturbing dream of the seductive Lena with a threatening reaping hook in her hand; Wick Cutter's attempted rape of Jim in Ántonia's bed. In contrast to "Elopement" and "The Burglar's Christmas," here Cather splits the erotic and the maternal sides of the mother between Lena and Ántonia, and Jim is drawn irresistibly toward Ántonia and the safety of a passionless relationship mediated by distance and memory.

The question of whether he "succumbs to immobilizing regressive needs" is complex, and the answer to it depends on an analysis of the relationship between author and narrator, which unfortunately is also extremely complex. Does Jim speak for Cather? Or is there ironic distance between author and narrator? The answer to both questions is yes. At times Jim is Cather's mask and spokesman, whereas at others she is ironically detached from him. This wavering distance between author and narrator makes settled interpretation difficult and probably accounts for the novel's conflicting readings; it's hard to locate Cather's point of view in this text. In the introduction Cather seems to make her separation from Jim Burden definitive by insisting that he, not she, wrote the narrative the reader is going to encounter. This unusual device, which Cather employs nowhere else, suggests that she wished to stress their separation. Her choice of a male narrator might at first seem further evidence of her wish to create a distinction between author and character, but this differentiation lessens when we note that many of the incidents of Jim's early years parallel hers. In addition, as we have seen, Cather frequently chooses male characters as masks, and since the Black Hawk years of Jim's acquaintance with Ántonia cover his adolescence, the period when Cather masqueraded as William, the sex difference between author and narrator does not seem that significant. Cather's paradoxical detachment from Jim and fusion with him continues throughout the text. At times she undercuts his perceptions; for example, the reader sees the irony when Jim first declares his superiority to the cowardly Black Hawk boys who fear the sensuous hired girls, and then flees from Lena Lingard to the celibate scholarly world ruled by the aptly named Gaston Cleric. But in the novel's conclusion Cather does not seem to question Jim's transformation of Ántonia into a "rich mine of life" nor challenge his view that in returning to Ántonia and childhood he is "coming home to [him] self" (p. 371). Does this mean that Cather is being both sexist and regressive here, viewing her heroine through the filter of a limiting female stereotype and celebrating the joys of returning to childhood? It does not seem to me that she is unthinkingly perpetuating and sanctioning limiting male views of women. First of all, Jim Burden is more the author's mask than a fully imagined male character, so in the novel's conclusion we are presented with a *woman's* construction of another woman's meaning, with Cather again resorting to camouflage when revealing her deepest preoccupations.[48] In addition, although the Earth Mother can be a limiting stereotype, the image of woman as possessing mythic powers of fertility and nurturance could be interpreted as Cather's re-claiming and reworking of a male-perpetuated stereotype which she uses to enhance rather than limit woman's dignity and stature.

The question of whether we should call this a regressive fantasy remains. Gelfant argues that "retrospection, a superbly creative act for Cather, becomes for Jim a negative gesture."[49] In this view, Cather is driven by the same urges as her narrator—to return to the past and retrieve the child's relationship with the mother—but she writes a novel from these urges, whereas the narrator is passive and empty, a "wasteland" figure.[50] Certainly Cather's satisfying of regressive urges in the creative process was a positive way of dealing with such impulses, but I would argue that Jim does the same. Finally he is not regressive in the sense that William was in "The Burglar's Christmas"; Jim, as Cather's fiction has it, does not merely narrate a story. He *writes the novel.* He thus is Cather's alter ego, the author compelled to create by the conflicts he cannot fully resolve in life, moved like Willa Cather to write by his yearning for a lost maternal figure, Ántonia Shimerda/Annie Sadilek.

After attempting a war novel in *One of Ours* (1921), inspired by the death of a nephew in World War I rather than a return of her youthful urge to write a "manly battle yarn," Cather returned to another version of *My Ántonia*'s compelling story in *A Lost Lady* (1923) where once again a male adolescent worships an idealized mother figure whom he views in terms of his own subjective needs.[51] But here Cather's control of authorial distance is consistent and unerring, as suggested by her decision to make Niel Herbert a limited center of consciousness within a third-person narration rather than a first-person narrator. The origin of this novel was also the loss of a maternal woman Cather had known in childhood. When she heard of the death of Mrs. Silas Garber, "a woman I loved very much in my childhood," she created the lovely, alluring, and finally desperate Marian Forrester whose decline parallels the decay of pioneer values in America.[52] The book embodies cultural as well as personal loss, reflecting the disaffection with modern American society that pervades Cather's fiction in the 1920s. Her famous statement that "The world broke in two in 1922 or thereabouts" embodies her repudiation of a present she saw as materialistic, spiritually bankrupt, and ignoble.[53] But although both *A Lost Lady* and *The Professor's House* (1925) reflect Cather's disaffection with the present, both novels make commitments to continuing and to accepting change, process, and life's inevitable disappointments. In dealing with the theme of loss in *A Lost Lady*, she turns once again to her most compelling preoccupation and deals with the child's search for the mother. But this novel both expresses these yearnings and examines them at the same time, with the omniscient author ironically undercutting the regressive impulses of the point-of-view character.

The union of the cultural and personal loss is embodied in the title. The "lost lady" is America's virgin land, raped and pillaged by men like Ivy Peters, the novel's Snopes-like villain who corrupts the spiritual and imaginative vision of the West's pioneers, draining the Forresters' marsh to make it commercially profitable. The "lost lady" is also the heroine and by extension the mother of earliest childhood whom we all must lose. In contrast to Ántonia, Marian Forrester is more erotic than maternal. Cather, aware of the sexual drive in the child's passion for the mother, adopts a male persona in order to explore this dynamic. Niel Herbert allows her to present the Oedipal drama in the conventional son/mother terms, and since the novel concerns the adolescent's unacknowledged desires for the mother figure, the male persona is consistent with her own posturing as William Cather during the same years. Niel Herbert is the youthful perceiver who first idealizes and romanticizes the lost lady, then viciously repudiates her. Unable to acknowledge his own unconscious sexual drives which would sully his idealized courtly lady, he reacts with excessive disgust and revulsion when he discovers that she satisfies her sexual needs with other men—first the animalistic Frank Ellinger, then the repulsive Ivy Peters to whom she turns after her husband dies. Furious that his idealized mother prefers life on any terms—as well as another man to himself—Niel is filled with "weary contempt" when Marian refuses to "immolate herself" after her husband's death and "die with the pioneer period to which she belonged" so that his memory of her can remain pure and unsullied (p. 169). Like Hawthorne's Young Goodman Brown or Aylmer, Niel cannot accept either woman's sexuality or her human limitations. To him Marian is either goddess or whore, Virgin Mary or sullied Eve. But as Cather shows us, such images are Niel's constructions built from his own desires and fears, not accurate interpretations of Marian Forrester. Although some readers have assumed that Cather repudiates Marian Forrester along with Niel, this is not the case. She delicately and consistently separates her point of view from his, ironically undercutting his perceptions by suggesting the unconscious motivations for his judgments.

The contrast between Niel's and Cather's perspectives can best be seen in the central scene where Niel, the courtly lover, pays what seems to be a religious pilgrimage to Marian Forrester, rising in the "unsullied" dawn to pick a bouquet of roses as his offering (p. 85). When he hears Frank Ellinger's laughter from her bedroom, his excessive response suggests the child's feelings of loss, anger, and betrayal when he realizes that the mother's sexual attentions are given elsewhere. He hurls the flowers in the mud, murmuring "'lilies that fester smell far worse than weeds'" (p. 87). Although Niel thinks that his motives are pure and intends that the flowers will give Marian a "sudden distaste for coarse wordlings like Frank Ellinger," Cather makes it clear that he is propelled by sexual desire and jealousy (p. 85). The pilgrim's destination, ironically, is the lady's bedroom which he hopes to reach "before Frank Ellinger could intrude his unwelcome presence," and the landscape through which he moves is erotically charged, reflecting his unacknowledged sexual design (p. 84). Although Cather is drawing on the same drives that spilled over in "The Burglar's Christmas," here she is in control—distanced, judging, separate from her adolescent viewer. She demonstrates both Niel's self-deception and his life-denying unwillingness to accept time, change, and sexuality, in the process providing the reader with a fuller portrait of Marian Forrester than Niel will ever see.[54]

In her next novel, *The Professor's House* (1925), Cather indulged in veiled autobiography, expressing her inner conficts once more through a male protagonist, Godfrey St. Peter, the middle-aged professor who unaccountably does not want to leave his familiar old house for the gleaming new one he has bought and which his wife loves. Unlike Niel or Jim, he does not worship an idealized mother figure, but he is obsessively attached to the attic room in his old house where he has written all his books, a room he shares only with the seamstress Augusta and her sewing dummies. As Leon Edel has noted, the professor's unreasoning, stubborn attachment to his womblike retreat suggests the child's wish to remain attached to the mother. Hence the novel's ending, where the professor accidentally almost suffocates in the room by overturning an oil lamp, is psychologically sound: "Appropriately enough, Willa Cather ends her story with the professor nearly suffocating in his room. To remain in the womb beyond one's time is indeed to suffocate."[55] Edel links the professor's excessive depression and infantile attachment to the room he must leave with the author's extratextual conflicts. The book reflects, he argues, Cather's depression and grief at the loss of Isabelle McClung, who after marrying Jan Hambourg could offer her friend neither her exclusive attention nor the protective attic room where Cather used to write. But as we have seen, the drives Cather was drawing on here antedate the relationship with Isabelle, although doubtless that loss was the immediate source for the novel.

The professor, Edel points out, "wants his mother to be both a mother and an erotic stimulus and above all he wants to possess her exclusively."[56] Hence he is another version of the regressive William. But from the beginning of the novel, Cather makes it clear that he can never attain these desires. *The Professor's House* is no unmediated authorial fantasy but a carefully crafted novel in which Cather both expresses regressive yearnings through her protagonist and analyzes them as the omniscient author. Fulfilling childish dreams for blissful union with a mother figure is impossible, she implies, for throughout the novel women are connected with disappointment, rejection, and loss. Even the two symbolic figures that could be idealized—the sewing dummies in the attic room which the professor could clothe or complete to suit the requirements of his imagination—are disturbingly indifferent. The first, called "the bust" because it is "richly developed in the part for which it was named," should represent maternal nurturance, but it is repeatedly disappointing: "Though this figure looked so ample and billowy (as if you might lay your head upon its deep-breathing softness and rest safe forever), if you touched it you suffered a severe shock, no matter how many times you had touched it before. It presented the most unsympathetic surface imaginable."[57] The second form, which suggests the erotic rather than the maternal aspect of the mother, having a "sprightly, tricky air," is similarly disappointing. Underneath the sprightly surface is a void: "It had ... no viscera behind its glistening ribs, and its bosom resembled a strong wire bird-cage ... she never fooled St. Peter" (p. 19).

St. Peter has been disappointed by women in life as well, for they inevitably fail to satisfy his needs. His wife and daughter Rosamund, like the first mannequin, are described as "hard"; their interest in material possessions disturbs him, but their real sin is their failure to be as emotionally giving as he would like. At the end of the novel, as the professor becomes increasingly enamored of his own childhood self, his "original ego," he associates women with the sexual urges that destroyed his inviolate childhood self in adolescence (p. 265). Although St. Peter feels that he is returning to his "first nature" in resurrecting the inviolate childhood self free from reliance on women for sexual or emotional gratification, Cather shows us through his continued barnaclelike attachment to his attic room that he is not inviolate and independent, but increasingly passive and dependent (p. 267). His needs for nurturance are disguised rather than eradicated. The professor is rescued from the death to which his regressive needs lead by the sewing woman Augusta, and Edel interprets this to mean that "a mother-figure has once more appeared upon the scene for the professor, who thus hangs on to his fixation even though it has brought him an immense threat. The book ends with the professor's problem unresolved."[58] My view differs. Just as Cather survived the loss of Isabelle, moving on in adult life despite its disappointments, so the professor commits himself to continuing. After his rescue, he realizes he must live without all the gratifications the child within would like. His savior Augusta is far from an indulgent maternal figure; she represents reality, not wish fulfillment ("She wasn't at all afraid to say things that were heavily, drearily true" [p. 280].) She represents the "bloomless side of life" that he had always "run away from," but now that he must face it, he "found it wasn't altogether repugnant" (p. 280). At the end of the novel, having accepted that adults at times have to live "without delight," St. Peter finally faces the future rather than the past.

Even more that *O Pioneers!* and *My Ántonia* with their archetypal female figures, *The Professor's House* could trouble a feminist reader. Once again Cather portrays women as seen in terms of male desires and fears; in addition, the professor's happiest human bond is with a male companion, Tom Outland, rather than with his wife. At first it seems we are in the classic masculine wilderness of the American novel, reading a text by Twain, Fitzgerald, or Hemingway that denigrates women and celebrates male bonding; at times it seems that the professor's deepest yearning is to light out for the territory with Tom Outland. But as I have been arguing, when we add a biographical and psychological component to the analysis, the assumption that Cather was either unthinkingly reflecting male views of women or strategically employing male themes in order to gain critical esteem must be challenged. As we have seen, by the time she wrote this novel, Cather had long abandoned her contempt for women. Her choice of male characters to explore sexual and emotional drives was necessitated by cultural and perhaps personal pressures to camouflage her own "unnatural" attachments, and perhaps also by an inner need to place the barrier of gender between herself and the female force she found so compelling. The fact that her portrayals of women at times parallel those created by male writers suggests that those archetypes are compelling and persistent in those people whose emotional and erotic needs remain directed toward women after childhood. Hence, I would argue, Cather's use of such recurring female images reflects her continuing emotional investment in women more than her indoctrination by patriarchal literature and culture.

The professor's idyllic bond with Tom Outland, which a feminist reader may find even more offensive than the images of women in this novel, is more difficult to explain satisfactorily. Why would Willa Cather celebrate male bonding? Since Tom gradually comes to represent the professor's "original ego," it seems that Cather was forced to create this masculine pairing by her original choice to cast St. Peter as male. And in fact St. Peter's friendship with Tom is only a mask for his deeper yearning to return to childhood and the maternal presence symbolized by his attic room.

In the next few years, Willa Cather became increasingly acquainted with the bloomless side of life. She and Edith Lewis were forced to leave their comfortable apartment when the building was torn down, and Cather—who hated rootlessness—was forced to live in a hotel for several years until the couple resettled. Her father died in 1927, a blow she found devastating; then her mother suffered a stroke which left her paralyzed until her death in 1931. The fiction Cather wrote during this period—*My Mortal Enemy* (1926), *Death Comes for the Archbishop* (1927), *Shadows on the Rock* (1931)—shows a turning away from human relationships and emotional turmoil for the calm, eternal consolations of religion, which provides her characters with the self-transcendence the land had offered Alexandra Bergson. Although these novels do not draw heavily on the themes discussed here, it is interesting to note that Cather's vision of Catholicism centers on the image of the Virgin, the eternally caring Mother who will not fail her human children. The solitary, aging archbishop finds his loneliness dissipated and "sense of loss . . . replaced by a sense of restoration" by her Presence, which offers his soul not life's bloomless side but a "perpetual flowering."[59]

Evidently the impersonal consolations of religion and the Virgin did not satisfy, for in her last works, Willa Cather turned more directly to her personal past for inspiration than she ever had before, drawing on memories of her own family and childhood rather than on acquaintances like Annie Sadilek or Mrs. Garber. The mother/daughter configuration is central in this late fiction, dominating "Old Mrs. Harris" and *Sapphira and the Slave Girl* (1940). But it appears in a new form here. Cather is no longer exploring a male persona's attachment to an idealized mother. In this fiction she throws away the masks: the daughter is female, not a disguised male; both daughter and mother are clear visions of Willa Cather and Virginia Cather; and the mother is now a complex human being with strengths and weaknesses, not the "good" or the "bad" mother of early childhood.[60] Cather's new interest in exploring her bond with her mother overtly as well as her ability to view her mother more objectively was connected with Virginia Cather's illness and death. As Edith Lewis observes, "the long illness of Mrs. Cather . . . had a profound effect on Willa Cather, and I think on her work as well."[61] The role reversal Cather experienced as she sat by her mother's bedside, mothering her weakened and helpless mother, enabled her to discard previous views of her mother which related to herself. She was now separate enough both to see her mother as a person and to acknowledge their similarities. Instead of fearing they shared the same identity, Cather could manage sympathetic identification with her mother: "She realized with complete imagination what it meant for a proud woman like her mother to lie month after month quite helpless."[62] Cather's new understanding coupled with the feelings of guilt, love, and loss roused by her mother's death prompted her to re-examine the mother/daughter relationship from a more objective perspective in the late fiction.

The beautifully crafted "Old Mrs. Harris" is her most autobiographical work (it could have been titled "Family Portraits," Edith Lewis commented).[63] The story explores the tensions and misunderstandings linking three women in the same household—the grandmother Mrs. Harris, her daughter Victoria Templeton, and her granddaughter Vickie, the three corresponding to Rachel Boak, Virginia Cather, and the adolescent Willa. Only the self-forgetful grandmother can transcend her own ego to sympathize with the other two, for both Victoria and Vicki are too self-absorbed to see or respond to others' needs. Grandma Harris's fatal illness they at first interpret only in terms of themselves until they are shocked by the old woman's un-complaining death. The triumph of the story is Willa Cather's handling of point of view. Although the author judges Vicki and Victoria for their self-absorption, she understands the reasons for it; each woman is given a complex and many-sided portrayal. When Victoria Templeton withdraws to her bed-room and lies there with camphor-soaked handkerchief around her head, the omniscient author offers the sympathetic insight into her predicament that Vicki—or her own adolescent self—does not possess. Victoria's seemingly self-indulgent withdrawal from the family conceals her despair at an un-wanted pregnancy. But Vicki, concerned only with herself and her imminent break from the family, is not privy to this insight that only comes with age. The story's moving portrayal of generational conflicts suggests that Cather's ability to achieve compassionate understanding of her mother came too late for life but not for art.

In her last novel, Cather returned even further into the past for creative inspiration, tapping memories of her Virginia childhood in *Sapphira and the Slave Girl*. The novel dramatizes the separation and eventual reconciliation between three pairs of mothers and daughters: the tyrannical Sapphira and her daughter Rachel, the Negro slave Old Till and her daughter Nancy, and Willa Cather and her own mother, whose reconciliation inspired the novel and is reflected in the other mother/daughter reunions. In her previous fiction, Cather had shown the daughter/artist drawing strength and inspira-tion from symbolic or distant mothers—Alexandra from the land, Thea from her womb/cave and the Indian women—and in interviews she acknowledged her creative debt to the pioneer mothers whose stories fired her imagina-tion.[64] It is fitting that in her last novel, Cather acknowledges her own mother's contribution to her creative imagination, for the book's unusual structure—novel followed by an autobiographical epilogue in which the center of consciousness is the five-year-old Willa—reveals that Virginia Cather provided her daughter with her last novel.

The fictional portion of the book, which is set in Virginia in the 1850s, had its origin in Cather's most intense and enduring childhood memory: the reunion of Old Till and her daughter Nancy, whose return from Canada the young child had witnessed. Sapphira Colbert, a strong, tyrannical south-ern lady, is the central character. Becoming unreasonably jealous of the slave girl Nancy Till whom she thinks her husband desires, Sapphira torments and persecutes the innocent girl; eventually she invites her husband's nephew for a visit in hopes that he will seduce—even rape—the slave girl. Her own daugh-ter Rachel Blake then opposes her mother's plan and helps Nancy escape to Canada. The vengeful Sapphira breaks all ties with her daughter, but the two women are finally reconciled when Rachel's own daughter dies and Sapphira is jolted from her self-absorbed pride by compassion. The novel suggests the harm women's erotic attachment to men brings to mother/daughter relation-

ships, since it is Sapphira's possessive feelings about her husband that prompt
her to throw Nancy in the path of her would-be rapist; she is Ceres abandoning Persephone to Pluto instead of searching for her. By contrast, the reunion
is solely a mother/daughter affair, with one daughter being sacrificed so that
the mother and grandmother can be reconciled. The fictional portion of the
novel ends with Sapphira asking Rachel and her daughter to spend the winter
with her.

Then Cather attaches the curious Epilogue in which the distinction between fiction and fact, art and life, is erased. Set in Back Creek twenty-five
years later, the Epilogue describes Nancy Till's poignant reunion with her
aging mother Old Till. Cather often added codas to her novels that take place
years later, but this is the only one that purports to be factual. Nancy and
Old Till, fictional characters in the novel proper, now become real people
Willa Cather knew as a child. Of course, an autobiographical fragment like the
Epilogue is a type of fiction, since the view of the past is filtered through
memory and shaped by imagination. But significantly, in letters to friends,
Cather insisted that the Epilogue was literally true.[65]

The Epilogue's imaginative center is the powerful memory that had
endured in her mind for over sixty years:

> Till had already risen; when the stranger followed my mother into the
> room, she took a few uncertain steps forward. She fell meekly into
> the arms of a tall, gold-skinned woman who drew the little old darky
> to her breast and held her there, bending her face down over the
> head scantily covered with grey wool. Neither spoke a word. There
> was something Scriptural in that meeting, like the pictures in our
> old Bible.[66]

The person responsible both for the child's interest in the two women and for
her witnessing this dramatic reunion was Virginia Cather. She had first stimu-
lated Willa's imagination by telling her stories about the escaped slave. "Ever
since I could remember anything, I had heard about Nancy. My mother
used to sing me to sleep with: *Down by de cane brake, close by de mill,
Dar lived a yaller gal, her name was Nancy Till*" (p. 281). Virginia Cather
continues to minister to her child's needs as the memory is unrolled. On the
day Nancy is to return to Back Creek, Willa is sick with a cold, but her
mother persuades the two women to stage their reunion at the Cather farm-
house so that the child can be included in the unfolding drama. Then she puts
Willa in her own bed so that she can watch the road from a good vantage
point and see Nancy as soon as the stage arrives. When that moment comes,
Virginia arranges a front-row view for her daughter:

> Suddenly my mother hurried into the room. Without a word she
> wrapped me in a blanket, carried me to the curved lounge by the

window, and put me down on the high head-rest, where I could look
out. There it came, the stage, with a trunk on top, and sixteen hoofs
trotting briskly round the curve where the milestone was.
[P. 281–82]

So, the Epilogue suggests, Virginia Cather's maternal concern for her
daughter's emotional and imaginative needs gave Cather the dramatic memory
from which she fashioned her last novel. The Epilogue thus both ends the
novel and, in a way, begins it. Set in the 1870s, it completes the story of
Sapphira and Rachel, Nancy and Old Till. But it also begins the story by
showing the psychological and emotional source for the novel the adult
woman would write in 1940. The insight Cather reveals into the sources
of her creativity, linked here with the mother/daughter relationship, is
startling and somehow very satisfying. *Sapphira*'s Epilogue is the right ending not only for Willa Cather's last novel but also for her entire literary
career.

## Notes

1. Judith Fetterley, *The Resisting Reader: A Feminist Approach to American Fiction* (Bloomington: Indiana University Press, 1978), p. viii.
2. For an example of this type of criticism pertaining to American fiction,
   see Judith Fryer, *The Faces of Eve: Women in the Nineteenth-Century
   American Novel* (New York: Oxford University Press, 1976).
3. Cheri Register, "Literary Criticism," *Signs: Journal of Women in Culture
   and Society* 6, no. 2 (Winter 1980):268–82.
4. Sandra Gilbert and Susan Gubar, *The Madwoman in the Attic: The
   Woman Writer and the Nineteenth-Century Literary Imagination* (New
   Haven: Yale University Press, 1979), pp. 45–92.
5. Gilbert and Gubar, *Madwoman*, pp. xi, 84.
6. Register, "Literary Criticism," p. 277.
7. David Stouck, *Willa Cather's Imagination* (Lincoln: University of
   Nebraska Press, 1975), p. 208.
8. For two brief discussions of the connection between Willa Cather's relationship with her mother and her fiction, see Jane Lilienfeld, "Reenter-
   ing Paradise: Cather, Colette, Woolf and Their Mothers," in *The Lost
   Tradition: Mothers and Daughters in Literature*, ed. Cathy N. Davidson
   and E. M. Broner (New York: Ungar, 1980), pp. 160–75; and G. B.
   Stewart, "Mother, Daughter and the Birth of the Female Artist,"
   *Women's Studies* 6, no. 2 (1979):127–45.
9. Quoted in Mildred Bennett, *The World of Willa Cather* (Lincoln: University of Nebraska Press, 1951; rpt. University of Nebraska Press,
   Bison 1961), p. 168.

10. The major sources for biographical information on Willa Cather and Virginia Cather are E. K. Brown, *Willa Cather* (completed by Leon Edel) (New York: Knopf, 1953); James Woodress, *Willa Cather: Her Life and Art* (New York: Pegasus, 1970); Edith Lewis, *Willa Cather Living* (Lincoln: University of Nebraska Press, 1953); Elizabeth Sergeant, *Willa Cather: A Memoir* (New York: Lippincott, 1953); and Bennett, *World of Willa Cather*.

11. Lewis, *Willa Cather Living*, p. 6.

12. Nancy Chodorow, *The Reproduction of Mothering: Psychoanalysis and the Sociology of Gender* (Berkeley: University of California Press, (1978), pp. 67–129 in particular; and Jane Flax, "The Conflict between Nurturance and Autonomy in Mother-Daughter Relationships and within Feminism," *Feminist Studies* 4, no. 2 (June 1978):171–91. Register describes the impact Chodorow's book has had on feminist literary criticism in her review essay.

13. I have discussed the cultural sources for her William Cather period more extensively in "Tomboyism and Adolescent Conflict: Three Nineteenth-Century Case Studies," in *Woman's Being, Woman's Place: Female Identity and Vocation in American History*, ed. Mary Kelley (Boston: G. K. Hall, 1979), pp. 351–72.

14. Lewis, *Willa Cather Living*, p. 13.

15. For some startling photographs of Cather during this period, see Bennett, *World of Willa Cather*.

16. Chodorow, *Reproduction of Mothering*, pp. 130–40.

17. A full discussion of Cather's early views of art and artists can be found in Bernice Slote's comprehensive introductory essays in Slote, ed., *The Kingdom of Art: Willa Cather's First Principles and Critical Statements 1893-1896* (Lincoln: University of Nebraska Press, 1966), pp. 3–114, hereafter referred to as *KA*.

18. *KA*, p. 423.

19. *KA*, pp. 158, 70.

20. William M. Curtin, ed., *The World and the Parish: Willa Cather's Articles and Reviews, 1893-1902*, 2 vols. (Lincoln: University of Nebraska Press, 1970), I:276–77.

21. A discussion of Willa Cather's college years that includes uncollected short fiction as well as views of classmates can be found in James Shively, *Writings from Willa Cather's Campus Years* (Lincoln: University of Nebraska Press, 1950).

22. The Pound letters are in the Manuscript Department, Perkins Library, Duke University. Because of testamentary restrictions, Willa Cather's letters cannot be quoted directly, so I am forced to resort to paraphrase and summary.

23. Carroll Smith-Rosenberg. "The Female World of Love and Ritual: Relationships between Women in Nineteenth-Century America," *Signs: Journal of Women in Culture and Society* 1, no. 1 (Autumn 1975): 1–29.

24. Lillian Faderman, *Surpassing the Love of Men: Romantic Friendship and Love between Women from the Renaissance to the Present* (New York: Wm. Morrow, 1981), pp. 273–353.
25. Willa Cather to Louise Pound, 15 June 1892.
26. All quotations are from stories available in Virginia Faulkner, ed., *Collected Short Fiction, 1892–1912* (Lincoln: University of Nebraska Press, 1965).
27. *KA*, pp. 437–41.
28. Willa Cather, *Not under Forty* (New York: Knopf, 1936), p. 85.
29. Quoted in Cather's Preface to *Alexander's Bridge* (Boston: Houghton Mifflin, 1922), p. vii.
30. Sergeant, *Willa Cather*, p. 60.
31. See both the Preface to the 1922 edition of *Alexander's Bridge* and "My First Novels: There Were Two," in *Willa Cather on Writing* (New York: Knopf, 1932).
32. *O Pioneers!* (Boston: Houghton Mifflin, 1913; rpt. 1941), p. 65. All future references in the text will be to this edition.
33. Bennett, *World of Willa Cather*, p. 208.
34. Sergeant, *Willa Cather*, p. 86.
35. "The Unity of Willa Cather's 'Two-Part Pastoral':Passion in *O Pioneers!*", *Studies in American Fiction* (Fall 1978):157–71.
36. Lewis, *Willa Cather Living*, p. 78.
37. Sergeant, *Willa Cather*, p. 215.
38. See her continuing use of this imagery in "Katherine Mansfield" in *Not under Forty*, pp. 123–47.
39. Bennett, *World of Willa Cather*, p. 195.
40. Ibid., p. 212; Sergeant, *Willa Cather*, p. 137.
41. Lewis, *Willa Cather Living*, p. 81.
42. *The Song of the Lark* (1915; reprint ed., University of Nebraska Press, 1978), p. 48. All future references in the text will be to this edition.
43. Ellen Moers, *Literary Women* (New York: Doubleday, 1976), p. 258.
44. Gilbert and Gubar, *Madwoman*, discuss the connections between women's use of the cave image and feminine oppression and creativity. Although often symbolizing female constriction and confinement, the womb/cave can also be "the place of female power" to which the woman artist retreats "to retrieve what has been lost," her creative power and matrilineal heritage (pp. 95, 99); Cather uses the womb/cave in the positive sense they describe in "The Parables of the Cave," pp. 93–104.
45. Adrienne Rich discusses the traditional association of femininity, creativity and pottery making in *Of Woman Born: Motherhood as Experience and Institution* (New York: Norton, 1976), pp. 96–102.
46. *My Antonia* (Boston: Houghton Mifflin, 1918; rpt. Houghton Mifflin, Sentry), p. 339. All future references in the text will be to this edition.
47. Blanche Gelfant, "The Forgotten Reaping-Hook: Sex in *My Antonia*," *American Literature* 43 (March 1971):63–64.

48. In an unpublished paper "*My Antonia*, Jim Burden, and the Dilemma of the Lesbian Writer," Judith Fetterley argues that "Jim Burden is Willa Cather's cover for her own lesbian sensibility" because she "wants to disguise . . . the fact of love between women."

49. Gelfant, *Reaping-Hook*, p. 64.

50. Ibid., p. 63.

51. *A Lost Lady* (New York: Knopf, 1923; rpt. Knopf, Vintage, 1972). All future references in text will be to this edition.

52. Bennett, *World of Willa Cather*, p. 69.

53. Prefatory Note to *Not Under Forty*.

54. Kathleen L. Nichols offers a perceptive analysis of the unconscious forces that distort Niel's vision in "The Celibate Male in *A Lost Lady*: The Unreliable Center of Consciousness," *Regionalism and the Female Imagination* 4, no. 1 (Spring 1978):13–23.

55. Leon Edel, *Literary Biography* (Toronto: Univ. of Toronto Press, 1957), p. 70.

56. Ibid., p. 68.

57. *The Professor's House* (New York: Knopf, 1925; rpt. Vintage ed., 1973), p. 18. All future references in the text will be to this edition.

58. Edel, *Literary Biography*, p. 70.

59. *Death Comes for the Archbishop* (New York: Knopf, 1927; rpt. Knopf, Vintage, 1971), p. 256.

60. The terms refer to the young child's "splitting" of the actual mother, who is at times both nurturant and rejecting, into an all-giving "good" mother and a cold "bad" mother. The split is reflected in the fairy-tale pattern of the fairy godmother and the witch. See Bruno Bettelheim, *The Uses of Enchantment: The Meaning and Importance of Fairy Tales* (New York: Vintage Books, 1977), pp. 66–73.

61. Lewis, *Willa Cather Living*, p. 156.

62. Ibid., p. 156.

63. Ibid., p. 6.

64. "I have never found any intellectual excitement any more intense than I used to feel when I spent a morning with one of those old women at her baking or butter making. I used to ride home in the most unreasonable state of excitement," Cather said in a 1913 interview (*KA*, p. 449).

65. Willa Cather to Dorothy Canfield Fisher, 14 October 1940 (Guy Bailey Memorial Library, University of Vermont).

66. *Sapphira and the Slave Girl* (New York: Knopf, 1940; rpt. Knopf, Vintage, 1975), p. 283. All future references in the text are to this edition.

# Cynthia Secor

# The Question of Gertrude Stein

Feminist criticism has taught us to question the heretofore unquestioned and unquestionable: to ask why the products of writing women have not been more carefully collected, preserved, and published; why in our western culture, until the nineteeth century, "author," the solemn title of authority, had been reserved almost exclusively for males. Feminist criticism leads us to ask, in this paper, with Gertrude Stein, why it is that in the twentieth century it should be a woman who does the serious thinking about literature.[1] This paper assumes with Stein that she has done the serious thinking about literature in this century. It takes for granted with her that in the nineteenth century women writers lacked self-confidence, whereas by the twentieth century it is the men who lack self-confidence.[2] As feminists we can say that men also lacked and continue to lack the profound marginality that characterized the angle of vision of a Jewish, lesbian woman born in Allegheny, Pennsylvania, in 1874. For the serious thinker, marginality to the dominant culture is as much a gift as a curse. As Stein would say, seeing is the thing.

We further agree with Stein that Americans can think anything about men and women, a sign of our self-appointed capacity to think and say anything about everything.[3] Gender is the most profound category of difference consistently recognized by diverse cultures at any given time, and over time. To be free enough to question gender is to be free enough to question whatever one fancies to question.

In recent times it would seem that questions are the domain of science and philosophy, representation the task of the artist, and stability the responsibility of church, government, and business. It is of more than passing interest, therefore, that if ever Gertrude Stein consciously trained to be an artist, she did so by unusual, but quite logical stages. As an undergraduate she studied philosophy at Harvard with Santayana and James; her postgraduate work was with the medical faculty at Johns Hopkins. For Stein, representation is the practice of either complex description or logical demonstration. Dying, Stein is reputed to have asked Alice Toklas, "What is the answer?" and, when Toklas was silent, to have continued, "In that case, what is the question?"[4] To face death with humor is admirable, but to face it with the methodological consistency characteristic of one's work and life is to simplify for future generations the primary critical task. We need only seek the question being asked, the proposition being demonstrated.

For the critic of the novel the questions are many. And interesting. What novels did she write? Why did she write when she did the texts she chose to call novels? What does one do with texts that appear to be prose narratives, but which stretch or dismiss classical definitions of the novel? Is a metaphysical poem with characters and action a novel if it is written in prose? What are the criteria for criticizing a novella that pauses in the middle to illustrate with itself the critical assumptions that underlie its composition? How does a novella or novel function that employs sequentially distinct styles, even genres? Is an autobiography a novel, if the author is the subject, but not the narrative persona? Is it permissible for a novelist to stop when she is finished regardless of the reader's expectation of formal closure? Is a children's story a novel if the author considers representation rather than realism as the criterion of reality? Are we prepared for a woman novelist to comment on the correlations among the psychosexual development of individuals, the aging process, international warfare, and the efficacy of prophecy—and call it a novel? In brief, are we prepared for Gertrude Stein?

As is often the case with a major woman writer, critics have been slow to read her thoroughly and carefully, quick to trivialize her effort, and even when entirely sympathetic and impressed, baffled as to how best to explain her achievement.

It has been reassuring for us that Jane Austen did not write about the Napoleonic wars, that George Eliot's novels, "baggy monsters" or not, did decidedly have beginnings, middles, and ends, and that Virginia Woolf, as she recklessly dissolved the boundaries between the fluid and the solid, stoutly retained the distinction between masculine and feminine. With Gertrude Stein, it is difficult to determine what if any rules of decorum are appropriate. It would appear to be in her nature to pose a problem, solve it to her own satisfaction, and then move on. This is perhaps the dynamic underlying her famous statement that she wrote for herself and strangers. It is probable that she will suffer the fate of all major writers, to be rediscovered endlessly by successive schools of critical practice. At the present moment, she is as susceptible to post-structuralist as to feminist analysis, the only variable being that the major post-structuralist critics are males who have not read her and the major feminist critics are women who are reading her.

The questions that interest me as a feminist critic are questions of character, voice, period, narration, entity, political consciousness, democratization of representation, permissible content, dismissal of gender as a fundamental category, rejection of myth as objective representation, and Stein's ultimate ability to represent economically the individual's state of mind as it correlates with the zeitgeist, national character, or what can only for lack of a better word be called mob psychology.

As I read chronologically through the texts that can be argued to be novelle, short stories, or novels, I am struck simply with the breadth of her work, the tenacity with which she set and solved ever more complex problems, problems that are at once philosophical, cultural, and literary. In her hands, the work has become text, and through her words, the inaudible, invisible, and devalued life of women has been given permanent representation in significant form.

Now, nearly thirty-five years after Stein's death, two aspects of her work continue to be problematic for critics and common readers alike. How she means and what she means remain open to question. This is a healthy state of affairs, for when a writer ceases to be questioned, a writer ceases to be read. "How she means" is problematic in the sense that much of the best of twentieth-century fiction is problematic, often deliberately difficult. The serious reader is expected to grapple with the significance of representation, the strategies whereby meaning is generated, the nature of voice, the structure of narration, and the possibility or impossibility of ascertaining definitively what is being expressed. "What she means" is problematic for many readers because she is deliberately writing beyond the patriarchal tradition and is, therefore, difficult to grasp until one understands that the male, as such, the masculine, the hierarchical, the phallic, the violent, the conflictual, the linear, the direct, and the masterful are not what she writes about. In her fiction, these attributes are present, but in no sense are they primary values.

For the purposes of this paper, I want to consider the narratives written before World War I as a significant cluster and those written between 1932 and 1942, that is, before and during the early years of World War II as a second significant cluster. It can be argued that the major works of these two periods reflect a shift in interest from character to narration, and that the impulse to work with the novel, a fully defined generic form, is a response to her own awareness of the growing tensions in the world around her. As a Jew, a lesbian, and an expatriate, she can be assumed to have had especially sensitive antennae. She used the novel as it has always been used, to create a fictional world, real for the reader, in which to represent the relations of individuals to society.

Leon Katz reports that beginning in the bleak winter of 1902, after her break with May Bookstaver, Stein embarked on an ambitious reading program which never faltered throughout the years in which she wrote *Q.E.D.*, *Three Lives*, *The Making of Americans*, "Ada," and *Tender Buttons*, which was completed in 1912. It was her intention "to read through English narrative writing from the sixteenth century to the present."[5]

The works written during this period show her in transition from the novel of the nineteenth century to the novel of the twentieth. *Q.E.D.* (1903) is traditional in form if not in content.[6] The lesbian triangle is handled as James might handle a triangle, sparsely, with emphasis on the moral dilemma: there is conflict in the traditional sense; the central character moves from innocence to experience; the resolution is impasse. The problem of voice is no problem, insofar as she appears to quote directly from life where ever useful. Protagonist, narrator, and author are of one opinion and, in effect, of one voice. The work is clearly an apprentice piece.

With *Three Lives* (1905-6), we are in the familiar realm of the novella. The protagonists are women, common women, in keeping with the naturalistic impulse of the novel of the period—a German housekeeper, a German servant girl, and a streetwise young Negro woman. The focus of each life is perhaps less common: the housekeeper has as the romance in her life a woman later involved with a shady doctor dealing in abortions; the servant girl marries only to fade out of existence as her role as mother is absorbed by her husband; and the streetwise young woman becomes involved with a young doctor in a debilitating relation that simply cannot for them be the right relation. It is in the latter story that Stein's interest in the representation of character leaves the nineteenth century behind. The individualized rhythm of the speaking voice becomes the medium for the representation of character. The individual character regardless of gender or ethnicity is shown in its singularity without recourse to stereotype or myth.

Plot is present in each of these three stories, but one does not experience it as a driving force, rather as a slender organizing principle. What is interesting is the female protagonist, who she is, and how she fares in the world. Character is given. In "The Gentle Lena," the central character simply gives way to a stronger one. There is no conflict to speak of. In "The Good Anna," there is a series of relations with romance as the organizing theme, but no essential conflict. As with Lena, the good Anna is observed. Melanctha is heard, and the distinction is startling. There is conflict, as in *Q.E.D.*, but the plot and the conflict fade into insignificance as the speaking voice becomes the vehicle of the central meaning. The characters of Jeff and Melanctha are represented in their spoken words, not by the content of their speech, but by the structure of their speech. There is conflict between them, but it is merely the scaffolding on which to construct the rhythm of their characters. The language in *Q.E.D.* is autobiographical. In "Melanctha," it is representational, rather than realistic.

The beginning and the end of "Melanctha" belong to the convention of the tale, the yarn; the middle is new, it establishes its own conventions. Years later Stein does the same thing when she begins *Mrs. Reynolds* with a set of details, the "descriptive residue,"[7] that establishes the conventional world of the novel for the reader, just before Stein departs it for the uncharted ground of the "new novel" she is writing. Again and again Stein will do this in her novels, novelle, and short stories, give us just enough of the conventions associated with the genre to convince us of what we are reading before she begins to stretch our capacity for seeing, hearing, and believing.

"Ada" (1908-12) demonstrates a related strategy. This novella within a few short pages uses sequentially three distinctly different styles, taking the reader from the fiction of realism to a fiction of poetic celebration. The reader is made to experience the radical transformation experienced by the female protagonist, as she moves from the world of heterosexuality to the world of lesbian companionship. Many years later in *Ida, A Novel*, Stein uses the same strategy, rendering the first half of this novel of identity and entity as a picaresque novel and the second as a stately epithalamion.[8]

*The Making of Americans* (1906-1911) shares with *Ida, a Novel* and *Mrs. Reynolds* the distinction of being one of Stein's three major novels. It is the first. In the tradition of the nineteenth century, it is a novel of the family. Meant as neither tragedy nor comedy, it is in the Shakespearian sense a chronicle or history. It is a history of a people. It is about the lives of the members of a German Jewish family come to America. It is about acculturation: "The old people in a new world, the new people made out of the old, that is the story that I mean to tell, for that is what really is and what I really know."[9] Already in these years Stein is struggling to create form adequate to represent the range of persons possible on earth, to show some of them as they combine individual nature, national character, and the imprint of geographical space. In a sense the variables are the same as George Eliot worked with in *Middlemarch*, but the product feels strange: it belongs to a new century, the character stands out more starkly than the environment, and the mind of the narrator is in the process of becoming more important than the character of the characters. Clearly, Stein the young novelist is engrossed in working out her personal definitions of personality, causality, and significance. The opening of *The Making of Americans* is a parable for her practice during this period—and perhaps for the remainder of her career: "Once an angry man dragged his father along the ground through his own orchard. 'Stop!' cried the groaning old man at last, 'Stop! I did not drag my father beyond this tree.'"[10] Like her angry man with his old father, Stein is about to drag the Anglo-American novel beyond the point it had been taken by Eliot, Hardy, Bennett, Galsworthy, and the others.

By the end of the composition of *The Making of Americans*, it is clear that the mind of the novelist has become a significant dimension of the structure of the work, not as narrator, but as composing force. Combined with this interest in the mind as composing force was Stein's conviction at that time that each man, woman, and child could and should be represented. Doubtless her ideas were sharpened by her careful reading of Otto Weininger's *Sex and Character*, a sexist, anti-Semitic work typical of much of the intellectual thinking and writing of the period.[11] As a woman and a Jew, she had to establish her practice well beyond the limits Weininger set. Genius had to be universal.

If there is a single lasting interest throughout her fiction, it is to demonstrate that the mind, the composing mind, is beyond gender and ethnic categories. In the mid-1930s, in *The Geographical History of America,* she pursues this proposition vigorously, examining in detail the distinction between the human mind and human nature, between entity and identity. This interest in the composing mind, this "real feeling for every human being,"[12] led inevitably to her passion for the word: "I had to capture the value of the individual word, find out what it meant and act within it."[13] These, she said, were the things that interested her up through the writing of *Tender Buttons.* And with *Tender Buttons* (1910–12) she broke completely with the form of the nineteenth-century novel, though not with the content of her own earlier fiction.

And it is with *Tender Buttons* that the tools of the feminist critic for the first time become as useful as those of the structural critic. In the previous works, one can trace her descent from George Eliot, exclaim over her honest and accurate depiction of lesbians, working women, abortion, women of easy virtue, and friendships between women. But it is with *Tender Buttons* that her narrative strategies depart radically from those of her predecessors. The content is familiar: a triangle of sorts, as in *Q.E.D.*, "Fernhurst," "Melanctha," and "Ada." Here Gertrude Stein ceases to live with Leo Stein and comes to live with Alice Toklas. The artifacts of domesticity, the parts of the female body, interpersonal relations, food, nursery rhymes, characters out of life and fiction, all are present, not as metaphors, symbols, or stereotypes, but as systems of meaning being explored within a common structure, and not sequentially as in "Ada," but simultaneously. Tender buttons are the nipples that give both nourishment and pleasure. The world portrayed in the work is one of feminine domesticity, female sensuality, and lesbian sexuality. It is a world of women, a pleasant world made up of objects, food, and rooms, but it is also a world that admits the violence of men, the disdain with which women can be treated, the disbelief that women can be enough for women, that men are not needed.

Published in June 1914, on the eve of World War I, this novel uses the conventions of seventeenth-century metaphysical poetry. Its celebration of the body becomes at its climax a celebration of the capacity we have for emotion, for "care," the tenderest mode of human feeling and behavior: "The care with which the rain is wrong and the green is wrong and the white is wrong, the care with which there is a chair and plenty of breathing. The care with which there is incredible justice and likeness, all this makes a magnificent asparagus, and also a fountain."[14] It is a secular metaphysic grounded in the traditional activities and attributes of women.

Why should Stein attempt a novel in the form of a metaphysical poem? Because it is within the conventions of the metaphysical poem to link the unlinkable so as to force meaning not otherwise obvious. Stein had at last in Alice Toklas found a loving companion and around them Western Europe, the patriarchal society in its most advanced industrial form, was about to explode. This work bridges the radical distance between personal happiness and impending public chaos. Two systems of experience are linked within a common system of meaning. Here personal happiness dominates; later when Stein comes to write *Mrs. Reynolds*, the balance will be more just. But again the public chaos will be gathered into the capacious mind of the domestically occupied Mrs. Reynolds. In Anglo-American fiction, the comparison is clearly with Mrs. Ramsey. War is human nature; the human mind alone keeps it in perspective.

*Tender Buttons* was one of those books that young writers read. It blasted open whole new spaces of meaning. Cocteau reported being thunderstruck by a single manuscript page that contained the simple observation, "Dining is west." For Stein, it ended the long period of portraits and characters, and cleared the way for the plays, the landscapes, and *Lucy Church Amiably*. The twenties were a peaceful time for Stein.

But slowly the times changed, the forces of violence began to build again. In 1927, the same year that she wrote *Lucy Church Amiably* and the light and playful *Four Saints in Three Acts*, Stein wrote *Patriarchal Poetry*. This work admits all the pain and ambiguity that is intentionally excluded from *Lucy Church Amiably* and *Four Saints in Three Acts*. This difficult and revealing work is a moving autobiographical account of the slow and painful process through which Stein's voice as a writer developed. It is about what it means to both love and reject the language and literature in which and with which you have grown up, to have gradually to remake that language so that you as a woman are no longer relational, subordinate, and subjugated.

During this prewar period two things seem to be happening. Stein becomes preoccupied with narration, with telling; and she becomes preoccupied with telling about herself. The autobiographical impulse and the impulse to explore the potential of the novel as a vehicle for narration seem equally strong. During the years 1932–40, she writes many novels, novelle, and short stories. She calls some of the latter novels because of the generic conventions used, even though their brevity approximates the short story or novella rather than the novel as we know it from earlier days.

Two novels written in 1932 demonstrate how diverse was the impulse to fictionalize her experience. *Marguerite; or A Simple Novel of High Life* is a dark and difficult work representing what it is to be a lesbian in Europe in the early thirties. This work was not published until the 1950s, well after Stein's death. In contrast, *The Autobiography of Alice B. Toklas*, published almost as soon as it was written, was an instant success and led to her now legendary tour of America. In effect, the theme of this work is her genius, her place among the greats of her own time and place. The theme is picked up again in *Everybody's Autobiography* (1936). What does it mean to be one of the minds genuinely representative of one's own time and to be capable of rendering the concerns of the age in significant form? In *The Autobiography of Alice B. Toklas*, three geniuses are identified: Gertrude Stein, Pablo Picasso, and Alfred Whitehead. In *Everybody's Autobiography*, there are two, herself and Einstein. By 1936 the Jewish question was again very much on her mind.

Throughout these years, beginning with "Composition as Explanation" (1926) through "Why I Like Detective Stories" (1937), Stein persistently writes about the process of composition, of narration, of telling. Some of the material was worked up as lectures for the American tour, some for magazine publication, and some as integral parts of the short fiction of the period, as in *The Superstitions of Fred Anneday, Annday, Anday; A Novel of Real Life* (1934). The stylistics she articulates anticipate many of the central concerns of the structuralist and post-structuralist critics. The examples used in these essays and the subject matter of the short fictions written during the same period are a delight for the feminist critic. Her concern is for mothers, daughters, granddaughters even, for the identity of wives, of lesbian partners, and the relation of all these to the children they bear, who observe them or fail to see them, as the case may be. Orphans too are present, that is, women without a concrete sense of their own heritage.

The most important work of the period is *The Geographical History of America or The Relation of Human Nature to the Human Mind* (1935). Alluded to in the opening pages of this essay, this work is an extended philosophic meditation, related in intention to *Patriarchal Poetry*. It represents, on the eve of World War II, Stein's understanding of what is permanent and what is central to human experience. It is as if she is preparing herself for the holocaust to come.

*Ida, A Novel* and *Mrs. Reynolds*, the second and third of Stein's major novels, seem almost to divide between them the themes that surfaced during the thirties. At first reading it seems strange that the two novels begun in 1940 should be so different, but it makes perfect sense if we remember Stein's penchant for posing questions, and never, never repeating herself. *Ida, A Novel* (1940) is intended as a portrait of the American woman, an American woman, any American woman, every American woman. Who is she? We follow her from birth through her middle years. The impulse to write the book is both personal and patriotic.

The feminist achievement of the work is that Ida is always Ida. In effect we follow the female protagonist as she wanders from place to place, from relation to relation, her husbands coming and going until one finally stays. The first half of the work closes with a statement about her marriage to

Andrew that stands in stark contrast to centuries of patriarchal literature: "For this there was a change, everybody changed, Ida even changed and even changed Andrew. Andrew had changed Ida to be more Ida and Ida changed Andrew to be less Andrew and they were both always together."[15] Lost entirely is the conventional sense of woman as wife and handmaiden, as a creature for whom marriage is fulfillment and destiny. Stein picks apart the conventions of the traditional novel, uses them in combination with other formal generic conventions, drops them out completely, or retains them in part as suits the problem she has set herself. Marriage is the subject of the second half of the novel, and Ida continues to become more and more herself.

*Mrs. Reynolds* (1940) in its own way is perhaps even more iconoclastic. The work is a *tour de force* in which Stein represents World War II as it is perceived by a middle-aged woman living peacefully in her village. Her dreams, her interest in prophecy, her conversations with husband and neighbors lead us to understand the dynamics of international conflict as they may be grounded in the childhood of national leaders, in the collective mind of those involved directly and indirectly in the conflict itself. As Stein says, "There is nothing historical about this book except the state of mind."[16]

From a feminist perspective the mode of narration is brilliant. Mrs. Reynolds speaks throughout to Mr. Reynolds, recounting each day her dreams, conversations, thoughts, and forebodings. It is as if Conrad had in *The Heart of Darkness* made his storyteller a wife and his circle of civilized listeners a single husband. The storyteller, the detecting mind, the adventurer returned is a woman, the listener a man. Playing as she does with a well-established nineteenth-century novelistic convention, Stein gives to the female the traditional role of maker and speaker and to the male the traditional role of vessel and recipient. Neatly and unobtrusively, Stein has reversed our assumptions about passivity and activity. To Mrs. Reynolds is assigned the traditional male prerogative of commenting on matters of religious, political, and military significance.

Thus, in the face of the deepening international crisis, Stein responded first by articulating the appropriate stylistic and philosophic framework and then by producing calmly the last two of her three major novels. In this context, it is important to remember why a novelist may pause to write either stylistic theory or traditional philosophy—to clear the vision, to sharpen the perspective.

*The Making of Americans, Ida, A Novel*, and *Mrs. Reynolds* are the most significant of her long prose narratives, both because of the complexity of the novelistic problems posed and because their scale permits us just comparisons with *Middlemarch* and *Portrait of a Lady*, that is, with novels of unquestioned importance, works that have earned a secure place in the canon of Anglo-American fiction. These three novels are complex statements about the relation of individual to society, culture, geography, and history. They are about the ecology of human life. Unpretentiously they trace the processes of acculturation, individuation, and symbiosis without ever losing the informing sense that the presence of life assumes the inevitability of death.

Feminists, Jews, and homosexuals were sent to the camps and ovens. Stein did not ignore the devastation; she faced it squarely in the novels. The human mind must comprehend and give perspective to human nature. She does not write directly about the experience (which but for luck, timing, and perhaps the direct intervention of Bernard Fay might have been hers), rather she writes in full knowledge of it. Violence, madmen, scapegoats, irrationality provide content for *Mrs. Reynolds*, as the French resistance provides content for *Yes Is For A Very Young Man*. Neither work, however, is about violence or resistance. These behaviors are by definition human nature, and it is the human mind that is Stein's concern, how the human mind composes, derives significance from the irrational, the ordinary, all that can be observed at any given moment from any given point of view.

From beginning to end, Stein as a writer creates out of what can only be called the confidence of women in the twentieth century. Her fundamental values are feminine, sensual, domestic, nurturing, and healing. She looks at the chaos of two world wars and responds with the simple directness of the Ladies Hospital Auxiliary or the League of Women Voters. During the first war, she and Toklas drove their Ford van from hospital to hospital for the American Fund for French Wounded, transporting supplies. During the second war, the two women, both Jewish aliens, now in their sixties, hid out in the French farming country where they had long had their summer home. Immediately after the liberation, they toured U.S. Army bases in Germany, and entertained in their home, helping the G.I.s to make the transition from war to peace, as in the earlier war they had helped many a homesick doughboy. In her work, as in her life, Stein created out of the fundamental female sense that the womb, the room, the nipples, the tender buttons, are a never-ending fount of life and nourishment. Her aesthetic begins, as all aesthetics begin, in our knowledge of the body, in the shapes and sounds of our first pleasure and pain. In the texts, despite her direct personal involvement in two wars and the loss in both of dear friends, the principal aesthetic at work is that of abundance, pleasure, and satisfaction. Tinged by fear at times, but never torn by despair or terror, the texts render unnecessary a distinction between the *texte de plaisir* and the *texte de jouissance*.[17] *Tender Buttons*, the most violent of the novels, culminates in intense joy that is but an aspect, a facet of the tender caring that informs the work. Stein's icon is the circle of roses: "rose is a rose is a rose is a rose." The world of her novels is fundamentally accepting and inclusive. Such are the fundamental, unassailable patterns of meaning that run through the forty-some years of her life as a producing writer. She like George Eliot before her takes St.

Therese as her patron saint, Jew and Protestant alike acknowledging no sectarian schisms in their quest for sisterhood, service, and authority.

Was Stein pleased with herself? Our final question. As usual she has herself already posed it, and provides our first answer. The lines are given to Susan B. Anthony in *The Mother of Us All* (1945-46), lest we, born after the first great wave of American feminism, forget our mothers. Anthony speaks with the simple, unassuming authority we imagine to have characterized those wise women of antiquity at whose feet Socrates sat.

> *Silence*
>
> Life is strife, I was a martyr all my life
> not to what I won but to what was done.
>
> *Silence*
>
> Do you know because I tell you so, or do
> you know, do you know.
>
> *Silence*
>
> My long life, my long life.
>
> *Curtain* [18]

As the curtain falls, we are left to our question, posed for us in the stark, unyielding language of the twentieth century, Do we know?

## Notes

I would like to thank my colleague Adrian Tinsley for her assistance and criticism in the preparation of this paper.

1. Gertrude Stein, *The Geographical History of America* (1936; reprint ed., New York: Vintage, 1973), p. 218.
2. Gertrude Stein, *Everybody's Autobiography* (1937; reprint ed., New York: Vintage, 1973), p. 5.
3. Stein, *Geographical History*, p. 214.
4. James R. Mellow, *Charmed Circle* (New York: Praeger Publishers, 1974), p. 468.
5. Leon Katz, Introduction to *Fernhurst, Q.E.D., and Other Early Writings*, by Gertrude Stein (New York: Liveright, 1971), p. xviii.
6. All dates in parentheses are dates of composition as listed in Appendix C, in Richard Bridgman, *Gertrude Stein in Pieces* (New York: Oxford University Press, 1970).

7. Jonathan Culler, *Structuralist Poetics* (Ithaca, N.Y.: Cornell University Press, 1975), p. 193.
8. Cynthia Secor, "Ida, A Great American Novel," *Twentieth Century Literature* 24, no. 1 (1978):106.
9. Gertrude Stein, *The Making of Americans* (1925; reprint ed., New York: Something Else Press, 1966), p. 3.
10. Ibid.
11. For a detailed analysis of the relation of these two works, read Leon Katz, "Weininger and *The Making of Americans*," *Twentieth Century Literature* 24, no. 1 (1978):8–26.
12. Gertrude Stein, "Afterward," in *What Are Masterpieces*, ed. Robert Bartlett Haas (New York: Pitman Publishing Corp., 1970), p. 99.
13. Ibid., p. 100.
14. Gertrude Stein, *Tender Buttons* (1914; reprint ed., New York: Haskell House Publishers, 1970), p. 78.
15. Gertrude Stein, "Ida," in *Gertrude Stein: Writings and Lectures 1909–1945*, ed. Patricia Meyerowitz (1941; reprint ed., Baltimore: Penguin, 1971), p. 388.
16. Gertrude Stein, *Mrs. Reynolds* (1952; reprint ed., Freeport, N.Y.: Books for Libraries Press, 1969), p. 267.
17. Culler, *Structuralist Poetics*, p. 190.
18. Gertrude Stein, "The Mother of Us All," in *Selected Operas and Plays of Gertrude Stein*, ed. John Malcolm Brinnin (1947; reprint ed., n.p.: University of Pittsburgh Press, 1970), p. 202.

# Mary A. McCay

## Fitzgerald's Women: Beyond Winter Dreams

Isabelle, Rosalind, Daisy, Nicole, Rosemary, Marcia, Josephine—their names run like a litany of beauty through the pages of F. Scott Fitzgerald's novels and short stories. Their lips dare kisses, and their ever-slim bodies promise pleasure. Yet there is, in Fitzgerald's characterization of them, an explicit criticism of their values, their way of life—not just of their wealth or their seductive games, but finally of what they think is important. Clearly this criticism is also implicit in Fitzgerald's treatment of his protagonists: Amory Blaine, Anthony Patch, Jay Gatsby, Dick Diver, and the various heroes who people the short stories. But the criticism of the women is different. There is about the men a sense, perhaps, of failed Romanticism, of misplaced dreams and ideals of struggling mightily for the wrong goal—or perhaps for the wrong woman. Towards his women, Fitzgerald has a highly critical attitude that often leaves them stripped to a core that is finally lacking in enduring values. He is harder on them then he is on his men. He judges them more severely— as if he secretly expected more of them at the outset but put them in a world that allowed them no theater for growth. They are stunted from the start by Fitzgerald's expectations on the one hand and by the world they live in on the other.

That world was early twentieth-century America, a world whose rich young men were jaded by war and by surfeit and whose women had very few channels to express themselves creatively. Perhaps that is why Zelda Fitzgerald went mad. There was no room for a woman's creative energy in the world of American men. She could watch them, envy them, but never emulate them. That world was not entirely of Fitzgerald's fictional making— he was as much a chronicler and a critic of the world in which he lived as he was an outsider longing for entrance into the palatial homes of America's wealthy. But Judith Fetterley isn't entirely wrong in faulting Fitzgerald for accepting too much of the myth of the American quest for wealth and status. Fitzgerald also does, at times, simply use women characters as objects of Romantic quest, as Fetterley asserts, as grails sought after by disadvantaged outsiders who are in search of the secret of affluent America.[1] However, Fetterley's evaluation is not complete because Fitzgerald's fiction, at its best, runs deeper than she describes. His women are seldom as passive as Fetterley implies, nor are they static seduction figures simply luring men to destruction.

Fetterley's criticism in her chapter on Fitzgerald in *The Resisting Reader* argues that Nick Carraway plucks Daisy Buchanan's petals until "there is nothing left but a denuded center."[2] This implies that Daisy and other Fitzgerald women have no function of their own but rather are objects either of quest or criticism. The evaluation certainly oversimplifies Fitzgerald's attempt to show that the emptiness of many women's lives, Daisy's included, leaves them with a nervous pointless energy that can only be destructive to themselves and others. They are not passive, their energy is abundant but unfortunately misdirected. Fetterley's criticism also denies Fitzgerald's honest attempt to find and maintain an enduring creative relationship with a woman in a world that was largely based on sham.

Fitzgerald himself was often seduced by the sham world of the rich—a world that alternately pampered and excluded him. It was a world that would not allow him entry until his first book was successful; and for Fitzgerald that exclusion was symbolized by Zelda Sayre's original refusal to marry him because he did not make enough money. He never forgot that insult, and it recurs again and again in his work. Nor did he ever forget that Zelda herself failed his expectations. His letters to her show a consistent strain of criticism of her empty values and her wasted life.

If Fitzgerald was often excessively critical of Zelda, he also used her experience and her ideas. Nancy Milford's careful study, *Zelda*, documents how Fitzgerald achieved much of his material at her expense. Sheila Graham's book, *The Real F. Scott Fitzgerald*, also reveals how Fitzgerald used Graham's experience and her imagination as a source for *The Last Tycoon*. How he used those women and their experience is the key to what Fitzgerald is saying about women. His quest is not, as Fetterley asserts, one for a romantic ideal, a grail quest for the unattainable, but rather a constant struggle to reconcile a world part of him felt should exist with a world he saw around him and for which another part of him longed.

The first world was the world of work—one he had seen in his mother's struggle to give her son the best. That struggle often embarrassed the young Fitzgerald—certainly his mother's dress and manners mortified him—but the older Fitzgerald, when he had a child of his own, recognized his mother's legacy. She had saved him from the South, his father's world, a world of passive attenuated creatures who could not exist outside the hothouse of their own environment—creatures who, as he began to see in Zelda, needed special soil to survive. His mother's legacy of struggle and work was the one he wanted to pass on to his own daughter and the one he more and more came to use as a standard for his women characters.

The other world was not so easily dismissed, however; and it is the one most Fitzgerald critics see when they evaluate him. It is the world of the fabulously wealthy, the irresponsible, the people who have little or no responsibility for their actions. It is the world of Nicole Diver, of Daisy and Tom Buchanan, of people whose money protects them from reality but also blinds them to it.

If one sees Fitzgerald only in terms of the selfish rich women—often modeled after Zelda—then one understands only half of the novelist. Certainly, enough has been done to show the relationship between his marriage to the wealthy Zelda Sayre and his work as a novelist of the wealthy. It is the other half, the working half, that should be given more attention because that side lets us see more clearly the reality of the Fitzgerald who, as the glitter paled from the women and the wealth of the rich, turned to hard work and struggle to survive.

To understand Fitzgerald's growing awareness of the world of work and to examine the characters in the light of that attitude, it is helpful to see his fictional women in the light of two important relationships in the novelist's own life. This, of course, excludes his relationship with Zelda which influenced his view of the world of the wealthy. That influence was, in many ways, negative as far as Fitzgerald's female characters are concerned. The two other women came to show the novelist ways of delineating female characters who represented the world of work and who were not destructive. The primary relationship is that with his daughter, Frances Scott Fitzgerald; the other is that with Sheila Graham which blossomed at the end of Fitzgerald's life when he was sick, used up, and on the verge of physical and emotional collapse.

Fitzgerald's letters to his daughter, written between 1933 and his death in 1940, show how closely the father monitored, criticized, and tried to influence the behavior of his child. At times the letters reveal an almost authorial pressure, as if the father were trying to create in the daughter the female character he could be proud of—something he had never achieved in his fiction. The father was especially caustic when he felt the daughter failed to measure up. He set very high standards for her. In one of his earliest letters, he establishes the criterion by which she will be judged: "I want you to be among the best of your race and not waste yourself on trivial aims. To be useful and proud—is that too much to ask?"[3] This standard is such that Scottie must find an objective, a goal, and work for it. When she fails, or is wasteful, or forgets the objective, her father takes her to task. He reminds her in November of 1936:

Now, insofar as your course is concerned, there is no question of
your dropping mathematics and taking the easiest way to go into
Vassar, and being one of the girls fitted for nothing except to reflect
other people without having any particular character of your own.
I want you to take mathematics up to the limit of what the school

offers. I want you to take physics and I want you to take chemistry. I
don't care about your English courses or your French courses at
present. If you don't know two languages and the ways that men
choose to express their thoughts in those languages by this time,
then you don't sound like my daughter. You are an only child, but
that doesn't give you any right to impose on that fact. [*Letters*,
p. 25]

Two things are important about this letter. First, Fitzgerald wants his
daughter to form her own character, not to become like so many women who
people his novels—empty, beautiful shells who must be filled up by men.
Second, he wants her to succeed in precisely those areas in which he failed,
mathematics and science.

He further admonishes her to be rigorous in the pursuit of her goal by
calling attention to the fact: "You are a poor girl, and if you don't like to
think about it just ask me. If you don't make up your mind to being that,
you become one of those terrible girls that don't know whether they are
millionairesses or paupers" (*Letters*, p. 26). He focuses constantly on the fact
that Scottie must prove herself, that she must not pose as a rich debutante.
He warns her: "The girls who were what we called 'speeds' (in our stone-age
slang) at sixteen were reduced to anything they could get at the marrying
time" (*Letters*, p. 28). It is a warning implicit in the criticism of all the
beautiful "speeds" who play with the affections of men in the pages of Fitzgerald's fiction. Her poverty and her father's backbreaking effort to make
enough money to provide her with a good education must act as restraints
on her youthful exuberance and also as spurs for her to work harder.

In 1938 when Scottie was studying for college boards to enter Vassar, she
broke curfew at Ethel Walker's and was asked to leave. Fitzgerald's response
was bitter, and in his wrath, he focused on Zelda's failure which he was afraid
Scottie might inherit. He accused his wife of tarnishing his dream: "She
wanted me to work too much for *her* and not enough for my dream. She
realized too late that work was dignity and the only dignity and tried to
atone for it by working herself, but it was too late and she broke and is
broken forever" (*Letters*, p. 46). Fitzgerald's bitterness against women without purpose finds full expression in the same letter; "I never want to see again
in this world women who were brought up as idlers. And one of my chief
desires in life was to keep you from being that kind of person, one who
brings ruin on themselves [*sic*] and others. . . . I have begun to realize that
you don't [want to reform]. You don't realize that what I am doing here is
the last tired effort of a man who once did something finer and better. There
is not enough energy, call it money, to carry anyone who is a dead weight
and I am angry and resentful in my soul when I feel that I am doing this"
(*Letters*, p. 47).

The focus of that angry diatribe is Scottie's failure to focus on her goal (getting into Vassar) and her refusal to work seriously toward that end. Scottie's behavior is certainly reminiscent of her father's at Princeton, but more significantly, it recalls Amory Blaine's in *This Side of Paradise*. He fails math and loses his position in the class. His life suddenly lacks purpose, and he loses touch with the goal he once entertained of being the president of the *Princetonian*. His life has lost its focus:

> What Amory did that year from early September to late in the spring was so purposeless and inconsecutive that it seems scarcely worth recording. He was, of course, immediately sorry for what he had lost.[4]

The loss of the goal, the sudden collapse of consequence and focus to his days make Amory's life useless. On the heels of this failure, Amory's father dies, and the young man is forced to reconsider his position. He is not nearly as wealthy as he thought he was. The European trips with Beatrice, the speculative failures of his father, and finally his mother's illness, all have depleted the once magnificent estate. Amory will have to work. It is this one fact that saves him from the parade of women he encounters whose empty lives would only destroy him. Isabelle, a "speed," tempts him, but her perception of the situation is limited by the narrowness of her own vision: "The future vista of her life seemed an unending succession of scenes like this: under the moonlight and pale starlight, and in the backs of warm limousines and in low, cosy roadsters stopping under sheltering trees—only the boy might change" (*TSP*, pp. 69-70).

Rosalind comes next, beautiful, empty, tempting. She turns down Amory's marriage proposal even though she claims to love him because he will have to work for a living and she wants to live a rich, carefree life. Perhaps her refusal is the best thing that happens to Amory in the novel. He is spared the consequences of his infatuation and will survive to become a person. Rosalind would certainly have destroyed any purpose he found in life.

Looking back on Fitzgerald's first novel in the light of his letters to his daughter when she was reaching the age of Isabelle, Rosalind, and Eleanor clarifies how truly contemptuous he was of useless women and focuses on what he feared about Scottie—her flings as a "wild society girl" (*Letters*, p. 48). He reminds her constantly to focus her goals: "Every girl your age in America will have the experience of working for a living. To shut your eyes to that is like living in a dream—to say 'I will do valuable and indispensable work' is the part of wisdom and courage" (*Letters*, p. 51).

That he wanted Scottie not to become simply an idler and that he found women idlers contemptible is clear in his consistent treatment of them throughout his work. The list of idle women is long: Judy Jones of "Winter

Dreams," whose pointless life eventually deprives her of her beauty; Gloria, who lives a purposeless, hedonistic existence in *The Beautiful and Damned*; and finally Gretchen of "Gretchen's Forty Winks." This story comically illustrates the importance for Fitzgerald of giving one's life meaning, of striving for a goal. Once again, it is the man who has the vision and the woman who would distract him. Gretchen and her friend, George Tompkins, try to drag Roger, Gretchen's husband, away from the pursuit of his dream, but he persists, finally drugging Gretchen so that he can finish his assignment. When Roger has won his contract, Gretchen awakes to find that her friend George, the idler, has had a nervous breakdown. Gretchen is ordered back to bed by the doctor because "'she's been under some strain,'"[5] and Roger is pronounced sane and healthy. His work has kept him fit.

Workers survive the rigors of life, whereas idlers and "speeds" succumb just as Zelda did. Eleanor in *This Side of Paradise* clearly repulses Amory with her mad behavior. She is a wild, reckless girl who has frightened Baltimore mothers with her shocking escapades. Fitzgerald finds that combination of recklessness and madness especially repugnant. Eleanor is "the last time that evil crept close to Amory under the mask of beauty" (*TSP*, p. 222). Her evil, as Amory comes to learn, is that she is weak. Her beauty had "too many associations with license and indulgence. Weak things were often beautiful, weak things were never good" (*TSP*, p. 280).

Fitzgerald, toward the end of his life, when Scottie was reaching maturity, wanted more than anything else for his daughter "to live more fully and richly than the majority of pretty girls whose lives in America are lop-sided, backward-looking, and wasteful" (*Letters*, p. 62). His daughter must be more than the empty heroines of his novels, or his most important message has been lost. The difference of course was that Fitzgerald offered Scottie something that he never allowed his women characters—an education and a chance to find her own metier.

Weakness masking itself as beauty and drawing brave young men to wreck like sirens—those women are Fitzgerald's true tormentors. They become clearly defined characters in *The Great Gatsby* and *Tender Is the Night*, but the figure is also there in Gloria of *The Beautiful and Damned*. She is a woman whose beauty hides her essential weakness; once her beauty is gone, she sinks, like Anthony, into a kind of mental and moral decay. Deprived of Old Patch's money, there is really nothing to live for.

Fitzgerald's next novel, his most critically successful, *The Great Gatsby*, is pervaded by a sense of lack of purpose. Nick, the narrator, a man with Fitzgerald's work values, watches as the waste of life consumes even the most purposeful—Gatsby himself. The hero comes to West Egg in the hope of claiming Daisy Buchanan—both the reason and the prize for his colossal efforts.

When Nick first meets Daisy on East Egg, her vague purposelessness is apparent. In a conversation with Jordan Baker who claims "'we ought to plan something,'" Daisy replies, "'All right . . . what'll we plan . . . what do people plan?'"6 Their pointlessness is further accentuated by Nick's sense of purpose. He reminds the reader that the events of the novel were "merely casual events in a crowded summer. . . . Most of the time I worked" (*GG* p. 56). Nick is, indeed, practically the only character in the novel who does work; and he is further separated from the aimless lives of the others by being, as he says himself, "one of the few honest people I have ever known" (*GG*, p. 60). His work and his honesty give him a perspective about the lives of the very rich. He judges them all and finds them all, except Gatsby, wanting. "They were careless people. . . . They smashed things up and then retreated back into their money or their vast carelessness, or whatever it was that kept them together and let other people clean up the mess they made" (*GG*, pp. 180–81).

Of course, Gatsby is spared that condemnation precisely because he has worked for his money. He has made money so that he could attain a colossal dream. He is truly Franklinesque in his goals, his schedule and his general resolves.

Contrasted to Gatsby, all the other characters pale. More importantly Daisy, the focus of his dream, pales. She cannot withstand the intensity of Gatsby's vision. She tries to modify it, to dampen the fire of his love by telling him: "'Oh you want too much! . . . I love you now, isn't that enough . . . I did love him once—but I loved you too'" (*GG*, p. 133). To her, the love of Gatsby is no different from the sordid love of her husband Tom, who shares his affection for her with various other women. Neither Buchanan can understand Gatsby's vision, nor can they, with all their money, create one for themselves. They can only destroy.

Finally, Daisy completely compromises any feeling she had for Gatsby by letting him take the blame for Myrtle Wilson's death. Daisy has, in fact, killed Tom's mistress, and yet she will allow everyone to believe it is Gatsby. She hides once again behind her money. Her life will simply be a constant repetition of Tom's affairs and her own unhappiness. She has neither the strength nor the courage to change her position. She is trapped in her need for money and comfort and in her failure to make something of her life. She could have done that with Gatsby.

Throughout the novel, Nick emphasizes this lack of definition among the women characters. He sees them as creatures blurred by the pointless round of parties and vacuous relationships. Myrtle's sister, Catherine, has "a blurred air to her face" (*GG*, p. 30); and all the women at Gatsby's parties look alike. There is even a set of twins to add to the sameness. One young man, Benny McClenahan, always attends Gatsby's parties with four girls: "They were never quite the same ones in physical person, but they were so identical one with another that it inevitably seemed they had been there before" (*GG*, p. 63).

When writing *Gatsby*, Fitzgerald focused on the "unfairness of a poor young man not being able to marry a girl with money."[7] Yet the girl with money is herself a trap. She will drag the hard-working young man away from his dream as Fitzgerald claimed Zelda dragged him so often away from his writing into pointless traveling, partying, and finally debauchery. Fitzgerald holds the woman responsible: Daisy for failing to live up to Gatsby's vision; Jordan Baker for failing Nick Carraway's test of virtue; Judy Jones for her pointless marriage, and for her loss of beauty destroying Dexter Green's winter dreams. The women live meaningless lives and have no reason to exist except that they are very rich. They are, like Mrs. Harold Piper of "The Cut Glass Bowl," a curse to those whose lives they touch.

In this short story, Fitzgerald carefully examines the effects of an empty life. His female protagonist, Evylyn Piper, turned down young Carleton Canby in 1892 in order to marry Harold Piper, whose prospects were better. At that time, Carleton gave Evylyn a wedding present which he said described her perfectly: he gave her a cut-glass bowl "that's as hard as you are and as beautiful and as empty and as easy to see through."[8] Throughout the story, the bowl haunts Mrs. Harold Piper. It figures in the reversal of her husband's fortunes and in the mutilation of her daughter, and it bears the tidings of her son's death. Evylyn cannot escape the connection. Her beauty and her emptiness have destroyed her home and family. Finally she loses even her beauty; and, when she tries to destroy the bowl, it takes her with it. Her life and the lives of her husband and children have been ruined by her emptiness. She has nothing to give. Nor can she finally deny that the bowl reflects her true personality.

The most keenly wrought analysis of the woman whose empty life destroys another is *Tender Is the Night*, written when Fitzgerald himself was undergoing the same debauch that precipitates Dick Diver's decline from eminent psychiatrist to wandering practitioner. The cause of his decline is, in Fitzgerald's eyes, Nicole—beautiful, rich, sick Nicole—whose illness becomes a challenge to the young psychiatrist who would make the beautiful shattered girl whole again. However, in focusing all his energies on her, in keeping her afloat, he himself loses touch with his early goals, and finally, his life becomes as empty as hers. He cannot stand the emptiness, the aimlessness, of the very rich—it destroys him. Nicole herself has been destroyed by that wealth and by her own beauty, a beauty that tempted her own father to ravish her. She is, as Dick first describes her, a "beautiful shell," and the young doctor puts all the energy and imagination he should be devoting to his own work into remaking her. She is, indeed, a product of his sweat.

More than being just a creation of her husband, Nicole is also the weak beauty who selfishly drains him of his energy. She "thought of him really as an inexhaustible energy, incapable of fatigue—she forgot the trouble she caused him at the moment when she forgot the troubles of her own."[9] When she comes to him during his own crisis, he lashes out against her irresponsible use of him: "I can't do anything more for you," he says, "I'm trying to save myself" (*TN*, p. 301). Nicole can no longer lean on Dick; she fights to free herself, to transfer her needs to another man. "She fought him [Dick] with her money and her faith that her sister disliked him and was behind her now; with the thought of new enemies he was making with his bitterness, and her quick guile against his wining and dining slowness, her health [gained at his expense] and beauty against his physical deterioration, her unscrupulousness against his moralities . . . and suddenly she achieved her victory" (*TN*, pp. 301-2).

After the confrontation, Dick "leaned his head forward on the parapet. The case was finished. Doctor Diver was at liberty" (*TN*, p. 301). At last he is free of Nicole, the woman he has married out of his own need to be near the very rich and the very beautiful. She is also, he learns, the woman who has tainted his goals and undermined his resolves. He should have left the battle when he first learned that Baby Warren wants to buy Nicole a doctor. He saw immediately that Baby was flawed: "there was something wooden and onanistic about her"; . . . she is, finally, "a trivial, selfish woman" (*TN*, pp. 152, 179). He should have seen that Nicole could not escape that. But he plunges ahead, like Gatsby, with a sort of romantic readiness, so he, like Gatsby, cannot be condemned. Nicole, however, can be and is.

Fitzgerald is, perhaps, more severely critical of Nicole than he is of any of his other women characters because her family uses its money to buy Dick for her and because she, knowing his resolve to live only on his own salary, convinces him to use her wealth for the family's comfort. Her most egregious error is that she, "wanting to own him, wanting him to stand still forever, encouraged any slackness on his part, and in multiplying ways he was constantly inundated by a trickling of goods and money" (*TN*, p. 170). Dick has no defense in his career, because Nicole's "income had increased so fast of late that it seemed to belittle his work" (*TN*, p. 170).

Finally, Dick's only salvation is to return to America without Nicole, to hide out in "one town or another." He doesn't answer when Nicole writes "asking him if he needed money" (*TN*, p. 315). Dick escapes Warren money and Warren corruption, but at the cost of his own dream—he will never finish his important medical treatise.

There is more hostility underlying *Tender Is the Night* than there is in any other work. Fitzgerald recognized its flaws, flaws produced by his own emotional state and by the tension between himself and Zelda. He wrote several letters to his editor, Maxwell Perkins, claiming that he was writing a novel called *The Boy Who Killed His Mother*.[10] The central idea is explicit in the title, and that hostility was carried over into *Tender Is the Night* in Fitzgerald's critique of women. The gold star mothers might represent a nobler age, but they also sent their sons out to get killed, just as the frontier mothers lied about the wolves at the door. Mrs. Speers uses the Divers to give her daughter Rosemary experience, but she fails to take the Divers into account. Women throughout the novel use men and then pass on to others. They are like the Amazons who could never "grasp the fact that a man is vulnerable only in his pride, but delicate as Humpty-Dumpty once that is meddled with" (*TN*, p. 177).

If Nicole represents for Fitzgerald the weakness inbred in the very rich who have no need to work, there is another character who, to a small extent, illustrates his attempt to create a woman who has goals and who takes control of her own destiny. Although he is not altogether successful in his characterization of Rosemary Hoyt, the budding young Hollywood success, she does work. Her work gives her definition and it gives her power. Dick is attracted to Rosemary because "she had been brought up to work" (*TN*, p. 40). Her mother, twice widowed, has ingrained in her the necessity of finding a goal and working toward it. When Mrs. Speers realizes that her daughter is infatuated with Dick Diver, she encourages her to pursue him: "You were brought up to work—not especially to marry. . . . Go ahead and put whatever happens down to experience. Wound yourself or him—whatever happens it can't spoil you because economically you're a boy not a girl" (*TN*, p. 40). Although there is much in Mrs. Speers's attitude to be criticized, Fitzgerald has given Rosemary the very tool she needs to pursue her own goals: she can be independent precisely because she earns her own money. Her freedom renews Dick's disgust with living on Nicole's wealth. It is Rosemary's arrival on the French Riviera that precipitates the change in Dick's attitude toward his bondage. The young actress has the hard fresh idealism that the doctor once possessed.

Rosemary's promise, the promise of the young who can succeed, is fulfilled for Fitzgerald in his daughter, Scottie. His last letters to her, rather than focusing on her failures, reveal real paternal pride. Scottie is beginning to succeed. His daughter, as he did at Princeton twenty years before, has written a musical and actually formed a club very much like Princeton's Triangle Club. Fitzgerald's daughter is working, writing, and succeeding— Fitzgerald praises her for her spunk. He fears, however, that she, like himself, might become too deeply involved and repeat his scholastic failure: ". . . to see a mistake repeated twice in two generations would be just too much to bear," he tells her (*Letters*, p. 86).

As much as his letter to Scottie warns caution, the extent of his admiration for his daughter is revealed in a letter he wrote to Zelda in March 1940.

There is, in this letter to his wife, not just praise of the hard-working daughter, but also explicit criticism of the wife who used up other people—as Nicole did in *Tender Is the Night*. He writes:

> I don't think that you fully realize the extent of what Scottie has done at Vassar. You wrote rather casually of two years being enough, but it isn't. Her promise is unusual. Not only did she rise to the occasion and get in young but she has raised herself from a poor scholar to a very passable one; sold a professional story at eighteen; and moreover in very highbrow, at present very politically minded Vassar she has introduced with some struggle a new note. She has written and produced a musical comedy and founded a club called the Omgim to perpetuate the idea." [*Letters*, pp. 141-42]

Contrasted to Scottie's achievement secured by hard work and the definition of goals is Zelda's failure. She has taken up more "working hours than one human being deserves of another" (*Letters*, p. 131). This statement Fitzgerald makes in reference to Zelda's dependence on her doctor. Certainly it is reminiscent of the writer's condemnation of Nicole. They are both beautiful, weak, dependent women.

Fitzgerald finally condemns Zelda while praising Scottie for having achieved those goals which he thinks important. "I think now you will always be a worker, and I'm glad. Your mother's utterly endless brooding over insolubles paved the way to her ruin. She had no education—not from lack of opportunity because she could have learned with me—but from some inner stubbornness" (*Letters*, p. 95).

The woman who works, the child who lives up to the expectations of the father and fulfills his long neglected dreams—that is the woman Scott Fitzgerald can love. The others, weak, beautiful temptresses, must be put aside. Although he never successfully purged himself of Zelda, he did find, in the last three years of his life, a woman who had her own dreams and her own work and who could love him without destroying him. That woman was Sheila Graham, the model for Kathleen in the unfinished novel *The Last Tycoon*. This last work shows the influence that the success of his daughter and the love of Sheila Graham had on his attitude towards women and on his writing.

The novel uses a female narrator, Cecilia Brady, home to Hollywood from Bennington College for the summer. She is the daughter of Pat Brady, a Hollywood producer and bitter enemy of the man Cecilia loves, Monroe Stahr. Cecilia becomes, like Nick Carraway before her, the moral focus of the book. Fitzgerald said in one of his notes on the book that he was writing it for Scottie, whose moral vision had, he perceived, grown over the last few years.[11]

Cecilia is in love with Stahr. She, like many others in Hollywood, is attracted to that part of the man that makes him different from most other producers. He had protected his studio people from the vicissitudes of Hollywood. "Through the beginning and the great upset, when sound came, and the three years of depression he had seen that no harm had come to them."[12]

As Cecilia's enchantment with Stahr grows, she becomes more and more critical of her father. She observes, on seeing Brady on a New York street when she didn't expect to, "I was aware of a bulky, middle aged man who looked a little ashamed of himself" (*LT*, p. 22). He was a man whose "strong will didn't fill him out as a passable man" (*LT*, p. 28). These remarks become moral judgments in the light of Brady's plots against Stahr. Cecilia's father represents Hollywood's underlying corruption of which Cecilia becomes increasingly aware. Stahr alone seems devoid of pretensions and of corruption. He rises above the clawing competition to give generously of himself to his people. He saves the job of a cameraman who has been put out of work by vicious rumors that he is going blind. Cecilia observes all of this and comes to see Stahr much as Nick Carraway sees Gatsby—"worth the whole damn bunch put together" (*GG*, p. 154).

Just as Fitzgerald is able to create in Cecilia a perceptive female narrator who is "of the movies, but not in them,"[13] he also, in his last effort, creates what he himself termed the "most glamorous and sympathetic of my heroines" (*Correspondence*, p. 547). *Sympathetic* is indeed the key word with which to describe Kathleen. Fitzgerald saw her as someone who could save the dying Stahr just as he saw Sheila Graham as someone who had the power to save him. In what precisely did this power rest? For both women it lay in the fact that they are *sui generis*—like Gatsby, they create themselves, then offer their love to others. The story of Kathleen's background in the novel is taken directly from the story Sheila Graham told Fitzgerald. She created a past to hide her poverty.

Graham's father died when she was an infant, and she grew up in a small basement apartment which her mother shared with a woman who took in washing. She was sent to an orphanage when she was six, only to return home at fourteen to care for her dying mother. In order to hide this reality, Graham created a world of Parisian finishing schools, presentations at court, and fabulously wealthy suitors (the last was a fact). Fitzgerald was fascinated by this imaginative, ambitious girl who always paid her own way. He saw in Graham's story the makings of a romantic imagination. She was intent on creating a future to fit the glorious past.

It is a tribute to Graham that Fitzgerald gave Kathleen a past as romantic as Graham's story. His heroine is mysterious—appearing during a flood at the studio floating on top of "the huge head of the Goddess Siva" (*LT*, p. 25). She is also like a vision out of the past: "not four feet away was the face of his [Stahr's] dead wife, identical even to the expression" (*LT*, p. 26). Sheila

Graham commented that, although she was not aware of it at first, her looks reminded Scott of Zelda.[14]

Fitzgerald, in creating Kathleen as a parallel of Sheila, praised Graham's strength, courage, and her romantic possibilities. She fascinated Fitzgerald because she was a woman who had the qualities of his best heroes. She gave him a model for a female character who could revitalize his fiction. In his notes on the character of Kathleen, he draws heavily on Graham's experience and on her vitality. Stahr "has an overwhelming urge towards the girl who promises to give life back to him. . . . She is the heart of hope and freshness" (*LT*, pp. 151-52). Unlike earlier heroines who are parasites on the dreams of men, Kathleen has a life of her own. She is independent, and that draws Stahr to her: "It was very seldom he met anyone whose life did not depend in some way on him or hope to depend on him" (*LT*, p. 152). Because of her vitality, Kathleen can save Stahr if he will let her: "'This is your chance, Stahr,'" he tells himself. "'Better take it now. This is your girl. She can save you, she can worry you back to life'" (*LT*, p. 115).

So the characters of Cecilia and Kathleen are inextricably intertwined with his daughter and his lover. Fitzgerald's need at the end of his life to find vitality that could give him life, to find purpose that could give him heart, drew him to Scottie who was fulfilling a promise he felt he never kept, and to Sheila Graham who had the drive, the power, and the vitality Zelda (and perhaps he himself) always lacked. In his growing awareness of their strengths, he found a source for fictional women he could respect.

## Notes

1. Judith Fetterley, *The Resisting Reader: A Feminist Approach to American Fiction* (Bloomington: Indiana University Press, 1978), p. 77.

2. Ibid., p. 85.

3. Andrew Turnbull, ed., *The Letters of F. Scott Fitzgerald* (New York: Dell Publishing Co., 1966), p. 21. All references to Fitzgerald's letters to his daughter are from this edition and are cited in the text as *Letters*.

4. F. Scott Fitzgerald, *This Side of Paradise* (New York: Charles Scribner's Sons, 1960), p. 98. All further references to *This Side of Paradise* are cited in the text as *TSP*.

5. F. Scott Fitzgerald, *Six Tales of the Jazz Age and Other Stories* (New York: Charles Scribner's Sons, 1960). Other stories in this collection are referred to in the text as *Six Tales*.

6. F. Scott Fitzgerald, *The Great Gatsby* (New York: Charles Scribner's Sons, 1953), p. 12. All further references to *The Great Gatsby* are cited in the text as *GG*.

7. Andrew Turnbull, *Scott Fitzgerald* (New York: Charles Scribner's Sons, 1962), p. 150.

8. F. Scott Fitzgerald, *Flappers and Philosophers* (New York: Charles Scribner's Sons, 1948), p. 97.

9. F. Scott Fitzgerald, *Tender Is the Night* (New York: Charles Scribner's Sons, 1962), p. 301. All further references to *Tender Is the Night* are cited in the text as *TN*.

10. Henry Dan Piper, *F. Scott Fitzgerald, a Critical Portrait* (New York: Holt, Rinehart & Winston, 1965), Ch. 10.

11. Ibid., p. 279.

12. F. Scott Fitzgerald, *The Last Tycoon* (New York: Charles Scribner's Sons, 1970), p. 27. All further references to *The Last Tycoon* are cited in the text as *LT*.

13. Matthew Bruccoli and Margaret N. Duggan, eds., *Correspondence of F. Scott Fitzgerald* (New York: Random House, 1980), p. 546. All further references to letters in this collection are cited in the text as *Correspondence*.

14. Sheila Graham, *The Real F. Scott Fitzgerald Thirty-Five Years Later* (New York: Grosset & Dunlap, 1976), p. 26.

# Judith Bryant Wittenberg

# William Faulkner:
# A Feminist Consideration

During the past four decades, critics attempting to come to terms with the "images of women" as portrayed in the fiction of William Faulkner have more or less arrayed themselves into two groups, those who see Faulkner's females as stereotypical and thus the author himself as either a misogynist or a gyneolatrist (more often the former) and those who regard those same females as complex and variegated and hence see the author as sympathetic to women, even, in a few rare instances, as a proto-feminist. This polarized situation in a field that shows signs, two decades after Faulkner's death, of approaching consensus on other issues has some intriguing aspects that perhaps reveal as much about critical trends and the critics themselves as they do about Faulkner's fictional women.

Maxwell Geismar was the first to raise the specter of misogyny that haunted Faulkner criticism until correctives began to appear in the late 1960s, deeming "the Female" as one of the "twin Furies" that preside over Yoknapatawpha and calling Faulkner's portraits of women a series of "female incubae."[1] Next came Irving Howe, who cited Faulkner's "inclination toward misogyny" and the "ferocity" of his portraiture of "the young American bitch" as indicating "a major failing as a novelist."[2] Leslie Fiedler, the best-known exponent of this critical view, called Faulkner a "serious calumniator of the female," delineated Faulkner's eight-point indictment against women, and divided his nubile female characters into mindless earth goddesses and bitchy nymphomaniacs.[3] The discussion of Faulkner's misogyny and the pejorative categorization of Faulkner's women informed several subsequent essays, all but one of them written in the 1960s, obviously a not-so-liberal decade in Faulkner criticism.[4] Related to the stereotypers are the archetypers who have seen Faulkner's women as manifestations of the eternal life-giving Earth or as incarnations of the Great Goddess and thus intimated that they regard the author as gyneolatrous rather than misogynistic.[5]

Interestingly, only one of these critics is a woman, and the fact that she is heavily indebted to Geismar and Fiedler for her typology and interpretations raises the issue of such criticism as an exercise at once patriarchal and projective. It has been suggested that Fiedler's categorizing is part of a larger tendency in male critics toward the "biological put-down" of women characters as well as women writers,[6] and the recurrent violation of Faulkner's fictional context by such critics in the pursuit of their misogynistic assessments implies the possibility that such willful misreadings are as often projective as inept, revealing the persistence of such visions in the critics' own psyches. Faulkner himself warned readers on at least two occasions of the dangers of confusing his characters' opinions with his own,[7] yet a number of the misogynist readings do precisely that, accepting the characters who make negative comments as "Faulknerian spokesmen." Another general problem with this critical position is its failure to give equal time to Faulkner's men,[8] or to consider the presence of explanatory or countervailing elements in each work of fiction that serve to qualify many of the superficially negative depictions of women.

A series of critical efforts to countermand the Fiedlerian viewpoint began in the late 1960s, undertaken almost to a person by women, though there are some ironies in that fact, considering that Faulkner's fiction does betray at one level an ambivalent attitude toward females and that he made some overtly bitter or implicitly patronizing comments about the sex in essays and interviews,[9] albeit perhaps on occasion with tongue in cheek. Possibly such female revisionists share a faint masochism in the same way the male critics are united by their unexamined patriarchal assumptions. Nevertheless, all of these essays, which range in stance from the cautious to the enthusiastic and in quality from poor to impressive, are significant for their attempts to subvert the reductivist placing of Faulkner's women in narrow categories and to show the author as far more aware of and sympathetic to the complexity of the female psyche than those who deem him a misogynist or gyneolatrist have allowed.

In one of the first of these corrective pieces, Dolores Brien made a number of points which merit consideration by anyone approaching this topic: that Faulkner's work reveals the devastating effect on both men and women of the myth of spotless southern womanhood, that the women in the novels are usually perceived through the eyes of the male characters, which largely accounts for deficiencies in their individualization, and that one can group Faulkner's male characters according to their attitudes toward women.[10] Two subsequent essays—Elisabeth Muhlenfeld's on *Absalom, Absalom!* and Judith Fetterley's on "A Rose for Emily"[11]—examine thoroughly Faulkner's portrayal in individual works of the way women are constricted or used by males and by the southern social system. Other essays and a book devoted to Faulkner's women have asserted the infinite variety of his depiction of females[12] and thus should inhibit future critical impulses toward negativism and restrictive categorization.

Although generalizing about Faulkner's female characters is not, as Ilse Lind asserts, "fruitless,"[13] it is certainly problematical. Creating any sort of taxonomy, even a complex one, is a transtextual exercise with a number of pitfalls, not least among them the fact that it necessitates a certain distortion of context. Women seemingly alike may play sharply differing roles in their respective narratives, roles qualified by technical elements such as tone and point-of-view, or by Faulkner's having balanced a female "type" with an equivalent male type, or her particular neurosis with a similar one in a male character, thus making it impossible to read any gender-based "message" into the presentation. Moreover, reappearing characters, such as Narcissa Benbow or Eula Varner, may be—or seem to be—quite different in their various fictional manifestations. Another problem is raised by the fact that there is no striking evolutionary pattern in the canon, despite the assertion by Fiedler and Guerard that Faulkner's "rehabilitation" of Temple Drake and Eula Varner in novels of the 1950s reflected a diminishing misogyny;[14] some of Faulkner's feministically most interesting women occur in his fiction of the 1920s and 1930s. Nor is there an artistic correlative, since compelling women characters are found as often in the weak novels as in the great ones.

The extraordinary multivalence of Faulkner's oeuvre as a whole and of each individual work within itself thus makes broad-based assessments hazardous and demands that they be somewhat tentative. One can nevertheless discern some general tendencies in Faulkner's portrayal of women and women-related issues that show him, on the whole, to be neither pro- nor anti-female, but rather an absorbed student of the endlessly variegated human scene.

Faulkner's first two novels, though troubling to the sensitive reader because of their depiction of the first of his series of "mindless cows" and "nubile bitches" and their continual, often pejorative generalizations about women, some by the narrator himself, also evince a number of characteristics that show one cannot simply dismiss them—or any of Faulkner's fictions—as dominated by a negative view of women. *Soldiers' Pay* contains the impressive Margaret Powers, one of Faulkner's most admirable characters—as fine in her way as Dilsey, the Faulknerian female most often invoked as an exemplar of selfless devotion to others, and more thoroughly and complexly depicted and thus more interesting than Dilsey. Margaret selflessly devotes herself to caring for the dying Donald Mahon, even to the point of marrying him, and gladly extends her nurturing to others in need; intelligent and thoughtful, she also serves as a mediator and an instructor, one who manages to change Gilligan's "fixed ideas about women."[15] But Faulkner does not idealize Margaret; he takes us inside her mind to show her struggles with guilt about her dead husband and suggests that she may have serious sexual problems.

In his next novel, *Mosquitoes*, Faulkner portrays two women artists, the poet Eva Wiseman and the painter Dorothy Jameson. Though Faulkner has been criticized for satirizing them,[16] he satirizes everyone in the novel, male or female; moreover, Eva makes a number of valuable contributions to conversations, serving as an intellectual complement to her perceptive brother, Julius.[17] Many of these bright and/or self-sufficient women live in large cities or come from outside the South, implying that, for Faulkner, detachment from the narrow world of a southern small town is necessary for the woman who desires an expanded range of intellectual and vocational options.

Within the restrictive middle-class world of Faulkner's Jefferson, the possibilities for women appear more limited, confined to a choice between spinsterhood or marriage and children, as the comments of Cecily Saunders and Pat Robyn, implicitly members of that middle-class world, and the experiences of the women characters in *Flags in the Dust*, Faulkner's first Yoknapatawpha novel, make clear. The women who evince the serenity of flowers, like Narcissa Benbow (or of cows, like Lena Grove and Eula Varner of later works), are those who accept their narrow options, whereas those who are flirtatious and sexual, like Belle Mitchell and her sister Joan, are at some unspoken level refusing to settle for drab routine and social inhibitions. Faulkner was obviously aware of the effects of a rigidly patriarchal social structure upon its female members. Even though his own status as a product of that structure sometimes led him to imply that it was more admirable to accept than to rebel, his awareness of its oppressiveness was responsible for a number of memorable portraits of women. The papier-mâché virgins and child-women are to be pitied as much as derided, for they have been offered few choices by their society. A number of the women in Faulkner's early fiction call their lovers "papa" and still others remain closely tied to their actual fathers, suggesting that at every level the patriarchy is a powerful force that inhibits their emotional and intellectual development.

Education is not an option for most of the women in Faulkner's fiction. Pat Robyn's dilemma is reminiscent of Maggie Tulliver's: her brother is soon to leave for Yale and she is desperate to go along, though he, like Tom Tulliver, shows little interest in her plight and she herself resignedly concedes, "I guess I'll have to get married and have a bunch of kids."[18] Narcissa Benbow stayed at home while her brother went to Sewanee and then to Oxford, and, although Caddy Compson early showed herself to be the most energetic, curious, and resourceful of the Compson children, it was Quentin who was given the opportunity to go to Harvard. It is hardly surprising that such women frequently become restless and dissatisfied, either finding an outlet in flirtation and promiscuity or internalizing the rigid values that constrict them and turning their hostility on women who seek some form of freedom, even if only a sexual one. Narcissa's cruel treatment of Ruby Lamar in *Sanctuary* is obviously grounded in her inability to come to terms with her own confused longings.

With education rarely available to the women of Faulkner's fictional world, their capacity to be economically self-sufficient is almost nonexistent. Those few who work do so out of economic or emotional exigency, rather than from dedication to an ideal of professional self-fulfillment; because of this and because the range of vocational possibilities is so slight, they usually find little or no satisfaction in their jobs. Very often, because of her economic dependency, a woman's only resource is her body, which she must use as, or exchange for, currency. The women in this category are usually poor whites, such as Ruby Lamar of *Sanctuary*, Everbe Corinthia of *The Reivers*, Mink's wife of *The Hamlet*, Laverne Shumann of *Pylon*, and Dewey Dell Bundren of *As I Lay Dying*, but they may be from the middle class as well—Narcissa Benbow in "There Was a Queen" and Eula Varner Snopes in *The Town* obviously perceive the offer of their bodies as a necessary response to real or figurative blackmail.

A woman's major and virtually only route to social status and/or economic security is marriage, a fact reflected in the desperate maneuvers of Sophonsiba Beauchamp and her brother Hubert in "Was." But here, too, as the hunting and cardplaying metaphors of "Was" suggest, she may be without choice, a mere pawn in a male exchange system similar to that of primitive societies, as Mrs. Maurier of *Mosquitoes*, Ellen Coldfield of *Absalom, Absalom!* and Eula Varner of *The Hamlet* all discover, and even then she may be asked, like Rosa Coldfield, for proof of her ability to perpetuate the male line before receiving her legal "reward." Once married, a woman can demonstrate her energies and talents by able housewifery, like that of Mrs. Varner in *The Hamlet*, or by competent clubwork, like that of Maggie Mallison of *The Town*, though she is equally likely to become a drab "grey wife."

Many of Faulkner's women, however, even the ones ostensibly most confined by the social system, experience a sort of "liberation" in the crucible of war or severe personal crisis which prompts the discovery and display of qualities of strength, resourcefulness, independence, and even tragic grandeur. Two old ladies, Rosa Millard of *The Unvanquished* and Miss Habersham of *Intruder in the Dust*, nurtured under the code of protective gallantry toward "ladies," not only show impressive courage but manage to turn the code upon itself, exploiting it in unexpected ways. Some of the women, like Drusilla Hawk of *The Unvanquished* or Linda Kohl of *The Mansion*, go bravely off to war themselves, proving their worth as fighting participants, though they pay a superficial price—the loss of outward traces of their femininity—and a deeper one—the espousal of a masculine code of violence to the point where they are willing to be implicated in peacetime killings. Other women remain at home during wartime, showing quiet endurance rather than active heroism, learning "masculine" skills and operating family enterprises. Still others are tested by domestic crises and emerge as in some respects admirable, even heroic, figures. In *The Town*, Eula Snopes chooses death rather than elopement with the man she has loved for nearly two decades "in order to leave her child a mere suicide for a mother instead of a whore;"[19] in *Pylon*, after the violent death of her husband, Laverne Shumann gives up her son to his grandparents in order that he have a more stable life; and in *The Wild Palms*, the dying Charlotte Rittenmeyer, recognizing perhaps that she has been wounded as much by her own flawed idealism as by Harry's blundering knife, pleads for his exculpation and succeeds in converting him to her passionate faith in undying love.

If Faulkner was an acute social analyst who understood the plight women (and men) are placed in by the restrictive values of a patriarchal society, he was also, despite his professed ignorance of Freudian psychology, an embryonic psychoanalyst, bringing to and displaying in his fiction a rich awareness of the complex functioning of the human psyche according to many of the principles enunciated by Freud. Of course many feminists have repudiated Freud as a Victorian male chauvinist, but if one accepts Juliet Mitchell's more tempered view of Freud as descriptive rather than prescriptive,[20] then Faulkner's use of psychoanalytical insights, particularly as they affect his portraiture and his male characters' view of women, can be viewed as impressive. At least three psychoanalytical precepts are relevant to a feminist assessment of Faulkner's work: the idea that any individual has the potential to contain traits of both sexes, the belief that a person's character is largely formed by his or her early experiences and family relationships, and the concept of projection, of one's "reality" as created out of one's own desires and fears.

Faulkner's fiction reveals throughout his sensitive perceptions of what one critic calls "the infinite shadings of the masculine and feminine in human beings."[21] From his very first novel, Faulkner shows the way biological gender is modified by emotional ambiguity and portrays a whole array of men with traits traditionally regarded as feminine and women with essentially masculine qualities. Although in some cases these opposite-sex traits undermine the character's attractiveness, in still other cases they increase it, so that one cannot make any sort of consistent value judgment about Faulkner's presentation. In *Soldiers' Pay*, for example, though Januarius Jones's effeminate appearance and Cecily Saunders's phallic legs are emblems of their larger distortions, Joe Gilligan's "feminine" intuition and maternalism are positive qualities, as is Margaret Powers's ability to be "one of the boys"—to an extent that almost prompts Joe to call her a "fellow."[22] In virtually every one of Faulkner's subsequent novels, one can find characters who contain traits of the opposite sex, usually one of each gender. In *Mosquitoes*, there is the effete Mr. Talliaferro and the masculine Mrs. Wiseman, the boyish Pat and her brother with a "feminine" jaw.[23] In *Flags in the Dust* and *Sanctuary*, Horace Benbow often seems more helplessly female than the women, especially the predatory Joan and the somewhat mannish Ruby. As a child, Caddy Compson shows a "manly" courage and audacity and wishes to be a king or general, and Quentin's feminine timidity renders him ineffectual, traits similar to those evinced by another young sister and brother, Judith and Henry Sutpen, during the scene in which they watch the naked blacks wrestle. The intuitiveness of Darl Bundren seems as feminine as his mother's harsh philosophizing is "masculine." In *The Wild Palms*, the plump convict appears womanly, and Charlotte looks mannish, her aggressiveness contrasting with Harry's passivity, a trait usually regarded as feminine.

Related to Faulkner's balancing of "masculinized" women with "feminized" men in individual works is his recurrent portrayal of pairs of men and women with similar psychological profiles, so that the reader's tendency to make judgments linked to one sex is controverted. In *Soldiers' Pay*, Margaret Powers and Joe Gilligan are both selfless nurturers, Cecily Saunders and Januarius Jones are both selfish flirts, and the young Emmy and Donald were both children of nature; in *Mosquitoes*, Mrs. Maurier and Mr. Talliaferro are alike in aging pathetically and spending time as the spiritual parasites of creative people; Horace and Narcissa Benbow of *Flags in the Dust* are similar in their ambivalent fascination-disgust with sexuality; both Mrs. Compson and her son Jason are selfish, immature, and paranoiac. In *Light in August*, Lena Grove and Joe Christmas are both products of an exploited childhood now restlessly on the move and aggressive in different ways; Joe can also be linked with Joanna as outlanders suffering from confused sexual self-images.

Also extensively employed by Faulkner is the psychoanalytical tenet that human beings are shaped in crucial ways by the experiences and relationships of their early years; thus even evil creatures have themselves been victimized at earlier stages and should elicit pity along with condemnation. Though Faulkner doesn't always provide complete data of this sort, he usually offers at least a modicum from which inferences may be drawn. This has feminist implications for all of the women characters usually singled out by critics as proof of Faulkner's "misogyny," most particularly for Temple Drake, who has been called a "Venus flytrap,"[24] a "death Goddess,"[25] a "violator,"[26] and a "trembling, sexless, ferocious bitch."[27] Of course Faulkner himself said that "no person is wholly good or wholly bad,"[28] a view that implies that a sympathetically psychoanalytical reading is as appropriate as one that is judgmentally moral, especially in the case of Faulkner's villainous women (and men—but many of these have already been the subjects of sympathetic criticism). Admittedly, Temple Drake is a destructive young woman, responsible directly or indirectly for the deaths of two men and perhaps for the "suicide" of Popeye, but it is important also to see her as a victim not only of rape, but also of her family and of the society of which she is a product. Faulkner tells us little about her family, other than the fact that it consists of a father and four brothers, but we can infer some of the difficulties she has had and continues to have with male figures. Her father is a judge—a towering symbol of the Code—and certainly Temple's confused attitudes toward both her patriarchal family and the patriarchal society are responsible for much of her destructive behavior.

Throughout the novel, Temple is alternately restricted and betrayed by her father and father surrogates. She has obviously received inadequate guidance, for she shows no sense of purpose and has a promiscuous streak that reveals a need to rebel against the forces trying to make her into a "lady." When we first see Temple, she is surrounded by a group of watching, taunting men who represent the voyeuristic, lustful members of the larger male world. When Gowan Stevens drunkenly crashes his car, she receives her first physical wound at the hand of a man, which is followed by a series of others, both physical and spiritual: the invocation of male categories for women, under which Popeye calls her a "whore" and Ruby labels her a "cheap sport," the spying on her by virtually all the members of the Old Frenchman group, Gowan's outright abandonment of her, her rape by Popeye, and her long imprisonment at the brothel in Memphis. This confusing mixture of restriction and betrayal is perhaps a continuation of familial patterns—her father "covers for her" in the newspaper but makes no determined effort to find and rescue her—and it certainly leaves her alternately rebellious and concilia-tory toward men. She taunts Gowan and, mentally, her father ("Daddy would just die") but then invokes the parent in the litanous "My father's a judge."[29] Her temporary anorexia, like her wishful visions of boyhood and chastity belts, reveals her basic dis-ease with sexuality, but at every juncture, she shows an acceptance of her plight if not actual complicity in it. In *Requiem for a Nun*, Temple intimates that her "evil" was motivated by rebelliousness toward her father and brothers, and possibly her implication in the deaths of Red and Goodwin, the two "real men" of the novel, was prompted by the same impulses in more exacerbated form. At the end of the novel, she leaves the courtroom physically surrounded by her father and brothers, as she has been emotionally surrounded by men throughout the course of the narrative. Although one cannot condone her actions, one can see them as involving an almost inevitable response to the conflicting messages she has received from a predominantly male world.

This discernment of the origins of emotional and behavioral patterns in early experiences or family dynamics can only increase one's sympathy for other Faulknerian women who seem mindless or destructive, as it does for Faulknerian men like Popeye, Joe Christmas, or Mink Snopes. Cecily Saun-ders, for example, is certainly erratic and selfish, but she is also to some degree the product of conflicting parental attitudes. The Saunderses alter-nately press her to marry and treat her like a child; not surprisingly, she vacillates between provocativeness and regressiveness. Narcissa Benbow, early forced by her own mother's death into being a mother to her brother, learned to be possessive about Horace and repressive of her own sexuality, psychological characteristics subsequently responsible for destructive actions and reactions. Caddy Compson, also virtually "motherless," cares for her brothers, becoming promiscuous only when she is taught to regard sex as dirty and thus herself as "bad." Her daughter Quentin has an equally deprived and chaotic childhood with similar results; when Quentin shouts at Jason, "You made me,"[30] she speaks, in a way, for all such young women, whose "bitchiness" is a response to circumstances. Mindlessness is another sort of reaction, and the bovine sexuality of Eula Varner in *The Hamlet* can also be seen—though our "seeing" in this case, as in that of Caddy, is filtered through the perceptions of some emotionally involved and thus less than objective male characters—as in some sense induced by her family situation. Eula's father is lazy, lustful, and adulterous, her mother is indifferent, and her brother so hypersensitive to her physicality that he betrays his own attraction to her. Surrounded by lust and unconcern in early pubescence, Eula absorbs her family's dominant traits and becomes what they perceive her to be. Eula is, like most of Faulkner's young "bitches" and "goddesses," invariably influenced, if not fully determined by, the examples of her parents and the messages she receives from them and from her immediate society.

Another psychoanalytical concept that affected Faulkner's portrayal of women is that of projection, the making of reality from desire. Faulkner spoke about this phenomenon in one of its major manifestations when he said, "That is a part of man's or woman's instinctive nature to have an object, an immediate object to project that seeking for love on."[31] Because he was male and most of his narrators, whether omniscient or individualized, are male, the "object" most often "projected" is female, which accounts for a number of qualities in those fictional female "objects"—unreality, mythicity, extremity of desirability or fearsomeness. If Heathcliff represents the male Other to the female imagination of Emily Brontë, all the hyperbolic women in Faulkner's fiction are the Others of the author, the narrators, or the characters. André Bleikasten has written of the way in which Caddy Compson is an empty signifier that speaks the desire of men, a "blank screen" onto which her brothers project their longings and fears, their love and hate.[32] M. D. Faber has asserted that Caddy exists only *in* the men, a "link to the disastrous introjection of the mother."[33] Thus Caddy is not fully recuperable as an autonomous character,[34] for she signifies only in and through her brothers. Virtually the same is true of Addie Bundren, because we see her almost solely through her children, husband, and neighbors, who are in some sense all emotionally and/or judgmentally focused upon her; or the woman in "Old Man," seen only through the tall convict, a product of his anxieties about women; or Eula Varner in *The Hamlet* and *The Town*, a figure raised in the first novel to mythic heights by the titillation of her male observers, or to sphinxlike enigma in the second by the perplexity of another group of males; or, to a lesser degree, Lena Grove and Laverne Shumann, both surrounded, assessed, and pursued by males, largely "made" from masculine responses.

In *Mosquitoes*, Faulkner's characters speak of writing itself as a product of male-originated desire for some elusive ideal woman, and the linkage of "making" women fictionally with "making" them sexually is an intriguing one. Even as Faulkner showed the process of desire-based projection at work inside his fiction, he was aware of its operation from without as enunciative. Though the "shape of love" usually takes a woman's form, it can also be masculine. The elusive empty centers in Faulkner's fiction—the nexuses around which the quest for possession and understanding revolve—are male in at least three instances. Donald Mahon is a silent object of fear or desire to three women and three men; the dead John Sartoris in *Flags in the Dust* becomes a compelling "image" to both Narcissa and Bayard, and Thomas Sutpen of *Absalom, Absalom!* is a figure who exists only in the discourse of the narrators who create him through their efforts to recreate the past; Faulkner shows projection operant in both men and women and makes it a metaphor for creation itself.

Related to the fact that Faulkner's women frequently exist only in the men is their lack of language, Logos, the Word—predominantly a male possession. As Gavin Stevens says in *The Mansion*, Helen left no recorded word, and so, too, are many of Faulkner's nonmythic figures "voiceless." In works narrated omnisciently, most of the women have little to say—Laverne is almost silent, as are the females in *Go Down, Moses*, and male words dominate *Light in August, The Hamlet*, and *Intruder in the Dust*. Moreover, women are frequently perceived to have, or themselves assert, a philosophical opposition to words, and much of the male rhetoric proves to be empty, as in the case of Gavin Stevens and Ike McCaslin, or destructive, as in the case of Mr. Compson of *The Sound and the Fury*. Certainly Faulkner's fiction reveals that women have good reason to be fearful of language, for it is often used to constrict or undermine them: the male obsession with a woman's "good name" hampers her natural impulses, and the assignment of labels such as "lady" or "bitch" or "whore" can have pernicious effects—a few of his women become actual whores only after having been named as such.

Again, however, the generalization must be qualified. Margaret Powers is articulate and thoughtful; she also succeeds in eliciting tales from other females, as at the moment when the previously silent Emmy pours forth the story of her youthful idyll with Donald. The women in *Mosquitoes* speak for themselves, though only Eva Wiseman has much of interest to say. *Flags in the Dust* is a pivotal text in this regard, for Aunt Jenny du Pre is both vocal and interested in words. She tells stories about the family past, recounts bawdy tales in a language of "forceful clarity and a colorful simplicity," generalizes about men, expresses her political views, and responds to the writing of others, especially newspaper accounts of "humanity in its more colorful mutations."[35] Moreover, the quality of her voice is close to that of the narrator's, mingling romanticism and irony as she alternately invokes the heroic past in a voice "proud and still as banners in the dust"[36] and deflates the pretentious behavior of those around her in a voice that is sharp and humorous. She becomes almost a narrator surrogate when the presentation shifts from his to hers with barely a change in tone, as in the graveyard scene, or when she forecasts the major events of the narrative.

A number of women in Faulkner's subsequent novels also have distinctive voices capable of "authoring" the past and affecting others. Rosa Coldfield is Faulkner's most memorable female storyteller, as she creates the first of the visions of Thomas Sutpen, but others, too, discover the satisfactions of narrative—Mrs. Hines of *Light in August* sees Joe Christmas's early history "whole and real" in the moment of recounting it, according to Gavin Stevens,[37] and Drusilla Hawk makes Civil War incidents come alive for her listeners: "We saw it, we were there, as if Drusilla's voice had transported us," says Bayard.[38] Still other women have effective vocal identities, like Linda Snopes Kohl of *The Mansion*, whose "dry harsh quacking voice,"[39] the badge of her heroism in the Spanish Civil War, she uses discursively, occasionally becoming as talky as Gavin Stevens. In *Requiem for a Nun*, Temple Drake Stevens's long night of suffering at the hands of her inquisitor, Gavin Stevens, culminates in a fully verbalized reconsideration of her actions in the recent and distant past; in so finding her voice, Temple perhaps also finds the capacity to start, as she says, a "new life,"[40] although the bitter irony of her tone suggests that the likelihood of such a possibility is dim. Perhaps the female speaker with the greatest impact is Charlotte Rittenmeyer, whose recurrent statements of passionate, if misguided, idealism manage both the outlook and actions of Harry Wilbourne and ultimately effect her own destruction; her voice, with its urgent message, dominates "The Wild Palms" portion of the novel, and she essentially "authors" the central events of the narrative. Thus in his early and late fiction alike, Faulkner presents women who make effective use of language, figures that contrast with and serve to offset the portrayals of those who are voiceless and consequently identified only in and through masculine discourse.

As even this brief survey makes clear, generalizations about Faulkner's women and Faulkner's presentation of gender-based issues are problematic, constantly qualified or undermined by the complexity of his vision and the multivalence of his texts. That his women are neither goddesses nor villains seems obvious, just as his men are neither simply heroic nor absolutely evil. The only real "villains" in the Faulknerian world are a restrictive society that is inadequately responsive to the needs and desires of its individual members and a nuclear family that fails its children by offering poor examples or providing inadequate affection—and their victims are both men and women. In *The Mansion*, a novel possibly intended by Faulkner to be his valedictory, two men and a woman comment sadly on the human condition. Miss Reba sympathizes with "every one of us. The poor son of a bitches," as do V.K. Ratliff and Gavin Stevens, echoing her view with their summary comment, "The poor sons of bitches."[41] The male words may be the last words, and their viewpoints the most prevalent in the Faulknerian universe, circumscribing the women and limiting their options, but as the fiction makes clear at every level, men and women alike are poor frail victims of being alive.

## Notes

1. Maxwell Geismar, *Writers in Crisis* (Boston: Houghton Mifflin, 1942), pp. 145, 169.

2. Irving Howe, *William Faulkner: A Critical Study*, 2d ed. (New York: Vintage, 1962), pp. 143, 141, 144.

3. Leslie Fiedler, *Love and Death in the American Novel* (New York: Criterion, 1960), pp. 333, 309, 310.

4. Samuel A. Yorks, "Faulkner's Woman: The Peril of Mankind," *Arizona Quarterly* 17 (1961):119–29; Katharine M. Rogers, *The Troublesome Helpmate: A History of Misogyny in Literature* (Seattle: University of Washington Press, 1966), pp. 252–57; Elmo Howell, "Inversion and the 'Female Principle': William Faulkner's 'A Courtship,'" *Studies in Short Fiction* 4 (1967):308–14; David M. Miller, "Faulkner's Women," *Modern Fiction Studies* 13 (1967):3–17; Albert J. Guerard, "Forbidden Games (III): Faulkner's Misogyny," in *The Triumph of the Novel: Dickens, Dostoevsky, Faulkner* (New York: Oxford University Press, 1976), pp. 109–35.

5. Karl E. Zink, "Faulkner's Garden: Woman and the Immemorial Earth," *Modern Fiction Studies* 2 (1956):139–49; David Williams, *Faulkner's Women: The Myth and the Muse* (Montreal: McGill-Queens University Press, 1977).

6. Kimberley Snow, "Images of Woman in the American Novel," *Aphra* 2 (1970):67.

7. Frederick L. Gwynn and Joseph L. Blotner, eds., *Faulkner in the University* (Charlottesville: University of Virginia Press, 1959), p. 93; Robert A. Jelliffe, ed., *Faulkner at Nagano* (Tokyo: Kenkyusha Ltd., 1956), p. 69.

8. Though Miller briefly discusses two categories of Faulknerian males, "seed-bearers" and "Prufrocks," in "Faulkner's Women," pp. 13–16.

9. See Carvel Collins, comp., *William Faulkner: Early Prose and Poetry* (Boston: Atlantic-Little, Brown, 1962), p. 115; James B. Meriwether and Michael Millgate, eds., *Lion in the Garden: Interviews with William Faulkner 1926–1962* (New York: Random House, 1968), pp. 45, 240.

10. Dolores E. Brien, "William Faulkner and the Myth of Women," *Research Studies* 35 (1967):132–40. Although the majority of her assessments seem valid, a number of others remain questionable.
11. Elisabeth S. Muhlenfeld, "Shadows with Substance and Ghosts Exhumed: The Women in *Absalom, Absalom!*" *Mississippi Quarterly* 25 (1972):289–304; Judith Fetterley, "A Rose for 'A Rose for Emily,'" in *The Resisting Reader* (Bloomington: Indiana University Press, 1978), pp. 34–45.
12. Linda Wagner, "Faulkner and (Southern) Women," in *The South and Faulkner's Yoknapatawpha: The Actual and the Apochryphal*, ed. Evans Harrington and Ann J. Abadie (Jackson: University Press of Mississippi, 1977), pp. 128–46; Ilse Dusoir Lind, "Faulkner's Women," in *The Maker and the Myth: Faulkner and Yoknapatawpha, 1977*, ed. Evans Harrington and Ann J. Abadie (Jackson: University Press of Mississippi, 1978), pp. 89–104; Sally R. Page, *Faulkner's Women: Characterization and Meaning* (Deland, Fla.: Everett/Edwards, 1972).
13. Lind, "Faulkner's Women," p. 91.
14. Fiedler, *Love and Death*, pp. 314–15; Guerard, *Triumph of the Novel*, p. 110.
15. William Faulkner, *Soldiers' Pay* (New York: Boni & Liveright, 1926), p. 161.
16. Brien, "William Faulkner," pp. 133–34.
17. See William Faulkner, *Mosquitoes* (New York: Boni & Liveright, 1927), pp. 181–83, 242.
18. Ibid., p. 124.
19. William Faulkner, *The Town* (New York: Random House, 1957), p. 340.
20. Juliet Mitchell, *Psychoanalysis and Feminism* (New York: Random House, 1974).
21. Lind, "Faulkner's Women," p. 102; though she sees Faulkner as having derived this from Louis Berman and Havelock Ellis rather than from Freud.
22. Faulkner, *Soldiers' Pay*, p. 303.
23. Faulkner, *Mosquitoes*, p. 46.
24. Snow, "Images of Women," p. 56.
25. Williams, *Faulkner's Women*, p. 130.
26. Fiedler, *Love and Death*, p. 313.
27. Howe, *William Faulkner*, p. 196.
28. Gwynn and Blotner, *Faulkner in the University*, p. 9.
29. William Faulkner, *Sanctuary* (New York: Random House, 1958), p. 29.
30. William Faulkner, *The Sound and the Fury* (New York: Cape & Smith, 1929), p. 324.
31. Gwynn and Blotner, *Faulkner in the University*, p. 95.
32. André Bleikasten, *The Most Splendid Failure: Faulkner's "The Sound and the Fury"* (Bloomington: Indiana University Press, 1976), pp. 56, 65.
33. M. D. Faber, "Faulkner's *The Sound and the Fury*: Object Relations and Narrative Structure," *American Imago* 34 (1977):327.

34. Although Eileen Gregory "recovers" Caddy insofar as is possible in her excellent essay, "Caddy Compson's World," in *The Merrill Studies in The Sound and the Fury*, comp. James B. Meriwether (Columbus: Chas. E. Merrill, 1970), pp. 89–101.

35. William Faulkner, *Flags in the Dust* (New York: Random House, 1973), pp. 33, 35.

36. Ibid., p. 20.

37. William Faulkner, *Light in August* (New York: Smith & Haas, 1932), p. 422.

38. William Faulkner, *The Unvanquished* (New York: Random House, 1938), p. 111.

39. William Faulkner, *The Mansion* (New York: Random House, 1959), p. 199.

40. William Faulkner, *Requiem for a Nun* (New York: Random House, 1951), p. 268.

41. Faulkner, *The Mansion*, pp. 82, 429.

# Mark Spilka

## Hemingway and Fauntleroy: An Androgynous Pursuit

*He was further harassed by a copy of the* Oak Park News *containing a feature article about his mother. It was headlined* LAUNCHES NEW CAREER AFTER RAISING FAMILY *and told of Grace Hall Hemingway's recent success as a landscape painter at the advanced age of fifty-two. "One might suspect," wrote the reporter Bertha Fenberg, "the mother of Ernest Hemingway, author of* The Sun Also Rises, *to be something of a harsh realist, but this very jolly woman laughs at the pessimism of 'these young writers" and expresses the sane belief that the pendulum is swinging back to normal. 'God's in his heaven, all's right with the world' is her way of expressing her own happy life." No doubt, said Ernest sourly, Grace wished that her son Ernie were Glenway Wescott or some highly respectable Fairy Prince with an English accent and a taste for grandmothers.*

Carlos Baker, *Ernest Hemingway: A Life Story*

*If the Castle was like the palace in a fairy story, it must be owned that little Lord Fauntleroy was himself rather like a copy of the fairy prince, though he was not at all aware of the fact, and perhaps was rather a sturdy young model of a fairy.*

Frances Hodgson Burnett, *Little Lord Fauntleroy*

*The dignity of movement of an ice-berg is due to only one-eighth of it being above water.*

Ernest Hemingway, *Death in the Afternoon*


I


In the summer and fall of 1958, Ernest Hemingway brought to rough completion a revised draft of a long novel called *The Garden of Eden* which he had begun in 1946 and then put aside to pursue other projects. It was the last full-length novel he would ever finish, and its subject—the sex-reversal experiments of two androgynous couples living in France in the 1920s—was itself something of a reversal for him.* His lifelong interest in forms of masculine heroism—bullfighting, deep-sea fishing, soldiering, boxing, lion-hunting—had apparently given way to a study of role reversals in marriage. Actually his interest in the androgynous makeup of men and women had begun much earlier and had almost ended where it began. In *The Sun Also Rises* (1926), mannish Lady Brett Ashley and unmanned Jake Barnes are unable to consummate their love, ostensibly because of the sexual wound Barnes has sustained in the war, but more importantly because Brett herself—wearing a man's felt hat over her boyish bob as she stands at the bar with other "chaps"—represents the arrival of the liberated woman of the 1920s, a type whose assumption of equality with men makes her much too difficult for Hemingway's heroes to handle. The question of equal strength between men and women in marriage was one Hemingway never could answer for himself, and when Brett puts the question of the love that might have been at the end of the novel—"Oh Jake . . . we could have had such a damned good time together"—Barnes replies with a dissenting "Yes . . . Isn't it pretty to think so?"

In his next novel, *A Farewell to Arms* (1929), Hemingway would establish the terms for that dissent. He would go back in time to the war that produced such desolate postwar lovers and would explore the "damned good time"—the romantic love—that was no longer available to them. And the androgynous nature of that love which in open and implicit ways this novel establishes would be the secret key to its dissolution. In *A Farewell to Arms*, Hemingway would say farewell also to those feminine aspects of his own makeup, which he had tried honestly enough to confront, and would evade the question of equal strength in marriage by passing off the failure of love onto external and extraneous causes. The hair-matching motif which

---

*Androgyny* in this essay refers nominally to a mixture or exchange of traditionally male and female traits, roles, activities, sexual positions. But more essentially, I am concerned here with the way women began to define maleness in the mid-nineteenth century as an expression or projection of their own wishes and desires whether for power or recognition, as in the "feminine" stage (Chapter V) of Elaine Showalter's feminine-feminist-female progression in *A Literature of Their Own*. As I argue in the pages ahead, Grace Hall Hemingway's "feminine" concept of her firstborn son's maleness was one such androgynous projection which was to affect his life and work profoundly, as were her own late-nineteenth-century "feminist" propensities in the androgynous household she established with her cheerfully cooperative husband Clarence. Their child-rearing experiments may be seen in this light as a peculiar blend of "feminine" and "feminist" propensities with an emerging postpioneer emphasis on outdoor skills for both sexes—which Clarence especially advocated.

begins in this novel—where Catherine Barkley offers to cut her hair short if Frederick Henry will let his grow long—would recur in later fictions: in *For Whom the Bell Tolls* (1940), where Maria's close-cropped hair matches Robert Jordan's; in the posthumously published "The Last Good Country," where Nick Adams's kid sister Littless cuts her hair to resemble his; and in *The Garden of Eden* itself, where one couple has short hair in common and the other long. But the essential terms of the androgynous dilemma and the essential failure to resolve it would remain unchanged.

It may be, of course, that *The Garden of Eden* manuscript probes deeper into that dilemma than we know. The manuscript is still not available to scholars. Though it resides in the Hemingway Collection at the Kennedy Library, now in Boston, it has been placed "off limits" by Hemingway's widow, Mary Welsh Hemingway. But one scholar, Carlos Baker, was allowed to read it in preparation for his biography of 1969, *Ernest Hemingway: A Life Story*; and another, Aaron Lapham, was able to read the opening and closing chapters and to scan the rest when the manuscript arrived in 1977 at the Kennedy Library, then in Waltham, Massachusetts.[1] From their reports of its contents and its quality it seems unlikely that it represents an advance in Hemingway's grasp and penetration of issues raised in the earlier fiction. Indeed, he seems here to concentrate merely on the excitement of matching hairstyles and experimental ways of making love, without giving any serious attention to motivations and emotions or to the basis for androgynous harmony; and the theme he arrives at—"the happiness of the Garden that a man must lose"—is a familiar one in his earlier fiction. It would serve as well, for instance, for *A Farewell to Arms*, where the loss of androgynous happiness initially occurs. It seems important, nonetheless, that Hemingway saw androgynous love as an edenic garden man must lose or leave, that he returned repeatedly to the problem of its transience, and that he tried to explore its childhood sources and its Parisian flowering in his closing years. Seen in this light, the familiar "bitches" and "dream girls" of his fiction become androgynous alternatives (destructive and redemptive) rather than chauvinist fantasies, and his strenuous defense of maleness becomes part of a larger struggle with his own androgynous impulses rather than a sustained form of homosexual panic. His quarrel with those impulses was a lifelong quarrel, and like all such conflicts, it began in childhood circumstances —to which— happily—we now have greater access.

## II

"As soon as it was safe for the boy to travel, they bore him away to the northern woods." So Carlos Baker begins his standard biography, omitting with iceberg aptness the reasons why "they"—Hemingway's parents—

proceeded with such undue haste to expose their firstborn son to outdoor life and concentrating instead on the fact of early exposure. So Hemingway himself would concentrate on Nick Adams's early years in northern Michigan without explaining how and why he got there. Thanks to Baker and other biographers, however, we can now attend more directly to such iceberg omissions. We can say, for instance, that Hemingway's parents belonged to pioneer families—Halls and Hancocks, Hemingways and Edmondses—going back through western settlement and the Civil War to the American Revolution; and that outdoor life was accordingly an imaginative extension of their common family dream. We can say, further, that the dream explains their own radical experiments in child-rearing; for if Grace and Clarence Hemingway were in many ways conventional suburbanites, one of the peculiar ways in which they extended family tradition was through child-rearing. The cottage they bought in northern Michigan soon after their marriage was for the wholesome outdoor upbringing of postpioneer children. There Clarence would teach his wife and four daughters, as well as his two sons, how to shoot, fish, boat, and swim; and as founder of the local Agassiz Club back home, he would teach his children also the naturalist lore his own mother had first taught him. The raising of tomboy girls as well as manly sons was part of the family plan, and Grace Hall Hemingway, the first girl in Chicago to ride the high cycle when she was twelve, was as keen for it as her husband. Indeed, her favorite daughter in this regard was Sunny, the most athletic tomboy of them all, and she reveled as much in the manly exploits of her first infant son as in the smocks and tresses she favored for his infant wear.

Her twinship experiments, in which she tried to match Ernest with his sister Marcelline, his elder by a year, have long been misunderstood as attempts to feminize or sissify her son. But androgynous dollhood comes closer to her apparent intention. Ernest and Marcelline were her twin Dutch dollies, boy and girl, and the Dutch length of their hair and their matching dresses were androgynous features. After infancy, moreover, it was the male side of the androgynous mixture that Grace endorsed. If Ernest had to wait until he was six for his first boy's haircut, Marcelline had to wait an extra year in kindergarten so that she and Ernest could enter first grade together. In the following summer, moreover, Marcelline's hair was cut short to resemble Ernest's. Her suffering from that tonsorial reversal must have deeply impressed her brother, who would later imagine a heroine raped and cropped by Spanish fascists. Marcelline was in fact recropped by an obliging older girlfriend when her summer haircut grew out unevenly. As punishment for that embellishment, her disenchanted mother made her wear one of her sister Sunny's baby bonnets to school until her hair grew out again. After two mortifying weeks, however, Marcelline's second-grade teacher intervened and convinced Grace to relent; a week later she promoted Marcelline to the third grade, where she belonged, and so for a time foiled the twinship plan. But not for long. Between seventh and eighth grades, both parents agreed that Marcelline should stay out of school for another year to avoid being "rushed through strenuous routines during the difficult maturing time of the early teens."[2] So again Ernest caught up with her, and they finished high school together. An observant boy, Ernest must have noted how each of his sisters spent a quiet year out of school during that "difficult" time when pubescent girls first menstruate. Neither he nor his baby brother Leicester would suffer that particular female shame.

The edge Grace gave to maleness was not uncommon among turn-of-the-century women with advanced ideas. As Elaine Showalter notes in *A Literature of Their Own*, women novelists in nineteenth-century England tended to project their desire for power and freedom onto model male heroes, like Dinah Craik's *John Halifax, Gentleman* (1858), whose pluck-and-luck progress "enabled them to think out their own unrealized ambitions."[3] Grace Hemingway was a staunch admirer of *Halifax*; and the traits exhibited by his kind—"The love of sports and animals, the ability to withstand pain, the sublimation of sexuality into religious devotion, and the channeling of sexuality into mighty action"—were those she also hoped to inculcate in her firstborn son, even as "mothers, sisters, and wives" in Victorian women's novels were always the inculcators and definers, "the source[s] of instruction" for the hero's "manly character."[4]

It was a character, moreover, that combined feminine with masculine propensities. Anyone familiar with Frances Hodgson Burnett's *Little Lord Fauntleroy* will recognize the fantasy projected here: an American boy (a younger Halifax) is raised by his widowed mother to be "brave, just, and true" like his dispossessed British father, and to make the world a better place to live in; he is open and sympathetic, affectionate and loving, but also fearless and able to withstand pain; a charming boy who calls his mother "Dearest," he is also possessed of "a fine, strong, straight little body" that his mother much admires; he loves sports and animals, helps the poor and unfortunate, and is remarkably considerate of others; at seven he becomes the legal heir to his British grandfather, the Earl of Dorincourt, with a great deal of future power for good or ill; and so great is his charm, he persuades the crusty, ill-natured earl to accept and love his widowed mother as well as himself. The novel and the play based upon it enjoyed enormous popularity in the late nineteenth century, especially with American mothers, who for a time dressed their sons in black velvet suits with lace collars and red neck-ribbons and arranged their hair in shoulder-length curls, and who had no doubt dressed them earlier in "gal's clothes" like Fauntleroy's when he was "knee-high to a grasshopper."[5]

Grace Hall Hemingway was one such mother in 1899, when her first male child was born. Indeed, even before he was born, she had dedicated him to making the world a better place to live in—quite possibly a place like England! Both her parents were British citizens who, like Frances Hodgson Burnett, had emigrated to America in mid-century, and she shared the American fantasy of a triumphant return to royal favor. One of the near-triumphs of her brief career in grand opera was an invitation to sing before Queen Victoria which conflicted with her travel plans. Sharing her father's interest in music, as in literature and religion, she had made her operatic debut in Madison Square Garden in 1896; but troubled with defective eyesight from a childhood disease, she could scarcely bear the glare of the footlights. While abroad with her father that summer, she decided to forsake her career, pass up her chance to sing before the queen, and return home to marry the young doctor, Clarence Hemingway, who had attended her dying mother in the previous year.

Grace's professional middle name was Ernestine, devised in honor of her British father, Ernest Hall. She would name her firstborn son Ernest Miller Hemingway in honor of her father and his brother, Miller Hall. Her identification of herself and Ernest with these successful businessmen and Christian gentlemen suggests the same projected desire for power and freedom that British and American women novelists of the nineteenth century sought in model heroes like Halifax and Fauntleroy. The projection helps to explain why Grace's androgynous ideal could blend so readily with her husband's pioneer ideal in the child-rearing experiments in northern Michigan, where Fauntleroy conjoined with still another literary fledgling, Huckleberry Finn, within an imagined child named Ernest Miller Hemingway.

Like other American boys, Ernest would prefer Huckleberry Finn, whose frontier antecedents were at least secure, to Fauntleroy, the "Fairy Prince" whose undeserved reputation as a prig and a sissy he spent a lifetime dodging and denying. But in fact his sense of manliness was as much infused with the Fauntleroy ideal inculcated by his mother as with the pioneer ideal she also furthered, but which his father especially advanced. Like Fauntleroy, he was an affectionate, tender-hearted, considerate child who wore Dutch locks and dresses and called his mother "Fweetie." At two he learned to sew and loved it; at two years and eleven months he also learned to load, cock, and shoot a pistol. Again like Fauntleroy (alias Huck Finn), he loved sports and animals, was "*fraid a nothing*," and was much admired by his mother for his manly little body.

The home he lived in, whether at Oak Park or at Walloon Lake in northern Michigan, was an androgynous household. Its chief breadwinner during his early years was his mother, who earned as much as a thousand dollars a month at music lessons and performances while her husband built his medical practice. Out of those earnings, moreover, she paid for a cook, nursemaid, and governess, and so carried out her own mother's farsighted advice in childhood, that she keep out of the kitchen and other such arenas as much as possible.[6] The family's chief menu-planner and food-gatherer, accordingly, was Ernest's father, who cheerfully served his wife and father-in-law, in whose home they initially lived, and gave household orders to the servants in his absence. Abba Hall, the reigning patriarch, presided over the family table, led them in prayers, and continued as chief household manager. Grace reigned beside him, his companion still in their common love of the arts and pieties. When Abba died in 1905, Grace continued her dominant role in a household now largely managed by her husband.

A tall, energetic, athletic woman who could kick as high as the ceiling, Grace learned outdoor skills from Clarence, learned also to make her own furniture, designed their summer cottage and second Oak Park home and the music studios and efficiency kitchens at each locale, began a new career in painting in middle age, traveled widely, wrote, lectured, sang and played the piano, taught music to all her children, learned to drive in her sixties, and kept up a vigorous correspondence all her life. A tall, energetic, athletic man, Clarence matched her in bustling activities. Along with his medical practice and his invention of medical instruments and remedies, his marketing and household management, he was a prodigious cook, a canner of foods garnered from the farm in Michigan, a maker of his own bullets and candles, an expert marksman, a skilled hunter and angler, and an accomplished naturalist. In his healing and nurturing capacities, moreover, he concerned himself with the children's diets, weaned them from their bottles, took them with him on his medical rounds, and along with nature lore and outdoor skills, taught them all—including Ernest—how to cook. Thus, if Grace initially bore and breast-fed all six children, recorded their early lives with loving care, and guided them in the arts, Clarence did more than his share of child-rearing and had strong ideas about it. He also believed as strongly as Grace in the simple Christian pieties his son would later find inadequate to the realities of modern life; but these maxims and homilies left both parents free, nonetheless, for those vigorous extroverted activities—games, picnics, parties, trips to plays, operas, and concerts in Chicago, farmwork and outdoor sports in Michigan—that characterized their family life.

In many ways these role-reversing, experimenting parents were objects of family pride; but they were also so far ahead of their time that the children were sometimes embarrassed by them. At Walloon Lake, for instance, the neighbors made jokes about the noisiness of their mother's singing, the disorderliness of her household, her shirking of conventional "responsibilities" which the hapless Clarence (as they saw him) had to assume. As Constance Cappel Montgomery observes in *Hemingway in Michigan*, Mrs. Hemingway was different "from the norm for upper-middle-class women of her day. She was, in essence, a frustrated career woman," and the role reversals which, in her neighbors' eyes, she forced upon her husband were seen as the unhealthy "source of all the family's troubles."[7]

This biased view of the family was one that Ernest was exposed to and eventually came to share—along with most of his past and present critics. Montgomery herself believes, for instance, that Grace's neglect of her kitchen duties "forced her husband into the kitchen," though in fact he loved to cook and to busy himself with household as well as with medical tasks. More recently, Scott Donaldson—who questions systematically each of the author's other views about his life—accepts at face value his estimate of his mother and of her "bullying" relations with his father.[8] The perpetuation of such attitudes has tended to obscure how ambivalent Ernest actually was about his parents' perplexing ways. In his private life, as in his fiction, he often proved to be a secret admirer of his mother's strengths and a secret emulator of his father's weaknesses.

Thus each of Hemingway's marriages in some way reflects his continuing attraction to his mother's traits and ways. As his sister Marcelline notes, Grace had taught all her children to admire red hair.[9] Not too unexpectedly, then, Hemingway's first wife, Hadley Richardson, was a redhead seven years older than Ernest, an accomplished pianist like Grace, and—again like Grace— an exceptionally generous woman. So generous in fact, that she was willing to furnish the nest egg that allowed them to live in Paris while Ernest began his writing career—even as Grace had backed Clarence while he began his medical practice, financed his refresher course in obstetrics, and furnished the money (apparently) for their summer cottage and (after her father's death) their second Oak Park home.

Hemingway's second wife, Pauline Pfeiffer, though only four years older than Ernest, proved even more strong-minded and generous than Hadley, from whom she took him away in an act of marital piracy in which Ernest— quite interestingly—proved even more craven than his father ever was with Grace. Pauline was also a devoutly religious woman, like Grace, and for a time Ernest earnestly espoused her Catholic faith. He also cheerfully accepted the economic benefits—trips to Spain and Africa, homes in Key West and Cuba—that she and her rich uncle Gus showered upon him or enabled him to afford. Whether consciously or not, then, Ernest seems to have looked in his first two marriages for generous older women who would do things for him, as Grace had always done substantial things for Clarence.[10]

It is a fact of some importance, moreover, that his next two wives, Martha Gellhorn and Mary Welsh, were professional journalists who continued to pursue their careers—Martha actively, Mary fitfully—in marriage. These obvious concessions to his mother's precedent suggest a curious kind of growth in Hemingway, a movement from maternally protective sponsors to more professionally independent-minded women. In Mary Welsh he even seems to have found a combination of independent strength in the two arenas, domestic and professional, in which his mother flourished. A tiny woman, Mary stood up to him in domestic conflicts as Clarence had supposedly failed to stand up to taller and more buxom Grace, and he admired her diminutive version of his mother's domestic valor. But then his lifelong attraction to strong women gives the lie to his supposedly lifelong hatred of his mother, whom he regularly classified as "an all-time, All American Bitch."[11] If such hatred is merely the obverse, not the opposite, of love, it testifies to the profound depth of his early attachment to Grace and to the continuing strength of that denied attachment. Her androgynous ways, like the submerged part of his famous iceberg, gave more substance and direction to his life and work than he was ever able to acknowledge, and not a little dignity—as his famous tagline "grace under pressure" so resonantly suggests.

## III

In a sense, Hemingway's life and work—his serial monogamy and the romantic books that came out of it, dedicated to discarded or discardable wives—can be described as a series of maternal intrusions upon idyllic pastoral romances with sisterly admirers. At some point in adolescence, he had turned from his mother to his sisters for affection and approval; and as we shall see, the rupture of such innocent sibling bonds by maternal interference or disapproval had become his paradigm for the loss of romantic love. But this is only to say that each of his four wives reflected sisterly as well as maternal traits. As with all men, he had learned to love in childhood through family romances, and those he enjoyed with his sisters were as crucial to his emotional growth and health as the early closeness with his mother. What seems interesting here, or at least unusual, is that the idyllic sisterly bonds involved selfless androgynous love, while the threatening maternal bond became identified with the need for independent selfhood as love's prerequisite. Hemingway's seesaw pursuit of these different love-modes had begun amid the threatening instabilities of expatriate life in postwar Paris. In that heady atmosphere, it was the maternal bond, the threat of destruction by a powerful woman, deeply loved, and the need for independent strength to avoid that fate, that surfaced first.

Thus his first important novel, *The Sun Also Rises*, is designed to show the impossibility of romantic love and marriage when women assume male prerogatives, when they become the wrong kind of androgynous woman, the bitch who destroys the man she loves—as Grace, in Ernest's eyes, had been destroying Clarence. Grace's British antecedents and confident ways may well account for his attraction to Lady Duff Twysden, prototype for the first and perhaps most famous bitch-heroine in his fiction, Lady Brett Ashley. His attraction to Duff, Harold Loeb's brief affair with her, and Hemingway's resultant jealousy and distaste for Loeb, are the well-known biographical facts behind the creation of his postwar novel of wasteland instabilities and betrayals.[12] The flavor of romantic impossibility that Eliot and Fitzgerald had introduced in *The Waste Land* (1922) and *The Great Gatsby* (1925) was a further inspiration as Hemingway tried to show "how it was" with such "lost generation" lovers. The flavor became his own, and the inventions he used to convey it were legitimately employed; but the differences between how it actually was and the events and circumstances of the novel were nonetheless considerable.

The most crucial exclusion, and the novel's most obviously determining circumstance, was Ernest's supposedly idyllic Parisian life with his first wife, Hadley, and their infant son Bumby. That iceberg omission accounts for Jake Barnes's bachelorhood, on the one hand, and his emasculating war wound on the other, as aspects of authorial frustration and desire. Jake's longing for Brett Ashley and his inability to act upon it, given the loss of part of his penis in World War I, are analogues for Hemingway's longing for Duff Twysden and his inability to act upon it out of loyalty to Hadley and Bumby. Though he had not yet betrayed Hadley with Pauline Pfeiffer when he began writing the novel, he had for some time wanted to be unfaithful, and the novel is a testament to the imminent disruption of his own romantic marriage by a type much like his mother.

Duff's fictional counterpart, Brett Ashley, may seem a far cry at first from Grace Hemingway. Her drinking, smoking, easy promiscuity, and inability to pray scarcely square with Oak Park pieties and proprieties. But these obvious departures from parental codes seem less substantial in the 1980s than they did in the 1920s. What comes through now is Brett's energy, confidence, experimental courage, as she stands at the bar in her mannish garb, claiming male privileges and freedoms, setting new feminine fashions. "She started all that," says Jake Barnes admiringly, with something like the Hemingway family pride in Grace's experimental ways.[13] Jake's attraction to this "damned good-looking" woman "built with curves like the hull of a racing yacht" (p. 22), his sportsman's appreciation of her athletic femininity, are sometimes forgotten in the emphasis on her bitchery and his self-betrayal in later chapters, and on her dissolute ways in early ones. That she is "one of us"—one of the stoic hedonists who are able to maintain some kind of personal integrity in a wasteland world—is, however, part of her initial attraction. She is a brave survivor, as pioneer women were brave survivors; and like Hemingway's grandmother Adelaide, who regretted only things she hadn't done, or like his mother Grace, who usually did or got what she wanted, Brett has "always done just what (she) wanted" (p. 184). The destructive consequences of that doctrine are averted, as the novel ends, when she decides *not* to do something she has wanted, not to be "one of these bitches that ruins children" (p. 243). A woman who learns from her mistakes, she also has the courage to risk mistakes worth making. Thus it is Brett, not Jake, who tests the limits of the stoic wasteland code they largely share, who realizes for herself that the bullfighter, Pedro Romero, should be left alone, that she cannot let her hair grow long and become the womanly woman he wants; and if it remains for Jake to perceive the implications of such lessons for himself, and to prick their shared illusion that romantic love would have worked for them—that they might have had "such a damned good time together" had he retained his penis—it is Brett who enables that perception.

The book ends on this androgynous impasse: Brett cannot go backward and become the younger and more womanly mate suitable to the novel's manliest hero, the young man from an older culture; nor can Jake move forward to acquire sufficient strength to curb her newfound power—or could not, even if he were whole and potent like Romero. These ironic implications are part of the book's strength as a cultural perplex, a dramatically posed dilemma; but they scarcely exhaust its iceberg implications and puzzlements.

Hemingway's choice of an emasculating war wound as a way of focusing on the postwar social and emotional ills is perhaps the greatest puzzlement. Its literary value is obvious: as with Eliot's sterile fisher king, or Lawrence's paralyzed aristocrat, Clifford Chatterley, it enables Hemingway to connect the war and the society that made it with one of its most damaging consequences: the breakdown in marital and romantic stability, the shattering of the old romantic love code. The iceberg omission here is the mass promiscuity promoted by the war: by the separation of lovers between home and battlefronts, by the sexual urgencies of imminent deaths and maimings, and by the new mobility and independence for women as well as men. The expatriate crowd in postwar Paris has survived such sadly "liberating" conditions and can no longer uphold the old romantic code. For this reason, the novel begins with the goading presence of an untested man, Robert Cohn, who still believes in chivalric romance, and who demonstrates through the folly of his beliefs and actions that romantic love, for this generation at least, is dead.

The puzzlement of Jake's war wound is not literary, then, but authorial. Why did Hemingway choose to place a character much like himself in such an embarrassing fix? He would become famous, in later years, for defending his virility, for boasting about his *cojones*, his manliness in sexual and valorous conjunction. Why this deliberate abnegation of the biological wherewithal of manhood? His own war wounds on the Italian front were leg wounds made by shell fragments and machine-gun bullets. From the fragment that lodged in his scrotum and from his related knowledge of a man who had lost the end of his penis, he began to wonder about the consequences of that loss. Such a wound would leave a man able to desire but unable to act on his desire, unable to control and effect its fulfillment. In Hemingway's world, it is the control of emotional consequences that proves impossible; and the emasculating war wound was one way to express that condition. So Hemingway could not act on his desire for Duff Twysden, given his love for Hadley and Bumby, without suffering ugly consequences. There were, however, still earlier loves on which he could not act.

One was with the American Red Cross nurse, Agnes Von Kurowsky, whom he had met in the Milan hospital where he recovered from his wounds. The relation seems to have been a chaste one, though he would imagine it quite otherwise when he came to write *A Farewell to Arms*. An older and wiser person than Ernest, Agnes had ended their brief romance by sending him home when the war ended and failing to follow after him as promised. This shattering of first romantic dreams at nineteen would be followed by his mother's ultimatum a few days after his twenty-first birthday, that he leave their summer cottage until such time as he learned—like Fauntleroy—to treat her with the consideration she had always given him. As we shall see, these sequential blows do more to explain Hemingway's personal sense of romantic impossibility, of wartime and postwar loss, than his frustrated desire for Duff Twysden.

At one point in the novel, Jake supposes that in loving him Brett "only wanted what she couldn't have" (p. 31). That supposition becomes far more interesting when applied to Jake himself: in loving Brett he too "only wanted what he couldn't have." Beyond Duff Twysden and Agnes Von Kurowsky, there is another bitch woman, Grace Hemingway, whose love and approval Ernest too once wanted and couldn't have, a woman who in fact threw him out of their summer cottage when he was twenty-one and unable himself to leave the maternal nest—though by insults, shirked responsibilities, and other cowardly passivities, he indicated readily enough his desire to leave it. Setting easy Freudian inferences aside, consider here the lack of independent strength, of manliness and self-respect, in Hemingway's ambivalent relations with his mother. He did not strike out for himself into a new career after the war; he nursed his wound for two years, played with the idle rich as paid companion in Toronto, bummed around with war buddies, holed up in Petoskey one winter and tried ineffectually to write: his mother had to throw him out into the "big world out there" he supposedly yearned to re-enter.[14] His regression at this time helps to explain why loners, men without women, appealed so to his hurt pride and offended love, why he wrote about them while at the same time living dependently with serial wives. His inability to control the emotional consequences of filial love, his rejection by his mother, is the secret of the bitch-heroine's threatening power. The emotional consequences of such a union are indeed beyond his control: like Jake Barnes, he lacks the wherewithal to keep the love he wants but cannot have.

It is male default, then, that accounts for the bitch-heroine's destructive potential in *The Sun Also Rises*. With the exception of Pedro Romero, all the men in the novel—like all the women—are sexual and emotional cripples like Barnes. His literal wound is the measure of their common inability to keep love and marriage intact and, in that sense, to control the emotional consequences of their own desires. As a stoic hedonist, Barnes attempts to restrain and subdue his own romantic yearnings; but the novel steadily documents his weakness, his emotional default, his closeness to the romantic fool Cohn in his secret feelings. "It is awfully easy to be hard-boiled about everything in the daytime, but at night it is another thing," says Jake at the end of Chapter IV. His nightly tears and fears prepare us for his abject actions, similar to Cohn's, in serving his lady-love at the expense of self-respect. At Pamplona he will betray his own ideals as an *aficionado*; he will pimp for Brett with Romero and then come running to Madrid when her affair with Romero ends and she calls for help. Hemingway's indictment of his own moral and emotional weakness—an indictment that explains why he succumbed so easily to Pauline Pfeiffer—is clear.

So also is the principle of self-respect by which men may at least begin to deal with women stronger than themselves. The only man in the novel who abides by that principle, and who is thus able to "pay the bill" with Brett and escape unscathed, is Pedro Romero. Still immersed in an older culture, still uncorrupted by the new one, Pedro can hold his own for a time with Brett and even benefit from their brief affair. Quite obviously, his professional authority as master of the bullring carries over into the bedroom and sustains him with that dangerous lady. For in the bullring, Pedro is his own man as well as Brett's admirer. Where Cohn and Barnes expend and degrade themselves for their beloved, he pays tribute without self-loss (p. 216). His manhood, his integrity, does not depend on a woman's favor or approval, but is independently achieved.

Interestingly, Hemingway's emphasis on such independent strength anticipates current feminist insistence that women too must have it, must not depend on men for self-definition. But for Hemingway, the new women of the 1920s, the Duff Twysdens and Brett Ashleys, had already defined themselves, as had Grace Hemingway before them, whereas men like his father and himself had somehow failed to do that and were accordingly unable to deal with those who had. When Brett Ashley enters a Paris bar surrounded by homosexuals, she indicates one threatening consequence of the new male default. When Robert Cohn batters his way to his own emptiness, he indicates another. Only on the fishing grounds at Burguete, where Jake enjoys the support of male friends and defines himself through outdoor skills, is he able to maintain a healthy measure of self-respect. At Pamplona, where he is merely a spectator sportsman, an *aficionado* subject to corruption by outsiders, his control of emotional consequences breaks down. The new woman takes over his domain and almost destroys it.

Actually she allows Romero to return, strengthened and intact, from his sexual initiation. A man who lives independently of women, he becomes the model for survival in a world where romantic love and marriage are no longer possible. But his limited success is the measure of everybody else's failure and of his own narrow escape. He can only survive by going it alone, by keeping free of women who destroy integrity. The novel ends, then, in a standoff between the new independent woman, the newly unmanned man, and the old independent man whose lonely courage he must learn to emulate.

## IV

If romantic love was dead for Hemingway in postwar Europe, the question of how and why it died still intrigued him. In his next novel, *A Farewell to Arms* (1929), he returned to the scene of the crime and tried to absolve it. Nominally, the determining circumstance for the novel was his brief Italian romance with Agnes Von Kurowsky. He had touched on it in *The Sun Also Rises*, where Brett Ashley had been a nurse on the Italian front, like Agnes, when she first met Jake Barnes. But aside from being British, Catherine Barkley—the new novel's heroine—bears little resemblance to Brett and perhaps even less to Agnes Von Kurowsky. Agnes had been a confident, flirtatious, popular young woman, several years older than Ernest, whom she fondly addressed as "Kid." Unlike Brett or Catherine, she had lost no previous lover through wartime disaster and was not ready to please his replacement. Catherine seems in this light more nearly like Hemingway's relatively sheltered and admiring first wife Hadley. In transplanting his idyllic marriage with Hadley to the Italian front, he was trying, apparently, to restore the iceberg omission from which *The Sun Also Rises* secretly proceeds and to explain to himself and the world, and perhaps even to Hadley, why all edenic loves must fail.

Frederic Henry, the new novel's hero, is accordingly older than Hemingway was in World War I and considerably more experienced. He has been on the Italian front for a much longer time than Ernest, who spent only a month there in 1918 before being wounded; and he undergoes the disastrous retreat from Caporetto, which occurred a year before Hemingway even reached Italy.[15] His war-weariness, out of which the early chapters are narrated, was a state of mind Ernest never felt; and his decision to make a separate peace, to say farewell to arms, was one Ernest never made. As we know from several sources, the wounded Ernest was an enthusiastic patriot, eager to return to the front—so eager that he returned too soon, came down with yellow jaundice, and had to be carted back to the hospital in Milan.[16] Thus, where Frederic Henry's disillusionment with the war occurs on the retreat from Caporetto, Ernest's was a postwar acquisition—much of it inspired by literary sources. He had absorbed his antiwar sentiments from postwar readings of poets like Owen and Sassoon and novelists like Ford and Dos Passos. What he had read squared, however, with the military histories which then absorbed him, and with what he had personally heard and seen at and behind the front; and it squared also with the disillusionment of his postwar return to Oak Park, where his own war stories had gradually palled and gone out of fashion—as he partly records in "Soldier's Home" (1924). In his long recuperation, in which he continued to wear his British cape and Red Cross uniform and his high military boots, he had even become a figure of fun to his neighbors.[17]

He also suffered the sequential blows of rejection by Agnes Von Kurowsky and his mother in these early postwar years. His embittered feelings about Agnes he would compress into the mean-spirited sketch, "A Very Short Story" (1924). His bitterness toward his mother took a more complex form. The incident at Walloon Lake that touched off her rejection had, in effect, crystallized their gradual disaffection since childhood. His sisters Ursula and Sunny had planned a secret escapade, a midnight picnic on a sandbar on Walloon Lake with several other young friends. They had invited Ernest and his war buddy Ted Brumback to accompany them. On the sandbar there was much innocent singing and mandolin strumming and perhaps some spooning with neighbor girls. When they returned at three in the morning, however, their escapade had been discovered, and the penalties were severe. The girls were forbidden late dates for the rest of the summer; Ernest and Ted were banished from the summer cottage; and Ernest then received his mother's famous letter of rejection, summarizing his regressive behavior since his return from the war.[18] Ernest suppressed that telling summary and remembered only the unfairness and apparent arbitrariness by which an innocent idyll had been punished. It was like the unexpected and arbitrary punishments his parents—and particularly his father—had often meted out to him throughout his childhood in a family where the discipline was strict, sudden, and largely unthinking. In fact, his mother had given much thought to this decision, which came only after persistent passive-aggressive goading on his part. But for better and for worse, the paradigm of the world's outlandish punishments for stolen pleasures had been firmly set.

On the Italian front, then, war-weary ambulance driver Frederic Henry meets a slightly addled British nurse named Catherine Barkley. Frederic—after Frédéric Moreau, the disillusioned hero of Flaubert's *L'Education Sentimentale*—was originally a younger and more excitable man named Emmett Hancock. "Emmett" probably comes from Emmett County, Michigan, where Hemingway summered as a boy; and "Hancock" decidedly comes from the revolutionary Hancock side of Grace's family. Thus the choice of "Frederic" over "Emmett" seems to confirm the shift from Hemingway's youthful enthusiasm for the war—still evident in the early Hancock fragment—to weary disaffection in the novel, whereas the choice of "Henry" over "Hancock" suggests an ironic play on Patrick Henry, who—unlike Frederic—died nobly for his country. Catherine in turn owes much to Emily

Brontë's addled heroine, Catherine Earnshaw Linton, who also identifies with a radically disaffected lover, dies in childbirth, and haunts him after death. She owes much more, however, to sheltered Hadley, who at twenty-nine was ready to break the world's jail with Ernest, escape to the freer life in Paris, and so make amends for past confinements.[19]

Having lost a sweetheart in the war to whom she failed to yield herself, Catherine is ready to make similar breaks and amends with Frederic. Her compensatory love will nonetheless prove selfless and will involve a lesson in caring, or as some critics call it, *caritas*, which might be better called a lesson in androgyny. Consideration for others—which Grace Hemingway expected of Ernest and taught him to show his sisters—is the Fauntleroy ideal endorsed by Christian gentlemen. For Ernest it was a feminine version of manly character, which helps to explain why Catherine is the exemplary "source of instruction" for Frederic in this novel. Their selfless love is formed in one hospital, moreover, and dissolved in another, in keeping with the author's childhood familiarity with his father's medical world, where male and female caring intermix, and with his own experience as a caring Red Cross corpsman who recovered from war wounds in a Milan hospital.

The first version of the novel begins, in fact, with Emmett Hancock's arrival at the Milan hospital; and in Book Two of the final version, Frederic Henry's love for Catherine Barkley begins there too. Until this point, Henry has taken Catherine as a windfall, a welcome change from the prostitutes he has known at the front and on leave. Unlike the younger Hancock, who had wanted a nurse "to fall in love with," the older Henry has "not wanted to fall in love with anyone."[20] But now, flat on his back in the hospital, he immediately falls in love with Catherine. Perhaps Hancock's eager expectation explains Henry's sudden reversal.

In the hospital, the wounded hero in both versions is in masterful command. Neither the porters nor the stretcher-bearers nor the elderly nurse they rouse know where to put him. He demands to be put in a room, dispenses tips to the porters and stretcher-bearers, tells the befuddled nurse she can leave him there to rest. He is nowhere more authoritative, interestingly, than when flat on his back and served by gentle attendants and adoring nurses; in previous chapters in the novel, he has been relatively restrained with peers and subordinates. Plainly his wounds, which certify his manliness and relieve him for a time from further heroism, are one source of his newfound authority. His position as the first and only male patient in a hospital overstaffed to serve him is another; and the author's early authority when surrounded by admiring sisters, both before and after his return from the war, is not irrelevant to it. In Henry's certified passivity, then, lies his greatest power; he has license to reign from his bed as Grace Hemingway reigned when served breakfast there by her husband Clarence—or as Joyce's Molly reigned when served by Leopold Bloom. In effect, he has finally arrived at something like a woman's passive power.

His feminization takes still other interesting forms. He is tenderized by love, made to care like the caring Catherine in whom his selfhood is immediately invested. In a discarded passage, he feels that he goes out of the room whenever she leaves.[21] More crucially, he is like a woman in the lovemaking that takes place in his hospital room at night. As no one has yet bothered to observe, he has to lie on his back to perform properly, given the nature of his leg wounds, and Catherine has to lie on top of him. This long-hidden and well-kept secret is one Hemingway returns to, apparently, in *The Garden of Eden*, one Mary Welsh Hemingway may imply about married love with Ernest in *How It Was*, one Ernest seems to imply in *A Moveable Feast* about himself and Hadley.[22] That—James-like—Hemingway could not articulate the secret indicates the force, not merely of censorship in the 1920s, but of chauvinist taboos against it. The interesting thing is that Hemingway—for whom the idea of female dominance was so threatening—could so openly imply the female dominant without being understood or held to his confession. Of course, the ministering Catherine in the ministerial position was more than he was willing, much less able, to specify; but for anyone interested in "how it was"—and we have since become interested to excess—that iceberg conclusion was there for the drawing—or the thawing. Happily we now have books and movies that sanction female mountings of receptive males. But that Hemingway could then overcome his own and everyone else's fear of female dominance—could give it tacit public expression—seems to me remarkable. Compare explicit sexual writers of the day like Joyce, who could imagine an abjectly transvestite Leopold but not a masterfully supine one; or Lawrence, for whom supineness was an unthinkable abandonment of ithyphallic powers! So Hemingway might also be supposed to have felt, but apparently did not; perhaps because, like the supine Frederic, the wounded hero, he already felt masterful enough to enjoy it; perhaps because he saw good androgynous women like Catherine as unthreatening to his essential maleness, in the initial stages of love, and to that side of the male ego—male identity—the bitch woman seemed so immediately to jeopardize.

In any case, Frederic Henry's power is never greater than in these hospital love scenes. Not only does he impregnate Catherine from his supine position, he is also delivered of his own shell fragments by the romantically named Dr. Valentini, who in turn offers to deliver Catherine's baby free. As the analogy between his operation and her Caesarian suggests, Catherine—lacking Valentini's assistance—cannot emulate Frederic's successful parturition. He undergoes and survives an ordeal by suffering to which Catherine in her comparable situation will succumb.

Meanwhile, their hospital-based love enters a mystic phase. Before the operation she effaces herself, says she'll do, say, and want anything he wants: "There isn't any me any more," she concludes. "Just what you want" (p. 106). Afterwards, in discussing why they needn't marry, she repeats her point: "There isn't any me any more. I'm you. Don't make up a separate me" (p. 115). Her declaration, like Catherine Earnshaw's famous pronouncement— "I *am* Heathcliff"—is a time-honored Christian-Romantic version of the union of two souls. The friendly priest at the front has predicted and blessed their union for the lesson in selfless caring it entails. But Catherine and Frederic are Romantics whose Christianity has lapsed: "You're my religion," she tells him now (p. 116), and so invokes a Romantic heresy, the religion of love, going back to the eleventh century. Lacking any connection with God or immortality, their atheistic faith will eventually fail them, leaving Frederic alone and bereft with the memories here recalled. But for a time they are fused in mystic selflessness.

The androgynous nature of their fusion is further developed when they flee to Switzerland and Frederic's turn as the caring, selfless partner begins. This idyllic phase has been anticipated by Frederic's loving description of the priest's home in Abruzzi, which he has failed to visit, but which he then imagines as a "place where . . . it was clear cold and dry and the snow was dry and powdery and hare-tracks in the snow and the peasants took off their hats and called you Lord and there was good hunting" (p. 13). Switzerland is like that, except for the hunting, which Frederic selflessly eschews. He has abandoned sports and war for a world circumscribed by love, and now reads about them somewhat wistfully in newspapers. The escaped lovers reside in the chalet near Montreux where Hemingway and Hadley once lived and which Ernest prized for its "ideal blend of wilderness and civilization."[23] In that idyllic region, the lovers read, play cards, stroll together in the powdered snow, stop at country inns, or visit the nearby village where Frederic watches with excitement while Catherine has her hair done at the hairdresser's. Later they decide that he must grow a beard, or better still, let his hair grow long while she has hers cut short to match it: then they will be alike, one person, as they are now one person at night (pp. 298–300). They settle, however, for the beard, which grows splendidly through the winter— like a gradually re-emerging form of male identity. In the spring, the rains come, washing away the powdered snow; they move to Lausanne so Catherine can have her baby at the hospital; and Frederic takes up boxing at the local gym.

Their edenic love dissolves when Catherine dies from her Caesarian operation and their child is stillborn. Supposedly she has been caught in that "biological trap" which, in its absurdity and futility, is the female equivalent for death on the modern battlefield; and certainly her death has been carefully foreshadowed in just these cosmic terms. You may enjoy edenic and androgynous bliss in this world, Hemingway surmises, but in the end "they" will take it from you. The punishment for stolen happiness is death. But since the same punishment is meted out to honest misery, and since death in childbirth has been unusual since the end of the nineteenth century, the novel's tragic resolution seems arbitrary to many readers. Catherine's small hips—that androgynous feature—may have determined her fate in more ways than one. The love she offers so absorbs male identity that she is as threatening to it, finally, as any bitch heroine; and though she dies bravely, like a true Hemingway hero, it may be that she is sacrificed to male survival.

Whatever the case, Hemingway bids farewell to androgynous love in this novel and turns for the next ten years to the problem of shoring up his own male identity. The legend of the hard-boiled "tough guy" writer begins with the sentimental dodge of Catherine's death. It was not of course the world but those stronger women—Agnes, Grace, and Pauline—who brought to an end the androgynous idylls in Milan, Michigan, and Paris; and in the African stories of the 1930s, we begin to see why this is so.

## V

Hemingway's dedications of his books offer a rich field for speculation. *The Sun Also Rises*, in which he predicts the end of his first marriage, was dedicated to his first wife Hadley. *A Farewell to Arms*, in which he mourns the loss of Hadley, was dedicated—not to his second wife Pauline—but to her rich uncle Gus. The book he would dedicate to Pauline was *Death in the Afternoon* (1932), a study in the ritual proving of manhood. Certainly his life with Pauline was given over to such ritual provings—hunting in Africa, fishing off Key West and Bimini, boxing on shore with all contenders—and was characterized also by insulating affluence. Not surprisingly, the African stories of this period reflect these personal themes. They are about cowardly or corrupted men who must achieve modes of integrity that ensure their independence from bitch women, whether rich or beautiful; and they inquire into the failure of love and marriage between bought husbands and wives. The relations between such men and women are brutally damaging; there is no room for the tenderness and consideration of the selfless love mode in *A Farewell to Arms*. In "The Short Happy Life of Francis Macomber" (1936), however, Hemingway returned to a notion he had touched on in *The Sun Also Rises*— that manly strengths acquired on ritual proving grounds are transferrable back into the wasteland world where marriages must be lived—and so defined what might be called his quasi-Lawrencean love mode.

Francis Macomber, the rich, cowardly, and dependent hero of this story, has bolted from a lion while on a hunting trip in Africa. His wife then cuckolds him with their stoic British guide. In his angry reaction to open shaming, Macomber then proves his manhood while hunting buffalo. But when a wounded buffalo suddenly charges and seems about to gore him, his wife shoots at the buffalo from the safety of a nearby car, using a significantly named 6.5 Mannlicher gun, and kills her husband instead of the buffalo. Since she has visibly resented Macomber's newfound courage, the guide attributes the accident to her unconscious desire to murder him. "He *would* have left you, too," he tells her, indicating that the husband's independent manhood—his happy life—had been assured before he died.[24] Earlier the guide had mused on Macomber's transformation: "Probably meant the end of cuckoldry too. . . . Be a damn fire eater now. . . . More of a change than any loss of virginity. Fear gone like an operation. Something else grew in its place. Main thing a man had. Made him into a man. Women knew it too. No bloody fear" (p. 33).

The principle of renewable and transferrable manhood is clear; but so too is the principle of female recalcitrance. If Macomber now has the personal integrity to stand up to his wife and if necessary to leave her, she has grown accustomed to her dominance, has hardened into it, and now acts unconsciously to preserve it. Her conscious impulse to save him has given way to her deeper impulse to destroy him.

This ambiguous ending, which both affirms transferrable manhood but denies its utility, is our clue to the problem Hemingway never solved. A man may leave his bitch-wife for a good androgynous woman like Catherine Barkley—one willing to die for his survival; but he cannot live with a bitch—a bad androgynous woman—without being killed himself. And yet a strong wife is the only kind worth having.

Hemingway's attraction to the type seems undeniable. His animus is not against Mrs. Macomber's strength, for example, but against her use of it: her apparently enameled cruelty, and her ultimate refusal to accept her husband's transformation. And even these judgments are ambivalently delivered. Thus the guide admires not only Mrs. Macomber's beauty but her brains; he knows that she is neither stupid (p. 8) nor insensitive. When she goes off to cry over Macomber's cowardice, she seems to him "a hell of a fine woman," one who understands, who is "hurt for him and for herself," and who knows how things really stand (p. 9). If he dislikes the hardened cruelty that follows, he knows that it began with male default (p. 8) and that she responds with innocent freshness to his own virile love (p. 27). And Hemingway himself writes of the marriage: "She had done the best she could for many years back and the way they were together now was no one person's fault" (p. 34).

Some critics take this statement as a lead to Mrs. Macomber's "shorter happy life" when she tries to save her husband and shoots at the buffalo.[25] But as the framing of her shot confirms—from the safety of the car, with a "manly" or "man-licking" gun—the statement merely distributes blame over time. As the story's opening action reveals, it was Macomber's initial cowardice and dependence that ensured his wife's dominance. As the story's closing action reveals, she now likes to dominate and—like Brett Ashley before her—is no longer able to change. True to its period, the story is not about mutual honoring and the tragic loss of selfless love, as some critics hold, but about independent manhood—which even cowardly "boy-men" may achieve—as a defense against ingrown bitchery or, if that fails, unhappy death.

In "The Snows of Kilimanjaro" (1936), there is no question of overcoming bitchery. The bought husband in this story has settled for a marriage of convenience and now wants only to die a happy death. A corrupted writer who has traded his talent for the comforts his rich wife provides, he is dying of a gangrenous infection appropriate to his moral sloth. He accordingly wants to work the fat off his soul, to recuperate his integrity by writing stories in his mind—the only way left to him—and thus make a last-ditch struggle against demeaning death. As his original name—Henry Walden—suggests, the writer Harry is a loner even in marriage. He calls his wife "this rich bitch, this kindly caretaker and destroyer of his talent" (p. 60); he curses her "damned money" (p. 58), tells her that he doesn't love her, and tells himself that he has always made love better when lying about it for his bread and butter (pp. 55, 61). But he also acknowledges to himself that it wasn't his wife's fault, that he had himself destroyed his talent "by not using it, by betrayals of himself and what he believed in, by drinking so much that it blunted his perceptions, by laziness, by sloth . . ." (p. 60). He admits, moreover, that each woman he has fallen in love with has been oddly richer than the last, that he has made his living with his penis rather than his pen (p. 60). Hemingway's harsh critique of this writer and his loveless marriage seems frankly self-directed. He too wants to work the fat off his soul, wants to leave Pauline behind by writing his lonely way toward death. As Carlos Baker surmises, he too was afraid he might die before he wrote "the things that he had saved to write until he knew enough to write them well" (p. 54); he too wondered if he had put them off because he couldn't write them.[26]

The story takes on an oddly autobiographical dimension, then, as Hemingway uses Harry's memories of these materials to show off, in effect, his unused wares, the things he might have written but never did. These writer's memories, arranged in five italicized passages of varying length and interspersed between roman passages on Harry's present siege with death, are about war blunders and peacetime follies Harry has witnessed in snowy alpine settings, the life in Paris where his writing career began in blessed poverty, the squelching of an old romance he hoped to revive, an innocent western murder, his own mercy killing of a dying friend. They are conveyed in rapid nonstop prose designed to challenge the stream-of-consciousness techniques of Hemingway's competitors, Faulkner, Woolf, and Joyce, in psychological resonance. This they fail to do. As autobiographical wares, they are even open to charges of self-pity and self-aggrandizement. But they are suitable to Harry's spiritual and moral efforts to go down fighting, that is to say, writing; and they apparently earn him an imagined plane trip—in roman prose to indicate its essential reality—over Mount Kilimanjaro.

Harry's imagined pilot, appropriately, is a bluff Britisher, like the guide in the Macomber story, and one can fantasize the male-chauvinist heaven these comrades approach as a series of bullrings, fishing and hunting grounds, boxing arenas and baseball diamonds just beyond the mountain's snowy crest. Hemingway himself had imagined heaven in just such terms toward the end of his marriage to Hadley. On 1 July 1925, in a boisterously funny letter to Scott Fitzgerald, he had defined its essential features: a bullring where Ernest holds tickets for the best seats; a trout stream outside it that only he can fish in; two lovely houses in town—one (where his wife and children live) for monogamous true love, the other for his nine beautiful mistresses; and a fine Spanish church to confess in as he goes from one house to the other. By the 1930s, however, the mortgage on one such heavenly home had been foreclosed. The rich bitch who accompanies Harry shoots well and makes love well, like Pauline, and she may even qualify as a hunting companion atop Kilimanjaro at some future date; but there is no longer any question of monogamous—or androgynous—true love.

## VI

Except among the tougher denizens of the lower classes. In *To Have and Have Not* (1937) Hemingway creates the only middle-aged love affair in his fiction—perhaps in all modern American fiction—between the smuggler Harry Morgan and his wife Marie. Described as "a big woman, long legged, big handed, big hipped, still handsome," an old man's felt hat "pulled down over her bleached blonde hair," Marie at forty-five enjoys her forty-three-year-old one-armed husband's lovemaking, cries at the Tartar beauty of his "goddamn face," loves to watch him move "like some kind of expensive animal," cares for him rather than their two daughters, and genuinely mourns his inevitably bloody death.[27] But Marie is as tough as her tough-guy husband; the bond between them is earthy and erotic, and her Molly Bloom-like soliloquies are charged with frank appreciations of his *cojones*. Her domestic functions and Harry's piratical tasks, his risky means of supporting his wife and children, are the forms that selfless consideration takes in this novel, and these roles are sharply separated. Harry is very much a loner in his work, moreover; so much so that his dying insight—"a man alone ain't got no bloody fucking chance" (p. 225)—is the novel's proletarian moral.

Plainly Hemingway admires this rough and ready man who kills when he needs to, which is often, smacks men who insult his wife, insults the rich when they deserve it, and loves monogamously. And in a novel notable for its sympathy for women with integrity, he admires Marie too. Harry and Marie are the only quasi-Lawrencean lovers in his fiction; they make a go of it while the rich people around them squabble viciously, betray each other, perform badly in bed, masturbate themselves to sleep, or commit suicide. And perhaps because of their earthy independence, Harry and Marie are also the only successfully androgynous lovers in Hemingway's fiction. She admires and emulates his masculine toughness; he admires and covets her bleached blond hair. In the novel's closing soliloquy, she describes that bleaching and their common excited response to it as the defining episode in their marriage (pp. 258-60). Harry's death is founded, then, in social rather than marital causes—perhaps because he spends so little time at home.

Hemingway's portrait of Marie is one of two significant tributes in his fiction to his own "old woman," his second wife Pauline, who had once bleached her hair for him with similarly exciting results.[28] The other is Pilar in *For Whom the Bell Tolls* (1940). "Pilar" was the secret nickname Pauline chose for herself when she first went after Ernest; it was the name also for the fishing boat, *The Pilar*, which he bought in 1934 and christened in her honor; and in both cases, the name derived from the shrine at Zaragoza in Spain, *Nuestra Señora del Pilar* (Our Lady of the Pillar), and from the fair for "Pilar" each October. The shrine consists of an image of the Blessed Virgin on a pillar of porphyry. The image suggests why the young girl Maria is the middle-aged Pilar's protégé in the novel: the victimized virgin who depends on the strong woman's support. Since the novel is dedicated to Hemingway's third wife, Martha Gellhorn, it suggests also that Hemingway felt that Martha—a St. Louis girl like his first two wives—was in some sense an extension of Pauline's beneficence.[29] But the ambitious Martha contributes only physical features to Maria; that "little rabbit" in her selfless caring for the novel's hero, Robert Jordan, is more like Hadley in Spanish guise. Having been raped and cropped by Spanish fascists, she is also more like Hemingway's "twin" sister Marcelline, whose hair was cropped by his mother to resemble his, one childhood summer, and who suffered for it, as we have seen, for some time after. So Maria is Grace's gift as well as Pauline's, in the novel's psychogenesis, and that strong woman Pilar may owe as much to Grace as she does to Pauline. She is the tough outspoken gypsy mother Ernest would have preferred, apparently, to the one he got, whom in many ways she nonetheless resembles.

Pilar's husband Pablo, for instance, has become a coward, whose lapse from leadership forces her to take control of their guerrilla band. Ernest's father Clarence was a coward, in his view, who was dominated by his wife— along with the rest of the family—and who committed suicide in 1928 to escape his many problems. Ernest had touched on that tragedy in "Fathers and Sons" (1933) but felt that he could not write about it directly. In *For Whom the Bell Tolls*, however, he found a way to deal with it. Thus Robert Jordan too has a cowardly father who committed suicide, and though Jordan can eventually forgive and understand him, he cannot forgive his failure to stand up to his bullying mother. The novel turns, dramatically, on the question of whether Jordan will take his own life, like his cowardly father, or die bravely as his grandfather the Indian fighter would have wished. At one point, Jordan wonders whether his grandfather's bravery has passed down to him intact through his father, or whether the bully in his mother has passed down to him to make up for what his father lacked (pp. 338-39). Like a Faulkner hero, he wants his grandfather with him, to talk to; and in the end, injured and alone, he does talk to his grandfather (p. 469) and decides to die bravely rather than shoot himself (p. 470) as he waits for the approaching fascist troops.

Meanwhile, he shares most of his problems with the bully Pilar, an older woman he openly cares for (p. 92). Though she has read death in his palm, she gives him Maria to love and protect, rewards him as they work together for a hopeless political cause. Apparently she believes, as they do, that a whole lifetime together may be concentrated into a few idyllic days. The setting is pastoral—the Spanish mountains covered with pine-needled forests—and the romance is a Spanish family romance. At one point Maria refers to the guerrilla band as a family, and Jordan concurs (p. 139). The assembled cast—or "this sentimental menagerie," as Pilar calls it (p. 140)—is about the size of a Hemingway family picnic in the Michigan woods. The old man Anselmo who later dies at the bridge is the surrogate grandfather; Pilar and Pablo are the strong mother and weak father; the boy Joaquin is the youngest brother; Jordan is the favored son, and Maria is his sisterly companion, his close-cropped twin in selfless androgynous love. "You could be brother and sister by the look," Pilar says of this pair. "But it is fortunate that you are not" (p. 67). At the end, Jordan will make much of their fortunate fusion: "If thou goest then I go, too. . . . Whichever one there is, is both. . . . You are me now" (p. 463). Meanwhile, "the earth moves" when they make love, and Pilar expounds that mystery for them (pp. 114-15), among many others. Indeed, it is her version of manly character—the Fauntleroy ideal of transmuted virility—which defines their relation and channels sexuality into something spiritually profound.

But it is not very profound. The fusion with nature, the Lawrencean part of the ideal, depends on the separate existence of integral beings, and the lovers' selfless union dissolves that vital independence. The lyric descriptions of the lovemaking are accordingly somewhat insipid in their breathless running participles. And the love itself is suspiciously wishful. At one point, Jordan even compares it with "the dreams you have had when someone you have seen in the cinema comes to your bed at night and is so kind and lovely" (p. 137). Maria is Jordan's film fantasy come true, and only the detailed violence and earthiness of guerrilla life keeps the wishful element subdued. But she is not an incredible character. Though less vividly realized than

Catherine Barkley or Marie Morgan, she is a credible type of unformed innocence. It is the love itself that seems incredible. It lacks what Marie Morgan, in her strong personal integrity, brings to her love for Harry; it lacks what Pilar provides as she blends with Maria in their common family romance. Pilar even tells Jordan that she could have taken him away from Maria when she was young (p. 156)—as Pauline took Ernest away from Hadley; and in fact the novel and the love it champions would have been more credible if Pilar were Jordan's lover at any age—as the balanced love in *To Have and Have Not* confirms. But that love was only briefly delineated, and Hemingway here separates what he could not for long unite—considerate androgynous love between partners of equal strength.

Interestingly, he introduces a perverse component into his dubious Spanish blend. Pilar's attraction to Maria is stronger than her attraction to Jordan; she is more jealous of Jordan than Maria, and though she explains this aspect of her fondness for Maria as something always present in human relations and therefore only incidental (pp. 154-55), she reminds us for a moment of another older woman in Hemingway's life, Gertrude Stein—whose writing he mocks in a later passage (p. 289). But finally she is jealous of Maria's youth, and that tip-off of things to come is our last clue to the dilution here of the androgynous ideal. Hemingway has begun to look to much younger women for sisterly admiration, adoring selfless ministration to his shaky male identity. In *Across the River and Into the Trees* (1950), he will push that middle-aged fantasy to its absurdly immature conclusion. Meanwhile in *For Whom the Bell Tolls*, his admiration for Pilar keeps his three-day dreamfloat on the ground. As Pilar says to Maria: "You will not be nineteen always" (p. 157).

## VII

But for middle-aged male fantasts, there is always a new crop of nineteen-year-olds; and their own emotional age may be said to be fixed—as Hemingway's apparently was—at about nineteen. That was the year of his war wound in Italy and of his hospital romance with Agnes Von Kurowsky, and to that year he returns emotionally, in *Across the River and Into the Trees*,[30] with the accumulated wishfulness of three more decades. In this nostalgic novel— dedicated nominally to his fourth wife, Mary Welsh, but implicitly to his nineteen-year-old Italian muse Adriana Ivancich—the aging Colonel Cantwell, who is likely to die at any moment from heart failure, takes the daughterly love of nineteen-year-old Countess Renata as a tribute to his continuing virility. She makes him work at being the good, gentle, and considerate man he can be, in the Fauntleroy tradition; makes him temper his brutal rage at the military blunders of all the commanders he has known in World War II;

and listens with fascinated admiration to all aspects of his manly life. But the mechanical oscillation between her lesson in redemptive gentleness and his in military wrath parodies rather than reconciles these opposing views of manly character, reduces them to middle-aged folly and bluster. The coarsening of Hemingway's sensibility in World War II to that of a war-lover whose boyhood enthusiasm has soured into grizzled rant is everywhere evident, as is the coarsening of his youthful androgynous charm with peers and elders into dutiful middle-aged gallantry toward a teenage fan. The novel is thus doubly insulated from the realities of postwar nostalgia it tries to recreate. Neither World War II nor the kinds of love that survived it are remotely touched by the Venetian tryst between the aging warrior and his precocious ward. It does not even help that Cantwell calls himself a "good boy" (pp. 165, 173) when he tries to be gentle; or that he sees in an old motor-boat like himself "the gallantry of the aging machine" (p. 52); or that, like Catherine Barkley, Renata wants to be him (p. 156) or one of his soldiers (p. 231) or his selfless server (p. 143); or that they "play" at exchanging identities (p. 261); or that their lovemaking is confined—since she is menstruating—to magical manipulations beneath a gondola blanket with his maimed but mysteriously potent hand ("I dreamed it was the hand of Our Lord," says Renata on p. 84), and is thus chastely religious; or, finally, that this caring sparing colonel, like Morgan and Jordan before him, goes off to die well alone. The attempt to deal lightly or wondrously or delicately with these androgynous gestures only heightens their tiredness and misapplication.

The bad critical reception of *Across the River and Into the Trees* so angered Hemingway that, like Macomber after the lion, he decided to prove himself again with a giant fish. His mother had died in 1951, and though he refused to go to her funeral, he recalled in a letter to Carlos Baker "how beautiful Grace had been when she was young before 'everything went to hell in the family,' and also how happy they all had been as children before it all broke up."[31] Two years earlier, she had sent him his baby books, which he read and responded to with real gratitude. His hostile feelings toward her were softening, and in the prizewinning novella, *The Old Man and the Sea* (1952), he seems to have broken through to something like his old childhood tenderness. The old man of the tale is genuinely rather than dutifully gentle, and his responses to the sea and its inhabitants have the lyric grace of a childhood fable. Indeed, the blend of gentleness and toughness in his makeup is designedly exemplary; his lonely pursuit of the giant fish begins and ends with the boy on shore who once accompanied him, but whose parents forbade it when the old man proved unlucky. Now he is proving himself lucky again for the boy's sake, teaching him the value of lonely stoic patience and loving regard for their common world, teaching him to withstand pain and privation, teaching him the dignity, finally, of significant defeat.

From his twenties onward, Hemingway had been calling himself Papa, in emulation of that Christian gentleman, his maternal grandfather and name-sake, "Abba" Ernest Hall.[32] He had written stories of parents and children from the child's point of view, and one—"Fathers and Sons"—from his own paternal point of view; and he had always been a kind fatherly travel guide to his readers, their paternal instructor in the empirical hows of sporting or expatriate or military life, the lay of landscapes, towns, cities, and the stoic wisdom needed for survival in such climes and times. In *Across the River and Into the Trees*, he had even allowed Papa Cantwell to exchange lessons in valor and tenderness with daughterly Renata. But *The Old Man and the Sea* was his first and best attempt to concentrate on a Papa-figure who is himself an example of gentle manliness.

For the first time, moreover, the world itself is conceived as feminine and in loving rather than threatening terms. "They" are no longer out there to break or kill impartially the good and the brave and the gentle, as in *A Farewell to Arms*. If there are harsh realities to confront, they take their place within a benignly feminine context. Thus, where younger fishermen call the sea *el mar* and see it "as a contestant or a place or even an enemy," the old man fondly calls it *la mar* and sees it always "as feminine and as something that gave or withheld great favors, and if she did wild or wicked things it was because she could not help them. The moon affects her as it does a woman, he thought."[33]

This may be the only place in Hemingway's fiction where he takes femi-nine behavior as a benign explanation of the world's arbitrariness, and allows for menstruation as its biocosmic source. Certainly it is the only place where he acknowledges the true sex of his chief rival, and from the token struggle with nature which so often absorbs him draws an implied parallel between Mother Nature and Mother Grace—and draws it, moreover, with renewed tenderness.

But *The Old Man and the Sea* is a fable for gentle men and boys. There is no brutality in it, and there are no women to complicate the lesson in how men must live. In *Islands in the Stream* (1970), the posthumously published manuscript from which *The Old Man* was extracted, bachelor father Thomas Hudson would give more direct lessons in manhood to his three visiting sons from within a similar male preserve; but in this realistic novel, there is plenty of male brutality within that preserve and not a little sexual bravado; and though Hudson himself refrains from both and is implicitly loving with his boys, his conduct elsewhere in the book—especially with women—is scarcely exemplary. Essentially he raises the visiting boys as Clarence Hemingway had raised Ernest and Leicester: as empirical novices in a simplistic world of externals, a world of physical adventures from which complicated questions about human relations are excluded or unasked. Ideally the moral lessons from that physical world should be transferrable to human relations; but since Hudson himself has failed to make that transfer, except with a servant, his anthropomorphized cats, and a few bar companions, we see quite otherwise. Hudson's attempt to play Papa in this novel is painfully shallow and unconvincing, as is his stoic grief after the convenient deaths of all three sons. But at least he makes the attempt, and the closing revelation—that he never understands anybody that loves him—is at least touching in its honesty.

## VIII

The last of the five baby books Ernest's mother had sent him in 1949 contains a letter he left for her shortly after his sixteenth birthday. He had shot a blue heron in violation of the game laws; the game warden's son had discovered it in his boat, and when the warden himself came after Ernest, he fled first to family friends at Horton Bay, then to his Uncle George's summer home in Ironton. In the letter, Ernest is very much his mother's son: he tells her how he had stolen back to their summer cottage at night to kill a chicken and pick some beans and dig some potatoes for her, assures her that the farm will be all right, and asks how long he should continue to hide at Uncle George's.

The game warden episode in Hemingway's adolescence had a curious resonance for him. He told several embellished versions of it to friends over the years, and his sisters Marcelline and Sunny, his brother Leicester, and his wife Mary have since provided four different versions of it in their books.[34] In January 1952, Hemingway began to write his own fictional version of the episode. He worked on it sporadically until 1958, then set it aside to complete his novel about androgynous couples in France in the 1920s, *The Garden of Eden*. "The Last Good Country" (1973), as the unfinished novella is now called, is also about an androgynous couple, a brother and sister, who like Hansel and Gretel run off to the woods together when the brother—Nick Adams—is pursued by game wardens.

The story of their flight is an odd mixture of Western melodrama and childhood fable; some critics call it puerile and sentimental, but even in its flawed and unfinished state, it may be the most genuinely tender and personally revealing story Ernest ever wrote. Nick Adams is a protective and caring brother; his sister Littless is similarly caring, and the intimacy between them seems to me refreshingly rendered. The two siblings characterize themselves as "criminals" who love each other and do not love "the others" in their family (pp. 57-58); they are "different from the others" in that they take risks and get into trouble (p. 99); they have a capacity for what their friend Mr. Packard calls "original sin" (p. 84)—doing things worth repenting and therefore having to cope with consequences; and as they flee through the northern Michigan woods, they cope rather well, as did Hemingway's pioneer ancestors. They are frontier throwbacks, then, and the bond between them—the wellspring of childhood affections—flows fresh and clear like the roadside spring they sit by as the story opens and the similar spring they later camp by in the forest.

It seems significant, moreover, that their flight to the woods repeats the flight of Catherine Barkley and Lieutenant Henry from Italy when they row at night across Lake Maggiore to Switzerland. Littless is like Catherine in many ways, and her portrait confirms the source of Hemingway's good androgynous heroines in his tender relations with admiring, caring, selfless sisters. Like Marcelline, Littless cuts her hair short to resemble her brother's; like Sunny, she hikes with him through the woods and shares his troubles; and like Ursula, who once ran off to Petoskey to be with Ernest, she arranges to run off with Nick. She hopes to prevent him from killing the game warden's son, their only likely tracker; but she also hopes to keep him from joining the Indian girl Trudy, now pregnant by him—and Nick confesses, in an interesting reversal of his attitudes in earlier tales, that he much prefers her to Trudy.[35] He wants to be a "good man" now, a good brother and a good friend, and his sister is plainly the agent of his redemption: she keeps the wellspring flowing fresh and clear.

Littless is like Catherine, then, in fleeing with Nick to their pastoral refuge for criminals and outsiders and cutting her hair short there. She is like her also when she insists they are having "a lovely time" (p. 71), or when she pretends to be an assistant to the Queen of the Whores in Sheboygan (p. 96), or imagines herself as his common-law wife (p. 104). She is in such respects the uninitiated good girl playing—as Catherine plays—with the terms of male privilege, questioning those dubious freedoms, offering redemptive love. Some critics take it for incestuous love and complain of "barely sublimated incest" and "mawkish" sentimentality";[36] but cheerfully indulged adolescent crushes in siblings are scarcely mawkish or incestuous: they are normal testings of love's limits and possibilities, and without them we could not love as adults. What Hemingway catches here, then, is his own adolescent family romance, when as a protective older brother his male identity was assured and he could indulge in androgynous play with admiring younger sisters. He had returned in his fiction to the adolescent wellsprings of his own gentle manliness—here credibly portrayed as Nick hunts, fishes, and cooks for Littless, beds with her in protective innocence, admires her delicate sleeping beauty, shares his literary aims with her, and at the end even reads to her from *Wuthering Heights*!

Their pastoral idyll is not, however, without neurotic drawbacks. Nick's murderous rage toward the game warden's son is like Hemingway's rage at this time at the encroachments—real and imagined—of critical biographers like Philip Young and Charles Fenton; and the portrait of Mrs. Adams, who allows the fictional wardens to encamp in her cottage, retires with a sick headache, and leaves the details of flight and safety to her children, continues the author's ingrown hostility toward his mother—who in fact drove the wardens off with a shotgun and sent Ernest explicit instructions for flight.[37] It is from their mother, moreover, as much as from the game wardens, that Nick and Littless wishfully flee. Both law and mother oppress them, and against such odds their forest idyll cannot last. But Hemingway leaves it intact, suspends it at the last point in his life where superior male strength could be legitimately secured, and turns once more, in *The Garden of Eden*, to the unresolved tensions of adult androgyny.

## IX

After 1958, as health and his capacity to write diminished, he grew increasingly paranoid and suicidal. Always precarious, often inflated, his sense of personal worth had been invested, like his father's before him, in professional and sporting activities rather than domestic (and in that sense maternal) relations; and when these worldly activities failed him, he had no way to hold his own in either realm. On the night after his return from the clinic where he had twice been taken for attempted suicide, Mary Welsh Hemingway sang out from her bedroom the opening phrases of an old Italian folk song, and Ernest joined her from his room in singing the succeeding phrases. Whether that attempted harmony reminded him of his mother's matchless singing, with which he had never harmonized, or simply of his lost youth in Italy, we will never know. By dawn the old androgynous Indian-fighter had decided—like his father before him—not to wait for the approaching fascist troops.

## Notes

1. Carlos Baker, *Ernest Hemingway: A Life Story* (New York: Bantam, 1970), pp. 577-78, 583-84, 605, 620, 684-85, 786; Aaron Lapham, "A Farewell to Machismo," *New York Times Magazine*, 16 October 1977, pp. 51-55, 80-82, 90-99.
2. Marcelline Hemingway Sanford, *At the Hemingways: A Family Portrait* (Boston: Little, Brown, 1962), p. 111. See pp. 109-12 for the full account of these episodes.
3. Elaine Showalter, *A Literature of Their Own* (Princeton, N.J.: Princeton University Press, 1977), pp. 136-37.
4. Ibid., p. 137.
5. Frances Hodgson Burnett, *Little Lord Fauntleroy* (London: Collins, 1974), p. 130.
6. Sanford, *At the Hemingways*, p. 54.

7. Constance Cappel Montgomery, *Hemingway in Michigan* (New York: Fleet, 1966), p. 72. See also pp. 71–72, 81.
8. Ibid., p. 71 (see also pp. 70, 81–82); Scott Donaldson, *By Force of Will: The Life and Art of Ernest Hemingway* (Harmondsworth: Penguin, 1978), pp. 14–15, 170–71, 189–90, 221, 290–96. See also Peter Buckley's view of Grace as a Victorian monster of willful make-believe and selfishly demanding love in *Ernest* (New York: Dial, 1978), Part Two.
9. Sanford, *At the Hemingways*, p. 62.
10. For Hadley's interesting view of her loss of Ernest to Pauline as a kind of beneficial transfer of maternal trust, see Alice Hunt Sokoloff, *Hadley: The First Mrs. Hemingway* (New York: Dodd, Mead, 1973), p. 92.
11. Baker, *Ernest Hemingway*, p. 589. See also pp. 437, 573, 601, 626.
12. For a brief account of the novel's origins, see Sheridan Baker, "Jake Barnes and Spring Torrents," in *Studies in "The Sun Also Rises,"* ed. William White (Columbus, Ohio: Charles E. Merrill, 1969), pp. 40–43.
13. Ernest Hemingway, *The Sun Also Rises* (New York: Scribner's, 1926), p. 22. Page numbers in the text are from this edition.
14. The phrase occurs in Sanford, *At the Hemingways*, p. 184. She notes his regression after the Toronto year on p. 201. See also Carlos Baker's account of these years, pp. 77–99.
15. For an account of these differences and of the novel's genesis, see Michael S. Reynolds, *Hemingway's First War: The Making of "A Farewell to Arms"* (Princeton, N.J.: Princton University Press, 1976).
16. See, for example, Henry Villard, "A Prize Specimen of Wounded Hero," *Yankee Magazine*, July 1979, pp. 134–35; and Baker, *Ernest Hemingway*, pp. 71–73.
17. Sanford, *At the Hemingways*, pp. 190–92.
18. She speaks, for example, of his loafing, pleasure-seeking, borrowing without returning, sponging off others, spending earnings on luxuries, trading on his good looks with "gullible little girls," insulting and shaming her, tongue-thrashing her, sneering at her advice, dismissing her as out-of-date, and bringing in friends who ignore her. 24 July 1920, Hemingway Collection, Kennedy Library, Boston, Mass.
19. Sokoloff, *Hadley*, p. 1. For Hemingway's use of Flaubert, see Edward Engelberg, "Hemingway's 'True Penelope': Flaubert's *L'Education Sentimentale* and *A Farewell to Arms*," *Comparative Literature Studies* 16 (September 1979):189–206. For the Hancock fragment, see Bernard Oldsey, "The Original Beginning," Appendix A, in *Hemingway's Hidden Craft: The Writing of "A Farewell to Arms"* (University Park: Pennsylvania State University Press, 1979), pp. 93–99.
20. Oldsey, "Original Beginning," p. 98; Ernest Hemingway, *A Farewell to Arms* (New York: Scribner's, 1929), p. 93. Page numbers to the novel appear hereafter in the text.
21. *A Farewell to Arms* manuscript, variant p. 206, Hemingway Collection: "And now that she was gone down the corridor, I felt as though all of

me was gone away with her." See also Reynolds, *Hemingway's First War*, p. 289.

22. For the most explicit confirmation, see Mary Welsh Hemingway, *How It Was* (New York: Ballantine, 1976), p. 467. For more implicit references, see pp. 298–99, 371; Baker, *Ernest Hemingway*, p. 685; and Ernest Hemingway, *A Moveable Feast* (New York: Bantam, 1965), pp. 20–21. Consider also Hemingway's supine grin when topped by Max Eastman in the Scribner office fight, Baker, *Ernest Hemingway*, p. 404; and Thomas Hudson's supine cat-cuddling in *Islands in the Stream* (New York: Scribner's, 1970), pp. 203–5 ff.

23. Baker, *Ernest Hemingway*, p. 112.

24. *The Short Stories of Ernest Hemingway* (New York: Scribner's, 1972), p. 26. Pages hereafter are in the text.

25. For this long-lasting controversy, see especially Warren Beck, "The Shorter Happy Life of Mrs. Macomber," *Modern Fiction Studies* 1 (November 1955):28–37; my response to it, *MFS* 6 (Winter 1960–61): 289–96; his response to my response, *MFS* 21 (Autumn 1975):377–85; and our final exchange, *MFS* 22 (Summer 1976):245–69.

26. Baker, *Ernest Hemingway*, p. 371.

27. Ernest Hemingway, *To Have and Have Not* (New York: Scribner's, 1937), pp. 116, 128, 258. Pages hereafter are in the text.

28. Baker, *Ernest Hemingway*, p. 781.

29. See Baker, *Ernest Hemingway*, pp. 379–80, for Pauline's tolerant accommodation of Martha as a "fixture" in their home. Page references in the text to *For Whom the Bell Tolls* are from the 1940 Scribner's edition.

30. Page numbers in the text are to the 1950 Scribner's edition.

31. Baker, *Ernest Hemingway*, p. 626.

32. Peter Griffin will develop in depth the relation between Grace and her father as it affected Ernest in a forthcoming biography for Dutton.

33. Ernest Hemingway, *The Old Man and the Sea* (New York: Scribner's, 1961), p. 21.

34. See Sanford, *At the Hemingways*, pp. 100–02: Madelaine Hemingway Miller, *Ernie: Hemingway's Sister "Sunny" Remembers* (New York: Crown, 1975), pp. 51–53; Leicester Hemingway, *My Brother, Ernest Hemingway* (Cleveland, Ohio: World, 1962), pp. 35–37; and Mary Welsh Hemingway, *How It Was*, pp. 287–88. See also Baker, *Ernest Hemingway*, pp. 31–33. The most reliable scource is Grace's letter to Clarence in Leicester's book.

35. For the Trudy passage—excised by Scribner's from the printed version—see "The Last Good Country," version 2, pp. 11–13, Hemingway Collection. Page numbers in the text are from *The Nick Adams Stories* (New York: Bantam, 1973).

36. See Robert O. Stephen, ed., *Ernest Hemingway: The Critical Reception* (New York: Burt Franklin, 1977), pp. 483, 487–89, 493.

37. See Leicester Hemingway, *My Brother*, p. 36.

# Cheryl A. Wall

# Zora Neale Hurston: Changing Her Own Words

The developing tradition of black women's writing nurtured now in the prose and poetry of such writers as Toni Morrison and Alice Walker began with the work of Zora Neale Hurston. Hurston was not the first Afro-American woman to publish a novel, but she was the first to create language and imagery that reflected the reality of black women's lives. Ignoring the stereotypes, social and literary, that her predecessors spent their energies rejecting, Hurston rooted her art in the cultural traditions of the black rural South. As a daughter of the region, she claimed these traditions by birthright. As an anthropologist, she reclaimed them through years of intense, often perilous, research. As a novelist, she summoned this legacy in her choice of setting, her delineation of character, and most devotedly in her distillation of language. Hers became the first authentic black female voice in American literature.

Despite this achievement, Hurston's work suffered years of obscurity and critical neglect. Ten years ago, outside of that small group of readers and scholars whose primary devotion is to Afro-American literature, few had even heard her name. Still fewer were able to read her work, as it had been out of print since long before her death in 1960. Today Hurston's work has been revived, her reputation restored. She is now considered one of the major writers to have emerged from the Harlem Renaissance. Moreover, hers is the pre-eminent achievement in Afro-American letters during the 1930s; five of her seven books were published in that decade. Two of these, the folklore collection, *Mules and Men* (1935), and the novel, *Their Eyes Were Watching God* (1937), are now recognized classics in the Afro-American canon. The novel is becoming a favorite in American literature and women's studies courses as well. Although very much of its time, *Their Eyes Were Watching God* is timeless. As Sherley Anne Williams has written, its heroine's "individual quest for fulfillment becomes any woman's tale."[1] Other scholars and critics have begun to analyze Hurston's fiction in numerous articles and essays. The fascinating but hitherto fragmented story of her life has been reconstructed in a meticulously researched biography. Although her work is not nearly as well known as it deserves to be, more people have read it in the last few years than in Hurston's lifetime. For general readers and scholars alike, Zora Neale Hurston has emerged as a writer who must be taken seriously.

The black consciousness and feminist movements spurred the rediscovery and reassessment of Hurston's work. Under this impetus, her work began to be reprinted in the 1960s; it garnered little attention initially, overlooked in the flood of books by black writers suddenly returned to print. More of her books became available in the 1970s, often republished with introductions by leading black scholars and critics. By this time, feminists were retrieving works by "lost" women writers, a category for which Hurston was eminently qualified. Hurston's strong, resilient female characters won further favor; the first anthology of her prose, edited by Alice Walker, carried the imprint of the Feminist Press. Walker, whose championing of Hurston has been unselfish and unstinting, surely spoke for others when she wrote, "I became aware of my need of Zora Neale Hurston some time before I knew her work existed."[2] Walker explained that she found in Hurston a conviction of "racial health"; Hurston's characters were invaluable because of their ability to accept and love themselves.

The critical perspectives inspired by the black consciousness and feminist movements allow us to see Hurston's writings in a new way. They correct distorted views of her folklore as charming and quaint, set aside misperceptions of her characters as minstrels caught, in Richard Wright's phrase, "between laughter and tears."[3] These new perspectives inform this re-evaluation of Hurston's work. She asserted that black people, while living in a racist society that denied their humanity, had created an alternative culture that validated their worth as human beings. Although that culture was in some respects sexist, black women, like black men, attained personal identity not by transcending the culture but by embracing it.

Hurston's respect for the cultural traditions of black people is the most important constant in her career. This respect threads through her entire oeuvre, linking the local-color short fiction of her youth, her ethnographic research in the rural South and the Caribbean (an account of her fieldwork in Jamaica and Haiti, *Tell My Horse*, was published in 1938), her novels, and the essays she contributed to popular journals in her later years. In all, she published more than fifty short stories and articles in addition to her book-length works. Because her focus was on black cultural traditions, she rarely explored interracial themes. The black/white conflict, which loomed paramount in the fiction of her black contemporaries, in Wright's novels especially, hardly surfaced in Hurston's. Poet and critic June Jordan has described how the absence of explicitly political protest caused Hurston's work to be devalued. Affirmation, not protest, is Hurston's hallmark. Yet, as Jordan argues, "affirmation of Black values and lifestyle within the American context is, indeed, an act of protest."[4] Hurston appreciated and approved the reluctance of blacks to reveal "that which the soul lives by" to the hostile and uncomprehending gaze of outsiders. But the interior reality was what she wished to probe. In that reality, blacks ceased to be "tongueless, earless, eyeless conveniences" whose labor whites exploited; they ceased to be mules and were men and women.

The survival of the spirit was proclaimed first and foremost through language. As a writer, Hurston was keenly sensitive to the richness of black verbal expression. Like Langston Hughes and Sterling Brown, she had no patience with theories of linguistic deficiency among blacks; she ignored racist assumptions that rural blacks spoke as they did because they were too stupid to learn standard English. Hurston, whose father was a Baptist preacher, was well acquainted with the tradition of verbal elegance among black people. From her father's example, she perceived how verbal agility conferred status within the community. His sermons had demonstrated as well the power of his language to convey the complexity of the lives of his parishioners. Early in her career, Hurston attempted to delineate "characteristics of Negro expression." She stressed the heightened sense of drama revealed in the preference for action words and the "will to adorn" reflected in the profusion of metaphor and simile, and in the use of double descriptives (*low-down*) and verbal nouns (*funeralize*). To her, the "will to adorn" bespoke a feeling "that there can never be enough of beauty, let alone too much." Zora Hurston shared that feeling, as the beautifully poetic prose of her novels attests. The collective folk expression was the soil that nourished the individual expression of her novels. After a lengthy dialogue with her homefolk, Hurston was prepared to change some words of her own.[5]

In one of her first published articles, Hurston declared:

> BUT I AM NOT tragically colored. There is no great sorrow dammed
> up in my soul, nor lurking behind my eyes. I do not mind at all. I
> do not belong to the sobbing school of Negrohood who hold that
> nature somehow has given them a lowdown dirty deal and whose
> feelings are all hurt about it. . . . No, I do not weep at the world—I
> am too busy sharpening my oyster knife.[6]

The exuberant tone of the assertions in "How It Feels to Be Colored Me" suggests that they were more strongly felt than reasoned. Hurston locates the source of her feelings in her childhood experiences in Eatonville, Florida, the hometown to which she often returned in fiction and fact. Eatonville was an all-black town, the first to be incorporated in the United States. Hurston remembered it as a place of possibility and promise. She revered the wit and wisdom of the townspeople, admired the originality of their culture and their moral and aesthetic values, saw in their language drama and the "will to adorn." Having been insulated from racism in her early years, unaware of racial distinctions until she was nine, she professed herself "astonished" rather than angered by discrimination. The lingering astonishment accounts perhaps for the shortcomings of the article as self and racial definition; Hurston relied on "exotic primitive" myths popular in the twenties to round out the explanation of herself and her people.

During this time Hurston was studying anthropology at Barnard under the tutelage of Franz Boas. This study complemented by her fieldwork in Florida and Louisiana allowed her to appreciate her past intellectually as well as intuitively. No longer were her homefolk simply good storytellers, whose values were commendable, superstitions remarkable, and humor penetrating. As such, they had been well suited for local-color fiction of the kind Hurston published in the 1920s. Now however, "they became a part of cultural anthropology; scientific objects who could and should be studied for their academic value."[7] The cultural relativity of anthropology freed Hurston from the need to defend her subjects' alleged inferiority. She could discard behavioral explanations drawn from racial mythology. Eatonville blacks were neither exotic nor primitive; they had simply selected different characteristics from what Ruth Benedict, another pioneering anthropologist trained by Boas, called the "great arc of human potentialities."

In possession of these liberating theories, Hurston set forth in 1927 on the first of a series of field expeditions. Not surprisingly her first stop was Eatonville, a site she confidently expected to yield a rich lode of material. When the results of her fieldwork were published in *Mules and Men*, she introduced the book by stating, "I was glad when somebody told me, 'you may go and collect Negro folk-lore.'"[8] Her attitude was not typical of a professional anthropologist and neither was her method. She immersed herself in the culture she studied. Sitting on the porch of Joe Clarke's store in Eatonville, later signing on at sawmill camps and apprenticing herself to hoodoo doctors, she became a member of each community she entered. Clearly her race and personal heritage gave her an entrée previous researchers lacked. Beyond that, Hurston felt herself part and parcel of the culture she investigated. The diligence and skill with which she pursued her studies enabled her to capitalize on these advantages.

*Mules and Men* holds the distinction of being the first collection of Afro-American folklore published by an Afro-American. It distinguishes itself in other ways. Alan Lomax called it "the most engaging, genuine, and skillfully written book in the field of folklore."[9] Unlike many of its predecessors, it presents the lore not to patronize or demean but to affirm and celebrate. Written for a popular audience, it is highly readable; after nearly half a century, it has lost none of its capacity to delight. *Mules and Men* contains seventy folktales, but it is more than a transcription of individual texts. As her biographer Robert Hemenway points out, Hurston adds an unifying narrative that provides contexts as well as texts. By showing when a story is told, how, and to what purpose, Hurston attempts to restore the original meanings of the tales. Folktales, she understood, serve a function more significant than mere entertainment; "they are profound expressions of a group's behavior."[10] They cannot be comprehended without reference to those whose values and beliefs they embody. Consequently, the tales in *Mules and Men* are not collected from faceless informants, but from real men and women whose lives readers are briefly invited to share. Sharing their lives more profoundly, Hurston was ultimately forced to confront the role of women in rural black life. Her response, necessarily personal and engaged, gave shape to her most successful fiction.

Hurston met the woman who most informed this response soon after she arrived in Polk County, Florida, in January 1928. The sawmill camp where Hurston settled was an even richer repository of the folktales, worksongs, blues and cries, proverbs, and sermons than Eatonville had been. And of the people who lived there, Big Sweet was the most memorable. Hurston devoted several pages of her autobiography, *Dust Tracks on a Road* (1942), to her friendship with this woman; the influence of Big Sweet is highly visible in characters in Hurston's novels. Although Hurston gives few details about her appearance, the woman's name, with its suggestions of physical power and sexual attractiveness, of strength and tenderness, aptly sums up her character. Significantly, Hurston hears her before she sees her, and it is her talk that attracts her attention. Big Sweet is "specifying," "playing the dozens" with an outmatched male opponent. Before a large and appreciative audience, she breaks the news to him "in one of her mildest bulletins that his pa was a double-humpted camel and his ma a grass-gut cow." This performance gives Hurston "a measure of this Big Sweet," and her judgment is soon verified by the opinions of others on the job. Though fearsome, Big Sweet is not feared as much as she is respected, because the community draws a distinction between meanness and the defense of one's integrity. Hurston sees the wisdom of acquiring her friendship and hence protection. Big Sweet becomes the author's guardian and guide. She identifies informants, awards prizes in "lying" contests, and eventually saves Hurston's life.[11]

In his article, "Negotiating Respect: Patterns of Presentation among Black Women," folklorist Roger Abrahams notes: "how women assert their image and values as women is seldom found in the folklore literature."[12] In keeping with this premise, Big Sweet contributes only two folktales to *Mules and Men*; neither focuses on female identity. The relative scarcity of woman-centered tales in the oral tradition must have been one of the revelations of Hurston's fieldwork. Although tales created by men about women, many of them virulently antifemale, exist in some quantity, tales about women told from a female point of view are rare.[13] Hurston's narrative strategy permits her to sustain a female perspective in her account of Big Sweet. Her presentation of the context as well as the text of the lore is crucial in this regard. In the general narrative of her experiences in Polk County and in her descriptions of the specific situations in which stories are told, Hurston shows how Big Sweet asserts and maintains her identity. From these descriptions, the reader can take her own measure of this woman.

The dramatic performance of Big Sweet's "specifying" is not recounted in *Mules and Men*; her entrance here is low-keyed. She tells her two tales, "Why the Mocking Bird Is Away on Friday" and "How the 'Gator Got Black," matter-of-factly, but the second is preceded by an exchange that reveals a bit of her mettle. Someone else has recited "How Brer 'Gator Got His Tongue Worn Out" which has reminded Big Sweet of the similar tale she knows. Thus the reader sees one way the lore is transmitted. Before she gets a chance to begin her story, however, Big Sweet is interrupted and must reclaim her place in the discussion. "When Ah'm shellin' my corn, you keep out yo' nubbins" wins her readmission and the tale is told. A bit later, as the others joke and lie good-naturedly, Big Sweet injects a personal and pointed warning to her lover not to repeat his infidelity of the night before. He appeals to the other men for assistance, but they cannot beat her "specifying." Her declaration of independence cuts right to the heart of the matter: "Lemme tell *you* something, *any* time Ah shack up wid any man Ah gives myself de privilege to go wherever he might be, night or day. Ah got de law in my mouth."[14]

Big Sweet's behavior conforms to a pattern Abrahams outlines. Respect in the black community is not a permanent given; it must constantly be earned and negotiated. For women, these negotiations usually occur, as in the scenes described above, when people are "just talking." No one, whatever her reputation, is beyond challenge. "Ideally a woman has the ability to *talk sweet* with her infants and peers but *talk smart* or *cold* with anyone who might threaten her self-image."[15] Big Sweet exemplifies this ideal. She uses "Little-Bit" as a term of endearment for the narrator Zora in *Mules and Men*, warns her that collecting songs from one of the men has provoked his lover's jealousy, and promises to defend her. A conversation between her and Hurston quoted in *Dust Tracks* further evidences her ability to "talk sweet." Not understanding why Hurston wants to collect "lies" (folktales), she pledges to aid her in doing so. Such conversations are held privately; the public smart talking she does earns Big Sweet respect. A crucial incident recounted in *Mules and Men* pits Big Sweet against her arch rival, Ella Wall, a woman whose feats are also chronicled by Leadbelly and other country blues singers. Ella Wall enters the camp "jook" (a combination dance hall, gaming parlor and bawdy house) and sends a bold message to Big Sweet's man. The two women exchange verbal insults and then physical threats, until the conflict is halted by the arrival of the white quarters boss. While Ella Wall is disarmed and thrown off the job, Big Sweet stands up to the white man and refuses to yield her weapon. Her erstwhile lover expresses the admiration of the group in a telling compliment: "You wuz noble! You wuz uh whole woman and half uh man."[16] Big Sweet's increased respect is not earned at the cost of her femininity. Her value as a woman is in fact enhanced by her fierce conduct. After the argument, her lover proudly escorts her home.

Zora Hurston knew that approval of Big Sweet was not shared by the world outside the lumber camp. The life of this hard-living, knife-toting woman was the stuff of myriad stereotypes. And Hurston seemed all too aware of this judgment when she wrote, "I thought of all I had to live for and turned cold at the thought of dying in a violent manner in a sordid saw-mill camp." A dramatic revelation follows: "But for my very life I knew I couldn't leave Big Sweet if the fight came. She had been too faithful to me."[17] Hurston vows to stand by her friend. Passages such as this have caused some critics to accuse Hurston of being condescending and self-serving in her presentation of the poor. She does seem to be playing to her audience here; *sordid* voices their opinion of the camp and its people. It does not express Hurston's view. Her problem was to legitimize Big Sweet's conduct without defending it or positing sociological explanations for it. Her solution was to identify the sources of its legitimacy within the folk culture itself. Characteristically, her approach was subtle and easily overlooked by the casual reader; it was deliberate nonetheless. Just before the fight scene, Hurston described the visit of a traveling preacher to the camp. His sermon, "Behold de Rib," is a variant of the creation myth; its text is Genesis 2:21, its subject is female equality.

"Behold de Rib" is one of the book's highlights. It captures the pithy logic of folk wisdom, the rhythmic cadence and vivid imagery of the down-home preacher, and a good measure of folk humor. The preacher begins by defining his terms: he instructs his congregants, "Behold means to look and see," and invites them to "look at dis woman God done made." Before focusing on woman, however, he pauses to consider God's previous handiwork and envisions the acts of creation. A cluster of visual images along with the repetition of the phrase "I can see" unify this section of the sermon/poem, as the preacher bears witness to what can be seen through the "eye of Faith." God emerges as regent and warrior, striding through space, wearing the elements as a helmet, blowing storms through his lips. To make a place for the world, he seizes "de mighty axe of his proving power" and opens a gash in "stubborn-standing space." To light the heavens, ". . . God shook his head/ And a thousand million diamonds/Flew out from his glittering crown/And studded de evening sky and made de stars."

This last is a familiar trope in black preaching and brings to mind James Weldon Johnson's poem, "The Creation." One notes that both speakers have an anthropomorphic conception of God, but in "The Creation" He is "lonely"; in his most stirring analogy the speaker compares Him to a "mammy" bending over her baby. A masculine, even martial, God presides over the world of sexual equality. Johnson's speaker ends his story before getting to what is the central event of "Behold de Rib." Here stars are lit especially to shine on sleeping man and emerging woman:

> So God put Adam into a deep sleep
> And took out a bone, ah hah!
> And it is said that it was a rib.
> Behold de rib!
> A bone out of a man's side.
> He put de man to sleep and made wo-man,
> And men and women been sleeping together ever since.
> Behold de rib!
> Brothers, if God
> Had taken dat bone out of man's head
> He would have meant for woman to rule, hah
> If he had taken a bone out of his foot,
> He would have meant for us to dominize and rule.
> He could have made her out of back-bone
> And then she would have been behind us.
> But, no, God Amighty, he took de bone out of his side
> So dat places de woman beside us;
> Hah! God knowed his own mind.
> Behold de rib!

The preacher has modulated to a comic key, deepening the humor by alluding to that most famous of folk sermons, "Dry Bones." Still, his message is a serious one, as is apparent in the conclusion when he calls on his listeners, male and female, to march to glory side by side "in step wid de host dat John saw." [18]

Its rhythm and imagery place "Behold de Rib" squarely in the tradition of black preaching, but its mesage is anomalous. Female equality was not, is not, a common subject in black sermons. Hurston had transcribed other sermons in her field notes, including the one that became the centerpiece of her first novel, *Jonah's Gourd Vine*. Her selection of "Behold de Rib" was deliberate and so was its placement in *Mules and Men*. It prepares the reader to accept and approve Big Sweet's actions in the conflict that follows. She is heroic, as any man who similarly defended his honor would be. Although Hurston draws no connection between the sermon and the struggle—here and throughout the book her method is presentational, not analytical—the reader's approbation of Big Sweet is won in part by the juxtaposition of the two scenes.

The portrayal of Big Sweet anticipates the process of self-discovery Hurston's fictional heroines undergo. Like her, they must learn to manipulate language. The novels disclose Hurston's awareness that women, like children, are encouraged to be seen but not heard. She knew that few women had joined the lying sessions on Joe Clarke's store porch in Eatonville; Big Sweet was one of a small number of female storytellers in the folklore collection. It was Big Sweet's talk though that first captured Hurston's attention. Her words were emblematic of her power, for they signaled her ownership of self. The ability to back up words with actions was a second indicator of an independent self. The care Hurston took to legitimize Big Sweet's behavior intimated the expected reaction to an assertive woman. Nevertheless, Hurston believed that individual black women could base their personal autonomy on communal traditions. In so doing, her characters achieved their status as heroines.

Lucy Potts Pearson is such a character. Although her husband John is its main protagonist, *Jonah's Gourd Vine* traces Lucy's coming of age as well as his. Loosely based on the lives of Hurston's parents, *Jonah's Gourd Vine* tells the story of Lucy and John's courtship and marriage, John's swift rise to prominence as a Baptist preacher, his equally swift fall resulting from his marital infidelities, Lucy's strength and perseverance, and the family's ultimate dissolution. All this takes place against a background of social and technological change occurring in the South around the turn of the century. These changes are subordinate to the cultural traditions that remain intact: the sermons and sayings, children's games and rhymes, hoodoo beliefs and practices. In the foreground are the experiences of John and Lucy. Lucy dies two thirds of the way through the novel, but her spirit hovers above it until the end.

That talk, and especially women's talk, is a major concern of the book is established on the very first page. Ned Crittenden accuses his wife, John's mother, of "always talkin' more'n yuh know."[19] Amy Crittenden is undaunted, "Ah changes jes ez many words ez Ah durn please!" (p. 17), but her ability to act on her words is limited. An ex-slave whose eldest son John is the child of her former master, Amy has been "freed" to a marriage with a ne'er-do-well sharecropper. Abused by a husband who is unable to "treasure" his children as she does, Amy must watch him hire John out to a white man, the equivalent of selling him into slavery. Amy's resistance is covert: she encourages her son to escape his stepfather's tyranny by seeking work on the plantation owned by his unacknowledged white father. John's return to the town of his birth adheres to the pattern of the young man arriving from the provinces. Every new thing, from shoes to trains, is a source of fascination. But the greatest fascination is with words. The verbal play of the plantation's children, the ribald ditties of youths, and the prayers and sermons of the elders spark John's imagination. To win Lucy's love, he must learn to speak for himself. Both lovers search for words that can express mutual affection and respect.

Their effort is complicated by class distinctions within the community. John is an "over-the-creek nigger" with no prospects. Lucy's father is a land-owner, and her mother has arranged for her to marry a well-to-do farmer when she is of age. John has no education. Lucy is the star pupil in her school, famed for the long recitations she commits to memory. Though attracted to Lucy from the first, John finds her difficult to approach:

> When the opportunity presented itself he couldn't find words. Handling Big 'Oman, Lacey, Semmie, Bootsie and Mehaley merely called for action, but with Lucy he needed words and words that he did not have. [P. 63]

Recognizing that Lucy will not be swayed by the charms that capture other girls' affection, John yearns to master her language. Lucy assures him that he can learn recitations better than she, and he enrolls in school. Neither realizes that the needed words cannot be found in textbooks. They can only be learned from a deeper engagement with the folk culture. John achieves this when he spends a time in a work camp, where "next to showing muscle-power, [he] loved to tell stories." Upon his return, he is prepared to court Lucy in the traditional style. This time she is the one who must master a new tongue.

Robert Hemenway has identified the folkloric origins of the courtship ritual John employs.[20] Organized around the riddle—"are you a flying lark or a setting dove?"—the ritual allows the questioner to ascertain a woman's availability and willingness to pursue romance. A problem arises in the novel because the woman-child Lucy (she is only fourteen) does not know how to respond to the question. She had begun the conversation gaily, coyly matching wits with John. But as John broached more substantive concerns, "Lucy suddenly lost her fluency of speech." John presses this point thus:

> "Lucy, you pay much 'tention tuh birds?"
> "Unhunh. De Jay bird say 'Laz'ness will kill you,' and he go to hell ev'ry Friday and totes uh grain uh sand in his mouf tuh put out de fire, and den de doves say, 'Where you *been* so long?'"
> John cut her short. "Ah don't mean dat way, Lucy. Whut Ah wants tuh know is, which would you ruther be, if you had yo' ruthers—uh lark uh flyin', uh uh dove uh settin'?"
> "Ah don't know whut you talkin' 'bout, John. It mus' be uh new riddle."
> "Naw 'tain't, Lucy. Po' me, Lucy. Ahm uh one wingded bird. Don't leave me lak dat, Lucy." [Pp. 124-25]

Far from new, the riddle is ancient and is meant to elicit a formulaic response. If Lucy wants to encourage John's advances, she should identify herself as a flying lark. Her ignorance of the proper answer imperils the future of the relationship. Lucy is resourceful enough to sift through her memory for plausible replies. She does not hit upon the correct one, but she does keep the conversation going. Her references to the jaybird, for example, demonstrates her awareness that the answer is to be found in folk traditions.

The reference is to a familiar folktale, a variant of which, interestingly, is recounted by Big Sweet in *Mules and Men*. Here it is beside the point, as John's quick rejoinder makes clear. He poses the riddle directly. Lucy's continued inability to respond calls forth a plaintive cry: "Po' me, Lucy. Ahm uh one wingded bird."

Although her book learning is commendable, Lucy is clearly not sufficiently conversant with the rituals of her own culture. This suggests an immaturity and lack of experience that would render her an unsuitable wife. The situation is saved only when Lucy helps John improvise a new ritual that can substitute for the old. The instrument is a handkerchief out of which John has crafted what Hurston calls "a love knot." The lovers hold opposite ends of it throughout the conversation, and when Lucy misses the riddle, she points John's attention to the knot. Regaining her ground, she asks John to state what is on his mind. Wary, he asks first for a kiss ("Kiss me and loose me so Ah kin talk.") The kiss unlocks the poetic power that characterizes John's speech for the rest of the novel:

> "Lucy, Ah looked up intuh Heben and Ah seen you among de
> angels right 'round de throne, and when Ah seen *you*, mah heart
> swole up and put wings on mah shoulders, and Ah 'gin tuh fly
> 'round too, but Ah never would uh knowed yo' name if ole Gab'ull
> hadn't uh whispered it tuh me." [P. 125]

Lucy has reconferred John's wings. Though not as thoroughly grounded in the folk culture as he, she is knowledgeable enough to induce him to state his proposal in terms they *both* can understand. When he does, she accepts.[21] Their acting out of the courtship ritual predicts a marriage between two active partners, both of whom are able to manipulate language and negotiate respect between themselves and with others. It does not, however, foretell a marriage between equals. The prerogatives of maleness ultimately undo the balance.

Although he continues to profess and feel love and respect for Lucy, John Pearson does not remain faithful to her. His philandering, which begins shortly after the marriage and continues until her death, not only causes her great emotional pain but frequently jeopardizes the well-being of the entire family. He struggles against his weakness, expresses remorse when he fails, yet lacks all insight into his behavior. A serious flaw in the novel is Hurston's failure to provide a compelling motivation for John's conduct. A reader may infer that John's irresponsibility is, at least in part, a legacy of slavery. The plantation owner's initial reaction to John is, "What a fine stud." He projects all of his sexual fantasies on to John, labeling him at one point "a walking orgasm. A living exultation." John's sexual misadventures never cease to enthrall this man, who aids him in escaping rather than standing up to their consequences. In a period of transition between slavery and freedom, John remains bound by the slaveholder's conception of black men.

Lucy is, by contrast, a new black woman. Whenever John is irresponsible, Lucy is prepared to compensate. What he lacks in ambition and initiative, she is more than able to supply. She had defied her family to marry him and remains steadfast in her love and loyalty. She even looks with compassion on John's struggle to conquer the "brute beast" within, a struggle that intensifies after he is called to the ministry. John's spiritual call is genuine, but his acceptance of it also permits him to design a self-image independent of the white world. His move to Eatonville has further encouraged this possibility. There he can assume his rightful role as leader, his talents can be given free rein. The canker that galls is his recognition that Lucy deserves much of the credit for his success.

John's fellows are not blind to this fact, and they enjoy baiting him with the knowledge: "Aw, 'tain't you, Pearson, . . . iss dat li'l' handful uh woman you got on de place" (p. 178). His resentment of his dependence on Lucy grows and expresses itself in his demand for her total dependence on him. A comparison of the following passage with the courtship ritual discussed above measures the damage the marriage suffers.

> "Lucy, is you sorry you married me instid uh some big nigger
> wid uh whole heap uh money and titles hung on tuh him?"
> "Whut make you ast me dat? If you tired uh me, jus' leave me.
> Another man over de fence waiting fuh yo' job." [P. 179]

John's reaction to Lucy's verbal play is a violent threat; he will kill her if she ever repeats that fanciful remark. He stakes out claims of ownership, vowing to be Lucy's first and last man. Calming himself, he asks why Lucy has said such a thing. Her response is telling: "Aw, John, you know dat's jus' uh by-word. Ah hears all de women say dat." Lucy is answering John in terms sanctioned by the folk culture, terms that allow for her autonomy. She is engaging in the same kind of verbal sparring the courtship ritual required. The "by-word" would permit Lucy to negotiate respect in this exchange too, but John is no longer concerned with Lucy's ability to participate in cultural traditions. He concedes that the expression is a common one, but forbids her to use it.

Lucy continues to be supportive of John's career. Through her maneuvering, John becomes pastor of a large church, moderator of the State Baptist Association, and mayor of Eatonville. He can never accept her assistance as a complement to his gifts. He accuses: "You always tryin' tuh tell me whut tuh do. Ah wouldn't be where Ah is, if Ah didn't know more'n you think Ah do. You ain't mah guardzeen nohow" (p. 189). John's real defense against what he perceives to be Lucy's domination is other women. Of course, she cannot retaliate in kind. Words are her only defense, righteous, chastising words that strike fear in John's heart but fail to make him change his ways.

The climactic exchange takes one back to the opening pages of the novel. In his home, though not outside it, John has come to resemble Ned Crittenden, telling his wife to shut her mouth. Like Amy, Lucy refuses to be silenced. Instead she reproaches John severely and claims rights for herself and her children. "Big talk," she tells him, "ain't changin' whut you doin'. You can't clean yo' self wid yo' tongue lak uh cat." For the first time in their marriage, John strikes his wife. This action, Hurston later suggested, prompted the novel's title. Taken from Jonah 4:6-10, the title refers to the gourd vine which grew profusely and gave the prophet shade. The next morning a worm attacked the vine and it withered. Thus did God punish his disobedient servant. To Hurston the Biblical story represented: "Great and sudden growth. One act of malice and it is withered and gone."[22] Slapping Lucy marks the beginning of the end for John; his public fortunes decline, and his private life falls into disarray. Years later he has no understanding of what has happened to him. It is literally the end for Lucy, who dies of an illness soon after. Unlike John, however, she has learned something from her experiences, a lesson she passes on to her favorite daughter. "Don't you love nobody better'n you do yo'self. Do, you'll be dying befo' yo' time is out."

Though Lucy's insight is personal, she has expressed it in the manner of a folk proverb. Throughout the novel, her speech is aphoristic. Sayings like the still current "God sho' don't like ugly" and the less familiar, more ingenious "God don't eat okra" (in other words, He doesn't like crooked, slick ways) roll easily off Lucy's tongue. She has mastered the language and absorbed much of the wisdom of her culture. In the end, she apprehends some of its limitations. She hears the silence where the sayings affirming female identity should be. She espies the untaught knowledge that no one can live through someone else and begins to teach it. Without her realizing it, the folk culture through her husband had assigned Lucy Pearson a "place"; she warns her daughter to be on guard against such a fate. Loving John too much, she has acquiesced in her own suppression. At her death, she remains on the threshold of self-discovery.

Although Lucy is the character who is given insight, the novel is less hers than John's. He becomes the central character because he serves the author's purposes beyond the demands of the plot. A contemporary reviewer rightly called *Jonah's Gourd Vine* a "talkfest," and a recent critic describes it as "a series of linguistic moments." Both discern that language is Hurston's priority. Published before *Mules and Men* though written afterward, the novel was Hurston's first opportunity to share at length the discoveries of her fieldwork. She incorporated so much of her research that one reviewer objected to her characters being mere pegs on which she hung their dialect and folkways.[23] The objection is grossly overstated, but it does highlight a problem in the book. Too often the folklore overwhelms the formal narrative. The novel is enriched nonetheless by its numerous examples of the

Negro's "will to adorn," many of the expressions coming directly from Hurston's notes. She believed resolutely that blacks aspired for and achieved beauty in their verbal expression. With extraordinary care, she sought to reproduce their speech exactly as it was spoken. Given these concerns, John Pearson's was necessarily the key role. As preacher, hence poet, he represented the verbal artistry of his people at its height. He became, in the words of critic Larry Neal, "the intelligence of the community, the bearer of its traditions and highest possibilities."[24] This profound engagement with his culture causes John's struggle to reconcile his physical and spiritual selves to take precedence over Lucy's effort to claim her autonomy. In Hurston's second and most compelling novel, the female quest is paramount. The heroine, through acquiring an intimate knowledge of the folk culture, gains the self-knowledge necessary for true fulfillment.

With the publication of *Their Eyes Were Watching God*, it was clear that Zora Neale Hurston was an artist in full command of her talent. Here the folk material complements rather than overwhelms the narrative. The sustained beauty of Hurston's prose owes much to the body of folk expression she had recorded and studied, but much more to the maturity of her individual voice. The language of this novel *sings*. Unlike Lucy, Janie, the heroine of *Their Eyes*, is a fully realized character. During the twenty-odd years spanned by the plot, she grows from a diffident teenager to a woman in complete possession of her self. Two recurring metaphors, the pear tree and the horizon, help unify the narrative. The first symbolizes organic union with another, the second, the individual experiences one must acquire to achieve selfhood. Early reviewers thought of the novel as a love story, but recent commentators designate Janie's search for identity as the novel's major theme. Following the pattern we have observed, Janie's self-discovery depends on her learning to manipulate language. Her success is announced in the novel's prologue when, as a friend listens in rapt attention, Janie begins to tell her own story.

The action of the novel proper begins when Janie is sixteen, beautiful, and eager to struggle with life, but unable to articulate her wishes and dreams. Her consciousness awakens as she watches bees fertilizing the blossoms of a pear tree. In the following passage, the narrative voice is not Janie's but the scene, like the novel as a whole, expresses her point of view:

> She was stretched on her back beneath the pear tree soaking in the alto chant of the visiting bees, the gold of the sun and the panting breath of the breeze when the inaudible voice of it all came to her. She saw a dust-bearing bee sink into the sanctum of a bloom; the thousand sister-calyxes arch to meet the love embrace and the ecstatic shiver of the tree from root to tiniest branch creaming in every blossom and frothing with delight. So this was a marriage!

> She had felt a pain remorseless sweet that left her limp and
> languid.[25]

The lyricism of the passage mutes somewhat its intensely sexual imagery. Still, the imagery is remarkably explicit for a woman novelist of Hurston's time. Janie's response to the scene and her acceptance of its implications for her own life are instructive: "Oh to be a pear tree—*any* tree in bloom!" Janie acknowledges sexuality as a natural part of life, a major aspect of her identity. Before she has the chance to act on this belief, however, her grandmother interposes a radically different viewpoint.

To Nanny, her granddaughter's nascent sexuality is alarming. Having been unable to protect herself and her daughter from sexual exploitation, Nanny determines to safeguard Janie. Janie must repress her sexuality in order to avoid sexual abuse; the only haven is marriage. Marriage had not been an option for Nanny, who as a slave was impregnated by her master; her mistress had forced her to flee with her newborn infant. Her daughter was raped by a black schoolteacher, convincing Nanny that male treachery knows no racial bounds. The world has thwarted her dreams of what a woman should be for herself and her daughter, "Ah wanted to preach a great sermon about colored women sittin' on high, but they wasn't no pulpit for me," but she has saved the text for Janie. She envisions her on the pedestal reserved for southern white women, far above the drudgery that has characterized Nanny's own life—the drudgery that has made the black woman "de mule uh de world." She arranges for Janie to marry Logan Killicks, an old man whose sixty acres and a mule constitute his eligibility. "The vision of Logan Killicks was desecrating the pear tree, but Janie didn't know how to tell Nanny that." So she assents to her grandmother's wish.

Joe Starks offers Janie an escape from her loveless marriage. He arrives just after Logan Killicks, despairing of his efforts to win his wife's affection by "pampering" her, has bought a second mule and ordered Janie to plow alongside him. Perceiving that Killicks's command threatens to reduce her to the status her grandmother abhorred, Janie decides to escape with Joe. Their marriage fulfills Nanny's dreams. Eventually it causes Janie to understand that the old woman's dreams are not her own. Initially though, Joe Starks cuts a fine figure. Stylishly dressed and citified, he is a man of great ambition and drive. He is like no *black* man Janie has ever seen. He reminds her vaguely of successful white men, but she cannot grasp the implications of the resemblance. She can appreciate his big plans and the élan with which he courts her. Tempering her reservations that "he did not represent sun-up and pollen and blooming trees," Janie resolves, "he spoke for far horizon. He spoke for change and chance" (p. 50).

It quickly becomes apparent that, like Nanny, Joe has borrowed his criteria for success from the white world. He takes Janie to Eatonville because there, he believes, he can be a "big ruler of things." His ambition is soon realized. He buys property and opens a store which becomes the town's meeting place. He decrees that roads be dug, a post office established, a street lamp installed, and town incorporation papers drawn. Already landlord, store-keeper, and postmaster, Joe runs for mayor to consolidate his power. After his election, he builds a large white house that is a travesty of a plantation mansion, and then furnishes it in the grand manner right down to brass spittoons. His brashness elicits equal measures of respect and resentment from the townspeople. As much as they admire his accomplishments, they take exception to his manner. One citizen's observation is widely shared: "he loves obedience out of everybody under de sound of his voice" (p. 78).

Everybody naturally includes Janie. Joe assigns her the role of "Mrs. Mayor Starks." She must hold herself apart from the townspeople, conduct herself according to the requirements of his position. Under no circumstances must she speak in public. Starks first imposes this rule during a ceremony marking the opening of the store. The ceremony has occasioned much speech-making, and toward the end, Janie is invited to say a few words. Before she can respond, her husband takes the floor to announce:

> Thank yuh fuh yo' compliments, but mah wife don't know
> nothin' 'bout no speech-makin'. Ah never married her for nothin'
> lak dat. She's uh woman and her place is in de home. [P. 69]

Joe's announcement takes Janie by surprise. Unsure that she even wants to speak, she strongly resents being denied the right to decide for herself. Joe's prohibitions increase. He forbids Janie to participate in the lying sessions held on the store porch; she is hustled inside when they begin. Janie loves these conversations and notes that Joe, while not deigning to join in, stays around to listen and laugh. Being forbidden to speak is a severe penalty in an oral culture. It short-circuits Janie's attempt to claim an identity of her own, robs her of the opportunity to negotiate respect from her peers. Barred from speaking to anyone but Joe, she loses the desire to say anything at all. "So gradually, she pressed her teeth together and learned to hush."

After seven years of marriage, Janie recognizes that Joe requires her total submission. She yields. As she does so however, she retains a clear perception of herself and her situation, a perception that becomes her salvation in the end. On one occasion after Joe has slapped her (for naturally, her submission has not slowed his verbal or physical abuse), she experiences the following revelation:

> Janie stood where he left her for unmeasured time and thought.
> She stood there until something fell off the shelf inside her. Then she
> went inside to see what it was. It was her image of Jody tumbled
> down and shattered. But looking at it she saw that it never was the

flesh and blood figure of her dreams. Just something she had grabbed up to drape her dreams over. In a way she turned her back upon the image where it lay and looked further. She had no more blossomy openings dusting pollen over her man, neither any glistening young fruit where the petals used to be. She found that she had a host of thoughts she had never expressed to him, and numerous emotions she had never let Jody know about. Things packed up and put away in parts of her heart where he could never find them. She was saving up feelings for some man she had never seen. She had an inside and an outside now and suddenly she knew how not to mix them. [Pp. 112–13]

Facing the truth about Joe allows Janie to divorce him emotionally. She accepts her share of responsibility for the failure of the marriage, knowing now that if Joe has used her for his purposes, she has used him for hers. Yet she understands that her dreams have not impinged on Joe's selfhood; they have been naive but not destructive. By creating inside and outside selves, she hopes to insulate the core of her being from the destructive consequences of Joe's dreams. She cannot claim her autonomy, because she is not yet capable of imagining herself except in relationship to a man. Still, she is no longer willing to jeopardize her inner being for the sake of any such relationship.

Janie remains content to practice a kind of passive resistance against Joe's tyranny until he pushes her to the point when she must "talk smart" to salvage her self-respect. For many years, Joe has forced her to clerk in the store, taking every opportunity to ridicule her for minor mistakes. As he grows older, he adds taunts about her age to his repertoire of verbal insults. Sensing that her womanhood as well as her intelligence is under attack, she retaliates: "Humph! Talkin' 'bout *me* lookin' old! When you pull down yo' britches, you look lak de change uh life" (p. 123). So unaccustomed is Joe to hearing his wife "specify" that he imputes nefarious motives to her words. Ill and suspicious, he hires a hoodoo doctor to counteract the curse he believes Janie is putting on him. No curse exists, of course, but Starks is dying of kidney disease and of mortal wounds to his vanity. As he lies on his deathbed, Janie confronts him with more painful truths. Again she reveals how well she comprehends the effect of his domination: "Mah own mind had tuh be squeezed and crowded out tuh make room for yours in me" (p. 133).

The attack on her dying husband is not an act of gratuitous cruelty; it is an essential step toward self-reclamation. Moreover, in terms of the narrative, the deathbed episode posits a dramatic break with Janie's past. She is henceforth a different woman. Independent for the first time in her life, she exults in the "freedom feeling." Reflecting on her past, she realizes that her grandmother, though acting out of love, has wronged her deeply. At base, Nanny's sermon had been about things, when Janie wanted to journey to the horizons in search of people. Janie is able at last to reject her grandmother's way and resume her original quest. That quest culminates in her marriage to Tea Cake Woods with whom she builds a relationship totally unlike the others she has had.

Tea Cake is a troubadour, a traveling bluesman, whose life is dedicated to joyful pursuits. With this character, Hurston explores an alternative definition of manhood, one that does not rely on external manifestations of power, money, and position. Tea Cake has none of these. He is so thoroughly immune to the influence of white American society that he does not even desire them. Tea Cake is at ease being who and what he is. Consequently, he fosters the growth of Janie's self-acceptance. Together they achieve the ideal sought by most characters in Hurston's fiction. They trust emotion over intellect, value the spiritual over the material, preserve a sense of humor and are comfortable with their sensuality. Tea Cake confirms Janie's right to self-expression and invites her to share equally in their adventures. She sees that he "could be a bee to a blossom—a pear tree blossom in the spring" (p. 161). Over the protests of her neighbors, she marries this man several years younger than she whose only worldly possession is a guitar.

They embark on a nomadic existence which takes them to the rich farmland of the Florida Everglades where both Tea Cake and Janie work on the muck and where both share household chores. Their cabin becomes "the unauthorized center of the job," the focal point of the community like the store in Eatonville. Here, however, Janie "could listen and laugh and even talk some herself if she wanted to. She got so she could tell big stories herself from listening to the rest" (p. 200). This is an important and hard-won accomplishment. Even Tea Cake, strongly idealized character though he is, has had difficulty accepting Janie's full participation in their life together. Zora Hurston knew that Tea Cake, a son of the folk culture, would have inherited its negative attitudes toward women. She knew besides that female autonomy cannot be granted by men, it must be demanded by women. Janie gains her autonomy only when she insists upon it. Under pressure, Tea Cake occasionally falls back on the prerogatives of his sex. His one act of physical cruelty toward Janie results from his need to show someone else who is boss in his home. In the main though, Tea Cake transcends the chauvinistic attitudes of the group. He largely keeps his pledge to Janie that she "partake wid everything."

The marriage of Janie and Tea Cake ends in the wake of a fierce hurricane that is vividly evoked in the novel. In the process of saving Janie's life, Tea Cake is bitten by a rabid dog. Deranged, he tries to kill Janie, and she shoots him in self-defense. Despite these events, the conclusion of *Their Eyes Were Watching God* is not tragic. For, with Tea Cake as her guide, Jane has explored the soul of her culture and learned how to value herself. This fact is underscored in the prologue and epilogue of the novel, sections set after Janie's return to Eatonville following Tea Cake's death. In the former, she tells her friend Pheoby: "Ah been a delegate to de big 'ssociation of life. Yessuh! De Grand Lodge, de big convention of livin' is just where Ah been dis year and a half y'all ain't seen me" (p. 18). Having been to the horizon and back, as she puts it, she is eager to teach the crucial lesson she has learned in her travels. Everybody must do two things for themselves: "They got tuh go tuh God, and they got tuh find out about livin' fuh theyselves" (p. 285). This is Janie's text; the sermon she preaches is the novel itself. She has claimed the right to change her own words.

Hurston was never to duplicate the triumph of *Their Eyes Were Watching God*. In her subsequent novels, she changed the direction of her work dramatically. *Moses: Man of the Mountain* (1939) is a seriocomic novel which attempts to fuse Biblical narrative and folk myth. *Seraph on the Suwanee* (1948) is a psychological novel whose principal characters are upwardly mobile white Floridians. Although Hurston's willingness to experiment is admirable, the results are disappointing. Neither of her new settings is as compelling as the Eatonville milieu. Though the impact of black folk expression is always discernible, it is diminished and so is the power of Hurston's own voice. In these novels, the question of female autonomy recedes in importance, and when it is posed in *Seraph*, the answer is decidedly reactionary. What is of interest in terms of this essay is Hurston's reworking of themes identified in her earlier work.

Hurston's Moses is a combination of Biblical lawgiver and Afro-American hoodoo man. He is officially a highborn Egyptian, but according to legend, he is a Hebrew; Moses neither wholly rejects nor accepts the legend. The uncertainties about his identity complicate his quest for fulfillment. That quest conforms in part to the pattern we have outlined. Moses becomes a great manipulator of language, and much of his authority derives from the power of his words. As an educated man, he has been taught the formal language of the Egyptian elite. He later spends many years with the Midianites in spiritual preparation for his divinely appointed task; this period is somewhat comparable to John Pearson's stay in the work camp and Janie's sojourn on the muck. With the Midianites, Moses adapts to the rhythms of a rural folk culture and learns to speak more colloquial English. The Hebrews speak in the black folk idiom, and when he becomes their leader, Moses masters their tongue. Moses is of course a man of action, and as befits a leader, he fights most often for the rights of those under his stewardship. Though he knows he would be more beloved as a king and more popular as a politician, Moses rejects the accouterments of power. He has as little use for class distinctions as Janie and Tea Cake. In Moses, Hurston developed a character who was already a certified hero, not only in the Judeo-Christian tradition, but according to her introduction, also among the peoples of Asia and Africa. What she adds are new points of emphasis, and these had precedents in her earlier work. The most important is implicit in her attempt to reconcile the Biblical Moses and her conception of Moses as conjurer. Hurston had been the first scholar ever to research hoodoo in America and had studied the more systematic religion of Vodun in Haiti. In both instances, she had noted the coexistence of seemingly antithetical religious beliefs in the lives of her informants. In *Moses: Man of the Mountain*, one looks in vain for a synthesis of the two belief systems to which the hero is heir. Hurston simply allows them to coexist. In a novel whose protagonist seeks and achieves cosmic fulfillment, the failure to explicate the spiritual sources of that fulfillment is serious indeed.

*Moses* is a very ambitious novel. If it fails in some respects, it succeeds in others. It offers a very effective satire on the transition from slavery to freedom for black Americans. Hurston drew on the long-standing identification of blacks with the enslaved Hebrews, the identification that had inspired the majestic spiritual "Go Down, Moses" and countless other sacred and secular expressions. Most dwelt on the sufferings of bondage and the joys of emancipation. Hurston's concerns were the responsibilities of freedom. In the novel, the people of Goshen are hesitant to rebel against slavery and unable to fully comprehend freedom. Hurston satirizes their ready assent to the commands of their slavemasters and their reluctance to follow Moses. She mocks the vainglory of self-appointed leaders and the failure of the people to understand the need for sacrifice. Their petty bickering and constant backbiting are also objects of her ridicule. Hurston's satirical sallies are invariably good-natured and often very funny. But her novel is not the serious statement about faith and freedom she seems to have intended.

Hurston did not publish another novel for nine years. In the interim, her political instincts grew markedly conservative. World War II and its Cold War aftermath hastened the rightward drift of her thinking. At the suggestion of her publisher, she revised the manuscript of *Dust Tracks on a Road* to eliminate sections critical of the American system; as it was published in 1942, her autobiography seemed a celebration of the American way. Through the decade, Hurston contributed a number of articles to the *American Mercury* and the *Saturday Evening Post* which developed patriotic themes. By the 1950s, her work was welcome in the pages of the *American Legion Magazine*. Not all of Hurston's articles were reactionary. Some applauded the achievements of blacks in various endeavors. Others reaffirmed her belief in the value of black folklore, though she had ceased her research in the field. A few pieces, written for *Negro Digest*, protested racism in diplomacy, publishing, and everyday life. On the whole, however, Hurston's political views, which she expounded more often in the 1940s than at any other time in her life, supported the status quo. The same charge might be leveled at her last work of fiction, *Seraph on the Suwanee*.

This novel restates the major themes of *Their Eyes Were Watching God*, perhaps in a misguided attempt to universalize them. Here the protagonist is Arvay Henson Meserve, who like Janie searches for self-identity. She is hindered in her quest by the deep-rooted inferiority she feels about her poor cracker background. For the wrong reason, she has come to the right conclusion. As Hurston depicts her, she is inferior to her husband Jim and the only identity she can attain is through accepting her subordinate role as his wife. Hurston endows Jim Meserve with a mixture of the attractive qualities found in Joe Starks and Tea Cake. He is more crudely chauvinistic than either of them, but this aspect of his character is treated with amazing tolerance. Early in the novel, Arvay reflects that if she married Jim, "her whole duty as a wife was to just love him good, be nice and kind around the house and have children for him. She could do that and be more than happy and satisfied, but it looked too simple."[26] The novel demonstrates that it is much too simple, but at the conclusion the happiness Arvay supposedly realizes is achieved on exactly these terms. The problem is Hurston's inability to grant her protagonist the resources that would permit her to claim autonomy. Although Arvay "mounts the pulpit" at the end of the novel, she has no words of her own to speak.

Ultimately, Arvay's weakness may be less a personal problem than a cultural one. Though black characters play minor roles in the novel, black cultural traditions permeate the narrative. They influence everyone's speech, so much so that at times the whites sound suspiciously like the storytellers in Eatonville. Jim relishes the company of his black employees, whom he treats in a disgustingly condescending manner; and one of his sons, after being tutored by a black neighbor, leaves home to join a jazz band. Unlike the earlier protagonists, Arvay cannot attain her identity through a profound engagement with the folk culture, because she has no culture to engage. The culture of the people Arvay despises has supplanted her own. Seen from this perspective, *Seraph on the Suwanee* is not as anomalous or as reactionary a work as it otherwise appears.

From any vantage point, however, it represents an artistic decline. Hurston was at her best when she drew her material directly from black folk culture; it was the source of her creative power. Throughout her career, she endeavored to negotiate respect for it, talking smart then sweet in her folklore and fiction, proclaiming its richness and complexity to all who would hear. Her most memorable characters are born of this tradition. In portraying them, she was always cognizant of the difficulties in reconciling the demands of community and the requirements of self, difficulties that were especially intense for women. The tension could not be resolved by rejecting the community or negating the self. Hurston challenged black people to dig deep into their culture to unearth the values on which it was built. Those values could restore the balance. They could give men and women words to speak. They could set their spirits free.

## Notes

1. Introduction to *Their Eyes Were Watching God* (Urbana: University of Illinois Press, 1978), p. xiv.
2. *I Love Myself When I Am Laughing . . . and Then Again When I Am Looking Mean and Impressive, A Zora Hurston Reader* (Old Westbury, N.Y.: The Feminist Press, 1979); the quotation is from Walker's introduction to Robert Hemenway, *Zora Neale Hurston: A Literary Biography* (Urbana: University of Illinois Press, 1977), p. xii.
3. "Between Laughter and Tears," review of *Their Eyes Were Watching God, New Masses* 23, no. 10 (5 October 1937):25.
4. June Jordan, "On Richard Wright and Zora Neale Hurston: Notes toward a Balancing of Love and Hatred," *Black World* (August 1974):5.
5. "Characteristics of Negro Expression," [1934]; in *Voices from the Harlem Renaissance* ed. Nathan Huggins (New York: Oxford University Press, 1976), pp. 224–27. The expression "changing words" appears in several of Hurston's works. I suspect it derives from a form of the word "exchange," in which the weakly stressed syllable has been dropped. J. L. Dillard identifies the dropping of such syllables as a common characteristic of Black English. See *Black English* (New York: Random House, 1972), p. 249.
6. *I Love Myself*, p. 153.
7. Hemenway, *Zora Neale Hurston*, p. 62.
8. *Mules and Men* (1935; reprint ed., Bloomington: Indiana University Press, 1978), p. 3.
9. Quoted in Robert Hemenway, "Are You a Flying Lark or a Setting Dove," *Afro-American Literature: The Reconstruction of Instruction* (New York: Modern Language Association, 1979), p. 132.
10. Hemenway, *Zora Neale Hurston*, p. 168.
11. *Dust Tracks on a Road* (Philadelphia: J. P. Lippincott, 1942; rpt. 1971), pp. 186–91.
12. *Journal of American Folklore* 88 (Jan.–March 1975):58.
13. Hurston first noted "this scornful attitude towards black women" in "Characteristics of Negro Expression," p. 234. For examples of sexism in folktales, see Daryl C. Dance, *Shuckin' and Jivin': Folklore from Contemporary Black Americans* (Bloomington: Indiana University Press, 1978), pp. 110–42.
14. *Mules and Men*, p. 134.
15. Abrahams, "Negotiating Respect," pp. 58–62.
16. *Mules and Men*, p. 162.
17. *Mules and Men*, p. 160.

18. *Mules and Men*, pp. 148–51.
19. *Jonah's Gourd Vine* (Philadelphia: J. P. Lippincott, 1934; rpt. 1971), p. 9. All further references to this work appear in the text.
20. Hemenway, "Flying Lark or Setting Dove," pp. 134–38.
21. See Hemenway, "Flying Lark or Setting Dove," pp. 139–47, for an extended gloss on this passage. The essay as a whole has influenced my reading of the novel.
22. Hemenway, *Zora Neale Hurston*, p. 192.
23. John Chamberlain, *New York Times*, 3 May 1934, p. 7; Hemenway, *Zora Neale Hurston*, p. 192; Andrew Burris, review of *Jonah's Gourd Vine, Crisis* 41 (1934):166.
24. Introduction to *Jonah's Gourd Vine*, p. 7.
25. *Their Eyes*, p. 24. All further references to this work appear in the text.
26. *Seraph on the Suwanee* (New York: Scribner's, 1948), p. 33.

# Sherley Anne Williams

## Papa Dick and Sister-Woman: Reflections on Women in the Fiction of Richard Wright

Lulu Mann, wife of the hero, Brother Mann, in Richard Wright's story, "Down by the Riverside,"[1] is a metaphor of the general representation of women in Wright's work. Lulu suffers quietly and dies as mutely as she has lived; she speaks nary a word in the story. To be sure, much of the heroic and tragic action of the story is occasioned by Lulu's sex and role: she is in the midst of a long and difficult childbirth and her husband makes a superhuman effort to get her to the hospital during a flood, rowing Lulu, their young son, and Lulu's mother across a flooded landscape against a treacherous current. "What if the levee break?" runs like a refrain through the first part of the story, reminding us that nature can be worked with, even manipulated, but is ultimately beyond human control. And Brother Mann must also brave fear-crazed white civilians and carelessly racist troops: "'. . . in times like these they'll shoota nigger down jus like a dog . . .'"

We infer something of the quality of Lulu's and Mann's relationship from his dogged and willing attempts to get her to the hospital. The only transportation available is a rowboat stolen from an especially racist white man. In order to get Lulu help, Mann must brave not only the hostile environment but the wrath of a white man and, possibly, the white man's law. His problem is compounded when he is forced, in self-defense, to kill the owner of the boat: to get Lulu to the hospital now almost certainly means his own death. Still, Mann persists in his efforts to save his wife's life. "He could not turn back now for the [safety of] the hills, not with Lulu in this boat. Not with Lulu in the fix she was in." It is this very selflessness that proves his undoing for even as he makes this decision, Lulu is already dead. All that he has willingly suffered on her behalf is for nothing. He continues to pay.

Mann is conscripted to work on the levee and when the levee breaks, he goes with another black man to rescue a last family from the rapidly approaching flood waters. We are not surprised that the family is that of the racist Mann has killed: Wright was first a naturalist, at his best depicting the relentless momentum with which chance can catch one. This incident is, in addition, yet another instance in which Mann, unlike Wright's later heroes—

indeed, the heroes of many naturalist novels—makes the human and selfless choice. He is unable, because of his own humanity, to escape the consequences of the actions set in motion by nature, on the one hand, and the inhuman racial system, on the other. He can neither kill nor abandon the racist's family. And, predictably, once safe in the hill camp for flood victims, the dead man's wife and son denounce our Mann. He is seized, but he chooses to die escaping rather than at the hand of the unjust justice ("'Did he bother you, Mrs. Heartfield?'" the white men ask. "'The little girl?'" whipping themselves up for a lynching: "'Did he bother you, *then*, Mrs. Heartfield?'") that he knows awaits him at the hands of the white legal system.

It is a classic story of black male heroism, much in keeping, as are all of Wright's short stories and his autobiographical narratives, with the sense of heroism in Afro-American traditions.[2] That sense of heroism is basically to fight, by whatever means are available, against the racism and exploitation that continues to victimize black and other ethnic groups in America. Wright's hero begins his struggle toward self-definition through his attempt to save his wife's life, but this attempt is pushed to the background as Mann's struggle with the environment, with the system and the white man are portrayed. The background is the classic place of women and male-female relationships in much of the tradition. Neither women characters nor "women's questions" figure centrally in Wright's fiction; when they appear at all, they are subsumed under larger political or philosophical themes. Lulu is not an identifiable personality but an occasion for the hero to demonstrate soul, his persistence and grace under pressure.[3]

The only physical description we are given of any of the black characters in the story is Lulu's. She is "a small woman with large shining eyes." Despite, perhaps because of, these few details, she remains anonymous behind her "thin black face." Though she herself is silent, women do in fact speak in the story. These are older women, but their voices seem to stand, at least in part, for the younger Lulu. Sister Jefferson suggests the prototypical strong-black-woman who goads others to action no matter how futile or self-destructive. She poses the central question of the story, "'Whutcha gonna do, Brother Mann?'" In her insistence that "'Yuh gotta do something, Brother Mann,'" she stands for generations of black women who have demanded that their men make a way for them in a racist society out of no way at all. Brother Mann rises to the occasion, responds to the demand, only to be cheated of success by the weakness of his wife's flesh, the narrow hips that will not allow his child to pass.

Grannie, Lulu's mother, attempts, in the name of Jesus Christ or his surrogate on earth, the white folks, to suppress any actions but the most conventional and acceptable to the white powers that be. She refuses, at first, to get into the boat that is their only hope of getting to safety because it was stolen from a white man. And though she does finally accompany Mann, it is obvious that the white folks are more terrifying to her than a mere flood could ever be.

I have felt at liberty to give "Down by the Riverside" this rather exaggerated reading because Lulu, Sister Jefferson, and Grannie, lightly sketched though they are, foreshadow black female characterizations in Wright's later work. The distinguishing characteristics of Granny and Sister Jeff, religion-haunted racial timidity and domineering strength, come to define Wright's view of the black matriarch—the most prevalent female character type in Afro-American literature. Lulu's condition and her silence suggest something of the link Wright is later to make between black women and a mindless sexuality that almost as much as racism is the bane of the black man's existence. This latter view is, of course, troubling, and Wright's handling of the matriarch figure, even at its most illuminating and provocative, is not without its problems. Rather than being merely another instance of the general male chauvinism pervasive in both Afro- and Anglo-American literature, Wright's female portraits are a part of a systematic presentation in the landscape he paints as backdrop for the actions of his heroes. His portraits of black women, often no more than cameos or vignettes, are some of the most compelling and complex in the literature and place him at the extreme edge of the tradition in a position that is both extremely sexist and racist. The claim here is not that Wright did not know black women, which in some very real sense he clearly did—after all, his mamma was one. Rather, Wright seldom loved his black female characters and never liked them, nor could he imagine a constructive role for them in the black man's struggle for freedom. Moreover, his fictional portrayals of black women justify, by implication, the hunger of his black heroes for that forbidden American fruit, the white woman, and the validity of his own use of the white woman as the ultimate symbol of the black man's freedom.

Richard Wright is the father of modern Afro-American literature. His most famous novel, *Native Son* (1940), is seen in some quarters as "the model"[4] for contemporary black novelists, his autobiographical narrative, *Black Boy* (1945), as the text that authenticates "the extraordinary articulate self that lies behind"[5] this most famous novel of black privation and rage. *Native Son* began an era of new realism in Afro-American fiction, as black writers, inspired by the thrilling example of Wright, exposed the filth, corruption, and depravity of urban slums that, together with American racism, stunted and deformed the blacks forced to live in them. In his nonfiction work, *Twelve Million Black Voices* (1941), *Black Power* (1954), and *White Man Listen!* (1957), Wright documented the social and psychological effects on and reactions of black and other Third World peoples forced to live under the oppression of internal and external colonialism. In doing so, he took upon himself the task of being spokesman for some twelve million black people in America. And if his art suffered, as some critics have charged, because of this political spokesmanship, he at least made it possible to admit, explore, and thus move beyond the almost elemental expression of rage that drives *Native Son* to its powerful climax. But Wright also fathered a bastard line, racist misogyny—the denigration of black women as justification for glorifying the symbolic white woman—and male narcissism—the assumption that racism is a crime against the black man's sexual expression rather than an economic, political, and psychological crime against black people—that was to flower in the fiction of black writers in the late sixties and early seventies.

Women are only supporting players with bit parts in Wright's fiction. The women in *Native Son*, for example, are all cardboard figures: the white woman, Mary Dalton, whom Bigger Thomas accidentally kills, was never meant to transcend the symbolism of American fruit forbidden the black man; and Bigger's girlfriend, Bessie, whom he murders with malice aforethought, represents nothingness, a meaningless void that Bigger's killings allow him to rise above. Bigger's mother and his sister represent modern versions of toming and accommodation. We excuse these characterizations within the context of the novel because of the power of Wright's psychological portrait of Bigger; this is Bigger's story, and not even the introduction of an articulate white male character, Bigger's lawyer Max who, in a twenty-page speech, attempts to summarize something of what Wright had rendered (often brilliantly and beautifully) in the preceding two hundred and fifty pages, can diminish Bigger's presence in the novel. Because the characterization of women in Wright's novels is so limited, one must turn to Wright's stories in order to understand both the range and the issues involved in these portrayals. Wright never, in his published work, moves beyond these early characterizations of black women.[6]

# I

The only published works in which women characters are protagonists, "Long Black Song" and "Bright and Morning Star," appear in *Uncle Tom's Children*, the short-story collection written while Wright was a member of the Communist party. In this first collection, Wright set out to explore the question, "What quality of will must a Negro possess to live and die with dignity in a country that denies his humanity?" The epigraphs at the beginning of the book tell us more about the context in which Wright tries to answer this question. The first is a definition of an Uncle Tom, "the cringing type of [freedman] who knew his place before white folk," a household word among post-Civil War Negroes that Wright states unequivocally "has been supplanted by a new [one] from another generation which says Uncle Tom is dead!" The lyrics from a popular song, "Is It True What They Say about Dixie?" make up the second epigraph. "Does the sun really shine all the time?/Do sweet magnolias blossom at everybody's door?/ . . . Do they laugh, do they love like they say in ev'ry song? . . ./ If it's true that's where I belong." The stories, then, are at once political and mythic in the sense that Wright is trying to establish images that will have as much currency and resonance as the sentimental and superficial ones that color white society's present views of the south and the Negro. In each of the five stories, a black man is called upon to defend himself, his family, his community against a hostile and racist environment. The heroes in the first three stories are forced by events beyond their control into essentially private rebellions against southern racism. Their acts of heroism, often nihilistic and pyrrhic, are also the means through which they achieve a measure of authentic self-consciousness—which of course the racist system must deny or destroy. In the final two stories, "Fire and Cloud" and "Bright and Morning Star," Wright is able to assimilate Marxist ideology into fiction and create characters whose struggles are symbolic of the entire community's and affirm the validity of collective action.

The central characters display an increasing level of political consciousness. Big Boy, the adolescent hero of "Big Boy Leaves Home," the first story in the collection, is an apolitical innocent upon whom consciousness, of a sort, is forced. Johnny Boy, in "Bright and Morning Star," the last story in the collection, is an organizer for the Communist party in rural Mississippi. The characterizations of women follow a similar pattern; in the early stories their condition initiates some action that significantly affects the life course of the protagonist. Once that course has been influenced, however, these female characters no longer figure in the story—consider the white woman who sees the naked Negro boys in "Big Boy" and thus precipitates murder and flight, or Lulu. Women characters have a more central role in later stories in the collection.

"Bright and Morning Star" is one of the most deft and moving renderings of a black woman's experience in the canon of American literature. Writing while he was still a staunch believer in communism as the hope of the world's oppressed, Wright was able to achieve in this story a synthesis of ideology and literary expression that he was only occasionally able to equal in later, longer works. The mute Lulu, the childish wanton Sarah in "Long Black Song," May, the stereotyped and scary wife of the hero in "Fire and Cloud": these characterizations of black women are somewhat redeemed in the character of Aunt Sue. Yet, paradoxically, Wright's loving characterization also reinforces the image of the black woman as a symbol of the reactionary aspects in Afro-American tradition implicit in the preceding three stories.

Aunt Sue is a blend of the mother of Afro-American ideal and the mammy of American experience. She takes in washing for a living, carrying the hundred-pound baskets on her head; her most characteristic pose—when she is not ironing—standing with her "gnarled black hands folded over her stomach," is one of familiar humbleness. This pose later helps her to hide a gun and so is akin to the minstrel mask and the vaudeville grin as one of the disguises forced upon black people and made "renegade" through sly acts of self-assertion.[7] Sue is, to use the jargon of the day, a "single" parent (I have often wondered what a double or triple parent looks like), a widow who has raised her sons, Sug and Johnny Boy, to manhood alone. She has struggled against being engulfed in poverty and racism, aided by her wits and, more importantly, an abiding faith in Jesus Christ as Lord of Heaven and Savior of the world. Personal service on whites, endurance, a necessary self-efface-ment, a truncated family structure—these factors so characterize our concep-tion of the so-called matriarch that they have in the aggregate almost the quality of archetype. Certainly the character of Aunt Sue approaches the ideal. Yet Sue is also a dynamic character who in Wright's treatment rises above the social definition of *mammy*.

When Sug and Johnny Boy enter manhood and "walk forth demanding their lives," Sue has the strength to let them go. Her heart follows them as they become organizers, for she loves, as mother must, but she loves without smothering. Her love for her sons leads Sue to embrace the work of the Party; the wrongs and sufferings of black men "take the place of Him nailed to the Cross as the focus of her feelings," giving meaning to her life of toil as Christianity had before. In the party, Sue becomes aware of a kind of personal strength and pride that no one, least of all herself, thought a "black woman . . . could have:" the will to work against the racist power structure. We understand, of course, that Aunt Sue has willingly subsumed her own aspirations, her own personality under first one man, Jesus Christ, then another, the wronged heroic Black Man, that she would consider the wrongs done to her as a black woman negligible compared to what black men suffer. She believes that righting the wrongs of black men will automatically eliminate her own exploitation. This elementary conception of black libera-tion does not trouble us unduly; Wright subtly implies his own deeper under-standing of the political situation of women when he explains why it is natural for Reva, a young white woman comrade, to trudge through a down-pour to deliver an urgent message—"Being a woman, Reva was not suspect; she would have to go." He probably takes a devilish delight in portraying that symbol of deadly femininity, the white woman, using her privileged position to strike at his white male oppressors.

Yet, despite the changes wrought in her attitude by the new light shed by the party, Sue never quite accepts its dictum that she "'not see white n [she] not see black.'" She cannot entirely discard the teachings of her experience: "'You can't trust ever white man yuh meet.'" Johnny Boy's position, "'Yuh can't judge folks by how yuh feel bout em n by how long yuh don knowed em,'" is, of course, the correct party line. And though in this instance, Sue proves correct (the informer is one of the newly recruited white party members), Sue's insistence upon "pitting her feelings against the hard necessity of his [Johnny boy's] thinking" symbolizes the hold that the old life and the old ways still have over her.

A white man posing as a friend of the little band of party members tricks her into revealing the names of the local group, even as Johnny Boy is captured by the sheriff's posse. Carrying a sheet for his burial, Aunt Sue gains access to the place where Johnny Boy is held captive, the place to which the informer must return to lay his information before the sheriff. Sue is forced to watch while Johnny Boy is tortured. She considers killing him to spare him pain, but chooses to wait and kill the informer and so save the lives of all the other comrades. She succeeds in killing the informer and is herself killed. She dies with a defiant cry, "'You didn't git what you wanted!'" on her lips.

That defiant cry is ironic for these are the words of defiance that precipitated the crisis in the first place. They reinforce the quality of noble hubris that is an important part of her characterization. "'Ah just want them white folks t try t make me tell *who* is *in* the party n who *ain*! . . . Ahll show em something they never thought a black woman could have,'" she tells Johnny Boy early on in the story. And she is given a chance to show that something. The sheriff and his men come looking for Johnny Boy and refuse to leave when she orders them out of her house. Despite her uppitiness, the sheriff seeks to be conciliating: "'Now Anty . . .'" he begins, only to be brought up short by Sue's retort, "'White man don yuh *Anty* me!'" She rejects the bogus conciliation and the counterfeit respect the title implies; and rejects also the *place* in which that title puts her. In the ensuing exchange of words with the white men, she further demonstrates her pride and courage: "'Twenty of yuh runnin over one ol woman! Now ain yuh white men glad yuh so brave?'" The sheriff slaps her, for she is not to him a woman, but a nigger woman, a beast of burden to be beaten when it proves recalcitrant. As Aunt Sue does: She refuses to tell them anything about Johnny Boy. Balked, the sheriff and his men start to leave. Sue, wanting to drive home her victory for she has shown that there is nothing they could do to her that she could not take, taunts them as they go out her door. "'Yuh didn't git wht yuh wanted! N yuh ain gonna nevah git it!'" This so enrages the sheriff that he beats her senseless.

While Sue is dazed from the assault, Booker, whom she suspects of being an informer, seduces her into telling the names of her comrades ("'Is yuh scared a me cause Ahm *white*?'" he demands indignantly; then, cleverly invoking her son's name, "'Johnny Boy ain like tha.'") Later, after Reva has confirmed her suspicions that Booker is the informer, Sue reflects, pinpointing her moment of transcendent strength as the moment of her blind fall. "She put her finger upon the moment when she had shouted her defiance to the sheriff, when she had shouted to feel her strength . . . If she had not shouted at the sheriff, she would have been strong enough to resist Booker; she would have been able to tell the comrades herself," instead of entrusting the task to the traitor.

But hubris is only the superficial flaw. The "fit of fear" that had come upon her when she regained consciousness and discovered herself looking into a white face was "a part of her life she thought she had done away with forever." But that part of her life, "the days when she had not hoped for anything on this earth," had been evoked through her singing of the old sorrow songs, the spirituals that she "'can't seem to fergit,'" in the first part of the story. And in singing, she has opened herself to both the tragic expression of pride and that old-timey fear. She sang for the traditional reason, "to ease the anxiety [about Johnny Boy's safety] that was swelling in her heart." She had thought that it meant no more than this when she sang now. But the events of the evening reveal that the songs are not, even now, an empty symbol. She has almost, without knowing it, called on Jesus; and He had not answered. This is the "deeper horror": the fight for black men's freedom had not truly replaced Christ in her heart. This realization mires her temporarily between two worlds, neither of which she seems able to abandon or live in.

In succumbing to the fit of fear induced by Booker's presence, Sue has in her own mind reverted to type, to the stereotypical image of the servile, cringing slave. And she is ashamed of herself and even more "shamed whenever the thought of Reva's love crossed her mind." In the white girl's trust and acceptance of her, Sue has found her first feelings of humanity, and Reva's love draws her toward a reintegration and reaffirmation with the peoples of the earth. Reva's relationship to Aunt Sue is a re-reading of the conventional one between mammy and mistress. It represents the ideal solidarity possible between black and white workers and the sisterhood between women workers. Moreover, the black mother and the white girl are bound together by their love for Johnny Boy. Reva's love for Sue, her faith in the old black woman, represent for Sue the promise of the party made real in a genuine human relationship. That love is likened to the light from the airport beacon in far-off Memphis that in the story becomes a metaphor for the new day that communism will bring.

Sue's pride before the white girl causes her to shield Reva from any knowledge of the mistake she has made, and this is consistent with the literal, denotative level of the story. Sue has already lost one son, Sug, to "the black man's struggle." He is in jail. Johnny Boy, she realizes during the sheriff's visit, is as good as gone; he will either be jailed, killed, or forced to flee because of his work with the party. Reva "was all she had left." Thus, when the young white girl comes to her house, after the sheriff and Booker have left, she cannot bring herself to reveal the full extent of her weakness. Reva's confidence ("'An Sue! Yuh always been brave. Itll be awright!'") seems to mock her. It also goads her into thinking of a way to rectify her mistake. Ironically, this deception recalls the outline of the old mammy-mistress relationship, for one of the unacknowledged but understood tasks of the old family retainers—whether "Aunty" or "Uncle"—was to guide their young charges through the shoals of adolescence, shielding them from as much unpleasantness as possible and ministering to their hurts when it was not possible to keep them from pain. This latent aspect of Sue's love for Reva is reinforced by the suggestion of Reva as a sleeping beauty at the end of Section V of the story. Reva has come to spend the night with Sue in case there is trouble. She stays, even though the trouble has already come. Sue, resolved upon a course of action, gets Johnny Boy's gun and a sheet. Reva is in the room "sleeping; the darkness was filled with her quiet breathing . . . [Sue] stole to the bedside and watched Reva. Lawd, hep her!" Sue then steals away on her deadly errand, leaving Reva asleep, Reva's trust in black people intact, her world unshaken.

Concomitant with re-reading the relationship between mammy and mistress is the explicit sanctioning of romantic love between black men and white women as a symbol of racial equality and economic justice. Long before Sue gives Johnny Boy up to physical death in the service of the party, she gives him up to Reva. "The brightest glow her heart had ever known was when she had learned that Reva loved Johnny Boy"—this despite the fact that she knows the two of them "'couldna been together in this here south,'" to put it mildly. (We cannot help but remember the fate of Big Boy and his friends, the mob in "Down by the Riverside"—"'Did he *bother* you Mrs. Heartfield? The Little girl? Did he *bother* you *then*?'") Yet Sue's approval of the match is used consistently to demonstrate that Sue has broken with her old outlook and embraced a new one, that she has broken with her old allies and found new ones. Sue never draws back from her approval of the match, whereas she early shows that she cannot accept all of the party tenets without reservation and her "Lawd hep"'s are a kind of subconscious refrain through much of the story. Sue's last thought as she starts out with her winding sheet is of Reva: "Lawd hep her! But maybe she was better off . . . she wont nevah know. Reva's trust would never be shaken." And as Sue starts across the fields holding the gun and the sheet against her stomach, "'Po Reva . . . po critter . . . Shes fast ersleep.'"

Reva is fast asleep to Johnny Boy's fate, to Sue's frailty, Sue's humanity, to the dark realities and hardships of black life. Despite the exigencies of life in the party, nothing has happened to disturb Reva's faith in human nature, the party, her belief in the perfectibility of the world. And it is as much to keep this white world intact as it is to redeem her own self-esteem that Aunt Sue sets out to hunt down the informer.

In "Bright and Morning Star," Wright articulates a dream of rapprochement between the old and the new Negro, between the generations spawned in the bloody reprisals of Reconstruction and the generation nurtured on radical ideology in the new century, between black woman and white. He uses "the most beloved and familiar character"[8] in American experience, the mammy, to inveigh against adherence not only to the substance but to the form of the folk culture, to urge a complete break with the old-fogeyish past. The hope implicit in the story—if this old woman can change, any one can—is never realized in portrayals of younger black women. Indeed, an episode from *American Hunger* (1977), the posthumously published sequel to *Black Boy*, illustrates how completely Wright came to equate black women and black culture with the reactionary and regressive.

Wright worked as a publicity agent for the Federal Negro Theatre in Chicago during the early thirties. His attempts to bring "adult" drama to Chicago audiences met with resistance from the black actors and actresses in the company. Wright recalls that he had "the skinny white woman who directed" the company replaced by "Charles DeSheim, a talented Jew," and the company's repertoire of "ordinary plays all of which had been revamped to 'Negro style' with jungle scenes, spirituals and all," exchanged for "serious" dramatic works. A controversy erupted over the company's repertoire. The blacks reject the "grim, poetical, powerful, one-acter dealing with chain gang conditions in the south," written by a white man[9] because they think it "indecent." As one actor in Wright's recollection put it, "'I lived in the south and I never saw any chain gangs.'" We share Wright's surprise and disappointment at this appallingly disingenuous statement, yet we also recognize in the actors' stammered responses to this opportunity to act out something of the painful realities of black experience a similarity to Richard's own response, earlier in the narrative, when the inpenetrable wall of racism opened suddenly and so unexpectedly that he could not believe the light when he saw it. In that earlier episode, he was immobilized by the responses that racism had forced him to internalize and so missed an opportunity for human interaction, human communication across the color line.

The stultifying, inhibiting effects of racism are a dominant theme in Wright's work, and we understand that racism has stunted the aspirations of these black performers. There is more than a hint of heroism in the young writer's challenging the former vaudevilleans to become actors and actresses. There is also an awful and poignant irony in the climax to the angry meeting that follows: Richard is denounced as an Uncle Tom by a black girl. Wright *has* played the "Uncle Tom" in a literal sense; he did tell the white director that the actors had started a petition demanding his removal. But Wright, of course, told DeSheim of the petition, not as an informing lackey, but out of a sense of loyalty to a fellow artist: Wright had suggested the play that caused the controversy just as he had suggested that DeSheim be hired. Wright has also tomed in a more subtle and more important sense: he had implied the superiority of a white writer's version of black life over that of numerous black playwrights who were then struggling against enormous odds to get their works produced. But the company, in rejecting an opportunity to engage audiences in serious considerations of Afro-American experience and Anglo-American racism, had implicitly endorsed a continuation of the self-parodies, the black-face burlesques of Shakespeare and Molière that had been their staple fare. Moreover, they accepted these burlesques as their "place before white folk" in the theater. One feels a kind of absolute truth in Wright's statement that the blacks "were scared spitless at the prospect" of being allowed out of that place. The actors were in fact able to rise above some, at least, of their fears for, as Constance Webb tells us in her official biography of Wright, "most of the difficulties were eventually smoothed over and the play went into rehearsal." And, when the play was banned as too "controversial," the actors and actresses continued to demand that they be allowed to perform it—though to no avail.[10] This is not, however, how the episode recorded in *American Hunger* ends.

After the angry meeting, a "huge" "fat" "black" woman, a *blues* singer "found an excuse to pass [Richard] as often as possible and she hissed under her breath in a menacing singsong: "'Lawd, Ah sho hates a white man's nigger.'" This is more than a vernacular restatement of the tragicomic tensions of the first denouncement, for this worrying of the line poses the issues at another level. The politics of encounter and confrontation—represented by Richard, the writer—challenges the politics of accommodation and accep- tance—represented by the anonymous "folk" singer. Though literature is routed, it is obvious that Wright, even in his apparent defeat, does not expect the blues to live. "I telephoned my white friends in the Works Progress Administration," he states blandly. "'Transfer me to another job,'" he tells them, giving us to understand that if he is a white man's nigger, he at least is nigger to a white man with clout: "Within twenty-four hours DeSheim and I were given our papers. We shook hands and went our separate ways." The exclusion, the actual suppression of factual information is obvious and, we must assume, deliberate. Wright, the rising young black intellectual, joins the progressive, creative white man, leaving the Negro actors (one almost wants to say "masses") to their childish and backward ways.

Wright did make some attempt to retrieve this implicit and surprising alliance: "I felt—but only temporarily—that perhaps the whites were right, that Negroes were children and would never grow up." Yet the image of the fat, black, blues-singing woman, hissing the hero (who, after all, is only championing what *ought* to be her own desire for adult Negro dramatics), threatening and intimidating young Richard to the point that he felt in danger of his life, leaves an indelible mark. This image of the black woman hissing down progressive ideas is twin to the one of Sue, standing at her ironing board, unconsciously singing the old sorrow songs, opening the door to the past that the new day ought to have closed.

Wright never again creates so complex and dynamic a female character as Aunt Sue, nor does a strong black woman again figure so centrally in a piece of Wright's fiction. Strength in black women is seen increasingly as emanating from a kind of religious hysteria—Cross Damon's mother in *The*

*Outsider* (1953),[11] for example, or Richard's grandmother in *Black Boy*. Religion does not ennoble these later characters as it had Sue. Whether they come to religion, as did Sue, because life was hard and the white man was hard with it (as Bigger's mother does in *Native Son*) or because they have been sexually betrayed by some black man, as Cross's mother does, these religious strong women are portrayed as ineffectual in the face of the poverty and racism of their lives and as unacknowledged allies of the society in keeping black men in their place. These are primarily older women, for power, even in such a limited form, is seldom a quality Wright associates with younger black women.

Sue is intuitively political rather than consciously so; the only other black female character who approaches Sue's level of political involvement is Sarah, wife of a communist organizer in *The Outsider*. She urges her husband to fight the party's decision that he stop organizing among the men on his job. The incident is meant to illustrate the brutal capriciousness of the party, the way it tramples over individual and small-group interests in the name of some vague, generalized "higher good." But the strident tones in which Sarah challenges her husband—"'What in hell did I marry, a Marxist or a mouse? Listen, nigger, you're going to *organize*, you hear?'"—identify her as a closet ball-breaker who, under the guise of supporting and encouraging the black man in his struggle to maintain his dignity, constantly forces him into situations where that dignity will be trampled, his life put in danger. The incident illustrates, too, the kind of perverted strength that, at best, characterizes Wright's women. Sarah, like Sister Jefferson, nags, goads a man into action because her status as a woman prevents her from acting on her own behalf. "'Men made themselves,'" a male character observes in the same novel, "'and women were made through men.'" Wright seems incapable of creating strong black women who are independent of the crutch of religion. Sarah, the militant communist, crushed by the deportation of her husband, the suicide of her best friend, announces "I'm going to confession." We, like Cross, did not even know she was Catholic. It is significant that what Sarah really wants, as she reveals under Cross's questioning, is a man. But she is "thirty-five years old," "pretty old for that," and "fat now." "[She's] no confidence in herself anymore." Confession, the church, represent a yearning to submit to a master, to be relieved of responsibility for her life. Sarah was, evidently, Wright's final word on the strong-black-woman, for such a character does not again appear in his fiction.

It is interesting that Sarah, like Sue, approves, at least at first, of Cross's love affair with the white woman, Eva Blount. When she withdraws her approval, it is because Cross has been revealed as an amoral killer, not because of race. Sarah's approval is not made much of, it is actually pooh-poohed, put down to her matchmaking instinct. This casual attitude toward the affair merely becomes another element in the bizarre world in which the hero moves.

White women in Wright are never more than cardboard characters. One can divide them into "red necks" who cry rape and cause the death of black men (seen most clearly in Mrs. Carlson in *The Long Dream*), and "sweet little girls" who symbolize a freedom beyond a black woman's wildest imaginings. Wright makes it clear in *The Long Dream* that he understands the historical basis and the present pathology of this fatal fascination:

> ... that white world had guaranteed [the black man's] worth in the most brutal and dramatic manner. Most surely he was something, somebody in the eyes of the white world or it would not threaten him [with castration and death]. He knew deep in his heart that there would be no peace in his blood until he had defiantly violated the line [touching a white woman] that the white world had dared him to cross under the threat of death.

Now, one has no quarrel with this rationale; it is as good as any, and Wright does correctly identify the black man's image of the white woman as an indication of the black man's "forced," "abnormal" development.[12] What does madden one is the way Wright uses these unflattering images of black women to justify the black man's surrender to this parthology.

## II

Sarah,[13] "a simple peasant woman" in the soberly lyrical story "Long Black Song," betrays her hard-working husband with a white gramophone salesman. Sarah's husband, Silas, discovers her infidelity, kills the white man, and is himself killed by a white lynch mob. The sensationalism of the story line is tempered by a spare lyrical style rarely effected in Wright's later work. There is something in its somber lyricism that calls to mind "Blood Burning Moon," Jean Toomer's tale of an interracial triangle.[14] The similarities go beyond style. The black men in both stories are responsible and independent: "'An next year,'" Tom Burwell boasts to Louisa in his wooing speech, "'I'll have a farm. My own.'" (p. 57). Silas boasts upon his return from town after selling his cotton for a good price: "'Ah bought ten mo acres o lan. Ahma have to git a man to hep me nex spring . . .'" They are also proud of their ability to act as (white) men, despite the obstacles in their way. "'My bales,'" Tom continues, "'will buy yo what y gets from white folks now. Silk Stockings an purple dresses— . . .'" (p. 57). And Silas continues, "'Ain't tha the way the white folks do? Ef yuhs gonna git anywhere yuhs gotta do jus like they do.'" Both men meet fiery ends because they will not allow white men to trample on their pride by exploiting their women sexually. This view, that the rape of a black woman is not so much an attack upon her person, an assault upon her honor as an affront to the masculinity of black men, is in keeping with the patriarchal tenets of the tradition. Wright, as we shall see, is an extreme case, even within the general paternalism of the tradition.

Rather than the lurid, gothic landscape of Toomer's south—"Up from the dusk the full moon came, blowing like a fired pine knot, it illumined the great door and shadowed the Negro shanties . . . the full moon in the great door was an omen. Negro women improvised songs against its spell" (p. 51)— Wright's southern landscapes, where they appear at all, are usually straight-forwardly hostile, or less often, as in "Long Black Song," sentimentally suggestive: "Sarah saw green fields wrapped in the thickening gloam . . . The after-glow lingered, red, dying, somehow tenderly sad. And far away, earth and sky met in a soft swoon of shadow." More important is the contrast between the two women who stand at the apex of the triangles. Louisa is a woman, both sexually and racially aware: "To meet Bob [Stone, the younger son of the white family for whom she works] in the canebrake as she was going to do in an hour or so was nothing new." On the other hand, in her womanliness, Louisa *feels*, correctly, that Tom's proposal is on the way. And she genuinely cares for both men: "By measure of that warm glow which came into her mind at the thought of [Stone] he had won her" (p. 51). Yet Tom Burwell "held her to the factory town more firmly than he thought . . . His black balanced and pulled against the white of Stone when she thought of them" (p. 52). Tom declares himself and makes it clear to her that she cannot have both Stone and himself. Given this kind of choice, Louisa's decision to have Tom carries all the more weight and Stone's refusal to accept her decision is all the more reprehensible.

Compared to Louisa, Sarah seems almost infantile in her behavior. She continually misreads the signs implicit in the white man's presence: "She looked at him; she saw he was looking at her breasts. He's just like a lil boy. Acks like he can't understand *nothin*!" She cannot see the economic trap posed by the installment plan the white salesman proposes for the purchase of the gramophone clock: "'It only costs fifty dollars'" [fully one-fifth of all that Silas has earned for the year's cotton crop!] "'. . . just five dollars down and five dollars a month,'" the white man urges. Sarah smiles, "the white man was just like a little boy. 'Jus like a chile.'" "Jus like a lil boy, jus like a chile" runs through Sarah's encounter with the white man. And she is, in some literal sense, correct. He is a college student working at a summer job.

Yet it is clear from the beginning of this encounter that the salesman represents something more than the stereotypically lusting white boy-man. His presence is heralded by a throb that Sarah at first thinks is an airplane. It turns out to be the throbbing engine of a car. These two ubiquitous sym-bols of the twentieth century usually spell trouble in the backwater world of southern Negroes and poor whites. And so it proves. The white man sells both time and timelessness—a gramophone with a clock built into it. We are, of course, aware, as perhaps Wright was only dimly so, that the gramophone made possible the preservation and perpetuation of Afro-American musical culture in the face of the fragmentation caused by industrialization and ubanization in the first half of the twentieth century. Indeed, music was one of the chief apolitical elements in the tradition holding blacks together as a group.

The clock and the gramophone are an intriguing symbol in this regard for what the white man sells Sarah is a kind of carrot-and-stick initiation into the twentieth century: a means of participating in the collective culture, and the instrument that has helped to alienate people from natural time and made them vulnerable to mechanization. And Sarah is enthralled by the music. She is totally puzzled, however, about the need for a clock. She and Silas "'git erlong widout time.'" They know when to get up because they "'git up wid the sun.'" They tell when it's night (a rather stupid question on the white man's part) because it gets dark when the sun goes down.

The discrepancy between Sarah's world and the world represented by the white man is further underscored by Baby Ruth who beats on an old discarded clock; the bang! bang! bang! of her destruction of the old timepiece punctuates the initial dialogue, almost as though the baby is trying to recall Sarah to a consciousness of her marriage and family. Wright uses this echo as an ironic sound effect to climax the sexual act between Sarah and the white man: "She rode on the curve of the white bright days and dark black nights . . . till a high red wave of whiteness drowned her . . . and boiled her flesh *bangbangbang*," fusing the romantic longings that have dominated Sarah's thoughts, the climax of the sex act, and the reality of Sarah's marriage in a cold and literal image that foreshadows how Sarah's world ends.

In the seduction scene itself, Sarah is clearly torn between her own aroused desires: "Where his hands held her breast the flesh seemed to knot . . . she felt his lips touching her throat and where he kissed it burned," and the racial implications of her act: "But he's a *white* man, a *white* man," she thinks. He's a white man, a white man is a minor, a very minor refrain, meant obviously (But he's . . . Naw Naw) to conjure up centuries of oppression and physical violation as a protection against the present weakness of the flesh. The spell does not work for Sarah. Or perhaps another spell is at work.

Wright has been careful to show that Sarah can control her sexual impulses. She has demonstrated sexual reserve prior to her marriage with Tom, a former suitor (thoughts of whom come to her mind throughout the story): "She had held Tom up and he had held her up; they had held each other up to keep from slipping to the ground there in the corn field." Or again: "She had closed her eyes and . . . gone weak in his arms and had felt that she could not breathe any more and had torn away and run run run home." A look at the response of Aunt Sue ("Bright and Morning Star") to the physical presence of a white man provides further insight into Sarah's ambiguous response to the white man's advances.

Aunt Sue, beaten senseless by a mob of white men, regained consciousness and saw a white face that for a moment she could not recognize. In her dazed condition, she felt "somehow that she existed only by the mercy of the white face . . ." The face had for her the fear of "all the white faces she had ever seen in her life . . . She stood stone still" (as Sarah is still when the white man's arms tighten around her). Sue accepted the white man's "presence because she felt she had to . . . It seemed that the white man towered over her as a challenge to her right to exist upon the earth." And finally—"She was speaking even though she did not want to; the fear of the white man had hold of her, compelled her . . ." as Sarah is compelled "to straighten" her body against the white man's and so rub against his length as he holds her, "or die." Implicit here is the idea that black women have been conditioned by the threat of physical force to an almost unconscious submissiveness in the presence of white men, and it is this threat that helps to make "seduction," rather than rape, possible between Sarah and the white man.[15]

This, perhaps, explains the actual seduction. It cannot account for Sarah's reaction after the seduction: she lies in bed, "conscious of herself all over, full of a vast peace." We will, for the moment anyway, take the fact that Sarah leaves incriminating evidence—the white man's hat, his soiled handkerchief—lying about for Silas to find, that she spends no time reflecting on her actions or planning, however crudely, what she will tell Silas about the gramophone, as hasty plotting, undercharacterization. This is, after all, one of Wright's early stories. But we must note that only Silas's almost casual threat of violence galvanizes Sarah to some sort of defense. Nor can Sarah understand, at least initially, the enormity of her betrayal. "She wanted to tell Silas," after he has discovered the hat and the handkerchief, put one and one together, and chased her from the house, "that there was nothing to be angry about, that what she had done did not matter; that she was sorry; that after all she was his wife and still loved him."

Sarah does eventually come to acknowledge and understand something of the consequences of her action. Her maturation makes "Long Black Song" the story of Sarah's initiation into black adult/woman-hood. As she hides in the darkness waiting for what the morning will bring, Sarah realizes that Silas is a good man, as good to her "as any black man could be to a black woman." In betraying him, she has betrayed a rare personage in early Afro-American experience, a black man who has succeeded in acquiring the legitimate economic means to care for his family almost as well as the average white man. And most significantly, she has betrayed the collective dream, the idea that given a decent chance at economic stability and upward mobility black people could build stable families and viable communities.

Sarah gains also an increased and, one hopes, more functional racial consciousness: "Silas would never forgive her for something like [her infidelity].

If it were anybody but a white man it would be different." And she begins to assume responsibility for her actions: "She should not have done that last night [had sex with the white man]. This was all her fault, 'Lawd if anything happens t im its mah blame.'" Her maturity comes too late. The white man, even as she acknowledges her guilt, has returned to collect the down payment on the gramophone, and Silas is about to confront him.

The growth of Sarah's character, however, is overshadowed by the greater development in the character of Silas. There is some suggestion of the petty bourgeoisie, the thrift and accommodationist rhetoric of Booker T. Washington, in the way he talks of his land and his emulation of the white man's economic practices. Economic security may have driven Sarah into his arms. Certainly her thoughts when he returns from town are not of her own actions but of what he might have brought her—the red calico she had asked for, it turns out, and a pair of high top shoes as a surprise. Yet under the goading of Sarah's infidelity, Silas grows before our eyes, not so much taking over the story from Sarah as shining her down. For in her descent into worldly knowledge, Sarah is only able to traverse so far: "'Lawd,'" she asks as she watches from afar while Silas awaits the white mob he knows will come to avenge the death of the white man he has killed, "'how could Silas want to stay there like tha [and fight it out with the mob]?'" She has no understanding of Silas's heroic vision.

Silas dies in "eager plumes of red." But Sarah's is the last action: "She turned and ran ... blindly across the fields crying" and the last words, "'Naw Gawd!'" We are left with a final image of a black man flung into a bloody and violent conflict with the racist society by the thoughtless action of his helpmate; our final image of the black woman is that of a flighty wanton who has carelessly tossed away her own honor and that of her husband—perhaps without even realizing that there is such a thing as racial or sexual honor—whose grasp of her husband's heroism, even though she has seen it in action, is still and at best, minimal. The message of the story, simply put, is that the black man must combat racist oppression without and treachery from the black woman within.

Wright later shows some understanding of the sexual harassment to which black women are often subjected by white men in "Man of All Work," (*Eight Men*, 1962), in which a black man poses as a woman in order to get a job and support his wife and family. But the coupling of a peasant mentality with an overriding sexuality as dominant characteristics of black women in the flower of their productive years appears again and again in his works:

There is Bess Moss, the daughter of Wright's landlady in *Black Boy*, who is "astoundingly simple yet vital in a way that [he] had never known." Young Richard is both attracted and repelied by her."What could I do with a girl like this? Was I dumb or was she dumb? I felt that it would be easy to have sex relations with her and I was tempted." But, he wonders, "could I even talk to her about what I felt, hoped? Could she even understand my life? What had I above sex to share with her, and what had she? But I knew that such questions did not bother her." Even so, "he kissed her and petted her. She was eager, childish, pliable . . ." Or the "nameless and illiterate black child with a baby" whose father she does not know in *American Hunger*: "She was not calculating; if she liked a man she just liked him. Sex relations were the only relations she had ever had; no others were possible, so limited was her intelligence." This time, young Richard is more repelled than attracted. "I wondered just what a life like hers meant in the scheme of things and I came to the conclusion that it meant absolutely nothing." But unlike the preceding episode, these reflections do not keep him from engaging in sex with the young woman.

Dot, Cross Damon's young mistress in *The Outsider*, while more complex, is still recognizable as the wanton. She is described as "a passionate child achingly hungry for emotional experience . . . He would try to talk to her and as he talked he could tell that she was not listening; she was pulling off her dress, slipping down her nylon stockings, stepping out of her nylon slip and panties." Though she is a passionate child, Dot has little of that "terrible simplicity" that chracterized Bess Moss and the nameless illiterate of Wright's early days in Chicago. During their first meeting, a secret erotic link springs up between Dot and Cross, but to admit this, Dot must also acknowledge that she allowed Cross, then a stranger, to fondle her breasts in public. She balances her moral notions with her emotional hungers by denying that she was aware of Cross's touch—this despite the fact that Cross has felt the proof of her arousal. And beneath her ardent denials, behind the shame and indigna- tion whenever he mentioned the incident, "there was a furtive sense of erotic pleasure." There is too in this characterization a certain mindless self-absorp- tion that makes communication impossible: "He came at last to believe that she accepted the kind of talk in which he indulged as a mysterious part of a man's equipment, along with his sex organs."

Cross does not see that Dot's response to "his emptying out of his soul the dammed up waters of reflections and brooding thoughts" is very similar to that of Gladys, his wife, in the early stages of their relationship when "he told her something important": "Her feminine instinct placed him at once in the role of a strong and reliable man and encouraged him to play it." Both women appear vulnerable at first. Gladys had simply clung to him, making no demands, imposing no condition, setting no limits. Dot is a younger version of Gladys just as she is a younger version of Cross's mother. The three are linked together by their common betrayer, Cross, the black man, a link that Wright makes explicit when Cross's mother upbraids him about Dot's pregnancy. Cross knows that as his mother speaks, she is "reliving her own experience, grieving over her thwarted hopes that had driven her into the arms of religion for the sake of her sanity." And Dot's vulnerability, as was Gladys's, is deceptively double-edged. Dot is not the nonentity that her name implies, rather she is "Miss Dorothy Powers," underage victim of his statutory rape.

Wright's description of Gladys makes clear why it is impossible for Cross ever really to relate to the three women. "When she spoke at all on general topics it was about how good it was to have someone to be with when the whole world was white and she was colored." Cross, inspired by an almost missionary zeal, "hungered for her as a woman of his own color who was longing to conquer the shame imposed upon her by her native land because of her social and racial origins." Gladys is crippled by color consciousness, a fact that in time Cross "grew to accept along with her womanness." Because she is crippled, she is incapable of ever understanding anything about him. When she denies him at the end of the novel, she is being quite literally correct for she has never known Cross.

What disturbs here is not so much the portraits themselves, for one cannot, *ought not*, deny the psychological ravages of racism or the tortured moral positions that the double standard imposes upon black women. Rather, the disturbing element is the implication that sex and sexuality somehow preclude black women's ever acquiring a deep understanding of the situation of black men. This implication is made explicit in *The Long Dream* (1958). Fish Tucker, the young hero of the novel, is attracted to Gladys because she looks like a white woman. Yet, even the almost white Gladys is afflicted with the black woman's lack of comprehension: "Didn't she know that black men were killed for riding in cars side by side with women of her color," Fish wonders as he drives her around their small southern community. "Or did she regard it all as a childish game? It was plain that he would have to educate her, tell her what the racial score was." Fish realizes that Gladys does not possess enough imagination to see herself or the life she lived in terms that white people saw black people. True to the heroic ideal, Fish himself "hotly rejected the terms in which white people weighed or saw him for those terms made him feel agonizingly inferior . . . he was astounded that Gladys could feel or sense none of this." Finally he concludes, "In a certain way she was mentally *blacker* than he was, though she looked whiter."

In *The Outsider*, Wright goes on to develop in the character of Eva Blount a soul mate for Cross Damon who is an outsider, not because he "was born black and poor, but because he had thought [his] way through the many veils of illusion." That Cross's soul mate is a white woman is supposed to be beside the point, for what stands between Cross and Eva is "a wall not of race but of mutual guilt, blood and false identity." And maybe for Cross, Eva's race is incidental. Certainly there seems to be only simple chauvinism and egomania in his acceptance of her: "Her soul was reaching toward him for protection for solace. Cross smiled, feeling that he was listening to her words as perhaps God listens to prayers. . . . A wave of hot pride flooded him. She was laying her life at his feet. With a gesture of his hand he could own her, shield her from the party, from fear, from her own sense of guilt." Yet Eva's white skin seems to be all that distinguishes her from the other women whom Cross has fled. Like Cross's mother, his wife, and his mistress, "Eva would never be able to comprehend that he was a lost soul spinning like a stray atom far beyond the ken of her mind. . . . She did not understand who or what he was or what he had done, could not believe it when she heard it." Rather than arousing contempt, her ignorance excites Cross's desire, ". . . he turned to her and took her in his arms and had her so slowly and so intensely and with a mounting frenzy of sensual greed . . ." The irony is that Cross finds Eva only to lose her. His deeds are so dark and terrible that even "this sweet girl" clinging to him could not absolve him of his guilt.

The loss of Eva underscores the central theme of the novel, that modern man, having thought himself through the many veils of illusion stands forever outside the possibility of human fellowship. Eva is the classic white woman, beautiful, delicate, helpless, a character seen fairly often in Afro-American fiction of the fifties and sixties, particularly in novels by black men. Invariably, the white woman's beauty, her sensitivity, her *whiteness* symbolize ultimate liberation and justify the denigration of the black woman.

One feels less churlish now than ten years ago in pointing out that there is something at least ironic, if not downright contradictory, in calling the murderer of a black woman a rebel of the ghetto as critics persist in doing with Bigger Thomas in *Native Son*. It is not simply that Bigger's murder of his girlfriend, Bessie (because she *might* tell the police about his murder of the white woman, Mary Dalton), compromises his claim to heroic status, but that murder—literally or figuratively—seems to be the only means that Wright has of dealing with black women in his work—when he can bring himself to deal with them at all. We know, of course, that black women are more than, other than, the weak mothers and whores portrayed in his work; know also that neither the imagery nor the author's stance is unique in the tradition. This discussion of an important subtext in Wright's work can even be seen as casting a deeper and truer light over his reputation, rather than diminishing it, for his place in the tradition does not depend upon these often scandalous portraits of black women. Yet, we must also acknowledge that insofar as Wright refused, by rehashing the old stereotypes, to engage with black women, he stunted his own artistic growth. His treatment of black women blinded him to the strengths of Afro-American traditions, the folk culture he thought could not survive outside the South, that even as he began his career as a writer was already being transformed in urban ghettos in the north and west. Only toward the end of his life did he awaken to the value of Afro-American popular music as something more than setting.

Having said all this, one is still left with the question, What does one do with a brother who don't love you, who even when he is "loving" you ain't liking you? In part we are answered by the works of black women writers—Ann Petry, Dorothy West, Gwendolyn Brooks, Paule Marshall, Lorraine Hansberry—who in the two decades following the publication of *Native Son* explored much the same urban landscape as Wright. The effects of racism are portrayed clearly and movingly, yet none of these writers sees black life so exclusively in terms of deprivation as Wright, nor do they carry on in their works the kind of covert sexism that is endemic to Wright's fiction. In part we are answered by the work of black feminist critics—Barbara Smith, Mary Helen Washington, Maria K. Mootry, and others—who are forcing the re-evaluation and reinterpretation of the entire canon of Afro-American literature so that it more accurately reflects the presence and role of women. And finally, and perhaps most effectively, we are answered by the silent sister-woman in our own hearts: Papa Dick is an example, chile, not a model for making a constructive start.

## Notes

1. Richard Wright, *Uncle Tom's Children: Five Long Stories*, (New York: Harper & Row, 1940). Originally published in 1938 by Harper's, the first edition included "Big Boy Leaves Home," "Down by the River-side," "Long Black Song," and "Fire and Cloud." "The Ethics of Living Jim Crow," an autobiographical sketch (parts of which were later incorporated in *Black Boy*, the story of Wright's childhood and adolescence in the South), and "Bright and Morning Star" were added to the 1940 edition. All quotes are from the 1940 version of the collection.
2. *Eight Men*, a short-story collection (Cleveland and New York: World Publishing Co., 1961); and *Black Boy* (New York: Harper & Row, 1945) and *American Hunger* (New York: Harper & Row, 1977), the autobiographical narratives.
3. I have adapted this definition of *soul* from Eleanor Traylor, who in turn adapted it from Ernest Hemingway's definition of courage.
4. Addison Gayle, Jr., *The Way of the New World* (Garden City, N.Y.: Anchor Doubleday, 1975), p. 209.
5. Robert B. Stepto, *From Behind the Veil* (Urbana: University of Illinois Press, 1979), p. 129.
6. Wright completed a novel "entitled *Little Sister* and then *Maud* (unpublished) . . . intended as a social commentary on the role of women in American society." Constance Webb, *Richard Wright* (New York: Putnam's, 1968) p. 408. I did not have access to this manuscript, but given Webb's description of the heroine—she "whitened her skin by

taking arsenic waters orally"—I cannot think that it would change substantially the cumulative portrayal of women in Wright's work.

7. The mask is one of the most ubiquitous symbols in Afro-American literature; see, for example, the Paul Laurence Dunbar poem, "We Wear the Mask," in *The Complete Poems of Paul Laurence Dunbar* (New York: Dodd Mead & Co., 1913); W. E. B. DuBois, *The Souls of Black Folk* (New York: New American Library, 1969); LeRoi Jones, "A Poem for Willie Best," in *The Dead Lecturer* (New York: Grove Press, 1964) pp. 18–27.

8. Webb, *Richard Wright*, p. 165.

9. *Hymn to the Rising Sun* by Paul Green.

10. Webb, *Richard Wright*, p. 113.

11. Richard Wright, *The Outsider* (New York: Harper & Row, 1953). All quotations are from this edition unless otherwise noted.

12. Ellen Wright and Michel Fabre, eds., *Richard Wright Reader* (New York: Harper & Row, 1978) p. 738.

13. Wright seems to have been particularly fond of three feminine names, "Sarah": the name of characters in "Long Black Song" and *The Outsider*; "Bess" or "Bessie": in *Black Boy* and *Native Son*, respectively; and "Gladys": Cross Damon's wife in *The Outsider*, and the name of the hero's girlfriend in *The Long Dream*.

14. Jean Toomer, *Cane* (New York: Harper & Row, 1969), pp. 51–70.

15. Much the same sort of rationale is offered by a white character in Ernest Gaines, *The Autobiography of Miss Jane Pittman* (New York: Dial Press, 1972), pp. 193–94. Miss Jane, an old ex-slave, greets this theory with incredulity: "'. . . ain't this specalatin?'" Certainly the theory is far more plausible in the case of Sarah and Aunt Sue than it is in Miss Jane's autobiography.

# Contributors

FRITZ FLEISCHMANN is currently an instructor in German at Simmons College. He has written for *Anglia, Amerikastudien/American Studies, New England Quarterly,* and *Great American Reformers.*

KAY S. HOUSE is professor of English at San Francisco State University. In 1968-69 she was the senior Fulbright professor to Italy, where she subsequently spent three years, teaching in Florence and Rome. A member of the Editorial Board for the Cooper Edition, she is presently editing *The Pilot* for the State University of New York Press. When she is not teaching, she farms land in Illinois.

NINA BAYM is professor of English and director of the School of Humanities at the University of Illinois at Urbana-Champaign. She is the author of *The Shape of Hawthorne's Career* (1976) and *Woman's Fiction: A Guide to Novels by and about Women in America, 1820-1870* (1978), as well as numerous scholarly articles and reviews on such American authors as Emerson, Thoreau, Melville, Poe, Cooper, Dickinson, Frost, and Henry James.

LAURIE CRUMPACKER is assistant professor of history and coordinator of women's studies at Simmons College. Coeditor of *The Journal of Esther Burr* (forthcoming from Yale University Press), she is currently writing about spiritual aspects in the work of Harriet Beecher Stowe and Sarah Orne Jewett.

GENE PATTERSON-BLACK is a member of the Academy of Independent Scholars, Boulder, Colorado. He has collaborated on a translation of Raymond Schwab's *La Renaissance Orientale* for Colorado University Press, and has written and lectured about John G. Neidhardt and the Oriental Renaissance. In collaboration with Sheryll Patterson-Black, he has compiled and published *Western Women in History and Literature: An Annotated Bibliography.*

ROLANDE BALLORAIN, Ancienne Elève de l'Ecole Normale Supèrieure de Sèvres, Agrégée d'anglais, is Professeur de Première Supèrieure at the Lycée

Fénelon, Paris VIè. She was an ACLS Fellow in 1973–74 and a visiting scholar at Smith College for three years. Her publications include *Le Nouveau féminisme américain* (Paris: Denoël, 1972), translations of and interviews with American writers, as well as articles on Henry James, Kate Millett, modern American women novelists, and women's movements in France and the U.S. She is currently working on *Childhood and Adolescence in American Fiction* and *Les Ecrivains américains du repli.*

JOHN W. CROWLEY, professor of English at Syracuse University, is the author of *George Cabot Lodge* and of numerous articles on Howells and other American writers. At present, he is writing a book on Howells as a psychological novelist.

NINA AUERBACH is associate professor at the University of Pennsylvania. She is the author of *Communities of Women: An Idea in Fiction* (Harvard University Press, 1978) and of *Woman and the Demon: The Life of a Victorian Myth* (Harvard University Press, 1982). She has also written numerous articles about nineteenth-century literature and culture.

ELIZABETH AMMONS, associate professor of English at Tufts University, is currently on leave with an NEH grant. She has published essays in *American Literature, Criticism,* and *Studies in American Fiction.* She is the editor of *Critical Essays on Harriet Beecher Stowe* (G. K. Hall, 1980) and the author of *Edith Wharton's Argument with America* (University of Georgia Press, 1980).

CAROL HURD GREEN is currently associate dean of the College of Arts and Sciences at Boston College. Coeditor of *Notable American Women: The Modern Period* (1980), she is now working on a book on American women in the arts and politics in the 1960s. Her particular interest is in the intersection of religious faith and political commitment in women's lives: a long-term project is a study of the work and writings of Dorothy Day.

SUSAN WOLSTENHOLME is assistant professor of English at Cayuga County Community College. She has published essays on Henry James and Kate Chopin.

SHARON O'BRIEN, associate professor of English at Dickinson College, teaches courses in American Studies and Women's Studies. Under an NEH grant, she is currently a Visiting Fellow at the University of Pennsylvania, where she is completing a literary and biographical study of Willa Cather that locates identity formation in a cultural and psychological context. Her articles on Cather have appeared in *Women and Literature* and *Studies in American Fiction.*

CYNTHIA SECOR, director of HERS Mid-Atlantic, has served on the editorial boards of the Feminist Press, *Signs, Women's Studies Newsletter,* and *Women's Studies Quarterly.* She has published articles on feminism, androgyny, Daphne Rooke, and Gertrude Stein.

MARY McCAY is presently teaching American literature at Emmanuel College. She has published articles in the *Dutch Quarterly Review of English and American Letters,* and has written on her experiences as a teacher at Walpole Prison for the *Boston Globe.* She is now at work on a book about writing for government.

JUDITH BRYANT WITTENBERG is assistant professor of English at Simmons College. She is the author of *Faulkner: The Transfiguration of Biography* (1981), as well as articles on Faulkner and Ellen Glasgow.

MARK SPILKA teaches English and Comparative Literature at Brown University, where he also helps to edit *Novel: A Forum on Fiction.* He is the author of *The Love Ethic of D. H. Lawrence* (1955), *Dickens and Kafka: A Mutual Interpretation* (1963), *Virginia Woolf's Quarrel with Grieving* (1980), and has edited two anthologies: *D. H. Lawrence: A Collection of Critical Essays* (1963) and *Towards a Poetics of Fiction* (1977). He is currently working on a book-length study of Hemingway's quarrel with androgyny.

CHERYL A. WALL, assistant professor in the Rutgers University department of English, was a Fulbright lecturer on American literature in 1978-79. A contributor to *American Women Writers, Notable American Women* and *Phylon,* she is currently completing a book on the Women of the Harlem Renaissance.

SHERLEY ANNE WILLIAMS is the author of *Give Birth to Brightness,* a study of heroic visions in the works of contemporary Afro-American authors; *The Peacock Poems,* nominated for a National Book Award, 1976; and *Some One Sweet Angel Chile* (1982). She is presently at work on a historical novel based on her popular short story, "Meditations on History." She teaches Afro-American literature and lives in San Diego, California.